Fourth Edition
MANAGERIAL ECONOMICS

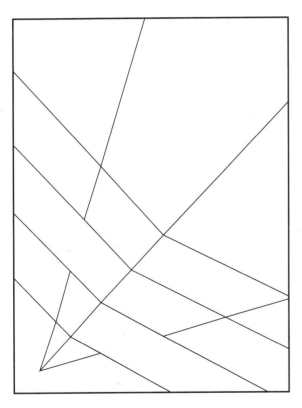

Analysis

Problems

Cases

Lila J.Truett
Professor of Economics
The University of Texas at San Antonio

Dale B. Truett
Professor of Economics
The University of Texas at San Antonio

COLLEGE DIVISION South-Western Publishing Co.

Cincinnati Ohio

Sponsoring Editor: James Keefe
Developmental Editor: Brigid Harmon
Production Editors: Mark Sears
Rhonda Eversole
Production House: Beckwith-Clark, Inc.
Cover/Internal Design: Lucy Lesiak Design
Marketing Manager: Scott Person

HT89DA

Library of Congress Cataloging-in-Publication Data

Truett, Lila J. (Lila Jean)
    Managerial economics : analysis, problems, cases / Lila J. Truett,
Dale B. Truett. — 4th ed.
        p.   cm.
    Includes index.
    ISBN 0-538-81285-0
    1. Managerial economics.   I. Truett, Dale B.   II. Title.
HD30.22.T78   1992
338.5'024658—dc20   91-30862
                                                                          CIP

2 3 4 5 6 7 MT 7 6 5 4 3 2
Printed in the United States of America

Preface

This book is designed primarily for use by business administration students who have done some introductory-level work in economics. As our title suggests, the objective of the book is to enhance students' understanding of the application of economic analysis to managerial decisions. We believe this goal can best be accomplished by providing a brief, clear statement of the principles of microeconomic decision making and supplementing this material with examples, problems, and cases that illustrate how such principles are applied.

Throughout the following chapers are numerical examples, applications, and minicases dispersed among discussions of decision criteria and rules. Chapters 2 through 15 end with questions and problems related to the materials covered. Answers to selected odd-numbered problems appear at the end of the book. In addition, we have provided integrating cases at the ends of the book's five major parts. Each case is somewhat longer than the typical end-of-chapter problem and combines a number of concepts developed in the preceding chapters.

STUDY GUIDE, INSTRUCTOR'S MANUAL, SOFTWARE, AND TEST BANK

Introduced with the third edition of the book, the *Study Guide* is a learning tool that complements the problem-solving approach employed in the text. Virtually all of the *Study Guide* problems have been classroom tested, and step-by-step solutions are provided at the back of the guide. A unique feature of the guide is a prompting device called "Getting Started," which verbally walks the student through the steps that must be taken to solve a specific type of problem. The *Study Guide* is closely tied to the book by means of a cross-referencing system that indicates the specific end-of-chapter problem or problems that are similar to a given *Study Guide* problem. Finally, for most chapters, the *Study Guide* contains a set of Hand-In Problems that can be used as out-of-class or homework assignments.

Solutions for the Hand-In Problems are found in the *Instructor's Manual*. Many of the Hand-in Problems are set up in a way that allows individual instructors to change the value of a key number to generate a variety of different answers. This enables them to vary the solutions from section to section of a given course or from one semester to another. The *Instructor's Manual* explains how to use this feature and provides some of the alternative values for the key numbers. The *Instructor's Manual* also contains step-by-step solutions to the end-of-chapter problems and all cases that appear in the book. We hope that instructors and students will use the problems and cases to the fullest possible extent: in our opinion, problem-solving experiences constitute the best way to develop an understanding of managerial economics.

The *Decision Assistant* is a software package that provides solution routines for various types of problems found in the text. These routines include maximization and minimization, linear programming, break-even analysis, and present value. In addition, the package contains both simple and multiple linear regression programs. Selected end-of-chapter problems in the book are identified as candidates for solution with the *Decision Assistant*. Adopters of the book can obtain the *Decision Assistant* from South-Western Publishing Company.

This edition of *Managerial Economics* is accompanied by an expanded *Test Bank*. The *Test Bank* includes a substantial number of problems that are similar to those found in the text and the *Study Guide*, as well as multiple choice and true/false questions. Note that the Hand-In Problems in the *Study Guide* can also be used as testing materials by changing the key numbers as explained here and in the *Instructor's Manual*.

■ ■ ■ ■ ■ ■ ■ ■ ■ **FOURTH-EDITION CHANGES**

This is the first edition of *Managerial Economics* that has undergone a significant organizational change. In response to user and reviewer suggestions, we have placed the demand estimation chapter (Chapter 3) immediately following the chapter on the economics of demand and revenues. While clearly it is not obligatory to move directly to statistics and estimation from the descriptive and theoretical material on demand, the widespread availability of microcomputers may inspire some instructors to do so. The *Decision Assistant* software described earlier contains a multiple regression program that supplements the demand estimation discussion in the text.

Other noteworthy changes in this edition include two completely new features within the body of each chapter—Managerial Perspectives and Numerical Examples. The Managerial Perspectives are high-interest, current illustrations of how real-world firms have addressed or failed to address issues and decision problems discussed in the book. The Numerical Examples are set off from the running text and call attention to the steps that must be taken to solve specific types of problems (arc elasticity, cost minimization, profit maximization, present value, etc.) that students will encounter repeatedly in the end-of-chapter and/or *Study Guide* problems. We believe that students can much improve their abilities to handle these related kinds of problems if they take the time to work through the Numerical Examples.

As in previous editions, we have provided a Glossary at the end of the book. This one is somewhat expanded, partially as a result of our decision to restyle the text with running definitions in the body of each chapter. The aim of the running definitions, of course, is to make it easier for students to learn the economic jargon so necessary to understanding the analytical side of our discipline. There is also a Mathematical Appendix at the end of the text that will serve as an important learning tool for many students.

Since the publication of the third edition of *Managerial Economics*, we have had the good fortune to be able to travel, study, and participate in economics conferences in a number of countries, ranging from the Soviet Union and China to England and South Africa. These experiences, coupled with consulting related to a broad range of industries, have much enhanced our understanding of business and public sector operations and decision making. We hope that what we have learned from these activities has helped to make this a better book, one that provides a unique, global perspective. The International Capsules introduced in the third edition to illustrate some of the dimensions of managerial economics in global business have been retained and reinforced by two new cases about manufacturing in China.

In response to user requests, other changes in the fourth edition include the addition of an appendix on basic demand and supply analysis (following Chapter 1) and broader discussions of the determinants of demand and elasticity in Chapter 2. Many new end-of-chapter problems have been added. Finally, the text has been thoroughly updated with many new references to current events and real-world examples.

▪ ▪ ▪ ▪ ▪ ▪ ▪ ▪ ▪ COURSE DESIGN

Our own experience in teaching managerial economics leads us to caution both students and professors that this book contains more material than can normally be covered in a three-hour, one-semester course. Where students can be expected to have no more than an average level of preparation in economic principles, it may not be possible to cover more than Chapters 1 through 6, 8, 9, 12, 16, and 17. Students with more advanced backgrounds may progress swiftly enough to allow inclusion of Chapters 7, 10, and 11 in the preceding list.

The book allows for some variation in emphasis. For example, to orient a course toward both private and public sector capital project analysis, Chapters 13, 14, and 15 could be substituted for the materials on demand estimation, forecasting, and complex pricing problems covered in Chapters

3, 10, and 11. For this kind of course, probably all of Part 5 should be covered.

For a two-course sequence, we suggest coverage of the basic materials (Chapters 1 through 6, 8, 9, 12, 16, and 17) in the first course. The second course, which might well be launched as an elective if it is not possible to include it in the core requirements of a program, could include linear programming (Chapter 7), advanced topics in pricing (Chapter 10 and its appendix), economic forecasting (Chapter 11), project analysis (Chapter 13, its appendix, and Chapter 14), and public sector decision making (Chapter 15).

■ ■ ■ ■ ■ ■ ■ ■ APPENDICES

As mentioned earlier, at the end of the book, we have provided a Mathematical Appendix that can be used either for student review or to give the course a more quantitative slant. A statistical appendix following Chapter 3 and one on compounding and discounting following Chapter 13 serve similar purposes. The appendices to Chapters 2, 4, and 10 deal briefly with topics that are either too difficult or too time-consuming, when fully developed, to be recommended as standard fare, unless the instructor has a special interest in them.

■ ■ ■ ■ ■ ■ ■ ■ ACKNOWLEDGMENTS

For our backgrounds in microeconomics, we certainly owe debts of gratitude to James Jeffers and Gerald Nordquist of the University of Iowa, H. H. Liebhafsky and Wendell C. Gordon of the University of Texas at Austin, and the late Cliff Lloyd. Our colleagues, Robert E. Langley and Vincent DiMartino, certainly are owed a debt of gratitude for their diligent work on the *Test Bank* and certain other materials. The faculty, staff, and students of the Division of Economics and Finance at the University of Texas at San Antonio helped us immeasurably while the book was in preparation. Thanks are due as well to all of the instructors at other institutions who took the time to provide their comments on previous editions and to the following reviewers whose helpful suggestions were incorporated into this edition.

Charles Callahan
SUNY College at Brockport

Robert Carbaugh
Central Washington University

Thomas Carroll
University of Nevada, Las Vegas

J.R. Clark
University of Tennessee, Martin

Bruce R. Domazlicky
Southeast Missouri State University

Leonard P. Lardaro
University of Rhode Island

Craig J. McCann
University of South Carolina

Walter E. Rice
California Polytechnic State University

Note to Students

In the short run (the present), playing your cards right gets you good grades. Over the long run (the future), playing them right can get you success. We want to help you do both, and we wrote this book with that in mind.

Your immediate problem is going to be to cope with the course that goes with this book. Here's how.

1. Read your assignments *before* your instuctor covers them in class. (If at first you do not understand the material, read through it again.)
2. Pay attention to the Numerical Examples that occasionally appear in the chapters. Work your way through them step-by-step with pencil and paper to make sure you understand them. It will help you to solve end-of-chapter, *Study Guide,* and exam problems.
3. Go down the list of questions at the end of each chapter. If there are some that you cannot answer, *review* the chapter and find the answer. Ask the instructor if you still are not sure.
4. Work *all* of the problems you are assigned, and do this *before* your instructor solves them for you.
5. When you think you understand a concept or method, make up a problem of your *own* (like the ones at the end of each chapter) and solve it.

We hope this book will help you develop useful skills for solving business or public economic problems or at least for evaluating the solutions or advice of others. These kinds of skills will likely be important to you long after your present course is over.

Much of what we discuss here is not too difficult if you put some thought into your study of it. One way to sharpen your economic IQ is to keep an eye on the news and on business periodicals such as *The Wall Street Journal* or *Business Week.* You will find, as we have, that the success or failure of many business undertakings hinges on how well management has understood many of the concepts we discuss in the chapters to follow. In fact we cite some experiences of real businesses in almost every chapter, and as you work your way through the book, we expect that you will develop some definite opinions about which firms have played their cards wisely and which ones have not. All of this, we hope, will help you to play yours well in the future.

Summary of Contents

Contents

P A R T 1

The Firm and Its Environment

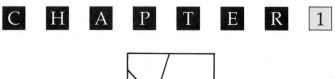

Introduction, Environment, and Methodology

Reminiscing about the 1980s, the vice-president of a midwestern building materials manufacturer noted that those years meant "going to work every day wondering if you would have a job after lunch."[1] Certainly the 1980s were difficult years, for although the United States and many other economies experienced a period of resurgence, the decade was marked by considerable corporate retrenchment, some spectacular bankruptcies, and a veritable onslaught of buyouts, mergers, and "raids." When the dust had settled, many companies had slashed costs and were running "mean and lean." More than two million employees had been eliminated from the ranks of the *Fortune* 500 firms.

As the 1990s unfolded, corporate managers continued to keep a wary eye on costs but were also on the lookout for new opportunities. Companies that had turned in good performances during the mid-1980s faced the specter of recession and falling profits and knew that they would have to keep a close eye on the bottom line. Management gurus were touting a reawakening of concern for employees, corporate customers, and consumers, but it was becoming clear that without strategies that would turn a reasonable profit, a kinder, gentler corporation might not be a surviving one.

While corporate economists have played substantial roles behind the scenes in much of the restructuring that has occurred, most of the space

■ ■ ■ ■ ■ ■
[1] "Management for the 1990s," *Newsweek* (April 25, 1988), p. 48.

allocated by the popular press to the field of economics and its leading personalities is focused on public policy prescriptions for dealing with such problems as inflation, unemployment, trade deficits, and the savings and loan debacle. These types of economic problems would be discussed in a *macro*economics course. This book is concerned with the economic decisions of firm managers, part of the traditional subject matter of *micro*economics. However, the difference between *managerial* economics and microeconomics lies primarily in the emphasis of the former on the practical application of well-known principles to economic problems faced by businesses.

Many large firms have turned to corporate managerial economists for help in making decisions that are critical to "the running of the business." More than a decade ago, *Business Week* summed up the emerging role of the managerial economist as follows:

> . . . companies across the country are now demanding less of the old-style corporate economist who churned out sweeping economic forecasts, which often were swept into the wastebasket, and are turning instead to the new-style economist who can ply his skills in such fields as econometrics and industrial economics to help shape company policy. Indeed, an increasing number of them have joined the team of top-level executives who map business strategy.[2]

Today, businesses continue to rely on managerial economics for answers to everyday questions that affect not only their performance, but also their relations with government and public and private interest groups. Even if one does not plan to become a managerial economist, understanding the decision-making approaches that managerial economics employs can yield great benefits in analyzing a wide variety of business problems.

■ ■ ■ ■ ■ ■ ■ ■ **MANAGERS AS DECISION MAKERS**

The managers of a firm are responsible for making most of the economic decisions—the type of product produced, its price, the production technology utilized, and the financing of production—that will ultimately result in profits or losses for the firm. The firm's manager or managers may or may not be its owner or owners; therefore the goals of the managers may not be quite the same as those of the owners.

Presently, a growing number of firms offer bonus plans (called *performance shares* or *performance units*) to their managers as incentives to maximize profits in situations where the managers do not initially have an

■ ■ ■ ■ ■ ■
[2] "Executive Clout for Economists," *Business Week* (February 13, 1978), pp. 58, 60.

ownership interest.[3] Moreover, if managers wish to retain their positions or to obtain better ones, they must ensure that their company maintains a satisfactory level of profits and, preferably, a high rate of profit growth.

In the case of a large corporation, some of the main decision makers for the firm usually include the chief executive officer, the president, the vice-president for sales, the vice-president for manufacturing, the vice-president for finance, the controller, and, ultimately, the board of directors and the stockholders. (The *controller* is the head accountant for the firm and is responsible for the collection of data regarding the firm's costs and revenues and for setting up its budgets, thereby performing a crucial role in the firm's decision-making process.)

The aforementioned managers usually take joint responsibility for decision making. Thus their fortunes or careers may rise or fall depending on the skill with which they interpret economic problems and the data and advice they receive from staff economists or economic consultants, financial analysts, and market researchers. We shall see that the managers' responsibilities, although centered around achievement of the firm's profit goal, have been expanded to include both liability for criminal offenses and damages that result from the activities of the corporations that the managers oversee. In the important area of antitrust liability, managers must blend their knowledge of economic decision making with that of law, in order to avoid decision errors that could prove disastrous for themselves and their firms.

In this book it is not our objective to teach you to become a chief financial manager, a controller, the head of a marketing department, or even a full-fledged corporate economist. What we shall attempt to do is to help you learn the economic principles that are relevant to decision making in all areas of firm management. An understanding of these principles will help the future firm manager know *which questions* to ask and thus *what data* are needed, as well as *what decision* to make once the data are obtained, in order to assist the firm in maximizing profits. If you do not eventually become a managerial economist, we hope that at least you will be able to communicate with economists and recognize when help from them can prove useful for problem solving.

The importance of utilizing economic principles in making managerial decisions is underscored by Small Business Administration statistics, which show that *50 percent* of all businesses fail within their *first two years* of operation and only *20 percent* survive for *five years*. We believe that the significance of these principles is further emphasized by the bankruptcy filings of such well-known companies as Foster Grant,[4] Eastern Airlines,[5]

■ ■ ■ ■ ■ ■

[3] See "Pay for Performance," *The Wall Street Journal*, April 18, 1990, pp. R7–R8; and "Executive Pay: How the Boss Did in '85," *Business Week* (May 5, 1986), pp. 48–58.

[4] "Foster Grant Runs for the Shade of Chapter 11," *Business Week* (September 3, 1990), p. 44.

[5] "Eastern May Be Worth More Dead Than Alive," *Business Week* (October 8, 1990), p. 44.

Wickes,[6] and Wheeling-Pittsburgh Steel,[7] as well as by some of the problems of other prominent firms, including General Motors,[8] Owens Corning,[9] Sears, Roebuck,[10] and even McDonald's.[11]

As indicated previously, we shall usually assume that the goal of a firm is *profit maximization*, or making the greatest possible total profit over some specified time period. The corresponding goal of the public sector manager is assumed to be the *efficient use of resources*. Arguments can be made and are made with regard to the accuracy of these assumptions. Nevertheless, we think they are useful assumptions. That is because we believe that even when a firm or agency has more complex objectives, managers benefit by knowing the difference between an efficient, or profit-maximizing, strategy and one that sacrifices some efficiency or profit in order to achieve other goals.

■ ■ ■ ■ ■ ■ ■ ■ OUR APPROACH TO PROBLEM SOLVING

Our emphasis here is on managerial problem solving, usually in a profit-maximizing context. In general, once managerial objectives are known, we take the following steps in arriving at a decision:

1. An *identification* of the problem or decision to be made;
2. A statement of *alternative solutions* to the problem;
3. A *determination of what data are relevant* to the decision, and an analysis of those data relative to the alternative solutions; and
4. The choice of *the best solution* consistent with our firm's or agency's objectives.

The time period under consideration will often be an important factor in our decision analysis. When decisions concern current operations and objectives are predetermined, alternatives may be very limited. In such cases step 2 may reduce to a simple statement of the conditions under which the objective will be met. For example, if management wishes to determine what rate of output per quarter will maximize profit from sales of a given product in a single market, there may be no alternative but to

■ ■ ■ ■ ■ ■

[6] See "Salvage Operation: How Team at Wickes Schemed and Cajoled to Restore Its Health," *The Wall Street Journal*, August 2, 1985, pp. 1, 14.

[7] "Wheeling-Pittsburgh Steel Corp. Files for Protection Under Bankruptcy Law After Union Vetos Plan," *The Wall Street Journal*, April 17, 1985, pp. 3, 4.

[8] "Smaller Giant: Huge GM Write-off Positions Auto Maker to Show New Growth," *The Wall Street Journal*, November 1, 1990, pp. A1, A6.

[9] "Max Weber is Out to Get Owens Corning in the Pink Again," *Business Week* (October 6, 1990), pp. 86, 90.

[10] "Can Ed Brennan Salvage the Sears He Designed?" *Business Week* (August 27, 1990), p. 34.

[11] "McDonald's Isn't Looking Quite So Juicy Anymore," *Business Week* (August 6, 1990), p. 30.

determine the output level that is consistent with this objective. However, if management wishes to decide which of a given set of investment projects will add the most to the value of the firm, a large number of alternatives may have to be analyzed. In general, the longer the time period in question, the greater the number of alternatives available to management.

The analyzing and choosing done in steps 3 and 4 rely heavily on standard and broadly accepted tools and criteria of economic analysis. As we progress through the definition of these tools and criteria and their application to specific economic problems of the firm, we shall develop rules for decision making that will be applied time and time again. In general, these rules have their foundation in what is known as *marginal* or *incremental analysis*. The underlying principle of the marginal or incremental approach is that changes in economic variables controlled by the firm (output, price, resource use, investment) should be undertaken anytime such changes add more to the firm's revenues than to its costs—in other words, anytime they add to profit. For public sector management, we extend this concept to the effect of changes in public output on *social benefits* and *social costs*.

■ ■ ■ ■ ■ ■ ■ ■   **BASIC CONCEPTS OF THIS BOOK**

This book is organized in a way that we hope will help you quickly master some key economic concepts and recognize relevant data for firm decision making. In fact, once Parts 1 and 2 are completed, virtually all of the tools and decision criteria necessary for the analysis of specific decision problems in the subsequent parts of the book will have been presented.

Since a firm's total profit during any time period is equal to its *total revenue* (sales) less its total costs, an accurate economic analysis of the demand for the product of a firm and its *cost* is crucial to the achievement of the firm's goal of profit maximization. In fact, inadequate record keeping, which precluded careful analysis of these two factors, was one of the reasons for the mid-1970s demise of retailer W. T. Grant.[12] In 1990, another big merchandising firm, Ames Department Stores (Ames, G.C. Murphy, and Zayre stores) was in deep financial trouble, in part because of poor record keeping at several hundred stores it had acquired when it bought another company.[13] Many other businesses have failed for similar reasons, while careful financial controls are a major factor in helping successful

■ ■ ■ ■ ■ ■

[12] See "Investigating the Collapse of W. T. Grant," *Business Week* (July 19, 1976), pp. 60–62.

[13] "They Took Their Shot At Being A Giant—and Missed," *Business Week,* May 7, 1990, p. 39.

firms (such as USX,[14] General Electric,[15] and IBM[16]) to generally remain profitable and expand.

Thus one of the first steps toward the development of a profit-maximizing strategy is to gain an understanding of the relationship between *demand* for a firm's output and the firm's revenue from sales. Chapter 2 is devoted entirely to a discussion of demand concepts, including (1) the relationship of price charged to quantity demanded, (2) the relationship of quantity demanded to total and incremental sales revenue, and (3) the effects on product demand of other variables, such as consumer income and prices of related goods. In Chapter 3, we turn to the empirical estimation of demand, relying primarily on modern statistical techniques that can be applied easily using a personal computer. Until recent years, small businesses rarely attempted statistical analysis of demand because most lacked computer facilities or the budget to hire consultants and mainframe time. Today, however, most businesses can do their own demand estimation.

Of course, large firms are performing more and more sophisticated demand analyses. For example, firms in the airline industry are using their computer systems to keep close tabs on air travel patterns and the effect of price changes on those patterns. As a result, they can adjust their fare structures quickly and precisely to adapt to changing markets.[17] A major producer of consumer goods, Procter & Gamble, also places a great deal of emphasis on market research and has been successful in tracking consumer demand.[18] On the other hand, firms in the U.S. auto industry have had to make painful adjustments to the production of small cars and increased competition from foreign car manufacturers because they did not correctly anticipate consumer demand for lighter-weight, high quality cars.[19]

Historically, some firms have placed major emphasis on obtaining a greater market share as a means of expanding profit.[20] Now, however, many firms are attaching increasing importance to *profit maximizing* and *flexible pricing* policies, as opposed to expanding sales volume. For exam-

■ ■ ■ ■ ■ ■

[14] "Big Steel is Hot Again," *Time* (February 13, 1989), p. 61.

[15] "The Best and Worst Deals of the '80s," *Business Week* (January 15, 1990), pp. 52–57; and "They Make Good Things for Flying," *Time* (May 2, 1988), p. 55.

[16] "What's Wrong at IBM?" *Business Week* (March 17, 1986), pp. 48–49; and "IBM: More Worlds to Conquer," *Business Week* (February 18, 1985), pp. 84–98.

[17] "Airlines Use a Scalpel to Cut Fares in the Latest Round of Price Wars," *The Wall Street Journal*, November 26, 1985, p. 31.

[18] "If You Are What You Eat, They've Got Your Number," *The Wall Street Journal*, August 31, 1989, pp. B1, B6; and "The Marketing Revolution at Procter & Gamble," *Business Week* (July 25, 1988), pp. 72–76.

[19] "A New Era for Auto Quality," *Business Week* (October 22, 1990), pp. 85–96.

[20] "GE's Wizards Turning from the Bottom Line to Share of the Market," *The Wall Street Journal*, July 12, 1982, pp. 1, 14; and "Corporate Strategists Giving New Emphasis to Market Share, Rank," *The Wall Street Journal*, February 3, 1978, pp. 1, 33.

ple, Procter & Gamble, mentioned earlier, has recently placed new emphasis on the profit goal. One company spokesman put it this way: "Before it had been share, share, share. We get the share, and the profits will follow." Now, however, he says the company is focusing more on profits.[21] To be a success at managing for profits requires a great deal of information, not only on markets and demand, but also on costs. This means that decision makers have had to increase their analytical skills as data collection and processing techniques have become more refined.

In Part 2 our emphasis shifts from demand and revenue analysis to the *costs* of the firm. Since profit maximization requires the greatest possible spread between total revenue and total cost, it is critical that managers understand how costs behave as output and sales of the firm change. Costs depend on the relationship between output and the inputs that are used to produce it.[22] For example, a manufacturing firm may purchase labor, machinery, raw materials, fuel, and managerial talent in order to make its product. In general, the firm's total cost will increase as output is increased, since more of these inputs will have to be bought to produce greater amounts of the product. Chapter 4 deals specifically with the way output varies as the amounts and kinds of inputs are changed. Our objective in Chapter 4 will be to determine for each possible output of the firm per given time period the combination of inputs that will minimize production cost. In Chapter 5 we show how the costs of the firm vary with its level of output, once the cost-minimization criteria of Chapter 4 are satisfied.

Finally, revenue and cost analyses are brought together in Chapter 6, where the criteria for profit maximization are fully developed. We shall demonstrate in Chapter 6, for example, that maximization of profit does not necessarily mean that sales are maximized or that unit costs are minimized. In fact, we will show that for profit maximization, a firm must produce up to the point where the *incremental profit* (additional revenue less additional cost) received from the production of one more unit of output is zero.

In addition to profit-maximizing decision rules, Chapter 6 includes a comparison of profit maximization with break-even analysis, another well-known business approach to managerial decision making, and a reconsideration of profit maximization as a "real world" managerial goal. Again,

■ ■ ■ ■ ■ ■

[21] "Can P&G Squeeze Profits Out of Orange Juice?" *Business Week* (January 23, 1989), p. 38.

[22] Lee Iacocca, Chairman of Chrysler Corp., showed a keen awareness of cost when he chided his suppliers for developing a parking-brake cable that would hold up at 60 degrees below zero. Reportedly, Iacocca asked "Why not 40 below? How many cars do we sell in Labrador? We've got to make sure we don't give our customers too much cost and not enough value." See "The Flashing Signal at Chrysler: Danger Dead Ahead," *Business Week* (June 18, 1990), p. 44.

once we reach this point in the book, most of the tools necessary for the analysis of the subsequent chapters will have been discussed and applied.

Environment of the Firm

Parts 3, 4, and 5 deal specifically with some special factors in the environment in which managers must make economic decisions regarding the firm. The environment of the firm contains many factors that the firm must analyze and successfully cope with in order to maximize profits. These factors include (1) variables that determine consumer demand for its product, such as consumer income; (2) the presence, prices, and advertising of competing products; (3) population growth; and (4) consumer tastes and preferences, as discussed in Chapter 2.

However, of particular importance to the firm in determining its pricing strategy is the *type of product market* within which it operates. In Chapters 8 and 9 we define four basic product market structures, focusing primarily on the number of firms in a given market and the corresponding relationship of that number to the notion of competition. Profit maximization is first examined in Chapter 8 under conditions of theoretically perfect competition and its antithesis—pure monopoly. Still, most firms are faced with situations lying somewhere between these two extremes. Therefore, profit-maximizing price and output decisions in these more realistic and complex settings are discussed in Chapter 9.

Special pricing and production decisions—such as those associated with the internal transfer of a product from one division of a firm to another, jointly produced products, and price discrimination among different groups of buyers—are considered in Chapter 10.

Another environmental factor that affects the firm's costs is the current state of technology, which helps to determine the opportunities for economies of scale in production, as discussed in Chapter 4. However, the firm's costs are also affected by the fact that some of its inputs are fixed in the short run and by input market structures with which the firm must deal, as discussed in Chapter 12.

When a firm's management is contemplating new investments, the environmental elements in the decision-making process become more complex. For example, some of management's investment alternatives may involve lines of production with which management is not familiar. Also, the longer time horizon relevant to this type of decision brings forth the possibility that many more variables may change than would be expected in a short-run analysis of current operations. The analysis of *capital projects* (investment undertakings), which is the subject of Chapters 13 and 14, involves expansion of our decision-making goals to handle both the larger number of alternatives available in the long run and the fact that profits attributable to a decision will flow into the firm over some future time period. Moreover, we shall develop means for taking into account the *risk* associated with various future alternatives for the firm and for adjusting our analyses for differences in risk between alternatives.

The final part of this book, Part 5, deals with interrelationships between government, or the *public sector*, and the firm. We first show, in Chapter 15, how our decision analysis can be modified to deal with managerial problems in public agencies and to develop rules for the efficient use of public sector resources. In Chapter 16 we consider government regulations as an element of the firm's environment and examine how profit maximization is affected by regulatory variables. These regulations affect both the pricing policies and the costs of the firm because the firm must meet numerous requirements regarding pricing, product safety, product quality, and plant safety.

Finally, in Chapter 17 we speculate about the future environment of the firm, focusing our attention on trends and impending changes that will likely affect the economic decisions of managers in years to come.

Other Tools Required in Decision Making

Besides the basic economic concepts and tools outlined in this chapter, other technical tools can greatly assist the manager in making decisions that will maximize firm profits. These tools include the calculus techniques of optimization (with or without a constraint), linear regression analysis, and linear programming.

A review of mathematical functions and graphs and an introduction to calculus are provided in the Mathematical Appendix at the end of the book. Optimization with calculus is covered in the appendix to Chapter 4 and in Chapter 6. Linear regression analysis, a statistical tool which assists the manager in estimating firm revenue and cost functions, is presented in Chapter 3 and its appendix. Chapter 7 discusses linear programming, a useful technique when a firm's relevant revenue and cost functions are linear but are subject to linear constraints that can be expressed in the form of inequalities. The general topic of forecasting techniques is examined in Chapter 11. Throughout the book are many numerical examples showing how to apply various analytical techniques. Be sure to work through these step by step as you read along; and remember, they can be used for review as well.

If mathematics is not your cup of tea, there is no reason to be discouraged. It is not necessary for you to master all of the quantitative tools we have mentioned before you can understand the basic economic principles involved in profit maximization or before you can find this book useful. Of course, various instructors will choose to place different emphases on the expertise you achieve in such methods. We believe, however, that a working knowledge of these tools will be very helpful to the business or public sector manager in economic decision making.

Appendix 1

Demand, Supply, and Market Price:
A Brief Review

The historian and philosopher Thomas Carlyle (1795–1881) once said that even a parrot could be taught to repeat "supply and demand" in response to any economic question. Thus, if we are to place ourselves at a level somewhere above the parrot, an understanding of the specifics of supply and demand analysis is warranted.

DEMAND AND THE DEMAND CURVE

In economic analysis, the term "demand" is used to refer to the various amounts of a good or service someone (a single consumer or a group of buyers) is both willing and able to buy at various possible prices. It is a functional relationship between a good's price and the quantity the buyer or buyers will take. When we are talking about the demand for a firm's product, we therefore mean the amounts of it that buyers will take at various possible prices. This kind of information is shown by either a *demand schedule* or a *demand curve* for the good. The amount that consumers will buy at any given price is usually called the "quantity demanded" of the good.

Let us assume for a moment that we are looking at the market demand for broccoli.[1] Table 1A–1 shows the amounts of broccoli consumers will purchase per month at various possible prices per bunch (bn.). (Broccoli is sold in bunches with an average weight of about one pound.) The

---

[1] In 1990, President George Bush made some disparaging remarks about broccoli. The result was that broccoli farmers sent tons of it to him to show their appreciation. See "You Can Slice It, Dice It, or Ice It, But to Some It'll Still Be the Pits," *The Wall Street Journal*, April 5, 1990, p. B1.

Table 1A–1   Demand for Broccoli

Price of Broccoli per Bunch (P_b)	Quantity Demanded of Broccoli per Month (Q_b)
$1.20	100,000
1.10	125,000
1.00	150,000
.90	175,000
.80	200,000
.70	225,000
.60	250,000
.50	275,000

amount people are willing and able to buy at any given price appears in the quantity demanded column, labeled Q_b. In Figure 1A–1, the same data are presented as a demand curve. The demand curve, D_b, is just a plot of the price and quantity-demanded data from the table, with price shown on the vertical axis and quantity demanded on the horizontal axis.

Note that the demand curve slopes downward to the right (has a *negative* slope). For most goods, we expect this to be the case, since at lower prices people will tend to buy larger amounts per time period. This inverse relation between a good's own price and the quantity demanded of it is a reflection of the *law of demand*. The law of demand simply states that both individuals and groups of consumers will generally increase their purchases of a good when its price falls and decrease their purchases when its price rises. It holds for most goods but cannot be proven to hold for all goods in all circumstances. For example, we know that snob appeal sometimes causes people to buy *more* of a good when its price rises (designer clothes, luxury cars). However, these cases are relatively rare.

Since the law of demand holds in Figure 1A–1, we can see that a fall in the price of broccoli will lead to increased purchases of broccoli by consumers. If the price falls from $0.80 per bn. to $0.70 per bn., consumers will increase their purchases from 200,000 bn. per month to 225,000 bn. Such a change (from point *A* to *B* in Figure 1A–1), which takes place when the good's own price changes and there is a movement *along* a given demand curve, is called "change in quantity demanded."

Behind the demand curve is a broader concept, the *demand function*. The demand function explicitly recognizes that consumers' purchases of a given item depend on other things besides its price. For example, how much broccoli consumers will buy probably depends not only on the price of broccoli, but also on the prices of other green veggies such as brussels sprouts or green beans. It may also depend on consumer incomes, since cheaper vegetables might be bought instead if consumers were closely watching their budgets. We can represent all this as a demand function

Figure 1A–1   Demand Curve for Broccoli

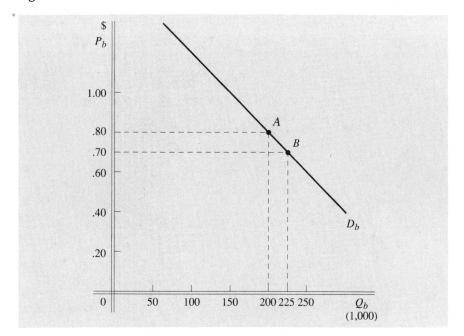

with the notational form $Q_b = f(P_b, P_v, I)$, where Q_b is the number of bunches of broccoli sold per month, P_b is the price of broccoli per bn., P_v is the average price per unit of competing veggies, and I is a measure of consumers' monthly income. The variables other than P_b on the right-hand side of the equation are called "determinants of demand."

In order to plot the demand curve as we did in Figure 1A–1, it is necessary that as we change the price of broccoli, other demand function variables such as the price of competing veggies and consumers' income remain constant. Why? Because the demand curve in the figure will *shift* if one of the other variables changes. Take income, for example. If income rises, some consumers who thought broccoli was too expensive for their dinner tables will decide to buy it. Thus at all possible prices there will be a greater demand for broccoli. In Table 1A–1 we would see a new column of data for quantity demanded, and in Figure 1A–1, the demand curve would shift to the right. Such a shift is illustrated in Figure 1A-2. This type of change is usually called a "change in demand." Thus *change in demand* is used to denote a shift in the demand curve, while *change in quantity demanded* refers to a movement along it. The latter would occur if the price of broccoli changed with income and the price of other green veggies remaining constant. This was implicitly assumed earlier when we changed the price of broccoli from $0.80 to $0.70 per bn. and noted the movement from A to B along the demand curve in Figure 1A–1. When we

Figure 1A–2   A Change in Demand for Broccoli

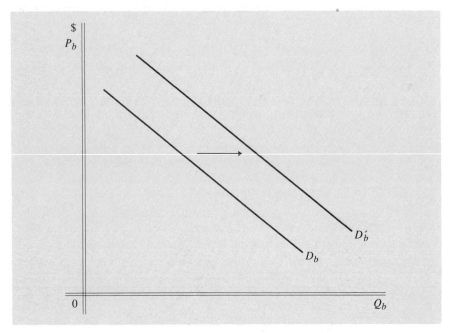

hold other variables constant while we change only one key variable, the phrase "other things equal" is often invoked to indicate that only *one* of the variables is being altered.

Since an increase in income—other things equal—will shift the demand curve to the right, a decrease in income will shift it to the left. This will be the case for most goods. (Exceptions will be discussed in Chapter 2.) If we consider the effect on demand for broccoli of a change in the price of other green vegetables (*substitutes* for broccoli) it is easy to see that the change in the price of a substitute will also shift the demand curve. In our example, if the prices of other green vegetables fall while consumer incomes remain constant, we can expect the demand for broccoli to decrease (demand curve for broccoli to shift to the left). Why? Because some consumers will substitute the other, now relatively cheaper, vegetables for broccoli. A change in the price of a substitute good will always shift the demand curve in the same fashion: to the right for an increase in the substitute's price and to the left for a decrease in the substitute's price. If a related good is a complement (something used *with* the good in question, rather than instead of it), the shift relation reverses. More will be said about this in Chapter 2.

The basics of demand analysis can be summarized as follows:

1. *Demand* is a functional relationship between the price of a good and the quantity demanded of it per time period.

2. The demand curve for a good normally slopes downward to the right, reflecting the law of demand.

3. A demand function states the relation between the quantity of a good consumers will buy and the values of several independent variables, including its own price, prices of related goods, income, and other relevant determinants of demand.

4. When a good's own price changes but other demand function variables remain constant, there is a *change in quantity demanded* (movement along the demand curve).

5. If one of the determinants of demand changes, the demand curve will shift (there will be a *change in demand*). The direction of that shift will depend on whether there is a direct or an inverse relation between that independent variable and consumers' purchases of the good in question.

■ ■ ■ ■ ■ ■ ■ ■ ■   SUPPLY AND THE SUPPLY CURVE

In economic analysis, the term *supply*, like demand, refers to a functional relationship. It is the relation between the various possible prices of a good and the *quantity supplied* by sellers of it per time period. Supply can also be represented as a schedule or a curve. For example, we might say that at a price of $.60 per bn. sellers of broccoli will be willing and able to bring to market a quantity supplied of 100,000 bn. per month. That would describe *one point* on their supply curve of broccoli. If they will bring to market 300,000 bn. at a price of $1.00 per bn., we have another point on their supply curve. Table 1A–2 is a supply schedule for broccoli, and Figure 1A–3 shows the broccoli supply curve. That curve has a positive slope (upward to the right), indicating that sellers will offer a larger quantity supplied at higher broccoli prices. We will often use upward-sloping supply curves in subsequent analyses, but occasionally we will consider circumstances where the supply curve does not slope upward. In the case

Table 1A–2   Supply of Broccoli

Price of Broccoli per Bunch (P_b)	Quantity Supplied of Broccoli per Month (Q_s)
$1.20	400,000
1.10	350,000
1.00	300,000
.90	250,000
.80	200,000
.70	150,000
.60	100,000
.50	50,000

Figure 1A–3   The Supply Curve of Broccoli

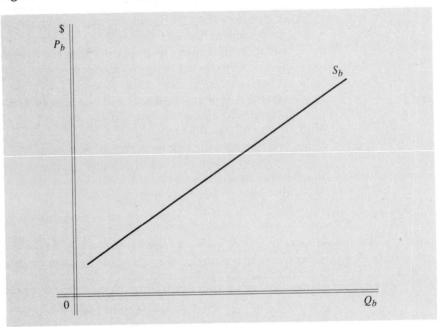

of broccoli, it would be easy to justify an upward-sloping supply curve, since production costs would be likely to go up as broccoli production increased and less-suitable land was brought into cultivation of broccoli.

Just as we noted the existence of a demand function behind the demand curve, there is a supply function behind the supply curve. That function relates the amount of a good sellers are willing and able to offer for sale to both its own price and other relevant independent variables known as the "determinants of supply." For broccoli, the supply function might be of the form $Q_s = f(P_b, P_v, IN_p)$, where Q_s is the number of bunches of broccoli sellers will bring to market per month, P_b is the price of broccoli per bunch, P_v is the price of an alternative product (something the producers might wish to supply instead of broccoli), and IN_p is an index of input prices. If one of the determinants of supply changes, the supply curve will shift. For example, a fall in the price of fertilizer might lead suppliers to be willing to grow and bring to market more broccoli per month at every possible broccoli price. Thus the supply curve of broccoli would shift to the right. Clearly, rising input prices would do the reverse.

■ ■ ■ ■ ■ ■ ■ ■   **DETERMINATION OF MARKET PRICE**

We are now ready to discuss the way supply and demand interact to determine market price. However, one caution is necessary. We will be assuming in what follows that the market in question (the broccoli market) is characterized by large numbers of sellers and buyers and that no individual firm or buyer in the market is powerful enough to affect the market price that is established. In other words, the going price that tends to hold for broccoli comes about as a result of the actions of the thousands of participants (buyers and sellers) in the market but not because any one of them is so large that he or she directly impacts the result. This is the condition known in economic theory as *perfect competition*. In a market characterized by perfect competition, the seller sees no need to lower the going price, since a large number of buyers are willing to pay that price. Similarly, the seller is aware that raising the price above the going level would result in zero sales, as the buyers know that a large number of sellers are willing and able to sell at the going price. For example, if broccoli is selling everywhere for $.80 a bunch, and seller Jilly Johnson decides she wants to charge $.85 per bn., a higher price will not result, because buyers will simply purchase 80-cent broccoli from the other sellers.

The "going price" we have mentioned is an *equilibrium* value toward which the actions of the multitude of sellers and buyers in the market will cause price to move. This can be explained easily if we combine the demand and supply curve diagrams introduced in the earlier figures into one graph, as in Figure 1A-4. Now, the upward-sloping supply curve of sellers intersects the demand curve of consumers at point *E*. Point *E* identifies the equilibrium values of both price and quantity demanded or

Figure 1A–4   Equilibrium in the Broccoli Market

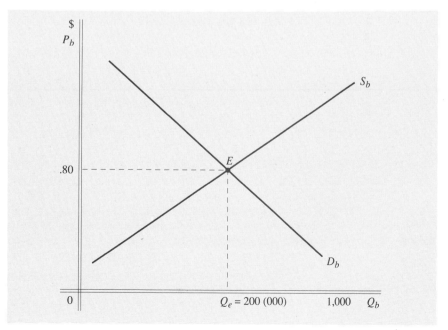

supplied, since if price is either greater or less than P_e, market forces will cause price to return to that level. Note, of course, that P_e is the only price that will equate the quantity demanded by buyers with the quantity supplied by sellers. This quantity, the equilibrium quantity, is labeled Q_e and conforms to 200,000, if the supply and demand curves are plotted from Tables 1A–1 and 1A-2.

The nature of the equilibrium at point E can be examined by asking what would happen if price were temporarily at some other value than P_e. In panel (a) of Figure 1A–5, suppose price is temporarily at P_H. This price is above the equilibrium price at E and results in a quantity supplied (Q_s) that exceeds quantity demanded (Q_d). As the diagram shows, there will be a surplus of broccoli in the market because sellers will want to sell more at price P_H than buyers will be willing and able to buy. Sellers will build up inventories of the stuff, and they will have to reduce price in order to get rid of it. Note that this will be true for any price above P_e. If, on the other hand, price is temporarily below P_e (as at price P_L in panel (b) of the figure), there will be a shortage of broccoli in the market, since quantity demanded (Q_d) will exceed quantity supplied (Q_s). Sellers will see their inventory levels drawn down and will be willing to increase quantity supplied only at higher prices. Consumers, as they become aware of the shortage, will be willing to pay higher prices. The result will be a tendency for price to rise until P_e is reached. Thus any price other than P_e is a disequilibrium price, which will bring on forces that will return the price to P_e and the quantity traded to an equilibrium volume of Q_e per month.

Figure 1A–5   Market Adjustment to Equilibrium

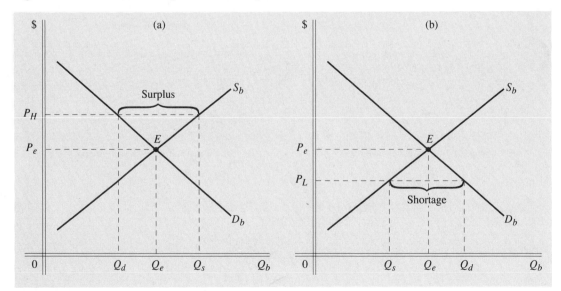

▪ ▪ ▪ ▪ ▪ ▪ ▪ ▪ ▪ ▪ CARRYOVER TO ANALYSIS OF OTHER MARKETS

Perfect competition is an idealized market structure that is only approximated by markets in the real world. Nonetheless, many markets tend to adjust in ways *similar* to those described in the perfectly competitive case, so it is frequently useful to think of the frictionless, self-regulating market of perfect competition as the point of departure for examining markets where, perhaps, sellers are not so numerous and adjustments are not so smooth or automatic. Even in those situations, we will have to ask what we think sellers will do in terms of quantity supplied at various prices and what the demand of consumers for their product looks like. The notions about demand and supply that have been reviewed here will enter the picture time and time again, and we will have to consider whether and how to modify them on a case-by-case basis.

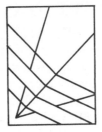

Revenue of the Firm

In his slapstick comedy, *Spaceballs*, Hollywood writer-producer-director-actor-comedian (did we leave anything out?) Mel Brooks, playing the great teacher "Yogurt," sets out to reveal the secret of The Force:[1] "Moichandising!" he declares to his young protégé in an accent betraying the urban East Coast, and goes on to reveal how high-powered marketing of toys, T-shirts, posters, and other products related to the movie will be a source of great wealth and power.

Certainly, marketing is important. Billions are spent on it each year, and broadcasters remind us annually how much it costs to buy an advertising minute during such spectacles as the Super Bowl. It seems that ads are showing up everywhere—not just on shopping carts and city buses but in church bulletins, on cash-register receipts, and now—whether by popular request or not—in some spots you cannot help but notice in washrooms at restaurants and other public establishments.[2]

What does the consumer want? Can you introduce new products that respond to consumer wants? Can businesses manipulate the wants of consumers? In the 1960s it was frequently argued that businesses could and did manipulate consumer wants.[3] An oft-cited example is the tailfins that appeared on certain automobiles just before the dawn of that decade—styling that served no purpose but was touted to consumers as the wave of the future. It was argued that such frills did not cater to any preexisting

---

[1] In his own inimitable fashion, Brooks had renamed it "The Schwartz."

[2] "Washroom Ads: 'Paid-for Graffiti,'" *Newsweek* (February 20, 1989), p. 42

[3] See John Kenneth Galbraith, "Time and the New Industrial State," *American Economic Review* (May 1988), pp. 373–382, as well as John Kenneth Galbraith and M. S. Randhawa, *The New Industrial State* (Boston: Houghton Mifflin, 1967), pp. 211–212.

want, but that the desire for tailfins was created in the consumer's mind by the producer. The producer was characterized as not caring much about what the consumer wanted and being interested only in what resulted in the greatest profit for the firm.

In the 1990s, while the emphasis on the bottom line remains very much alive, some businesses are coming around to the view that the bottom line will not look good if consumers' wants are not carefully attended to. Ford Motor Company Chairman Donald E. Petersen is reported to have said, "If we aren't customer-driven, our cars won't be either." Thus Ford and many other companies have solicited consumer input, not only regarding how satisfied customers are with the products and services they have chosen to buy, but also to determine what they want to see in the way of new products and product improvements. Ford, for example, now surveys about 2.5 million customers per year and has invited customers to "focus groups" that try to unravel design problems and anticipate consumer preferences.[4]

Despite the new attention businesses are paying to consumer wants, there is evidence that consumers are far from satisifed with what they are getting. A survey of American consumers done on behalf of *The Wall Street Journal* in 1989 found that only 5 percent believed business was "listening to them and striving to do its best." Consumers' attitudes were summed up by this quote from a 32-year-old professional in the computer industry:

> I live in the best country on the face of the earth, so I guess I'll put up with high prices, mediocre quality, and poor service.[5]

If consumers feel this way about American business, it presents business managers with both a challenge and an opportunity. Clearly, satisfied customers are beneficial to managers and their firms. Likewise, customer satisfaction is one of the ingredients that can make for a healthy bottom line. But businesses cannot afford blind pursuit of revenue enhancement, either through better marketing or improved customer satisfaction strategies, to the exclusion of other considerations.

In the final analysis, it is the difference between revenue and *cost* that determines a firm's profits; therefore the decisions that affect *both* of these factors are critical to business operations. It is no cause for amazement, then, that firms exert so much effort and expense trying to increase revenue while attempting to keep costs at as low a level as possible, *given a particular level of output*. Still, it is clear that without a market for its product, a firm will not be successful—no matter how low its costs. Accordingly, we emphasize the importance of managerial decisions relating to demand for a firm's product by discussing first how the firm manager should cope

■ ■ ■ ■ ■ ■

[4] "King Customer," *Business Week* (March 12, 1990), pp. 88–94.
[5] Alix M. Friedman, "Most Consumers Shun Luxuries, Seek Few Frills but Better Service," *The Wall Street Journal*, September 19, 1989, p. B1.

with both external and internal factors that affect dollar sales and, ultimately, the firm's success or failure. As we shall see early in this chapter, the term for total dollar sales is *total revenue* in the language of economists, and it will be our main focus for the present. Later, in Chapters 4 and 5, we will address the issue of cost, examining both the nature of the production process and its relation to the expenses the firm incurs in supplying output to its customers.

■ ■ ■ ■ ■ ■ ■ ■ ■ ADVERTISING, CONSUMER DEMAND, AND BUSINESS RESEARCH

The fact that U.S. corporations now spend $8 to $10 billion per year on network television advertising certainly suggests that they believe consumer demand for their products will be significantly affected as a result.[6] However, it should also be clear that advertising is not the only factor affecting the quantity that consumers demand of a particular product. In spite of advertising, consumers preferred "old" Coca Cola (now Classic Coke) to "new" Coke, and the RCA video disc player was a flop. Also, much to its dismay, top management in the automobile industry has discovered that many consumers now prefer Japanese cars to those produced by U.S. firms. In fact, General Motors is so concerned about what factors influence the demand for its automobiles that it invests money in a statistical analysis department, whose task, among other things, is to estimate the impact of various factors such as advertising, price, and personal income on the quantity of GM cars that potential consumers will purchase. Ford, too, has engaged in expensive research programs to determine both what consumers want to see in new cars and what they dislike about existing products.[7] Thus successful firm managers cannot simply assume that advertising expenditures will solve all revenue problems; they must recognize that diverse factors affect product sales.

In fact, while consumers sometimes are entertained by whimsical and amusing ads, there is growing evidence that advertising that is offensive or out of place can create quite a backlash. *Time* magazine reported in 1989 that consumers were putting up substantial resistance to advertising shorts run in movie theaters:

■ ■ ■ ■ ■ ■

[6] "'Ad Space' Now Has a Whole New Meaning," *Business Week* (July 29, 1985), p. 52.

[7] "King Customer," *Business Week* (March 12, 1990), pp. 88–94. Research by General Motors on automobile demand has been going on for many years. An interesting older study of automobile demand done by one of their economists is H. F. Gallasch, Jr., "Elasticities of Demand for New Automobiles" (Societal Analysis Department, Research Laboratories, General Motors Corporation, Warren, Michigan, May 21, 1976).

> Many are starting to rebel, and hoots and howls are common when commercials flash onto screens in New York City, where ticket prices run as high as $7.50.[8]

Similarly, *Business Week* reported in 1990,

> . . . ad executives say the hostility now is greater than ever before. "I have never seen such a volume and intensity of troubles with advertising," says . . . a retired chairman of Foote, Cone, and Belding Communications, Inc.[9]

In the face of all this, firms are becoming more and more interested in marketing in a much broader sense—the entire process of moving goods from the producer to the consumers. This far more inclusive view of marketing stresses the importance of determining consumer attitudes and wants and then analyzing the profitability aspect of proposed goods and services. As *Business Week* noted many years ago, firms have learned that decisions involving new products require

> . . . conducting preliminary research, market identification, and product development; testing consumer reaction to both product and price; working out production capacities and costs; determining distribution; *and then deciding on advertising and promotion strategies.* [Emphasis added.][10]

A recent development in consumer market research is called "VALS"—the consumer Values and Lifestyles program of SRI International (formerly Stanford Research Institute). This methodology divides consumers into categories based on their self-images, goals, and the products they use.[11] It looks at "who consumers are, how they live, what they buy—and more important, why they buy it."[12] This approach to consumer research is more comprehensive than the old one of looking only at demographic characteristics of consumers—age, education, income, and number of children, for example. Researchers are finding that consumers who used to have similar buying patterns now are parts of many different groups with diverse needs and interests. While the preceding steps are still important, a new wave in businesses' efforts to attract the consumer directs attention to service and customer satisfaction. Naturally, this strategy will require

---

■ ■ ■ ■ ■ ■

[8] "Hoots and Howls at Ads," *Time* (September 18, 1989), p. 70.

[9] "Consumers Are Getting Mad, Mad, Mad, Mad at Mad Ave.," *Business Week* (April 30, 1990), p. 70.

[10] "How GM Manages Its Billion Dollar R&D Program," *Business Week* (June 28, 1976), p. 54.

[11] Karen Malkowski, "Company Zestful in Targeting ZIP Code Areas," San Antonio *Express-News*, April 14, 1991, pp. 1-G, 2-G; and James Atlas, "Beyond Demographics," *The Atlantic* (October 1984), pp. 49–58.

[12] "Wizards of Marketing," *Newsweek* (July 22, 1985), p. 42.

continuing emphasis on the wants and preferences of consumers as well as a great deal of research on how to attract—and keep—customers.

Understanding what economists are saying about these issues requires that you comprehend their special terminology and the precise definitions they attach to everyday expressions such as "changes in demand." Therefore we shall first define *demand* and other revenue terms in our language. Later in this chapter, we provide some insights into what things influence the demand for a firm's product and how to deal with them, so that with proper management of these factors and their costs, the firm can achieve maximum profits. Most important, we hope that when you finish this chapter you will have gained a great respect for the power that consumers have in determining the success of an enterprise.

■ ■ ■ ■ ■ ■ ■ ■   THE DEMAND FUNCTION

A **demand function** states how each of a number of relevant variables affects the amount of a good or service consumers will buy during some time period.

The **demand function** for a firm's product (or service) relates the quantities of a product that consumers would like to purchase during some specific period to the variables that influence a consumer's decision to buy or not to buy the good. Such variables often include the price of the product, the prices of other related goods, consumers' incomes, the season of the year, and dollars spent on advertising. For example, the quantity of a particular brand (Brand X) of microwave oven purchased by consumers during a year may be a function of the price of the oven, the price of a competing brand of oven, the number of women who work outside the home, consumer annual disposable income, and dollars spent yearly on advertising. We could represent this relationship in functional notation as

$$Q_x = f(P_x, P_y, E_w, I, A),$$

where

Q_x = quantity demanded per year of Brand X,
P_x = price of Brand X,
P_y = price of Brand Y,
E_w = number of women who are employed,
 I = average annual household disposable income, and
 A = dollars spent per year on advertising.

When the firm plans its operations, it would be useful for it to know the exact functional relationship between the quantity demanded of its product (Q_x) and the independent variables (P_x, P_y, E_w, I, and A) that affect that quantity. We should note, however, that some of the independent variables in the demand function are completely beyond the control of the firm. The firm cannot significantly affect average household annual income or the number of women employed, even though its managers certainly should recognize how changes in these variables affect the quantity it can sell of its product. The firm may also not be able to affect the price of a competing good. Advertising and the price set for the firm's product, on the other hand, are variables controlled by management.

The price that the firm charges for its product is one of the variables that the firm can usually control. Therefore the firm often finds it particularly useful to give special attention to the relationship between quantity demanded over some specific time period and possible prices that the firm might charge during that period. The graphical representation of this relationship between price and quantity demanded is called the **demand curve**.

A **demand curve** is a curve or line showing the relation between the quantity demanded per time period of a good or service and various possible prices of that good or service

For example, assume our hypothetical demand function for Brand X microwave ovens purchased per year had the following specific relationship:

$$Q_x = 26,500 - 100P_x + 25P_y + .0001E_w + 2.6I + .02A$$

and that $P_x = \$400$, $P_y = \$500$, $E_w = 40,000,000$, $I = \$10,000$, and $A = \$50,000$. Solving for Q_x (the number of Brand X microwave ovens purchased per year), by letting the independent variables take on these values, we find that

$$Q_x = 26,500 - 40,000 + 12,500 + 4,000 + 26,000 + 1,000$$
$$= 30,000 \text{ ovens per year.}$$

If all of the independent variables remain at the values just stated, the firm will sell 30,000 microwave ovens per year.

If we hold all the variables except Q_x and P_x constant, we can graph the demand curve for Brand X ovens as shown in Figure 2–1. With all variables except P_x and Q_x held constant, the demand function becomes $Q_x = 70,000 - 100P_x$, which is the equation for the straight line plotted in the figure.

Change in demand refers to the shift in a demand curve that occurs when a demand function variable other than the own price of the item in question changes.

Change in Demand

If one of the variables held constant when we drew the demand curve should change, the demand curve shifts. We call this event a **change in demand**. For example, if average household income falls to $5,000 or rises to $15,000, the demand curve drawn in Figure 2–1 will shift, as shown in Figure 2–2. A change in demand, therefore, refers to a shift in the demand curve—as contrasted with a **change in quantity demanded**, which refers simply to a change in the amount of a good or service that consumers are willing to purchase over some time period *because of a change in the price* of the good. The behavior of consumers in the latter situation is represented by a different point on the same demand curve. A change in quantity demanded as P_x changes from $400 to $500 is illustrated in Figure 2–3.

Change in quantity demanded refers to a movement along the demand curve for a given good or service in response to a change in its own price.

Figure 2–1   Demand Curve for Brand X Microwave Ovens

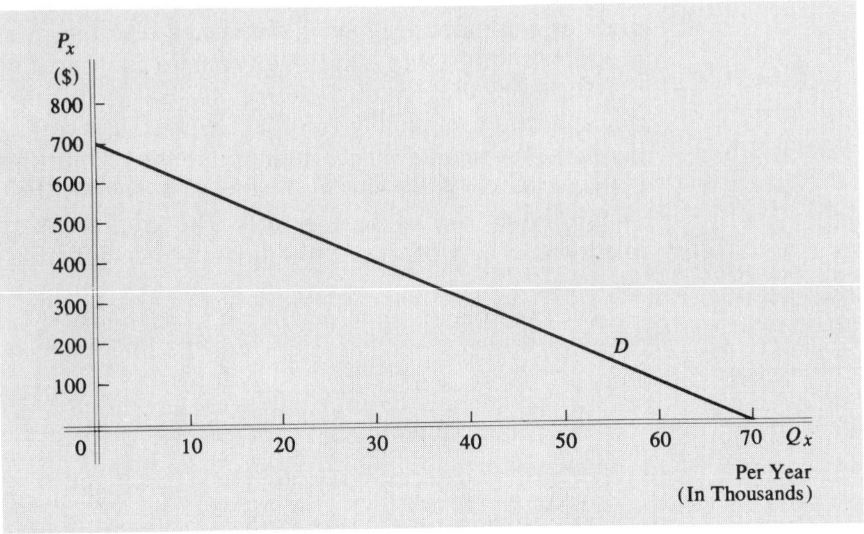

This graph depicts the demand curve, D, for Brand X microwave ovens. P_x represents the price of an oven, and Q_x is quantity demanded of ovens (in thousands) per year. At a price of $700 apiece, no ovens would be purchased. If the ovens were given away, 70,000 would be demanded per year.

Figure 2–2   Changes in Demand

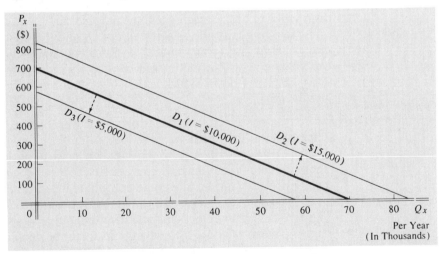

A change in income will cause the demand curve for Brand X microwave ovens to shift. If income increases from $10,000 to $15,000, demand will increase. If income decreases from $10,000 to $5,000, demand will decrease.

Figure 2–3   Change in Quantity Demanded

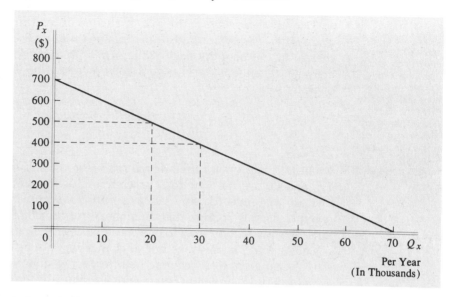

A change in the quantity demanded of microwave ovens occurs if there is a change in the price of the ovens. For example, if the price falls from $500 to $400, the quantity demanded will increase by 10,000 ovens per year.

Demand and Revenue

Total revenue is the total dollar sales of a firm during some particular time period. It is equal to the price of the product multiplied by the quantity sold.

The **total revenue** (total dollar sales) of a firm is directly related to the demand for the firm's product. In fact, if we know the demand curve for a firm's product and the price set by the firm, we can determine the firm's total revenue, which is just price times quantity demanded. Total revenue, then, is a function of price and quantity demanded, or $TR = g(P, Q)$. Since price is a function of quantity sold, we can write price in terms of quantity and then write total revenue as a function only of quantity sold. Thus, for our microwave oven manufacturer,

$$P_x = 700 - .01Q_x \quad \text{and} \quad TR = P_xQ_x = (700 - .01Q_x)(Q_x) = 700Q_x - .01Q_x^2.$$

Average revenue is the revenue received per unit of product sold. It is equal to total revenue divided by quantity sold and is equal to price if all units are sold at the same price.

Average revenue is total revenue divided by quantity demanded, or *price.* [$AR = TR/Q = (P \times Q)/Q = P$, where AR is average revenue, TR is total revenue, Q is quantity demanded, and P is price.] We should note that this result (that average revenue is equal to price) requires that all buyers be charged the same price for the product, which we shall assume is the case throughout most of this text. The special case of multiple prices for a single product will be discussed in Chapter 10. For the microwave

Marginal revenue is the rate of change of total revenue from selling one more unit of the product. **Arc marginal revenue** gives the average rate of change of total revenue with respect to quantity sold over some range of output.

oven demand curve, the *AR* formula is the same as the price equation we employed to get total revenue. In other words, $AR = P = 700 - .01Q_x$.

Marginal revenue is the rate of change of total revenue with respect to quantity sold; it indicates how total revenue will change if there is a change in the quantity sold of the firm's product. An approximation of marginal revenue is the change in total revenue divided by the change in quantity sold, or

$$\text{Arc } MR = \frac{\Delta TR}{\Delta Q} = \frac{TR_2 - TR_1}{Q_2 - Q_1},$$

where TR_1 and Q_1 are the original total revenue and level of output, and TR_2 and Q_2 are the new total revenue and level of output, respectively. The arc marginal revenue value is only an approximation of marginal revenue. That is because this value measures the *average* rate of change of total revenue with respect to quantity sold over the range of output under consideration. This average rate of change will not be exactly equal to the rate of change of total revenue with respect to quantity at *some particular output level* if this rate of change is different for different levels of output. We shall call this approximation **arc marginal revenue**, since it measures the average rate of change of total revenue with respect to quantity sold over some range of output or over some arc.[13]

The three fundamental revenue concepts are **total revenue**, **average revenue**, and **marginal revenue**, where:
Total revenue
$= P \times Q$.
Average revenue
$= TR/Q = P$.
Marginal revenue
$= \frac{\Delta TR}{\Delta Q}$.

The relationships between the total revenue, average revenue, and marginal revenue functions for the manufacturer of Brand *X* microwave ovens are illustrated in Figure 2–4 and Table 2–1. Total revenue is depicted in the lower graph, while marginal revenue and average revenue are depicted in the upper graph. Geometrically, average revenue at some quantity is the slope of a line drawn from the origin to the point on the *TR* curve corresponding to that level of output. The average revenue in Figure 2–4 is always decreasing, as can be seen from a comparison of the slopes of line segments *OA* and *OB* in the lower graph. We should emphasize that since the *AR* curve gives the relationship between price and quantity demanded for a firm, the *average revenue curve is also the firm's demand curve.*

■ ■ ■ ■ ■ ■
[13] Technically, marginal revenue at a particular output level is the value of the derivative of the total revenue function with respect to quantity, dTR/dQ, at that point. Thus, for the manufacturer of Brand *X* microwave ovens discussed above,

$$TR = 700Q_x - .01Q_x^2, \text{ and}$$
$$MR = dTR/dQ = 700 - .02Q_x.$$

At an output level of 30,000 units, marginal revenue is $100. However, between $Q_x = 20,000$ and $Q_x = 30,000$, *arc* marginal revenue is $200, since $\Delta TR = \$2,000,000$ and $\Delta Q_x = 10,000$ (as shown in Table 2-1).

Figure 2–4   Geometrical Relationships Among Average Revenue, Marginal Revenue, and Total Revenue for Brand X Microwave Ovens

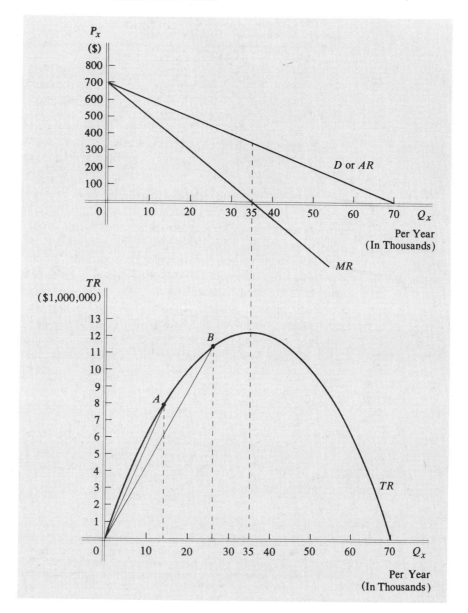

This graph depicts the geometrical relationships among average revenue (AR), marginal revenue (MR), and total revenue (TR) for Brand X microwave ovens. Marginal revenue is zero at a quantity of 35,000 ovens per month—the same point where total revenue is at a maximum. With a linear, downward-sloping demand curve, MR reaches zero at a quantity level (35,000 units) one half as large as that where average revenue is zero.

Table 2–1   Relationships Among Price, Total Revenue, and Arc
Marginal Revenue for Brand X Microwave Ovens

Price of X (Average Revenue)	Quantity of X Demanded	Total Revenue (P × Q)	Arc Marginal Revenue $\left(\frac{\Delta TR}{\Delta Q}\right)$
$700	0	0	
			$600
600	10,000	$ 6,000,000	
			400
500	20,000	10,000,000	
			200
400	30,000	12,000,000	
			0
300	40,000	12,000,000	
			−200
200	50,000	10,000,000	
			−400
100	60,000	6,000,000	

Marginal revenue at some particular quantity is the slope of the TR curve at that quantity of output. In Figure 2–4, marginal revenue is also always decreasing and is equal to zero when total revenue reaches a maximum, at $Q_x = 35,000$.[14] Moreover, as long as the AR curve is linear, the MR curve will be linear with a slope twice as steep as the AR curve and will thus intersect the quantity axis at a level of output half as large as that at the point where the demand curve intersects the same axis.[15]

Both Figure 2–4 and Table 2–1 illustrate that as long as price must decrease in order for the firm to increase the quantity demanded of its product, marginal revenue is less than price. Marginal revenue is less than price because we are assuming that to sell a larger quantity, the firm must

■ ■ ■ ■ ■ ■
[14] For TR to be at a maximum (or minimum) at a specific level of output, dTR/dQ must be equal to zero. Thus,

$$\frac{dTR}{dQ} = MR = 700 - .02Q_x = 0,$$

$$- .02Q_x = -700, \quad \text{or}$$
$$Q_x = 35,000.$$

The second derivative

$$\frac{d^2TR}{dQ^2} = \frac{dMR}{dQ} = -.02,$$

which is less than zero so that the second-order condition for a maximum is satisfied.

[15] If $TR = 700Q_x - .01Q_x^2$, then $AR = TR/Q = 700 - .01Q_x$ and, as stated above, $MR = 700 - .02Q_x$. The slope of the marginal revenue curve is $-.02$, which is twice as steep as the slope $(-.01)$ of the average revenue curve. In more general terms, if

$$AR = a - bQ, \quad \text{then}$$
$$TR = aQ - bQ^2, \quad \text{and}$$
$$MR = a - 2bQ.$$

The slope of the marginal revenue curve is $-2b$, which is exactly twice the slope of the average revenue curve.

lower its price on *all* units sold. Hence, if the firm in Table 2–1 wishes to sell 30,000 units rather than 20,000, it must lower the price—from $500 to $400—on *all 30,000* of the units. Therefore the firm gives up the opportunity to sell the first 20,000 units at a price $100 higher.

We can show the effect of this price decrease on the revenue from the first 20,000 units sold as follows:

Gain in revenue from sale of an additional
   10,000 units = 10,000 × $400   = $4,000,000
Loss in revenue from sale of first 20,000 units
   at $400 rather than $500 = 20,000 × (−$100) = −$2,000,000
Net increase in total revenue $2,000,000

$$\text{Marginal revenue} = \frac{\Delta TR}{\Delta Q} = \frac{\$2,000,000}{10,000} = \$200.$$

If the firm did not have to lower price to sell a larger quantity, the demand curve would be a horizontal line and price would equal marginal revenue, as shown in Figure 2–5.[16]

Figure 2–5   Horizontal Demand Curve ($P = MR$)

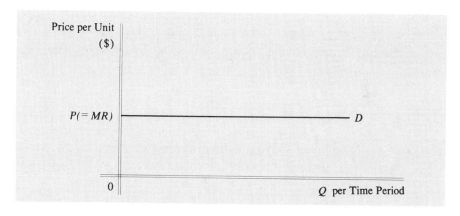

D is a horizontal demand curve. A firm can sell as many units of its product as it wishes to at the going market price. Price and marginal revenue are equal.

■ ■ ■ ■ ■ ■
[16] If $TR = P \times Q$, then

$$MR = \frac{dTR}{dQ} = P + Q\left(\frac{dP}{dQ}\right),$$

using the product rule for differentiation. If price does not change as quantity sold changes, $(dP/dQ) = 0$, and $MR = P$.

The relationships among demand and total and marginal revenue will be discussed later in this chapter. Moreover, in Chapter 6 we shall see that marginal revenue plays a very important role in helping the firm locate its profit-maximizing level of output.

Firm Demand Versus Industry Demand

The demand function that we have been discussing relates the quantity purchased of a particular brand of microwave oven (Brand X) to other variables. Since there is more than one brand of microwave oven available, we could also talk about the factors that determine the total number of microwave ovens (all brands) purchased during a year. This relationship is the *industry demand function*—as contrasted with the demand function for Brand X microwave ovens, which is the demand function for a firm. Many of the same variables will appear in the industry demand function as in the demand function of the firm, although their coefficients will usually be different. For example, the price of Brand Y will affect the industry quantity demanded, but its coefficient will probably be negative, indicating that an increase in P_y will *decrease* the total quantity of microwave ovens demanded. In addition, we would expect that the coefficients of (1) the number of women employed variable and (2) the average household annual income variable will be larger in the industry demand function than in that of the firm, which indicates that a change in either one of these variables will have a greater effect on the *total quantity demanded* of microwave ovens than on the quantity demanded of Brand X. The size of the coefficient of the advertising dollars variable will depend on the extent that firm advertising serves to increase overall quantity demanded of microwave ovens—as opposed to merely increasing the quantity demanded of the microwave ovens of one firm at the expense of the sales of another firm.

Although most of the demand functions presented in this chapter are demand functions for the product of a *firm*, the concepts discussed can generally be applied to either industry or firm demand functions.

■ ■ ■ ■ ■ ■ ■ ■ ■ DETERMINANTS OF DEMAND

The **determinants of demand** for a given good or service are demand function variables other than its own price.

It is usual to refer to any demand function variable that will cause a demand curve to shift as a **determinant of demand**. In other words, for Brand X microwave ovens, all of the variables on the right-hand side of the demand function equation except P_x are determinants of demand.

The determinants of demand are what cause consumers to change their view of how much they will buy of a given good or service at all possible prices that could be charged for it. Exactly what they are will depend on the good in question. For example, how many ice-cold drinks you want to buy at various possible prices is likely to depend on how hot

Numerical Example: The Demand for Draperies

Alicia Gartiz has estimated the following demand function for economical draperies sold by her firm, Pleats, Inc.:

$$Q_d = 1,200 - 20P_d + .1I + .08A,$$

where

Q_d = quantity demanded of pairs of drapes
P_d = price per pair of drapes
I = per capita income in the market area
A = her firm's advertising expenditure.

All data are on a monthly basis. The current values of the income and advertising variables are, respectively, $1,200 per month and $4,000 per month.

1. Assuming the above values for I and A remain constant, what is the equation of the demand curve for Pleats, Inc.'s drapes?
2. If Alicia wished to obtain the maximum monthly sales revenue, given the data above, what price would she charge and what would the revenue be?

Answer

1. Substituting the stated values into the demand function, we have $Q_d = 1,200 - 20P_d + .1(1,200) + .08(4,000)$, or $Q_d = 1,640 - 20P_d$.
2. The maximum total revenue will occur at the midpoint of the demand curve, where MR is zero and $Q_d = 820$. There, P_d will be $41. Total revenue will be $41(820) = $33,620. From the stated demand curve, $P_d = 82 - .05Q_d$, and, since MR will have the same intercept as AR on the vertical axis but be zero at the quantity corresponding to the midpoint of AR, $MR = 82 - .1Q_d$. This relationship holds because the MR curve's slope is twice as steep as that of the AR curve. Setting MR equal to zero locates maximum TR, or $82 - .1Q_d = 0$, so $Q_d = 820$. By substitution, $P_d = 82 - .05(820) = 41$.

the weather is. It would therefore be reasonable to include some measure of this (degrees Fahrenheit or Celsius) in the demand function for ice-cold drinks. But the weather is not likely to have a significant effect on your demand for ham sandwiches or pizza, and one would not likely include a weather variable in the demand functions for them.

If we tried to list all possible determinants of demand for goods and services, we would probably have a very long list. The following, however, are some of the most widely applicable:

1. Consumer incomes
2. Prices of related goods and services
3. Consumer tastes
4. Number of consumers in the market
5. Credit terms on loans
6. Advertising

We will consider each of these in turn, starting with two that are almost universally important, income and prices of related goods. Normally, as consumers' incomes increase, they tend to purchase more goods and services. If an individual consumer purchases more of a good when his or her income increases, that good is said to be a **normal good** with respect to income. If the reverse occurs, the good is an **inferior good**. It is often argued that hamburger is an inferior good for many people, since they will consume less hamburger and more of other meats (steaks, roast beef) if their incomes increase. In a demand function, a negative sign on the coefficient of the income variable indicates an inferior good, while the coefficient of the income term for a normal good will be positive. For a normal good, an increase in income will shift the demand curve to the right, while a decrease in income will shift it to the left. The reverse occurs for an inferior good.

The relation of the quantity purchased of a given good to the price of a related good depends, in a very basic sense, on whether the two are substitutes or complements. In the case of **substitute goods**, one can be used in place of the other and will, in fact, be substituted if one becomes relatively cheaper than the other. For example, frozen yogurt and ice cream are substitutes, and if the price of frozen yogurt drops while that of ice cream does not, some people will purchase yogurt instead of ice cream. In the demand function for ice cream, the coefficient of the price of the related good, frozen yogurt, would have a positive sign, indicating that a rise in the yogurt price would lead to greater quantity sold of ice cream, while a fall in the yogurt price would do the reverse. Likewise, one would expect a demand function for frozen yogurt to include the price of ice cream as an independent variable, with the coefficient taking a positive sign to indicate the substitute nature of the relation between the two goods. An increase in the price of a substitute, then, will shift the demand curve for a given good to the right, while a decrease in the price of a substitute will do the reverse.

For **complementary goods**, goods that are used together, the coefficient of the related good's price will be negative. For example, lettuce and salad dressing are complementary goods. If lettuce prices rise dramatically (as they have when freezing weather in California, Florida, and Texas has

A **normal good** displays a positive relation between consumer purchases and income.

An **inferior good** displays a negative relation between consumer purchases and income.

A **substitute good** is a good that can be used in place of some other good.

Complementary goods are generally used with one another.

spoiled winter crops), people will buy less lettuce *and* less salad dressing. Thus the price of lettuce is a determinant of the demand for salad dressing. Lettuce price would appear in a demand function for salad dressing with a negative coefficient in front of it, since an increase in that price would lead to a reduction in purchases of dressing (demand curve for dressing shifts to the left).

Clearly, consumer tastes can serve as a determinant of demand also, but they are not always easy to measure. Sometimes a proxy variable for them can be used; for example, percent of consumers in a given age group or ethnic group. If a given good appeals to the particular preferences of teenagers, the percentage of teenagers in the market area might serve as a good proxy for taste in the demand function. Number of consumers in the market is also an important determinant of demand. Clearly, the demand curve for any good or service will shift to the right if more consumers enter the market for it. A good example would be the demand for housing in Florida, which has increased dramatically as older people from all parts of the United States have decided to retire there.

The remaining items on our determinants-of-demand list are credit terms and advertising. Credit terms (availability of loans as well as the interest rate on them) are especially important demand function variables for *durable goods*—goods that last a long time and for which purchases can be postponed for some length of time. Examples are houses, cars, and large home appliances like washers and dryers. The housing market reacts greatly to changes in availability of home mortgages and changes in mortgage interest rates. If interest rates increase or loans simply become difficult to qualify for, the demand for both new and used homes will fall. Likewise, people will postpone new car purchases if credit terms are unfavorable, and automobile manufacturers are well aware that sales can be stimulated by offering buyer incentives in the form of easy credit terms. Advertising, too, can shift the demand curve, and firms spend huge sums on it in attempts to do so. Normally, we expect increases in advertising expenditure by an individual firm to lead to a rightward shift of the demand curve for its product. However, in the face of competing advertising by rival firms, it is possible for this impact to be canceled out.

■ ■ ■ ■ ■ ■ ■ ■   **A NOTE ON DETERMINANTS OF SUPPLY**

Determinants of supply are those variables other than a good's own price that change the quantity of the good sellers are willing and able to sell.

A supply function relates the amount that sellers will offer of a good to the independent variables that determine it. For example, a supply function for frozen yogurt might include as independent variables the price of frozen yogurt, the prices of the inputs used to make the yogurt, the prices of alternative products, and the number of suppliers in the market. The **determinants of supply** are those variables other than a good's own price that will increase or decrease the quantity of the good sellers are willing and able to sell. Besides the variables already mentioned, these might include government tax or subsidy policies, technology, and producer expectations about future market conditions.

If all of the determinants of supply remain constant, we can identify the supply curve of a given good as the curve or line showing the quantity of it that sellers will place on the market at various possible prices. The supply curve of a seller may slope upward to the right, indicating that the quantity supplied is a rising function of price. It probably does slope upward in many cases. (Figure 1A–3, in the appendix to Chapter 1, shows an example of an upward-sloping supply curve.) Later, when we examine market structures, more will be said about supply. However, the focus of the present chapter is demand, not supply, and it will be sufficient at this point to note that movements along a supply curve for a given good (changes in quantity supplied) take place when, other things equal, the price of the good itself changes. The entire supply curve will shift, however, when one of the determinants of supply changes. (If you are unfamiliar with basic demand and supply analysis, read the appendix that follows Chapter 1.)

■ ■ ■ ■ ■ ■ ■ ■ ■ ## ELASTICITY OF DEMAND

The managers of a firm must pay close attention to the responsiveness of the quantity demanded of its product to various factors, for only by understanding these relationships can they hope to make reliable predictions of sales. As we stated previously, the quantity demanded of a firm's product is determined both by factors outside the firm's control and by factors such as price and advertising, which are often within its control. The ability to predict revenue is crucial, for without an adequate level of sales relative to costs, the firm cannot be successful.

One measure of such responsiveness that is feasible if the demand function for the firm's product is known is merely to substitute different values for the independent variables in that function and then solve for the resulting quantity demanded and total revenue. However, it is also often useful for a firm to know the relative responsiveness of quantity demanded of its product to changes in the values of the variables that it knows affect that demand. Roughly speaking, the relative responsiveness of quantity demanded of Brand X to a change in some variable Z is defined as the percentage change in Q_x divided by the percentage change in Z, or

$$e_z = \frac{\text{percentage change in } Q_x}{\text{percentage change in } Z}.$$

This responsiveness is called the *elasticity of demand* for Product X with respect to variable Z.

Arc versus Point Elasticity

Point elasticity of demand (for X) with respect to Z refers to the elasticity of demand *given* (or at) some specific value for Q_x and Z. Since the point elasticity of demand formula usually involves the use of partial derivatives, we shall place our discussion of such elasticities in footnotes and concentrate on *arc elasticity* in the text. The arc elasticity of demand with respect to variable Z refers to the average responsiveness of Q_x to a change in Z between two different values of Z, Z_1 and Z_2. The formula for arc elasticity of demand with respect to Z is given by[17]

$$e_z = \frac{\Delta Q_x}{\dfrac{Q_{x_2} + Q_{x_1}}{2}} \div \frac{\Delta Z}{\dfrac{Z_2 + Z_1}{2}}, \quad \text{or} \quad \frac{\Delta Q_x}{\Delta Z} \cdot \frac{Z_2 + Z_1}{Q_{x_2} + Q_{x_1}}.$$

Since with arc elasticity we are trying to measure the average responsiveness of Q_x to changes in Z *over some range of* Z, we use an average of the first and second values of both Q_x and Z.

For example, let us examine the elasticity of demand of Brand X microwave ovens with respect to P_x. The demand function given earlier in this chapter was

$$Q_x = 26,500 - 100P_x + 25P_y + .0001E_w + 2.6I + .02A,$$

and we said that if $P_x = \$400$, $P_y = \$500$, $E_w = 40,000,000$, $I = \$10,000$, and $A = \$50,000$, then $Q_x = 30,000$.[18] The arc price elasticity of demand between $P_x = \$400$ and $P_x = \$500$ is given by

$$e_p = \frac{\Delta Q_x}{\Delta P_x} \cdot \frac{P_{x_2} + P_{x_1}}{Q_{x_2} + Q_{x_1}} = \frac{Q_{x_2} - Q_{x_1}}{P_{x_2} - P_{x_1}} \cdot \frac{P_{x_2} + P_{x_1}}{Q_{x_2} + Q_{x_1}} = \frac{-10,000}{100} \cdot \frac{900}{50,000} = -1.8.$$

The preceding equation assumes that $P_{x_2} = \$500$ and $P_{x_1} = \$400$, or that a price *increase* has occurred. However, a price decrease over this same range would also result in an elasticity coefficient of -1.8. This result holds because if price falls from $500 to $400, then the change in price will

■ ■ ■ ■ ■ ■

[17] The general formula for point elasticity of demand for good X with respect to variable Z is

$$e_z = \left(\frac{\partial Q_x}{\partial Z}\right)\left(\frac{Z}{Q_x}\right), \quad \text{or} \quad e_z = \left(\frac{dQ_x}{dZ}\right)\left(\frac{Z}{Q_x}\right),$$

if Q_x is a function solely of Z.

[18] At that point, the price elasticity of demand for Q_x is given by

$$e_p = \left(\frac{\partial Q_x}{\partial P_x}\right)\left(\frac{P_x}{Q_x}\right) = -100\left(\frac{400}{30,000}\right) = -1.33.$$

be −$100 and the change in quantity demanded will be +10,000. Therefore the only change in the elasticity calculation occurs in the signs of the numerator and denominator of $\Delta Q_x / \Delta P_x$.

We shall examine the concept of price elasticity of demand further in the next section.

Price elasticity of demand measures the degree of responsiveness of quantity demanded to a change in the price of a good or service. It is the ratio of the percentage change in quantity demanded to the percentage change in price.

Price Elasticity of Demand

The **price elasticity of demand** measures the relative responsiveness of quantity demanded of a product to a change in its price. As indicated in the previous section, the arc price elasticity of demand is given by

$$e_p = \frac{\Delta Q_x}{\Delta P_x} \cdot \frac{P_{x_2} + P_{x_1}}{Q_{x_2} + Q_{x_1}} .$$

We also found that e_p was equal to −1.8 between $P_x = \$400$ and $P_x = \$500$. This arc elasticity value means that over the interval between $P_x = \$400$ and $P_x = \$500$, a *1.0 percent increase* in P_x will result, on the average, in a *1.8 percent decrease* in quantity demanded.

As has been stated repeatedly, since the price of a firm's product is normally at least one of the variables in the demand function for its product over which the firm has some control, the price elasticity of demand is of far more than casual interest to the firm. Moreover, once the firm knows the price elasticity of demand for its product at some point (or over some price range), it also knows something about the behavior of its total revenue at that point (or over that price range). This fact is important because total revenue is one of the two factors (cost is the other) that determine a firm's total profit.

Since price and quantity usually move in opposite directions, the sign of e_p is usually negative, as we found above. Therefore, we shall classify e_p according to its *absolute value* (or absolute size, disregarding the negative sign). We denote the absolute value of something by two vertical lines, ||. We say, then, that if $|e_p|$ is less than one, the quantity demanded is *inelastic* with respect to price. If $|e_p|$ is greater than one, the quantity demanded is *elastic* with respect to price. If $|e_p|$ is equal to one, the quantity demanded is *unitary elastic* with respect to price. These classifications seem reasonable if we reflect that when $|e_p|$ is greater than one, or elastic, it means that quantity demanded changes by a greater percentage than the percentage change in price. This occurrence means that quantity demanded is very responsive to a change in price; that is, it is elastic. On the other hand, if $|e_p|$ is less than one, it means that quantity demanded changes by a smaller percentage than the percentage change in price and therefore is relatively unresponsive or inelastic.

We use the same terminology in everyday life. If the waistband of a pair of slacks stretches (that is, if it is responsive to a pull), the waistband is said to be elastic. However, a cold iron rod is not very responsive if someone tries to stretch it. Thus the rod is said to be inelastic.

In the case where $|e_p|$ is greater than 1, we saw that quantity demanded would change by a large percentage relative to the percentage change in price. A change in price would result in a more-than-proportional change in quantity demanded. In this case we would expect that the firm might be inclined toward price decreases. However, both cost and revenue changes must be considered, as we shall see in the next two sections of the chapter.

Note that quantity demanded usually falls when price is increased, regardless of whether demand is elastic or inelastic. Accordingly, quantity demanded rises when price is decreased—for either elastic or inelastic demand. It is the relative, or *proportional*, changes in quantity demanded and price that are important in determining the elasticity of demand.

Two extreme cases occur when $e_p = 0$ and $e_p = -\infty$. If $e_p = 0$, then the price elasticity of demand is completely inelastic and a change in price will not affect quantity demanded. The demand curve in this case is a vertical line, as in Figure 2–6, panel a. If $e_p = -\infty$, then the price elasticity of demand is infinitely elastic, which means that if a firm raises price above the going market price, it will lose *all* of its sales. In this case the demand curve is a horizontal line (see Figure 2–6, panel b). These cases (where demand is either totally inelastic or infinitely elastic) are rarely found in the real world. For example, there is a price at which most people could not even afford necessities, such as medical treatment. Still, we do associate the horizontal demand curve with the perfectly competitive firm; and the demand for some products, such as table salt, over at least some price ranges is highly inelastic.

Of course, demand curves are not necessarily straight lines. For example, the demand curve shown in Figure 2–7 has the property that the elasticity of demand (in absolute value) is equal to 1.0 at all points on the curve. In this case quantity demanded will change by an exactly offsetting proportion as a result of a price change. Few, if any, demand curves in the real world are unitary elastic at *all* prices. However, a curve such as that shown in Figure 2–7 could represent the quantity of money demanded for transactions purposes (such as paying bills and buying goods) at various prices. Many economists have argued that this relationship is unitary elastic with respect to changes in the general level of prices. Other types of *nonlinear* (curved) demand curves would also be possible.

Determinants of Price Elasticity of Demand

The same factors that determine the size of changes in quantity demanded in response to a price change also affect the price elasticity of demand. For example, the *greater the number of substitute goods* that are available, the higher the price elasticity of demand. If the price of one of the products

Figure 2–6   Two Extreme Measures of Elasticity

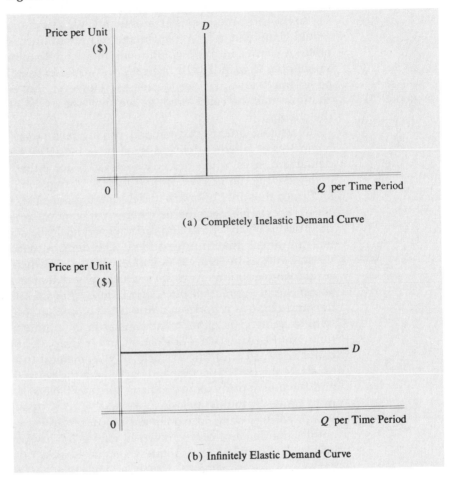

(a) Completely Inelastic Demand Curve

(b) Infinitely Elastic Demand Curve

A completely inelastic demand curve is depicted in panel a. The quantity demanded will not change in response to a change in price. Panel b shows an infinitely elastic demand curve. In this case, a firm can sell as many units of its product as it wishes to at the going market price, but it will sell zero units at a higher price.

increases while those of goods that are substitutes for it remain the same, we would expect consumers to switch some of their spending on the first product to purchases of the substitute goods. The greater the number of alternative goods available, the greater the opportunities for substituting spending on a product whose price has risen to purchases of a similar item whose price has remained the same.

Second, the price elasticity of demand will be higher the greater the *proportion* that spending on the item is of *consumers' total income*. Consumers usually do not spend a large fraction of their incomes on table salt.

Figure 2–7   A Unitary Elastic Demand Curve

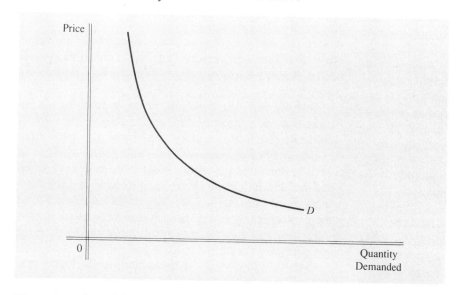

D is a unitary elastic ($|e_p| = 1$) demand curve. Unitary elastic demand curves have the property that total revenue ($P \times Q$) is the same for all prices.

Consequently, even a substantial percentage increase in the price of table salt is unlikely to have a major effect on their budgets if they continue purchasing the same amount of table salt as before. Third, e_p at a given point in time will depend on *consumer expectations* regarding future price changes. If a grocery store has soda pop on sale for a week, consumers will likely purchase more of it during that week if they believe that the price will return to its original level at the end of the week than if they believe that the price cut is a new "permanently" low price.

Finally, the price elasticity of demand will be greater the longer the time period allowed consumers to adjust their spending habits. During longer time periods consumers gain more information about the availability of alternative products, and additional substitute products are often developed. Purchases of smaller cars in response to gasoline price increases in the early 1970s are one example. In addition, consumers learned to develop new habits such as car pooling or using mass transit in response to an increase in gasoline prices.

Price Elasticity of Demand and Total Revenue

Finally, as we have already stated, the firm can know immediately whether its total revenue, or total sales dollars, will change in a positive or negative direction as a result of a proposed price change if it knows whether the price elasticity of demand for its product over the relevant range is inelastic, elastic, or unitary elastic. If demand is *inelastic* with respect to price, and price is lowered, total revenue will *decrease*. That is because quantity demanded will *not* increase *by a large enough proportion* to counteract the effect of a lower price received from each unit sold. The opposite effect occurs (for the same reason) when price is raised; that is, total revenue increases.

For example, the price elasticity of demand for basic household telephone service is probably inelastic. Unless the basic rate would increase drastically (such as a 100 percent increase), probably few people would have their phones removed. We might consider the frequent requests of Southwestern Bell for higher basic rates in Texas as evidence that Bell may believe that the demand for such service is inelastic.[19] However, AT&T seems more interested in keeping rates on interstate long-distance phone calls relatively low, indicating that the company may believe the demand for such service to be significantly more elastic than the demand for basic local telephone service.

On the other hand, if demand is price *elastic* and price is lowered, total revenue will *increase*—an effect opposite to that obtained when demand is price inelastic. This result occurs because quantity demanded will increase by a sufficiently large percentage to more than make up for the lower price received on each unit sold. An example of this phenomenon might be the special price reductions offered periodically by restaurants. Another example might be the reduced prices of airline tickets when advance purchase requirements are met. Correspondingly, if demand is elastic and price is increased, total revenue will decrease. Finally, if demand is unitary elastic, a change in price will not affect total revenue, since price and quantity will change in equal proportions and therefore have exactly offsetting effects. These results are summarized in Table 2–2.

This information regarding price changes and total revenue can be very significant for the firm. For example, suppose that an ice-skating rink finds that quantity demanded by skaters is such that the rink is not being used close to its capacity level and that the (absolute value of the) price elasticity of demand is greater than 1. In such case the rink should strongly consider lowering its price, since a large portion of its costs (like interest on money borrowed to finance the rink purchase and electricity to cool the ice) won't change very much. A similar situation could occur for a movie-theater owner, which may help to explain the practice by theaters of offering matinee showings at bargain prices. A smart firm attempts to estimate the price elasticity of demand at different times of the day and for different movies. Movie theaters do, then, attempt to take advantage

▪ ▪ ▪ ▪ ▪ ▪

[19] See "Bell Tolls Again for Texas Users," *San Antonio Express-News*, April 2, 1985, p. 14-A; and "Repealed Phone Tax Still Collected," *San Antonio Express-News*, May 16, 1986, p. 1-B.

Table 2–2   Summary of Relationship Between Price Elasticity of Demand and Total Revenue

e_p	Classification	*Effect of Price Change on Total Revenue*
$\|e_p\| > 1$	Elastic	Increase in price lowers *TR*. Decrease in price raises *TR*.
$\|e_p\| < 1$	Inelastic	Increase in price raises *TR*. Decrease in price lowers *TR*.
$\|e_p\| = 1$	Unitary Elastic	Price change does not affect *TR*.

of such differences to some extent with special afternoon rates and different rates for different movies.

Price Elasticity of Demand, Average Revenue, and Marginal Revenue

Now that we know the relationships among e_p, price changes, and the effect on total revenue, we can discern the relationships among e_p, price changes, average revenue, and marginal revenue. Figure 2–4, showing the relationships among the latter three variables, is reproduced in Figure 2–8. In addition, the relationships among e_p and average revenue and marginal revenue are indicated. Where $|e_p| > 1$, marginal revenue is *positive*, since a decrease in price increases total revenue. Where $|e_p| = 1$, marginal revenue is *zero*, since a decrease in price will not change total revenue. Finally, if $|e_p| < 1$, *marginal revenue is negative*, since a decrease in price will decrease total revenue.[20]

■ ■ ■ ■ ■ ■

[20] We can also derive another relationship between e_p, marginal revenue, and price. If

$$TR = P \cdot Q,$$

$$MR = \frac{dTR}{dQ} = P + Q\,\frac{dP}{dQ}\text{ , or}$$

$$MR = P\left(1 + \frac{Q}{P} \cdot \frac{dP}{dQ}\right).$$

However, $\dfrac{Q}{P} \cdot \dfrac{dP}{dQ}$ is equal to $1/e_p$, so $MR = P(1 + 1/e_p)$.

As noted in a previous section of this chapter, if the demand curve is a horizontal line, price is equal to marginal revenue. We can now prove this statement with the use of the relationship developed above. Since we know that $e_p = -\infty$ if the demand curve is horizontal, then in this case

$$MR = P(1 + 1/-\infty) = P(1 + 0) = P.$$

If $-\infty < e_p < 0$,

$$MR = P[1 + \text{some negative number}],$$

so $MR < P$, as already discussed in this chapter. Finally, if $e_p = 0$,

$$MR = P(1 + 1/0) = \infty.$$

Figure 2–8 Relationships Among Total Revenue, Marginal Revenue, Average Revenue, and Price Elasticity of Demand

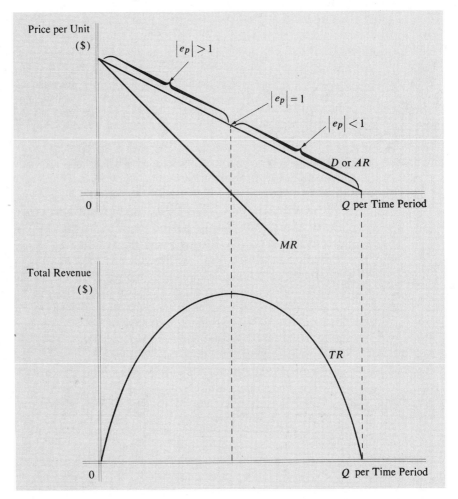

These graphs depict the relationships among total revenue (*TR*), marginal revenue (*MR*), average revenue (*AR*), and price elasticity of demand. When *MR* is positive, *TR* is rising and $|e_p|$ is greater than one. When *MR* = 0, *TR* is at a maximum and $|e_p| = 1$. When *MR* is negative, *TR* is falling and $|e_p|$ is less than one.

Nevertheless, a firm should not base its pricing decisions solely on the manner in which price affects total revenue; its costs must also be considered. When the price elasticity of demand is *inelastic*, the decision rule is straightforward: *raise price*. In this case total revenue will increase; and since quantity sold will decrease, total costs should at worst remain the same, resulting in an increase in total profit. In the case of *elastic* demand, the situation is more complicated. A *decrease* in price will *increase* total revenue, but the resulting increase in sales will likely increase total costs to some extent. *If* total revenue *increases by a greater amount than total costs*, then total profit will increase and price should be *lowered*. If a price *increase decreases total revenue by a smaller amount than it decreases* total costs, then price should be *raised*. We shall reserve further discussion of the costs of the firm, however, until a later chapter.

Firms are now becoming far more concerned about pricing policies than they have been in the past. At the retail level this has become readily apparent as three major new pricing approaches have become popular. These are *yield management, price matching*, and *everyday low pricing*. The first strategy uses computer software to track sales volume and market conditions so that the firm can raise prices when demand increases and lower them when it slacks off.[21] It has been used extensively by the airlines and by large hotel chains. Basically, successful yield management depends on ascertaining how consumer demand differs over time as well as among consumers. That is also the case with price matching. Stores employing it have found that few consumers actually take advantage of the offer to match competitors' prices. *The Wall Street Journal* reports that according to a pricing expert at UCLA,

> . . . price-matching policies actually give merchants "a way to keep prices a little higher for loyal customers while giving a lower price" to new customers the store is trying to attract.[22]

As we will see in a later chapter, both yield management and price matching are special cases of market segmentation—basically, dividing up markets into segments with different elasticities of demand.

The third new approach, everyday low pricing, has both a demand and a cost element. While firms, such as Sears, that have adopted the strategy expect it will enlarge their customer base, they also expect to reap cost savings from reductions in advertising and related expenditures. *Business Week* and Sears' major rival provide the following observation:

> Everyday low pricing requires efficient operations to maintain profit margins. "If you can't be a low-cost player, forget it," says Bernard F. Brennan, chairman of Montgomery Ward & Co. Ward's, which has reduced operating costs by $100 million annually since 1985, began everyday low pricing in 1987.[23]

■ ■ ■ ■ ■ ■

[21] See "No Cheap Hotel Room: Blame Yield Management," *The Wall Street Journal*, Nov. 4, 1988, p. 81; and "Computers Permit Airlines to Use Scalpel to Cut Fares," *The Wall Street Journal*, February 2, 1987, p. 25.
[22] "Who Wins With Price-Matching Plans," *The Wall Street Journal*, March 16, 1989, p. B1.
[23] "Little Prices are Looking Good to Big Retailers," *Business Week* (July 3, 1989), p. 44.

Numerical Example: Elasticity and the Straight-Line Demand Curve

Where is the range of elastic demand on the demand curve having the equation $Q_d = 8,000 - 50P$?

Answer. Demand is elastic from $Q_d = 0$ up to the midpoint quantity (where $MR = 0$) on the straight-line demand curve. Thus it will be elastic in the range $Q_d = 0$ up to $Q_d = 4,000$. From the equation, we can determine that $50P = 8,000 - Q_d$, and $P = 160 - .02Q_d$. Thus the elastic range can be stated in terms of price as that from $P = 160$ to $P = 80$. Of course, right at the midpoint, where $P = 80$ and $Q_d = 4,000$, there will be unitary elasticity.

Managerial Perspective: Building a Business on e_p: The Saga of Southwest Airlines

Herb Kelleher, CEO of Southwest Airlines, tells the story more or less this way: Along about 1972, the founders of Southwest Airlines believed something that the industry leaders, as well as the CAB (Civil Aeronautics Board, which then was in charge of regulating U.S. air transportation), scoffed at. It had to do with how the low- and middle-income consumer felt about air travel. According to Kelleher, the CAB and the major airlines managers believed that air travel was largely reserved for people who had the ability to pay high fares—the rich and those flying on business budgets—while the average American would choose car travel over air travel for most needs. Ordinary people, they argued, viewed air travel as a luxury good and would not increase their purchases of it very much if prices were reduced any feasible amount from those then prevailing.

Mr. Kelleher and his associates believed the opposite—that lower fares would result in large increases in the quantity of air travel purchased by the general public: "We were certain that demand was much more elastic than any of them believed it to be." Because at that time the CAB regulated all interstate fares in the United States and did not permit price competition, Kelleher says the only way his group could test their proposition was to establish an *intra*state airline in a market area large enough to make bargain air travel attractive to the consumer. That, he notes, had to be either California or Texas. They chose Texas. Southwest began by flying routes between the three large Texas cities, Dallas, Houston, and San Antonio. They offered "no frills" service. Refreshments never got fancier than peanuts and a drink, and there was only one class of seating, with no reserved seats. Ticket counters issued simple cash register receipts along with a reusable plastic boarding pass. In short, service was unpretentious, but the airline got the passengers to their destinations efficiently and *very* cheaply.

Consumer response to Southwest's low fares was tremendous. For a brief period, there was intense competition from Braniff on the intrastate routes, but Southwest persevered and kept to its game plan. It let consumers know that failure of Southwest would lead to the return of high fares in Texas, and they responded by being remarkably loyal to the firm. Southwest survived and has remained profitable. The price competition that was begun by Southwest and other upstarts in the industry led eventually to a new era in air transportation, with more discount fares, huge increases in traffic, and the eventual phaseout of the CAB. By 1990, however, mergers, bankruptcies, and buyouts had significantly reduced competition.

■ ■ ■ ■

References: Based on a speech by Herbert D. Kelleher at The University of Texas at San Antonio, March 1990. For more on Southwest, see "Southwest Airlines: Flying High with 'Uncle Herb,'" *Business Week* (July 3, 1989), pp. 53–55.

Income Elasticity of Demand

The **income elasticity of demand** is measured by the ratio of the percentage change in quantity taken of a product to the percentage change in income.

Income elasticity of demand measures the relative responsiveness of the quantity purchased of a product to changes in income. The arc formula for income elasticity of demand of Q_x is

$$e_I = \left(\frac{\Delta Q_x}{\frac{Q_{x_2} + Q_{x_1}}{2}} \right) \div \left(\frac{\Delta I}{\frac{I_2 + I_1}{2}} \right) = \frac{\Delta Q_x}{\Delta I} \cdot \frac{I_2 + I_1}{Q_{x_2} + Q_{x_1}}$$

$$= \frac{Q_{x_2} - Q_{x_1}}{I_2 - I_1} \cdot \frac{I_2 + I_1}{Q_{x_2} + Q_{x_1}} .$$

As stated earlier, in our microwave oven example, when $P_x = \$400$, $P_y = \$500$, $E_w = 40{,}000{,}000$, $I = \$10{,}000$, and $A = \$50{,}000$, then Q_x is equal to 30,000. When all of the above independent variables except income (I) remain constant, and I increases to $\$12{,}000$, then Q increases to 35,200.

Thus e_I between $I = \$10,000$ and $I = \$12,000$ is given by[24]

$$e_I = \frac{5,200}{2,000} \cdot \frac{22,000}{65,200} = .88.$$

Since the above income elasticity of demand is greater than zero, we can say that Brand X microwave ovens are *normal goods*. In our previous discussion of determinants of demand, normal goods are defined as products for which the quantity demanded increases as income increases (and vice versa). If $e_I > 1$, then the product is a normal good that is also a *superior good*. Such a value for e_I means that the quantity demanded of superior goods increases more than proportionally to the percentage increase in income. Such goods are also often called *cyclical normal goods*, since the quantity purchased of them varies proportionally more than income does over the business cycle. If the e_I is negative, it means that the quantity demanded of a good *decreases* as income *increases*. We call these products *inferior goods*.

Knowing the approximate income elasticity of demand for its product over the relevant region, a firm can estimate how a change in income will affect the quantity demanded of that good or service and can plan its production accordingly. This information is crucial to firms such as those in the automobile or appliance industries, where the demand for their products is very much affected by changes in the level of income. For example, consider the drastic production cutbacks in the automobile industry during 1991 and the early 1980s, when national income in *real terms* (that is, adjusted for price increases) was falling. The recessions also similarly affected the home-appliance industry.[25]
home-appliance industry.[25]

The income elasticity of demand has also been a useful concept in describing one of the problems of firms in the agriculture industry in the

■ ■ ■ ■ ■ ■

[24] The point formula for income elasticity of demand is

$$e_I = \frac{\partial Q_x}{\partial I} \cdot \frac{I}{Q_x}.$$

In our microwave oven example, the point income elasticity of demand where $P_x = \$400$, $P_y = \$500$, $E_w = 40,000,000$, $I = \$10,000$, $A = \$50,000$, and $Q_x = 30,000$ is given by

$$e_I = 2.6 \times \frac{10,000}{30,000} = .87.$$

[25] See, for example, Gregory A. Patterson, "Big Three U.S. Car Output To Sink to a 33-Year Low," *The Wall Street Journal*, April 11, 1991, p. A2; and Ralph E. Winter, "Recession Hits Major-Appliance Makers, Causing Layoffs; Recovery Isn't in Sight," *The Wall Street Journal*, June 23, 1980, p. 12. The boom in single-family housing in 1986 also favorably affected the appliance industry. See "Consumers May Be Ready to Put on Their Shopping Shoes," *Business Week* (May 19, 1986), p. 34.

United States during at least part of the twentieth century. The problem arises because the income elasticity of demand for agricultural products is less than 1—a fact that means the quantity demanded of agricultural products does not increase by as great a percentage as the percentage increase in income.

Cross Price Elasticity of Demand

Cross price elasticity of demand is measured by the ratio of the percentage change in quantity demanded of a product to the percentage change in price of a related product.

The **cross price elasticity of demand** for Product X with respect to the price of Product Y is a measure of the relative responsiveness of quantity demanded of Product X to changes in P_y. The arc cross price elasticity of demand formula is

$$e_{xy} = \frac{\dfrac{\Delta Q_x}{Q_{x_2} + Q_{x_1}}}{\dfrac{\Delta P_y}{P_{y_2} + P_{y_1}}} = \frac{\Delta Q_x}{\Delta P_y} \cdot \frac{P_{y_2} + P_{y_1}}{Q_{x_2} + Q_{x_1}} = \frac{Q_{x_2} - Q_{x_1}}{P_{y_2} - P_{y_1}} \cdot \frac{P_{y_2} + P_{y_1}}{Q_{x_2} + Q_{x_1}}$$

For our microwave oven demand function, when $P_x = \$400$, $P_y = \$500$, $E_w = 40,000,000$, $I = \$10,000$, and $A = \$50,000$, then Q_x is equal to 30,000 (as stated previously). If P_y decreases to \$400, then Q_x decreases to 27,500 units. Therefore, between $P_y = \$500$ and $P_y = \$400$,[26]

$$e_{xy} = \frac{-2,500}{-100} \cdot \frac{900}{57,500} = .39.$$

If, as in the preceding situation, the cross price elasticity of demand is positive, we say that the two goods are *substitute goods*. A positive value for e_{xy} means that an increase in P_y will result in an increase in Q_x (and vice versa), which indicates that an increase in P_y causes some customers to purchase Brand X instead of Brand Y (and vice versa). If e_{xy} were negative, it would indicate that an increase in the price of Good Y would decrease the quantity purchased of Good X. In this case Good X and Good Y are said to be *complementary goods*. As stated previously in our discussion of determinants of demand, complementary goods are, generally speak-

■ ■ ■ ■ ■ ■

[26] The formula for point cross price elasticity of demand is

$$e_{xy} = \frac{\partial Q_x}{\partial P_y} \cdot \frac{P_y}{Q_x} .$$

At the point where $P_x = \$400$, $P_y = \$500$, $E_w = 40,000,000$, $I = \$10,000$, $A = \$50,000$, and $Q_x = 30,000$,

$$e_{xy} = 25 \left(\frac{500}{30,000} \right) = .42.$$

ing, goods such that having more of one (at least to a point) increases the enjoyment a consumer obtains from the second. Examples of complementary goods are CDs and CD players, hamburger and hamburger buns, and gasoline and automobiles. If $e_{xy} = 0$, we say that the goods are *not related*.

Cross price elasticity information can be useful to the firm in several ways. If the firm produces two related goods or services, it is beneficial for it to be able to estimate how a change in the price of one will affect the quantity demanded of the other. For example, Procter & Gamble would like to know the effect of a price decrease for Crest toothpaste on the quantity demanded of the other brands of toothpaste that the company sells. A second situation in which cross price elasticity information is helpful occurs when another firm selling a related product has changed, or is expected to change, the price of that good or service. Thus Ford would like to know the impact of General Motors' rebates on the quantity sold of Ford vehicles.

Finally, a third situation in which cross price elasticity information could be of critical importance is if the firm were defending itself in an antitrust case by demonstrating (1) that its product has a positive cross price elasticity relationship with other products, therefore (2) that there are recognized substitutes for the product, and (3) that it accordingly does *not* have a monopoly. This type of approach was quite helpful to du Pont in defending itself in a famous antitrust case.[27] Du Pont had nearly 75 percent of the market for cellophane wrapping materials. However, the company successfully argued that the relevant market was the entire market for flexible packaging materials, including waxed paper and aluminum foil; it supported its position by showing that there were positive cross price elasticities between cellophane and these products and that therefore the products were substitutes. When the total market for flexible packaging materials was considered, du Pont had a much smaller market share.

Other Elasticity of Demand Concepts

As we stated when the concept of elasticity (of demand) was introduced, we can use an elasticity coefficient to indicate the relative responsiveness of the quantity demanded of a product to a change in any variable that may affect it. In our microwave oven example, we could also talk of the advertising elasticity of demand and of the employment (of women) elasticity of demand. For some products, population growth and, hence, the population elasticity of demand might be significant. The wise firm will try to discover the values of those elasticities that it believes are important factors affecting its revenue.

■ ■ ■ ■ ■ ■

[27] See *United States* v. *E. I. du Pont de Nemours and Co.*, 351 U.S. 377, 100 L. Ed. 1264, 76 S. Ct. 994 (1956).

Managerial Perspective: Some Dimensions of the Demand for Automobiles

Automobiles are a fixture of the American way of life, and it seems Americans are always interested in the attributes and prices of new cars. Economic studies of their demand for automobiles have produced some interesting results. First, there is a marked difference between demand for new cars in the aggregate and the demand for a given model of car. Second, consumers can always purchase a used car instead of a new one, so there is a substitute relationship not only between different makes of new cars but also between new and used.

The market demand for new automobiles has been estimated in a number of well-known studies. At different points in time and with different sets of data, these always seem to show the same result—that the price elasticity of demand for new cars is relatively low, usually around -1.1 to about -1.4. What this means is that when automobile manufacturers use rebates (a form of price cut) to help dealers entice customers to buy new cars, they realize very little, if any, increased revenue from those sales. However, the law of demand still works, so they do increase quantity sold and, therefore, reduce inventories. Since the automobile industry has long been dedicated to the "model year" concept of product development (introducing new models of most lines in the autumn each year), getting rid of excess inventory of this year's models is very important, especially if the release of next year's is not far off. Thus there is a pattern of rebating and offering other incentives at the end of each model year, even though it does not bring in big increases in revenue for the manufacturers.

While the elasticity of the aggregate demand for new cars is low, that for a specific model is much higher. This results from the fact that all cars are substitutes for one another, and some models of certain cars are very close substitutes for specific models of others. For example, a study published in 1983 found that the own-price elasticity for a Chevrolet Impala was -14.79 and that for a Ford Mustang was -8.42. The same study also found a cross-price elasticity of $+19.30$ for a Chevrolet Impala with respect to the price of a Pontiac Catalina, a close "cousin" of the Impala. Thus manufacturers (and dealers) can get buyers to switch purchases from one make of car to another by lowering price.

It has recently been noted that in the face of steep price increases by automobile manufacturers many consumers who did not view used cars as a close substitute for new ones have changed their minds. This change has probably been accelerated by the increasing availability of very-low-mileage used cars from corporate fleets and those marketed by car rental companies. Many cars offered by these sources are in nearly new condition and are sold with warranty terms that are quite comparable to those offered by new car sellers. Thus one variable that may have deterred many buyers from considering used cars close substitutes for new cars (risk of costly repair bills) has been largely eliminated.

■ ■ ■ ■

References: F. Owen Irvine, Jr., "Demand Equations for Individual New Car Models Estimated Using Transaction Prices with Implications for Regulatory Issues," *Southern Economic Journal* 49 (January 1983), pp. 764–782; H.F. Gallasch, Jr., "Elasticities of Demand for New Automobiles" (Societal Analysis Department, Research Laboratories, General Motors Corporation, Warren, Michigan, May 21, 1976); "With Deals This Good, Why Settle for New?" *Business Week* (July 3, 1989), p. 81.

Much of the information needed for demand studies can be obtained from Bureau of the Census data on population, income, and already existing businesses. Such reports can frequently be found in local libraries. Local planning authorities and trade associations are other important sources of information. In addition, consulting firms in the area of market research will be happy to supply and/or analyze data, for a fee. A more thorough discussion of demand estimation and forecasting techniques will appear in Chapters 3 and 11.

■ ■ ■ ■ ■ ■ ■ ■ **SUMMARY**

Elasticity of Demand, Revenue, and the Firm

In this chapter we have emphasized one of the two most critical factors for the success of a firm: the demand for its product. We have defined the *demand function* as the mathematical relationship that indicates how the quantity demanded of a firm's product over some time period is affected by variables such as the price of the good (or service), prices of other goods, income of consumers, and advertising expenditures. The *demand curve* gives the relationship between the quantity demanded of a good and its price. The demand curve is obtained from the demand function by holding all variables (except price and quantity demanded) constant at some level. Those variables held constant when the demand curve is obtained are called *determinants of demand*. We noted that a change in a good's own price will cause a movement along its demand curve but that a change in one of the determinants of demand (income, prices of related goods, and tastes, for example), will shift the entire curve.

We also related the demand curve to the total revenue, average revenue, and marginal revenue functions. *Total revenue* relates total sales dollars received by the firm to quantity sold. Total revenue is equal to price times quantity purchased and can be derived from the equation for the demand curve. *Average revenue* is obtained by dividing total revenue by quantity sold and is equal to price. The average revenue curve, therefore, is the demand curve. *Marginal revenue* is the rate of change of total revenue with respect to quantity sold and is, consequently, the slope of the total revenue function. *Arc marginal revenue* is the average rate of change of *TR* with respect to some change in quantity sold, or

$$\text{Arc MR} = \frac{\Delta TR}{\Delta Q}$$

We have emphasized that the profit-maximizing firm is concerned about the responsiveness of the quantity demanded of its product to changes in other variables—such as the price of the good or service, the prices of related goods, and the income of consumers. The measure of responsiveness that we have utilized here is *elasticity* of demand, which is given by

$$\frac{\%\ \text{of change in quantity demanded}}{\%\ \text{change in a specific related variable}}.$$

In this chapter we discussed three types of elasticity of demand—*price*, *income*, and *cross price*. We classified price elasticity of demand according to whether it was *elastic*, *inelastic*, or *unitary elastic*; and in each case we related price changes to total revenue and marginal revenue. Given the income elasticity of demand, we classified a product as being either a *normal* (including superior) *good* or an *inferior good*. Using the cross price elasticity of demand between one product and another product, we can classify the two goods as *substitutes* or *complements*. We also demonstrated in each case various ways such information can be useful to the manager.

Before a firm commits much time and money to a given line of product or type of service, it should gather enough information to substantiate its belief that a sufficient market exists for the item it wants to sell. Once it has established that the market does exist for its product and therefore has gone into business, the wise firm will use its knowledge of the concepts we have discussed in this chapter to gather and analyze the information that will enable it to predict and increase its revenue. Thereby it will be well on its way toward maximizing profit.

In the next two chapters we will discuss production and the cost of production—the other major factor determining the degree of success or failure of an enterprise.

■ ■ ■ ■ ■ ■ ■ ■ ■ ■ ■ ■ ■ **Questions** ■ ■ ■ ■ ■ ■ ■ ■ ■ ■ ■ ■ ■

1. Define total revenue, marginal revenue, and average revenue. Why is knowledge of each of these elements important for the firm?
2. Define price elasticity of demand. How is e_p related to total revenue for a firm?
3. Explain what is meant by the *determinants of demand*.
4. Discuss two situations in which knowledge of the income elasticity of demand is helpful.
5. What factors do you think affect the price elasticity of demand?
6. Which demand curve do you think would generally be less price elastic—that for a firm's product or that for an industry's product? Why?
7. What is the relationship between goods that are substitutes? Between goods that are complements? How is the classification of goods in this manner related to cross price elasticity of demand?
8. What is the value of marginal revenue when total revenue is maximized?

■ ■ ■ ■ ■ ■ ■ ■ ■ ■ ■ ■ ■ **Problems** ■ ■ ■ ■ ■ ■ ■ ■ ■ ■ ■ ■ ■

1. The table that follows gives price and corresponding quantity demanded data for a firm.
   a. Complete the table by finding total revenue and arc marginal revenue.
   b. Plot the demand curve, the total revenue curve, and the arc marginal revenue curve. Note that the *arc marginal revenue between two levels of output should be plotted midway between the two levels.*
   c. Find the price elasticity of demand between $P = \$35$ and $P = \$30$ and between $P = \$15$ and $P = \$10$. In which price range is it more elastic?

P	Q	TR	ARC MR
$40	0		
35	5		
30	10		
25	15		
20	20		
15	25		
10	30		
5	35		
0	40		

2. Barker Cement Company is considering lowering the price on an 80-lb. bag of cement from $3 to $2. Presently, Barker sells 10,000 bags of cement per week, and its market analysts believe the price elasticity of demand to be −2 over this price range.
   a. If Barker Cement Company lowers the price, will its total revenue increase, decrease, or remain unchanged? Why?
   b. What will be the new level of quantity demanded? Of total revenue?

3. a. Complete the following table by finding total revenue and price.

P	Q	TR	ARC MR
120	0	0	
			105
	10		
			75
	20		
			45
	30		
			15
	40		
			−15
	50		

   b. How would marginal revenue and price be related if price were constant? How are they related when price must decrease for quantity demanded to increase?

4. Jennie's Healthfoods now sells 2,000 lbs. of passion fruit per week at a price of $1.40 per lb. An economist has reported to management that the arc elasticity of demand for the fruit over the price range $1.40 to $1.20 per lb. is −2.0. If Jennie lowers her passion fruit price to $1.20 per lb., determine the following:
   a. How many lbs. of passion fruit will she sell per week?
   b. How much will her total revenue (TR) from passion fruit sales change?

5. Zeerok shoe company has hired a consultant to estimate the elasticity of demand for its most awesome basketball shoe. At present, Zeerok is charging $90 for a pair of the shoes. The consultant estimates that the arc price elasticity of demand for them is −1.40 for a price cut of $10.

   Currently, Zeerok is selling 20,000 pairs of the shoes per week at its 90-dollar price. If the consultant is correct and the company cuts its price from $90 to $80 per pair,
   a. What will be the new sales quantity per week of Zeerok's awesome shoe?
   b. Calculate the change in Zeerok's total revenue from sales of the shoe that follows from the change in part a.

6. International Video Machines, Inc., is a manufacturer of a video-recording device. The firm is considering lowering the price of its

product from $800 to $600. The company's market analysts have estimated the price elasticity of demand to be -2 over this price range. Presently, this firm sells 1,000 video recorders per month.

a. What will be the new quantity sold if the price is lowered to $600?

b. What will be the new level of total revenue in part a?

c. What additional information does International Video Machines, Inc., need to know before it can determine whether or not a price decrease will increase the firm's profit?

d. Suppose that after International Video Machines lowers its price, its competitor, Videoview, lowers the price of its machine from $900 to $800. The cross price elasticity of demand between the quantity sold of International Video Machines' video recorders and the price of Videoview's machine is .5. What will be the effect of Videoview's price decrease on the quantity sold by International Video Machines? (Use the quantity you found in part a as Q_1. Round your answer to the nearest whole number.)

7. A manufacturer of stuffed animals, Texas Teddy Bear, Inc., is trying to determine the price of its stuffed animals (all sell at the same price) during the upcoming Christmas season. In the past the price of its stuffed animals has been $10, but the firm is getting worried because of the popularity of space toys. The firm has produced some new stuffed animals in an effort to increase its share in the toy market, but it is also considering a price decrease to $8. Texas Teddy Bear's market research department has estimated the price elasticity of demand for the firm's stuffed animals to be -1.5. The estimated quantity that would be sold this Christmas season (October–December) at a price of $10 is 40,000.

a. How many stuffed animals would be sold at a price of $8 if e_p were -1.5?

b. What would be the effect on the firm's total revenue if the price were lowered to $8?

8. Dirt Cheap Records, Inc., estimates its price elasticity of demand to be -4. Currently, DCRI sells 1,000 records per week at a price of $5 each. If DCRI lowers its price to $4,

a. What will happen to total revenue? How do you know?

b. What will be the new quantity sold?

9. Brand X auto manufacturer has just lowered the price of its new car by $2,000 (from $12,000 to $10,000), and Brand Y is concerned about the effect this action will have on the quantity demanded of its cars. At the old price, Brand Y sold 10,000 cars per month. If the cross elasticity of demand of Ys cars relative to Xs prices is 1.5, what will be Ys new quantity sold?

10. Charles Sr., an East Coast fast-food chain, has been considering a price cut in its 1/4 lb. hamburger, the Astroburger. Currently, Astroburgers sell for $1.89, and Charles is selling 220,000 of the burgers per week.

Charles's research department has suggested reducing the price of the Astroburger to $1.65 and estimates that the arc elasticity of demand for the product is −1.80 over the range of the proposed price change.

a. If the research department is correct, what will be the weekly quantity sold of the Astroburgers after the price cut occurs?

b. What will be Charles's new total revenue from Astroburger sales?

Charles's major competitor, Mindy's, sells the Superburger, which is a close substitute for the Astroburger. Mindy's Superburger sells for $1.79, and, before Charles's price cut, 160,000 were sold per week. If the arc cross-price elasticity of demand between the Superburger and the Astroburger is +2.20 over the range of the Charles price change:

c. Calculate the change in the quantity sold of Mindy's Superburger that occurs when Charles cuts the price of the Astroburger.

d. Calculate the dollar amount of change in Mindy's total revenue following the price cut by Charles.

The following problems require calculus:

11. If $P = 120 − 1.5Q$ is the equation for the demand curve, find the corresponding total revenue function, marginal revenue function, and average revenue function.

12. The statistics department of an appliance manufacturer has estimated that the demand function (number purchased annually) for their (Brand X) automatic washer is as follows:

$$Q_x = 197{,}000 − 100P_x + 50P_y + .1I + .02A + 10{,}000P_L,$$

where

P_x = price of the company's washer,
P_y = price of a major competitor's washer,
I = average household income,
A = annual dollars spent on advertising, and
P_L = cost of doing one load of wash in a self-service laundry.

a. If $P_y = \$300$, $I = \$10{,}000$, $A = \$200{,}000$, and $P_L = \$.30$, find the price elasticity of demand between $P_x = \$350$ and $P_x = \$400$. (When $P_x = \$400$, with the values of the other variables as given above, then $Q_x = 180{,}000$.)

b. Is e_{p_x} elastic, inelastic, or unitary elastic? Why? If the price is cut, does total revenue increase, decrease, or not change?

c. Find the income elasticity of demand for Q_x, given $P_x = \$400$. The other variables are as given in part a. Interpret your answer—i.e., what does it say, if anything, about the demand for Brand X washers?

13. Alpha Company has estimated that the demand curve for its product is represented by the equation $Q = 2840 - 20P$, where Q is the quantity sold per week and P is the price per unit.
   a. Based on the estimated demand curve, write the equations for Alpha's
      (i) Average revenue,
      (ii) Total revenue, and
      (iii) Marginal revenue.
   b. What will be the maximum total revenue per week that Alpha can obtain from sales of its product? (Give the exact dollar amount and explain how you determine it.)
   c. Calculate the point price elasticity of demand for Alpha's product when $Q = 1,600$. Is demand elastic or inelastic at this quantity? How do you know?
   d. Calculate the *arc* price elasticity of demand for Alpha's product between $Q = 1,000$ and $Q = 1,100$. Interpret your result and relate it to what will happen to total revenue if Alpha is initially at $Q = 1,000$ and decides to cut price to increase its sales from 1,000 to 1,100 units.

14. A mathematical demand function for new Cadillacs sold per year for a dealer is as follows:

$$Q_c = 200 - .01P_c + .005P_L - 10P_g + .01I + 003A,$$

   where

$$P_c = \text{average price of Cadillacs,}$$
$$P_L = \text{average price of Lincoln Continentals,}$$
$$P_g = \text{price of gasoline,}$$
$$I = \text{average family income, and}$$
$$A = \text{dollars spent annually on advertising.}$$

   a. Find the point price elasticity of demand if $P_c = \$25,000$, $P_L = \$20,000$, $P_g = \$1.00$, $I = \$15,000$, and $A = \$10,000$.
   b. Is the price elasticity of demand elastic, unitary elastic, or inelastic? Why?
   c. Find the arc cross elasticity of demand for Cadillacs and Continentals between $P_L = \$20,000$ and $P_L = \$22,000$. (All other figures except Q_c remain the same as in part a.)
   d. Are Cadillacs and Lincolns substitutes or complements? Why?

15. Paradise Lake, Inc., is a developer of lakefront properties. Through statistical research, Paradise Lake has estimated the annual demand function for its lots to be as follows:

$$Q_L = 3,500 - .5P_L + .2P_C + .03I + .01A,$$

where

Q_L = number of Paradise Lake's lots purchased per year,
P_L = price of a Paradise Lake lot,
P_C = price of a competing land company's lots,
I = average annual household income, and
A = annual amount spent by Paradise Lake on advertising.

a. Find the income elasticity of demand for Paradise Lake's lots where P_L = \$10,000, P_C = \$8,000, I = \$12,000, and A = \$4,000.
b. Are these lots a normal good or an inferior good? Why?
c. What does your answer in part a tell Paradise Lake about the demand for its lots?
d. Find the price elasticity of demand for Paradise Lake's properties at the same point as in part a.
e. Is the price elasticity of demand for Paradise Lake's properties elastic, inelastic, or unitary elastic? How do you know?
16. Smooth Sailing, Inc., has estimated the demand function for its sailboats (quantity purchased annually) as follows:

$$Q_s = 73{,}000 - 40P_s + 20P_x + 15P_y + 2I + .1A + 10W,$$

where

P_s = the price of Smooth Sailing sailboats,
P_x = the price of Company X's sailboat,
P_y = the price of Company Y's motorboat,
I = per capita income in dollars,
A = dollars spent on advertising, and
W = number of favorable days of weather in the southern region of the United States.

a. Suppose that P_s = \$9,000, P_x = \$9,500, P_y = \$10,000, I = \$15,000, A = \$170,000, and W = 160. Find the price elasticity of demand at that point.
b. Is e_p elastic, inelastic, or unitary elastic in part a? Why?
c. What information does your answer in part a give Smooth Sailing that would be useful if the company were considering changing its price?
d. Find the cross price elasticity of demand for Smooth Sailing sailboats relative to Brand X sailboats between P_x = \$9,500 and P_x = \$10,000. Are the two boats substitutes or complements?
e. Find the income elasticity of demand for Smooth Sailing sailboats at the point given in part a. Are the boats a normal good or an inferior good? Why?

17. A firm's demand function for product X has the following equation:

$$Q_x = 1420 - 20P_x - 10P_y + .02I + .04A,$$

where

Q_x = number of units of X sold per week,
P_x = the price charged per unit of X,
P_y = the price charged for a related good, Y,
I = per capita income in the market area,
A = the amount spent per week on advertising.

Suppose the firm spends $1,200 per week on advertising, that P_y is $40, and that income in the market area is $8,000 per capita.

a. Write the equation of the demand curve for product X.
b. Briefly explain how product X is related to product Y, given the equation for the demand function. (Is Y a substitute or a complement, and how can you tell?)
c. Given the stated values of the other independent variables in this problem, calculate the point price elasticity of demand for X at P_x = $50.
d. Given the stated values of P_y, I, and A, at what price and quantity demanded will total revenue from sales of X be maximized? What will the maximum revenue be?

This problem can be solved with Decision Assistant.

18. Debra Ann Jones is the president of a successful merchandising operation, the DAJ Merchandising Corporation. In college, Debra received an electrical engineering degree with a minor in business administration. This combination provided her with excellent insight into the consumer electronic market. Debra had researched this market previously and determined that a very handsome profit could be made by concentrating on "hot, new consumer electronic items," such as electronic toys, telephones, and other novelties. Debra's research also revealed that quick reactions were the highest priority for success. That is, a firm had to spot a new product, buy the marketing or production rights, produce the product, and then sell it on a national scale before copies could be cheaply produced and sold. This marketing concept of striking quickly also enabled Debra to generate quick profits, and more attention was given to maximizing DAJ's revenue than to any other long-term consideration.

Debra has just been presented with one of those "hot items" she feels sure will add to the firm's success. The product is an electronic address book that can hold up to 50 names, addresses, and telephone

numbers. As an additional unique feature it includes a voice synthe-
sizer that "reads" any name, address, or telephone number stored in
the device.

DAJ's marketing department has been hard at work to determine
a demand function for the electronic address book. The best estimate
of demand is determined by the following equation:

$$P = 500 - .25Q,$$

where P is the price to be charged and Q is the quantity demanded
per month.

a. Use the Max/Min tool in the *Managerial Economics Decision Assistant*
   to see if you can assist Debra in determining the exact price DAJ
   should charge for the electronic address book if it wishes to maximize its total monthly revenue. Also determine the estimated total
   dollar sales per month assuming a total revenue maximizing price.

b. An alternative demand function has been proposed by several
   members of the marketing department. Determine the revenue
   maximizing price and quantity if the second demand function is
   given by the following equation:

$$P = 450 - .3Q,$$

where P is the price to be charged and Q is the quantity demanded
per month.

■ ■ ■ ■ ■ ■ ■ ■ ■ ■ **Selected References** ■ ■ ■ ■ ■ ■ ■ ■ ■ ■

Mansfield, Edwin. *Microeconomics: Theory and Applications*, 7th ed. New
    York: W. W. Norton, 1991, Chapters 3–5.
McCloskey, Donald N. *The Applied Theory of Price*, 2d ed. New York:
    Macmillan, 1985, Chapters 1–7.
McGuigan, James R., and R. Charles Moyer. *Managerial Economics*, 5th ed.
    St. Paul, Minn.: West, 1989, Chapter 7.
Nicholson, Walter. *Intermediate Microeconomics*, 5th ed. Chicago: The Dry-
    den Press, 1990, Chapters 3–6.

Appendix 2

Theory of Consumer Behavior

In Chapter 2 we looked at the relationship between price, quantity demanded, and total revenue. We also examined the concept of elasticity, and saw how it could be used to depict the effects of changes in variables such as income and the prices of related goods on the quantity demanded of a product.

It is also often useful to be aware of the notions about consumer behavior that lie in the background of the demand curve. In order to grasp the theory of consumer behavior put forth by economists, we must first recognize that the primary goal of consumers is assumed to be the maximization of their *utility* or *satisfaction*. In other words, consumers wish to achieve the greatest satisfaction possible within the bounds of their budget constraints.

CARDINAL UTILITY APPROACH

Early theories of consumer behavior implicitly assumed that personal utility or satisfaction could be measured in exact units of measurement, called *utils*, just as we measure length, temperature, and volume in inches, degrees, and liters. John and Sue Brown could say, for example, that they received 200 utils of satisfaction from an Anthony's super deluxe pizza and 50 utils of satisfaction from a bag of buttered microwave popcorn. With this type of measurement system, called a *cardinal* measurement system, we could say that John and Sue received four times as much satisfaction from a super deluxe pizza as from a bag of popcorn.

The *total utility* associated with a good or service is the total amount of satisfaction that the consumer obtains from the good or service. We can calculate marginal utility in the same way that we calculate other marginal values. *Arc marginal utility* is the addition to total utility provided by another unit of a good or service. For example, suppose your total utility is 1,500 utils. Someone gives you two bags of popcorn, and as a result, your total utility jumps to 1,600 utils. The marginal utility of a bag of popcorn in this case is equal to

$$\frac{\text{change in total utility}}{\text{change in bags of popcorn}} = \frac{100}{2} = 50 \text{ utils.}$$

In general, the arc marginal utility of a good, Good X, is given by $MU_x = \Delta TU_x/\Delta X$, where MU is marginal utility and TU is total utility.

Economists have shown, and we can easily see, that given a cardinal utility function, consumers will maximize their satisfaction by dividing their budget among goods and services so that the marginal utility per additional dollar cost of another unit of each of these products is equal. For example, if you are dividing your monthly entertainment budget between pizza and compact discs, you will maximize your utility only if the

$$\frac{MU_{pizza}}{P_{pizza}} = \frac{MU_{CD}}{P_{CD}},$$

where

$$MU_{pizza} = \text{the marginal utility of a pizza,}$$
$$MU_{CD} = \text{the marginal utility of a compact disc,}$$
$$P_{pizza} = \text{the price of a pizza, and}$$
$$P_{CD} = \text{the price of a compact disc.}$$

Let us suppose that the price of a pizza is \$5.00, the price of a compact disc is \$10.00, the marginal utility of a pizza is 300 utils, and the marginal utility of a compact disc is 500 utils. In this case,

$$\frac{MU_{pizza}}{P_{pizza}} = \frac{300 \text{ utils}}{\$5.00} = 60 \text{ utils per additional dollar,}$$

while

$$\frac{MU_{CD}}{P_{CD}} = \frac{500 \text{ utils}}{\$10.00} = 50 \text{ utils per additional dollar.}$$

Here,

$$\frac{MU_{pizza}}{P_{pizza}} \quad \text{is greater than} \quad \frac{MU_{CD}}{P_{CD}},$$

(60 is greater than 50).

Thus, to maximize your utility, you must reallocate your spending so that more pizza and fewer compact discs are purchased. For example, suppose you buy one less compact disc and two more pizzas. As a result, you will have a net gain of 100 utils for the same amount of money, as shown below.

Buy one less compact disc:

$$\text{Change in utility} = -500 \text{ utils}$$

$$\text{Change in spending} = -\$10.00$$

Buy two more pizzas:

$$\text{Change in utility} = (2 \times 300) = 600 \text{ utils}$$

$$\text{Change in spending} = (2 \times \$5.00) = \$10.00$$

Net effect of budget reallocation:

$$\text{Net change in utility} = -500 \text{ utils} + 600 \text{ utils} = +100 \text{ utils}$$

$$\text{Net change in spending} = -\$10.00 + \$10.00 = \$0$$

Do these results mean that you should buy all pizzas and no compact discs? Certainly not! As you begin to purchase more pizzas and fewer CDs per month, you will probably find that the marginal utility of another pizza will fall, while that of another CD will rise. This phenomenon results from the *principle of diminishing marginal utility*, which states that as more and more units of a good or service are consumed, total utility may increase, but after some point the *marginal utility* of another unit will begin to fall.

Thus, as you begin to reallocate your monthly budget so that you are purchasing more pizzas and fewer compact discs, we would expect the marginal utility of another pizza to fall and that of another CD to rise. As a result, you would eventually reach a combination of pizzas and compact discs where your utility would be at a maximum, given your budget. This point might occur, for example, where the $MU_{pizza} = 275$ utils and the $MU_{CD} = 550$ utils, so that

$$\frac{MU_{pizza}}{P_{pizza}} = \frac{275}{\$5} = \frac{MU_{CD}}{P_{CD}} = \frac{550}{\$10} = 55 \text{ utils per } \$1.00.$$

At this point there is no way that you can reallocate your spending between these two goods and increase your total utility.

■ ■ ■ ■ ■ ■ ■ ■ ■ ORDINAL UTILITY THEORY

In recent years economists have placed increasing emphasis on the fact that the amount of utility a consumer receives from a particular combination of goods and services is a subjective phenomenon. Moreover, it may be quite difficult for the consumer to develop a utility function with cardinal measurements of utility even for himself or herself. Furthermore, twentieth-century economists have found that the important conclusions of their theory of consumer behavior could be derived from an *ordinal* utility function, which has the benefit of being much easier to construct.

An ordinal utility function does not require precise measurements of the actual utility received from a good or service; it requires only that consumers be able to state whether they prefer one combination of goods to another or are indifferent between them. A consumer who is *indifferent* between the two sets of goods likes them both equally well; they both yield the same amount of satisfaction. Two additional assumptions that economists make in the ordinal utility approach are (1) that consumers are consistent in their rankings and (2) that a consumer also prefers more to less of a good in the *relevant range* of choice. The first assumption means that if you prefer three hamburgers to four tacos but you prefer four tacos to two hot dogs, then you must also prefer three hamburgers to two hot dogs. The second assumption means that if someone offered you a choice between two hamburgers and three hamburgers for free, you would always choose three hamburgers.

Given these assumptions, we can construct an ordinal utility function for a consumer. All that is required is that the consumer tell us how he or she would rank combinations of goods and services in order of preference. We then can assign utility numbers to these combinations, following the rule that if one combination of goods and services is preferred to a second, then the first combination must have a higher utility number than the second. If a consumer is indifferent between two combinations of goods and services, they must have *the same* utility number assigned to them.

After the consumer's utility function has been constructed, we can draw indifference curves based on that data. An *indifference curve* shows various combinations of two goods and services that a consumer is indifferent between. Of course, each combination of goods and services on an indifference curve must have the same utility number assigned to it.

For example, Figure 2A–1 shows two indifference curves for combinations of compact discs and pizzas. The number of compact discs purchased per month is shown on the vertical axis and the number of pizzas on the horizontal axis. Each indifference curve represents a different level of utility. Points *A, B,* and *C* in the diagram indicate that this consumer is indifferent between ten compact discs and one pizza, six compact discs and three pizzas, and three compact discs and six pizzas.

We should pause here for a few moments to note some properties of indifference curves. First, indifference curves must have a *negative* slope— that is, they must slope downward to the right. This characteristic is the direct result of our assumption that a consumer always prefers more to less of a good. If some of one good is given up, more of the second good

Figure 2A–1   Indifference Curves for Pizzas and Compact Discs

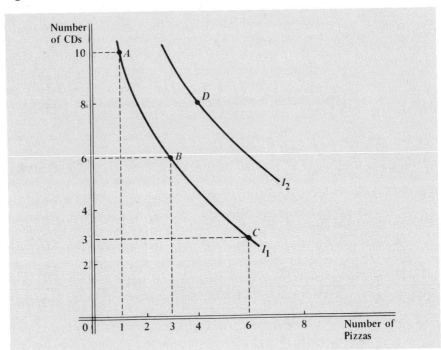

must be obtained for the consumer to remain at the same level of satisfaction and vice versa. Second, indifference curves cannot intersect. If they did intersect, that would mean that the combination of goods and services at the point of intersection gave a consumer two different levels of utility, which is impossible!

Third, higher (farther to the right) indifference curves must represent higher levels of utility. We can see why this relationship must hold by comparing points B on I_1 and D on I_2 in Figure 2A–1. Point D represents a combination of pizzas and compact discs that contains more of both goods than does B. Since a consumer prefers more to less of a good, I_2 must represent a higher level of satisfaction than does I_1.

■ ■ ■ ■ ■ ■ ■ ■ ■ **MARGINAL RATE OF SUBSTITUTION**

Points A, B, and C in Figure 2A–1 can be used to illustrate the marginal rate of substitution, a term that plays an important role in modern consumer theory. The *marginal rate of substitution (MRS)* indicates the rate at which a consumer is willing to substitute one good for another. In other words, it is the rate at which the consumer can substitute one good for another while remaining at the same level of satisfaction (on the same indifference curve). It is also equal to (-1) multiplied by the slope of the indifference curve at the relevant point. In general, we can write the marginal rate of substitution of Good X for Good Y as $MRS = (-1) \Delta Y / \Delta X$, where Good Y is on the vertical axis and Good X is on the horizontal axis.

In Figure 2A–1, the marginal rate of substitution between points A and B is equal to

$$(-1) \frac{\text{change in number of compact discs}}{\text{change in number of pizzas}} = (-1) \frac{(-4)}{2} = 2.$$

In other words, between points A and B the consumer will maintain the same level of utility by giving up two CDs in exchange for another pizza. Between points B and C, the MRS is equal to

$$(-1) \frac{\text{change in number of compact discs}}{\text{change in number of pizzas}} = (-1) \frac{(-3)}{3} = 1.$$

Between points B and C the consumer is willing to trade only one compact disc for one pizza.

The change in the MRS between points A and B and points B and C illustrates the principle of diminishing marginal rate of substitution. A *diminishing marginal rate of substitution* of Good X for Good Y means that as consumers obtain more of Good X relative to Good Y, they are willing to give up less of Good Y to get one more unit of Good X. This principle is related to the notion of diminishing marginal utility, as we shall see shortly.

When we move from one point to another on an indifference curve, the amount of utility that we lose by giving up some of one good must be exactly offset by the utility we gain from getting more of the second good. Thus for two goods, X and Y, along an indifference curve,

(2A–1)
$$\Delta Y \cdot \frac{\Delta TU}{\Delta Y} + \Delta X \frac{\Delta TU}{\Delta X} = 0.$$

By subtracting $\Delta X(\Delta TU/\Delta X)$ from both sides of equation (2A–1), we obtain

(2A–2)
$$\Delta Y \cdot \frac{\Delta TU}{\Delta Y} = -\Delta X \cdot \frac{\Delta TU}{\Delta X}.$$

Dividing both sides of equation (2A–2) by $\Delta TU/\Delta Y$, we get

(2A–3)
$$\Delta Y = -\Delta X \cdot \dfrac{\dfrac{\Delta TU}{\Delta X}}{\dfrac{\Delta TU}{\Delta Y}} .$$

Finally, dividing both sides of equation (2A–3) by $-\Delta X$, we find

(2A–4)
$$-\dfrac{\Delta Y}{\Delta X} = \dfrac{\dfrac{\Delta TU}{\Delta X}}{\dfrac{\Delta TU}{\Delta Y}} .$$

The left-hand side of equation (2A-4) is equal to the *MRS* of Good X for Good Y. The right-hand side is equal to MU_x/MU_y. Thus we have shown that

(2A–5)
$$MRS = -\dfrac{\Delta Y}{\Delta X} = \dfrac{MU_x}{MU_y} .$$

If we think for a minute, equation (2A–5) makes a lot of sense. It states that the rate at which a consumer is just willing to trade Good Y for Good X is equal to the ratio of the marginal utility of Good X to that of Good Y. If the MU_x is 50 units and the MU_y is 100, then the consumer would be willing to trade one unit of Y for two of X, or

$$MRS = \dfrac{1}{2} = \dfrac{MU_x}{MU_y} .$$

Note that the consumer will give up less of the good with the higher marginal utility in exchange for the good with the lower marginal utility. In other words, the rate at which the consumer will trade Good Y for Good X *varies inversely* with the ratio of the marginal utility of Y to the marginal utility of X. Thus

$$MRS = (-1)\dfrac{\Delta Y}{\Delta X} = \dfrac{MU_x}{MU_y} , \; not \; \dfrac{MU_y}{MU_x} .$$

■ ■ ■ ■ ■ ■ ■ ■ CONSUMER EQUILIBRIUM

A consumer will maximize his or her satisfaction by allocating purchases in order to be on the highest indifference curve possible given the budget available. In Figure 2A–2 we see three indifference curves: I_1, I_2, and I_3. A consumer's budget line, denoted by $Y'X'$, is also drawn.

We can derive the equation for the consumer's budget line as follows. First assume that our consumer has B_o dollars to spend on goods X and Y. Then the maximum amount that the consumer can spend on each good is given by

(2A–6)

$$P_y \cdot Y + P_x \cdot X = B_o,$$

where

$$P_y = \text{the price of Good } Y$$
$$Y = \text{the quantity purchased of Good } Y,$$
$$P_x = \text{the price of Good } X, \text{ and}$$
$$X = \text{the quantity purchased of Good } X.$$

Equation (2A–6) states that the price of Good Y multiplied by the quantity purchased of Good Y plus the price of Good X multiplied by the quantity purchased of Good X is equal to B_o.

To get equation (2A–6) in a form where it can be graphed easily, as in Figure 2A–2, we first subtract $P_x \cdot X$ from both sides of the equation, obtaining

(2A–7)

$$P_y \cdot Y = B_o - P_x \cdot X.$$

Figure 2A–2   Consumer Equilibrium

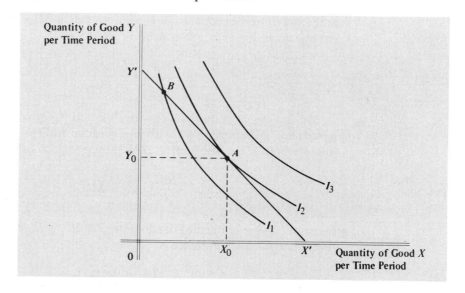

Now, dividing both sides of this equation by P_y, we get

(2A–8)
$$Y = \frac{B_o}{P_y} - \frac{P_x}{P_y} \cdot X.$$

Equation (2A–8) is in the familiar linear form of $Y = a + bX$. The Y-axis intercept, Y' in Figure 2A–2, is equal to B_o/P_y. That is the number of units of Y that can be purchased if the consumer's entire budget is spent on Good Y. Similarly, the X-axis intercept, X' in Figure 2A–2, is given by B_o/P_x.

The slope of the consumer's budget line is equal to $-P_x/P_y$. In other words, the rate at which a consumer can trade off spending on one good for spending on another is given by the ratio of their prices. More specifically, $\Delta Y/\Delta X$ along the budget line is equal to $-P_x/P_y$.

As we can see from Figure 2A–2, the consumer will maximize his or her satisfaction at point A, on indifference curve I_2, by purchasing Y_o units of Y and X_o units of X. At this point, indifference curve I_2 is just tangent to the consumer's budget line.

Our consumer could, of course, manage to spend the entire budget by purchasing the quantities of Goods X and Y denoted by point B on indifference curve I_1. However, I_1 represents a lower level of utility than does I_2, so the consumer could do better than this point. On the other hand, no points on indifference curves higher than I_2 can be achieved with this budget. Consequently, this consumer will find that utility is maximized at point A, given the budget line.

Since the consumer's budget line must be tangent to the relevant indifference curve at the utility-maximizing point, the slope of the budget line and the slope of the indifference curve must be equal at that point. We just found the slope of the budget line to be $-P_x/P_y$. The slope of the indifference curve is equal to $(-1) MRS = -MU_x/MU_y$. Thus the consumer will maximize his or her satisfaction only if

(2A–9)
$$-\frac{P_x}{P_y} = -\frac{MU_x}{MU_y}.$$

We can easily show that equation (2A–9) is equivalent to the utility-maximizing rule developed with the cardinal utility approach. First, we multiply both sides of equation (2A–9) by $-MU_y$ to find

(2A–10)
$$\frac{MU_y}{P_y} \cdot P_x = MU_x.$$

If we now divide both sides of equation (2A–10) by P_x we obtain our earlier utility-maximizing condition:

$$\frac{MU_y}{P_y} = \frac{MU_x}{P_x}.$$

DERIVING A DEMAND CURVE

We now need go only one short step further to derive a consumer's demand curve for a product. This process is illustrated in Figure 2A–3, which shows two budget lines for Jim Bob, who is dividing his lunch-money budget between fajita tacos and slices of pizza. He can get either one *a la carte* at a shopping mall where he works. Initially, the price of a taco is $1, the price of a slice of thick, Sicilian pizza is $2, and Jim Bob has $20 a week to spend on lunches. (He drinks water for free.) This relationship is depicted by budget line $Y'X'$. With these prices and a budget of $20, Jim Bob will maximize his satisfaction at point A by purchasing ten tacos and five slices of pizza.

Suppose that the price of pizza falls to $1. The new budget will now be given by $Y'X''$. At the new price Jim Bob can now buy 20 rather than 10 slices of pizza if he spends all of his money on pizza. However, if he spends all of his budget on tacos, he can buy only the same number as before (20). With the new, lower price for pizza, Jim Bob will maximize his satisfaction by purchasing eight tacos and twelve slices of pizza, as shown in Figure 2A–3 at point B. As depicted in Figure 2A–4, we now have two points on Jim Bob's demand curve for pizza, given that the prices of other products and his budget in dollar terms remain the same.

Figure 2A–3   Effect of a Price Change

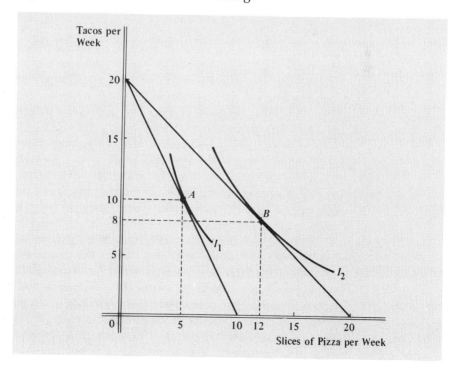

Figure 2A–4   Demand Curve for Pizzas

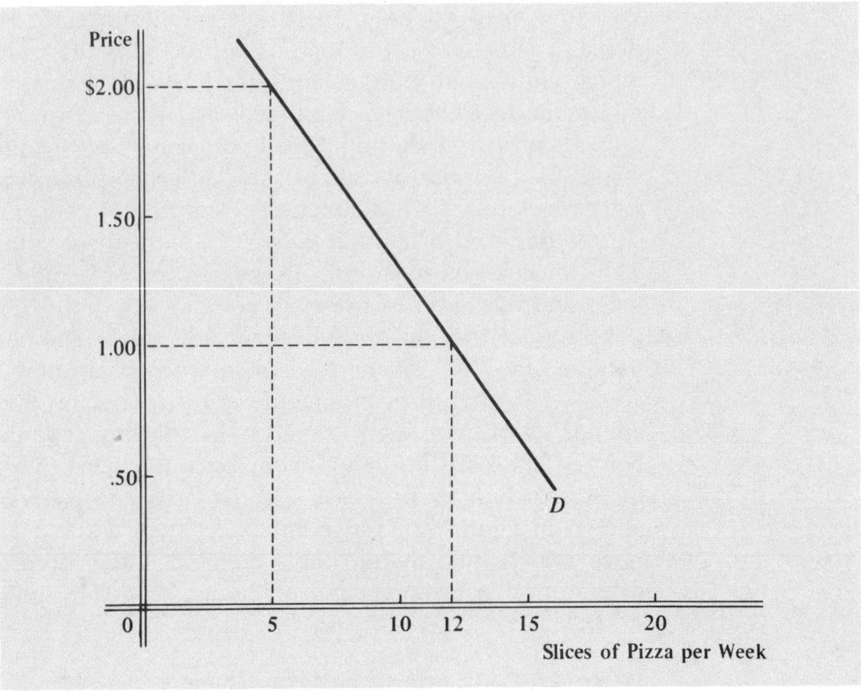

At a price of $2 Jim Bob will purchase five slices of pizza per week, whereas at a price of $1 he will purchase twelve slices of pizza per week.

We can separate the effect of the price change on the quantity purchased of pizzas into two parts: the (real) income effect and the substitution effect. The *income effect* occurs because if the price of a good or service purchased by a consumer changes, it has an effect on the consumer's *real* budget or income—what that dollar budget can purchase. In Jim Bob's case, when the price of a slice of pizza falls, his real income rises (by $1 times the five slices of pizza he previously purchased). He can now buy ten slices of pizza for the same amount of money as he paid for five slices at a price of $2. The *substitution effect* occurs because the price of a slice of pizza is cheaper relative to the price of a taco than it was before.

Figure 2A–5 shows how the price effect can be separated graphically into the two parts. Lines YX' and YX'' are the two budget lines from Figure 2A–3. Initially, Jim Bob purchases ten tacos and five slices of pizza per week, as shown at point A. After the decrease in the price of pizza, Jim Bob purchases eight tacos and twelve slices of pizza per week, at point B. Line RS is drawn parallel to the new budget line, $Y'X''$, but tangent to the original indifference curve, I_1. Consequently, line RS has the same price ratio (its slope) as the new budget line, but it allows the consumer to

Figure 2A–5   Income and Substitution Effects

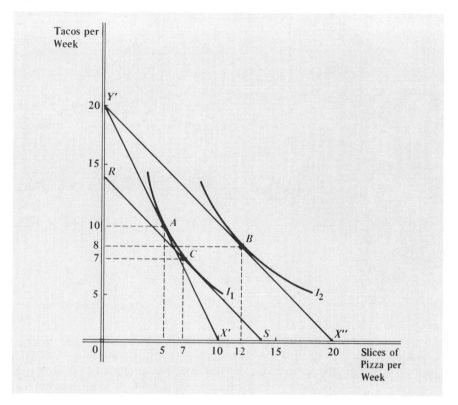

achieve only the same level of satisfaction as before the price decline. In this sense, budget line *RS* keeps the consumer's real income constant.

With budget line *RS*, Jim Bob will maximize his satisfaction by purchasing seven tacos and seven slices of pizza per week, at point *C*. The decrease by three units in the number of tacos purchased and the two-slice increase in the quantity of pizza purchased between points *A* and *C* show the substitution effect at work. The price ratio of the two goods has changed, but real income has remained constant.

The movement from point *C* to point *B* shows the income effect at work. The increase in real income Jim Bob experiences as a result of the fall in the price of pizza results in his purchasing five additional slices of pizza and one additional taco over what his position would be allowing for the substitution effect alone.

The substitution effect is always negative. That is, an increase in the price of a good or service relative to the prices of other products will always have a negative impact on our purchases of it. The opposite effect happens for a price decrease. The income effect may be either positive or negative, depending on whether a product is a normal or inferior good. In the preceding case, both tacos and pizza are normal goods.

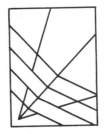

Topics in Demand Analysis
and Estimation

The primary objective of this chapter is to deal with the question of how the firm's managers can obtain information sufficient to put into operation the demand concepts we will repeatedly utilize in our discussions of revenue, profit maximization, and product markets. Obviously, *the more closely the firm can estimate demand conditions for its product, the more likely it is to determine correctly its profit-maximizing rate of output and price, or whether to produce a particular product at all*. The importance of accurate demand estimation is underscored by the results of a recent study that examined sales forecasts for 63 start-up computer software firms. The survey found that 43 percent of the companies' estimates of first-year sales were off by at least 30 percent; 77 percent of the companies' estimates were incorrect by at least 10 percent. On the average, the companies *overestimated* their first-year sales by 28 percent.

While the companies spent an average of $38,000 on demand estimation, the amount that they spent on these estimates had little relationship with the accuracy of the forecast. However, the accuracy of the forecasts did have a close relationship with how important firm owners *thought* it was to have accurate sales forecasts.[1] Ironically, an otherwise unnecessary business failure is likely to be the result of this lack of concern on the part of new firm owners.

■ ■ ■ ■ ■ ■
[1] "Sales Projections: Facts or Wishful Thinking?" *The Wall Street Journal*, July 2, 1989, p. B3.

Even well-established businesses have problems estimating the demand for their product or products. For example, RCA introduced its SelectaVision videodisc (CED) player in 1981. This machine had absorbed 15 years and $150 million in development costs. In 1984 RCA stopped production of the CED player after losses of $580 million. The company overestimated the demand for its players in the first few years after they were introduced because it did not foresee how rapidly the prices of videocassette recorders would fall during that period and the extent of consumer loyalty to the VCRs. Ironically, RCA finally abandoned the players just as their sales were rapidly increasing. Firm officials decided that sales would not grow sufficiently to make continued production of the players profitable.[2] That decision may have been RCA's second mistake, since the sales of videodiscs also fell dramatically when production of the players stopped. Over a longer time horizon, the combined production of players and discs may have become quite profitable.

Another example of incorrect market analysis is afforded by Ford Motor Company, which lost $250 million during the three years that it produced the Edsel. Today, U.S. automakers are still having trouble competing with cars made by foreign companies.[3]

Even "Big Blue" (International Business Machines) is not immune to marketing blunders. Although IBM spent $40 million on the *promotion alone* of its home computer, PCjr, production of the PCjr was discontinued only slightly more than a year after it was introduced in late 1983. Sophisticated users were turned off by its limited capabilities, and casual consumers were unhappy with its relatively high price compared with the prices of other home computers.[4]

The extent to which demand is *actually analyzed* varies greatly from firm to firm. One reason for this is market structure (firms that are perfectly competitive are unlikely to view demand estimation as a very significant activity since they do not have a sufficient market share to significantly affect the market price of their product). Another reason is lack of expertise or lack of the resources to obtain such expertise.

Thus demand estimation by firms runs the gamut from rough, rule-of-thumb decision making and "educated guesses" to the development of complicated econometric models relating a large number of variables to

■ ■ ■ ■ ■ ■

[2] See "Pioneer Electronics Videodisk Business Grows in Consumer Area That RCA Quit," *The Wall Street Journal*, January 9, 1985, p. 6; "CBS Will End Its Production of Videodisks," *The Wall Street Journal*, July 10, 1984, p. 8; "Slipped Disc," *Time* (April 16, 1984), p. 47; and "RCA's Rivals Still See Life in Videodiscs," *Business Week* (April 23, 1984), pp. 88–90.

[3] See "Will Japan Do To Europe What It Did to Detroit?" *Business Week* (May 7, 1990), pp. 52–53; "Motor City Madness," *Business Week* (March 6, 1989), pp. 22–23; "Ford Offers New Incentives to Spur Sales," *The Wall Street Journal* (March 30, 1989), p. B1; "Why Detroit Is Still Hooked on Sales Gimmicks," *Business Week* (May 19, 1986), p. 50; and "A Gallery of Goofs," *Time* (July 22, 1985), p. 51.

[4] "How IBM Made 'Junior' an Underachiever," *Business Week* (June 25, 1984), pp. 106–107.

the quantity demanded of a given product. We shall begin with a discussion of market surveys and then consider statistical estimation of demand functions and techniques for the generation of market data.

■ ■ ■ ■ ■ ■ ■ ■ **MARKET SURVEYS**

Many larger firms are able to allocate a substantial portion of resources and managerial effort to the task of demand analysis. More complicated demand functions involving variables other than price can be estimated from market data, and surveys or experiments can be undertaken to obtain a profile of consumer preferences. Generally, management can place a good deal more confidence in the results of a well-designed market experiment than in the results of a survey (that is, a questionnaire either filled out by respondents or administered by an interviewer), since the former provides information on how consumers *actually* react to certain changes, while the latter tells only how consumers *think* they will react *if* certain changes take place.

Surveys *can* be quite useful when questionnaires do not call for very fine discrimination by the respondents. For example, one might successfully survey consumer preferences regarding small cars versus large cars, since consumers may be able to differentiate easily between the two. However, it might be much more difficult for a consumer to determine whether a reduction in price of, say, 3 percent would be a sufficient incentive to buy a car this year instead of waiting until next year.

In addition to being limited in terms of what kind of information can be determined, large-scale market surveys can be quite expensive. Some years ago, for example, Clairol, Inc., undertook a consumer survey related to four of its hair-care products. The approach used combined advertising of the products with a mail questionnaire and a sweepstakes.[5] In other words, attention was drawn to the products in the *process* of administering the survey.

To conduct the survey, Clairol had to stand the expense of five full pages of color advertisements in each of four nationally circulated women's magazines, as well as $22,000 in sweepstakes prizes for respondents and all promotional and research expenses. (However, we should note that the purposes of the survey were probably dual: to advertise four of Clairol's products *and* to sample consumer preferences.)

Only three questions were asked about each product, and all of the questions related to product differentiation rather than to price. (Example: Why do you think Nice 'n Easy sells the most?

■ ■ ■ ■ ■ ■
[5] See *Family Circle* (February, 1977), pp. 1–4.

1. It leaves hair looking natural.
2. It leaves hair looking healthy.
3. It's easy to use; you just shampoo it in.

To the extent that customers participated in the survey, Clairol saved the cost of a stamp per response by having its respondents supply their own postage stamps on the mail-back questionnaires. However, management also obviously believed that the sweepstakes prizes were necessary to get a large number of responses.

It is clear that small businesses cannot undertake such ambitious campaigns as Clairol did to measure subjective perceptions of product traits. Nor is it necessary, as historical market data or data from smaller-scale market surveys or experiments can be utilized. Using some form of statistical analysis, small businesses, as well as Clairol's researchers, could examine the data that they obtained. We discuss one type of statistical technique, *linear regression analysis*, in the following section.

■ ■ ■ ■ ■ ■ ■ ■ DEMAND ESTIMATION WITH REGRESSION ANALYSIS

Regression analysis is a statistical technique used to "fit" an equation to empirical data in order to estimate the relationship between a dependent variable and one or more independent variables. In demand estimation, when regression analysis is employed, the dependent variable is the quantity of some product purchased or sold per unit of time; and the independent variables usually include such items as price of the product, prices of related goods (substitutes or complements), consumer income, advertising expenditure, and credit terms. The regression equation is usually linear or log-linear (a form in which the natural logarithm of the dependent variable is usually a linear function of the logs of the independent variables).[6] If there is more than one independent variable, the equation-fitting technique is called *multiple regression.*

Figure 3–1 provides a simple vehicle for explaining what regression analysis does. Suppose the quantity of frozen bagels sold is envisioned to be affected solely by the price of the bagels. In order to estimate monthly demand, we obtain data from a group of supermarkets (of about the same size and located in similar neighborhoods) over a period of time short enough so that any other factors that might affect bagel purchases will remain constant.

The points labeled Y_1, Y_2, etc., in panel (a) of Figure 3–1 represent the price-quantity observations we obtained from the data on supermarket sales of bagels (each Y_i is a price-quantity sold combination that existed at

■ ■ ■ ■ ■ ■
[6] We discuss natural logarithms in the appendix to this chapter.

Figure 3–1 Price and Quantity-Sold Observations and Corresponding Regression Line

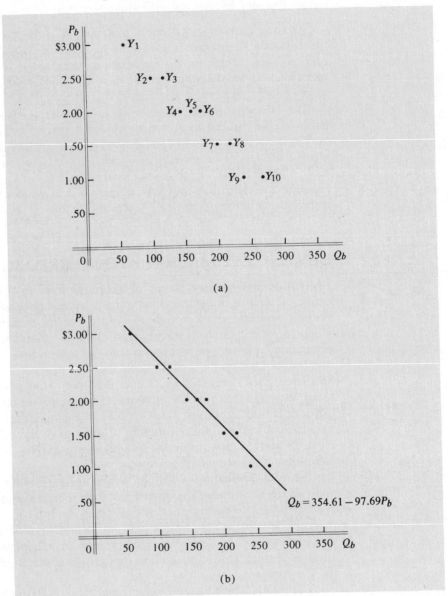

(a)

(b)

In panel (a), data are plotted showing different prices charged for bagels and corresponding quantities sold by a firm. In panel (b), a regression equation, $Q_b = 354.61 - 97.69P_b$, has been estimated. This equation represents the best linear approximation of the relationship of quantity sold of bagels to bagel prices.

some point in time in *one* of the supermarkets). Thus panel (a) of Figure 3–1 constitutes a scatter diagram of the relationship of the quantity of bagels sold to price per package of bagels. We can see that the set of points forms a kind of band that slopes downward to the right.

Using a linear regression model, a statistician can estimate a straight-line demand function, given a set of data points such as those in Figure 3–1, in a way that will ensure a statistical "best fit" to the scatter diagram. In panel (b) of Figure 3–1, the line drawn through the scatter diagram is a *regression line* representing the best linear approximation of the relationship of quantity sold of bagels to bagel prices. It is a best fit in the sense that the sum of the squares of the horizontal distances between the observed data points and estimated points lying on the regression line have been minimized.[7]

There are many computer programs available that perform the task of calculating the regression line when raw data on observed points are fed into the computer. The multiple linear regression demand function estimated by the computer will be of the form

$$Q_d = a + bX_1 + cX_2 + \ldots + nX_n,$$

where Q_d is the dependent variable and the X_i are the independent variables. For our scatter diagram in panel (b) of Figure 3–1, the regression equation turns out to be $Q_b = 354.61 - 97.69P_b$ which, given the current set of data, is the best linear approximation of the demand curve for bagels. (Here, Q_b is the number of 16-ounce packages of bagels sold per week in a supermarket of given size and characteristics, and P_b is the price of a package in dollars.)

The closer the observed data points lie to the regression line, the more confidence we can have in the predictive accuracy of the regression model. A measure of how closely the estimated relationship reflects or accounts for the variation in the observed data is R^2, the *coefficient of determination*. Briefly, R^2 measures the proportion of the total variation in the dependent variable that is "explained" by the variation of the independent variable(s). For our bagel model, the R^2 of 0.97 indicates that 97 percent of the variation in bagel quantity sold is "explained" by the variation of bagel prices.

The word "explained" is placed inside quotation marks because a large (close to 1.00) R^2 does not necessarily mean that variation in the independent variable(s) *caused* the variation in the dependent variable. Large R^2s are merely indications that the independent variables are *correlated* with the dependent variable; that is, the independent variables "vary together" with the dependent variable.

■ ■ ■ ■ ■ ■

[7] The *horizontal* distances are minimized because we are placing the *dependent* variable, Q_b, on the horizontal axis, as is customarily done for demand functions in economics.

The values of R^2s that are obtained in regression analysis vary widely (theoretically, from 0.00 to 1.00). When an estimate of a demand function using linear regression analysis has been obtained, it is then important to analyze the statistical significance of both the corresponding R^2 and the estimated coefficients of the independent variables. These topics are discussed more carefully in the appendix to this chapter.

One needs a course in advanced statistics to understand thoroughly the regression model and to learn how to interpret the obtained results. Nevertheless, the manager of a firm is often able to hire the expertise necessary to perform a statistical demand analysis and to establish a degree of confidence in its predictions. The cost of such a study can be quite small if the manager has kept accurate records of the relevant data. Furthermore, without too much effort, the manager can learn enough about statistics to be able to communicate with such experts and to utilize effectively the results of their analyses in making pricing and output decisions. We turn now to some actual cases of demand estimation utilizing regression analysis.

Examples of Regression Studies

It is difficult to obtain regression studies of demand that have been prepared by private firms, because firms generally avoid making public any information that might prove useful to competitors. Moreover, it is only on rare occasions that small firms will engage the expertise necessary to execute a soundly constructed regression analysis of demand. Because of such limitations, available studies tend to deal with product demand at fairly high levels of aggregation. Nevertheless, we shall discuss three such studies in the following pages.

Chow: The Demand for Automobiles

The demand for automobiles in the United States has been examined numerous times. A classic regression analysis is that done by Gregory Chow and published in 1960.[8] Chow's estimated automobile demand function is

$$X_t = -0.7247 - 0.048802P_t + 0.025487I_{e_t},$$

where

X_t = The per-capita stock of automobiles at the end of time period t, given in hundredths of a unit,

─────────

∎ ∎ ∎ ∎ ∎ ∎

[8] See G. C. Chow, "Statistical Demand Function for Automobiles and Their Use for Forecasting," *The Demand for Durable Goods*, edited by A. C. Harberger (Chicago: University of Chicago Press, 1960), p. 158.

P_t = an automobile price index, and
I_{e_t} = expected per-capita income.

The R^2 for Chow's equation is 0.895.

Since the coefficient of P_t is negative while that of I_{e_t} is positive, the equation indicates that an increase in automobile prices will reduce X_t, whereas an increase in expected income will increase X_t—which is as we would expect. As we learned in Chapter 2, it is possible from Chow's equation to calculate price and income elasticities of demand for *car ownership* when P_t and I_{e_t} are specified.[9] For the year 1960, Chow computed these elasticities to be about − 0.6 and + 1.5, respectively. Thus Chow's study supports the hypothesis that auto sales are much more likely to respond to increases in expected consumer income than to price reductions. Subsequent studies, some a good deal more complicated than Chow's, tend to support his results.[10] The generally low price elasticities may explain automakers' past reluctance to reduce list prices, even though they have been known to offer sizable rebates when caught with large inventories in periods of declining expected real consumer incomes. (The rebates and other incentives offered consumers during the 1980s and early 1990s are a case in point).[11]

In a more recent study involving the automobile industry, Carlson and Umble estimated the following demand function:

$$D_t^i = \beta_0 + \beta_1 Y_t^D + \beta_2 P_t^i + \beta_3 G_t + \beta_4 Z_t^E + \beta_5 Z_t + \epsilon_t$$

■ ■ ■ ■ ■ ■
[9] For example, if P_t = 120.0 and I_{e_t} is $600, then

$$X_t = -0.7247 - 0.048802(120.0) + 0.025487(600)$$
$$= 8.71126.$$

Thus

$$e_p = (\partial X_t / \partial P_t) \cdot P_t / X_t = -0.048802 \, (120/8.71126)$$
$$= -0.672261,$$

or approximately −0.67.
Also,

$$e_I = (\partial X_t / \partial I_t) \cdot I_{e_t} / X_t = 0.025487 \, (600/8.71126)$$
$$= 1.755452,$$

or approximately +1.76. Chow estimates that the price and income elasticities of demand for *new cars* is −1.2 and +3.0, respectively.

[10] For example, see H. F. Gallasch, Jr., "Elasticities of Demand for New Automobiles," Societal Analysis Department, Research Laboratories, General Motors Corporation, Warren, Michigan (May 21, 1976). However, Gallasch obtained estimates of price elasticity of demand between −1.6 and −1.3 and of income elasticity of demand of +1.0.

[11] See Joseph B. White, "Stumbling Auto Makers Face Tough '91," *The Wall Street Journal*, January 7, 1991, p. B1; "Motor City Madness," *Business Week* (March 6, 1989), pp. 22–23; and "Detroit's Sad New Year," *Newsweek* (February 15, 1982), p. 68.

where

D^i = the demand for car of size i;

Y^D = real (adjusted for inflation or deflation in the economy) disposable income, seasonally adjusted and adjusted for population size;

P^i = the average car price (adjusted for general inflation or deflation in the economy) for size i;

G = gasoline price (not adjusted for general price changes);

Z^E = a dummy variable to indicate periods of gasoline shortages;

Z = a dummy variable to indicate United Auto Worker strikes; and

ϵ = an error term.[12]

Carlson and Umble found that of the independent variables, disposable income appeared to have the greatest impact on the demand for automobiles. The coefficient of the automobile price variable was also statistically significantly different from zero, with the expected negative sign. The coefficient of the gasoline price variable was statistically significant and positive in the estimated demand equations for subcompact and compact cars, significant and negative in the equation for standard full-size cars, and not significantly different from zero in the equation for luxury cars. The coefficient of the variable for gasoline shortages was statistically significant and positive in the estimated equation for subcompact cars, not significantly different from zero in the equation for compact cars, and significant and negative in the equations for the other models.

Harp and Miller: The Demand for a New Convenience Food

Regression analysis can also be applied to the estimation of demand for a *new* product. The easiest way to approach this problem is to examine data for goods that are close substitutes for the new product in question. Since only about 10 percent of new products introduced survive one year, it is important for firms to have an estimate of the potential demand for a new product.[13] In research done under the auspices of the U.S. Department of

■ ■ ■ ■ ■ ■
[12] See Rodney L. Carlson and M. Michael Umble, "Statistical Demand Functions for Automobiles and Their Use in Forecasting in an Energy Crisis," *Journal of Business* Vol. LIII (April 1980), pp. 193–204.

[13] See H. H. Harp and M. Miller, "Convenience Foods: The Relationship Between Sales Volume and Factors Influencing Demand," *Agricultural Economic Report No. 81*, Economic Research Service, U.S. Department of Agriculture, revised October 1965.

Agriculture, H. H. Harp and M. Miller provide a regression equation that is an estimate of the demand function for a new convenience food.[14] The Harp and Miller equation is in log form and relates annual sales in 100 million serving units of product to nine independent variables. The equation is

$$
\begin{aligned}
\log Y = {} & -0.6 - 0.60 \, (\log X_1)^2 - 0.85 \log X_2 \\
& + 0.28 \, (\log X_3)^2 + 0.31 \log X_4 \\
& + 0.65 \log X_5 - 0.16 \, (\log X_5)^2 \\
& + 0.44 \log X_6 + 0.23 \log X_7 \\
& - 0.58 X_8 + 0.33 X_9
\end{aligned}
$$

where the variables are defined in the following manner:

Y = sales in units of 100 million servings,
X_1 = cents per serving of convenience foods,
X_2 = percentage market share of convenience foods that are close substitutes for the new one,
X_3 = cents per serving of fresh or home-prepared foods,
X_4 = cents per serving of highest volume near-substitute convenience food,
X_5 = importance of convenience food group in question in the consumer purchase pattern,
X_6 = index of availability in supermarkets,
X_7 = sales of highest volume competing good, and
X_8, X_9 = dummy variables to adjust for unusually high or low predicted sales.

In the equation used above, the *coefficients* of the independent variables (like X_2, X_4, X_6, and X_7), which are expressed in log form and are not squared, give estimates of their respective elasticities of demand. In other words, when the dependent variable and the independent variables are in log form, a *constant* elasticity of demand is estimated for each of the independent variables.[15] Since variables X_3 and X_4 refer to the cost of

■ ■ ■ ■ ■ ■

[14] *Ibid.*

[15] For example, suppose we have a hypothesized demand function,

$$
Q_d = a X_1^{b_1} X_2^{b_2}
$$

which in natural log form is

$$
\log Q_d = \log a + b_1 \log X_1 + b_2 \log X_2.
$$

The estimated b_i values give us estimates of the elasticity of demand with respect to X_1 and X_2, respectively.

(continues)

substitutes for the new convenience food, the positive values of the estimated coefficients of the terms involving those variables support our expectations that they would have positive cross price elasticities of demand. Variables X_1 and X_2, respectively, relate to the cost of the new convenience food and the market share of competing foods. As we would expect, we find that the estimated coefficients of the terms involving those variables are negative, indicating negative elasticities of demand with respect to X_1 and X_2.

Regression analysis is a powerful tool on which a large proportion of market research studies are based. If sufficient data can be obtained without unreasonable expense, a firm's management might be wise to undertake demand estimation using the regression approach whenever it is uncertain about the demand and revenue situation it faces. However, the regression model and its results must be carefully examined to ensure that the functional relationship specified is one that constitutes a reasonable depiction of the actual demand situation.

Since, as was stated earlier, variables that are related statistically do not necessarily have a cause-effect relationship to one another, management must always be careful in its use of statistically estimated demand functions. Moreover, important variables may have been excluded. In the Harp and Miller study, for example, an R^2 of 0.87 was obtained for the regression equation stated previously. However, the authors cautioned that their model is limited by the exclusion of three variables—product quality, brand promotion (advertising), and product life cycle.

Wilson: The Demand for Electricity

An example of an estimated demand function that has an unclear interpretation is the following:

$$Q = 21{,}737 - 1{,}178P + 144G - 1.370Y + 47.9R + 0.069C$$

◼ ◼ ◼ ◼ ◼ ◼

[15] (concluded) To see why this is so, recall that the elasticity of demand with respect to variable Z is given by

$$e_z = \frac{\partial Q_d}{\partial Z} \cdot \frac{Z}{Q_d}$$

If we examine the elasticity of demand with respect to X_1, we find

$$\frac{\partial Q_d}{\partial X_1} = ab_1 X_1^{b_1-1} X_2^{b_2}, \text{ and}$$

$$e_{x_1} = ab_1 X_1^{b_1-1} X_2^{b_2} \cdot \frac{X_1}{Q_d}$$

$$= ab_1 X_1^{b_1-1} X_2^{b_2} \cdot \frac{X_1}{a X_1^{b_1} X_2^{b_2}}$$

$$= b_1, \text{ since } X_1^{b_1-1} \text{ times } X_1 = X_1^{b_1}.$$

A similar result holds for X_2.

where

> Q = quantity of electricity demanded by households,
> P = Federal Power Commission's computed typical bill for 500 kilowatt-hours in the corresponding (to the household) city,
> G = price of natural gas in cents per therm,
> Y = median annual family income,
> R = average number of rooms per housing unit, and
> C = number of degree days.[16]

As we would expect, the coefficient of the price variable is negative, which indicates negative price elasticity of demand. The coefficient of the gas price variable is positive, which indicates both a positive cross price elasticity of demand and that gas and electricity are substitutes, which is also as we would expect.

However, the sign of the income variable coefficient is *negative*, which indicates a negative income elasticity of demand and implies that as incomes rise, people use *less* electricity. While it seems realistic to hypothesize that the income elasticity of demand is quite small (at least at high income levels), it is difficult to think of a reason why it should be negative. The problem may be the way in which the study was set up—it covered a cross section of 77 cities during one time period. It is possible that the negative income elasticity coefficient resulted because many of the higher income households were in areas where a large percentage of homes were heated by natural gas rather than by electricity.

Also, the coefficient of the house size variable was not significantly different from zero at the 10 percent level of statistical significance (those of the other variables were significant). The R^2 was only .52. Thus the researcher in this case perhaps should have tried to change the estimated demand function to see if a regression relationship could be obtained without the problems mentioned previously. For example, a variable could be added that would indicate whether or not most homes in a particular area were heated with gas or electricity. Such matters are discussed in greater detail in the appendix to this chapter.

■ ■ ■ ■ ■ ■ ■ ■ ■ ■ ■ **MARKET EXPERIMENTS**

Where there is uncertainty about product demand and the data required to perform a regression analysis are not available, it may be possible or desirable to conduct a market experiment that will generate such data. In a market experiment, those variables that are anticipated to be determinants of the quantity sold of a product are changed by the seller. For

■ ■ ■ ■ ■ ■

[16] John W. Wilson, "Residential Demand for Electricity," *Quarterly Review of Economics and Business* Vol. 11 (Spring, 1971), pp. 7–22.

example, if management believes the quantity of its product that can be sold is primarily a function of price and advertising, it can adjust (change) these two variables over a certain period of time or across different markets and study the relationship of these variables to quantity sold.

Market experiments, although useful, are inherently risky and expensive. For example, an experiment in which price is increased could lead to both a temporary reduction in revenues and a permanent loss of customers to rival firms. If the experiment includes increases in advertising, additional costs will be incurred. Another problem is that there are almost always some relevant variables that the experimenters cannot control (income, tastes, and prices of related goods). Finally, because of their expense, the size and duration of market experiments are usually limited; therefore such experiments may not generate a sufficiently large number of observations to allow much confidence in their results.

An example of the pitfalls of market experiments is provided by the introduction of "no-frills" fares in the airline industry during 1975.[17] At the request of National Airlines, the Civil Aeronautics Board (CAB) permitted experimentation with discount fares (reductions of up to 35 percent) on selected routes for a period of about ten weeks. National's competitors on the routes, Eastern Airlines and Delta Airlines, also were allowed to try out the lower fares, although they were opposed to the experiment.

When the experiment was over, National claimed to have exhaustively studied the effects of the fares on passenger traffic (quantity sold) and revenues, and its experts concluded that both the number of passengers and the sales revenues on the routes increased substantially because of the lower fares. While National claimed the thrift fares increased its revenue by $4 million over the trial period, Eastern and Delta claimed that their revenues fell (Eastern by over $500,000). Moreover, National engaged in a vigorous advertising campaign emphasizing the thrift fares. Thus the increases in traffic it experienced may well have been at the expense of the other two airlines, even though National claimed that 56 percent of the passengers it carried at thrift fares were new passengers who would not otherwise have flown.[18] However, National did decide to end the no-frills fares—at least with the 35 percent discount—in the spring of 1976.[19]

With CAB approval, the airlines continued experimenting with their fare structures in the late 1970s and early 1980s. On December 31, 1984, the CAB completely lost its power to control routes and fares as provided for in the Airline Deregulation Act of 1978.[20]

■ ■ ■ ■ ■ ■

[17] "National Says 'No Frills' Air Fare Helps, but Eastern Counters that Loss Resulted," *The Wall Street Journal*, July 8, 1975, p. 7.

[18] *Ibid.*

[19] Todd E. Fandell, "National to End 'No-Frills' Fare: TWA Will File for 2% Domestic Increase," *The Wall Street Journal*, March 22, 1976, p. 2.

[20] See "The CAB Flies into the Sunset Today," *The Wall Street Journal*, December 31, 1984, p. 8; and "CAB Flies into the Sunset, 'Closed Forever,'" *San Antonio Express News*, January 1, 1985, p. 1-C.

Since that time there has been a great deal of competition among the airlines with respect to fares as well as other promotional items, including frequent-flyer bonuses and discounts on hotels and car rentals. New airlines entered the industry, but a signifiant number of companies have declared bankruptcy. Some of the remaining airlines are having trouble making a profit.[21] However, in recent years the airline industry has become more consolidated, as airlines have either gone out of business or merged with other airlines, and ticket prices have started to increase once again.[22] Moreover, with the help of computers, airlines are able to track travel patterns more closely now than in the past. As a result, companies receive quicker feedback on their pricing experiments and are better able to design their fare structures to fit the market.[23]

■ ■ ■ ■ ■ ■ ■ ■   **SUMMARY**

Techniques of Demand Estimation

This chapter has examined several techniques of demand analysis and demand estimation. At the beginning of the chapter, we discussed *market surveys*, devices through which firms question customers about their preferences or their probable reaction to certain changes, such as changes in the price of a good. Although a market survey is certainly one method of obtaining information about consumer tastes and spending, we pointed out that consumer surveys do not guarantee sufficiently detailed or reliable data to present a firm with a precise estimate of its demand function.

Linear regression analysis, one of the main statistical techniques that a firm can use to estimate its demand function, was also examined. We discussed the interpretation of the estimates of the coefficients of the independent variables in the demand function as well as that of the coefficient of determination, R^2. We pointed out that even though a given firm's management may not have the expertise to carry out a statistical

■ ■ ■ ■ ■ ■

[21] See "All Lorenzo Needs Now Is a Few Billion More in Assets," *Business Week* (April 23, 1990), p. 33; "Ailing Pan Am Still Relying on Asset Sales," *The Wall Street Journal*, March 12, 1990, p. A4; "Braniff Files For Protection From Creditors," *The Wall Street Journal*, September 29, 1989, pp. A3, A14; "Super Savings in the Skies," *Time* (January 13, 1986), pp. 40–45; "Behind the Rise and Fall of Air Florida," *Business Week* (July 23, 1984), pp. 122–125; "Earning Wings the Hard Way," *Time* (February 3, 1986), p. 56; and "Up, Up and Away?" *Business Week* (November 25, 1985), pp. 80–94.

[22] "One Sure Result of Airline Deregulation: Controversy About Its Impact on Fares," *The Wall Street Journal*, April 19, 1990, pp. B1, B4; and "Skies Are Deregulated, But Just Try Starting a Sizable New Airline," *The Wall Street Journal*, July 19, 1989, pp. A1, A8.

[23] "Air Ticket-Pricing Gets Overhaul," *San Antonio Express-News*, April 8, 1991, p. 1-C; "Computers Permit Airlines to Use Scalpel to Cut Fares," *The Wall Street Journal*, February 2, 1987, p. 25; "Airlines Use a Scalpel to Cut Fares in the Latest Round of Price Wars," *The Wall Street Journal*, November 26, 1985, p. 31; and "Finding the Best Air-Travel Deal Gets Harder as Restrictions Grow," *The Wall Street Journal*, March 31, 1986, p. 21.

Managerial Perspective: *Peter Rabbit*, *Fatal Attraction*, and Market Experiments

Recently, Waldenbooks, the largest bookseller in the United States, began a market experiment with certain books. Waldenbooks negotiated an agreement that in exchange for not returning certain unsold books to the publisher, it could initially purchase these books at cheaper-than-usual prices. To be included were some children's books such as *Peter Rabbit* and *The Wind In The Willows*, some former bestsellers such as *Eat to Succeed*, and some art books.

Waldenbooks planned to keep track of the time each of these books spent on the shelf in its stores. If a book was not sold within 60 days, its price would be lowered. If it remained unsold for 90 days, the price would be lowered again. After 120 days, the price might be lowered for a third time, depending on the original price of the book. The in-store location of a book would change as each price reduction was made; presumably it would be displayed more prominently as a sale or bargain book. Dara Tyson, senior manager for public relations and promotions at Waldenbooks, described the program as "very revolutionary. It represents value and spontaneous buying."

Although Waldenbooks recognized that the new policy might reduce profit margins on these books, it anticipated that volume—and, correspondingly, inventory—turnover would increase sufficiently so that there would be a net positive effect on total profit. Some competing bookstore owners predicted that the new plan would not work and offered such comments as "I don't think the public can be fooled," and "If they don't want to buy a book, they won't, regardless of the price."

The authors have not seen a report on the results of this particular experiment; however, they have noted the presence of "bargain" books at a number of bookstores in recent years.

Waldenbooks was not the only company engaged in market experiments. Movie studios such as Paramount were conducting market experiments with home videos. While Paramount was pricing videotapes of some hit movies, such as *Fatal Attraction*, at $89.95, it listed others—*Top Gun*, for example—at $26.95. Disney took a similar approach when it set the list prices of *Lady and the Tramp* and *Good Morning Vietnam* at $29.95. While Paramount sold 500,000 copies of *Fatal Attraction* the first three months after its release, Disney sold 2 million copies of *Good Morning Vietnam* in the *first month* after its release. Disney figured that it had to sell 1.6 million copies of the movie at the lower price for it to make a greater profit than at a price of $89.95. (However, the expected sales volume at a price of $89.95 was not specified.) By September 1988, customers had purchased 3 million copies of *Top Gun* and 3.2 million of *Lady and the Tramp*. *E.T.* was expected to be a sure winner at $24.95.

Still, deciding which movies will have a sufficiently high price elasticity of demand for the cheaper prices to be profitable is not always easy. According to Robert Klingsmith, president of Paramount's video division, "It should be highly repeatable family fare that has comedy, music or action-adventure. Heavy drama like *Fatal Attraction* isn't the kind of program you put on TV every Saturday night for family viewing."

■ ■ ■ ■

References: "Waldenbooks to Cut Some Book Prices in Stages in Test of New Selling Tactic," *The Wall Street Journal*, March 29, 1988, p. 32; "Sales Can Soar, If the Price Is Right," *The Wall Street Journal*, September 23, 1988, p. 19. Also see "Movie Studios Produce Uneven Picture With Efforts to Win More Video Buyers," *The Wall Street Journal*, June 6, 1990, pp. B1, B4.

demand estimation procedure, it is possible to hire someone to perform such an analysis; we noted that without a great deal of study, one can gain enough knowledge of statistics to interpret and utilize the results of such an investigation.

Finally, we pointed out that if the firm does not have sufficient data available for statistical demand analysis, it may wish to conduct market experiments by changing price and/or the amount of advertising and recording the corresponding quantity sold. However, we also cautioned that market experiments may be costly, especially in terms of lost sales.

We have emphasized both in this chapter and in Chapter 2 the importance of a firm's knowing the demand function for its product. Without such insight on the part of the firm, profit maximization would be the result of sheer luck. However, the firm must decide *how much* data it will obtain and in what ways that data will be gathered, taking into consideration both the cost and the accuracy of the information. The firm should always be aware of the value of keeping records of prices charged, advertising expenditures, and corresponding quantities sold; these statistics comprise one source of information regarding its demand.

In the next two chapters, we turn our attention to production and cost. As we shall see later, two elements are essential if a business firm is to maximize its profit: an accurate analysis of the demand for the product and efficient production of that good or service.

■ ■ ■ ■ ■ ■ ■ ■ ■ ■ ■ ■ ■   **Questions**   ■ ■ ■ ■ ■ ■ ■ ■ ■ ■ ■ ■ ■

1. What is a market survey? What are some of the problems associated with the use of market surveys to estimate the demand for a firm's product?
2. What information is obtained through the use of linear regression analysis?
3. Discuss market experiments: what they are, how they may be used, and any drawbacks that they might have.
4. Explain how a hotel in Miami Beach might estimate the demand for its rooms. Be specific, including a description of what variables you would consider and why, as well as any other relevant information as to how you would conduct the experiment.
5. Using linear regression analysis, Estate Lighting Company estimated its demand function for a particular chandelier with the following results:

$$Q_E = 995 - 2.51P_E + 1.78P_C + 0.05I,$$

where

Q_E = quantity sold per year of the Estate Lighting chandeliers.
P_E = price of the Estate Lighting chandelier,
P_C = price of a competing firm's chandelier, and
I = average annual household income.

a. How can Estate Lighting use this information to find its price, income, and cross price elasticities of demand?
b. What would an R^2 of 0.84 indicate?
c. Can you think of a potentially important variable that Estate Lighting has ignored in its demand analysis?

6. In the Wilson article cited in this chapter, (page 84), a log (base 10) form of the demand function for electricity was also estimated with the following results:

$$\log_{10} Q = 10.25 - 1.33 \log_{10} P + 0.31 \log_{10} G - 0.46 \log_{10} Y \\ + 0.49 \log_{10} R - 0.04 \log_{10} C, (R^2 = 0.566),$$

where

Q = quantity demanded (kilowatts) of electricity,
P = cost of the Federal Power Commission's typical bill for 500 kilowatt-hours per month,
G = average price of natural gas (cents per therm),
Y = median annual family income,
R = average size of housing units, and
C = degree days.

a. What does each of the estimated coefficients represent in the above demand function? Interpret the economic significance of each of them.

b. What does a value of $R^2 = 0.566$ mean?

■ ■ ■ ■ ■ ■ ■ ■ ■ ■ Selected References ■ ■ ■ ■ ■ ■ ■ ■ ■ ■

Brennan, Michael J., and Thomas M. Carroll. *Preface to Quantitative Economics & Econometrics*, 4th ed. Cincinnati: South-Western, 1987.

Johnston, J. *Econometric Methods*, 3d ed. New York: McGraw-Hill, 1984.

Mirer, Thad W. *Economic Statistics and Econometrics*. New York: Macmillan, 1983.

Verleger, Philip K., Jr. "Models of the Demand for Air Transportation," *The Bell Journal of Economics and Management Science*, Vol. III (Autumn, 1972), pp. 437–457.

Appendix 3

Linear Regression Analysis

In this appendix we shall try to aid the interested student in achieving a better understanding of how a linear regression model is constructed and how it can be interpreted.

THE LINEAR REGRESSION MODEL AND UNDERLYING ASSUMPTIONS

If a researcher uses linear regression analysis, the assumption is made that two variables, Y and X, are related in the following manner:

(3–1)
$$Y_i = \alpha + \beta X_i + \epsilon$$

which states that Y is a linear function of X plus an error term.[1] Researchers usually include an error term in a regression model because they believe that while *on the average*, $Y = \alpha + \beta X$, there may also be other variables representing less important factors affecting Y that are left out of the regression model. Also, there may be measurement errors present. Another way to state what we have just said is that it is assumed that

(3–2)
$$\mu_{YX} = \alpha + \beta X,$$

where μ_{YX} is the *mean or average* value of Y given a particular value for X, α is the Y-axis intercept, and β is the slope of the function.

[1] We shall discuss only the case of one independent variable and one dependent variable. The case of more than one independent variable (multiple linear regression) is conceptually quite similar. For information on multiple linear regression, see the sources listed at the end of this appendix.

For example, suppose a supermarket has sold milk at a price of $.80 per half gallon for only four weeks and that during week 1, week 2, week 3, and week 4, it sold 100, 80, 90, and 110 cartons of milk, respectively. The average value of Y or Q_d, given X, or $P = \$.80$, is

$$\frac{100 + 80 + 90 + 110}{4} = \frac{380}{4} = 95.$$

Thus the mean, μ_{YX}, of Y *given* X is found by adding up all of the Y values corresponding to that particular X value and dividing by the number of observations. Thus

$$\mu_{YX} = \frac{\sum\limits_{i=1}^{n} Y_i | X}{n},$$

where n is the number of observations of Y associated with that particular value of X.

In order to compute some of the statistics and to interpret the statistical significance of the results obtained in most linear regression analyses done in the area of economics, the following additional assumptions must usually be made:

1. The error term, ϵ_i, is a random variable with a normal (bell-shaped curve) distribution.
2. The mean or expected value of ϵ is zero. We write this as $E(\epsilon) = 0$. This assumption means that while some values of ϵ may be positive, some negative, and others zero, the *average* value of ϵ is zero.
3. The *variance* of the ϵ_i terms *given each X value* is assumed to be the same and equal to σ_{YX}^2. We find the variance, σ_{YX}^2, by finding

$$\sum\limits_{i=1}^{n} \frac{(Y_i - \mu_{YX})^2}{n}.$$

Thus we sum the squared differences or deviations of each Y value from its mean, μ_{YX}, given a particular X. For our milk example,

$$\sigma_{YX}^2 = \frac{(100 - 95)^2 + (80 - 95)^2 + (90 - 95)^2 + (110 - 95)^2}{4}$$

$$= \frac{25 + 225 + 25 + 225}{4} = \frac{500}{4} = 125.$$

The *standard deviation* is given by $\sqrt{\sigma_{YX}^2} = \sqrt{125}$, which is approximately equal to 11.18 in the milk-carton example. We also assume that $E(\epsilon_i\epsilon_j) = 0$, where i *does not equal* j, which means that ϵ_i and ϵ_j are not related. Also, $E(\epsilon_i\epsilon_i) = \sigma^2_{YX}$.

4. *In economic research we usually assume that* X is a random variable with a normal distribution. (In a controlled experiment, the X values could be fixed.)

Estimators of the Slope and Intercept Terms

If we could observe all of the combinations of X and Y that have occurred in the past or would occur in the future for all possible values of X, our task of finding α and β or "fitting" the relationship hypothesized in equation 3–1 would be made much easier. All of these observations of X and Y are called the *population*. Unfortunately, in economics we usually cannot observe the entire population because obtaining all of the data is either impossible or too expensive. Thus we must make do with a *sample* (which we assume is randomly drawn) from the population data. This situation is one in which we must rely a great deal on the laws of statistics.

In the real world, therefore, our task is to find an estimate of α and β in equation 3–1 from a sample of data. Thus we want to find

(3–3)
$$Y_c = a + bX,$$

where a and b are estimates of α and β, respectively, and Y_c is the computed value of Y given a particular value of X and our estimated relationship. Then

$$Y_i = a + bX_i + e_i,$$

where e_i is the error term for our estimated relationship and is an estimate of ϵ_i, the population error term. Thus

$$Y_i - Y_c = e_i.$$

We would like our estimates of α and β to have at least two characteristics. First, if we took repeated samples and estimated α and β for each sample, we would like the mean or expected value of a to be equal to α and the mean or expected value of b to be equal to β. In other words we want $E(a) = \alpha$ and $E(b) = \beta$. In this case we say a and b are *unbiased estimators*. Second, we would like the values of a and b, which are found from each sample, to vary as little as possible among the samples. Thus we want σ^2_a and σ^2_b to be minimized.

Furthermore, we want our regression equation to be such that the sum of the squared error terms, $\Sigma^n_{i=1}e^2_i$ (*where n is the number of sample observations*), is minimized. We want to minimize the sum of the *squared* error terms because if our assumptions are correct, the sum of the error terms themselves should equal zero. It turns out that if we use a mathematical method to find a and b, which minimizes Σe_i^2, these estimators of α and β will also have the other two desirable properties (unbiasedness and minimum variance) mentioned previously. These estimators are

(3–4)
$$a = \overline{Y} - b\overline{X},$$

and

(3–5)
$$b = \frac{\sum\limits_{i=1}^{n} (X_i - \overline{X})(Y_i - \overline{Y})}{\sum\limits_{i=1}^{n} (X_i - \overline{X})^2},$$

where $\overline{Y}$ is the average or mean value of Y for the *whole sample* and $\overline{X}$ is the average or mean value of X for the sample.[2] The term $\overline{Y}$ is somewhat different from the term μ_{YX} discussed earlier, which is the *population mean of Y, given a specific X value*. It is also different from μ_Y, which is the *population mean* of all the Y values. We usually cannot observe the popu-

■ ■ ■ ■ ■ ■

[2] We can derive a and b in the following manner. Recall that

$$e_i = Y_i - Y_c = Y_i - a - bX_i.$$

Then

(3–6)
$$\sum_{i=1}^{n} e_i^2 = \sum_{i=1}^{n} (Y_i - a - bX_i)^2.$$

We wish to find values of a and b such that Σe_i^2 is minimized. To minimize Σe_i^2, we take the first (partial) derivatives of equation 3–6, with respect to a and b and set them equal to zero to satisfy the first order conditions.

(3–7)
$$\frac{\partial \Sigma e_i^2}{\partial a} = -2 \sum_{i=1}^{n} (Y_i - a - bX_i) = 0$$

and

(3–8)
$$\frac{\partial \Sigma e_i^2}{\partial b} = -2 \sum_{i=1}^{n} X_i(Y_i - a - bX_i) = 0.$$

Simplifying equations 3–7 and 3–8, we obtain the *normal equations*

(3–9)
$$\sum_{i=1}^{n} Y_i = na + b \sum_{i=1}^{n} X_i$$

and

(3–10)
$$\sum_{i=1}^{n} X_iY_i = a \sum_{i=1}^{n} X_i + b \sum_{i=1}^{n} X_i^2.$$

When equations 3–9 and 3–10 are solved simultaneously, we obtain

$$a = \overline{Y} - b\overline{X}$$

and

$$b = \frac{\sum\limits_{i=1}^{n} (X_i - \overline{X})(Y_i - \overline{Y})}{\sum\limits_{i=1}^{n} (X_i - \overline{X})^2}.$$

lation means, so we must therefore "make do" with the sample means. We call the estimators a and b for α and β, respectively, which can be found from equations 3–4 and 3–5, given above—the *least squares estimators* because they minimized Σe_i^2. We can also say that a and b are the *best linear unbiased estimators* (BLUE) because they have the additional two desired properties of minimum variance and unbiasedness. If the sample we take has n observations (values of X and Y), we can easily use an electronic calculator to compute a and b:

(3–4′)
$$a = \frac{\Sigma Y}{n} - b\frac{\Sigma X}{n},$$

and

(3–5′)
$$b = \frac{n\Sigma XY - \Sigma X\Sigma Y}{n\Sigma X^2 - (\Sigma X)^2},$$

where the sums are taken over the n sample observations.

Table 3A–1 gives an example of a sample of milk prices and quantity sold data collected by our supermarket. Notice that there are *six* observations, so $n = 6$. Given the information in Table 3A–1, we find

$$
\begin{aligned}
b &= \frac{n\Sigma XY - \Sigma X\Sigma Y}{n\Sigma X^2 - (\Sigma X)^2} \\[6pt]
&= \frac{6(480) - 700(4.30)}{6(3.19) - (4.30)^2} \\[6pt]
&= \frac{2880 - 3010}{19.14 - 18.49} \\[6pt]
&= \frac{-130}{.65} \\[6pt]
&= -200,
\end{aligned}
$$

and

$$
\begin{aligned}
a &= \frac{\Sigma Y}{n} - b\frac{\Sigma X}{n} \\[6pt]
&= 116.67 - (-200)(.72) = 260.67.
\end{aligned}
$$

Thus our estimated demand function is $Y_c = 260.67 - 200X$. In order to check casually to see how closely our estimate of the demand function reflects the actual sample points, we compute Y_c at $X = \$.70$ and find $Y_c = 120.67$. In this case the error, e_i, which is equal to $Y - Y_c = 120 - 120.67 = -0.67$. Similarly, at $X = \$.90$, we find $Y_c = 80.67$ and $e_i = 80 - 80.67 = -0.67$. The sample points and the estimated demand function are shown in Figure 3A–1.

Table 3A–1   Data for Milk Demanded Problem

Quantity Demanded Y	Price of Milk X	XY	X²
160	$.50	80	.25
140	.60	84	.36
120	.70	84	.49
110	.80	88	.64
90	.80	72	.64
80	.90	72	.81
$\Sigma Y = 700$	$\Sigma X = \$4.30$	$\Sigma XY = 480$	$\Sigma X^2 = 3.19$
$\dfrac{\Sigma Y}{n} = 116.67$	$\dfrac{\Sigma X}{n} = .72$	$(\Sigma X)^2 = 18.49$	

Figure 3A–1   Sample Points and $Y_c = a + bX$

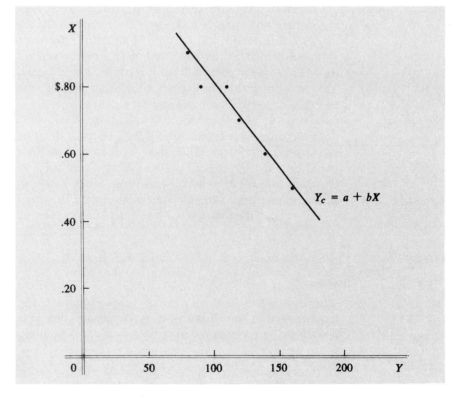

The sample points indicating the quantity demanded of milk and corresponding prices and the estimated demand function are shown here.

Interpretation of the Regression Statistics

Our casual observation indicated that our estimated regression equation "fairly closely" approximated the actual Y_i values in the sample. However, we usually wish to determine, using standard statistical measures, how closely an estimated function fits the sample data and what inferences we can draw from the estimate, which is based on the *sample*, regarding the *population* (quantities that would be demanded at *all possible prices*). Thus we shall discuss statistics that give us an indication of the statistical significance of the coefficient estimates and of the coefficient of determination, R^2; finally, we shall discuss a statistic that will allow us to find a confidence interval for Y, given X.

Statistical Significance of Estimates of α and β

First, let us examine the statistical significance of an estimate, b, of a coefficient, β, of the independent variable, X. Frequently in regression analysis, one of the prime concerns of the statistician is to determine whether or not the *actual* coefficient is different from zero (and sometimes whether it is positive or negative). This information is very important because it indicates the relationship between the independent variable and the dependent variable, which is the relationship the researcher is primarily interested in, in that type of situation. It turns out that we can use a statistical test to tell us whether or not we can reject the hypothesis (called the *null hypothesis*) that the coefficient in question is equal to zero (or some other number), *given a particular level of probability or chance that we are rejecting the hypothesis when it is true.*

To set up this test, we must calculate a *t statistic*. The *t* statistic has a distribution similar to the normal (bell-shaped) distribution when the sample size is large, and either the *t* distribution or the normal distribution could be used to analyze the statistical significance of the coefficients in this case. However, when the sample size is small, perhaps less than 40 observations, the *t* statistic should be used.

The *t* statistic that we need to calculate is given by

(3–11)
$$t = \frac{b - \beta}{\hat{\sigma}_b} ,$$

where b is the estimate of β and $\hat{\sigma}_b$ is the estimate of the standard deviation (square root of the variance) of b. We already know for our example that $b = 200$. The formula for $\hat{\sigma}_b$ is

$$\hat{\sigma}_b = \sqrt{\hat{\sigma}_b^2} = \sqrt{\frac{\hat{\sigma}_{YX}^2}{\Sigma(X - (\overline{X})^2}} .$$

The term $\hat{\sigma}^2_{YX}$ *is called the estimated standard deviation of the regression* or the *estimated standard error of the estimate*. We can find $\hat{\sigma}^2_{YX}$ from the following relationship:

(3–12)

$$\hat{\sigma}^2_{YX} = \frac{1}{n-2} \Sigma (Y - Y_c)^2.$$

Since $Y - Y_c$ represents the "error," or difference between the *actual* value of Y or and our *estimate* of Y or Y_c, it is easy to see how $\hat{\sigma}^2_{YX}$ got its name. The YX subscript indicates that we estimated the functional relationship between Y and X, or $Y = f(X)$. The term $n - 2$ represents *degrees of freedom* which, briefly, indicate the number of elements or values that can vary freely in computing t. We get six degrees of freedom from the sample observations ($n = 6$) for computing $Y - Y_c$, but we lose two degrees of freedom because a and b—which we use to find Y_c—are already determined by the regression equation. Thus for our example the degrees of freedom equal 4.

In Table 3A–2 we give the original sample values of X and Y and the computed values for $(X - \overline{X})$, $(X - \overline{X})^2$, Y_c, $(Y - Y_c)$, and $(Y - Y_c)^2$. Thus we can find

$$\hat{\sigma}^2_{YX} = \frac{1}{n-2} \Sigma (Y - Y_c)^2 = \frac{1}{4} (202.694) = 50.674.$$

Table 3A–2   Calculations for $\hat{\sigma}^2_{YX}$

Quantity Demanded Y	Price of Milk X	$X - \overline{X}$*	$(X - \overline{X})^2$	Y_c	$Y - Y_c$	$(Y - Y_c)^2$
160	$.50	−.22	.048	160.67	−.67	.449
140	.60	−.12	.014	140.67	−.67	.449
120	.70	−.02	.000	120.67	−.67	.449
110	.80	.08	.006	100.67	9.33	87.049
90	.80	.08	.006	100.67	−10.67	113.849
80	.90	.18	.032	80.67	−.67	.449
			$\Sigma(X - \overline{X})^2 = .106$			$\Sigma(Y - Y_c)^2 = 202.694$
			$\hat{\sigma}^2_{YX} = \dfrac{\Sigma(Y - Y_c)^2}{n-2} = 50.674$			

* Recall from Table 3A–1 that $\overline{X} = \dfrac{\Sigma X}{n} = .72$.

Now we can find

$$\hat{\sigma}_b = \sqrt{\frac{\hat{\sigma}_{YX}^2}{\Sigma(X - \bar{X})^2}} = \sqrt{\frac{50.674}{.106}}$$

$$= \sqrt{478.057} = 21.86.$$

The calculated value for t now becomes

(3–13)
$$t = \frac{b - \beta}{\hat{\sigma}_b} = \frac{-200 - \beta}{\hat{\sigma}_b}$$

$$= \frac{-200 - \beta}{21.86}$$

If we wish to test the hypothesis that $\beta = 0$, we substitute $\beta = 0$ into equation 3–13 and obtain

$$t = \frac{-200}{21.86} = -9.15.$$

To interpret this value for t, we must look at a table for the t distribution. A partial t table is given in Table 3A–3. Each value of t given in the table indicates the probability for ϕ degrees of freedom that t would be greater than the value given, assuming the hypothesis used to calculate t is true. A corresponding interpretation holds for t being less than (minus one) times the value given in the table. Thus from Table 3A–3 we see that for $n = 4$ degrees of freedom, the $P(t > 2.132) = .05$ or 5 percent. Also,

Table 3A–3   The t Distribution

ϕ Degrees of Freedom	γ 5 Percent	γ 1 Percent
1	6.314	31.821
2	2.920	6.965
3	2.353	4.541
4	2.132	3.747
5	2.015	3.365
6	1.943	3.143
7	1.895	2.998
8	1.860	2.896
9	1.833	2.821
10	1.812	2.764

Source: R. A. Fisher, *Statistical Methods for Research Workers,* 14th ed. (New York: Hafner Press, 1972), abridged from Table IV.

the $P(t < -2.132) = .05$ or 5 percent, where P stands for the probability or chance of some event occurring. The statement $P(t > 2.132) = .05$ means that in only 5 out of 100 times (on the average) would we calculate a t value greater than 2.132 *if the null hypothesis were true.* A similar interpretation holds for the figures in the 1 percent column.

The kind of probability statements given above are called *one-tailed tests* because they indicate the probability of t being *greater than* some number or the probability of t being *less than* some number if we consider $P(t < -2.132)$. If we wish to find the probability that t lies outside the interval given by plus or minus the t value given in the table, we must multiply the stated probability percentage by two (there is a $.05 + .05$ probability that t will be in either "tail"). Thus

$$P(t > 2.132 \text{ or } t < -2.132) = .10$$

for four degrees of freedom. We call this probability statement a *two-tailed test.* We could also state that the

$$P(-2.132 < t < 2.132) = .90,$$

since the probability of t being *outside* an interval plus the probability of t being inside the interval must equal 1.00.[3]

Now let us examine the t statistic that we computed for b, based on the null hypothesis that $\beta = 0$. In this case our computed value for $t = -9.15$. We see from Table 3A–3 that for four degrees of freedom,

$$P(t < -3.747) = .01, \text{ and}$$

since our computed value for t is *smaller* than -3.747, we can say that the chances are less than 1 in 100 that we would obtain a t value of -9.15 if the null hypothesis were true. Therefore, we can reasonably reject the null hypothesis and accept the hypothesis that β is less than zero. Another way of stating our conclusion is to say that b is significantly less than zero at the 1 percent level of significance.

We can also compute a t statistic for a, the estimate of the Y-axis intercept. The computed value of t for a is given by

(3–14)
$$t = \frac{a - \alpha}{\hat{\sigma}_a},$$

■ ■ ■ ■ ■ ■

[3] The probability of a *certain* event occurring is 1.00; the probability of an *impossible* event occurring is 0; and the sum of the probabilities of individual events occurring, *one and only one of which must and can occur* (but is not predetermined to occur), must be 1.00.

where

(3–15)
$$\hat{\sigma}_a = \sqrt{\hat{\sigma}_a^2} = \sqrt{\frac{\hat{\sigma}_{YX}^2 \Sigma X^2}{n\Sigma(X - \overline{X})^2}}.$$

From Tables 3A–1 and 3A–2, we can find

$$\hat{\sigma}_a = \sqrt{\frac{50.674(3.19)}{6(.106)}}$$

$$= \sqrt{254.167}$$

$$= 15.94.$$

If our null hypothesis is $\alpha = 0$ and our alternative hypothesis is $\alpha > 0$, then

$$t = \frac{260.67 - 0}{15.94}$$

$$= 16.35$$

From Table 3A–3 it is obvious that we can reject the null hypothesis that $\alpha = 0$ and can accept the alternative hypothesis that $\alpha > 0$; we can say that a is significantly greater than zero at the 1 percent level of significance.

The Coefficient of Determination: R^2

Another measure of the statistical significance of the regression line that we have found from the sample points is the coefficient of determination, or R^2. To understand what R^2 represents, note first that we may separate the deviation of the actual Y values from the *sample mean* into two parts in the following manner:

(3–16)
$$Y - \overline{Y} = (Y - Y_c) + (Y_c - \overline{Y}).$$

(Total
Deviation)   (Unexplained
Deviation or
Error)   (Explained
Deviation)

The term $(Y_c - \overline{Y})$ represents the portion of the deviation of the Y values which is "explained" by the regression equation that was obtained from the sample points. You should recall that $Y - Y_c = e_i$. It is also true, given our assumptions at the beginning of this appendix, that

(3–17)
$$\Sigma(Y - \overline{Y})^2 = \Sigma(Y - Y_c)^2 + \Sigma(Y_c - \overline{Y})^2.$$

$\Sigma(Y - \overline{Y})^2$ is called the *total* sum of squares, $\Sigma(Y - Y_c)^2 = \Sigma e_i^2$ is the *unexplained* sum of squares, and $\Sigma(Y_c - \overline{Y})^2$ is the *explained* sum of squares. If we divide equation 3–17 by $\Sigma(Y - \overline{Y})^2$, we obtain

(3–18)

$$1 = \frac{\Sigma(Y - Y_c)^2}{\Sigma(Y - \overline{Y})^2} + \frac{\Sigma(Y_c - \overline{Y})^2}{\Sigma(Y - \overline{Y})^2} .$$

R^2 is defined as

(3–19)

$$R^2 = \frac{\Sigma(Y_c - \overline{Y})^2}{\Sigma(Y - \overline{Y})^2} ,$$

or the ratio of the explained sum of squares to the total sum of squares. When the *unexplained* deviation equals zero, $Y = Y_c$ and

$$R^2 = \frac{\Sigma(Y_c - \overline{Y})^2}{\Sigma(Y - \overline{Y})^2} = \frac{\Sigma(Y - \overline{Y})^2}{\Sigma(Y - \overline{Y})^2} = 1.$$

When the *explained* deviation equals zero, $Y_c = \overline{Y}$ and

$$R^2 = \frac{0}{\Sigma(Y - \overline{Y})^2} = 0.$$

Consequently, the *maximum* value that R^2 can be is one, and the minimum value that R^2 can be is zero.

In Table 3A–4 we have computed the values for the total sum of squares, the unexplained sum of squares, and the explained sum of squares for our example. Thus we can find

$$R^2 = \frac{\Sigma(Y_c - \overline{Y})^2}{\Sigma(Y - \overline{Y})^2} = \frac{4,336}{4,533.334} = 0.956.$$

Table 3A–4   Analysis of Variance

Y	$Y - \overline{Y}$*	$(Y - \overline{Y})^2$	Y_c	$Y - Y_c$	$(Y - Y_c)^2$	$Y_c - \overline{Y}$*	$(Y_c - \overline{Y})^2$
160	43.33	1,877.489	160.67	−.67	.449	44	1,936
140	23.33	544.289	140.67	−.67	.449	24	576
120	3.33	11.089	120.67	−.67	.449	4	16
110	−6.67	44.489	100.67	9.33	87.049	−16	256
90	−26.67	711.289	100.67	−10.67	113.849	−16	256
80	−36.67	1,344.689	80.67	−.67	.449	−36	1,296
		$\Sigma(Y - \overline{Y})^2 = 4,533.334$			$\Sigma(Y - Y_c)^2 = 202.694$		$\Sigma(Y_c - \overline{Y})^2 = 4,336$

* Recall from Table 3A–1 that $\overline{Y} = \dfrac{\Sigma Y}{n} = 116.67$.

Therefore the regression line we estimated from sample points can account for almost 96 percent of the variation in the observed values of Y.[4] In the case where X and Y can both vary (as we have assumed here is true), the correlation coefficient, R, which is the square root of R^2, also can be interpreted as a measure of the degree of *covariability* of X and Y (of the extent to which X and Y vary together).[5]

Confidence Interval for Y

Suppose we wish to make a prediction regarding an individual Y value—such as a prediction about the quantity demanded of milk when the price of milk = $1.00. Usually, we would like to have some objective measure of the confidence we can place in our prediction, and one such measure is a *confidence interval* constructed for Y.

A confidence interval for a predicted Y, *given a value for X*, can be constructed in the following manner. We first find the value of a t statistic for Y where

(3–20)

$$t = \frac{Y - Y_c}{\hat{\sigma}_{YX} \sqrt{1 + \dfrac{1}{n} + \dfrac{(X - \overline{X})^2}{\Sigma(X - \overline{X})^2}}}$$

■ ■ ■ ■ ■ ■
[4] An R^2 value adjusted for degrees of freedom is often computed as

$$R'^2 = 1 - \frac{\dfrac{\Sigma(Y - Y_c)^2}{n - 2}}{\dfrac{\Sigma(Y - \overline{Y})^2}{n - 1}},$$

$$= 1 - \frac{\Sigma(Y - Y_c)^2}{\Sigma(Y - \overline{Y})^2} \cdot \frac{n - 1}{n - 2},$$

where $n - 2$ is the degrees of freedom of $\hat{\sigma}^2_{YX} \left[= \dfrac{\Sigma(Y - Y_c)^2}{n - 2} \right]$ and $n - 1$ is the degrees of

freedom of $\hat{\sigma}^2_Y = \dfrac{\Sigma(Y - \overline{Y})^2}{n - 1}$. This latter term loses one degree of freedom because $\overline{Y}$ is

fixed. For our example,

$$R'^2 = 1 - \frac{202.694}{4,533.334} \cdot \frac{5}{4}$$

$$= 1 - 0.054$$

$$= 0.946.$$

In our case R'^2 is quite close to R^2; and, in general, they will be very close when the degrees of freedom are large.

[5] This matter is discussed extensively in Taro Yamane, Statistics: *An Introductory Analysis*, 3d ed. (New York: Harper and Row, 1973), Chapter 15.

with $n - 2$ degrees of freedom. We also know that

$$P(-t_{.05} < t < t_{.05}) = .90,$$

which means that

(3–21)

$$P\left[-t_{.05} < \frac{Y - Y_c}{\hat{\sigma}_{YX}\sqrt{1 + \dfrac{1}{n} + \dfrac{(X - \overline{X})^2}{\Sigma(X - \overline{X})^2}}} < t_{.05}\right] = .90.$$

Multiplying both sides of the inequality by $\hat{\sigma}_{YX}$ times

$$\sqrt{1 + \frac{1}{n} + \frac{(X - \overline{X})^2}{\Sigma(X - \overline{X})^2}}$$

we obtain

$$P\left[-t_{.05}\hat{\sigma}_{YX}\sqrt{1 + \frac{1}{n} + \frac{(X - \overline{X})^2}{\Sigma(X - \overline{X})^2}} < Y - Y_c\right.$$

$$\left. < t_{.05}\hat{\sigma}_{YX}\sqrt{1 + \frac{1}{n} + \frac{(X - \overline{X})^2}{\Sigma(X - \overline{X})^2}}\right] = .90,$$

or

$$P\left[Y_c - t_{.05}\hat{\sigma}_{YX}\sqrt{1 + \frac{1}{n} + \frac{(X - \overline{X})^2}{\Sigma(X - \overline{X})^2}} < Y < Y_c\right.$$

$$\left. + t_{.05}\hat{\sigma}_{YX}\sqrt{1 + \frac{1}{n} + \frac{(X - \overline{X})^2}{\Sigma(X - \overline{X})^2}}\right] = .90.$$

If we wish to find the 90 percent confidence interval for quantity demanded (or Y) at a price of \$1.00 (or $X = \$1.00$) for our preceding example, we first compute

$$Y_c = 260.67 - 200(1.00) = 60.67.$$

From Table 3A–3 we find $t_{.05}$ for four degrees of freedom $= 2.132$. We know $\hat{\sigma}_{YX} = \sqrt{50.674} = 7.119$. Finally, we compute

$$\sqrt{1 + \frac{1}{n} + \frac{(X - \overline{X})^2}{\Sigma(X - \overline{X})^2}}$$

$$= \sqrt{1 + \frac{1}{4} + \frac{(1.00 - .72)^2}{.106}} = \sqrt{1.25 + \frac{.078}{.106}}$$

$$= \sqrt{1.986} = 1.409.$$

Consequently, the 90 percent confidence interval for Y, given $X = \$1.00$, is given by

(3–22)

$$P[60.67 - 2.132(7.119)(1.409) < Y < 60.67 + 2.132(7.119)(1.409)]$$
$$= P(60.67 - 21.38 < Y < 60.67 + 21.38) = .90,$$

or

$$P(39.29 < Y < 82.05) = .90.$$

We can interpret our confidence interval (3–22) as follows: if we were to select 100 samples and construct 100 corresponding confidence intervals for $X = \$1.00$, we should expect that 90 out of 100 of those confidence intervals will contain the actual value of Y corresponding to $X = \$1.00$.

Notice that the term

$$\sqrt{1 + \frac{1}{n} + \frac{(X - \overline{X})^2}{\Sigma(X - \overline{X})^2}}$$

gets *larger* as the given X value $\left[\text{in the numerator of } \dfrac{(X - \overline{X})^2}{\Sigma(X - \overline{X})^2}\right]$ gets farther and farther away from the sample mean, $\overline{X}$. Consequently, the farther the given X for which we wish to predict Y is from $\overline{X}$, the wider the confidence interval for Y for a given probability level, and our prediction of Y is less reliable. This last statement is particularly relevant if the given X value is outside the range of the sample observations.

Possible Problems in Linear Regression

Several problems may occur in linear regression analysis. If there is more than one *independent* variable, two of these variables may be so closely related that estimation of the relationship between these variables and Y is made very difficult. This is the problem of *multicollinearity*.

Another problem may occur when the ϵ_i terms are not statistically independent. In this case $E(\epsilon_i \epsilon_j) \neq 0$, for $i \neq j$, σ_b will usually be *underestimated*, and the statistical significance of b will be *overestimated*. This problem is called *autocorrelation*.[6]

A third problem may occur if the variance of ϵ_i is not the same for each value of X. In this situation we have the problem of *heteroscedasticity*.

■ ■ ■ ■ ■ ■
[6] One common statistic that can be used to test for the presence of autocorrelation is the Durbin-Watson statistic, computed as follows:

$$d = \frac{\displaystyle\sum_{t=2}^{n} (e_t - e_{t-1})^2}{\displaystyle\sum_{t=1}^{n} e_t^2},$$

(continues)

Finally, the fourth problem that we shall mention is that of *identification*. When we attempt to estimate a demand function, we must assume that all variables other than price or other independent variables included in the model that affect quantity demanded are held constant, so that the demand function is stable over that period. Figure 3A–2 illustrates the results we could get if the demand curve were shifting or if both the demand and the supply curves were shifting while the sample observations were gathered.

We shall leave a discussion of possible solutions to these problems to more advanced statistics texts.[7] At this point, we merely wish to warn our readers that such problems might occur.

■ ■ ■ ■ ■ ■ ■ ■ **LOGARITHMIC TRANSFORMATIONS**

In this last section, we shall discuss logarithms. Since *linear* regression analysis can be used only for the direct estimate of linear relationships between two (or more) variables, logarithmic transformations are often a useful means of changing a nonlinear function, which we cannot directly estimate, into an equivalent linear relationship, which we can.

Before we discuss this procedure, we shall first briefly explain what a logarithm is. The *logarithm* of a number is the power to which *another* number, called the base, must be raised in order for the whole term to be equal to the original number in question. Thus, since $3^2 = 9$, we can say that $\log_3 9 = 2$, where 3 represents the base. We can also say that $\log_2 16 = 4$, since $2^4 = 16$. In this case, 2 is the base. In general we can say that $\log_a N = x$, which means that $a^x = N$. Two bases that are commonly used are the base 10 and the base e. Logs taken to the base 10 are called *common* logarithms and are often used in computations. Logs taken to the base e are called *natural* logarithms, where e is approximately equal to 2.718. The base e is often used in studies involving growth or decay over

■ ■ ■ ■ ■ ■

[6] (concluded) where the subscript t refers to time period. Durbin and Watson computed values for d_L and d_U such that:

if $d < d_L$, reject the hypothesis that there is no autocorrelation and accept the alternative hypothesis of *positive* autocorrelation;

if $d > 4 - d_L$, reject the hypothesis of no autocorrelation and accept the alternative hypothesis of *negative* autocorrelation;

if $d_U < d < 4 - d_U$, do not reject the hypothesis of no autocorrelation;

otherwise, the test is inconclusive.

See J. Durbin and G. S. Watson, "Testing for Serial Correlation in Least-Squares Regression," *Biometrika*, vol. 37 (1950), pp. 409–428, and vol. 38 (1951), pp. 159–178.

[7] See J. Johnston, *Econometric Methods*, 3d ed. (New York: McGraw-Hill, 1984), Chapters 6–12, for a more detailed discussion of these problems and possible solutions. Also see Yamane (note 5), Chapter 23.

Figure 3A–2   Effect of a Shifting Demand Curve

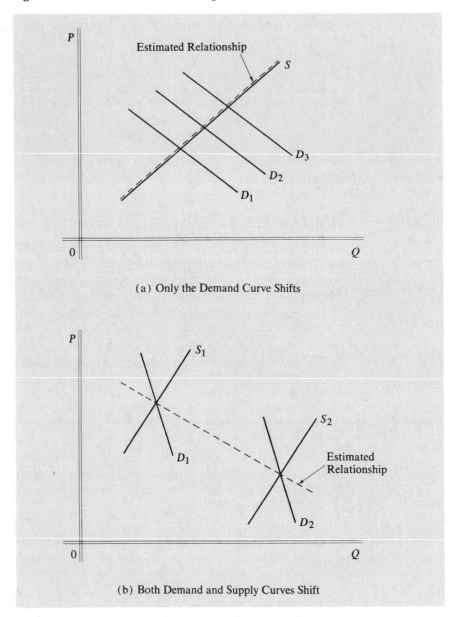

(a) Only the Demand Curve Shifts

(b) Both Demand and Supply Curves Shift

If the demand curve shifts over the period for which the demand function is being estimated, identification of the relationship becomes a problem. If only the demand curve shifts, as in panel (a), the supply curve may be estimated. If both the demand and the supply curves shift, as in panel (b), identification of which relationship (if any) is being estimated becomes more difficult.

time, since an amount A_o growing constantly at rate r for t time periods is equal to A_t, where

$$A_t = A_o e^{rt}.$$

The following rules hold for logarithms to *any base*, although we shall state them in terms of logs to base e.

1. Log of a Product

$$\log_e (XY) = \log_e X + \log_e Y.$$

The log of the product of two numbers is equal to the sum of the logs of each number.

2. Log of a Quotient

$$\log_e \left(\frac{X}{Y}\right) = \log_e X - \log_e Y.$$

The log of the quotient of two numbers is equal to the log of the denominator of the original fraction subtracted from the log of the numerator.

3. Log of a Number Raised to an Exponent

$$\log_e (X)^n = n \log_e X.$$

The log of a number raised to an exponent is the exponent multiplied by the log of the number.

4. $\log_e e = 1$, since $e^1 = e$.

As indicated above, logarithms, especially natural logarithms, are frequently used to transform nonlinear relationships into equivalent linear relationships, which can then be estimated using linear regression analysis. For example, suppose we wish to estimate α, β_1, and β_2 in the following hypothetical demand function:

$$Q_d = \alpha P^{\beta_1} Y^{\beta_2} e^\epsilon,$$

where

Q_d is quantity demanded per time period of a product,
P is price per unit of this product,
Y is income, and
ϵ is an error term.

We can transform this expression into a linear function by taking the logs of both sides of the equation as follows:

$$\log Q_d = \log \alpha + \beta_1 \log P + \beta_2 \log Y + \epsilon.$$

As we stated and proved earlier in Chapter 3, β_1 and β_2 represent the price and income elasticities of demand, respectively. Thus this type of demand function has constant elasticities of demand.

■ ■ ■ ■ ■ ■ ■ ■ ■ SUMMARY

The Linear Regression Model

In this section we shall summarize our assumptions regarding the linear regression model and the statistics that we have discussed.

A. Assumptions
1. The two variables Y and X are related in the following manner:

$$Y_i = \alpha + \beta X_i + \epsilon_i,$$

where ϵ_i is the population error term.
2. The error term ϵ_i is a random variable with a normal distribution.
3. The mean or expected value of ϵ is zero.
4. The variance of ϵ *for each* X value is the same. Also, $E(\epsilon_i \epsilon_j) = 0$, where i *does not equal* j, which means that ϵ_i and ϵ_j are not related.
5. X and Y can both vary.

B. The Regression Model
From a sample of values for X and Y, we wish to estimate a and b such that

$$Y_c = a + bX,$$

where the expected value of a equals α $[E(a) = \alpha]$, and $E(b) = \beta$. The best linear unbiased estimators of a and b are given by

$$a = \overline{Y} - b\overline{X},$$

and

$$b = \frac{\Sigma(X - \overline{X})(Y - \overline{Y})}{\Sigma(X - \overline{X})^2} = \frac{n\Sigma XY - \Sigma X \Sigma Y}{n\Sigma X^2 - (\Sigma X)^2},$$

where $\overline{Y}$ is the mean value of Y $(= \Sigma Y_i/n)$ for the sample, $\overline{X}$ is the mean value of X $(= \Sigma X_i/n)$ for the sample, and n is the number of observations in the sample. Each sum is to be taken over the sample observations.

C. Tests of Statistical Significance
1. Test for b.

$$\text{Compute } t = \frac{b - \beta}{\hat{\sigma}_b} \text{,}$$

$$\text{where } \hat{\sigma}_b = \sqrt{\frac{\hat{\sigma}_{YX}^2}{\Sigma(X - \overline{X})^2}}$$

$$\text{and } \hat{\sigma}_{YX}^2 = \frac{\Sigma(Y - Y_c)^2}{n - 2} \text{.}$$

The degrees of freedom are given by $n - 2$. We can use a table for the t distribution to decide whether or not to reject a null hypothesis regarding β.

2. Test for a.

$$\text{Compute } t = \frac{a - \alpha}{\hat{\sigma}_a} \text{,}$$

where

$$\hat{\sigma}_a = \sqrt{\frac{\hat{\sigma}_{YX}^2(\Sigma X^2)}{n\Sigma(X - \overline{X})^2}} \text{,}$$

and then use a t-table to test a null hypothesis regarding α.

3. The Coefficient of Determination: R^2.

$$R^2 = \frac{\text{explained sum of squared deviations}}{\text{total sum of squared deviations}}$$

$$= \frac{\Sigma(Y_c - \overline{Y})^2}{\Sigma(Y - \overline{Y})^2} \text{.}$$

Briefly, R^2 gives a measure of how much of the variation in Y can be accounted for by the variation in X, according to the estimate of the relationship between the two variables. A large R^2, however, does not mean that a change in X *caused* a change in Y but merely that the two variables vary together.

4. Confidence Interval for Y Given X.
The 90 percent confidence interval for Y given X can be found by computing

$$P\left[Y_c - t_{.05}\hat{\sigma}_{YX} \sqrt{1 + \frac{1}{n} ; \frac{(X - \overline{X})^2}{\Sigma(X - \overline{X})^2}} < Y \right.$$

$$\left. < Y_c + t_{.05}\hat{\sigma}_{YX} \sqrt{1 + \frac{1}{n} + \frac{(X - \overline{X})^2}{\Sigma(X - \overline{X})^2}} \right] = .90,$$

for $n - 2$ degrees of freedom.

▪ ▪ ▪ ▪ ▪ ▪ ▪ ▪ ▪ ▪ ▪ ▪ Problems ▪ ▪ ▪ ▪ ▪ ▪ ▪ ▪ ▪ ▪ ▪ ▪ ▪

1. Given the following sample points for sales of milk and corresponding prices for the supermarket mentioned in the appendix:

Quantity Demanded (Y)	Price of Milk (X)
240	$.20
230	.30
200	.40
160	.50
150	.50
140	.60
120	.70
110	.80
90	.80
80	.90

a. Find the least squares estimators a and b of α and β, where

$$Y_i = \alpha + \beta X_i + \epsilon_i,$$

and

$$Y_c = a + bX.$$

b. Compute the R^2 for the regression line that you found above.
c. Test the hypotheses that $\alpha = 0$ and that $\beta = 0$.
d. Compute the 90 percent confidence interval for Y, given $X = \$.50$.
e. Would you expect the estimates of α and β to be more reliable for a small sample or a large sample? Why?

This problem can be solved with Decision Assistant.

2. Connie Jefferson is the primary flower retailer in her home town of San Flores. Connie has watched the sales volume of her favorite flower, the yellow rose, change over the past ten weeks. The changes are due to

an experiment that Connie is conducting. She has been told she could sell more roses by reducing the price, and Connie tends to agree. In her experiment, Connie has set out to determine the relationship between the price charged for yellow roses and the quantity demanded. Over the last ten weeks, Connie has carefully tracked the selling price of her roses and the quantity sold. Her data is as follows:

Week	Price (in dollars)	Quantity Sold
1	30	50
2	8	270
3	10	240
4	27	90
5	25	110
6	21	130
7	12	200
8	15	190
9	19	160
10	20	150

a. Use the Bivariate Linear Regression tool in the *Managerial Economics Decision Assistant* to assist Connie in the following:
  (i) Determining the relationship between price and quantity demanded using regression analysis. (Determine the demand function.)
  (ii) Graphing the relationship between price and quantity demanded.
  (iii) Determining R^2. What does this answer mean? How reliable is your estimate of the demand function?
b. (Requires prior completion of Chapter 2 in the textbook.) Using the demand function you helped Connie determine in part a, assist her in the following:
  (i) Determining the total revenue, average, and marginal functions for the demand function of yellow roses.
  (ii) Obtaining graphic representation of those three functions.
  (iii) Determining the revenue-maximizing quantity and price. What total revenue will be generated given this price?

■ ■ ■ ■ ■ ■ ■ ■ ■ ■   **Selected References**   ■ ■ ■ ■ ■ ■ ■ ■ ■ ■

Johnston, J. *Econometric Methods*, 3d ed. New York: McGraw-Hill, 1984.
Mansfield, Edwin. *Statistics for Business and Economics*. New York: W. W. Norton, 1980.

Mendenhall, William, and James E. Reinmuth. *Statistics for Management and Economics*, 3d ed. Belmont, California: Duxbury Press, 1978.

Yamane, Taro. *Statistics: An Introductory Analysis*, 3d ed. New York: Harper and Row, 1973.

Integrating Case 1A

Are There Two Markets for Microwave Ovens?[1]

Master Cook, Inc. (MCI), which manufactures microwave ovens, is trying to determine its optimal pricing strategy. In the past MCI has been manufacturing a deluxe model of oven for people in the upper-middle-income bracket. The demand function of people (in this category) for the deluxe model is given by

$$Q_H = 60,000 - 50P_H + 25P_C + 10E_{W_H} + .14I_H + .0001A_H,$$

where

Q_H = annual sales (number of units) of the deluxe model,
P_H = price of the deluxe model,
P_C = price of a competing-brand oven,
E_{W_H} = number of women (in 1,000s) employed whose families are members of this income bracket,
I_H = average annual income of families in this bracket, and
A_H = annual dollar expenditures on advertising for the high-priced model.

Currently, P_H = \$600, P_C = \$500, E_{W_H} = 5, I_H = \$40,000, A_H = \$500,000, and Q_H = 48,200.

For several years after the deluxe model was introduced, demand grew rapidly. Now, however, MCI believes that the market for this model is fairly well saturated and that prospects for future growth in sales are limited. (Note the small size of the coefficients of I_H and A_H.)

■ ■ ■ ■ ■ ■

[1] For an article on microwave oven sales, see "Microwave Oven Sales Lose Some Speed," *Business Week* (July 31, 1978), pp. 99–100.

Consequently, MCI is trying to determine if its profits would be greater if it added a second model—less elaborate, but cheaper—to its product line. Some researchers in the marketing department have argued that there exists a large potential market among middle- and lower-middle-income consumers if MCI were to develop a substantially cheaper model that performed the basic function of fast cooking. In fact, the researchers were so convinced such a market existed that they mailed a questionnaire to 10,000 families living in the suburbs of several large U.S. cities. They selected residents of housing developments populated primarily by people in the target income bracket.

From the 5,000 questionnaires that were returned and from U.S. government statistics indicating the number of families in the target income range, the market researchers estimate that the demand function for the cheaper microwave oven is

$$Q_L = 34,800 - 100P_L + .05E_{W_L} + .7I_L,$$

where

Q_L = annual sales (number of units) of the lower priced model,
P_L = price of lower priced model,
E_{W_L} = number of women (in 1,000s) in the labor force whose families are members of these income brackets, and
I_L = average annual income of families in the target income range.

Currently, E_{W_L} = 40,000 and I_L = $16,000.

■ ■ ■ ■ ■ ■ ■ ■ ■ ■ ■ ■ ■ **Questions** ■ ■ ■ ■ ■ ■ ■ ■ ■ ■ ■ ■ ■

1. If management is prepared to design a microwave oven specifically for the moderate-income market, how can it use the estimated demand curve for the lower priced product to assess the relationship of its pricing decision to quantity sold and to the behavior of sales revenue? Suppose the managers were particularly interested in the following possible sales prices:

   P_L = $480, $450, $425, $400, $375, $350, $325, $300, $275, $250, $225, $200, and $175.

   What would be the estimated quantity sold at each price, and how would total revenue and arc marginal revenue vary from price to price?

2. Over what price range is the estimated demand for the low-priced oven *elastic*? Is it *inelastic* at any price or prices? If so, which?

3. What is the income elasticity of demand for this product between $I_L = \$16,000$ and $I_L = \$18,000$? (Assume $P_L = \$400$ and $E_W = 40,000$.) What do you think the prospects are for future sales growth as income rises? Why?

4. What is the effect of employed women on the quantity demanded of this product? Be sure that your answer is complete and precise.

5. What other variables (not in the estimated demand function for the cheaper model given above) might affect the demand for this product? How might the firm obtain information on their effects on demand after the new model is introduced?

6. Suppose that the additional cost incurred by MCI as a result of producing more of the cheaper models is $95 per oven over its feasible range of output. Can you determine from the table you constructed in Question 1 the optimal quantity of this oven for MCI to produce? Why? (We shall discuss this issue carefully in Chapters 4, 5, and 6.)

Integrating Case 1B

Omega Distributing Company I

Omega Distributing Company specializes in supplying laundry and cleaning products to chain grocery stores. One of the products it sells is a fabric softener marketed under the brand name Blast. Although the product has generated substantial net revenues for Omega, management is unsure of its pricing and advertising strategies and has undertaken, with the cooperation of some retail stores, to conduct a statistical analysis of demand for the product in its market area.

Omega's analysts believe that the principal determinants of consumer purchases of Blast are (1) the price charged for Blast, (2) the price of Cloud (a competing brand of softener sold by a rival firm), and (3) advertising expenditures on Blast. The following data were collected from a group of representative stores.

$Q =$ Weekly Quantity of Blast Sold (hundreds)	$P_b =$ Price of Blast (dollars)	$P_c =$ Price of Cloud (dollars)	$A =$ Advertising dollars (ten thousands)
1027	1.45	1.42	3.97
1204	1.29	1.45	4.54
974	1.47	1.39	3.77
1111	1.33	1.43	3.29
1042	1.44	1.40	3.49
1304	1.32	1.47	4.27
1054	1.33	1.38	4.11
997	1.35	1.37	3.50
1223	1.31	1.43	3.97
1247	1.30	1.44	3.88
1049	1.46	1.43	3.99
1250	1.27	1.47	4.54
972	1.47	1.38	3.75
1184	1.32	1.46	3.31
1054	1.43	1.41	3.49

In the table, the price of Cloud is the retail price charged consumers, while the price of Blast is the price Omega charges its customers. However, since the retailers use markup pricing, the price charged by Omega does determine what consumers pay for Blast.

Omega's analysts hypothesized that a linear demand function of the following form would describe the relation between quantity sold and the set of independent variables shown in the table:

$$Q = B_0 + B_1(P_b) + B_2(P_c) + B_3(A)$$

Using multiple regression analysis and the data in the table, they estimated the values of the coefficients B_0 through B_3 to be the following:

$$B_0 = -820$$

$$B_1 = -689$$

$$B_2 = 1,972$$

$$B_3 = 18 \quad \text{(all rounded to the nearest whole number)}$$

■ ■ ■ ■ ■ ■ ■ ■ ■ ■ ■ ■ ■ ■ **Questions** ■ ■ ■ ■ ■ ■ ■ ■ ■ ■ ■ ■ ■ ■

1. Assume that Omega's analysts found no statistical reason to reject the regression results or any of the estimates of the coefficients of the demand function. Management asks what the demand function indicates about how the sales volume of Blast is related to its price, the price of Cloud, and advertising expenditures on Blast. Duncan Haynes, a member of the team that carried out the study states that a number of important conclusions can be drawn by setting each of the variables in the table equal to its mean value and determining the quantity sold that the demand model estimates. He says that the signs of the estimated coefficients and the elasticity of the sales quantity with respect to each of the independent variables will indicate that Omega should consider some alterations in its current pricing and advertising strategies.

    Using the mean values of the independent variables in the table with the estimated regression equation, determine what strategy changes Duncan would be likely to suggest.

    This exercise should be carried out only by students who have access to a computer and a multiple regression program and have the statistical background to interpret the results.

2. Using the data obtained by Omega and the form of regression equation given above, estimate a linear regression equation for Omega's sales volume of Blast. Check to see whether your results agree with the linear function estimated by Omega's analysts. Interpret the results of the equation with regard to (a) overall goodness of fit and (b) significance of the estimated coefficients of the independent variables.

P A R T 2

Production, Cost, and Profit Maximization

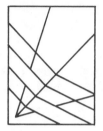

Theory of Production

The basic function of a firm is that of readying and presenting a commodity or service for sale—presumably *at a profit*. When the firm's activities center around a tangible product rather than a service, the firm may merely obtain the item from another enterprise and sell it to a third party, or it may also undertake the partial or complete (from raw materials) manufacture of that item. We shall use the term "production" in a broad sense so that it refers to all of the procedures that a firm may go through to present its good or service for sale.

Not long ago, the popular press was bemoaning the advent of the "hollow corporation" in the United States.[1] In the sense used here, a *hollow corporation* is one that has shifted its manufacturing base overseas or buys many parts and intermediate products abroad while maintaining its management base in the United States. In the mid-1980s, it seemed clear that American manufacturing companies were going to have to achieve more efficient production methods in order to be internationally competitive and bolster manufacturing activity and employment in their home country. Fortunately, it appears that many U.S. businesses have responded to that challenge.

When making product decisions, a firm's management must consider both *what* is to be produced and *how* to produce it. Companies that are successful over long periods of time usually have performed outstandingly well in both of these areas. General Motors is a firm that has in the past achieved long-run success attributable at least in part to careful product design and efficient organization of production. However, in recent years

------

[1] "The Hollow Corporation," *Business Week* (March 3, 1986), pp. 57–85.

the automaker's attempts to more fully automate its plants with robots have run into difficulties. GM's Japanese competitors, with less automation, high productivity, and their just-in-time inventory system, have been able to achieve lower costs both in their U.S. and in their Japanese plants.[2] Product quality also became a problem at GM, and the company's share of the U.S. new-car market declined from 44 percent to only 33 percent.[3]

In the eight-year period from 1982 to 1990, GM sunk over $3.5 billion into a new division, Saturn, to produce the Saturn automobile with production technology and organizational approaches that were, in many instances, completely new to the company. The subsidiary is said to have a "dream plant," located in Spring Hill, Tennessee. New production methods include "lost foam casting," which improves the precision of cast metal parts and reduces machining costs by as much as 30 percent. There are innovative assembly lines that allow for the manufacturing of both automatic and manual transmissions in any sequence, and materials and subparts flow smoothly from one part of the plant to another. Even loading docks have been placed at critical distances from the points where materials will be used.

Industrial giants such as GM are not the only organizations that have been revamping production processes. Small steel mills such as North Star Steel in Minneapolis have been able to produce some types of steel more efficiently than have the large ones. Their efficiency is partly the result of modern equipment, including the electric arc furnace and the continuous caster, and a successful effort to keep overhead low and improve intraplant communication.[4]

America's business schools also have been responding to the challenge in manufacturing. Donald P. Jacobs, Dean of Northwestern University's Kellogg School has said,

> . . . we take the threat to our manufacturing competitiveness very seriously. For the first time in our history we have . . . a triple "M," a masters of management in manufacturing. . . . But what shocked us is that we don't even have a brochure out explaining the program and we've already had 800 requests for information.[5]

■ ■ ■ ■ ■ ■

[2] "Auto Makers Discover 'Factory of the Future' Is Headache Just Now," *The Wall Street Journal*, May 13, 1986, pp. 1, 12.

[3] "Here Comes GM's Saturn: More Than a Car, It Is GM's Hopes for Reinventing Itself," *Business Week* (April 9, 1990), pp. 56–62.

[4] See "U.S. Minimills Launch a Full-Scale Attack," *Business Week* (June 13, 1988), pp. 100–102, and "Small Is Beautiful Now in Manufacturing," *Business Week* (October 22, 1984), pp. 152–156. National Steel, one of the healthiest of the major U.S. steel companies, in the mid-1980s sold a half interest to a Japanese steel company, Nippon Kokan (NKK). The Japanese firm quickly found 300 practices that needed to be changed to cut costs at National. See "National Steel's New Game Plan Is Made in Japan," *Business Week* (June 3, 1985), p. 78.

[5] "Shifting the Focus at B-Schools," *New York Times*, December 31, 1989, p. 4F.

Today's business publications are full of stories about trends toward "smart factories," "work teams," "concurrent engineering," "flexible manufacturing," and the "quest for quality" in U.S. industry.[6] Computer-integrated manufacturing (CIM) and computer-aided design (CAD) are two tools that have helped firms to both be more efficient and respond quickly to market changes. However, as the examples just cited have shown us, no mechanical or electronic device will substitute for careful, efficient, on-the-ball management. Making the right choices at the right time, simplifying and reorganizing production for greater efficiency, and producing products that are qualitatively equal to or better than imported alternatives depend on people skills, not just automation or robotics. In fact, General Motors is said to have benefited more from the management techniques it learned from Toyota in its California joint venture (Geo) than from what it found out about Japanese robotics or factory automation.[7]

In Chapter 2, we discussed the necessity of producing a product for which a sufficient market could be obtained. In the next two chapters, we shall discuss how a firm's manager can use economic principles to ensure that its product is produced at the lowest possible cost, *given a certain desired level of output.*

As we discuss production, it will be helpful to distinguish between two general categories of time periods—the long run and the short run. The **long run** is distinguished from the short run by being a period of time long enough for all inputs, or factors of production, to be variable as far as an individual firm is concerned. The **short run**, on the other hand, is a period so brief that the amount of *at least* one input is fixed. Certainly the length of time necessary for all inputs to be variable may differ according to the nature of the industry and the structure of the firm. For example, the long run for General Motors would likely be a greater length of time than that for a firm specializing in temporary office help. In a practical sense, economists think of the long run as a planning period involving decisions regarding investment in new plant and equipment, while the short run involves operations from existing plant and equipment.

> In the **long run** all inputs are variable, whereas in the **short run** some input or inputs are fixed.

■ ■ ■ ■ ■ ■ ■ ■ ■ **THE PRODUCTION FUNCTION AND THE LONG RUN**

We shall begin our discussion by concentrating on the production function. Briefly, a **production function** is a mathematical statement of the way that the quantity of output of a particular product depends on the use of

> The **production function** is a statement of how inputs can be combined to get various quantities of output of some given product.

■ ■ ■ ■ ■ ■
    [6] See "Making It Better," *Time* (May 8, 1989), pp. 142–148; "The Payoff From Teamwork," *Business Week* (July 10, 1989), pp. 56–62; and "Smart Factories: America's Turn," *Business Week* (May 8, 1989), pp.142–148.
    [7] "Downsizing Detroit: The Big Three's Strategy for Survival," *Business Week* (April 14, 1986), p. 87.

specific inputs, or resources. In the long run, it is possible to vary the amount of each input that is included in the function and therefore to use virtually any combination of the inputs to obtain output. For each possible combination of inputs, the production function indicates the *maximum quantity of output that can be produced*. For example, one production function might be $Q = L^2 + 2KL$, where Q equals quantity of output, K is quantity of capital, and L is quantity of labor. Another production function might be $Q = 10K^{1/2}L^{1/2}$. Table 4–1 gives some approximate quantities of output for the latter production function corresponding to different amounts of capital and labor. We say that the production function indicates *maximum* quantities that can be produced with each combination of inputs because we assume *all* inputs are being utilized efficiently; that is, none are idle or wasted. In other words, no workers are playing cards when they are supposed to be tightening bolts on an assembly line.

In general, we can represent the production function for a firm as

$$Q = f(a,b,c, \ldots ,z),$$

where a, b, c, . . . ,z are amounts of various inputs and Q is the level of output for a firm. Although a firm usually has more than two types of inputs and a more general case can be handled mathematically without too much difficulty, we shall restrict our discussion to a situation in which there are only two inputs. Thus we shall use a production function of the form

$$Q = f(a,b),$$

where a and b are factors of production and Q is quantity of output. We are limiting our discussion to the two-input case because it can be illustrated easily and because all of the economic principles that we derive from this case apply to a more general case as well. The production function relationship $Q = f(a,b)$ can be graphed as a surface in three-dimensional space so that the surface generally reaches higher altitudes

Table 4–1   Values of Q, K, and L for the Production Function $Q = 10K^{1/2}L^{1/2}$

K	Output Quantity (Q)				
5	22.36	31.62	38.73	44.72	50.00
4	20.00	28.28	34.64	40.00	44.72
3	17.32	24.49	30.00	34.64	38.73
2	14.14	20.00	24.49	28.28	31.62
1	10.00	14.14	17.32	20.00	22.36
	1	2	3	4	5	L

as the quantities used of inputs *a* and *b* increase (see Figure 4–1). Such a function indicates that a greater level of output can be achieved with greater amounts of the inputs—an assumption that seems realistic.

Isoquants and the Marginal Rate of Substitution

As we shall see later, the economic way of looking at the most efficient (that is, the cheapest) combination of two inputs that will produce a particular level of output is most easily understood if we first visualize the production surface in Figure 4–1 as consisting of a series of isoelevation contours (lines of equal height above the *ab* plane), each of which corresponds to a particular level of output (see Figure 4–2).

Now, imagine that these contours have been projected down into the *a*, *b* (input) plane (see Figure 4–3). These contours, which are called **isoquants** (meaning, literally, *equal quantity*), give the various combinations of inputs *a* and *b* that would enable a firm to produce a particular level of output. Thus each isoquant corresponds to a specific level of output and

> An **isoquant** is a contour line that shows the various combinations of two inputs that will produce a given level of output.

Figure 4–1   The Production Function

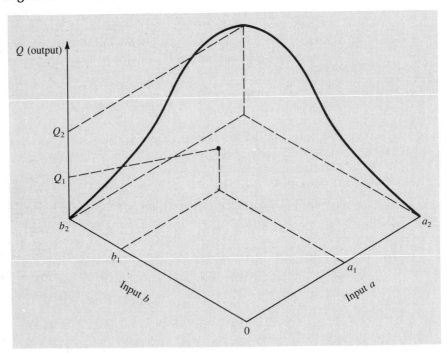

Figure 4–1 depicts a production function—the relationship between the quantity produced (*Q*) and the quantities utilized of two inputs, *a* and *b*. For example, with a_1 of input *a* and b_1 of input *b*, Q_1 units of output can be produced. A similar explanation holds for a_2, b_2, and Q_2.

Figure 4–2   Iso-Quantity Contours on the Production Surface

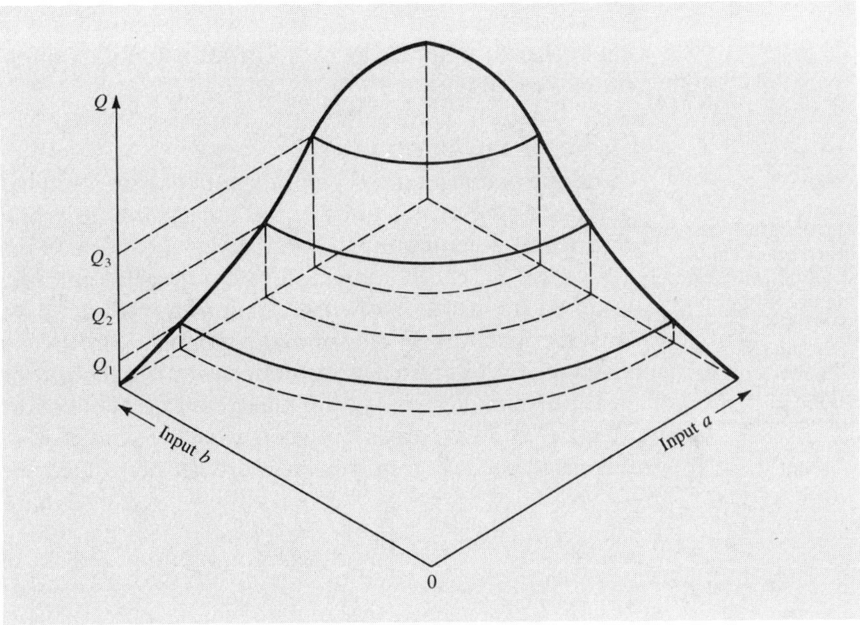

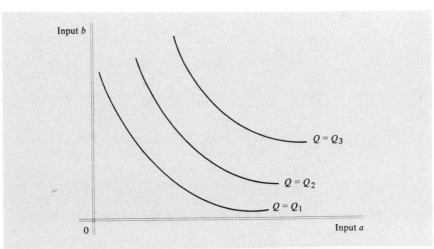

The iso-quantity contours depict various combinations of inputs a and b that can be used to produce levels of output equal to Q_1, Q_2, and Q_3, respectively.

Figure 4–3   Isoquant Curves

The iso-quantity contours depicted in Figure 4–2 are projected onto the input (a,b) plane in Figure 4–3. Here, they are called isoquants.

shows different ways, all technologically efficient, of producing that quantity of output. As we proceed northeastward from the origin, the output level corresponding to each successive isoquant increases because, as we stated earlier, a higher level of output usually requires greater amounts of the two inputs.

Slope of an Isoquant

The margin in the left column reads: The **marginal rate of (technical) substitution (MRS)** is the negative of the slope of an isoquant and shows how much of one input can be substituted for another, output constant.

The slope of an isoquant is significant because it indicates the rate at which factors a and b can be substituted for each other while a constant level of production is maintained. Specifically, the slope of an isoquant in Figure 4–3, or $\Delta b/\Delta a$, can be obtained by finding the amount of input b that can be given up if one more unit of input a is added while output is held constant, keeping Q constant. Economists call the negative of this term $(-\Delta b/\Delta a)$ the **marginal rate of (technical) substitution (MRS)** of input a for input b. In Figure 4–4 the marginal rate of substitution between points C and D is 3, whereas between points E and F it is 2/3. The MRS has decreased because inputs a and b are *not* perfect substitutes for each other.

Figure 4–4   Diminishing Marginal Rate of Substitution

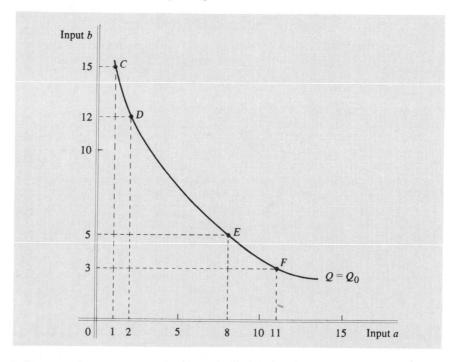

In Figure 4–4 the marginal rate of substitution of input a for input b decreases as the amount of input a used relative to input b increases. Between points C and D, $MRS = -(\Delta b/\Delta a) = -(-3/1) = 3$. Between points E and F, $MRS = -(-2/3) = 2/3$.

Therefore, as more of input *a* is added, less of input *b* can be given up in exchange for another unit of input *a* while keeping the level of output unchanged.

In Figure 4–5 we find an isoquant corresponding to an output level of 20 units for the production function illustrated in Table 4–1. That table indicated that 20 units of output could be produced in the ways shown here:

Level of Output (Q)	Amount of Capital (K)	Amount of Labor (L)
20	4	1
20	2	2
20	1	4

The two inputs involved are capital, measured on the vertical axis, and labor, measured on the horizontal axis. The marginal rate of substitution of labor for capital between points A and B is equal to $-(\Delta K/\Delta L) = -(-2/1) = 2$. Between points B and C, the marginal rate of substitution is equal to $-(\Delta K/\Delta L) = -(-1/2) = 1/2$. In this case also, the marginal rate of substitution is decreasing, and the inputs (capital and labor) are imperfect substitutes.

Figure 4–5 An Isoquant for 20 Units of Output

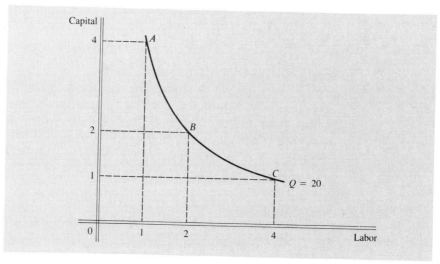

Figure 4–5 depicts an isoquant for 20 units of output. That level of output can be produced using 4 units of capital and 1 of labor, 2 units of capital and 2 of labor, or 1 unit of capital and 4 of labor.

Relation of MRS to Marginal Product of Inputs

The marginal rate of substitution $-(\Delta b/\Delta a)$ is equal to the ratio of the *arc* marginal product of input *a* to the *arc* marginal product of input *b*. Explained briefly, the arc marginal product of an input is the average change in output resulting from a unit increase in that input, holding the other input(s) constant. Thus $MP_a = \Delta Q/\Delta a$ and $MP_b = \Delta Q/\Delta b$. Along an isoquant, the *increase* in quantity resulting from the addition of input *a* must be exactly offset by the *decrease* in quantity from a reduction in input *b*, or $\Delta Q = 0 = MP_a(\Delta a) + MP_b(\Delta b)$. Thus $MP_a(\Delta a) = -MP_b(\Delta b)$, and dividing both sides by $\Delta a(MP_b)$, we obtain the following equation:[8]

$$\frac{MP_a}{MP_b} = -\frac{\Delta b}{\Delta a}, \quad Q \text{ constant.}$$

If we think about it, it must be the case that the rate at which one input can be substituted for another, while maintaining the same level of output, is inversely related to their relative productivities. For example, if 1 unit of capital will add 20 units of output per hour and 1 unit of labor will add 10 units of output per hour, then we can substitute 2 units of *labor* for 1 unit of *capital*. This relationship holds, since one unit of labor is only *half* as productive as one unit of capital in this case ($MP_L = 10 = \frac{1}{2}MP_K$). Thus

$$MRS = -\left(\frac{\Delta K}{\Delta L}\right), \quad Q \text{ constant} = -\left(\frac{-1}{2}\right) = \frac{1}{2} = \frac{10}{20} = \frac{MP_L}{MP_K}.$$

We shall discuss the concept of the marginal product of an input in greater detail later in this chapter.

Substitutability of Inputs

Three general types of shapes that an isoquant might have are shown in Figure 4–6. In Figure 4–6, panel (a), the isoquants are right angles, indicating that inputs a and b must be used in fixed proportions and therefore are *not substitutable*. An example of this type of situation would be yeast and flour for a specific type of bread. Tires and a battery for an automobile would be another example. In any such case of nonsubstitutable inputs,

---

[8] Precisely, in calculus terms, the slope of an isoquant is db/da, with quantity constant. We can find the slope of the isoquant by first finding the total differential of the production function. If $Q = f(a,b)$, then the total differential is $dQ = (\partial Q/\partial a)da + (\partial Q/\partial b)db$. Along an isoquant, $dQ = 0$, since quantity of output does not change and so $(\partial Q/\partial a)da + (\partial Q/\partial b)db = 0$. Solving for db/da, we find $db/da = -(\partial Q/\partial a)/\partial Q/\partial b)$, the slope of the isoquant. Finally, $\partial Q/\partial a$ is the marginal product of input *a*, and $\partial Q/\partial b$ is the marginal product of input *b*; so $db/da = -MP_a/MP_b$.

Figure 4–6   Substitutability of Inputs

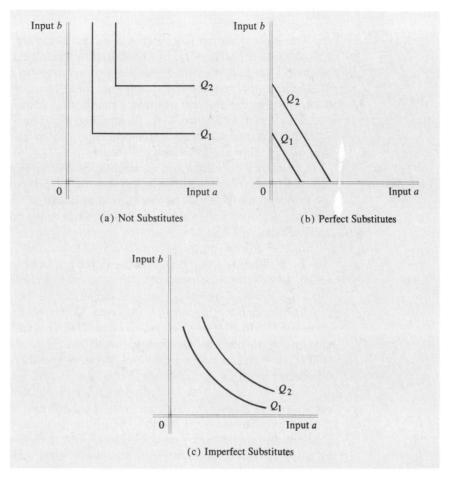

(a) Not Substitutes

(b) Perfect Substitutes

(c) Imperfect Substitutes

Panel (a) depicts the case of two inputs that are not substitutable. In this case one particular combination of inputs is required to produce a specific level of output. Output cannot increase without increased quantities of both inputs. Panel (b) depicts the case of two inputs that are perfect substitutes. They can be substituted for each other at a contant rate while the firm maintains the same level of output. Panel (c) depicts the case of inputs that are imperfect substitutes. They can be substituted for each other at changing rates, while the firm maintains the same level of output.

the *MRS* will be zero, since when an additional unit of *a* is used, there is no amount of *b* that can be given up if output is to remain constant.

The other extreme case—where inputs *a* and *b* are *perfect* substitutes—is shown in Figure 4–6, panel (b). In this case input *a* can be substituted for input *b* at a fixed rate, as indicated by the straight-line isoquants (which have a constant slope and *MRS*). In the area of baking, honey and brown sugar are often nearly perfect substitutes. Natural gas and fuel oil are close substitutes in energy production.

The most common situation is depicted in Figure 4–6, panel (c) (and was discussed previously). In this situation the inputs are *imperfect substitutes*, and the rate at which input *b* can be given up in return for one more unit of input *a* while maintaining the same level of output (the *MRS*) diminishes as the amount of input *a* being used increases (observe points C, D, E, and F in Figure 4–4). In farming, combines and labor for harvesting grain provide an example of a diminishing *MRS*; and, in general, capital and labor are imperfect substitutes.

The choice of which input combination to use is easy in the cases of inputs that are not substitutable and inputs that are perfect substitutes. In the first situation, there is no decision to be made. An automobile requires one engine, one transmission, and four wheels; no other combination of these inputs will do.

In the case of perfectly substitutable inputs, it is easy to calculate which, if either, of the two inputs is cheaper relative to its productive ability. For example, suppose 10,000 cubic feet of natural gas can produce the same amount of energy as one barrel of oil. Furthermore, suppose that 1,000 cubic feet of natural gas costs $3.30 and that one barrel of oil costs $36.00. In this case (all other factors being equal) a firm would use natural gas to produce its energy, since 10 x $3.30 = $33.00 (the cost of 10,000 cubic feet of natural gas) and $33.00 is less than $36.00 (the cost of one barrel of oil).

Since the decision-making process is relatively simple in cases where inputs are not substitutable or are perfect substitutes, we shall concentrate most of our attention on the case of inputs that are *imperfect substitutes*. Determining the cheapest combination of inputs that will enable a firm to produce a given level of output is somewhat more complicated in the last case, as we shall see shortly.

Least Cost Combination of Inputs

Once we have established the *technical* (physical) trade-off possibilities between inputs *a* and *b* in production, in order to make an *economic* (profit-maximizing) decision on their employment we still need to consider the rate at which they can be exchanged in the firm's budget. To aid our thinking in this regard, economists have developed the concept of the **isocost** (equal cost) **line,** which shows all combinations of inputs *a* and *b* that can be employed for a given dollar cost. Therefore the equation for an isocost line is of the form

An **isocost line** shows the various combinations of two inputs that can be bought for a given total dollar cost.

$$C_0 = P_a(a) + P_b(b)$$

where C_0 is the firm's total cost of inputs for some specific time period, P_a and P_b are the prices of input a and input b, respectively, and a and b represent the physical quantities of the two inputs. Verbally, the isocost equation states that when the firm's total cost is C_0 the price of input a times the *amount* of input a purchased (used) plus the price of input b times the *amount* of input b purchased (used) must equal C_0.

In Figure 4–7 we have drawn isocost lines for $C_1 = \$50$, $C_2 = \$80$, and $C_3 = \$100$, where $P_a = \$5$ and $P_b = \$10$. Note that these three isocost lines are *parallel*. They must be parallel because the slope of each line is equal to $-P_a/P_b$, or $-5/10 = -1/2$.[9] Note that the slope of an isocost line must be equal to $-P_aP_b$, since that represents the rate at which input a can be substituted for input b while maintaining the same level of cost. In our example above, if $P_a = \$5$ and $P_b = \$10$, then we can substitute 2 units of a for every 1 unit of b while maintaining the same cost level. Thus $\Delta b/\Delta a$, cost constant $= -P_a/P_b = -\$5/\$10 -1/2$.

The b axis intercept for each isocost line is equal to C_i/P_b, since dividing the total amount of expenditure by the price of an input will give the

Figure 4–7   Isocost Curves

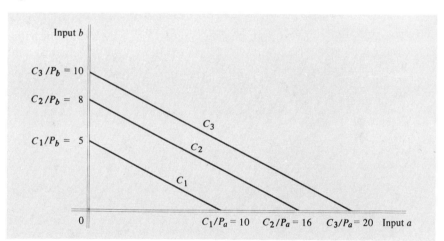

Figure 4–7 shows three isocost lines for inputs a and b. C_1, C_2, and C_3 represent cost levels of \$50, \$80, and \$100, respectively. The price of input a, P_a, is assumed to be \$5; and the price of input b, P_b, is assumed to be \$10. If the firm wishes to maintain a cost level of $C_1 = \$50$, it can use \$50/\$5 = 10 units of input a or \$50/\$10 = 5 units of input b. It can also use the other combinations of inputs a and b depicted by C_1.

■ ■ ■ ■ ■ ■

[9] If the equation for an isocost line is $P_a(a) + P_b(b) = C_0$, then the slope of the isocost curve (when b is on the vertical axis) can be found by solving for b and observing the resulting coefficient of a. Thus, $P_b(b) = -P_a(a) + C_0$, and $b = -(P_a/P_b) a + C_0/P_b$. Therefore, as long as P_a/P_b remains constant, the slopes of the isocost curves will remain the same.

maximum amount of the input that can be purchased if no other input is purchased. Thus, for C_1, the b intercept is $C_1/P_b = 50/10 = 5$. For C_2 it is $C_2/P_b = 80/10 = 8$. Similarly, the a intercept is $C_1/P_a = 10$ in the case of isocost line C_1, and it is $C_2/P_a = 16$ for isocost line C_2.

To obtain the combination of inputs a and b that will enable a firm to produce the *greatest output* for a *given cost* (or what is the same thing, to produce a *given* output at the lowest possible cost), the firm owner must employ the two inputs in such a manner that the isocost line corresponding to the given level of expenditure (cost) touches the highest isoquant possible. Such a point will occur where the isocost line is just *tangent* to an isoquant, and the point of tangency will identify the input combination that is most economical (see Figure 4–8). This result requires that the slopes of the isoquant curve and the isocost line be equal at that point, or $-P_a/P_b = \Delta b/\Delta a$ when output is held constant.[10] We call this combination of inputs the **least cost combination of inputs.** (We should note here that this formula for the least cost combination of inputs is valid only if the firm can assume that P_a and P_b are constant. We shall discuss this matter further in Chapter 12.)

> A **least cost combination of inputs** requires that the marginal product per additional dollar spent on each input be equal. This condition will hold at the point of tangency between an isocost line and an isoquant.

Figure 4–8   A Least Cost Combination of Inputs

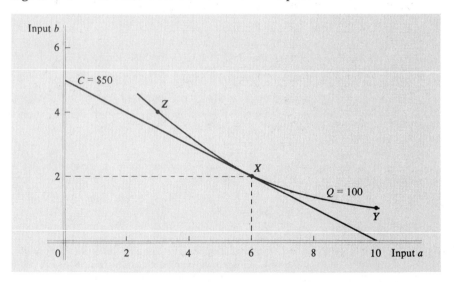

A least cost combination of inputs will be found where an isocost line ($C = \$50$) is tangent to an isoquant curve ($Q = 100$). In this case the cheapest way to produce 100 units of output is with 6 units of input a and 2 units of input b. This combination of inputs will also yield the greatest output (100 units) for a cost of $50.

■ ■ ■ ■ ■ ■
    [10] A least cost combination of inputs requires that $-P_a/P_b = db/da$ when Q is held constant, using calculus terms.

In Figure 4–8 if $P_a = \$5$ and $P_b = \$10$, then $-5/10$ (or $-1/2$) must be equal to $\Delta b/\Delta a$ at point X, where 6 units of input a and 2 units of input b are employed at a total cost outlay of $50 to produce 100 units of output. The same quantity of output could be produced using other combinations of a and b; for example, $a = 10$ units and $b = 1$ unit (point Y) or $a = 3$ units and $b = 4$ units (point Z), but they would cost more ($60 and $55, respectively). Moreover, there is no way to produce a quantity greater than 100 units with a cost limitation of $50. Thus, at point X the firm is producing 100 units of output in the cheapest manner possible or, alternatively, producing the greatest level of output possible for $50 cost.

Since $-\Delta b/\Delta a$ (the MRS) along the isoquant is equal to MP_a/MP_b, it must also be true that for the firm to be using the least cost combination of inputs,

$$\frac{-P_a}{P_b} = -\frac{MP_a}{MP_b}$$

Rearranging terms and dividing by minus one, we can see that this condition also requires that[11]

$$\frac{MP_a}{P_a} = \frac{MP_b}{P_b}.$$

This equation states that for the firm to be employing the *least cost* combination of inputs a and b, the *additional output obtainable from spending another dollar on input* a *must equal the additional output obtainable from spending another dollar on input* b. If this relationship did not hold, the firm would be better off purchasing either less of the input with a lower additional output per additional dollar expenditure or more of the input with a greater additional output per additional dollar expenditure, or both. For example, if the firm has two inputs—capital and labor—and if $MP_L = 5$, $P_L = \$5$, $MP_K = 40$, and $P_K = \$25$ (all in per-hour terms), then

$$\frac{MP_L}{P_L} = \frac{5 \text{ units}}{\$5} < \frac{MP_K}{P_K} = \frac{40 \text{ units}}{\$25},$$

or 1 unit per $1 is less than 1.6 units per $1. In this situation the firm would be better off using less labor and more capital.

For example, suppose that the firm used 5 fewer units of labor and 1 more unit of capital. Assuming that each of the 5 units of labor removed

■ ■ ■ ■ ■ ■

[11] Given $-P_a/P_b = -MP_a/MP_b$, we can multiply both sides of the equation by $(-MP_b)$ and obtain $MP_b \cdot (P_a/P_b) = MP_a$. Dividing both sides of the equation by P_a, we obtain $MP_b/P_b = MP_a/P_a$.

had the same marginal product, the results that follow would be obtained. From using 5 fewer units of labor:

Change in cost = $-5 \times \$5 = -\$25$ per hour

Change in output = -5×5 units = -25 units per hour

From using 1 more unit of capital:

Change in cost = $1 \times \$25 = \$25$ per hour

Change in output = 1×40 units = 40 units per hour

Net change in cost = $\$0$

Net change in output = $+15$ units per hour

Thus, by substituting 1 unit of capital for 5 units of labor, the firm would obtain an additional 15 units of output per hour without incurring any additional cost.

However, the firm would probably not find it in its best interest to fire all its workers and utilize *only* capital. Why not? The reason is that as more and more capital is substituted for labor, the marginal product of capital will most likely fall and the marginal product of labor will rise. This phenomenon occurs because the inputs are not perfect substitutes, and, as stated previously, in this case the marginal rate of substitution will vary as more of one input is used relative to another input.

This point is easy to understand if we visualize a plumbing contractor who has the job of digging a trench for a waterline. The use of some capital equipment, such as trenching machines and jackhammers, may be less costly than using all labor. Nevertheless, at the extreme it is hard to imagine trenching machines and jackhammers running themselves in a very productive fashion—some amount of labor will be required for a least cost combination of inputs.

Example of a Production Problem

Now let us consider a more realistic situation that a manager might face. Alert Concrete Company is considering modernization of its concrete-batching plant. Presently, it takes two workers to operate the plant at a rate of 30 yards of concrete batched per hour. If a third worker is employed in batching, output will increase to 40 yards per hour.

The result that can be obtained by modernizing the plant and retaining only two workers is an output rate of 45 yards per hour. The wage rate of the workers is $6.40 per hour, and management estimates that the additional costs associated with the modernization of the plant (depreciation, fuel, opportunity cost of funds, etc.) will be $14,400 per year, based on 265 working days of 8 hours each. Should the company hire an additional worker or should it modernize the plant?

To answer this question, the firm must get all of the figures on the same *per-unit basis,* such as per hour or per year. All of the figures given in the preceding two paragraphs are on a *per-hour* basis except for the cost of modernizing the plant. Therefore we shall transform the latter figure. If plant modernization will result in costs of $14,400 per year, based on 265 working days of 8 hours each, the *per-hour* cost of plant modernization is $14,400 divided by 2,120, or $6.80. (The figure 2,120 is 265 times 8, the total number of hours the plant is in operation per year.)

Now, to determine whether Alert Concrete should hire another worker or modernize its plant, we must compare marginal product per hour relative to cost per hour for a third worker versus modernizing the plant. For a third worker, $MP_L/P_L = 10/\$6.40 = 1.6$ units per additional dollar spent. For modernizing the plant, $MP_K/P_K = 15/\$6.80 = 2.2$ units per additional dollar spent. Thus the firm would get the most additional output per additional dollar spent by modernizing the plant.

We should point out, however, that the firm might want to go beyond our simple least cost rule and consider over what period of time it would desire to produce a higher level of output and how much higher that output should be. That is because modernizing the plant would give the firm less flexibility in regard to level of cost relative to level of output than would hiring another worker. Additionally, the firm would need to consider how wage rates might rise in the future relative to unit costs for modernizing the plant.

Economic Region of Production

Finally, we should emphasize that there are certain combinations of inputs that the firm should not use in the long run *no matter how cheap they are* (unless the firm is being paid to use them). These input combinations are represented by the portion of an isoquant curve that has a positive slope. A positively sloped isoquant means that merely to maintain the *same level* of production, the firm must use more of *both* inputs if it increases its use of one of the inputs. What is happening in this situation is that the marginal product of one input is negative; using more of that input would actually cause output to *fall* unless more of the other input were also employed.

This situation is illustrated in Figure 4–9. Point C on I_0 marks the spot where $MP_b = 0$. Beyond that point (greater amounts of b) on I_0, the MP_b is negative. We can see that beyond point C, if we use more of input b, we must also use more of input a to maintain the same level of output. At point D, the MP_a is 0, and if a greater quantity of input a is used, its marginal product becomes negative. At point E on I_1, the MP_b is zero; and at point F, the MP_a is zero. Lines such as 0X and 0Y, which connect the points on the isoquants where the marginal product of each respective

Figure 4–9   The Economic Region of Production

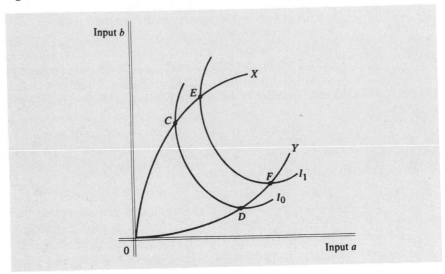

Ridge line $0X$ connects the points where the MP_b is zero. Ridge line $0Y$ connects the points where the MP_a is zero. A profit-maximizing firm will try never to produce using input combinations outside the ridge lines.

The **economic region of production** is the range in an isoquant diagram where both inputs have positive marginal product. It lies inside the **ridge lines**.

input becomes zero (MP_b for $0X$, MP_a for ($0Y$), are called **ridge lines**.[12] They bound the **economic region of production**, since the marginal product of one input is negative outside the ridge lines.

Expansion Path of the Firm

The **expansion path** is the path of least-cost input combinations in the isoquant diagram that occurs as the firm expands its long-run output at *given* input prices.

Given fixed input prices and our assumption about the slope of the isoquants (diminishing marginal rate of substitution), and if we assume the isoquant is a *smooth* curve, there will be one least cost combination of inputs for each level of output. The line connecting all such points is called the **expansion path** of the firm (see Figure 4–10). As we shall see later, the point that the firm finally chooses when it maximizes profit will depend on revenue considerations as well as on cost.

Returns to Scale

Returns to scale measures the effect on output of increasing all of the inputs in a production function by the same proportion (e.g., doubling all inputs).

Returns to scale is a term that refers to how output changes when *all* inputs are increased by the same multiple (e.g., doubled or tripled). If output increases by a greater multiple than that by which the inputs are increased, then *increasing* returns to scale are present. If output increases

■ ■ ■ ■ ■ ■
[12] Ridge line $0X$ connects points where the isoquants are vertical ($MP_a/MP_b = MP_a/0 = \infty$), and ridge line $0Y$ connects points where the isoquants have a zero slope ($MP_a/MP_b = 0/MP_b = 0$).

Numerical Example: The Least Cost Input Combination

Letterperfect, Inc. is now providing word processing services to its customers using ABM 286 computers. It leases the computers from ABM for $100 per month each and can lease more for this same amount. Letterperfect's business has increased, and it is planning to lease an additional computer. The ABM representative has told management that if it leases a new PS386 computer, word processing output on that machine should be about 54 standard pages per day— a high figure for their type of business. The new computer leases for $140 per month.

If Letterperfect's past experience indicates that an additional ABM 286 model yields 40 standard pages per day, should management lease the new computer or just another unit of the 286 model? Explain, relating your answer to the least cost input rule. (Assume 20 work days per month.)

Answer. Relate pages per additional machine (marginal product) to the respective machine's price. On a monthly basis, this would be 800 pages for the ABM 286 and 1080 pages for the PS386. So

$$\frac{MP_{ABM}}{P_{ABM}} = \frac{800}{100}; \quad \frac{MP_{PS}}{P_{PS}} = \frac{1080}{140}$$

$$8 > 7.71$$

Since the MP of $1 worth of the ABM 286 model exceeds the MP of $1 worth of the PS386 model, there is no reason to lease the newer model computer. The old model, while less productive per unit, provides more bang for the buck!

by the same multiple, *constant* returns to scale are present. Finally, if output increases by a smaller multiple, *decreasing* returns to scale are present.

For example, suppose a firm's production function is given by $Q = 2K^2 + LK + L^2$, where K is the quantity of capital and L is the quantity of labor. If the firm uses 5 units of labor and 5 units of capital, output equals 100. If labor and capital are both doubled to 10 units each, $Q = 400$, which is more than double the original quantity. In this case the firm has increasing returns to scale. On the other hand, if the firm's production function is $Q = 10K^{1/2}L^{1/2}$, and $L = 2$ and $K = 2$, then $Q = 20$. If capital and labor are doubled (to 4 units each), $Q = 40$, which is exactly double the original

Figure 4–10 The Expansion Path

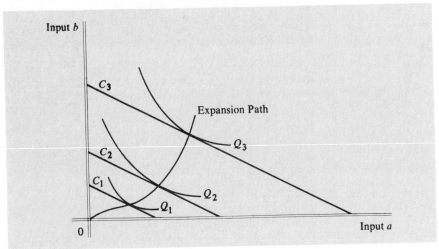

The expansion path connects least cost combinations of inputs for different levels of output. It is assumed that the input price ratio is constant.

level of output. In this case the firm has constant returns to scale. Finally, if the firm's production function is $Q = 100 + 5K + 10L$, and $L = 5$ and $K = 5$, then $Q = 175$. If labor and capital are doubled to 10, $Q = 250$, which is less than double the original output level. In this case the firm faces decreasing returns to scale.

As we shall see in Chapter 5, if a firm has increasing returns to scale, its cost per unit of output will decline as output increases. On the other hand, if a firm has decreasing returns to scale, its cost per unit of output will increase as output increases. Finally, if a firm has constant returns to scale, its cost per unit of output will remain constant.

The nature of its returns to scale is very important to a firm, not only because of the way returns to scale affect its own costs, but also because of the way in which such returns affect the firm's ability to compete with other firms of various sizes in the same industry. It's likely that three firms among those most aware of this principle are General Motors, Ford, and Chrysler, since it has long been argued that increasing returns to scale is an important phenomenon in the automobile industry.[13] However, the nature of returns to scale in this industry may be changing as production shifts to smaller cars.[14]

■ ■ ■ ■ ■ ■

[13] See *Administered Prices: Automobiles*. Report of the Subcommittee On Antitrust and Monopoly of the Committee of the Judiciary, United States Senate, Eighty-Fifth Congress, Second Session, November 1, 1958, especially pp. 13–16.

[14] See "Two Sides of a Giant: GM Can Learn a Few Lessons from its Dynamic European Offshoot," *Time* (February 19, 1990), pp. 68–70; "Is Your Company Too Big?"   (continued)

■ ■ ■ ■ ■ ■ ■ ■ ■ TOTAL PRODUCT CURVES AND THE SHORT RUN

The **total product function** of a variable input indicates the maximum output that can be obtained from different amounts of the input, while all other inputs are kept fixed.

The **average product** of a variable input is equal to total product divided by the number of units of the input in use.

The **marginal product** of a variable input is the rate of change of total product with respect to the input, all other inputs kept fixed. **Arc marginal product** is an approximation to marginal product over some range of output and is equal to the change in total product divided by the change in the variable input.

Although all inputs are variable in the long run for a firm, they usually are *not* all variable in the short run. We have defined the short run as a period of time sufficiently brief so that at least one input is fixed; in this section we shall assume that input b is the fixed input. Since we are treating input b as being fixed, we shall make use of a function that relates total output to levels of input a only. Accordingly, we shall define the **total product function** of input a (TP_a) as the function that indicates the maximum level of output possible with various amounts of input a and a fixed amount, b_0, of input b, so that $TP_a = f(a, b_0)$. We can also define the **average product** of input a as the total product of a divided by the quantity of a in use, or $AP_a = TP_a/a$. Finally, the marginal product of input a gives the rate of change of total output with respect to changes in input a. As has already been indicated, arc marginal product of input a is defined as the average addition to total product obtained by adding one more unit of input a, or $\Delta TP_a/\Delta a$. As arc marginal revenue was an approximation to marginal revenue, so is **arc marginal product** of input a an *approximation* to the marginal product of input a. That is because arc marginal product of input a measures the average rate of change of total output with respect to input a over *some range* of values for input a, rather than measuring the rate of change at a *single value* for input a.[15] The *short-run product functions* of the firm are

Total product = total output per time period related to different amounts of a variable input;

Average product = output per unit of variable input; and

Marginal product = rate of change of output as variable input increases.

As we have already seen, managers of the profit-oriented firm are deeply interested in how its output will vary with respect to the quantity used of an input. The reason, of course, is that such information is essential for determining the profit-maximizing level of output.

Law of Diminishing Returns

Figure 4–11 demonstrates the relationships among total product, average product, and marginal product. At point A, marginal product (which is the slope of the total product curve) reaches a maximum, and beyond that

■ ■ ■ ■ ■ ■

[14] (concluded)   *Business Week* (March 27, 1989), pp. 84–94; John Koten, "Ford Decides Bigness Isn't a Better Idea," *The Wall Street Journal*, September 16, 1981, p. 25; and "Small Is Beautiful Now in Manufacturing," *Business Week* (October 22, 1984), pp. 152–156.

[15] Technically, the marginal product of input a is given by $dTP_a/da = \partial Q/\partial a$, where input b is held constant at some level, b_0.

Managerial Perspective: Changing Production Functions in U.S. Manufacturing

The whole world knows that U.S. manufacturing has been on the defensive for several decades. Faced with increasing foreign competition of ever-higher quality, U.S. firms used to run to Washington for restrictions against imports of foreign goods. While this approach is not entirely a thing of the past, many American firms have come around to the view that the best defense is a good offense.

Recent examples of firms that have taken the offensive in manufacturing include one very small firm in the steel industry and one very large firm that makes automobiles. Tiny Nucor Corporation in late 1989 began to ship steel from its revolutionary thin-slab plant and created quite a stir in the steel industry. Nucor had revised the production function for making flat-rolled steel sheets in a way that will change the face of its industry for years to come. The process, which creates a much thinner piece of steel for the rolling mill than any previous technology, has reduced the number of worker hours required per ton of sheet steel by 75 percent. All of the big U.S. steel producers are studying the technology carefully, and Nucor reports that experts from Russia, China, and India have visited its plant. It is clear that new capital-labor combinations have entered the production function for steel, and these will alter firms' decisions markedly in the future.

At the other end of the size spectrum, Ford Motor Company chose to spend upwards of a billion dollars on a new breed of engine plant. Located in Romeo, Michigan, the plant focuses on a modular engine design which reduces parts by 25 percent. Flexible manufacturing techniques at the new plant allow for the production of more than a dozen different sizes of engines on the same production line. The engines have many interchangeable parts, and alternators, smog pumps, and other self-contained units are bolted directly onto the engine block rather than requiring complicated brackets. The plant can be shifted to the manufacture of smaller, more fuel-efficient engines very quickly, should government regulations require it. Reportedly, the new approach has reduced the retooling costs for new V-8 engines from a typical $500 million figure to about $60 million.

∎ ∎ ∎ ∎

References: "Big Steel is Facing David vs. Goliath Test," *The Wall Street Journal*, Oct. 17, 1989, p. A16; and "A Dozen Motor Factories—Under One Roof," *Business Week* (November 20, 1989), pp. 90, 94.

Figure 4–11   Total Product, Average Product, and Marginal Product Curves

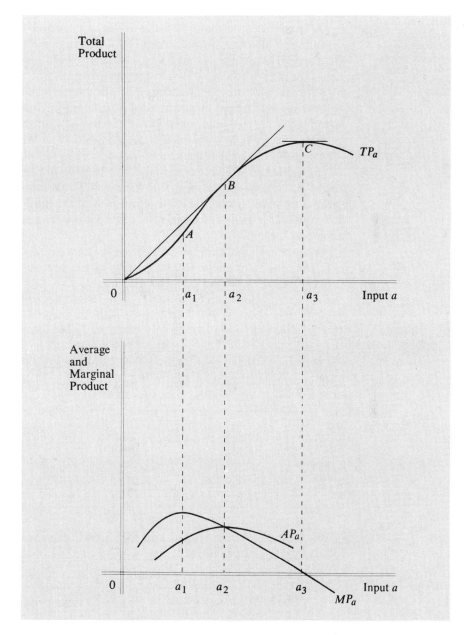

Figure 4–11 depicts the relationships among the total product (TP_a), average product (AP_a), and marginal product (MP_a) of input a. The TP_a is at a maximum when $MP_a = 0$. Also, $MP_a = AP_a$ when AP_a is at a maximum.

The **law of diminishing returns** states that in the short run the marginal product of a variable input will eventually fall as output is increased.

point, diminishing returns to input a set in. The portion of the marginal product curve after point A illustrates the economic **law of diminishing returns** (or diminishing marginal productivity). This law asserts that if equal increments of one variable input are added while keeping the amounts of all other inputs fixed, total product may increase; but *after some point, the additions to total product* (the marginal product) *will decrease.* This law merely recognizes the fact that inputs are usually not perfect substitutes. For example, in farming, the first unit of labor, when combined with some machinery and a field of wheat, might increase total product significantly. After some point, however, the next unit of labor will surely increase the total bushels of wheat produced by a smaller amount than did the previous unit of labor employed.

Examples of the law of diminishing returns are shown in Tables 4–2 and 4–3, which are derived from Table 4–1. In Table 4–2, diminishing returns to factor L set in after the first unit of L is added (input K is fixed at 1 unit). Diminishing returns to K also set in after the first unit of K is added in Table 4–3.

The AP_a, which for a particular amount of input a is given by the slope of a line segment extending from the origin to the point on the total product curve corresponding to that quantity of the input, reaches the maximum at point B in Figure 4–11, where line segment OB is tangent to TP_a. At this point, $MP_a = AP_a$, since MP_a for some amount of input a is

Table 4–2   Total, Average, and Marginal Product of Input L, Given $K = 1$

L	TP_L	AP_L	Arc MP_L
0	0	—	
			10.00
1	10.00	10.00	
			4.14
2	14.14	7.07	
			3.18
3	17.32	5.77	
			2.68
4	20.00	5.00	
			2.36
5	22.36	4.47	

Table 4–3   Total, Average, and Marginal Product of Input K, Given $L = 4$

K	TP_K	AP_K	Arc MP_K
0	0	—	
			20.00
1	20.00	20.00	
			8.28
2	28.28	14.14	
			6.36
3	34.64	11.55	
			5.36
4	40.00	10.00	
			4.72
5	44.72	8.94	

given by the slope of the line tangent to TP_a at the corresponding output level. Total product attains its maximum at point C, where the total product curve reaches its peak. Since the slope of the total product curve is zero at this point, MP_a must also be zero. This relationship becomes obvious if we recognize that if TP_a is at a maximum, then at that point the addition of another unit of input *a* will not change the level of total output produced. By definition, however, this fact means that MP_a is zero.

Average-Marginal Relationship

Because of the **average-marginal relationship**, an average curve cannot rise unless the related marginal curve is above it; the average cannot fall unless the marginal is below it.

In Figure 4–11, there is an important quantitative relationship between the average and marginal product curves for the variable input *a*. Note that when MP_a falls, it passes through the maximum point of the AP_a curve. When an average curve has a maximum point, the corresponding marginal curve will pass through that point. This is because of a mathematical property known as the **average-marginal relationship.** The reason the AP_a is rising to the left of its maximum is that the amount added to total product by the next unit of input is greater than the average product of previous units. This *causes* the average to rise. To the right of the maximum of AP_a, an additional unit of input *a* adds less to total product than the average amount added by previous units, thereby lowering the average. In short, anytime a marginal curve is *above* its corresponding average curve, the average curve will be rising; anytime the marginal is *below* the average, the average will be falling. You can verify this numerically by looking at Table 4–4, where data on TP_a, AP_a, and MP_a are shown.

In Table 4–4, when the second and third units of *a* are added to the production process, the average product of *a* rises, since the marginal product of the additional unit is greater than the previous average in both instances (200 > 100, and 300 > 150). However, beyond *a* = 3, average

Table 4–4 Total, Average, and Marginal Product of *a* for a Case Where AP_a Has a Maximum

Units of a (a)	TP_a (Q)	AP_a (Q/a)	MP_a (ΔQ/Δa)
1	100	100	
			200
2	300	150	
			300
3	600	200	
			140
4	740	185	
			100
5	840	168	
			60
6	900	150	

product declines. This is because the marginal product of each additional unit is lower than the average of all the previous units (140 < 200, 100 < 185, and 60 < 168).

The average-marginal relationship holds even if the average curve does not have an extreme value (maximum or minimum). For example, if you review Tables 4–2 and 4–3, you will see that the average product of the variable input always falls in those tables. This is because the marginal product (shown in the right-most column) is always less than the average. If you go back to Chapter 2, you can verify that the relationship also holds for marginal revenue and average revenue. In fact, the average-marginal relationship is not restricted to economics. You may note that if you have a "B" overall grade average (3.0 on a 4-point system) but only manage to turn in a "C" performance for this term, your average will fall. On the other hand, if this turns out to be an "A" term for you, your average will rise. The average-marginal relationship will turn up again in the next chapter, which is on cost.

Production in the Short Run Versus the Long Run

We can contrast a short-run situation of one fixed input and one variable input with the long-run situation (all inputs are variable) by utilizing the isoquant map in Figure 4–12. Points A, B, C, and D represent least *cost* combinations of inputs a and b required to produce the levels of output represented by I_1, I_2, I_3, and I_4, respectively. Assume the firm has been operating at point C (with b_0 units of b and a_0 units of a) and that b is fixed in the short run. In the short run, therefore, the firm must operate along the line b_0b_0, and its costs for producing any output level different from that of I_3 will be greater than would be necessary with the optimal combination of inputs.

As we discussed earlier in this chapter, point E on I_1 illustrates a point at which the combination of a and b is especially undesirable—where the marginal product of one input (b) is negative. This result is clear if we observe that I_1 has a positive slope at E—which indicates that if more of input b is used in production, more of input a must also be used to maintain the *same* level of output. Similarly, the marginal product of input a is negative beyond point F on I_1. The profit-maximizing firm would not plan to be in a position where the marginal product of an input is negative unless the firm were paid for using the input.

In Figure 4–12, if input b was fixed as far as expenditure was concerned but *not fixed in its utilization,* and if the firm desired to produce the quantity represented by I_1, the *short-run* best combination of inputs would be achieved by utilizing input b only to the point where its marginal product became zero. That is because decreases or increases in the *use* of this input will have no effect on expenditures for it in the short run. This position is represented by point G. One example of such a reduction in utilization of an input that is relatively fixed in expenditure is the closing off of dining

Figure 4–12   Effect of a Fixed Input on Cost on Production

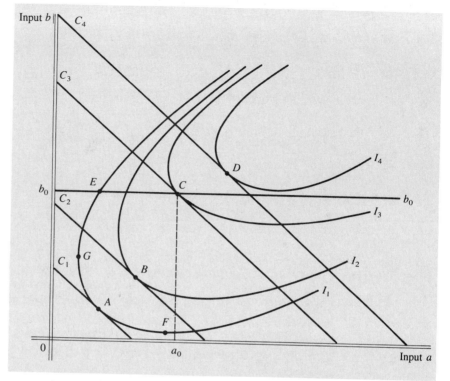

The input combination of a_0, b_0 is the least cost combination of inputs for the output level represented by I_3. However, if input b is fixed at b_0 in the short run, the costs of the firm will be higher at any other level of output than they would be with a least cost combination of inputs.

areas in a restaurant during less busy periods when they are not needed for seating. A smaller number of servers are able to give good service to a given number of people if the people are seated in an area that is not so large. Another example is the shutting down of one assembly line in a factory or the shutting down of one plant of a firm with multiple plants.[16]

Optimal Use of Variable Inputs in the Short Run

We shall leave a thorough discussion of the optimal use of variable inputs for a later chapter. Here we shall merely state that such optimal use requires that a variable input be employed up to the point where the additional revenue brought into the firm by the last (or next) unit of that

■ ■ ■ ■ ■ ■

[16] See "GM Will Shut 4 Assembly, Body Plants for up to 2 Weeks Due to Big Inventories," *The Wall Street Journal*, March 10, 1986, p. 3.

Numerical Example: Relation of Average and Marginal Product to Total Product

Complete the table below, assuming that the firm is in the short run and that L is the only variable input.

Units of L	TP_L	AP_L	Arc MP_L
0	0	—	
2		80	
4	340		
			70
6			

Answer. a. The first missing TP_L is 160, which is $AP_L(L)$, or 80(2). The second missing TP_L is 480, which is obtained by multiplying the given MP_L of 70 times the change in L of 2, and adding on to the previous TP_L of 340, or 70(2) + 340 = 480. This follows from the definition $MP_L = \Delta TP_L/\Delta L$. So, $MP_L(\Delta L) = \Delta TP_L$.

b. The missing AP_L values are 340/4 = 85 and 480/6 = 80, since $AP_L = TP_L/L$.

c. Since $MP_L = \Delta TP_L/\Delta L$, the missing MP_L values are 160/2 = 80 for the change from $L = 0$ to $L = 2$ and 180/2 = 90 for the change from $L = 2$ to $L = 4$.

Marginal revenue product of an input is the rate of change of total revenue with respect to change in a variable unit.

input is just equal to its marginal cost, or the cost of that additional unit. We call this additional revenue the **marginal revenue product of an input;** it is equal to the marginal (physical) product of the input times the additional net marginal revenue (marginal revenue net of raw materials or components cost) that the firm can obtain from output produced. If we state this principle for input a, the firm would employ input a until

$$MRP_a \equiv (MP_a \cdot NMR) = MC_a,$$

where MRP_a is the marginal revenue product of input a, MP_a is the marginal (physical) product of input a, NMR is the net marginal revenue obtained from each additional unit of output, and MC_a is the marginal cost of input a.

Managerial Perspective: Getting "People Power" Into the Manufacturing Process

"You have a friend in the business," trumpets one ad from Gateway 2000, a Sioux City manufacturer of IBM-compatible personal computers. In fact, Gateway 2000 computers are very nice, and what you are now reading was originally written on one. As of 1990, Gateway was a very successful company, selling thousands of computers per week. Gateway attributes at least a part of its success to the way it assembles components from many suppliers into a top-quality, competitively priced PC. Each PC is assembled by a single person who is responsible for his or her own quality control and rewarded according to how satisfied customers are with the product. Thus production workers are not doing just the monotonous, routine installation of a single part on a fast-moving assembly line.

Replacing assembly-line manufacturing with processes that yield more employee involvment with the product is not new, but it is certainly receiving more attention recently, as companies place increased emphasis on both quality and efficiency. Volvo pioneered the break with the assembly line in the auto industry, and in 1987 its chairman, Roger Holtback, dedicated a new plant in Uddevala, Sweden by assembling a Volvo 740 *all by himself.* Holtback reportedly said, "It started nicely, but it wouldn't have been delivered to a customer." Volvo does not anticipate having individual workers assemble an entire car; at Uddevala it uses teams of from seven to ten workers. The reason for Volvo's approach has to do with the Swedish work force, which is highly educated and independent-thinking. Management at Volvo believes that monotonous, assembly-line work produces high absenteeism and poor quality from a work force that is looking for a challenge in what they do.

The teamwork approach to manufacturing has been breaking out in the United States as well. Xerox has formed employee teams to encourage cooperation on the shop floor and spur innovation and problem solving. *Business Week* reports that in 1989, numerous U.S. corporations were using the work-team approach: Boeing, Caterpillar, Digital Equipment, General Electric, and General Motors, to name a few. Procter & Gamble is reported to have started using work teams as early as 1962. The name of the game in the team strategy is similar to that at Gateway—pride in accomplishment, greater worker satisfaction, higher quality, and increased productivity.

Approaches that increase employee involvement are not without critics. From the management side there are warnings that it is not for everybody and that while it may instill craftsmanship, it is not as efficient as assembly-line production. From the labor side come complaints that management uses the teamwork concept to erode the collective bargaining system and to introduce changes that yield more for the company than for its production workers. But the teamwork and employee involvement approaches appear to be here to stay, and in many industries, production in the twenty-first century is unlikely to be accomplished the same way it was during much of the twentieth.

■ ■ ■ ■

References: *Computer Shopper* (March 1990), p. 32; *PC Magazine* (May 15, 1990), pp. 129–32; "Volvo's Radical New Plant: The Death of the Assembly Line?" *Business Week* (August 28, 1989), pp. 92–93; "The Payoff From Teamwork," *Business Week* (July 10, 1989), pp. 56–62; and "Making It Better," *Time* (November 13, 1989), pp. 78–81.

■ ■ ■ ■ ■ ■ ■ ■ SUMMARY

Production and the Firm's Profit

We have repeatedly emphasized that only two main factors are of concern to the profit-maximizing firm: *revenue* and *cost*. In this chapter we have shown that if its profit is to be at the maximum level, the firm must be using a combination of inputs that will minimize cost *at the optimal level of output*. Production at the lowest possible cost *for a given level of output* requires that the additional output that would be obtained per additional dollar spent for another unit of one input is equal to that obtained per additional dollar spent for every other input. We called this a *least cost combination of inputs*.

While deriving the condition for achieving the least cost combination of inputs, we developed the concepts of the production function, isoquant and isocost curves, and the marginal rate of substitution of one input for another. The *production function* indicates the maximum quantities of output a firm can produce using various combinations of inputs. An isoquant curve shows different combinations of two inputs that can be used to produce a specific level of *output*, whereas an isocost curve indicates different combinations of two inputs that can be utilized for a given dollar cost. The *marginal rate of substitution* is the negative of the slope of an isoquant curve, and it indicates the rate at which one input may be substituted for another while the same level of output is maintained. The least cost combination of inputs for a particular level of output is located where an isocost curve is tangent to the isoquant curve corresponding to that level of output. At this point, the marginal rate of substitution equals the ratio of the input prices, or

$$\frac{MP_a}{MP_b} = \frac{P_a}{P_b} .$$

The set of all least cost input combinations makes up the *expansion path* of the firm.

It is also important for a firm to be aware of the *returns to scale* of operations so that the firm can estimate how its unit costs will be affected as it expands or contracts its scale of operations. If the firm has *increasing returns* to scale, an increase in its scale of operations will more than proportionally increase its output and thereby lower unit costs. If the firm has constant returns to scale, an increase in its scale of operations will increase output by the same proportion, and unit costs will remain constant. Finally, with decreasing returns to scale, an increase in the scale of the operations of a firm will increase its output by a smaller proportion, so that unit costs will increase.

We also pointed out that in the short run, some inputs a firm employs are fixed (at least in regard to cost outlay), so the firm may not be able to achieve the least cost combination of inputs at its optimal level of output at all times. This latter possibility emphasizes the importance to the firm of predicting accurately what its profit-maximizing level of output will be in the future. Fulfillment of the desire of the profit-oriented firm to produce at least cost (*given* the level of output) requires that it be able to at least estimate parts of its production function and future input prices.

In the short run, the profit-oriented firm should be aware of how its output varies with respect to changes in the amount of its variable input or inputs. In this connection we introduced the following terms: total product, average product, and marginal product. The *total product* of a variable input indicates the maximum output that can be obtained from different amounts of one variable input, keeping all other inputs fixed. The *average product* of a variable input is obtained by dividing total output by the number of units of the input in use. The *marginal product* of an input is the rate of change of total product with respect to changes in the amount of the input. The *law of diminishing returns* states that the marginal product of an input will decrease after some point.

To maximize profit in the short run, the firm should employ a variable input (say, input *a*) up to the point where the additional revenue that another unit of input will bring in is just equal to its cost, or where the marginal revenue product of input *a* equals its marginal cost ($MRP_a = MC_a$). Even though the *cost* associated with the fixed inputs of a firm may be fixed in the short run, their *utilization* may not be fixed. In this case the firm should avoid using so much of a fixed input that its marginal product becomes negative.

In the next chapter, we relate level of cost directly to level of output for a firm. We shall also discuss several cost concepts that the profit-maximizing firm must understand and be able to utilize.

■ ■ ■ ■ ■ ■ ■ ■ ■ ■ ■ ■ **Questions** ■ ■ ■ ■ ■ ■ ■ ■ ■ ■ ■ ■ ■

1. What is a production function? How does it differ from a total product function?
2. What condition(s) must be satisfied for a firm to achieve a least cost combination of its inputs? Why can't the firm always attain a least cost combination of inputs in the short run?
3. Does the obtaining of a least cost combination of inputs assure a firm that it is maximizing profit? Why or why not?
4. Compare the concepts of diminishing marginal productivity and decreasing returns to scale.
5. Define isoquant and isocost curves. Why would information given by these two curves be useful to the firm?
6. What are ridge lines? What is their significance to a firm?
7. Explain the meaning of the expansion path for a firm. What might cause it to change?

■ ■ ■ ■ ■ ■ ■ ■ ■ ■ ■ ■ **Problems** ■ ■ ■ ■ ■ ■ ■ ■ ■ ■ ■ ■ ■

1. Yolanda Von Sweeny owns an art factory in Palermo, Italy. She is thinking of expanding her exports of large-size paintings of picturesque Italian cityscapes. She has had little difficulty recruiting new artists to Palermo to work a 40-hour week in the factory. The weekly wage is now up to 672,000 lira, which translates to $480 in U.S. currency, and she thinks she can hire as many artists as she needs for that rate. An additional artist normally adds 96 paintings per week to the output of the factory. However, Yolanda has been approached by a Hong Kong dealer who is selling remarkable computerized robots that can closely duplicate the work of some of her current artists. A robot can paint 210 pictures per week and has a daily operating and financing cost of $168 (U.S. currency) per operating day. Regardless of whether she uses the robots or additional artists, Yolanda plans to operate the factory only 5 days per week.
   a. Employ the least cost input rule to determine whether Yolanda should consider buying the robots. (It will be easier if you use dollars rather than lira.)

b. Given the current daily cost of robots, what artist wage would make Yolanda indifferent between employing the robots and hiring more artists?

c. What other considerations might influence Yolanda's decision?

2. Suppose a firm has the total product curve below, assuming that input L is its only variable input and that Q = output per time period.

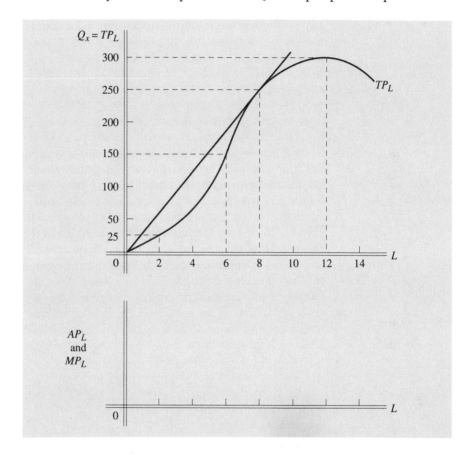

(Note: Plot MP_L values at the mid-point of each ΔL that you use to determine them.)

a. In the quadrant below the given diagram, sketch the curves of marginal product and average product of input L. (Provide an appropriate scale on the vertical axis.)

b. What is the maximum value of AP_L?

c. Can you employ geometry to determine the value of MP_L when it is maximum? (Hint: Draw a tangent to TP_L at its inflection point and evaluate its slope.)

3. Diamond Brewery is reevaluating its optimal combination of inputs as a result of recent union-negotiated wage rate increases. At the present time, the *MP* of labor on the production line is five cases of beer per hour and the wage rate is $6. The *MP* of capital is ten cases of beer per hour, and the price of a unit of capital's services for one hour is $10. Is the combination of inputs at Diamond optimal? Why or why not?

4. State whether each of the following production functions exhibits increasing, constant, or decreasing returns to scale.
   a. $Q = 100,000 + 500L + 100K$
   b. $Q = .01K^3 + 4K^2L + L^2K + .0001L^3$
   c. $Q = 50K^{1/2}L^{1/2}$
   d. $Q = .001M + 50,000$
   e. $Q = 15K + .5KL + 30L$
   f. $Q = AK^{1-a}L^{2a}, a > 0$

5. Shiney Apple Co. can use either labor or a combination of labor and machines to pick apples. Labor can be obtained very cheaply—the going rate is $7 per hour, while the cost (depreciation, gasoline, maintenance, etc.) of using a machine for one hour is $30. The firm is currently using only labor to pick apples, reasoning that labor is cheaper in dollars per day than the machine. In the present situation, the marginal product of an additional unit of labor is 4 bushels of apples per hour, while the additional product contributed by an apple-picking machine is 40 bushels per hour. You are hired by the firm managers as a consultant to advise them on whether or not to purchase such a machine. What recommendation do you make? What additional data might you also want to take into consideration?

6. Use the following table to complete this problem.

MP_L	L	Q	AP_L
	0	0	—
	5	20	
8.0			
	10		
	15	90	
	20	110	
	25		5.0
2.0			
	30		
	35	140	

a. Complete the table, given that L is labor units, Q is units of output per day, and that L is the only variable input.

b. Suppose the firm is producing between 90 and 110 units of output per day and that the price of a unit of input L is $40. If at that level of production the marginal product of its only fixed input, capital, is 24 units of output per day, should it consider adding to its capital equipment if the price of a unit of capital is $120? Explain.

7. The following table gives the quantities of output that can be produced with different amounts of capital and labor utilized by a firm.

Units of K	Units of Output						
6	122	174	213	244	274	300	
5	112	158	194	224	250	274	
4	100	142	173	200	224	244	
3	87	122	150	173	194	213	
2	71	100	122	142	158	174	
1	50	71	87	100	112	122	
0	1	2	3	4	5	6	Units of L

a. What are the returns to scale for this firm over the range of capital and labor shown in the table? Why?

b. Compute the marginal product and average product of capital for $L = 3$ units as K varies from 1 unit to 6 units.

c. Compute the marginal product and average product of labor for $K = 1$ unit as L varies from 1 unit to 6 units.

d. Suppose the firm is producing 87 units of output using 1 unit of capital and 3 units of labor. The cost of a unit of labor is $10, and the cost of a unit of capital is $20. Is the firm using a *least cost* combination of inputs? Why or why not?

8. A small local plumbing contractor is trying to decide whether to rent a backhoe or to hire more labor for an especially large plumbing job. The contractor estimates that 600 tons of dirt and rocks must be dug and moved. It is believed that a backhoe could move 10 tons of dirt per hour and would cost $30 per hour to rent (including the operator). On the average a worker can move 1 ton of dirt per hour, and the wage rate is $4.50 per hour.

a. Should the contractor rent a backhoe or hire enough workers to do the job? Why?

b. Suppose the backhoe could be rented on a full eight-hour day basis only (a full day would be charged for any partial days). Would this change your answer in part a? Why or why not?

9. A total product curve for input *a* is drawn in the following diagram:

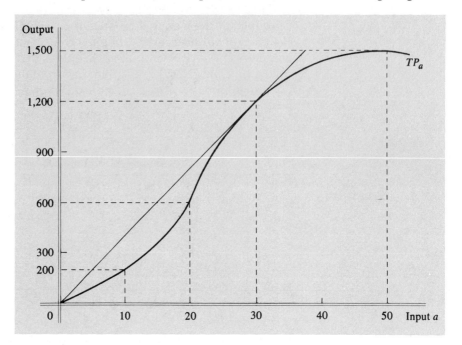

a. Find the average product of input *a* at amounts of *a* equal to 10, 20, 30, and 50 units.
b. Find the marginal product of *a* between 0 and 10 units, 10 and 20 units, 20 and 30 units, and 30 and 50 units.
c. Sketch the average and marginal product curves for *a*, and label the axes appropriately.
d. Where is AP_a at its maximum? Where is MP_a at its maximum?
e. At what point do diminishing returns to input *a* set in?

10. Use the isoquant diagram on the next page to fill in the blank spaces in the statements below.
a. At point ____ the total product of input *a* will reach its maximum when input *b* is fixed at b_1.
b. Point ____ and point ____ represent least cost combinations of inputs, given the isocost curves drawn in the diagram.
c. With expenditures limited to the level represented by isocost curve

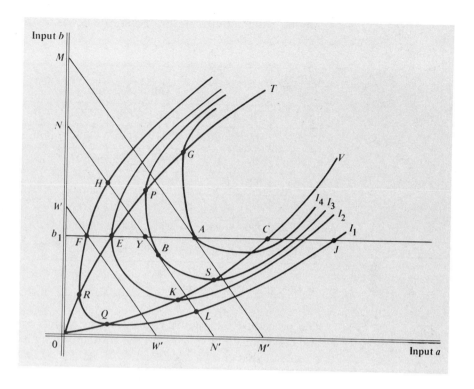

NN', a firm would produce at point ____ in the short run where $b = b_1$. In the long run, with the same budget, it would produce the level of output represented by isoquant ____ .

d. On I_1, the marginal product of b equals zero at point ____ ; at point ____ on the same isoquant, the marginal product of a equals zero.

e. In the short run, with plant size b_1 (and fixed in utilization at b_1), output level I_1 could be produced at point ____ or at point ____ . However, the cost-minimizing firm with plant size b_1 (but not fixed in utilization) would choose to produce I_1 at point ____ .

11. An automobile manufacturer is considering buying a robot to paint automobiles. One robot can paint 40 cars an hour and costs $12,000 a year (based on 240 working days of eight hours each). A person can paint 60 cars an hour and costs $11.50 per hour. Should the firm

purchase the robot or hire a person if it wishes to maximize profit? Why?

12.

Units of K	Units of Output						
7	70	140	210	280	350	420	490
6	60	120	180	240	300	360	420
5	50	100	150	200	250	300	350
4	40	80	120	160	200	240	280
3	30	60	90	120	150	180	210
2	20	40	60	80	100	120	140
1	10	20	30	40	50	60	70
0	1	2	3	4	5	6	7 Units of L

The preceding table gives corresponding values for amounts of labor and capital used by a firm and the corresponding maximum quantities of output that can be produced.

a. Complete the following table when capital is fixed at 4 units.

Units of L	TP_L	AP_L	Arc MP_L
1			
2			
3			
4			
5			
6			

b. If the cost of a unit of capital's services (P_K) is $30 and the cost of a unit of labor's services is $10, is $K = 4$ and $L = 3$ a least cost combination of inputs? Why or why not?

c. Given the information in part b and in the table, what is the cheapest way this firm can produce 120 units of output?

d. Does the production function depicted in the table have constant, increasing, or decreasing returns to scale? Why?

e. What happens to the marginal product of labor as the amount of capital used by the firm increases? Why?

The following problems require calculus:

13. A production function for a firm has the relationship given below between the level of output (Q) and the levels of capital (K) and labor (L).

$$Q = 4KL + 3L^2 - (1/3)L^3$$

   a. Find the isoquant equation for $Q = 100$.
   b. Derive the expression, or function, that gives the slope of the isoquant (in terms of quantities of K and L).
   c. Derive the marginal product of labor function from the preceding production function if K is fixed at 5 units.
   d. If K is fixed at 5 units, where do diminishing returns to labor set in?

14. A given firm has the following simple short-run total product function:

$$Q = 400L - 0.5L^2,$$

where

$$L = \text{units of labor}$$
$$Q = \text{output per month.}$$

   a. What is the equation for the firm's average product?
   b. What is the equation for its marginal product?
   c. At what level of labor use is marginal product zero?
   d. What is the firm's maximum output per month?

15. Suppose a firm has the following production function:

$$Q = 12KL + KL^2 - (1/12)KL^3$$

If the firm is operating in the short run and capital (K) is fixed at $K = 4$, determine the following:
   a. The maximum output that the firm can produce when $K = 4$;
   b. The level of use of input L where AP_L is at a maximum;
   c. The output level where diminishing marginal returns to input L occurs.

16. Toadhall Company has the following total product function with input Z as its only short-run variable input:

$$Q = 160Z + 18Z^2 - (1/3)Z^3$$

   a. At what Z value will the MP_Z for this firm equal zero?
   b. What will be the maximum short-run output the firm can produce?

c. What is the numerical value of the marginal product of Z (MP_Z) when that concept is at its maximum?

d. At what Z value will the average product of Z be maximized?

■ ■ ■ ■ ■ ■ ■ ■ ■ ■ **Selected References** ■ ■ ■ ■ ■ ■ ■ ■ ■ ■

Bilas, Richard A. *Microeconomic Theory*, 2d ed. New York: McGraw-Hill, 1971, Chapter 6.

Hyman, David N. *Modern Microeconomics*, 2d ed. Homewood IL: Richard D. Irwin, 1988, Chapter 6.

Lyons, Ivory L., and Manuel Zymelman. *Economic Analysis of the Firm.* New York: Pitman, 1966, Chapter 15.

McCloskey, Donald N. *The Applied Theory of Price*, 2d ed. New York: Macmillan, 1985, Chapter 11.

McGuigan, James R., and R. Charles Moyer. *Managerial Economics*, 4th ed. St. Paul, Minn.: West, 1989, Chapter 11.

Pindyck, Robert S., and Daniel L. Rubinfeld, *Microeconomics*. New York: Macmillan, 1989, Chapter 6.

Appendix 4

Mathematics of Determining the Least Cost Combination of Inputs

We can mathematically solve for the least cost combination of inputs to produce a given level of output or (what is essentially the same sort of problem) to find the combination of inputs that will maximize output subject to the condition that only a particular level of cost be incurred by the firm. Mathematical methods often have the advantage of being simpler and more precise than graphical techniques.

The simplest mathematical technique *if* the cost and production functions are mathematically simple is that of substitution. For example, assume that our production function is

(4-1)
$$Q = L^2 + 5LK + 4K^2,$$

that the price of a unit of labor services and a unit of capital services is $5 and $10, respectively, and that our cost limitation is equal to $1,000 per time period. Our goal, then, is to find the quantities of K and L that will maximize output (Q) subject to the condition that

(4-2)
$$5L + 10K = 1,000.$$

If we solve equation 4-2 for L in terms of K and substitute in equation 4-1, we obtain

(4-3)
$$L = 200 - 2K,$$
$$Q = (200 - 2K)^2 + 5(200 - 2K)K + 4K^2,$$
$$Q = 40,000 - 800K + 4K^2 + 1,000K - 10K^2 + 4K^2,$$

and

(4-4)
$$Q = 40,000 + 200K - 2K^2.$$

Using the first order condition for an extremum, we find dQ/dK and set it equal to 0, as shown in the equation

(4-5)
$$dQ/dK = 200 - 4K = 0$$

Solving equation 4-5 for K, we find $K = 50$, and substituting in equation 4-3, we find $L = 100$. The second order condition for a maximum is also satisfied.

If the functions are such that the substitution method is difficult, the Lagrangian multiplier method is useful. The Lagrangian multiplier method essentially involves adding the constraint (in a form in which it will equal zero when it is satisfied) to the original function to be maximized or minimized. Then, through creation of a new independent variable (the Lagrangian multiplier), the satisfaction of the constraint becomes a first order condition for a new function.

Using our production function in equation 4-1, we obtain a new, augmented function to be maximized:

(4-6)
$$Z = L^2 + 5LK + 4K^2 + \lambda(1,000 - 5L - 10K)$$

Here, the Greek λ is the Lagrangian multiplier. In this form, λ is readily interpretable as the marginal effect on the production function (on output) of relaxing the cost constraint.

Now, applying the optimizing conditions for a function of more than one independent variable, we find the following first order conditions:

(4-7)
$$\partial Z/\partial L = 2L + 5K - 5\lambda = 0,$$

(4-8)
$$\partial Z/\partial K = 5L + 8K - 10\lambda = 0,$$

and

(4-9)
$$\partial Z/\partial \lambda = -5L - 10K + 1,000 = 0.$$

Note that we are treating λ the same way as any regular independent variable. Solving equations 4–7 through 4–9 simultaneously, we find $L = 100$, $K = 50$, and $\lambda = 90$.

■ ■ ■ ■ ■ ■ ■ ■ ■ ■ ■ ■   **Problem**   ■ ■ ■ ■ ■ ■ ■ ■ ■ ■ ■ ■

1. A firm's production function is given by $Q = L^2 + 10LK + K^2$, and its cost function is given by $TC = 5L + 20K$. What is the maximum quantity the firm can produce for $1,150 cost? What quantities of capital and labor should it utilize?

CHAPTER 5

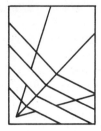

Cost of Production

Cost, as we have repeatedly emphasized, is one of the two major factors with which profit-maximizing firms *must* deal wisely. Successful managers are certainly aware that it is the *level of cost relative to revenue* that determines the firm's overall profitability.

One of the most memorable things about the airline industry in the 1980s was the number of companies in trouble. This list included Continental, Eastern, Pan American World Airways, and Braniff, to name a few.[1] However, Northwest Airlines did quite well while its competitors were having difficulties.

Before the airlines were deregulated in the United States, some companies, protected by high fares and limited competition, were not as careful about costs as they might have been. However, Northwest strove to control costs and increase productivity to obtain even greater profit. When deregulation did occur, Northwest was considered to be the most efficient of the major airlines.[2] As a result, the firm was in far better shape to cope with the fierce competition that gripped the airline industry in the 1980s. In the latter part of the 1980s American Airlines was in a strong position as a result of developing the airline industry's best computer

■ ■ ■ ■ ■ ■

[1] See "All Lorenzo Needs Now Is a Few Billion More in Assets," *Business Week* (April 23, 1990), p. 33; "Ailing Pan Am Still Relying on Asset Sales," *The Wall Street Journal*, March 12, 1990, p. A4; "Pan Am Seeks Chapter 11 Shield, Gets UAL-Backed Cash Infusion," *The Wall Street Journal*, January 9, 1991, p. A3; "Braniff Files For Protection From Creditors," *The Wall Street Journal*, September 29, 1989, pp. A3, A14; and "Braniff Hopes to Shrink Itself Into a Charter," *The Wall Street Journal*, November 8, 1989, p. A8.

[2] "At Northwest Airlines, Emphasis on Keeping Costs Low Pays Off," *The Wall Street Journal*, October 31, 1983, pp. 1, 12. Also see "U.S. Seeks Delay in Northwest Air, Republic Merger," *The Wall Street Journal*, February 19, 1986, p. 6.

reservation and yield-management systems. Union concessions also helped to lower American's costs below those of United and Delta.[3]

The movie industry affords us another example of how important efficient operation is to a firm's success. Paramount Pictures is a company that has been known for careful cost management. It is also the producer of such successful films as *Raiders of the Lost Ark* and *Terms of Endearment*. However, behind the scenes of these popular films some tough decisions were made.

For example, when George Lucas and Steven Spielberg first brought *Raiders of the Lost Ark* to Paramount, it was estimated that the *opening scene alone* would cost $25 million. However, Michael Eisner, then president of Paramount, insisted that the entire movie be produced for $20 million, and the final cost was actually less than that. According to Eisner, "You've got to . . . pretend you're playing with your own money."[4] Because Paramount keeps its costs per film relatively low, it is able to produce a greater number of films each year than many other studios. As a result, its chances of producing a hit are also greater.

More recently, low-budget filmmakers have become a significant force in the movie industry. They typically produce movies for much less than half the average cost of a major-studio film ($15.8 million), yet they have achieved some spectacular successes.[5]

Remanufacturing is a cost-saving approach that is becoming more and more popular—and *profitable*—for many things, including automobiles, robots, airplane engines, and telephones. Remanufacturing involves using both old and new parts to make a piece of equipment "as good as new" again. Using this approach, the remanufacturers can sell their products for far less than the corresponding new items and still make a substantial profit. For example, a remanufactured bus with a new body can be sold for about $110,000 compared with a price of $170,000 for a new one. That difference represents a 35 percent savings.[6]

It is clear that careful cost management can be critical to a firm's survival. In addition to the examples just mentioned, the automobile, steel, computer manufacturing, and many other industries have vividly illustrated this fact. Thus a major emphasis of many U.S. firms in the 1980s was on controlling costs.[7] According to *Business Week*:

■ ■ ■ ■ ■ ■

[3] "American Aims For the Sky," *Business Week* (February 20, 1989), pp. 54–58.

[4] "Hollywood's Penny Pinchers," *Newsweek* (April 9, 1984), p. 83.

[5] See "A Down-Home Movie Mogul," *Newsweek* (January 12, 1987), p. 41; "Lights! Camera! Cut the Budget!" *Time* (March 30, 1987), p. 57; and "Studio Commandos," *Newsweek* (May 12, 1986), pp. 58–59.

[6] "A Growing Love Affair with the Scrap Heap," *Business Week* (April 29, 1985), pp. 69–72.

[7] See, for example, "Companies vs. Costs," *Newsweek* (March 17, 1980), p. 76; and "'What If' Help for Management," *Business Week* (January 21, 1980), pp. 73–74.

. . . companies across the country are focusing on one of the basics of business: making a better product faster and cheaper. They are recognizing that the best-conceived strategic plans or marketing analyses are useless if products are too costly to produce or too shoddy to sell. And they are putting in corporatewide programs aimed at spotting every quick and lucrative fix available to increase manufacturing productivity at the lowest possible cost.[8]

If a firm can reduce its unit costs over those of comparable firms in its industry, it has a head start in making a profit—either by selling its product at the same price as its rivals and reaping the benefits of a greater price-cost differential or by being able to lower price and successfully capture a larger market share.

■ ■ ■ ■ ■ ■ ■ ■ ■ ## TYPES OF COSTS

Explicit costs are those costs of production that involve a specific payment by the firm to some person, group, or organization outside the firm.

There are many different types of costs that a firm may consider relevant under various circumstances. Such costs include historical costs, opportunity costs, fixed costs, variable costs, incremental costs, private costs, and social costs. **Historical costs** or **explicit costs** are costs of the firm for which *explicit payment* has been made sometime in the past or for which the firm is committed in the future. These are the costs that a financial accountant attempts to record as data and are gathered for the firm's income statement.[9] Examples of explicit costs include wages and salaries, rent, materials costs, depreciation, the amount paid for a machine, and interest payments. The obvious advantage of restricting cost figures to those based on historical costs is that of objectivity—records of transactions should exist from which the figures can be verified.

Implicit costs are the costs of using firm-owned resources. They are opportunity costs that cannot be accounted for by payments to outsiders. These costs represent opportunities that a firm gives up by using a resource in one way rather than another.

However, most economists consider the concept of explicit or historical costs to be too narrow when estimating the total costs of the firm, and they would include *implicit opportunity costs* that the firm incurs as well as explicit costs in the firm's cost figures. **Implicit costs** are those that do not involve actual payment by a firm to factors of production but nevertheless represent costs to the firm in the sense that in order to use certain inputs in the production process, the firm has had to abandon opportunities to use them elsewhere.

■ ■ ■ ■ ■ ■

[8] "Business Refocuses on the Factory Floor," *Business Week* (February 2, 1981), p. 91.

[9] The Securities Exchange Commission in the past required that some firms adjust their cost figures to reflect the current value of assets used in the production process. See Fredrich Andrews, "Replacing Cost Accounting Plan Adopted by SEC," *The Wall Street Journal*, March 25, 1976, p. 6. The Financial Accounting Standards Board in late 1986 issued a new statement that relieved these companies of this requirement. They still are encouraged to provide this information on a voluntary basis. See *Management Accounting* (January 1987), p. 9, and FASB No. 82.

For example, let us suppose that John and Ruth Brown (1) have opened a delicatessen in a building that they own in a shopping mall; (2) have invested $20,000 of their own financial capital in it; and (3) consider its management to be John's full-time job. A monthly income statement such as might be prepared by an economist is shown in Table 5–1. Notice that both explicit and implicit costs are included.

The first part of the income statement is straightforward, resulting in an income figure consistent with that found by using currently accepted accounting principles. From that amount, however, we have subtracted amounts for the firm owners' implicit opportunity costs—estimated rental income that the firm's owners could have earned on the building by leasing it to another business, the monthly salary that John could expect to make if he worked for someone else, and an expected return on the $20,000 capital if invested elsewhere (with equal risk). Note the presence of the words *expected* or *estimated* in the list of opportunity costs. Such words reflect the fact that the firm must estimate what revenue its resources listed above would bring in if they were employed according to the *next best* opportunity. This nonobjectivity of the implicit cost figures bothers some accountants and is the main reason that such figures are not generally acceptable in financial statements for use by stockholders or investors. Still, if implicit costs are positive, actual economic costs for a firm will be larger than accounting costs, and therefore economic profit generally will be smaller than accounting profit. Thus the inclusion of implicit costs is important for managerial decision making by a firm's owner(s) because it helps the owner(s) to better understand the economic implications of the demands that the firm is placing upon *all* resources.

Fixed costs are costs that do not vary with the level of output in the short run.

We shall now briefly consider the other cost items listed at the beginning of the chapter. **Fixed costs** are those costs that are fixed in the short

Table 5–1

John and Ruth's Deli
Statement of Economic Profit
for Month Ended July 31, 1991

Total Revenue (sales)		$120,000
Less Cost of Goods Sold		84,000
Gross Profit		$ 36,000
Less Operating Expenses		30,000
Operating (accounting) Net Income		$ 6,000
Less		
Implicit Rental Income	$2,000	
Implicit Salary Income	2,600	
Implicit Interest Income	160	4,760
Economic Profit		$ 1,240

Variable costs are costs that increase or decrease as a firm's output increases or decreases.

Semivariable costs are costs that are fixed over some ranges of output and variable over others.

Incremental cost is the additional cost that a firm will incur if it undertakes one more activity, or if it takes one course of action rather than another.

The **private costs** of a firm include all of the costs of resource use, both explicit and implicit, the firm must bear to produce its output.

The **social costs** of a firm are the private costs of the resources that the firm uses plus any additional costs imposed on society by the firm's operation.

run and therefore do not vary with the level of output produced by the firm during that time period. **Variable costs** are those costs that do vary with the level of production of the firm. Note that *in the long run, all costs of the firm are variable*. It is possible to distinguish a third category, **semivariable costs,** which are fixed over some ranges of output and variable over others. Two examples might be a firm's water bill and the wages paid to supervisors. For simplicity we shall assume that all short-run costs fall into one of two categories—fixed or variable—and that *all* cost items are variable in the long run.

Incremental costs associated with some decisions by the firm are the additional costs that a firm would incur if it took one course of action rather than another. In many instances the profit-maximizing firm owner makes decisions based on a comparison of incremental revenue and incremental costs. We shall discuss this topic further in Chapter 6.

Finally, the **private costs** of a firm are the sum of the explicit and implicit costs that it incurs, as we have already discussed. The **social costs** of a firm are those that society in general bears because of the firm's activities. Social costs would include the private costs of a firm, since presumably all of the firm's resources could be used elsewhere in producing goods of value to (at least some members of) society. However, social costs would also include costs paid for by society but not by the firm, even though such costs were a result of production by the firm. Examples might include air, water, and noise pollution. A firm could, in addition, generate *negative* social costs (social benefits) such as the beauty of a well-kept golf course and the resultant increase in the values of surrounding properties. Most people would be pleased that an exclusive country club had decided to locate near their property—even if they wanted only to sell that property for a profit. Social costs are important considerations in economic decision making (and law making) by society in general. However, since the part of social cost that is not included in private cost is not usually considered by the *profit-maximizing* firm in its decision-making process, it will generally be ignored in our discussion of the firm. We shall now turn to a more detailed discussion of the firm's private costs.

■ ■ ■ ■ ■ ■ ■ ■ ■   ## COSTS IN THE LONG RUN

Long-run total cost is the minimum economic cost of producing each possible level of output when the time period is sufficiently long to change all inputs of the firm's production function.

Once we know the production function [as in Chapter 4, we shall continue to use $Q = f(a,b)$] for a firm's product and the prices and quantities of its inputs, a and b, for each level of output, we can then easily discover how total costs vary with the level of output. In Figure 5–1, panel (a), we have shown a series of least cost points (A, B, C, D, and E) corresponding to different levels of production; and in Figure 5–1, panel (b), we have graphed corresponding output levels and **long-run total costs** (*LTC*). Note that we are again assuming that both inputs, a and b, are variable so that

Managerial Perspective: The Cost of Being Your Own Boss

Many people dream of owning their own business—being their own boss, gathering the respect of the community as a successful business person, and, certainly, making a lot of money. In a recent article, however, *Business Week* may have brought some of these dreamers back to reality with a discussion of "sweat equity." Sweat equity is the value that people build in a business (or home) by investing their time and, usually, plenty of hard work and brainpower as well.

A three-year study by the National Federation of Independent business found that 53 percent of the owners of firms that had been in business for 18 months spent 60 or more hours a week in that endeavor. For some, the time commitment was even more substantial: 11 percent of those who started their own company and 14 percent of those who bought companies reported spending 80 or more hours a week in managerial duties. However, recent studies indicated that less than 20 percent of executives in big corporations spent that much time on the job. Moreover, almost 20 percent of new business owners claimed to be working additional part-time or full-time jobs as well.

When one considers the preceding data regarding the expenditure of managerial blood, sweat, and tears along with the fact that only 20 percent of all businesses survive for five years, it is clear that owning your own business is not an easy road to riches. While we certainly do not wish to discourage any budding entrepreneurs, they cannot make an economic decision regarding a new enterprise without counting the considerable cost in their own time and energy.

■ ■ ■ ■

References: "Like 60-Hour Weeks? Try Your Own Business," *Business Week* (August 10, 1987), p. 75; Geoffrey Leavenworth, "Small Business: Still a Gamble," *Texas Business & Texas Parade* (June 1978), p. 65.

LTC in Figure 5–1, panel (b), is applicable only when the firm can achieve the optimal input combination for its desired level of output. In other words, the firm must be operating on its expansion path [line *0X* in Figure 5–1, panel (a)]. Thus *LTC* in Figure 5–1, panel (b), must be the long-run total cost curve of the firm. As stated in Chapter 4, the least cost combination of inputs for each level of output requires that

$$\frac{MP_a}{P_a} = \frac{MP_b}{P_b} = \cdots = \frac{MP_n}{P_n},$$

Figure 5–1   Variation of Total Cost

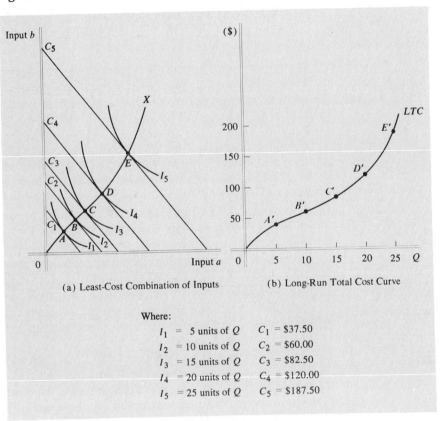

(a) Least-Cost Combination of Inputs

(b) Long-Run Total Cost Curve

Where:

I_1 = 5 units of Q	C_1 = $37.50	
I_2 = 10 units of Q	C_2 = $60.00	
I_3 = 15 units of Q	C_3 = $82.50	
I_4 = 20 units of Q	C_4 = $120.00	
I_5 = 25 units of Q	C_5 = $187.50	

Least cost combinations of inputs for levels of output corresponding to I_1, I_2, I_3, I_4, and I_5 are given by points A, B, C, D, and E, respectively, in panel (a). These points then determine corresponding points (A', B', C', D', and E', respectively) on the long-run total cost curve (LTC), in panel (b).

Long-run average cost is equal to long-run total cost divided by the level of output. It measures cost per unit of output when all inputs are variable.

Long-run marginal cost is the rate of change of long-run total cost as the level of output changes.

for all inputs of the firm, where MP_i is the marginal product of input i and P_i is the price of input i (and assumed to be constant).

Long-run average cost (or per-unit cost) at some output level Q can be found by dividing LTC by Q, or $LAC = LTC/Q$. Geometrically, LAC for a particular level of output is the slope of the line segment drawn from the origin to LTC at the same level of output. The long-run average cost curve corresponding to LTC in Figure 5–1, panel (b), is drawn in Figure 5–2. **Long-run marginal cost,** or the rate of change of long-run total cost with respect to output, at a particular quantity of output is given by the slope of the total cost curve at that output level.[10] In discrete terms, *arc*

▪ ▪ ▪ ▪ ▪

[10] For example, at Q_1 this slope is equal to the slope of a line tangent to LTC at LTC_1; and, mathematically, LMC_1 is equal to $dLTC/dQ$ at Q_1.

Figure 5–2   Deriving Average Cost from the Total Cost Curve

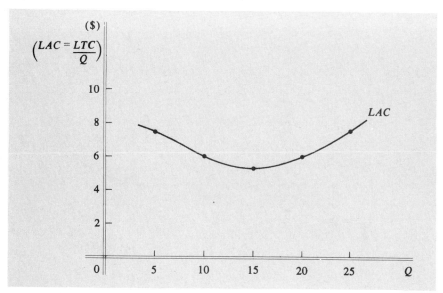

The long-run average cost curve can be derived from the long-run total cost curve by dividing each *LTC* figure by the corresponding quantity of output.

marginal cost is an approximation to marginal cost and is the *average rate of change* of total cost with respect to the quantity of output *between two levels of output*. Arc *LMC* can be found by dividing the change in total cost by the change in the quantity of output, or arc $LMC = \Delta LTC / \Delta Q$. The *LTC* curve drawn in Figure 5–1, panel (b), has first decreasing, then increasing, marginal cost.

   The relationships among long-run total, average, and marginal costs for the long-run total cost curve in Figure 5–1, panel (b), are further demonstrated in Figure 5–3. We observe that *LMC* is decreasing until $Q_1 = 10$, at which point the *LTC* curve has its smallest slope. Minimum *LAC* is reached at $Q_2 = 15$, where a line drawn from the origin to point LTC_2 is just tangent to *LTC*, since this is the least steeply sloped line that can be drawn from the origin to a point on *LTC*. At Q_2 also, marginal cost equals average cost = \$5.50, since long-run marginal cost is by definition the slope of a line tangent to *LTC* at the point under consideration. These numerical relationships among long-run total cost, long-run average cost, long-run marginal cost, and arc long-run marginal cost are also summarized in Table 5–2. Note that both the data in this table and the per unit curves in the lower panel of Figure 5–3 are consistent with the average-marginal relationship. Thus the *LMC* curve passes through the minimum of the *LAC* curve.

   It should be emphasized, however, that the cost curves discussed previously give the firm information on costs when the *lowest possible* cost

Figure 5–3   The Relationships Among Total Cost, Average Cost, and Marginal Cost

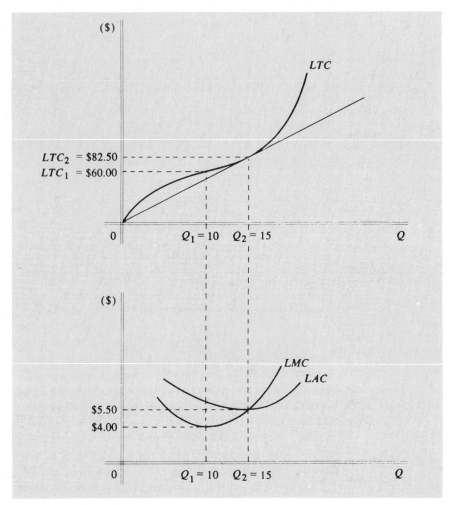

Figure 5–3 depicts the relationships among long-run total cost (*LTC*), average cost (*LAC*), and marginal cost (*LMC*). *LMC* reaches its minimum where the slope of *LTC* reaches its smallest value. *LMC* is equal to *LAC* when *LAC* is at a minimum.

for a particular level of output can be achieved, *given current input prices*. These cost curves assume that the firm can vary all inputs and thus achieve a least cost combination of inputs for every possible level of output. It follows that they are relevant *only* for long-range planning by the firm regarding level of production, size of plant, and other similar decisions. In the next section we shall discuss the short-run cost situation of the firm.

Table 5–2   Summary of Numerical Values for LTC, LAC, LMC, and Arc LMC^*

Q	LTC	LAC	LMC	Arc LMC
0	$ —	Undefined	$10.00	
5	37.50	7.50	5.50	$ 7.50
10	60.00	6.00	4.00	4.50
15	82.50	5.50	5.50	4.50
20	120.00	6.00	10.00	7.50
25	187.50	7.50	17.50	13.50

* These relationships are easily derived mathematically. The total cost function drawn in Figure 5–1, panel b, is given by $LTC = 10Q - .6Q^2 + .02Q^3$. The long-run average cost function is given by $LAC = LTC/Q = 10 - .6Q + .02Q^2$. The long-run marginal cost function is obtained by taking the derivative of LTC with respect to Q, $LMC = dLTC/dQ = 10 - 1.2Q + .06Q^2$. LMC reaches its minimum when $dLMC/dQ = -1.2 + .12Q = 0$, or $Q = 10$. At this point, $LMC = 10 - 1.2(10) + .06(100) = \$4.00$. LAC reaches its minimum where $dLAC/dQ = -.6 + .04Q = 0$, or where $Q = 15$. At this point, $LAC = 10 - .6(15) + .02(15)^2 = \$5.50$.

■ ■ ■ ■ ■ ■ ■ ■   **COSTS IN THE SHORT RUN**

Total fixed cost is the private economic cost of the firm's fixed inputs in the short run. The TFC curve is a horizontal line since these costs do not vary with the level of output in the short run.

Short-run total variable cost is the sum of all private economic costs of the firm that vary with its level of output in the short run.

Short-run total cost includes all of the private economic costs of the firm in the short run. Short-run total cost is equal to total fixed cost plus short-run total variable cost.

In the short run, *at least one* input is fixed, so a firm may not be able to achieve the best combination of inputs for its desired level of output. In Figure 5–4, panel (a), input b is fixed at b_0. Thus, in the short run, the least cost combination of inputs can only be achieved for the level of output associated with I_3, since this is the only point on b_0 that is also on the expansion path for the firm, given current input prices. If the firm should desire to produce any other level of output in the short run, it must do so at a greater cost than it could achieve with an optimal combination of inputs. In Figure 5–4, panel (b), the STC curve associated with input b fixed at b_0 is higher than the long-run total cost curve (LTC) at all output levels except for Q_3. Moreover, in general, short-run costs will be greater than long-run costs except for those output levels for which the fixed inputs are at their optimal levels. In Figure 5–4, panel (a), if input b were fixed at b_1 units, short-run total cost would be greater than the lowest possible cost for every output level except Q_2 [see Figure 5–4, panel (b)].

Because of the presence of both fixed and variable costs in the short run, we can identify seven different types of short-run cost curves: total fixed cost, total variable cost, total cost, average fixed cost, average variable cost, average total cost, and marginal cost. The relationships among these curves are illustrated in Figure 5–5. **Total fixed cost** (TFC) is a horizontal straight line at an amount equal to $P_b \cdot b$ if input b is fixed. **Short-run total variable cost** (TVC) is given by $P_a \cdot a$, where a is the variable input. **Short-run total cost** (STC) is the summation (vertical) of TFC and TVC (or $STC = TFC + TVC$).

Numerical Example

Given the following diagram:

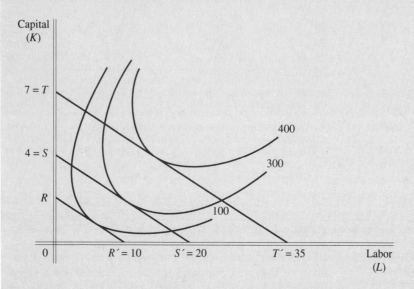

If the price of a unit of labor, P_L = $50, complete the following.

a. At an output of 400, TC = _____ .
b. The price of a unit of capital, P_K = _____ .
c. The maximum number of units of capital that could be purchased with a budget represented by line RR' is _____ .
d. From the three outputs shown, the lowest average cost obtainable is _____ .

Answer: a. TC = $1,750, which is the value of the budget on line TT', or the same as $L(P_L)$ = 35($50).

b. P_K = $250. Anywhere along TT', for example, $1,750 is spent. This includes point T, where K = 7. Thus P_K = $1,750/7 = $250.

c. At point R, K = 2. Anywhere along RR', TC = $500 = $L(P_L)$ at R' = 10($50). Since P_K = $250, only two units of K can be bought with the budget represented by RR'.

d. Minimum AC for these outputs occurs when Q = 300 and AC = $1,000/300 = $3.33. The other two ACs are $500/100 = $5.00 and $1750/400 = $4.38, respectively, for the 100 and 400 output levels.

Figure 5–4   Short-Run Costs and Production

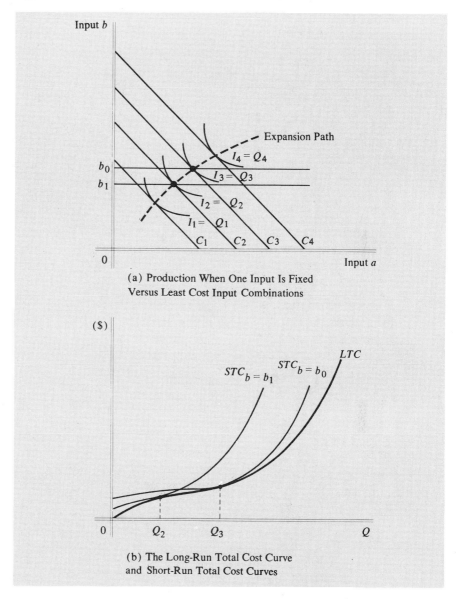

(a) Production When One Input Is Fixed
Versus Least Cost Input Combinations

(b) The Long-Run Total Cost Curve
and Short-Run Total Cost Curves

The expansion path of the firm determines the long-run total cost curve (*LTC*). However, in the short run, the firm may not be able to achieve a least cost combination of inputs. For example, if input *b* is fixed at b_0 in the short run, the total cost curve appropriate for various levels of output will be $STC_{b=b_0}$. It will represent a least cost combination of inputs at Q_3 only. At other levels of output, $STC_{b=b_0}$ is greater than *LTC*. A similar explanation holds if input *b* is fixed at b_1.

Figure 5–5 Graphical Relationships Among the Short-Run Cost Curves

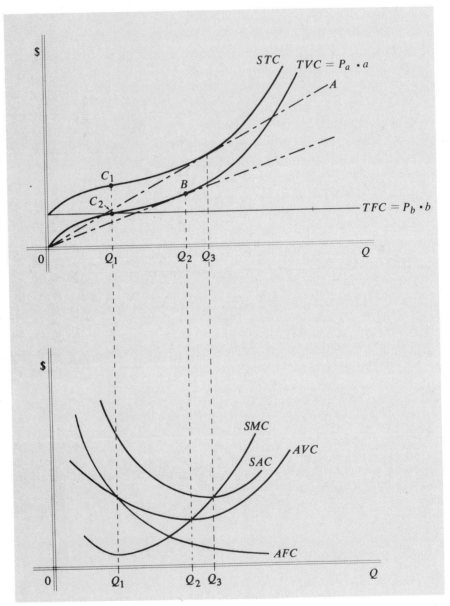

In Figure 5–5 it is assumed that input b is fixed and that input a is variable. Total fixed cost (TFC) is equal to the price of input b (P_b) multiplied by the quantity of input b. Total variable cost (TVC) is equal to $P_a \cdot a$. Short-run total cost (STC) is equal to $TVC + TFC$. Average fixed cost (AFC) is equal to TFC/Q. Average variable cost $(AVC) = TVC/Q$. Short-run average cost (SAC) is equal to $STC/Q = AVC + AFC$. Short-run marginal cost (SMC) is equal to the slope of the STC curve. SMC is equal to AVC and SAC at their respective minimum points.

Average fixed cost
is fixed cost per
unit of output in
the short run. Average fixed cost is
equal to total fixed
cost divided by the
level of output.

**Short-run average
variable cost** is the
variable cost per
unit of output produced in the short
run. It is equal to
short-run total variable cost divided
by the level of
output.

**Short-run average
total cost** is the
cost per unit of
output in the short
run. It is equal to
short-run total cost
divided by the
level of output. It
is also equal to average fixed cost
plus short-run average variable cost
for each level of
output.

**Short-run marginal
cost** is the rate of
change of *either*
short-run total cost
or short-run total
variable cost as the
level of output
changes in the
short run.

Directing our attention to unit costs, we observe that **average fixed
cost** (AFC) is found by dividing a given dollar amount of fixed cost by
larger and larger levels of output. Thus, it approaches, but does not reach,
zero (the quantity axis) and is the shape of a rectangular hyperbola.[11]
Short-run average variable cost (AVC) is found by dividing short-run total
variable cost by the corresponding level of output ($TVC/Q = AVC$). **Short-
run average total cost** (SAC) can be found by dividing short-run total cost
by the level of output or by adding AFC and AVC ($SAC = STC/Q = AFC
+ AVC$). As indicated in our discussion of long-run costs, unit (average)
costs for a particular level of output can be obtained geometrically by
finding the slope of a line segment extending from the origin to the point
on the total cost curve corresponding to that quantity of production. The
same procedure can also be used to find AFC and AVC from the TFC and
TVC curves, respectively. Thus in Figure 5–5 short-run average cost at Q_3
is the slope of line segment OA.

   Short run marginal cost is defined in the same manner as marginal
cost is defined in the long run: the rate of change of short-run total cost
with respect to the level of output. Arc short-run marginal cost between
two levels of output can be found by dividing either the change in short-
run total cost or the change in short-run total variable cost by the change
in quantity (arc $SMC = \Delta STC/\Delta Q$ or $\Delta TVC/\Delta Q$). Since fixed cost does not
change in the short run, the changes in STC and TVC must be equal.
Therefore arc short-run marginal cost measures the average rate of change
in total cost with respect to changes in the level of output in the short
run.[12] Table 5–3 gives a numerical illustration of all of the short-run cost
functions.

Table 5–3   A Numerical Example of the Relationships Among Short-
Run Cost Curves

Q	TFC	TVC	STC	AFC	AVC	SAC	SMC	Arc SMC
0	$1,000	$ —	$1,000	$ —	$ —	$ —	$ 80	
5	1,000	275	1,275	200.00	55.00	255.00	35	$ 55.00
10	1.000	400	1,400	100.00	40.00	140.00	20	25.00
15	1,000	525	1,525	66.67	35.00	101.67	35	25.00
20	1,000	800	1,800	50.00	40.00	90.00	80	55.00
25	1,000	1,375	2,375	40.00	55.00	95.00	155	115.00
30	1,000	2,400	3,400	33.33	80.00	113.33	260	205.00

■ ■ ■ ■ ■ ■

[11] A rectangular hyperbola is given by the functional form $XY = a$ where a is a constant.
[12] Instantaneous short-run marginal cost (or short-run marginal cost at some level of
output) is obtained by finding $dTVC/dQ$ or $dSTC/dQ$ and is the slope of both the short-run
total cost and the short-run total variable cost curves. For example, if $STC = 1,000 + 80Q -
6Q^2 + .2Q^3$, then $TVC = 80Q - 6Q^2 + .2Q^3$ and $SMC = dSTC/dQ = dTVC/dQ = 80 - 12Q
+ .6Q^2$. Table 5–3 gives a numerical illustration of all of the short-run cost functions.

Finally, we observe in Figure 5–5 that *SMC* reaches its minimum where *STC* and *TVC* reach their respective flattest points—that is, where their slopes are least (at C_1 and C_2). Also, *AVC* reaches its minimum where the slope of a line segment from the origin to a point on the *TVC* curve is at its minimum (at point *B* in Figure 5–5). At this point, *AVC* = *SMC*, since both are equal to the slope of *0B*, which is tangent to *TVC* at quantity Q_2. For the same reasons, *SAC* reaches its minimum at Q_3, and *SMC* = *SAC* at that point. Notice that *SAC* reaches its minimum later (at a larger quantity) than *AVC* because of the presence of fixed costs. In addition, the *SMC* passes through the respective minima of *AVC* and *SAC*, in keeping with the average-marginal relationship.

It should be readily apparent that costs need not always vary with output according to the relationships hypothesized in Figure 5–5. In fact it is often assumed in managerial accounting, at least in the relevant range of production in the short run, that average variable cost (and therefore marginal cost) is constant. Appropriate cost curves, given the assumption of constant unit variable costs, are shown in Figure 5–6. This assumption greatly simplifies analysis of the costs and consequently of the corresponding profit-maximizing position of the firm. Moreover, for many firms in the short run and over relatively small ranges of production, such an assumption is probably a fair approximation of reality.

■ ■ ■ ■ ■ ■ ■ ■ ■   RELATIONSHIP OF SHORT-RUN COST CURVES TO SHORT-RUN PRODUCT CURVES

The total product, average product, and marginal product curves discussed in Chapter 4 are closely related to total variable cost, average variable cost, and marginal cost in the short run. We can demonstrate the reason this statement is true in the following manner. First, assume we have a general production function of the type used in Chapter 4.

$$Q = f(a,b),$$

where *a* and *b* are inputs, *Q* is output, and input *b* is *fixed* in the short run at 4 units. We shall assume that the corresponding total product of *a*, average product of *a*, and marginal product of *a* are as given in Table 5–4.

Turning to the cost curves, we recall from Figure 5–5 that short-run total cost is composed of total fixed cost plus total variable cost, or

$$STC = TVC + TFC.$$

Also, total fixed cost is equal to $P_b \cdot b$, and total variable cost is equal to $P_a \cdot a$, where P_a and P_b are the prices of inputs *a* and *b*, respectively, and

Figure 5–6   Short-Run Cost Curves with Constant Average Variable
Cost

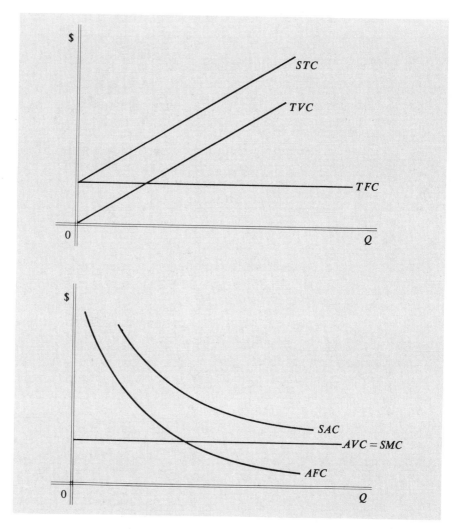

If average variable cost (*AVC*) is constant, *STC* and *TVC* are straight lines. *AVC* = *SMC* in
this case.

a and *b* are the quantities of the inputs. We have stated that *b* is fixed at
4 units and that P_b is equal to $50. Thus, since both P_b and *b* are fixed,
total fixed cost is a horizontal line at $P_b \cdot b$ = $50 x 4 = $200, as shown in
Figure 5–7.

Total variable cost (= $P_a \cdot a$) is derived from the TP_a curve by multiplying each amount of input *a* by P_a and plotting the obtained *TVC* value
against its respective *Q* value (*Q* on the horizontal axis), as shown in

Table 5–4 Relationships Between Productivity of Variable Input and Short-Run Cost Curves*

Input a (Units)	Input b (Units)	Output (Q) (Units)	AP_a	Arc MP_a	Arc SMC	AVC	AFC	SAC	TVC	TFC	STC
0	4	0	—	5	$ 7.20	—	—	—	0	$200	$200.00
2	4	10	5	15	2.40	$7.20	$20.00	$27.20	$ 72.00	200	272.00
4	4	40	10	10	3.60	3.60	5.00	8.60	144.00	200	344.00
5	4	50	10	4	9.00	3.60	4.00	7.60	180.00	200	380.00
6	4	54	9	2	18.00	4.00	3.70	7.70	216.00	200	416.00
7	4	56	8			4.50	3.57	8.07	252.00	200	452.00

* P_a is $36, and P_b is $50.

Figure 5–7   Short-Run Total Cost, Total Variable Cost, and Total Fixed Cost

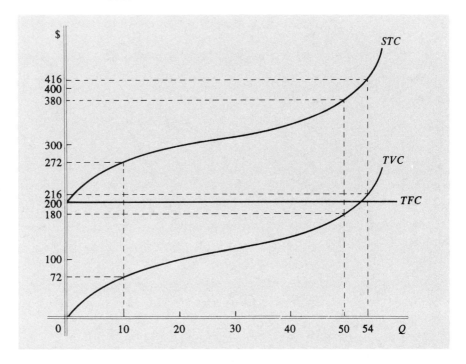

Since input b is fixed at 4 units and $P_b = \$50$, $TFC = P_b \cdot b = \$200$. $STC = TVC + TFC$.

Figure 5–8. (In Figure 5–8 we have assumed that P_a is $36.) For example, at $Q = 50$ units, a is equal to 5 units, and TVC is equal to $\$36 \times 5 = \$180$. At $Q = 54$ units, a is equal to 6 units, and TVC is equal to $\$36 \times 6 = \$216$.

We can also analyze the relationships of the AP_a curve and the MP_a curve to the average variable cost, short-run average total cost, and short-run marginal cost curves. We know that

$$SAC = \frac{STC}{Q} = \frac{TFC}{Q} + \frac{TVC}{Q} = AFC + AVC.$$

If

$$TFC = P_b \cdot b \qquad \text{and} \qquad TVC = P_a \cdot a,$$

then

$$AFC = \frac{P_b \cdot b}{Q} \qquad \text{and} \qquad AVC = \frac{P_a \cdot a}{Q}.$$

Figure 5–8   Relationship Between Total Product of Input a and Total Variable

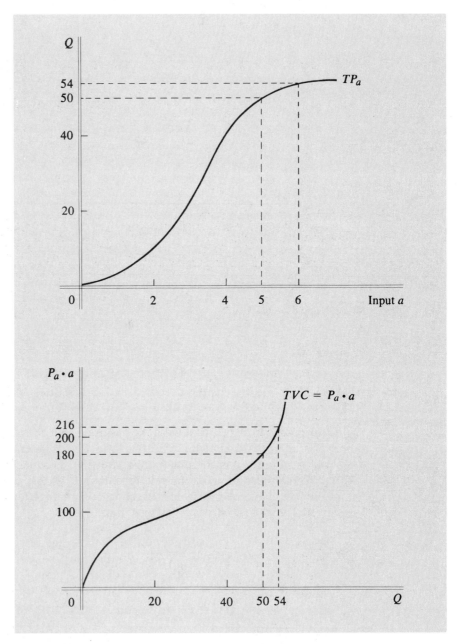

The productivity of a variable input and short-run costs vary inversely. If input a is the only variable input, $TVC = P_a \cdot a$. Note that the more steeply sloped the TP_a curve, the less steeply sloped the TVC curve (or the greater the MP_a, the smaller the SMC).

Therefore

$$SAC = \frac{P_b \cdot b}{Q} + \frac{P_a \cdot a}{Q} .$$

As shown in Figure 5–5, the average fixed cost curve is a rectangular hyperbola, since $P_b \cdot b$ is constant. Some points on the AFC curve for TFC = \$200 are shown in Figure 5–10. Since $AVC = (P_a \cdot a)/Q$, we can write

$$AVC = \left(\frac{a}{Q}\right) P_a = \frac{1}{(Q/a)} \cdot P_a = \frac{1}{AP_a} \cdot P_a = \frac{P_a}{AP_a} .$$

Therefore AVC is equal to P_a/AP_a where AP_a is the average product of input a. In other words, AVC is the reciprocal of AP_a, multiplied by P_a (see Figure 5–9). Again, we have assumed $P_a = \$36$. For example, at $Q = 10$ units, AP_a is equal to 5 units and $AVC = P_a/AP_a = \$36/5 = \$7.20$. At $Q = 50$, AP_a is equal to 10 units and $P_a/AP_a = \$36/10 = \$3.60$. The SAC curve is shown in Figure 5–10 as the vertical summation of AFC and AVC.

Figure 5–9   Relationship Between Average Product of a and Average Variable Cost

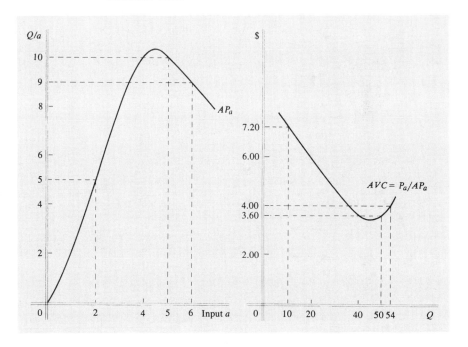

The greater the average product of the variable input (input a), the smaller AVC. For example, when the amount of input a is 2 units, $AP_a = 5$ units. $AVC = P_a/AP_a = \$36/5 = \$7.20$. When 5 units of input a are utilized, then $AP_a = 10$ units and $AVC = \$3.60$.

Finally, we will consider the relationship between the marginal product of input a and short-run marginal cost. In Chapter 4 we said that arc $MP_a = \Delta Q/\Delta a$, and in this chapter we have said that arc $SMC = \Delta STC/\Delta Q = \Delta TVC/\Delta Q$. We know that $TVC = P_a \cdot a$ (as long as P_a remains constant). Then arc $SMC = (\Delta a/\Delta Q)\, P_a = [1/(\Delta Q/\Delta a)] \cdot P_a = (1/\text{arc } MP_a) \cdot P_a$, where MP_a is the marginal product of input a. Thus SMC is the reciprocal of the marginal product of a multiplied by P_a, or P_a/MP_a, as shown in Figure 5–11.[13]

Figure 5–10   Short-Run Average Cost, Average Variable Cost, and Average Fixed Cost

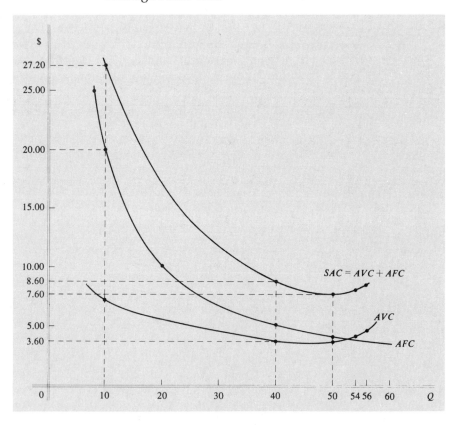

Short-run average cost (SAC) is equal to $AVC + AFC$. For example, at 10 units of output, $AVC = \$7.20$, $AFC = \$20.00$, and $SAC = \$7.20 + \$20.00 = \$27.20$.

■ ■ ■ ■ ■ ■
[13] In calculus terms, $MP_a = \partial Q/\partial a$ and $SMC = (\partial a/\partial Q) \cdot P_a$, so $SMC = (1/MP_a) \cdot P_a$.

Figure 5–11   Relationship Between Marginal Product of a and Short-Run Marginal Cost

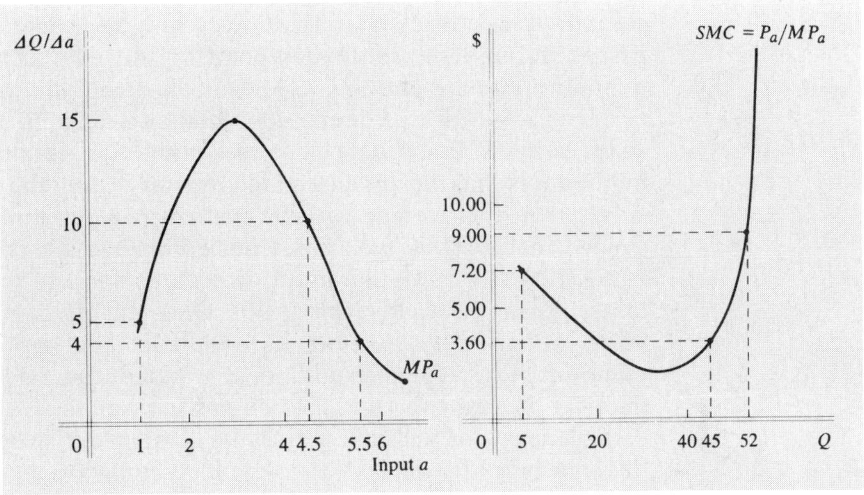

The greater the marginal product of a variable input, the lower the short-run marginal cost (*SMC*). For example, the marginal product of the first unit of input a is 5 units. The marginal cost of those first 5 units of output is equal to $P_a/MP_a = \$36/5 = \$7.20$. The marginal product of the fifth unit of a is 10 units. *SMC* at this point (between 40 and 50 units of output) = $3.60.

These relationships seem reasonable if one thinks about them for a moment. Suppose the average worker on a soda pop assembly line turns out 4 cases of soda an hour and the hourly cost of one worker is $6.00. The *average variable cost* per case of soda must be $P_a/AP_a = \$6.00/4$ cases = $1.50 per case. If the *marginal product* of an additional worker is 3 cases per hour, then the *marginal cost* of another case of soda will be $P_a/MP_a = \$6.00/3$ cases = $2.00 per case.[14]

By examining Figures 5–7, 5–9, and 5–11, we can observe that the productivity of an input and costs vary inversely. Other things being equal, the greater the productivity of a variable input, the lower the short-run costs of a firm. The lower the productivity of an input, the higher the short-run costs of a firm. For example, in Figure 5–9, when the AP_a is equal to 5 units, average variable cost is equal to $7.20. When AP_a is doubled to 10 units, *AVC* is cut in half. In Figure 5–11, when the MP_a is

■ ■ ■ ■ ■ ■

[14] We are temporarily ignoring the cost of additional containers and other materials. In reality the per-case amounts of these items would be added onto the *AVC* and *SMC* figures. We discuss the matter of component costs more thoroughly in Chapter 12.

5 units, *SMC* is equal to $7.20. When MP_a decreases to 4 units, *SMC* rises to $9.00.

Figure 5–12 shows the relationship between the short-run marginal cost curve and the *AVC* and *SAC* curves. Note that the rising *SMC* curve passes through the minimum point of the *AVC* curve as well as the minimum point of the *SAC*. This is in keeping with the *average-marginal relationship*, which was discussed in the preceding chapter and mentioned again earlier in this chapter. The reason the *AVC* is falling to the left of its minimum is that the amount added to total cost by the next unit of output is less than the average variable cost of previous units. In the case of a single variable input, we can say this occurs because the marginal product of additional units of that input exceeds its average product, causing *AP* to rise. Rising *AP* yields falling *AVC*. Once the *MP* of the input falls below its *AP*, *AP* will fall; therefore *AVC* will rise. This happens to the right of minimum *AVC*, where an additional unit of output adds more to total cost than the average variable cost of previous units. If input *a* is the only variable input, it will follow that the output level where *SMC* = *AVC* is the *same* output where $MP_a = AP_a$, or that *minimum AVC* corresponds to *maximum* AP_a.

Figure 5–12   Relation of SMC to AVC and SAC

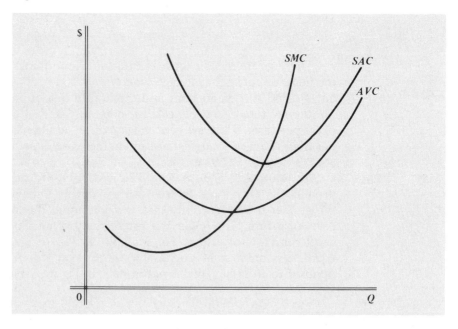

A marginal curve will always pass through the extreme value of the corresponding average curve. Thus, as it rises, *SMC* passes through the minimum of *AVC* *and* through the minimum of *SAC*.

Numerical Example: Relation of Short-Run Product to Cost

The following data pertain to Dynamo Corporation, a small firm that employs college students to do fast-food delivery using bicycles. Each employee must furnish his or her own bicycle. Naturally, there is no allowance for fuel. Complete the last column of the table, assuming that each additional worker is paid $6 per hour and that marginal product is measured in deliveries per hour.

Number of Workers	Arc Marginal Product of a Worker	Marginal Cost
0		
1	5	
2	8	
3	6	
4	4	
5	2	

Answer: The easiest way to obtain marginal cost from these data is to use the relation $SMC = P_a/MP_a$, where a is the variable input. Thus, for the first worker, we have $SMC = (\$6/5) = \$1.20$, and for the second, $SMC = (\$6/8) = \$0.75$. For the third, fourth, and fifth workers, the respective SMCs are $\$1.00$, $\$1.50$, and $\$3.00$. If you use $SMC = \Delta TVC/\Delta Q$, you will obtain the same results.

■ ■ ■ ■ ■ ■ ■ ■ ■   RELATION OF SHORT-RUN TO LONG-RUN AVERAGE COSTS

Once again we emphasize that for any given output, short-run total cost (and therefore short-run average cost) is unlikely to be as low as the level achievable when *all* inputs are variable. Typically, only one of all possible output levels attainable in a short-run setting will be characterized by cost data equal to long-run least possible cost for that level of output, and short-run total cost will exceed long-run total cost for all other possible short-run outputs. (An exception, discussed on p. 189, is the case in which all inputs are not divisible.)

In Figure 5–4 we indicated the relationship between short-run total cost curves and the long-run total cost curve. In Figure 5–13 the relationship between short-run average cost curves and the long-run average cost curve is demonstrated. Notice that the long-run average cost curve is an

Figure 5–13   Relationship Between Short-Run Average Cost Curves
and the Long-Run Average Cost Curve

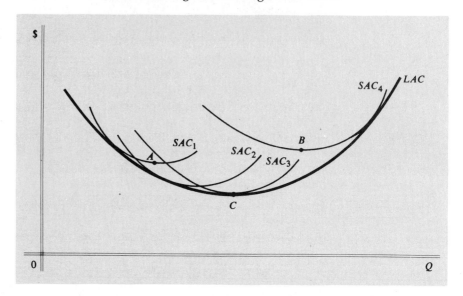

Each point on the long-run average cost curve (*LAC*) represents a least cost combination of
inputs and a point on one short-run average cost curve.

Economies of scale
are technological
and organizational
advantages that ac-
crue to the firm as
it increases output
in the long run.
Economies of scale
reduce long-run
average costs.

**Diseconomies of
scale** are techno-
logical and organi-
zational disadvan-
tages that the firm
encounters as it in-
creases output in
the long run. Dise-
conomies of scale
increase long-run
average costs.

envelope curve for the short-run average cost curves. In other words, it is
made up of points that indicate the lowest unit costs obtainable for each
level of output. We further observe that such points are not necessarily
the minimum points of the short-run average cost curves. In fact, for
outputs smaller than that corresponding to the minimum point of the
long-run average cost curve, the short-run average cost curves are tangent
to the long-run curve to the *left* of their respective minimum points. This
occurs because of the existence of **economies of scale,** which means that
smaller unit costs can be obtained by producing with a larger size plant
than by producing at the minimum short-run average cost corresponding
to a smaller plant size. (See point *A* in Figure 5–13.) The opposite result
occurs if **diseconomies of scale** are present, so that it is cheaper to produce
beyond the point of minimum short-run average cost corresponding to a
smaller plant than by producing at the minimum short-run average cost
point corresponding to a larger plant. (See point *B* in Figure 5–13.) Only
at the minimum point of the long-run average cost curve, where constant
returns to scale are obtained, can the firm produce a given level of output
most cheaply by producing at the minimum point of a short-run average
cost curve. (See point *C* in Figure 5–13.) The regions of economies of scale,
diseconomies of scale, and constant returns to scale are summarized in
Figure 5–14. Economies and diseconomies of scale occur because of the

Figure 5–14   Long-Run Average Cost and Returns to Scale

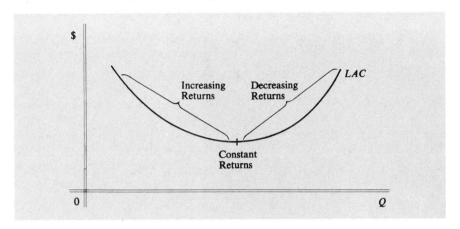

When the firm experiences increasing returns to scale, *LAC* declines. When the firm has constant returns to scale, *LAC* is constant. When the firm has decreasing returns to scale, *LAC* is increasing.

nature of the firm's production function and are *not* caused by changes in external data such as input prices. Thus they are sometimes called *internal* economies and diseconomies.

We should point out that drawing the *LAC* curve as a smooth, U-shaped curve implies that all inputs are perfectly divisible. In reality, all inputs are not necessarily infinitely divisible. For example, there are a limited number of sizes of blast furnaces readily available. When inputs are indivisible, the firm's long-run average cost curve merely consists of those points on the short-run average cost curves corresponding to the sizes of plant that are available that represent the lowest unit cost possible for each level of output. This situation produces a scalloped long-run average cost curve, such as that shown in Figure 5–15.

■ ■ ■ ■ ■ ■ ■ ■ ■   CHOOSING THE OPTIMAL PLANT SIZE: AN EXAMPLE

To get an idea of the type of analysis a firm must go through in trying to determine its optimal plant size, consider once more the case of John and Ruth Brown and their delicatessen, discussed at the beginning of this chapter. In Table 5–5 the income statement presented in Table 5–1 is reproduced with some additional information. Suppose that the deli, by selling 20,000 meals per month, is operating near its capacity level and that the Browns are contemplating expanding their restaurant.

In fact, assume that John and Ruth are considering two possibilities for expansion. The first possibility would involve building an addition

Figure 5–15   Long-Run Average Cost Curve when Four Plant Sizes
Are Available

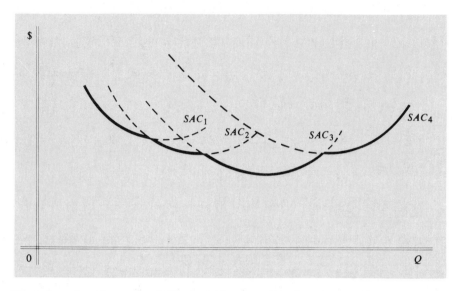

If only four plant sizes are available, the *LAC* curve will be determined by finding the plant
size with the lowest per-unit costs for each level of output. SAC_1, SAC_2, SAC_3, and SAC_4 are
short-run average cost curves corresponding to the four plant sizes. The long-run average
cost curve is the heavy black line.

Table 5–5

John and Ruth's Deli
Statement of Economic Profit
for Month Ended July 31, 1991

Total Revenue (20,000 meals @ average price of $6.00)		$120,000
Less		
Cost of Goods Sold (food and beverages—20,000 meals @ $4.20)		84,000
Gross Profit		$ 36,000
Less		
Operating Expenses		
Fixed	$20,000	
Variable (20,000 meals @ $0.50)	10,000	30,000
Operating (accounting) Net Income		$ 6,000
Less		
Implicit Rental Income	$ 2,000	
Implicit Salary Income	2,600	
Implicit Interest Income	160	4,760
Economic Profit		$ 1,240

onto the original deli, so that the back wall would extend further into the mall parking area. This plan would increase the deli's capacity by 50 percent to 30,000 meals per month and would involve an initial outlay of $60,000 for construction and equipment. John and Ruth have $20,000 additional money of their own that they could invest, and they know where they can borrow the remaining $40,000 at 9 percent interest. *If the expanded restaurant were to operate at capacity, its income statement (with additional information) would be like that presented in Table 5–6.*

The second expansion possibility involves buying the small vacant building adjoining the deli in the mall. This additional area would double the deli's capacity to 40,000 meals per month, and the Browns could get a good deal on the building, so that the initial outlay necessary for the building, remodeling, and equipment would be only $100,000. Again, the Browns could put up $20,000 of their own money and borrow the remaining $80,000 at 9 percent interest. If the restaurant were to follow this expansion plan *and were to operate at capacity,* John and Ruth expect that their monthly economic profit statement would be similar to that presented in Table 5–7. Note that if the Browns expand the restaurant to double the capacity, they *do* expect to be able to take advantage of some economies,

Table 5–6

John and Ruth's Deli
Statement of Economic Profit
for Month Ended _____
(At Capacity Under Expansion Plan 1)

Total Revenue (30,000 meals @ average price of $6.00)		$180,000
Less		
Cost of Goods Sold (food and beverages—30,000 meals @ $4.20)		126,000
Gross Profit		$ 54,000
Less		
Operating Expenses		
Fixed	$29,000	
Variable (30,000 meals @ $0.46)	13,800	42,800
Operating Net Income		$ 11,200
Less		
Explicit Interest Expense		300
Accounting Net Income		$ 10,900
Less		
Implicit Rental Income (existing building)	$ 2,000	
Implicit Salary Income	2,600	
Implicit Interest Income	320	4,920
Economic Profit		$ 5,980

Table 5–7

John and Ruth's Deli
Statement of Economic Profit
for Month Ended _____
(At Capacity Under Expansion Plan 2)

Total Revenue (40,000 meals @ average price of $6.00)		$240,000
Less		
Cost of Goods Sold (food and beverages—40,000 meals @ $4.10)		164,000
Gross Profit		$ 76,000
Less		
Operating Expenses		
Fixed	$35,500	
Variable (40,000 meals @ $0.40)	16,000	51,500
Operating Net Income		$ 24,500
Less		
Explicit Interest Expense		600
Accounting Net Income		$ 23,900
Less		
Implicit Rental Income (existing building)	$ 2,000	
Implicit Salary Income	2,600	
Implicit Interest Income	320	4,920
Economic Profit		$ 18,980

such as greater volume buying of both food and other operating supplies and more efficient use of equipment.

If John and Ruth think they have a high probability of being able to sell 40,000 meals per month, then obviously they should decide in favor of the larger expansion plan. However, suppose that they expect to be able to sell only 29,000 meals per month for the next few years. Then, assuming they cannot take advantage of volume food buying at that level of business under either plan, they expect monthly results under each expansion plan to be similar to those computed in Tables 5–8 and 5–9. In this case, without additional factors to consider, it appears that John and Ruth should select the smaller expansion plan.

Nevertheless, the Browns may well wish to consider some additional factors before they make their final decision. For example, they would perhaps wish to consider a longer time horizon than three or four years, especially if they expect sales to continue expanding. As they expand the time period under consideration, the second plan may look more and more desirable. The Browns would also want to consider the risks associated with each expansion plan in the event that their projected levels of sales are incorrect. They should also consider their possibilities for expanding their restaurant *after* they have already used the first expansion

Table 5–8

John and Ruth's Deli
Statement of Economic Profit
for Month Ended _____
(At 29,000 Meals Under Expansion Plan 1)

Total Revenue (29,000 meals @ average price of $6.00)		$174,000
Less		
Cost of Goods Sold (food and beverages—29,000 meals @ $4.20)		121,800
Gross Profit		$ 52,200
Less Operating Expenses		
Fixed	$29,000	
Variable (29,000 meals @ $0.46)	13,340	42,340
Operating Net Income		$ 9,860
Less Explicit Interest Expense		300
Accounting Net Income		$ 9,560
Less		
Implicit Rental Income (existing building)	$ 2,000	
Implicit Salary Income	2,600	
Implicit Interest Income	320	4,920
Economic Profit		$ 4,640

Table 5–9

John and Ruth's Deli
Statement of Economic Profit
for Month Ended _____
(At 29,000 Meals Under Expansion Plan 2)

Total Revenue (29,000 meals @ average price of $6.00)		$174,000
Less		
Cost of Goods Sold (food and beverages—29,000 meals @ $4.20)		121,800
Gross Profit		$ 52,200
Less Operating Expenses		
Fixed	$35,500	
Variable (29,000 meals @ $0.40)	11,600	47,100
Operating Net Income		$ 5,100
Less Explicit Interest Expense		600
Accounting Net Income		$ 4,500
Less		
Implicit Rental Income (existing building)	$ 2,000	
Implicit Salary Income	2,600	
Implicit Interest Income	320	4,920
Economic Profit		$ (420)

plan. We shall further discuss the techniques John and Ruth should use in this type of analysis in Chapters 13 and 14. They would also be wise to consider the results after changing their price structure and probably should do some investigation of the demand function of their deli's product. These topics are discussed at length in Chapters 2, 3, 6, 10, and 11.

Managerial Perspective: Lean, Mean, and Green

It hardly seemed worth bothering. The blades on the saws in Georgia Pacific sawmills could be made half as thick as they were before, thanks to a new, stronger metal alloy used to make the blades. Yet that smaller blade will result in 800 additional railcars of Georgia Pacific products each year rather than sawdust on the mill floor.

And Georgia Pacific is not alone in its effort to reduce waste. Companies all over the United States are finding that they must become more efficient if they are to survive in the international market environment in which they find themselves. Rockwell International found that by investing in an $80,000 laser to etch contract numbers on communications sold to the Pentagon, the company could save not only $4,000 annually in direct labor cost, but—much more important—$200,000 per year in inventory holding costs. Through automation of its refineries, weeding out unprofitable service stations, and modernizing high-volume stations, Exxon has been able to increase the volume sold through the stations by one-third. The paper industry and the steel industry have also been heavily involved in an effort to become more competitive by closing plants, restructuring, and layoffs. As a result, productivity in manufacturing grew at an annual rate of almost 4 percent between 1981 and 1987, a great improvement over the 1.3 percent rate of growth that prevailed between 1973 and 1981.

Of course, cost-cutting that is not carefully planned and thought through can be harmful to a firm's health. General Motors' problems with its new automated, state-of-the-art plants have been well publicized. Certainly, firms must be careful not to reduce plant capacity to such an extent that they lose market share when the demand for their products increases. Nor can they afford to ignore product development and quality control and improvement. One company recently supplied Ford Motor Company with 1.6 million oil pump parts without a single defect. According to its president, the company found that quality control that once was believed to be impossible is now necessary for survival. Xerox found that quality improvements could save as much as $2 billion on sales of $10 billion, certainly a significant figure. David Kearns, chief executive officer of Xerox, stated, "Over the years, you grow up thinking that the greater quality you give a customer, the higher the price. We now know that's not true. Quality drives costs down." The cost saving comes because doing it right the first time is often cheaper than repairing manufacturing defects and working to regain loyalty from dissatisfied customers.

Companies are finding that being "green" is profitable as well. Measures to improve the environmental impact of their products help companies to avoid obvious costs like fines and lawsuits. However, environmentally responsible policies can result in lower production and marketing costs as well. In 1989, Exxon endured an avalanche of bad publicity, not to mention more than $3 *billion* in environmental charges, as a result of the Valdez oil spill. ARCO Chemical found that it could reduce its energy costs by 35 percent by using a new, more efficient plant. Union Carbide recycled or sold 82 million pounds of waste in the first six months of 1989, generating $3.5 million in revenue and saving $8.5 million of disposal costs. By getting workers on the shop floor to buy into the notion of reducing hazardous wastes, General Electric was able to trim waste oil at an aircraft engines plant by 20 percent.

Clearly, careful cost management has become imperative for successful companies as they enter the twenty-first century, and environmentally sound policies with respect to resource use and disposal are a part of this mandate as well.

■ ■ ■ ■

References: "America's Leanest and Meanest," *Business Week* (October 5, 1987), pp. 78–80; "The Productivity Paradox," *Business Week* (June 6, 1988), p. 104; "U.S. Parts Makers Just Won't Say 'Uncle,'" *Business Week* (August 10, 1987), p. 76; "Culture Shock at Xerox," *Business Week*," (June 22, 1987), p. 110; and "The Greening of Corporate America," *Business Week* (April 23, 1990), p. 100.

■ ■ ■ ■ ■ ■ ■ ■ ■ ■   ## ESTIMATION OF COST

One of the tasks with which a profit-maximizing firm manager must contend is that of estimating what the costs of the firm will or should be for different levels of output. For example, strong financial controls and cost estimation have contributed significantly to the profitability of the General Electric Company; the lack of such controls has hurt Westinghouse.[15] In Detroit, Ford and General Motors make cost calculations to fractions of a cent.[16]

■ ■ ■ ■ ■ ■

[15] "The Opposites: GE Grows While Westinghouse Shrinks," *Business Week* (January 31, 1977), pp. 60–66.
[16] "Detroit's New Appetite for Electronic Controls," *Business Week* (August 29, 1977), p. 66.

There are two general methods of estimating costs: one is through utilization of historical cost data, and the second is through utilization of estimates by engineers. Managers who choose the historical cost method try to estimate future costs from data about actual costs incurred by the firm in the past. These historical cost figures must be adjusted to include opportunity costs and to take into consideration any changes in input prices or technology that will affect a firm's costs. An attempt should be made to separate short-run cost data from long-run cost data. Such an analysis will necessitate a study of those cost-output combinations that were obtained with a least cost combination of inputs and those that were not. Moreover, an attempt must be made to match historical costs with the appropriate level of output. Some costs, such as certain maintenance and repair expenses, may not always be incurred by the firm at the same time that the responsible level of output was produced. Finally, historical cost figures must also be adjusted for inflation if they are to be useful in estimating future costs.

Once the historical cost figures have been adjusted, firm managers can use various methods to estimate a firm's cost function or functions. We shall briefly discuss three of them here—the high-low method, the visual-fit method, and the regression method. To use the high-low method, one merely draws a straight line connecting the highest and lowest cost figures on a scatter diagram showing the adjusted historical cost data, as demonstrated in Figure 5–16. Employing the visual-fit

Figure 5–16   High-Low Method of Cost Estimation

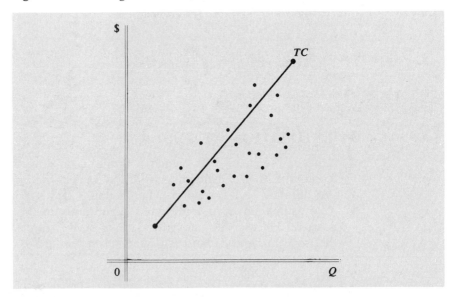

The high-low method of cost estimation involves drawing a total cost curve by connecting the lowest level of cost with the highest level of cost.

method, one draws a line through points on a scatter diagram that appears to be most representative of (or "best fits") the underlying cost data. This method is illustrated in Figure 5–17. The third method, regression analysis, requires the use of more sophisticated statistical techniques to estimate the cost function and the correlation of cost with the level of output. This method, although more precise, is also more difficult to use. It was discussed in Chapter 3 and its appendix in connection with demand estimation.

Finally, the method involving engineering cost estimates has an advantage in that the cost figures obtained in this manner should already be based on current technology and current prices. Also, there should not be the problem of separating long-run and short-run cost figures nor the problem of matching costs incurred with the relevant levels of production. However, engineering cost estimates are still only that—*estimates*. The better the engineers understand the nature of a firm's production relationships and the more closely they can estimate future prices, the more nearly accurate their cost estimates will be. Even these figures, however, must still be adjusted to reflect implicit or opportunity costs.

Thus it is evident that the estimation of a firm's costs is rarely a simple task. Still, the difficulty of estimating a firm's costs does not diminish the importance of that information to the firm managers. Managers face the job of finding a proper (profit-maximizing) balance between more precise information regarding the firm's costs and the corresponding cost of obtaining it and less reliable, but cheaper, information.

Figure 5–17   Visual-Fit Method of Cost Estimation

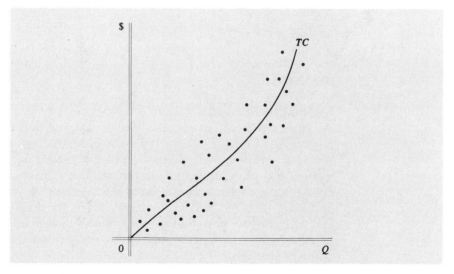

The visual fit method of cost estimation involves sketching that total cost curve which appears to "best fit" the historical cost data.

> **Managerial Perspective:** Estimating Product Cost
> The Modern Way
>
> Computers invaded industry decades ago, and they are now a common fixture on production lines as well as in corporate offices. What everyone has learned is that these wondrous information processors are only as good as the software designed to run them. Often the capabilities of computers are underutilized because no one has developed appropriate applications programs. Computer-aided design (CAD) and computer aided manufacturing (CAM) are examples of fields in which there has been an outpouring of software development.
>
> Now comes the Parts Cost Estimating (PCE) program. This new breed of software utilizes a base of existing knowledge in specific types of manufacturing to generate cost estimates for yet-to-be-built products. Thus, once the CAD folks have come up with a design, the PCE people can check out its likely production cost. The brainchild of Geoffrey Boothroyd, a professor at the University of Rhode Island, the first PCE program was for machining parts made of metal. However, modifications of the program can handle parts made by injection molding, bending of sheet metal, forging, and other methods. The PCE program calculates how long certain operations will take, how much material they use, and finally their cost.
>
> ■ ■ ■ ■
>
> Reference: "Software That Tells You How Much That New Widget Will Cost," *Business Week* (April 4, 1988), p. 63.

■ ■ ■ ■ ■ ■ ■ ■ **SUMMARY**

Costs and the Firm

We have repeatedly emphasized the crucial role that costs play in determining the profitability of the firm. The profit-oriented firm manager must consider both opportunity costs and explicit costs in order to use time, money, and physical resources economically. Obviously, a firm does not always have totally accurate information about its costs; but it is very important that it have reliable *estimates* of its fixed costs, of how its costs vary with respect to output over the relevant range of production, and of whether or not its costs would be lower (and if so, how much) with a different size plant.

We have discussed three general types of cost classifications in this chapter: (1) *explicit,* or *historical,* costs and *implicit,* or *opportunity,* costs; (2)

fixed and *variable* costs; and (3) *private* and *social* costs. Explicit costs are costs for which the firm has made direct payment or will make direct payment in the future and are the basis for most accounting cost figures. Opportunity costs are costs that the firm incurs by utilizing its resources in one activity when such resources could also be used in another manner, even though no explicit payment is being made by the firm for their use. Examples of such resources are the owner-manager's time and money. A consideration by the manager of both the explicit and implicit costs of a firm is necessary to ensure that *all* of the firm's resources are being used to maximize profits. Thus *economic costs* include both explicit and implicit costs. Fixed costs are costs that do not vary with the level of a firm's output in the short run, whereas variable costs do vary with the level of output. By classifying costs in this manner, a firm manager can separate opportunities and decisions relevant to the short run from opportunities and decisions that are relevant to long-run planning. Private costs are costs that a firm incurs, whereas social costs are those borne by society as a whole. A classification of costs as to which are private and which social is most useful for decisions involving social policy.

Next, we discussed the long-run costs of a firm, all of which are assumed to be variable and are derived by finding a series of least cost combinations of inputs. The long-run costs were discussed in terms of *total cost, average cost,* and *marginal cost*. Long-run total cost is all of the costs that a firm incurs, given that the firm is producing with the optimal input mix. Average cost is the average cost per unit of output, or *LTC/Q*. Marginal cost is the rate of change of total cost with respect to the level of output.

Because of the existence of fixed costs in the short run, short-run costs must be discussed in terms of *total cost, total fixed cost, total variable cost, average total cost, average fixed cost, average variable cost,* and *marginal cost*. The definition of each of these terms is similar to that for corresponding long-run terms (total, average, or marginal). We also demonstrated the close relationships between short-run product curves and cost curves.

Moreover, we discussed the relationships among short-run average cost, long-run average cost, and returns to scale. We also gave a simple example of some of the analysis that a profit-maximizing firm manager should undertake when determining the optimal plant size for the firm.

Finally, we ended this chapter with a brief discussion of cost estimation techniques. The two general types of methods used are the historical cost method and the engineering cost method, and data used in both methods usually require some adjustments. Obtaining information about a firm's costs can be an expensive project for a manager, who must determine when (and how much of) that expense is in the best interests of the firm.

As those who operate successful businesses understand, in order to be profitable, a firm must produce a good or service that people desire, market it well, and price it correctly, *in addition to* keeping its unit costs low relative to those of other firms in the same industry.[17] In the next chapter we shall discuss how the profit-maximizing firm determines its optimal level of output (and price), given its cost and revenue data.

■ ■ ■ ■ ■ ■ ■ ■ ■ ■ ■ ■ ■ **Questions** ■ ■ ■ ■ ■ ■ ■ ■ ■ ■ ■ ■ ■

1. Define and compare historical costs, accounting costs, opportunity costs, economic costs, private costs, and social costs.
2. Why is it important that a firm owner consider opportunity costs when making economic decisions regarding the firm? Give some examples of opportunity costs.
3. What is a least cost combination of inputs? How do such input combinations relate to the long-run total cost curve for a firm?
4. What is the difference between the long run and the short run for a firm? How do the firm's costs differ in the two time periods?
5. How are the short-run average cost curves and the long-run average cost curve related?
6. Why can arc short-run marginal cost be found by finding either ($\Delta STC/\Delta Q$) or ($\Delta TVC/\Delta Q$)?
7. How do returns to scale affect the shape of the long-run average cost curve?

■ ■ ■ ■ ■ ■ ■ ■ ■ ■ ■ ■ ■ **Problems** ■ ■ ■ ■ ■ ■ ■ ■ ■ ■ ■ ■ ■

1. a. Complete the following table, which gives short-run cost data for a firm.

Q	STC	TFC	TVC	SAC	AFC	AVC	Arc SMC
0	10,800		0	—	—	—	
1,000			1,000				
2,000			1,600				
3,000			2,400				
4,000			3,600				
5,000			5,000				
6,000			7,200				

■ ■ ■ ■ ■ ■
[17] See, for example, "Kodak Chief Is Trying For the Fourth Time, To Trim Firm's Costs," *The Wall Street Journal*, September 19, 1989, pp. A1, A8.

b. Sketch the cost curves, given the data that you have computed in the preceding table.
2. a. In the following table, complete the cost data for a firm.

Q	STC	TFC	TVC	SAC	AFC	AVC	Arc SMC
0			0	—	—	—	
1					120		20
2							16
3							12
4							16
5							21
6							29

b. Sketch the cost curves, given the data in part a.
3. Given that $Q = f(a,b)$, as shown in the diagram on the next page, and that $P_a = \$1$ and $P_b = \$2$, answer the questions in parts a through e.
a. If $b_3 = 450$ units of input b, what is the total cost of producing 300 units of output?
b. What is the long-run *average* cost of producing 300 units of output? Is this consistent with point H′ in the lower diagram?
c. Assuming the curve in the lower diagram *is* long-run average cost, how many units of a is a_1 equal to in the upper diagram?
d. What is the dollar amount of TC_2?
e. If $a_4 = 1,400$ units and $Q_4 = 400$ units, find average cost at point J in the upper diagram.
4. Complete the following table, given that the price of input a is constant and that a is the only variable input. (Hint: The price of input a and total fixed cost can be determined from the information given in the table.)

Input a (Units)	Q (Output in Units)	Arc MP$_a$	Arc SMC	AVC	SAC
0	0			Unde-fined	Unde-fined
1	5		$10.00	$10.00	$30.00
2	20				
3	40				
4	55				
5	65				

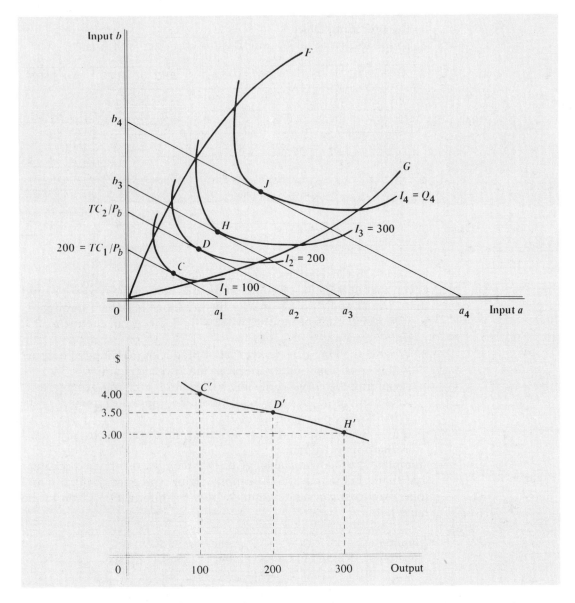

5. Exclusive Excavating Corporation digs holes. Its only variable input is labor, and each worker must bring his or her own shovel. Each worker costs $100 per day, and Exclusive's total fixed cost per day is $300. The following table contains some of the company's daily production and cost data.
   a. Complete the table.
   b. Where is *SMC* at a minimum? Where is MP_L at a maximum?

SMC	MP$_L$	Q	L	TVC	SAC
		0	0	0	—
		40	2		12.50
4.00		100	4		
		150	6		
		190	8		
5.88		224	10		
		254	12		5.91
		274	14		
		284	16		

6. Given the following diagram and the information that input a is the only variable input, answer the questions in parts a through d.

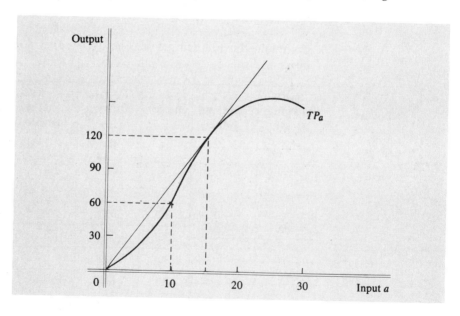

a. What is the maximum value of AP_a?
b. At approximately what quantity of input a will MP_a be at a maximum?
c. If P_a is $96, what is the minimum AVC?
d. If P_a is $96 and TFC is $4,800, find STC and SAC at an output level of 60 units.

7. Complete the following table, assuming that the firm is in the short run, that input a is the only variable input, and that P_a, the price of input a, is fixed.

Input a (Units)	Output (Units)	AP_a	Arc MP_a	Arc SMC	AVC	AFC	STC
0	0	—			$ —	$ —	
			5.0	$ 40.00			
2	10				40.00		
				22.22			
4		7			28.57		
			10.0				
6	48					14.00	
				50.00			
8	56	7			28.57		
10		6					
			1.5	133.33			
12	63				38.10		

* Take note in your calculation of marginal product that Δa is 2 units of a between output values.

8. Complete the following table, assuming that L is the only variable input and that its price, P_L, is fixed.

SMC (Marginal Cost)	MP_L (Marginal Product)	L (Input)	$TP_L = Q_X$ (Output)	TVC (Total Variable Cost)	STC (Total Cost)
		5	100	200	600
		10	200		
		15	450		
		20	550		
4.00	10				
		25	600	1,000	
		30	625		
10.00	4				
		35	645		
		40	660		2,000

a. Now calculate the following:
   (i) Average fixed cost at an output of $Q = 200$.
   (ii) Average product of L at an output of $Q = 600$.
b. Suppose total fixed cost is increased by 25 percent. Which of the numbers in the table would change? Why?

9. The following data represent the quantities of product X that can be obtained from various combinations of two inputs, Y and Z.

Units of Input Y	Output of Product X					
6	122	205	277	345	408	468
5	112	190	256	317	374	429
4	100	168	228	283	334	383
3	86	145	197	245	289	331
2	70	119	160	200	236	270
1	50	84	114	142	167	191
0	1	2	3	4	5	6	Units of Input Z

a. How will the long-run average cost curve for the production of X behave? Explain how you know from the given data.

b. Suppose the price of a unit of Y is $14 and that of a unit of Z is $12. Do one unit of Y and two units of Z constitute a least cost combination of inputs for an output of 84 units of product X? Explain why or why not.

c. Suppose input Z is fixed at Z = 4. Complete the following table, assuming the same production function and input prices. (Assume also that no output can be obtained if Y = 0.)

SMC	MP_Y	Output of X	Input of Y	AP_Y	AVC	STC
		0	0	—	—	

10. In the following table, assume that L is the only variable input and that P_L, the price of a unit of labor, is fixed.

a. Given that L is labor units and Q is units of output per time period, complete the table.

MP	L	Q	STC	AFC	AVC	TVC	MC
	0	0	120	—	—	0	
	2	20		6		160	
	4	60					
	6	90				480	
	8	110					
	10	125					

b. Explain what a 25 percent increase in total fixed cost would do to the concepts listed in the table.

11. Suppose a firm has two inputs, a and b, and that b is fixed in the short run. Its short-run total product is described by the following table.

a	Q = Output
0	0
2	50
4	120
6	180
8	230
10	270
12	300

a. Fill in the table below, assuming that the price of a unit of input a is $40.

SMC	MP_a	Output (Q)	Input of a	AP_a	AVC	STC
			0			
						744

b. What will be the value of average fixed cost when output is at a level of $Q = 180$? How do you know?

c. Suppose the price of a unit of b is fixed, and that the amount employed of b is constant at $b = 12$. How much is the firm paying per unit of b? (What is b's price?) Explain how you know.

The following problems require calculus.

12. Suppose the total cost function is $550 + 9Q - .15Q^2 + .005Q^3$.
    a. Find the marginal cost, average variable cost, average cost, and the average fixed cost functions.
    b. Sketch the functions that you derived in part a.
    c. At what level of output does the SMC reach its minimum? AVC? AFC?
    d. Find SMC and AVC when AVC is at its minimum.
13. A firm has the following short-run total cost function:

$$STC = \$1{,}000 + 240Q - 4Q^2 + (1/3)Q^3.$$

    a. Write equations for the firm's SMC, AVC, and SAC.
    b. Determine the output level at which SMC will be minimized.
    c. Determine the output level at which AVC will be minimized.
14. Suppose a firm has the following total cost function:

$$STC = 300 + 40Q - 8Q^2 + (2/3)Q^3$$

    a. Write equations for
       i) Average fixed cost
       ii) Average variable cost
    b. What will be the value of short-run average cost when $Q = 60$?
    c. Write the marginal cost equation for this firm.
    d. What will marginal cost be when $Q = 20$?
    e. For this firm, what will be the dollar value of AVC at its minimum?
15. Juno Corp. has the short-run total cost function

$$STC = TFC + TVC = 800 + 60Q - 4.5Q^2 + 0.15Q^3,$$

where Q is output. Answer the following:
    a. What is the dollar value of average fixed cost at an output of 20 units?
    b. At what level of output will marginal cost be at its minimum?
    c. What will be the value of average variable cost when it is at its minimum?

■ ■ ■ ■ ■ ■ ■ ■ ■ ■ **Selected References** ■ ■ ■ ■ ■ ■ ■ ■ ■ ■

Cookenboo, Leslie, Jr. "Production Functions and Cost Functions: A Case Study," *Crude Oil Pipe Lines and Competition in the Oil Industry.* Cambridge, Mass.: Harvard University Press, 1955.

Leftwich, Richard H., and Ross D. Eckert. *The Price System and Resource Allocation*, 9th ed. Hinsdale, Ill.: The Dryden Press, 1985, Chapter 10.

Mansfield, Edwin. *Microeconomics: Theory and Applications*, 7th ed. New York: W. W. Norton, 1991, Chapter 7.

McGuigan, James R., and R. Charles Moyer. *Managerial Economics*, 5th ed. St. Paul, Minn.: West, 1989, Chapter 12.

Moore, Frederick T. "Economies of Scale: Some Statistical Evidence," *Quarterly Journal of Economics* 78, no. 2 (May 1959), pp. 232–236.

Moroney, John R. "Cobb-Douglas Production Functions and Returns to Scale in U.S. Manufacturing Industry," *Western Economic Journal* 6, no. 1 (December 1967), pp. 39–51.

Nicholson, Walter. *Microeconomic Theory*, 3d ed. Chicago: The Dryden Press, 1985, Chapter 8.

Some International Dimensions of Demand, Production, and Cost

As a business firm develops its strategy regarding product lines, organization of production, and efficiency in the use of its resources, its managers frequently perceive that there are opportunities to sell in markets other than those of its home country. In addition, foreign sales of a product are often followed by a managerial decision to produce that product at a foreign location or, in some cases, to *purchase* certain component parts from foreign suppliers. Although these options are available to firms of all sizes, those that have been most successful in pursuing them are large multinational corporations, many of which are headquartered in the United States. Some examples are General Motors, Ford, and Chrysler, large drug manufacturers such as Eli Lilly, and chemical companies such as Celanese.

THE BASIS FOR INTERNATIONAL TRADE

In order to understand why firms enter international markets, we must first look at the economic rationale underlying foreign trade. Economic theory argues that international trade occurs because of country-to-country differences in relative prices. More precisely, it is argued that a country will export goods that are relatively cheap in its home market and import those that are relatively expensive. A simple example will help to illustrate this point.

Suppose we consider two countries, the United States and Germany, both of which produce two goods: white table wine and Cheddar cheese. Assume at first that there is no trade between the two countries. Each will be willing to give up some of one of the two goods only if it gets a suitable amount of the other in return. Thus we are examining a basis for two-way trade, where each country both exports to and imports from the other.

Of course, in this example and in international trade generally, each country's internal prices will be stated in its own currency. This will not deter us from identifying goods that are relatively cheap or relatively expensive, since the relative value of any good can be measured in terms of how much of some other good must be given up in order to obtain it. Let us suppose that in Germany a bottle of white table wine sells for 20 marks, while a pound of Cheddar cheese sells for 10 marks. In other words, a bottle of wine is worth two pounds of cheese. Now suppose that in the United States either one bottle of wine or one pound of cheese can be bought for $3.00. Thus a bottle of wine is worth only one pound of cheese to U.S. consumers. In relative terms, then, wine is expensive in Germany, while cheese is expensive in the United States.

Table I-1 summarizes the price information. How can we determine whether two-way trade will occur? The answer is that we must know the *exchange rate* between marks and dollars in order to analyze this situation. For example, suppose that in the market for currencies, a dollar can be obtained for 4 marks. The exchange rate is thus 4 marks per dollar, or $0.25 per mark (the mark is 1/4th of a dollar). As Table I-2 shows, the German internal prices of wine and cheese (20 marks and 10 marks, respectively) translate into $5.00 per bottle for wine and $2.50 per pound for cheese. On the other hand, the U.S. internal prices ($3.00 for either good) translate into 12 marks for either wine or cheese. German consumers will find U.S. wine attractive at 12 marks per bottle, since equivalent German wine costs 20 marks. Likewise, U.S. consumers will be attracted by the price of German cheese—$2.50 per pound—since equivalent U.S. cheese costs them $3.00 per pound. Thus we do have a basis for two-way trade at the exchange rate of 4 marks per dollar. Germany will export cheese, and the U.S. will export wine.

The importance of the exchange rate cannot be overstressed. If, in the example just cited, the exchange rate had been 3 marks per U.S. dollar, the dollar price of German cheese would be 10/3 or $3.33 per

Table I–1 Local Currency Prices of Wine and Cheese in Germany and the United States

	Price of:	
	---	---
	Wine in Local Currency	Cheese in Local Currency
Germany	20 marks	10 marks
United States	$3.00	$3.00

Table I–2 Translation of Internal Prices to Foreign Currency

| | Money Price of Product in: | | | |
| | Marks | | Dollars | |
Country	Wine	Cheese	Wine	Cheese
Germany	20	10	5.00	2.50
United States	12	12	3.00	3.00

pound, while German wine would be priced at 20/3 or $6.67 per bottle. Thus U.S. consumers would not wish to buy either product from Germany, since both would be cheaper produced in the United States ($3.00 per unit). However, German consumers would find both U.S. products attractive. There would be a basis for one-way trade, but not for two-way trade.[1]

Why Relative Prices Differ

Until the last 20 years or so, the most widely accepted explanation for international dif-

■ ■ ■ ■ ■ ■
[1] One-way trade is not feasible for very long. In this example, the desire of Germany to buy both wine and cheese from the United States would flood the currency markets with marks and cause the price of the mark to fall until some German goods became attractive to American buyers.

ferences in relative prices was variation in production costs from country to country. Thus, in our example, it would be argued that production costs for cheese were lower in Germany than in the United States, while for wine the reverse was true. The supposed reason for the lower production costs was said to be relative abundance or scarcity of resources. The relative production cost explanation (called the Heckscher-Ohlin theorem after the two Swedish economists who developed it) was widely accepted, since it seemed to do a good job of explaining why countries with an abundance of unskilled labor (Latin American countries, India, and some Asian countries) tended to export products that required relatively large doses of labor to produce. Of course, it also seemed to explain why industrialized countries such as the United States, Japan, and Germany tended to export goods that required relatively large amounts of capital goods to produce. However, the production cost approach did not seem to explain why most of world trade occurs *among* the industrialized countries, all of which are relatively capital abundant. One answer was put forth by Staffan Linder, who argued that different relative prices might well depend as much on demand as on cost of production.

Linder looked at modern trade patterns and observed that the lion's share of world trade is carried out by the industrialized countries (United States, Japan, Western Europe) trading among themselves. These countries both import and export large amounts of manufactured goods, and all of them have an abundance of capital equipment, skilled labor, and advanced technology. Since all of them can supply manufactured goods at relatively low costs of production, why do they trade so much with one another? Linder reasoned that the explanation could be found in overlapping patterns of demand. The industrialized countries in general have large internal markets and relatively affluent consumers. Thus products that can be sold in one of them can probably be sold in all of them. If a company introduces a battery-powered electric face scrubber in the United States, it probably will find a market for that product in Germany and France. However, it is unlikely to find much of a market for it in Peru. Many other U.S. products might be successfully marketed in a country like Peru, but the *range* of products Peruvians will buy is much smaller than the range of products that can be sold in Western Europe.

Different intensities of demand certainly can account for different relative prices, even if production costs are the same in the United States as in Europe. For example, if Germans become absolutely wild about designer sweatsocks, the relative price of these garments may become much higher in Germany than it is in the United States, opening up an opportunity for U.S. manufacturers to sell them in Germany.

THE PROBLEM OF TRADE BARRIERS

Today's world is full of pitfalls to international trade that make it imperative for a company entering a foreign market to proceed with caution. One commonly encountered problem is trade barriers. These take two forms: tariffs and nontariff barriers. Import tariffs are taxes levied on imported goods. They are frequently used to protect home industries from foreign competition. Sellers of an imported good simply view the import tariff as an additional cost of production, and they are willing to supply the imported good only at a price that will cover the costs of production *including* the tariff.[2] Thus the tariff raises the price of the imported good and may actually make it impossible for the imported good to compete with equivalent locally produced goods. In many developing countries, local manufacturing is protected by very high import tariff rates—perhaps 100 percent or more of the invoice price of the imported article. In effect, these tariffs totally prohibit the importation of many kinds of goods (automobiles and television sets, for example).

Nontariff barriers may actually prohibit imports in a more decisive fashion than do import tariffs. Two examples of these devices are the *import quota* and the *import license*. An import quota is a limitation on the physical amount of a particular good that will be allowed to enter the country. For example, if Pulistonia decides to establish an annual import quota of 200 motorcycles, then no more than 200 motorcycles will be allowed to enter the country each year. This has a more certain effect than a tariff, since a tariff pushes price up but does not specifically limit quantity. Presumably, anyone wishing to pay the tariff can still import the good. Quotas are usually accompanied by a licensing system, since the government must keep track of the quantity of imports and determine who gets to do the importing. Thus Pulistonia would require a license to import motorcycles and devise some means for dividing the quota among the licensees (auctioning off the licenses, for example, or giving them only to in-laws of government officials).

Licensing often occurs even when there is no quota. In other words, under a system that appears to rely mainly on import tariffs for protection, a license may also be required to import a particular item and thereby enjoy the privilege of *paying* the tariff. Mexico has employed such a system in the past; the government simply refused to give out licenses whenever it wished to prohibit the importation of some particular good. During the 1960s, Mexico had an elaborate system of tariffs on automobiles; the rates were meaningless, however, since almost no one could get a license to import a car anyway.

These are not the only kinds of trade barriers firms encounter when they attempt to enter a foreign market. Frequent restrictions are placed on size and labeling. (Example: "Do not send product in quart bottles, we allow only liters," or "Do not label product on the side, only on the bottom.") A firm may also find that government agencies are allowed to purchase its product only if locally produced output is nonexistent, regardless of price differentials between the two. In fact, something like the latter restriction is used by many state governments in the United States ("Buy American" laws). The moral is that no firm should seriously consider entering a foreign market without first determining the nature and extent of trade barriers found in that market. This may require considerable research at significant expense, but it is *absolutely necessary*. If insurmountable trade barriers are present, a firm may have to choose between giving up a specific foreign market or entering it by investing in production facilities located there.

Analyzing Foreign Demand

Whether a firm is considering export or foreign production, an important step in its decision process will be the assessment of potential foreign demand for its product. For a product that has been successful in

■ ■ ■ ■ ■ ■
[2] Economic theory shows that the price paid by consumers in the importing country will rise by less than the amount of the tariff if foreign supply is not infinitely elastic.

the home market, the firm might simply choose to look for foreign markets where consumer preferences are likely to be similar to those in its own country. If its product is not unique, there are likely to be other firms already selling in the chosen foreign market. Statistical data on production, consumption, and imports in that market may make it possible for the firm to estimate a market demand function for the product or at least estimate the rate of growth of demand. (Statistical procedures for demand estimation were discussed in Chapter 3.)

Rapid growth of demand is one indicator that a foreign market is ripe for entry. However, even if data on a firm's product are not available, an assessment of potential demand can be made from other information on the characteristics of the foreign market. For example, for many countries, data on population, per capita income, and income distribution are easily obtained. As Staffan Linder suggested, for certain manufactured goods it would be important to identify sizable markets where the middle class is large and per capita income is relatively high. Although this set of circumstances seems to describe the industrialized countries only, it also applies to the urban middle-class consumers found in many of today's developing countries (Brazil and Mexico, for example). Moreover, a firm might find that a smaller country constitutes a feasible export market simply because there is no local production of its product.

Data Sources

To make an evaluation of foreign demand requires knowledge of basic sources of secondary data (data not directly gathered by the firm). The U.S. Department of Commerce produces many publications that contain data on foreign markets, including not only data on U.S. exports by commodity and country (Report FT 447), but also an international marketing information series. The latter provides (1) global market surveys covering 15 or more countries for certain target industries or products; (2) foreign country market surveys covering leading industrial sectors in a single country; (3) "Overseas Business Reports" including background data and economic conditions for both industrialized and developing countries; and (4) a variety of other valuable information on foreign economic trends and new developments in world trade. There is also a great deal of basic data available from international agencies such as the United Nations, the Organization of American States, and the Organization for Economic Cooperation and Development (for industrialized countries).

The governments of most industrialized countries and many of the developing countries provide data on their own production, consumption, and foreign trade. In fact, these are the basic sources of much of the statistical data published by the international agencies. Statistics vary widely in terms of both availability and accuracy. For some countries, there is a great deal of lag in data publication, so that the latest available information may pertain to the economy of five years ago rather than that of the present. Other countries do not even gather economic and demographic data on a regular basis. For example, it was reported in 1984 that Oman had never taken a census and that the People's Republic of China did not take a census between 1953 and 1982.[3]

Where secondary data are not available, a firm may have to either collect its own information or rely on expert opinion regarding a foreign market opportunity. It

■ ■ ■ ■ ■ ■

[3] For more on sources of secondary data, see Edward W. Cundiff and Marye Tharp Hilger, *Marketing in the International Environment* (Englewood Cliffs, N.J.: Prentice-Hall, Inc., 1984), especially pp. 199–203.

may be relatively easy to have survey research done on a potential market in an industrialized country, although pitfalls related to cultural and language differences must be avoided. (Do not ask about the size of a car "trunk" in a country where the luggage compartment is called a "boot.") In a developing country, the obstacles to market research may be substantial, since many consumers will not have telephones or even access to reliable mail service. The best sources of information in such cases may be local experts such as consultants, industry colleagues, or economic officers assigned to embassies or consulates.

Product Adaptation

Analysis of the need for product adaptation often goes hand in hand with analysis of foreign demand. Product adaptation means changing the product to fit the characteristics of the foreign market environment. It may involve production costs. For example, electrical appliances presently manufactured for 110-volt current in the home market may have to be redesigned for 220-volt current in the foreign market. Sometimes product adaptation has more to do with how the product is *presented* to potential buyers in the foreign market than with its physical characteristics. A case in point is the Chevrolet Nova, a car that was produced and sold by General Motors in a number of countries. The name of the car presented a problem in the Spanish-speaking world, since *no va* in Spanish means "it won't run." There are other cases in which cultural norms make product adaptation imperative. For example, one U.S. candy manufacturer reportedly planned to introduce a chocolate candy with peanuts into the Japanese market. Fortunately, the firm found out in time that an old Japanese belief held that eating peanuts with chocolate would

cause nosebleeds.[4] In a case like this, it would probably be advisable to develop a new product aimed at local tastes and preferences rather than attempt to change the perception of the existing product.

It is clear that the product adaptation question has at least three dimensions: (1) change in the physical attributes of the product; (2) change in buyer perception of the product; and (3) development of an entirely new product for foreign consumers. While the second item has mainly to do with marketing, the economics of production is of substantial importance for the other two. Production can take place, in whole or in part, either at home or in a foreign location.

Producing in a Foreign Country

Having examined various dimensions of identifying a foreign market for a product, the time has come to consider what it means to produce a product in a foreign location. There are numerous advantages to such a strategy, but it is an arena into which a firm should enter only after a good deal of careful study.

The decision to produce abroad is usually made either for reasons of cost or for political reasons. When a firm produces in its home market and exports to a foreign market, its production costs are determined by resource prices in its home country. To sell abroad, it must also pay transportation costs and any other costs incurred in getting the good to the foreign market. In the foreign location, the firm may find that certain resources are lower priced than at home. This could be reason enough to consider producing all or part of the good in the

◼ ◼ ◼ ◼ ◼ ◼
[4] Philip R. Cateora, *International Marketing* (Homewood, Ill.: Irwin, 1983), p. 270.

foreign country rather than at home. However, political factors may also determine the location of production.

Many developing countries provide incentives for firms to invest in production facilities. These range from tax breaks and loan guarantees for foreign investors to provision of plant space in government-sponsored industrial parks. Often such incentives are coupled with barriers against importation of finished products, so that the only access to the country's market is through local production or assembly of the final product. To some extent, firms in industrialized countries are pushed into establishment of foreign production facilities when they realize that their only hope for gaining a foothold in a potentially large foreign market is through such investments.

The Product Cycle
Where costs rather than government policies determine foreign investment, the development of foreign production facilities often follows the pattern described by the *product cycle* theory of international trade. This theory, popularized by Raymond Vernon of Harvard University, argues that new product development takes place in advanced, industrialized nations. The firm that develops such a product is likely to be its first producer, and the product is aimed first at consumers in the home market. Once the product is successful, the firm may look to foreign markets for increased sales. It may also try to reduce costs by seeking foreign sources of certain parts, even though final production still occurs at home. Finally, it may decide to set up a foreign subsidiary to manufacture the good. If foreign production proves cheaper than home country production, the firm may choose to shut down its home country facilities. The result is that the home country

then becomes an *importer* of the very product that it first exported.

The product cycle theory seems to provide a reasonable approximation of how U.S.-based multinational corporations have expanded into overseas production, especially in Europe and parts of Asia. Here, costs rather than government policies attracted the firms' investments. In situations like these, deciding whether or not to set up foreign plants is based rather straightforwardly on the kinds of cost analyses firms are familiar with from their operations at home. If long-run production costs are minimized by producing in the foreign location, and if investing there does not appear to be overly risky, then foreign production may well be the strategy to choose.

Analysis of Foreign Costs
In comparing foreign costs with those at home, it is important to be aware of political or environmental differences that may make the total cost of inputs higher than their nominal price. For example, seemingly lower labor costs often make foreign production appear to be attractive, but firms have learned that low wage rates may be offset by both lagging worker productivity and government requirements for such benefits as social security, medical services, paid holidays, and severance pay. In terms of the production analysis presented in Chapter 4, this means that the marginal product of labor is lower in the foreign location than at home and that the price of foreign labor is actually much higher than its wage rate implies. Further, the cost of foreign labor may escalate rapidly if a politically powerful union can make unwarranted demands on foreign-owned firms.

Other dimensions of foreign cost analysis include the availability of raw materials and intermediate goods, added costs related to communications and transportation, the costs of training and work-force development, and the cost implications of such government policies as restrictions on employment of non-native personnel. Costs for the firm can be substantially increased if it must purchase inputs from local suppliers who are either inefficient or corrupt. Tariffs against imported inputs may have been put in place to forward the interests of such producers at the expense of both consumers and foreign investors. The costs of transporting inputs within the foreign country may not be comparable with those at home, and communications may not measure up to those in the home country (in some countries telephone service is unreliable). Nationalistic fervor often leads to the passage of labor laws that discriminate against the employment of foreign technicians and managers and cause firms to employ less-experienced or less-qualified local personnel.

The foregoing are just a few of the issues a firm must investigate before taking as bold a step as investing in foreign production facilities. Thus analysis of foreign production costs requires perhaps even more scrutiny than analysis of foreign demand.

■ ■ Questions and Problems ■ ■

1. How are relative prices related to the basis for international trade?
2. Given the table in the next column:
   a. Explain why the data *do* provide a basis for two-way trade between Greece and Belgium. (Assume labor costs reflect relative prices in each country.)

| | Units of Labor Required to Produce One: | |
	Tablecloth	Barrel of Wine
Greece	10	5
Belgium	4	4

   b. Which good will be exported by Greece? Why?
   c. Assume that the numbers in the table represent domestic prices (in drachmas for Greece and francs for Belgium) instead of labor costs. If one drachma = one franc is the exchange rate, will two-way trade occur? (If *yes*, explain why. If *no*, tell what would have to take place in order for two-way trade to occur.)

■ ■ ■ Selected References ■ ■ ■

Ethier, Wilfred. *Modern International Economics.* New York: Norton, 1983.

Cundiff, Edward W., and Marye Tharp Hilger. *Marketing in the International Environment.* Englewood Cliffs, N.J.: Prentice-Hall, 1984.

Keegan, Warren J. "Multinational Product Planning: Strategic Alternatives," *Journal of Marketing* 33 (January 1969), pp. 58–62.

Linder, Staffan B. *An Essay on Trade and Transformation.* New York: Wiley, 1961.

Vernon, Raymond. "International Investment and International Trade in the Product Cycle," *Quarterly Journal of Economics* 80, no. 2 (May 1966), pp. 190–207.

Profit Analysis of the Firm

Throughout this book we are assuming that the primary concern of the firm is its level of profit. Some firms may have other subsidiary goals, such as a large volume of sales or a good company image. We assume, however, that any such concerns are *definitely secondary* in nature to the concern for generating profits, and we recognize that often the attention paid to such secondary goals merely reflects the impact company officials believe such variables may have on future company profits. Thus assuming that the overriding goal of the firm is **profit maximization**—obtaining the greatest economic profit possible—we shall direct our attention to decision rules for determining the corresponding optimal price and level of output for the individual firm.

Although profit maximization is the primary goal of a firm, we do not mean to suggest that the firm maximize profit with no regard for legal or ethical considerations. The firm that wishes to remain a successful and responsible part of our society in the long run must consider the ethical ramifications of its actions. Henry Ford II once remarked:

> There is no such thing as planning for a minimal return less than the best you can imagine—not if you want to survive in a competitive market. It's like asking a professional football team to win by only one point—a sure fire formula for losing. There's only one way to compete successfully—all out. If believing this makes you a greedy capitalist lusting after bloated profits, then I plead guilty. The worst sin I can commit as a businessman is to fail to seek maximum long-term profitability *by all decent and lawful means* [emphasis added]. To do so is to subvert economic reason.

Maximizing profit is an obligation that corporate managers have to the company's shareholders, but it is also an obligation to society. If the firm is not maximizing profits, scarce resources are typically being wasted. Yet, as Mr. Ford intimated, both the business enterprise and society are benefited in the long run only when the goal of maximum profit is achieved by "decent and lawful means."

Managerial Perspective: The Fall and Resurrection of "The Steel"

It was March, 1986. Walter Williams had just been given the job of chief executive officer of Bethlehem Steel, an honor that less courageous men would have refused. Called "The Steel" by its employees, the company had enjoyed four straight years of losses, was anticipating a fifth, and had only a few month's worth of cash available. Its stock price had fallen to an all-time low value.

Bethlehem was not prepared for the 1982 decrease in steel demand, the worst in 40 years, coupled with an influx of high-quality and low-cost Japanese steel. To make matters worse, Bethlehem was inefficient and the quality of its steel was poor. Campbell Soup, Caterpillar, and Firestone were among the customers that almost abandoned Bethlehem.

Williams's predecessor had cut 39,000 jobs, closed some steel mills, spent several billion dollars rehabilitating others, and implemented stronger accounting controls. Williams sold 16 operations, unrelated to the mills (for example, a plastics company), got wage concessions from the workers, and worked to improve the quality of the steel and the productivity of the mills. In fact, Bethlehem was able to reduce by 50 percent the number of worker hours required to make a ton of steel; some mills' productivity exceeds that of their Japanese counterparts. These efforts were rewarded when Bethlehem had record profits in 1988, with the highest profit per ton of the U.S. mills. (Bethlehem was also helped when the demand for steel increased that year.)

In mid-1989, however, "The Steel" had not completely conquered its problems. Substantial expenditures were still needed to further modernize the mills and meet a huge unfunded pension liability. Rising wage rates were making further productivity increases imperative. Bethlehem's labor costs were 18 percent greater than mills in Japan and five times those in South Korea; meanwhile, the Japanese mills continued their pursuit of increased productivity. Only another recession would properly test the newly achieved profitability of The Steel.

During the first part of 1991, the United States economy was again mired in a recession. In late December of 1990, Bethlehem was the first steel producer to cut a planned 8 percent increase in flat-rolled steel prices to 4 percent. Still, Bethlehem's management believed the firm would be able to weather the storm more easily than it had in the 1980s.

■ ■ ■ ■

References: "Forging the New Bethlehem," *Business Week* (June 5, 1989), pp. 108–110; "Low Demand, Flat-Rolled Profits," *Business Week* (January 14, 1991), p. 76.

To understand the importance of the profit-maximizing guidelines presented in this chapter, we must first recognize the fact that things can go sour—even for a firm that has apparently established itself. For example, why did W. T. Grant Company, the seventeenth-largest retailer in the United States with sales of $1.6 billion and $38 million in profits in 1972, file for bankruptcy in October 1975? Was it the result of calamitous factors external to the firm? *Apparently not.* Significantly, there are indications that during Grant's rapid expansion years from 1969 to 1973, the company exercised little control over accounts receivable, cost of goods sold, and inventories. Moreover, the company apparently did not keep accurate records of how individual items were selling and at what prices and costs.[1]

More recently, Allied Stores Corporation and Federated Department Stores, Incorporated, filed for protection under Chapter 11 of the Bankruptcy Code; at the time, it was the largest bankruptcy filing of retail stores in history. These companies include such venerated retailers as Abraham & Straus, Bloomingdale's, Rich's, Burdines, Lazarus, Jordan Marsh, and Bon Marché.[2] Lack of effective cost management and marketing seems also to have played a significant role in the recent problems of General Motors, John Deere, and Sears, to cite further examples.[3]

If a firm knows little about both the demand for its product or products and its costs, it has, as a result, slight opportunity for effective manage-

■ ■ ■ ■ ■ ■

[1] See "Investigating the Collapse of W. T. Grant," *Business Week* (July 19, 1976), pp. 60–62.

[2] "It'll Be A Hard Sell," *Business Week* (January 29, 1990), pp. 30–31; and "Bankruptcy Petition Brings Fresh Risks for Allied, Federated," *The Wall Street Journal*, January 16, 1990, pp. A1, A6.

[3] See "Two Sides of a Giant," *Time* (February 19, 1990), pp. 68–70; "GM's Bumpy Ride on the Long Road Back," *Business Week* (February 13, 1989), pp. 74–78; "GM Gets Back in High Gear," *Newsweek* (February 20, 1989), p. 39; "Will the Big Markdown Get the Big Store Moving Again?" *Business Week* (March 13, 1989), pp. 110, 114; "Shaking Sears Right Down to Its Work Boots," *Business Week* (October 17, 1988), pp. 84, 87; "Now Sears Has Everyday Low Profits, Too," *Business Week* (August 21, 1989), p. 28; "The Big Store's Big Trauma," *Business Week* (July 10, 1989), pp. 50–55; "As John Deere Sowed, So Shall It Reap," *Business Week* (June 6, 1988), pp. 84–86.

ment and probably little chance for survival, not to mention success. A 1985 article in *The Wall Street Journal* put it bluntly:

> Accountants see it all the time—management by ignorance. An owner doesn't realize his business is in trouble until it is too late. "Many businesses go under," says Aubrey D. Boutwell, a CPA in Pascagoula, Miss., "and owners don't even know what their problems are. All they know is they end up with no money and can't pay their bills."[4]

Effective use of the profit-maximizing decision rules that we will discuss requires that a firm be able to estimate its revenue and cost over the relevant ranges of production. Later in the chapter we shall examine break-even analysis, a modification of the more traditional economics of profit maximization.

■ ■ ■ ■ ■ ■ ■ ■ ■ **PROFIT MAXIMIZATION**

The decision rule for profit maximization can be explained by using either total or marginal curves, and we shall do both in this chapter. In the simplest terms, total profit is equal to total revenue minus total cost. In Chapter 2 total revenue was defined as the total sales of a firm, equal to the price multiplied by the quantity sold of each product. Chapter 5 explained that the total cost of a firm includes both explicit and implicit, or opportunity, costs. Thus we can define **total profit** as the "pure" or "economic" profit remaining after all explicit and implicit costs—including a normal or average return for the funds invested in this business—have been subtracted from total revenue.

Total profit or economic profit for a firm is equal to total revenue minus total cost, where total cost includes all opportunity costs associated with the firm's activities.

In Figure 6–1 we have drawn a total revenue curve, a total cost curve, and a total profit curve. Since we are assuming that the goal of the firm is to maximize profit, we wish to establish a decision rule that will enable the firm to find that output level and price which will make total profit (that is, total sales revenue less total cost) the greatest amount possible. In Figure 6–1 the profit-maximizing output is Q_3.

Notice that at Q_3, the slopes of the total revenue and total cost curves are equal, and the slope of the total profit curve is zero. In Chapter 2 we pointed out that the slope of the total revenue curve at a particular output level is marginal revenue at that level of output; and, correspondingly, we stated in Chapter 5 that the slope of the total cost curve is marginal cost. In the same manner, the slope of the total profit curve is **marginal profit**, or the rate of change in the total profit of the firm with respect to output.[5] Marginal profit can be approximated by $\Delta T\pi/\Delta Q$, or the change in total profit divided by the change in quantity produced between two levels of output. This latter value we call *arc marginal profit*, as it gives the average

Marginal profit is the rate of change of total profit with respect to changes in the level of output.

■ ■ ■ ■ ■ ■

[4] "Watch the Numbers to Learn if the Business Is Doing Well," *The Wall Street Journal*, August 26, 1985, p. 17.

[5] Mathematically speaking, marginal profit is the derivative of the total profit function with respect to quantity, $dT\pi/dQ$.

Figure 6–1   Total Revenue, Total Cost, and Total Profit

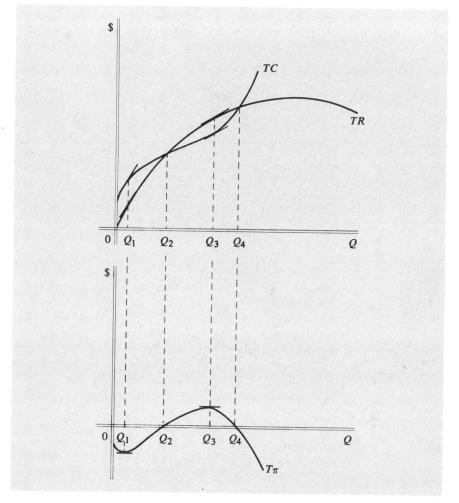

Total profit ($T\pi$) will be maximized at the level of output where total revenue (TR) minus total cost (TC) is at its greatest positive level. At this point, the slope of the TR curve (marginal revenue) will equal the slope of the TC curve (marginal cost).

rate of change of total profit with respect to output *between two levels of output*. Marginal profit can also be found by subtracting marginal cost from marginal revenue. Therefore, at Q_3 in Figure 6–1, marginal revenue equals marginal cost, marginal profit is zero, and total profit is at a maximum. In Figure 6–2 we have sketched the marginal revenue, marginal cost, and marginal profit curves corresponding to the total revenue, total cost, and total profit curves in Figure 6–1.

It is not a coincidence that marginal revenue and marginal cost are equal where profit is maximized. We have already stated that $MR = MC$

Figure 6–2   Marginal Revenue, Marginal Cost, and Marginal Profit

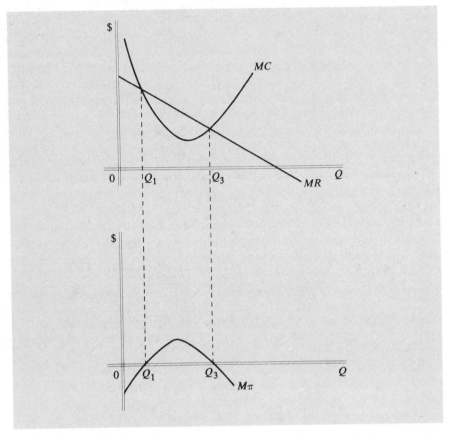

Total profit is maximized at Q_3, where marginal profit ($M\pi$) is equal to zero, and MC is greater than MR at higher levels of output. At Q_1, $M\pi$ is equal to zero, but MC is less than MR at higher levels of output. In this case the firm will increase profit by expanding output.

means $MR - MC$ [or marginal profit ($M\pi$)] is zero at that level of output. Recall that marginal revenue is the additional revenue from selling another unit of output. Marginal cost is the cost of producing another unit of output. As long as the additional revenue from producing another unit is greater than the cost of the unit (that is, if marginal profit is positive), the firm will find it profitable to expand its output.

For example, if the marginal revenue from producing another television set is $200, and the set's marginal cost is $100, the firm will add $100 to profit by producing the TV. Even if the marginal revenue of a television set were $175 and the set's marginal cost were $174, the firm would still add $1 to profit by producing the TV. On the other hand, if the marginal revenue from producing another TV is $160 and the TV's marginal cost is

$180, the firm's profit will decrease by $20 if it produces another TV. Only when the additional revenue from producing another unit of output is equal to its cost will profit be maximized.

If marginal profit is zero at a particular level of output (like Q_3 in Figure 6–2), that fact *may* be an indication to the firm that at larger output levels, *marginal profit* will be *negative* and total profit will consequently decline. However, we can also observe that $MR = MC$ and $M\pi = 0$ at Q_1 in Figure 6–2. At this point, total profit reaches a relative *minimum* and will increase if the level of output is increased. Thus the decision rule that the firm should follow to maximize total profit is that it should produce at the level of output where $MR = MC$ ($M\pi = 0$) and MR is below MC at higher output levels.[6] The firm can find its corresponding profit-maximizing price by substituting in that level of output for quantity demanded in its demand function or by dividing the corresponding total revenue by that quantity.

In Figure 6–3 we demonstrate both the relationships among average revenue, average cost, and average profit and the relationships among marginal revenue, marginal cost, and marginal profit. *Marginal profit* is maximized at Q_1, where the difference between MR and MC is the greatest positive amount. **Average profit** is maximized at Q_2, where the difference between AR (price) and AC is the greatest positive amount. However, *total profit* for the firm is maximized at a level of output (Q_3) that is *greater than* either Q_1 or Q_2. In other words, total profit is usually maximized not where average or unit profit is maximized, but rather at a higher level of output. We can find total profit at Q_3 by multiplying $A\pi_3$ by Q_3. Total profit is also equal to ($P_3 - AC_3$) multiplied by Q_3, since P_3 (or AR_3) minus AC_3 must equal $A\pi_3$. Total profit is, therefore, identical in value to the area of

Average profit is the profit per unit sold. It is equal to total profit divided by quantity of output. It is also equal to price minus average cost.

■ ■ ■ ■ ■ ■

[6] The condition that MR be below MC at higher levels of output is merely a statement in economic terms of the mathematical second order condition for a maximum, given in the Mathematical Appendix to this book. The first order condition for maximum total profit is that the first derivative of the total profit function be equal to zero. If

$$T\pi = TR - TC,$$

then the first order condition is that

$$\frac{dT\pi}{dQ} = \frac{dTR}{dQ} - \frac{dTC}{dQ} = MR - MC = 0,$$

or

$$MR = MC.$$

The second order condition is that

$$\frac{d^2T\pi}{dQ^2} = \frac{dMR}{dQ} - \frac{dMC}{dQ} < 0,$$

which requires that marginal revenue be less than marginal cost at higher levels of output.

Figure 6–3 Relationships Among Marginal Revenue, Marginal Cost, and Marginal Profit and Average Revenue, Average Cost, and Average Profit

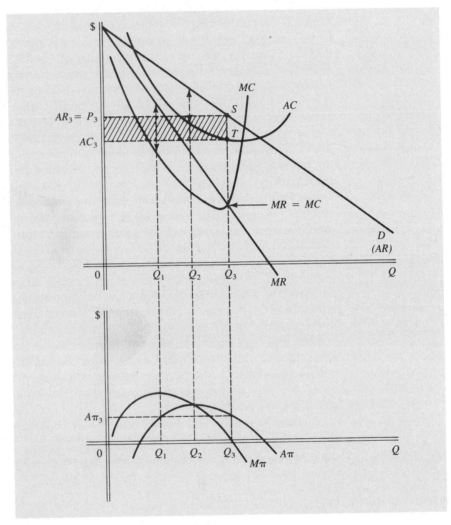

Marginal profit ($M\pi$) is maximized where $MR - MC$ is at its greatest positive level, at Q_1. Average profit ($A\pi$) is maximized at Q_2, where $AR - AC$ is greatest. However, total profit is maximized at Q_3, where $MR = MC$, $M\pi = 0$, and $MR < MC$ at higher levels of output.

rectangle P_3STAC_3; and, given the curves drawn in Figure 6–3, this area will be greatest at Q_3. An understanding of these relationships will be quite helpful in Part 3 of this text.

In Table 6–1 we can see once again how our $MR = MC$ decision rule can be utilized by the firm to maximize profit. Between 5 and 10 units of

Table 6–1   Revenue, Cost, and Profit Maximization

Q	P	TR	TC	Tπ	Arc MR	Arc MC	Arc Mπ
0	200	0	200	−200			
5	190	950	1,200	−250	190	200	−10
10	180	1,800	2,050	−250	170	170	0
15	160	2,400	2,450	−50	120	80	40
20	140	2,800	2,700	100	80	50	30
25	120	3,000	2,850	150	40	30	10
30	105	3,150	2,950	200	30	20	10
35	93	3,255	3,055	200	21	21	0
40	80	3,200	3,180	20	−11	25	−36

output, marginal profit is zero; but marginal cost is falling below marginal revenue, so marginal profit is positive at higher levels of output. Profit is maximized between 30 and 35 units of output, where marginal revenue and marginal cost are again equal and marginal profit is zero. Beyond 35 units of output, marginal revenue falls below marginal cost, and marginal profit becomes negative. Thus, to summarize what we have been saying, the firm should expand its output up to the point where the production of additional units would *add more to the firm's costs than to its revenues.*[7]

■ ■ ■ ■ ■ ■

[7] Using calculus, a firm manager can find the precise level of output that would maximize total profit if the firm's total revenue and total cost functions are known. For example, suppose the firm's total revenue function is

$$TR = 100Q - 2Q^2$$

and the total cost function is

$$TC = 30 + 120Q - 5Q^2 + (1/12)Q^3.$$

The total profit function would then be given by total revenue minus total cost or

$$T\pi = -(1/12)Q^3 + 3Q^2 - 20Q - 30.$$

To find the level of output that would maximize total profit, we find the marginal profit function, set it equal to zero, and solve for the quantity of output. Therefore

$$M\pi = \frac{dT\pi}{dQ} = -(1/4)Q^2 + 6Q - 20 = 0.$$

To solve this equation, we first multiply both sides by −4 and then factor:

$$Q^2 - 24Q + 80 = 0$$

and

$$(Q - 20)(Q - 4) = 0.$$

Thus, at $Q = 20$ and at $Q = 4$, marginal profit is zero.

(continued)

Numerical Example: Algebra of Profit Maximization

A firm has the following total and marginal cost functions, where Q is output per week:

$$STC = 500 + 20Q + .05Q^2$$
$$SMC = 20 + .1Q$$

What will be its profit-maximizing output, assuming it faces a fixed market price of $40 for its product? How much will the maximum profit be?

Answer. To find the profit-maximizing quantity, set marginal profit or $(MR - MC)$ equal to zero.

$$40 - 20 - .1Q = 0$$

Thus

$$20 = .1Q,$$

and

$$Q = 200.$$

Profit equals

$$TR - STC = \$40(200) - 500 - 20(200) - .05(40,000)$$
$$= 8,000 - 500 - 4,000 - 2,000$$
$$= \$1,500$$

We can tell that a profit *maximum* occurs at $Q = 200$ since at higher levels of output MR is less than MC.

At this point, we should take note of one more qualification to our profit maximization decision rule. The firm maximizes profits by producing where $MR = MC$ (with marginal revenue thereafter *below* marginal cost)

■ ■ ■ ■ ■ ■
[7] (concluded)   Nevertheless, we must still check the second order condition for a maximum to see if profit is maximized at either $Q = 4$ or $Q = 20$. The second derivative of $T\pi$ is

$$\frac{dM\pi}{dQ},$$

and

$$\frac{d^2T\pi}{dQ^2} = \frac{dM\pi}{dQ} = -.5Q + 6.$$

At $Q = 4$ the second derivative is positive, so $T\pi$ is minimized at that level of output. At $Q = 20$ the second derivative is negative, so profit is maximized at that level of output.

as long as price is greater than or equal to average variable cost. If price is less than average variable cost, the firm should not produce at all—even in the short run.

For example, suppose a restaurant has fixed costs of $4,000 per month and has an average price of $4.00 and an average variable cost of $4.50 for each meal served. If the restaurant operates for a month selling 10,000 meals, its total sales revenue will be $40,000 and its total variable cost will be $45,000. In this case the firm's revenues will not cover $5,000 of its variable costs or *any* of the $4,000 fixed costs, so the firm will be losing $9,000 per month (see Table 6–2). If the firm did not produce at all, the most it could lose would be the $4,000 per month fixed cost. Therefore the firm will minimize its loss by temporarily shutting down. Firms frequently make this choice during recessionary periods, when demand falls but is expected to increase in the future. Of course, a firm would go out of business permanently if it were not able to increase revenue or reduce costs enough so that it could eventually make a normal return or a profit.

On the other hand, if the average price of a meal were $4.60, the average variable cost were $4.40, and the firm were to sell 9,000 meals, then the firm's total revenue would be $41,400, its total variable costs would be $39,600, and its total loss would be $2,200 (see Table 6–3). This

Table 6–2   Total Loss for a Restaurant When Price Is Less Than Average Variable Cost

Total Sales (10,000 meals @ $4.00 each)	$40,000
Less:	
Total Variable Cost	
(10,000 meals @ $4.50 each)	45,000
	($ 5,000)
Less:	
Total Fixed Cost	4,000
Net Income (loss)	($ 9,000)

Table 6–3   Total Loss for a Restaurant When Price Is Greater Than Average Variable Cost But Less Than Average Total Cost

Total Sales (9,000 meals @ $4.60 each)	$41,400
Less:	
Total Variable Cost	
(9,000 meals @ $4.40 each)	39,600
	$ 1,800
Less:	
Total Fixed Cost	4,000
Net Income (loss)	($ 2,200)

last example illustrates the principle that in the short run, it is in the firm's best interests to continue to operate as long as it can cover its variable costs and make something toward covering its fixed costs. In the long run, of course, the firm presumably would require that all of its economic costs be covered if it is to stay in business. An exception to this principle would be owner-managed enterprises where an opportunity-cost loss of the owner's time and/or money is accepted in return for the pleasure of owning the business and "being your own boss." However, this type of owner violates our profit maximization assumption; therefore we shall disregard this possibility throughout the remainder of the book. The **profit-maximizing rule** (or **loss-minimizing rule**) is that a firm produce up to the point where marginal profit is zero, as long as price is at least as great as average variable cost in the short run or as great as long-run average cost in the long run. This point will be where marginal revenue is equal to marginal cost.

The **profit-maximizing rule** is to produce up to the point where marginal revenue is equal to marginal cost and at higher output levels marginal revenue is less than marginal cost, as long as price is greater than or equal to average variable cost in the short run or long-run average cost in the long run.

Managerial Perspective: Road to Riches or Ruin?

"Don't worry, honey. In three years, we will need people to help us carry the money."

It was 1981, and Julian Carnes, Jr., had signed a technical licensing agreement with Concrete Coring Company, a developer of tools to drill and cut concrete. By June, 1989, Mr. Carnes, a professional engineer and military officer, was preparing to dissolve his firm. He had invested $50,000 of his own savings, borrowed from the Small Business Administration, borrowed from his parents, borrowed against his life insurance, used money set aside for his son's college education, and mortgaged his home. Both he and the business had filed for protection from creditors under Chapter 11 of the Federal Bankruptcy Code.

What went wrong? Nothing so simple as no demand for the product. The sales of Carnes Enterprises rose steadily from its founding in 1981 until 1986, when a New Zealand firm agreed to take over the company's operations and many of its obligations. Consider, however, that Mr. Carnes started up in the fall, certainly not the peak season for construction. Moreover, he started the business with unnecessarily expensive equipment, and enough of it—plus enough employees—to meet a demand that didn't develop until the third year of operations. Since he had invested heavily in training three of the workers, Carnes faced the dilemma of laying them off and losing his investment in their training or keeping them and continuing to pay their high wages. Since the firm was undercapitalized for such high fixed costs and low sales in the early months, Carnes Enterprises quickly ran into a cash flow problem, which required the borrowing of additional funds and higher interest costs. It also made the mistake of "borrowing" from employee withholding, only to incur penalties and additional interest charges when it could not pay the Internal Revenue Service on time. To add to the company's trouble, one contractor that had awarded Carnes a large subcontract canceled the job when the work was half completed. Carnes sued the contractor for reimbursement, but the contractor filed for protection under Chapter 11 of the Bankruptcy Code.

As a result of the cash flow problems, Carnes could not maintain his equipment properly and was not able to keep crucial spare parts on hand in case of a breakdown. Therefore, jobs took twice as long as they should have, greatly increasing the firm's costs. Customers began to think that maybe the firm would not be around too long and put off paying their bills as long as they possibly could. Average collection time on receivables rose dramatically. The upshot of all of these problems was that the firm realized a profit in only one year, 1983.

Julian Carnes, Jr., was able to find a new job quickly after the New Zealand company took over operations. However, he must still contend with paying off the mortgage on his house and meeting certain other obligations for which he is personally liable as a result of the firm. Although Mr. Carnes would do things differently if he were to begin a new business, he has not lost his enthusiasm for being an entrepreneur: "I'd go back to owning a business in a minute," he admits.

■ ■ ■ ■

Reference: "Success Comes Too Late for a Small Firm," *The Wall Street Journal*, June 12, 1989, p. B1.

■ ■ ■ ■ ■ ■ ■ ■ BREAK-EVEN ANALYSIS

Break-even analysis is in some respects a simplification of profit-maximization analysis. In a typical break-even problem, a constant price, a constant average variable cost, and a specific level of fixed costs are assumed; and the resulting level of output (or sales) necessary for the firm to cover its total costs (to break even) or to cover its total costs and achieve a target level of income is then obtained. With these assumptions we can derive the formula for break-even output quite easily. To break even, a firm's revenue must equal its costs, or

(6–1)
$$TR = TC = TVC + TFC.$$

Numerical Example: Profit Maximization, Tabular Data

Complete the following table and find the profit-maximizing output, assuming total fixed cost is $400.

Arc MR	Q	P	TR	TVC	Arc MC
	0	100	0	0	
95					60
	10	95	950	600	
	20	90	1,800	1,000	
75					60
	30	85	2,550		70
65	40	80	3,200		
	50	75	3,750	3,150	

Answer. The missing *MR* values are 85 and 55, each obtained by calculating $\Delta TR/\Delta Q$. The missing *MC* values are 40 and 85, each obtained by calculating $\Delta TVC/\Delta Q$. Finally, the missing *TVC* values are 1,600 and 2,300, each obtained by multiplying the relevant *MC* by ΔQ and adding on the ΔTVC to the preceding *TVC* value.

Profit is maximized where, for an increase in Q, MC > MR. This occurs at Q = 30, since increasing Q to 40 would result in MC = 70, but MR = 65. Profit is TR − TC = 2,550 − 1,600 − 400 = 550.

We can write total revenue as price times quantity ($P \times Q$) and total variable cost as average variable cost times quantity ($AVC \times Q$), so that equation 6–1 becomes

(6–2)
$$P(Q) = AVC(Q) + TFC.$$

If we subtract $AVC \times Q$ from both sides of equation 6–2, we obtain

(6–3)
$$P(Q) - (AVC)(Q) = (P - AVC)(Q) = TFC.$$

Dividing both sides of equation 6–3 by $(P - AVC)$, we get the formula for break-even point quantity, which is

(6–4)
$$Q_{BEP} = \frac{TFC}{P - AVC}.$$

The term $(P - AVC)$ is called the *unit contribution margin*, since it indicates the contribution that each unit sold will make toward covering fixed cost and, eventually, generating profit.

To see how break-even analysis is used, assume that the Magic S (for "magic sandwich") is a fast-food restaurant that specializes in submarine sandwiches. The Magic S has fixed costs per month of $40,000. Most of the revenue for this firm is derived from its featured meal: a hot submarine sandwich, small drink, and french fries for $4.00. The average variable cost of the meal is approximately constant at $2.40 over the relevant range of production. To find out how many of the specials the Magic S must sell per month to break even, we substitute these figures into equation 6–4 and obtain

$$Q_{BEP} = \frac{\$40,000}{\$4.00 - \$2.40} = 25,000 \text{ specials.}$$

Moreover, we could find out how many specials the Magic S would have to sell to make a target income of, say, $24,000 per month by substituting fixed costs plus $24,000 in place of merely fixed costs and obtain

$$Q = \frac{\$64,000}{\$1.60} = 40,000 \text{ specials.}$$

The assumptions of a constant price and constant unit variable cost enable us to graph the total revenue and total variable cost curves for the Magic S as straight lines, and we obtain a graphical solution for the break-even quantity for the Magic S, as shown in Figure 6–4. The break-even point is, of course, where the total revenue curve cuts and rises above the total cost curve. We can translate break-even quantity to break-even dollar sales merely by multiplying break-even point quantity by price. For the Magic S, break-even point dollar sales are $25,000 \times \$4.00 = \$100,000$.

Moreover, if we multiply both sides of our break-even point quantity formula (equation 6–4) by price, we can derive the break-even dollar sales formula, which is

$$P(Q_{BEP}) = \frac{P(TFC)}{(P - AVC)} = \frac{TFC}{[1 - (AVC/P)]} = \frac{TFC}{\text{contribution margin ratio}}$$

Note that $[1 - (AVC/P)]$ is called the *contribution margin ratio*, since this term is the ratio of the unit contribution margin to price. The contribution margin ratio indicates the fraction of the price of each unit sold that contributes to covering fixed cost and, eventually, generating a profit. Break-even dollar sales could thus be found graphically by using dollar sales, rather than units sold, along the horizontal axis.

Firms often use break-even analysis to determine expected profits under several different, but presumably feasible, alternatives being considered—with various prices, for instance, or different unit variable costs, different fixed costs, or some combination of those possibilities. For ex-

Figure 6–4   Break-Even Quantity for the Magic S

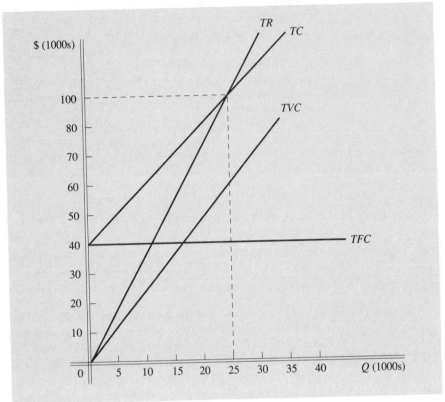

Total cost (TC) is equal to TVC + TFC. The break-even level of output occurs where total revenue (TR) = TC, at an output level of 25,000 specials per month.

ample, suppose an electric motor manufacturing company has current plant capacity of 1 million motors per year. Unit variable costs associated with this plant are $10, and fixed costs are $1 million. The current capacity number of motors can be sold for $20 each. The firm is considering expanding and modernizing its plant facilities so that the current capacity will be doubled. Under this proposal, unit variable costs would be expected to decrease to $5, and fixed costs would be expected to increase to $2 million. The firm estimates that it could sell 1.5 million motors at a price of $15.

Two things in which the motor company would be vitally interested are the quantities required to break even for both the present plant and the proposed plant and the expected profits from each plant. Break-even points for the two plants are found as follows:

$$\text{Present plant: } Q_{BEP} = \frac{1,000,000}{10} = 100,000 \text{ motors;}$$

$$\text{Proposed plant: } Q_{BEP} = \frac{2,000,000}{10} = 200,000 \text{ motors.}$$

The expected profits from each plant would be the following:

Present Plant

Quantity Sold:	1,000,000	
Price: $20		
Total Revenue:		$20,000,000
Less:		
Total Variable Costs:		10,000,000
		$10,000,000
Less Fixed Costs		1,000,000
Net Income Before Taxes		9,000,000

Proposed Plant

Expected Quantity Sold:	1,500,000	
Price: $15		
Total Revenue:		$22,500,000
Less:		
Total Variable Costs:		7,500,000
		$15,000,000
Less Fixed Costs		2,000,000
Expected Net Income Before Taxes		$13,000,000

Thus our data indicate that expected profits would be greater with the larger plant. Nevertheless, before it makes a final decision on so significant a matter, the firm might want to consider expected profits with an intermediate-sized plant. It might also want to consider expected profits from using different prices with each sized plant. Further, the risk associated with each plant should be taken into account (see Chapter 14).

A person considering starting a new enterprise could also find break-even analysis a useful tool in obtaining a rough estimate as to whether or not the business could reasonably be expected to be successful under any of several proposed plans.[8] For example, suppose that our Magic S sandwich place has not yet been built and that the prospective owners believe that they cannot expect to sell 25,000 submarine specials per month. The prospective owners could, among other things, consider the feasibility of lowering fixed costs by building a smaller establishment or of increasing demand by offering a greater variety of sandwiches. They could also consider increasing quantity demanded by lowering price.

■ ■ ■ ■ ■ ■
[8] For example, see "Tigers, A Volcano, Dolphins, and Steve Wynn," *Business Week* (November 20, 1989), pp. 70–71; and "Vacancy Signs Are Lit, But More New Hotels Are on the Way," *Business Week* (March 17, 1986), pp. 78–79.

■ ■ ■ ■ ■ ■ ■ ■ **PROFIT MAXIMIZATION VERSUS BREAK-EVEN ANALYSIS**

Break-even analysis in its most sophisticated usage is a simplified approximation to profit maximization. In traditional profit maximization analysis, the firm presumably knows its revenue and cost functions and chooses to produce at the level of output and charge the price that will maximize profits (where marginal revenue equals marginal cost). Price and average variable cost are *not* required to be constant.

On the other hand, when it uses break-even analysis, a firm *usually assumes* a constant price and a constant average variable cost in the relevant range of production and recognizes explicitly or implicitly a capacity limitation. The firm then solves for the quantity of sales necessary to break even or to achieve some target level of income.[9]

The firm may use break-even-type analysis to reach a fairly close approximation to profit maximization by considering expected profits under a variety of alternatives. Such alternatives would include various prices, different-sized plants, and different levels of advertising expenditures. However, if the firm has enough information regarding the preceding variables to approximate the results achieved using profit maximization analysis, it would most likely be easier for the firm to construct total revenue and total cost functions corresponding to its best information and to produce where marginal revenue equals marginal cost (and marginal revenue is falling below marginal cost).

Break-even analysis offers some advantage over traditional profit maximization analysis when the information available to the firm regarding its future costs and revenues is seriously limited and a rough approximation to profit maximization is the best that the firm owner may reasonably expect to accomplish. If more detailed information is available, then profit maximization is more efficient.

■ ■ ■ ■ ■ ■ ■ ■ **INCREMENTAL PROFIT ANALYSIS**

Incremental profit is equal to incremental revenue less incremental cost resulting from a specific change in the activity of a firm.

Incremental profit analysis is simply a variation of traditional profit maximization and represents a quite useful way of thinking about a current or prospective sales order, change in equipment, or other activity of the firm. All that is required for incremental profit analysis is that the firm ask itself whether the sales order, equipment change, or other activity contributes (or will contribute) more to total revenue than to total cost—that is, whether its contribution to the total profit of the firm will be

■ ■ ■ ■ ■ ■

[9] It is possible to use nonlinear total revenue and cost functions (price and average variable cost are not constant) in break-even analysis. However, this approach is not used frequently.

positive. When the firm considers whether or not the incremental profit is positive, it should ignore all revenue that will be obtained and all costs that will be incurred by the firm regardless of the decision it makes on the matter under consideration. In other words, it merely considers the **incremental revenue** and *incremental cost* pertaining to the activity being considered.

Incremental revenue is the additional revenue that a firm will receive by undertaking a particular project.

When examining the incremental costs associated with a particular undertaking, a firm usually must distinguish between direct and indirect costs. *Direct costs* associated with a particular product or activity are costs that can be obviously and physically identified with that product or activity. *Indirect costs*, while they may be associated with a product or activity, generally must be allocated on some basis, since the precise amount required for (or associated with) each line of endeavor is less clear. For example, the cost of materials or intermediate products that physically make up a final product is a direct cost. The cost of the labor required to process and/or assemble these materials is also a direct cost. On the other hand, the cost of warehouse storage space that is shared by several products is an indirect cost. Direct costs associated with an activity will be incremental costs, while indirect costs frequently will not.

The use of incremental profit analysis can be illustrated with the example of a retail firm that sells three brands of appliances—Brand *X*, Brand *Y*, and Brand *Z*. Table 6-4 shows total revenue, total direct costs, and total indirect costs attributed to each product line. In this case, indirect costs are assigned to each product line according to the proportion that total revenue from each line's sale is of the total revenue of the firm.

After a quick glance at Table 6–4, it appears that Brand *Z* is subtracting from the total profits of the firm by the amount of the net loss attributed to it ($5,000). However, a more in-depth analysis is required before that conclusion is justified. This analysis should include answers to such questions as how much, if any, will indirect costs be lowered if the firm no longer carries Brand *Z*? Is there another, more profitable, brand of merchandise that the firm could carry rather than Brand *Z*? For example, if the indirect costs will be unchanged if the firm no longer carries Brand *Z* (or a third product line) and if the firm has no more profitable brands that it can sell in place of Brand *Z*, then total profits of the firm would actually be *reduced* by $15,000 if the firm were to drop Brand *Z*! Let's see why this

Table 6–4   Revenue and Costs for an Appliance Store

	Brand X	Brand Y	Brand Z
Total Revenue	$150,000	$100,000	$50,000
Total Direct Costs	60,000	50,000	35,000
Total Indirect Costs	60,000	40,000	20,000
Net Income (loss)	$ 30,000	$ 10,000	$(5,000)

is so. If the $20,000 of indirect costs assigned to Brand Z would be incurred even if the firm did not carry a third brand of appliance, then the sale of Brand Z *does contribute* $15,000 toward covering those costs.

Nevertheless, the firm should be careful to consider its alternatives in both the long run and the short run. In the long run, it may be possible for the firm to eliminate the $20,000 of indirect costs if the firm does not sell a third brand of appliance. It may also be possible to become a dealer in a more profitable third brand. Moreover, dropping Brand Z may increase the revenue from sales of Brand X and Brand Y. Thus the firm must consider how its decision about Brand Z will affect both long-run and short-run revenue and cost. Still, all of these deliberations are merely utilizing a version of the profit maximization rule, which states that the firm should continue to produce as long as marginal revenue is greater than marginal cost and should not produce when marginal revenue is less than marginal cost.

Continental Airlines made explicit use of incremental profit analysis in adjusting certain parts of its fare structure in 1982.[10] There is also evidence that restaurants use incremental profit analysis when determining their price structure."[11]

■ ■ ■ ■ ■ ■ ■ ■ ■ **SUMMARY**

Profit Maximization and the "Real" World

We have assumed that the goal of the firm is to maximize its profits. Accordingly, in this chapter we have developed a decision criterion that, when followed, will ensure profit maximization. That criterion is to *produce up to the point where marginal revenue equals marginal cost, subject to the conditions that marginal revenue is less than marginal cost at higher levels of output and that price is at least as great as average variable cost.* If price is less than average variable cost, the firm should at least temporarily shut down.

In reality a firm manager does not always have precise information regarding the firm's costs and revenue and obtaining such information may be costly. In this situation a firm manager often uses break-even analysis to determine what level of output is necessary for the firm to break even or to achieve a target level of income. When using this type of analysis, the firm manager assumes that price and average variable cost are constant, a simplification that is *not* necessary with traditional profit

■ ■ ■ ■ ■ ■
[10] "Most Big Airlines Cut Intercontinental Fares," *San Antonio Express*, February 10, 1982, p.1B.
[11] See "With Liquor Sales Slipping, Restaurants Try Fancier Desserts and Higher Prices," *The Wall Street Journal*, June 14, 1985, p. 23.

Managerial Perspective: Earnings versus Cash Flow

"Earnings, Schmernings—Look at the Cash" read the headline in a recent *Business Week* article. The point of the article was that a single-minded emphasis on a firm's net income was shortsighted. The cash flow of a firm is its net cash receipts over the period in question. The cash flow of a firm will be affected by the net income of a firm, but the two figures are typically not equal to one another.

Accounting net income reflects total sales less total accounting costs. However, the cash flow to the firm may be something entirely different for the period. For one thing, most firms allow some customers to purchase their goods on credit. As a result, the total dollar sales of the firm for a particular period, say a month, and the cash collected by the firm from those sales may differ by a substantial amount. The credit sales may be reflected merely by an increase in accounts receivable. On the other hand, the firm may have some cash receipts from collections of accounts receivable from sales in prior months. In turn, the firm may purchase some inputs on credit; thus the variable input costs for the period may not always be reflected immediately in cash outflows. On the other hand, the firm may have to pay the entire purchase price for a new machine at the time it is acquired, and a cash outflow equal to the entire cost of the machine will be incurred immediately. The entire amount paid for the machine will not be reflected as a cost in the firm's income statement for the period, however; it will be written off as depreciation over a period of time that reflects the expected life of the machine. Thus, in those later periods, depreciation will be a cost item that does not represent a cash outflow. On the other hand, debt payments (not including interest payments) represent outflows of cash that are not costs, although they may very well be related to costs incurred in the past.

Three categories of net cash flows can be distinguished for the firm. The broadest classification is operating cash flow (OCF)—the net cash flow from the ordinary operations of the firm, but before repayments of debt and interest are made. The second concept of cash flow is the one that is commonly referred to when the term "cash flow" is used. It includes net income adjusted for such things as changes in accounts receivable and accounts payable, plus accounting charges to net income (e.g., depreciation, depletion, or amortization expenses) that do not require the current use of cash. The third category of cash flow is perhaps most important for the firm's viability: the *free* cash flow, or what remains after essential capital expenditures have been made and dividends have been paid.

A firm with free cash flow can decide to pay additional dividends, pay off debt, or buy back shares, among other things. Because a firm with free cash flow can develop a cushion of cash assets as a reserve against a temporary decline in sales, it is less vulnerable to the movements of the business cycle. Firms that have no free cash flow may not be able to make principal and interest payments on their debt during periods of temporary declines in sales; thus they may find their very existence in jeopardy.

Net income may not always reflect accurately the growth in assets of a firm. For example, amortization is a write-down of intangible assets such as goodwill. (Goodwill is the difference between what a company paid for an asset and its book value.) Accounting rules require that goodwill be written off over a period of years, whether or not the asset's market value is declining. Furthermore, tangible assets that are being depreciated may actually be increasing in value.

The *Business Week* article concludes with this comment:

> The case for cash flow doesn't mean that profits are passé. For most investors, net income will remain the handiest snapshot of a company. Even so, following the cash as it flows through a company . . . "gives you insight into the quality of earnings." Indeed, if profits are soaring, but the cash flow isn't, a company's good fortunes may prove to be short-lived.

■ ■ ■ ■

Reference: "Earnings, Schmernings—Look at the Cash," *Business Week* (July 24, 1989), pp. 56, 57.

maximization techniques. In these circumstances the formula for break-even output is

$$Q_{BEP} = \frac{TFC}{P - AVC}.$$

The manager may use break-even analysis to determine approximately the profit-maximizing price and level of output by considering expected profits under a variety of alternatives (such as various prices, different plant sizes, and different levels of advertising expenditures).

However, break-even analysis offers some advantages over traditional profit maximization analysis only when the information available to the firm manager regarding the firm's costs and revenues is quite limited and a rough approximation to profit maximization is the best that can be expected. Still, the firm manager may find that the firm falls far short of profit maximization unless some reliable estimates of its revenue and costs relative to the level of output can be obtained. The wise firm manager, therefore, must attempt to gain such information about its costs and the demand for its product up to the point where the expected cost of obtaining additional information is greater than the expected benefits of such information. Some techniques of demand estimation were discussed in Chapter 3. Cost estimation techniques were briefly summarized in Chapter 5.

Finally, we discussed incremental profit analysis—a variation of traditional profit maximization analysis that is useful to the firm manager when he or she is analyzing such problems as accepting an additional sales order, trading in a piece of equipment, adding or dropping a product line, or similar alternatives. We stated that the profit-oriented manager should accept an alternative as long as its *incremental revenue less incremental cost (its marginal profit)* is greater than zero.

In the next chapter, we shall discuss linear programming—a profit maximization technique the firm can use when its revenue and cost functions and any other constraining functions are linear.

■ ■ ■ ■ ■ ■ ■ ■ ■ ■ ■ ■ ■ ■ **Questions** ■ ■ ■ ■ ■ ■ ■ ■ ■ ■ ■ ■ ■

1. What do we mean when we say that the goal of a firm is profit maximization?
2. Is the assumption of profit maximization a realistic goal? Why or why not?
3. Compare break-even analysis and (the more traditional) profit maximization. How are they alike? How are they different?
4. What is incremental profit analysis? Give several examples of situations in which it would be useful.

■ ■ ■ ■ ■ ■ ■ ■ ■ ■ ■ ■ ■ ■ **Problems** ■ ■ ■ ■ ■ ■ ■ ■ ■ ■ ■ ■ ■

1. Complete the following cost and revenue table and indicate the profit-maximizing output and price.

Q	Arc MR	TR	P	Arc MC	AFC	AVC	SAC	TC
0			21		—	—	—	
	20			25				
1					28			
	18			15				
2								
	16			11				
3								
	14			5				
4								
	12			4				
5								
	8			6				
6								
	6			11				
7								
	4			19				
8								

2. Penny Car Rental has fixed costs per month of $300,000 and variable costs per car rented per day of $6. If Penny charges $30 per day to rent a car, how many car-rental days (the number of cars rented times the number of days each is rented) must Penny have each month to break even? To make $60,000 before taxes?

3. Complete the following cost and revenue data and find the profit-maximizing price and output.

Q	P	TR	Arc MR	Arc MC	TFC	AVC	Arc Mπ
0	$5.00	0				—	
			$4.90	$3.00			$1.90
10		49					
				1.00			
20		96			60		
				1.00			
30		135					
				.50			
40		160					
				1.00			
50		175					
				1.50			
60		180					
				2.00			
70		175					
				3.00			
80		144					
				4.50			
90		90					
				7.00			
100		10					

4. A firm making sofas has the following income data for one week:

Sales (50 sofas at $1,000)		$50,000
Less cost of goods sold:		
Variable manufacturing costs	$20,000	
Fixed manufacturing costs	5,000	25,000
Gross margin		$25,000
Less selling and administrative expenses:		
Variable	$10,000	
Fixed	5,000	15,000
Net income		$10,000

a. Find the firm's break-even quantity.

b. Find the firm's new break-even output if it builds a new plant that will raise fixed manufacturing costs to $10,000 but decreases variable manufacturing cost to $300 per unit. Assume average variable selling expenses, fixed selling expenses, and selling price remain the same.

5. In the following table, complete the cost and revenue data for a particular model of side-by-side refrigerator-freezer sold in a department store. What is the profit-maximizing price and output?

P	Q	TR	Arc MR	Arc MC	AFC	TVC	TC	Arc Mπ
900	0				—			
				500				
875	10							
				400				
850	20							
				350				
800	30							
				300				
750	40				150			
				250				
675	50							
				200				
600	60							
				180				
500	70							
				200				
400	80							
				300				
200	90							

6. For the month of October, the Crossroads Diner had the income situation shown in the table.

Crossroads Diner
Income Statement
for Month Ended October, 1991

Gross Sales (10,000 meals @ average price of $6.00)		$60,000
Less Cost of Goods Sold:		
Cooks	$ 9,000	
Servers, etc.	9,500	
Food	21,000	
Utilities (prorated—food service)	900	
Depreciation (prorated—kitchen, dining area, and equipment)	4,500	44,900
Gross Margin		$15,100
Less Administrative and Selling Expenses:		
Monthly Advertising Expense	$ 6,900	
Transportation Expense	1,500	
Office Salaries and Supplies	3,000	
Utilities (prorated—office)	600	
Depreciation (prorated—office)	600	12,600
Operating Income		$ 2,500
Less Interest Expense		6,000
Net Income (Loss)		($ 3,500)

a. Compute the number of meals that the diner would have to sell monthly to break even. You may assume in this part that average variable costs and average revenue per meal are constant. *Do state whether and why you classify each cost item* (or some portion thereof) *as variable or fixed.*

b. What implicit costs do you think would have been incurred by the owners of the Crossroads Diner but are not presented in the (accounting) income statement?

c. As the economic consultant for the Crossroads's owners, what suggestions can you make to help them improve their income from the diner? *Tell why* you think each of your suggestions will be helpful.

7. The next table gives monthly sales and cost data for a bicycle manufacturer.
   a. Complete the table.
   b. What is the profit-maximizing price and level of output for the firm? Why?

Price	Quantity	Total Revenue	Marginal Revenue	Marginal Cost	TVC	AFC	Marginal Profit
$200	0				$0	—	
190	1,000				150,000		
	2,000	360,000			290,000	6.00	
170	3,000				420,000		
160	4,000				540,000		
				100			
150	5,000						
				80			
140	6,000						
				75			
130	7,000						
				80			
120	8,000						
			30	100			
	9,000						
			10				
	10,000				1,095,000		
90	11,000				1,235,000		

8. The annual income statement shown at the top of the next page is for Alamo Chemical Company, which produces slug and snail bait. Of the $300,000 advertising expense, $250,000 is variable, and all but $100,000 of the travel expense is variable. Alamo considers $50,000 of the office salaries to be variable.

a. Find the break-even quantity for Alamo Chemical.

b. Alamo is considering installing some new machinery that would raise its fixed manufacturing costs to $1,000,000. This machinery would lower the direct labor cost to $.15 per bag and double the

Sales (1,000,000 two-pound bags @ $5)		$5,000,000
Less Cost of Goods Sold:		
Direct Labor	$700,000	
Direct Materials	350,000	
Variable Overhead	150,000	
Fixed Overhead	600,000	1,800,000
Gross Margin		$3,200,000
Less Administrative and Selling Expenses:		
Sales Commissions (@ $.50 per bag)	$500,000	
Travel Expenses	600,000	
Advertising Expense	300,000	
Office Supplies	10,000	
Office Salaries	90,000	1,500,000
Net Operating Income		$1,700,000
Less Interest Expense		500,000
Net Income Before Taxes		$1,200,000

firm's capacity to 2,000,000 bags. (Presently, the firm is operating at capacity.) Interest expense would also increase to $1,000,000. *The firm believes it can sell to the new capacity level if it lowers price to $4.50 per bag.* Other average variable costs and fixed costs would not change.

Do you recommend that Alamo install the new machinery? Why or why not? What will be its expected new level of net income before taxes if the machinery is installed and the price lowered to $4.50?

9. Mueller Brewery manufactures a full-flavored, dark German beer. Shown in this problem is Mueller's income statement for a month earlier this year.

Sales (100,000 cases @ $7 per case)		$700,000
Less Cost of Goods Sold:		
Direct Materials (nonreturn bottles)	$195,000	
Direct Labor	210,000	
Fixed Manufacturing Expenses	50,000	455,000
Gross Margin		$245,000
Less Administrative and Selling Expenses:		
Delivery Expenses	$ 30,000	
Sales Commissions	50,000	
Advertising Expenses	10,000	
Travel Expenses	5,000	
Fixed Administrative and Selling Expenses	10,000	105,000
Net Income Before Taxes		$140,000

a. Find the number of cases of beer Mueller's must sell per month to break even.

b. Mueller expects to sell, on the average, 100,000 cases per month for the rest of the year. Its capacity is 120,000 cases per month. Because of a strike by brewery workers in a foreign country that usually does not import Mueller's beer, a major hotel chain in that country has made an all-or-nothing offer to import 40,000 cases per month for the next three months at a price of $5.75 per case. Mueller's can supply from inventory only 30,000 of the total additional cases required for the three-month period because it did not anticipate receiving such an order. There will be no delivery expense, sales commissions, travel expense, or advertising expense connected with this order. Should Mueller agree to supply the hotel chain with the beer? *Why or why not?*

10. Kokkakola Co. is a firm located in Athens, Greece, that produces a popular soft drink normally sold in single-serving cans. Because of government price controls, it knows that the wholesale price it can charge for the drink is 80 drachmas per can. Its market studies show there is nothing to be gained by charging less. If Kokkakola's total cost function per month in drachmas is

$$TC = 8,000,000 + 20Q + .0001Q^2,$$

and its marginal cost therefore is

$$MC = 20 + .0002Q,$$

determine
a. how many cans of the drink it should sell,
b. how much its total monthly profit will be.

11. A firm estimates the following demand information for daily sales of its product, where Q is the quantity sold and P is the price:

$$Q = 136 - 0.4P$$

$$P = 340 - 2.5Q$$

$$MR = 340 - 5Q$$

a. If its marginal cost is described by the function

$$MC = 40 - 10Q + Q^2,$$

what will be its profit-maximizing output and price?

b. Suppose the total cost function from which the above marginal cost was derived is

$$TC = 3{,}000 + 40Q - 5Q^2 + (1/3)Q^3,$$

and determine how much profit the firm will have per day.

12. Squiggly Wiggly Corp. sells fishing worms in the wholesale market. The company has monthly fixed costs of $1,960, and it sells worms for $5.00 per gallon.
   a. If its AVC is constant at $2.20 per gallon of worms, how many gallons will it have to sell in order to break even?
   b. Suppose Squiggly Wiggly desires to have an economic profit of $12,000. If the costs given above are the total economic costs of the firm, what monthly quantity of worm sales will yield the desired profit? (Round to nearest gallon.)

The following problems require calculus.

13. A firm has the following total revenue and total cost functions:

$$TR = 21Q - Q^2$$

$$TC = \frac{Q^3}{3} - 3Q^2 + 9Q + 6$$

   a. At what level of output does the firm maximize *total revenue?*
   b. At what level of output does the firm maximize *total profit?*
   c. How much is the firm's total profit at its maximum?

14. Find the maximum profit for a firm if its total revenue function is $TR = 50Q - Q^2$ and its total cost function is $TC = 100 - 4Q + 2Q^2$.

15. Suppose a firm's estimated demand curve has the equation

$$Q = 220 - P,$$

and its total cost function is

$$TC = 1{,}000 + 80Q - 3Q^2 + (1/3)Q^3$$

   a. Write an equation for the firm's total revenue function.
   b. Determine the *output level* and *price* that will maximize profit (or minimize short-run loss) for the firm.
   c. Calculate the firm's economic profit or loss at the optimum point.

(Note: The following problem also requires use of the Lagrangian multiplier technique, discussed in the appendix to Chapter 4.)

16. Lone Star Instruments, Inc., makes two deluxe printing models of calculators—a scientific model and a business and financial model. The demand function for the scientific model is

$$Q_S = 20,000 - 100P_S,$$

where
$$Q_S = \text{annual quantity demanded of the scientific model,}$$

and
$$P_S = \text{price of the scientific model.}$$

The demand function for the business and financial model is

$$Q_B = 50,000 - 400P_B,$$

where
$$Q_B = \text{annual quantity demanded of the business and financial model,}$$

and
$$P_B = \text{price of the business and financial model.}$$

The total cost function for LSI is given by

$$STC = \$100,000 + 25Q,$$

where
$$Q = Q_S + Q_B.$$

LSI also has a capacity limitation of 17,500 calculators per year.
   a. Find the profit-maximizing quantity and price for each model of calculator.
   b. Solve for the Lagrangian multiplier. What does its value tell you?

17. Suppose a firm has the following short-run total cost function:

$$STC = 4,850 + 40Q - 1.5Q^2 + 0.04Q^3,$$

where Q is output, and the constant in the equation represents total fixed cost. Answer the following:

a. What is the dollar value of average fixed cost at an output of 25 units?
b. At what level of output will marginal cost be at a minimum?
c. At what level of output will *AVC* be at a minimum?
d. If the firm has a fixed product price of $190 per unit, at what level of output will it choose to operate, and what will be its economic profit or loss?

18. Traumco sells a specialized medical monitoring device. It estimates the monthly quantity demanded to be represented by the equation

$$Q = 350 - .25P, \text{ where } P \text{ is price.}$$

Its monthly cost function is

$$STC = 20,000 + 200Q - 9Q^2 + (1/3)Q^3.$$

Determine the profit-maximizing quantity sold and price for the monitor. How much will the maximum monthly profit be?

These problems can be solved with Decision Assistant.

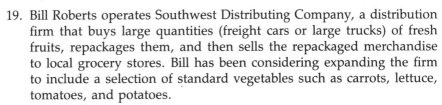

19. Bill Roberts operates Southwest Distributing Company, a distribution firm that buys large quantities (freight cars or large trucks) of fresh fruits, repackages them, and then sells the repackaged merchandise to local grocery stores. Bill has been considering expanding the firm to include a selection of standard vegetables such as carrots, lettuce, tomatoes, and potatoes.

   Carrots: Bill has determined the total revenue function for carrots is given by the equation

$$TR = \$100Q - \$0.5Q^2,$$

where Q represents the quantity of bushels of carrots sold. The total cost function for carrots is given by the equation

$$TC = \$1,500 - \$10Q + \$.05Q^2,$$

where Q represents the quantity of bushels of carrots purchased.
   Lettuce: Bill has determined the total revenue function for lettuce is given by the equation

$$TR = \$200Q - \$0.5Q^2,$$

where Q represents the quantity of crates of lettuce sold.

The total cost function for lettuce is given by the equation

$$TC = \$1{,}500 - \$20Q + \$.05Q^2,$$

where Q represents the quantity of crates of lettuce purchased.

Tomatoes: Bill has determined the total revenue function for tomatoes is given by the equation

$$TR = \$350Q - \$0.5Q^2,$$

where Q represents the quantity of flats of tomatoes sold.
The total cost function for tomatoes is given by the equation

$$TC = \$1{,}500 - \$35Q + \$.05Q^2,$$

where Q represents the quantity of flats of tomatoes purchased.

Potatoes: Bill has determined the total revenue function for potatoes is given by the equation

$$TR = \$450Q - \$0.5Q^2,$$

where Q represents the quantity of sacks of potatoes sold. The total cost function for potatoes is given by the equation

$$TC = \$1{,}500 - \$45Q + \$.05Q^2,$$

where Q represents the quantity of sacks of potatoes purchased.

Use the Max/Min tool in the *Managerial Economics Decision Assistant* to determine profit-maximizing quantity and price for each of the products (carrots, lettuce, tomatoes, and potatoes).

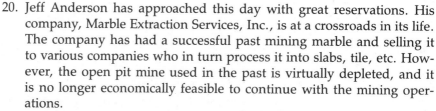

20. Jeff Anderson has approached this day with great reservations. His company, Marble Extraction Services, Inc., is at a crossroads in its life. The company has had a successful past mining marble and selling it to various companies who in turn process it into slabs, tile, etc. However, the open pit mine used in the past is virtually depleted, and it is no longer economically feasible to continue with the mining operations.

Jeff has researched the possibilities of moving the operations and has been fortunate to locate a suitable area that has been tested and found to contain an excellent grade of marble. A long-term lease has been signed on the property, and now all that remains is to determine the type of mining operation to be used at the new site. Great advances in automation have occurred in the mining industry since the original mining operation commenced, and Jeff is now faced with a decision that will affect the company's fortunes for the next 25 years.

The director of mining operations, Mike Wilson, has studied various options concerning the new facilities. From his study he has determined there are three possibilities which will be consistent with the site itself and with the grade of marble being mined.

Plant A is highly automated with some of the latest electronic and robotic equipment in the industry. The average variable cost for extracting a ton of marble is estimated to be $500 per ton. Fixed cost, mostly due to the price and quantity of equipment, is estimated to be $3 million per year.

Plant B is slightly less automated and therefore relies on more labor in the mining process. Fixed costs are estimated to be $2 million per year. Average variable costs will be approximately $750 per ton.

Plant C relies on the more traditional, labor-intensive methods of marble mining and has the lowest fixed costs of $1 million per year. Estimated average variable costs are $1,000 per ton.

The director of marketing, Anne Stephens, has studied the marketplace for the type of marble to be mined and determined the average price for marble of similar quality is $2,000 per ton.

a. As an economist for the company, you have been asked to provide an analysis of each plant. The Break-Even Analysis tool in the *Managerial Economics Decision Assistant* can be used to evaluate the profitability of each plant type. What is the break-even quantity for each type of plant?

b. In addition to other information you consider important, Jeff specifically wants the answers to the following questions.

   i) At each of the following production levels, what level of profit would be generated by each plant?

   > 5,000 tons per month
   > 4,000 tons per month
   > 3,000 tons per month
   > 2,000 tons per month
   > 1,000 tons per month

   ii) Assuming that Anne Stephens is predicting the higher volume of 5,000 tons per month, which plant should be used? Under what conditions would your answer change? Be specific and give reasons for your logic.

■ ■ ■ ■ ■ ■ ■ ■ ■ ■ ■ **Selected References** ■ ■ ■ ■ ■ ■ ■ ■ ■ ■ ■

"Airline Takes the Marginal Route," *Business Week* (April 20, 1963), pp. 111–114.

Cyert, R. M., and C. L. Hedrick. "Theory of the Firm: Past, Present, and Future: An Interpretation," *Journal of Economic Literature* X, no. 2 (June 1972), pp. 389–412.

Dean, Joel. "Measuring Profits for Executive Decisions," *Accounting Review* (April 1951).

Enke, Stephen. "On Maximizing Profits: A Distinction Between Chamberlin and Robinson," *American Economic Review* XLI (September 1951), pp. 566–578.

Lyons, Ivory L., and Manuel Zymelman. *Economic Analysis of the Firm: Theory and Practice*. New York: Pitman, 1966, Chapters 4 and 6.

Nicholson, Walter. *Microeconomic Theory: Basic Principles and Extensions*, 3d ed. Chicago: The Dryden Press, 1985, Chapter 9.

Williamson, O. F. "The Modern Corporation: Origins, Evolution, Attributes," *Journal of Economic Literature* XIX (December 1981), pp. 1537–1538.

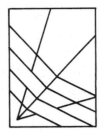

Linear Programming and the Firm

In the preceding chapters, we have discussed optimizing decisions made by the firm regarding demand, production, cost, and profit-maximizing output and price, using techniques that depended upon the mathematics of calculus. In this chapter we shall discuss some of those decisions, using the tools of a different branch of mathematics—that of **linear programming.** Linear programming is a mathematical decision-making tool for optimization problems with a linear objective function and linear constraints that are in the form of inequalities.

RELATIONSHIP BETWEEN LINEAR PROGRAMMING AND CALCULUS TECHNIQUES

As one should expect since we are including a discussion of decision making using both tools in this book, calculus and linear programming *each* have areas of applicability where the other cannot be used. For example, linear programming can be used only when the relevant functions or relationships involved are linear.[1] This restriction means the cost, revenue, and total profit functions must all be graphed as straight lines as long as only one independent variable is involved. If there is more than one independent variable, no variable (X_i) must be raised to a power other

[1] There is a branch of mathematical programming—nonlinear programming—for which the linearity assumption is not required. However, that topic is too advanced for this book.

than 1 or multiplied by any other variable. Thus all functions must be of the form $Y = a_0 + a_1X_1 + a_2X_2 + \ldots + a_nX_n$, where the a_i are constants. Linear programming techniques require constant returns to scale, constant marginal productivity of a variable input (if we are using short-run cost functions), constant input prices, and constant output prices.

Obviously, such requirements are not necessary for the application of calculus techniques, since many of the functions that we used in the production and cost chapters were *not* linear; and, indeed, over wide variations in levels of output, these relationships are probably nonlinear for most firms. However, as we indicated in our discussion of break-even analysis, over small variations in levels of production, the assumption of linearity may be realistic.

On the other hand, linear programming can be utilized in situations where certain constraints or limitations faced by the firm can be expressed in terms of *inequalities*, whereas the traditional calculus techniques can be used only when these constraints can be expressed as *strict* equalities. Thus, for example, it is easy to see the usefulness of linear programming in a situation in which a firm has certain capacity limitations such that it may utilize either none of a particular input or various amounts of it up to some maximum amount available. A firm may wish to maximize short-run profit, subject to some minimum requirement on dollar sales. A manufacturing firm may wish to minimize the cost of producing a good, subject to certain minimum safety and/or quality requirements. Later in this chapter, we discuss a marketing problem that involves linear programming, and there are also many uses for linear programming in the area of finance. For example, a firm may wish to maximize the expected return on its investment portfolio, subject to certain minimum constraints on the amounts held of certain types of assets.

The use of linear programming (and calculus) by a firm implies, however, that fractional solution values for the decision variables at the optimal point are acceptable and that, if necessary, the decision maker can round to the profit-maximizing whole number. In cases where such an assumption is unwarranted, a more complex procedure—integer programming—may be necessary. This technique is beyond the scope of this book, but further reading may be done in sources listed at the end of this chapter.

■ ■ ■ ■ ■ ■ ■ ■   **THE PRIMAL PROGRAM**

Each linear programming problem has two programs: the *primal program* and the *dual program*. The primal program explicitly states the objective of the firm and its constraints and is, therefore, easier to understand. For this reason we shall begin this chapter with an example of a primal maximization program, leaving a discussion of the dual program for later.

Profit Maximization with Input Constraints

As we have already stated, frequently a firm wishes to maximize profit but is constrained because there are maximum amounts available of certain inputs. For example, suppose a winery produces two products—white wine and champagne. In the short run, the firm has three capacity limitations: fermenting capacity, bottling capacity, and champagne purifying capacity. For those who are not familiar with the production processes involved in making champagne, we should explain that champagne requires a double fermentation. This double process is done so that the partially fermented grape juice, along with some grape pulp, is sealed in bottles and allowed to undergo further fermentation to acquire the bubbles and effervescence characteristic of champagne. The champagne mixture is then partially frozen so that the bubbles will not escape when the bottles are unsealed and the sediment is removed. By this means, the champagne is purified and then rebottled.

The maximum amount of initial fermenting capacity becoming available in casks is 600 units each week, the maximum amount of bottling capacity available per week is 500 units, and the maximum amount of champagne purifying capacity available each week is 150 units. Production of one bottle of champagne requires three units of fermenting capacity, two units of bottling capacity, and one unit of champagne purifying capacity. Production of one bottle of white wine requires only one unit of fermenting capacity and one unit of bottling capacity. These relationships are summarized in Table 7–1.

The Graphical Solution

In Figure 7–1 we have graphed three straight lines indicating the *maximum* amounts of white wine and/or champagne the firm can produce, *given* the three input constraints. These three straight-line relationships were derived in the following manner from the information presented in Table 7–1. First, consider the constraint on fermentation. If we were to express the information relevant to that constraint presented in the table as a mathe-

Table 7–1   Input Requirements for Producing White Wine and Champagne

Input	Units of Input Required per Bottle		Maximum Number of Units of Input Available
	Champagne	*White Wine*	
Fermentation	3	1	600
Bottling	2	1	500
Champagne Purifying	1	0	150

Figure 7–1   Maximum Quantities of White Wine and Champagne that Can Be Produced, Given Fermenting, Bottling, and Champagne-Purifying Constraints

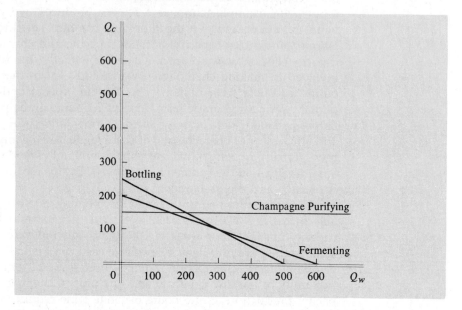

The bottling constraint indicates the maximum quantities of champagne and wine that can be produced with current bottling capacity. The champagne-purifying and fermenting constraints have similar interpretations.

matical relationship, we could state that three times the number of bottles of champagne produced plus one times the number of bottles of white wine produced must be less than or equal to 600 units, which is the maximum available amount of inputs required for fermentation. In mathematical notation

$$3Q_c + Q_w \leq 600,$$

where Q_c is the number of bottles of champagne and Q_w is the number of bottles of white wine. Thus this mathematical relationship summarizes the fermentation constraint because it combines the information that (1) it takes three units of fixed fermentation input to produce one bottle of champagne, (2) it takes one unit of fixed fermentation input to produce one bottle of white wine, and (3) a maximum of 600 units is available. In a similar manner, we can derive mathematical expressions for the other two constraints, which are presented in Table 7–2.

If we remove the inequality sign from each of these constraints, thus making them strict equalities, we obtain the relationships which indicate the *maximum* quantity of champagne and/or wine that could be produced

Table 7–2   Mathematical Expressions of the Fermenting, Bottling, and Champagne-Purifying Constraints

Fermenting	$3Q_c + Q_w \leq 600$
Bottling	$2Q_c + Q_w \leq 500$
Champagne Purifying	$Q_c \leq 150$

under each constraint if all available units of the input were utilized. These equations are presented in Table 7–3 and are the equations for the straight-line functions graphed in Figure 7–1.

Note that when we consider only one constraint, the firm may be able to produce any one of a wide variety of combinations of wine and champagne and still satisfy the constraint. For example, the firm could produce 200 bottles of champagne and no wine *or* 600 bottles of wine and no champagne and still meet the fermenting constraint.

However, the firm must satisfy *all* of the constraints and, consequently, is able to produce only those combinations of champagne and wine that are in (including the boundary) the region of the graph in Figure 7–1 that is within all three constraints. We have indicated this region in Figure 7–2 with a heavy black boundary and diagonal lines. The combinations of champagne and wine in this region make up the *feasible region* of production.

Given these constraints, the firm can produce any combination of wine and champagne that is within the feasible region of production. However, we have assumed that the firm wishes to produce that combination of products that will *maximize its profit* (or minimize its loss). To achieve this goal, the firm needs to know the *profit contribution* (price less average variable cost) per unit for each product that it produces. Assume that the profit contribution per bottle of champagne is $2.50, whereas the profit contribution per bottle of white wine is $1.00. With this information the firm can use *isoprofit curves* to graphically find its optimal quantities of wine and champagne. Similar to other economics curves with an iso-prefix, an **isoprofit curve** indicates the various combinations of two products which will yield *equal profit* for the firm. (Recall from Chapter 4, for example, that an *isocost* curve indicates the combinations of two inputs that are of *equal cost*.)

An **isoprofit curve** indicates the different combinations of two products that will result in equal profit for the firm.

In Figure 7–3 we have graphed three isoprofit curves and the feasible region from Figure 7–2. We were able to obtain the equation for each

Table 7–3   Equations Expressing Maximum Quantities of Wine and Champagne that Can Be Produced Under Each Constraint

Fermenting	$3Q_c + Q_w = 600$
Bottling	$2Q_c + Q_w = 500$
Champagne Purifying	$Q_c = 150$

Figure 7–2   Feasible Region of Production of Wine and Champagne

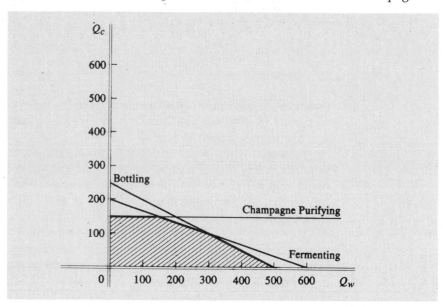

The feasible region of production, indicated by the diagonal lines, represents the quantities of wine and champagne that the firm can produce with its current capacity.

isoprofit line by substituting different values for total profit contribution (πC) in the following function:

$$\pi C = \$2.50Q_c + \$1.00Q_w.$$

This function states that the total profit contribution of the firm must be equal to $2.50 times the number of bottles of champagne produced plus $1.00 times the number of bottles of wine produced. By substituting $375 for πC, we can find the equation that indicates the different combinations of wine and champagne that will result in a $375 level of profit contribution. To derive the equations for the other isoprofit curves, we do the same thing for $\pi C = \$550$ and $\pi C = \$650$. (The amounts $375, $550, and $650 were picked because they involved combinations of champagne and wine that were near the boundary of the feasible region.)

If the firm is to maximize profit, it must be on the highest isoprofit curve possible, given its constraints. In Figure 7–3 we observe that the isoprofit line for $\pi C = \$550$ just touches an outside corner (point A) of the feasible region; therefore a profit contribution level of $550 is the greatest amount that the firm can achieve, given its capacity constraints. Point A also indicates the profit-maximizing combination of champagne and wine

Figure 7–3   Isoprofit Lines and the Feasible Region of Production

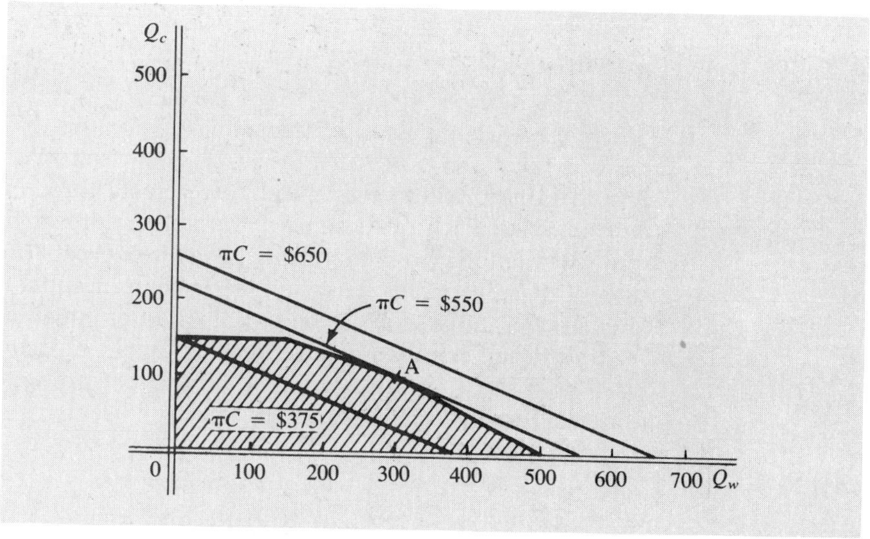

The equation for each isoprofit curve is obtained by substituting each respective level of profit contribution in the equation

$$\pi C = \$2.50 Q_c + \$1.00 Q_w,$$

where πC is the total profit contribution, Q_c is the number of bottles of champagne, and Q_w is the number of bottles of wine. The isoprofit curve for $\pi C = \$550$ just touches an outside corner (point A) of the feasible region, and it indicates the profit-maximizing quantities of champagne and wine.

that the firm should produce in this situation—100 bottles of champagne and 300 bottles of wine. Note that while point A is the optimal point, the firm still has some excess champagne purifying capacity.

The Algebraic Solution Method

The graphical method of finding the profit-maximizing combination of products is quite useful for illustration. However, algebraic methods are more precise and more practical when the number of decision variables is greater than two, because graphing is difficult when there are more than two variables. There are a variety of algebraic methods in use, and often these operations would be performed by a computer. Consequently, in this book we shall discuss only one of the simplest algebraic procedures.

As indicated in the preceding paragraph, the objective function (or goal) of the firm is to maximize

$$\pi C = \$2.50 Q_c + \$1.00 Q_w,$$

subject to the following constraints (see Table 7–2):

$$\text{Fermenting} \qquad 3Q_c + Q_w \leq 600,$$

$$\text{Bottling} \qquad 2Q_c + Q_w \leq 500, \text{ and}$$

$$\text{Champagne purifying} \qquad Q_c \qquad \leq 150.$$

To solve this problem algebraically, we create three new variables called *slack variables*. Each of these slack variables represents excess capacity in some area, and since there cannot be *negative* excess capacity, the value of each of these variables must be greater than or equal to zero. The values of Q_c and Q_w must likewise be greater than or equal to zero.

Since each slack variable represents excess capacity in some area, we place one slack variable in each of the preceding constraints, which changes it to an equality:

(7–1)
$$3Q_c + Q_w + S_F = 600,$$

(7–2)
$$2Q_c + Q_w + S_B = 500,$$

and

(7–3)
$$Q_c \qquad + S_P = 150.$$

In this case S_F represents excess fermenting capacity, S_B represents excess bottling capacity, and S_P represents excess champagne purifying capacity. The addition of these slack variables transforms these constraints into equalities because the amount of a particular kind of input used in producing champagne and wine, plus the excess capacity left over, must equal the total available amount of the input.

Before proceeding any further, we should note that in this case corners of the boundary (also called *extreme points*) of the feasible region occur (1) where two constraints intersect, (2) where a constraint intersects either the horizontal or vertical axis, or (3) at the origin. Therefore, at any extreme point, at least *two* of the five variables (Q_c, Q_w, S_F, S_B, and S_P in the constraint equations) must be zero. It is also true in the general case with m constraints and n decision variables that the number of *zero-valued* variables must be great enough so that the number of *nonzero-valued* variables is no greater than the number of constraints. Usually, if there are m constraints, there will be m variables that are nonzero.

To draw each constraint line, we assumed that all available capacity of the corresponding input was being utilized. This means that along a capacity constraint line, the value of the corresponding slack variable is zero. Thus, in Figure 7–4, at point A, Q_c, and Q_w are zero; at point B, Q_w and S_P are zero; at point C, S_P and S_F are zero; at point D, S_F and S_B are zero; and at point E, S_B and Q_c are zero.

Figure 7–4   Constraints and the Boundary of the Feasible Region

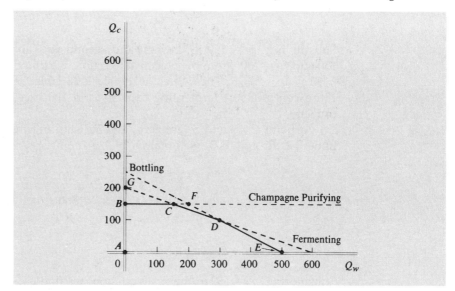

Points A, B, C, D, and E mark the corners of the boundary of the feasible region of production. Points G and F lie outside the feasible region.

Observe that not all points where two of these variables are zero are *necessarily* part of the feasible region. For example, at point F, S_P and S_B equal zero, but point F is not part of the feasible region because it is outside the fermenting constraint. At point G, Q_w and S_F are zero, but point G is also outside the feasible region.

Furthermore, *at least one* of the extreme (boundary corner) points of the feasible region will mark a profit-maximizing combination of champagne and wine to be produced. (If a constraint happens to coincide with an isoprofit curve, then two extreme points, both on the constraint, and all points in between, will be equally profitable.) Therefore, by solving the constraint equations for Q_c and Q_w at each extreme point of the feasible region and determining the corresponding πC from the objective function, we can discover the optimal combination of champagne and wine.

As long as the profit contribution per unit of output is positive, we can ignore the origin, since at that point, $Q_c = 0$, $Q_w = 0$, and $\pi C = 0$. At point B, S_P and Q_w are zero, and substituting those values into equations 7-1 through 7-3, we obtain the following equations:

$$3Q_c + S_F = 600,$$

$$2Q_c + S_B = 500,$$

and

$$Q_c = 150.$$

Substituting $Q_c = 150$ in the first and second equations, we obtain $S_F = 150$ and $S_B = 200$. From the objective function, we find that $\pi C = \$2.50(150) + \$1.00(0) = \$375$. The values of the slack variables tell us that there are 150 excess units of fermenting capacity and 200 excess units of bottling capacity.

At point C, S_P and S_F are zero, and substituting these values in equations 7–1 through 7–3, we obtain

$$3Q_c + Q_w = 600,$$
$$2Q_c + Q_w + S_B = 500,$$

and

$$Q_c = 150.$$

Substituting $Q_c = 150$ in the first equation, we find $Q_w = 150$. Substituting $Q_c = 150$ and $Q_w = 150$ in the second equation, we find $S_B = 50$. From the objective function, we find $\pi C = \$2.50(150) + \$1.00(150) = \$525$.

At point D, S_F and S_B are zero, and substituting those values into equations 7–1 through 7–3, we obtain:

$$3Q_c + Q_w = 600,$$
$$2Q_c + Q_w = 500,$$

and

$$Q_c + S_P = 150.$$

Subtracting the second equation from the first, we obtain $Q_c = 100$. Substituting $Q_c = 100$ in either of those equations, we find $Q_w = 300$. Substituting $Q_c = 100$ in the last equation, we get $S_P = 50$. From the objective function, we find $\pi C = \$2.50(100) + \$1.00(300) = \$550$.

At point E, Q_c and S_B equal zero, and in a manner similar to that used for the other points, we obtain $Q_w = 500$, $S_F = 100$, $S_P = 150$, and $\pi C = \$500$.

The information that we have obtained by examining each of the boundary corners of the feasible region is summarized as follows:

Point A
$Q_c = 0, Q_w = 0$
$S_F = 600, S_B = 500, S_P = 150$
$\pi C = 0$

Point B
$Q_w = 0, S_P = 0$
$Q_c = 150, S_F = 150, S_B = 200$
$\pi C = \$375$

Point C
$S_F = 0$, $S_P = 0$
$Q_c = 150$, $Q_w = 150$, $S_B = 50$
$\pi C = \$525$

Point D
$S_F = 0$, $S_B = 0$
$Q_c = 100$, $Q_w = 300$, $S_P = 50$
$\pi C = \$550$

Point E
$Q_c = 0$, $S_B = 0$
$Q_w = 500$, $S_F = 100$, $S_P = 150$
$\pi C = \$500$

As we have already found graphically, the optimal combination of champagne and wine is given by point D, where $Q_c = 100$, $Q_w = 300$, and $\pi C = \$550$—the highest profit contribution level obtainable by this firm.

How did we know that points A, B, C, D, and E made up the boundary corners of the feasible region, as opposed to points like F and G? Before we solved for the values of the nonzero slack variables, the only way we could tell was from the graph. *After* we solved for the values of the nonzero slack variables, we could tell because the values of those variables were positive. At points such as F and G, the value of at least one slack variable will be negative, meaning that at least one constraint is being violated. For example, at point G, $S_P = -50$, meaning that the purifying constraint has been violated. However, it is often helpful to use a graph together with the algebraic method of finding the profit-maximizing point in order to locate more easily the corners of the feasible region boundary (as long as the number of decision variables is not too large).

We now turn to an example of the primal program in a cost minimization problem.

Example of a Linear Programming Cost Minimization Problem

Linear programming is quite useful for certain types of cost minimization decision problems, as well as for profit maximization problems, so long as the linearity requirement is met. For example, suppose that a manufacturer of high quality (and relatively high priced) speakers for stereo component systems is trying to decide on the optimal combination of advertisements in two magazines. The cost per ad in the first magazine is $500, while the cost per ad in the second magazine is $400. The firm has certain minimum quantities of different types of people whom it wants to reach through these advertisements. Specifically, it wants to reach at least 600,000 people under 50 years of age, at least 180,000 people with annual incomes of $40,000 and over, and at least 260,000 people who already own stereo systems.

The firm believes that no person subscribes to both magazines, as the characteristics of people who read the first magazine differ significantly from the characteristics of those who read the second magazine. Accordingly, the firm believes that each ad placed in the first magazine will reach 20,000 *new* readers who are less than 50 years old, 15,000 new readers who have annual incomes of at least $40,000, and 10,000 new readers who already have stereo systems. The corresponding figures for the second magazine are believed to be 30,000 new readers under 50 years of age, 5,000 with incomes of $40,000 and over, and 10,000 who already own stereo systems.

The objective of the stereo speaker manufacturer is to minimize the cost of the advertisements while fulfilling the minimum goals for reaching each type of audience. Thus our linear programming problem becomes this: Minimize $C = \$500Q_1 + \$400Q_2$, where Q_1 is the number of advertisements placed in the first magazine and Q_2 is the number of advertisements placed in the second magazine, subject to the following constraints:

Age	$20,000Q_1 + 30,000Q_2 \geq 600,000,$
Income	$15,000Q_1 + 5,000Q_2 \geq 180,000,$ and
Stereo ownership	$10,000Q_1 + 10,000Q_2 \geq 260,000,$

where

$$Q_1 \text{ and } Q_2 \text{ are } \geq 0.$$

The first constraint states that 20,000 times the number of ads placed in the first magazine (which will equal the number of people less than 50 years old reached by that magazine) plus 30,000 times the number of ads placed in the second magazine (which should equal the number of people under 50 years old reached by the second magazine) must be greater than or equal to 600,000, the *minimum* number of people under 50 years of age which the speaker manufacturer wishes to reach. The second and third constraints have similar interpretations. Note that the constraint inequalities in this minimization problem are in the form of greater-than-or-equal-to constraints, whereas in the maximization problem they were less-than-or-equal-to constraints. This difference occurs because in the first case the constraints are placing a limit on making something *larger,* while in the second case they are placing a limit on making something *smaller.* The constraints and the feasible region for the stereo speaker manufacturer are graphed in Figure 7–5, and the respective extreme points are designated by points *A, B, C, and D.*

Using the algebraic method developed in the previous section, we use slack variables to transform the constraints into strict equalities as follows:

(7–4)
$$20,000Q_1 + 30,000Q_2 - S_A = 600,000,$$

(7–5)
$$15,000Q_1 + 5,000Q_2 - S_I = 180,000,$$

Figure 7–5   Constraints and the Feasible Region for Advertisements in Two Magazines

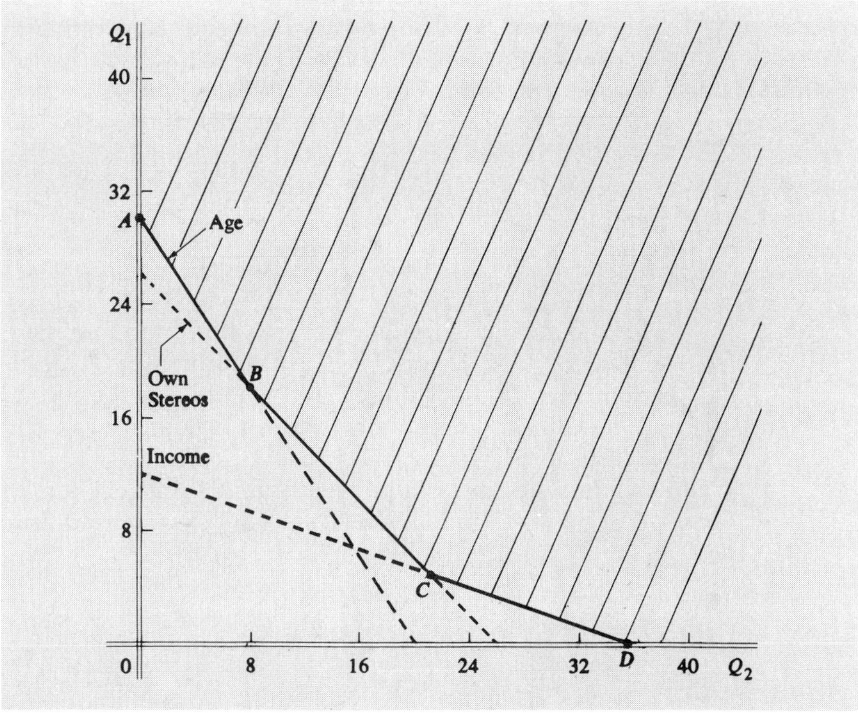

In this case the feasible region, denoted by the diagonal lines, is above *ABCD*.

and

(7–6)

$$10{,}000Q_1 + 10{,}000Q_2 - S_O = 260{,}000.$$

Here, the slack variables represent the *additional* people reached by advertisements in a particular classification above the minimum number required. As before, the values of all variables must be greater than or equal to zero.

We now examine each boundary corner point. At point A, S_A and Q_2 are equal to zero. Substituting these values into the constraint equations 7–4 through 7–6, we obtain:

$$20{,}000Q_1 \qquad\quad = 600{,}000,$$

$$15{,}000Q_1 - S_I = 180{,}000,$$

and

$$10{,}000Q_1 - S_O = 260{,}000.$$

From the first constraint, we find $Q_1 = 30$, and substituting for Q_1 in the second and third constraints, we find $S_I = 270,000$ and $S_O = 40,000$. From the objective function, we obtain $C = \$500(30) + \$400(0) = \$15,000$.

At point B, S_A and S_O are zero, and substituting these values into the constraint equations, we obtain the following:

$$20,000Q_1 + 30,000Q_2 \quad = 600,000,$$

$$15,000Q_1 + \quad 5,000Q_2 - S_I = 180,000,$$

and

$$10,000Q_1 + 10,000Q_2 \quad = 260,000.$$

By subtracting twice the third equation from the first equation, we obtain $10,000Q_2 = 80,000$ or $Q_2 = 8$. Substituting for Q_1 in the third equation, we find $Q_1 = 18$. Substituting for Q_1 and Q_2 in the second equation, we find $S_I = 130,000$. From the objective function, we can obtain $C = \$500(18) + \$400(8) = \$12,200$.

In a similar fashion, we can find the values for Q_1, Q_2, S_A S_I, S_O, and C at points C and D. Our results are summarized as follows:

Point A
$Q_1 = 30$, $Q_2 = 0$, $S_A = 0$
$S_I = 270,000$, $S_O = 40,000$
$C = \$15,000$

Point B
$Q_1 = 18$, $Q_2 = 8$, $S_A = 0$
$S_I = 130,000$, $S_O = 0$
$C = \$12,000$

Point C
$Q_1 = 5$, $Q_2 = 21$,
$S_A = 130,000$
$S_I = 0$, $S_O = 0$
$C = \$10,900$

Point D
$Q_1 = 0$, $Q_2 = 36$,
$S_A = 480,000$
$S_I = 0$, $S_O = 100,000$
$C = \$14,400$

Thus the firm will minimize its advertising cost, given these constraints at point C, where $Q_1 = 5$, $Q_2 = 21$, and $C = \$10,900$. Therefore the firm should advertise 5 times in the first magazine and 21 times in the second magazine. In Figure 7–6 we have graphed the boundary of the feasible region and the isocost curve for $C = \$10,900$, and we have indicated the optimal values of Q_1 and Q_2.

Summary of Primal Program Solution Procedure

The steps that should be followed to obtain the optimal solution to a primal program using a combination of graphical and algebraic methods are summarized as follows:

1. Set up the objective function and the constraints in mathematical notation.

Figure 7–6   The Least-Cost Combination of Advertisements in Two Magazines

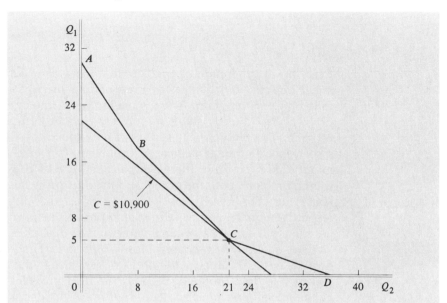

The firm will minimize advertising cost at point C, with 5 advertisements in the first magazine and 21 in the second magazine.

2. Graph the constraints by considering them to be strict equalities and determine the extreme points of the boundary of the feasible region, recalling that the values of all slack variables and the quantities produced of the products must be greater than or equal to zero. Moreover, these corner points must include *the* optimal point or at least *one of a set* of equally optimal points. If the constraints cannot be graphed easily, go to the third step, using the algebraic technique described earlier to examine each point where the number of nonzero variables is at least no greater than the number of constraints.

3. Using the algebraic technique described earlier, examine each of the extreme points in turn, solving for the quantities of each of the products and the slack variables at each point and the resulting level of profit contribution or cost in order to determine at which point profit will be maximized or cost will be minimized. (It will often be helpful to graph an isoprofit/isocost curve that falls near the outermost/innermost boundary of the feasible region as an aid in eliminating some extreme points from consideration without having to solve the constraint relationships for each point algebraically.)

In the next section, we examine the nature of the dual programs in the two examples of the optimization problems presented previously.

■ ■ ■ ■ ■ ■ ■ ■ ■ **THE DUAL PROGRAM**

Every linear programming problem that involves maximizing or minimizing an objective function has a corresponding linear programming problem called the *dual* program. As we have indicated, the original programming problem that directly states the objective of the firm is called the *primal* program. For every primal *maximization* problem, there can be constructed a corresponding dual *minimization* problem; conversely, for every primal minimization problem, there can be constructed a corresponding maximization problem. Both the primal and the dual programs will give the same values for the *decision variables* in the *primal* objective function at their respective optimal points. Also, the optimal value for the primal objective function will equal the optimal value for the dual objective function.

The dual program is useful for two reasons. First, it may be easier to find the optimal values of the decision variables in the primal program by solving the dual program. Second, the dual program gives an imputed value of the opportunity cost to the firm of the decision variables in the primal objective function and of the constraints.

Dual Minimization Problem

Consider the primal maximization problem that we discussed earlier in this chapter. The primal objective function that the firm wished to maximize was

$$\pi C = \$2.50Q_c + \$1.00Q_w,$$

where Q_c and Q_w were the quantities of champagne and wine, respectively, to be produced by the firm, and \$2.50 and \$1.00 were their respective profit contributions per unit. This objective function was to be maximized subject to the following constraints (see Table 7–2):

Fermenting	$3Q_c + Q_w \leq 600,$	
Bottling	$2Q_c + Q_w \leq 500,$ and	
Champagne purifying	$Q_c \qquad \leq 150,$	

where Q_c and Q_w are ≥ 0.

The corresponding dual program is concerned with finding the *minimum* values which can be assigned to the three inputs represented by the capacity constraints and still account for *all* of the unit profit contribution of each product. These minimum values of the fixed inputs represent their marginal value or opportunity cost to the firm in terms of the profit contribution which results from their use by the firm.

Thus the dual objective function that the firm wishes to minimize in this case is

$$C = 600V_F + 500V_B + 150V_P,$$

where C is the total opportunity cost to the firm of the three resources, V_F is the marginal opportunity cost of the fixed resources used in fermentation, V_B is the marginal opportunity cost of the fixed bottling resources, and V_P is the marginal opportunity cost of the fixed champagne purifying resources. The coefficients 600, 500, and 150 represent the total available amounts of fixed resources used in fermenting, bottling, and champagne purifying, respectively.

As should be expected, the constraints set limits on the values to be assigned to the three resources, and these limits are stated in terms of the unit profit contribution of each product. Accordingly, the constraints are

(7–7)
$$3V_F + 2V_B + V_P \geq \$2.50,$$

and

(7–8)
$$V_F + V_B \geq \$1.00.$$

These two constraints state that the sum of the marginal value or opportunity cost of each input times the amount of that input used to produce a unit of a particular product must be greater than or equal to the unit profit contribution for that product. Thus the first constraint applies to champagne and indicates that three units of the fixed fermenting resource, two units of the fixed bottling resource, and one unit of the champagne purifying resource are needed to produce one bottle of champagne with unit profit contribution of $2.50. A similar interpretation can be made of the second constraint, which applies to wine.

Since it is difficult to graph in three-dimensional space (V_F, V_B, and V_P necessitate three dimensions), we shall solve the dual program algebraically. First, as with the primal, the inequalities must be transformed into equalities by adding new variables, as shown below:

$$3V_F + 2V_B + V_P - L_c = \$2.50,$$

and

$$V_F + V_B - L_w = \$1.00,$$

where L_c and L_w are greater than or equal to zero. In this case L_c represents the *net* opportunity cost to the firm of producing champagne, and L_w

represents the *net* opportunity cost of producing wine.[2] If, for example, L_c were positive, it would indicate to the firm that the opportunity cost of the resources used in producing a bottle of champagne was greater than its unit profit contribution. In this case the profit-maximizing firm would not produce *any* champagne and the optimal Q_c would be zero. A similar interpretation holds for L_w.

Unfortunately, if we do not already know the optimal Q_c and Q_w (and since we cannot easily eliminate any *un*feasible solutions by graphing), we have ten possible solution points to consider.[3] Recall that at any boundary corner of the feasible region, there will be *at least* a sufficient number of zero-valued variables in the constraint equations so that the number of remaining variables is equal to (or possibly less than) the number of constraints. We have listed the results for all ten possibilities as follows:

Point 1
$V_F = 0, L_c = 0, L_w = 0$
$V_B = \$1.00, V_P = \$.50$
$C = 600(0) + 500(\$1.00) + 150(\$.50)$
   $= \$575$

Point 2
$V_B = 0, L_c = 0, L_w = 0$
$V_F = \$1.00, V_P = -\$.50$
Not a feasible solution, $V_P < 0$

Point 3
$V_p = 0, L_c = 0, L_w = 0$
$V_F = \$.50, V_B = \$.50$
$C = 600(\$.50) + 500(\$.50) + 150(0)$
   $= \$550$

Point 4
$V_F = 0, V_B = 0, L_c = 0$
$V_P = \$2.50, L_w = -\$1.00$
Also not a feasible solution, as
   $L_w < 0$

Point 5
$V_F = 0, V_B = 0, L_w = 0$
Impossible—violates the second
   constraint

Point 6
$V_F = 0, V_P = 0, L_c = 0$
$V_B = \$1.25, L_w = \$.25$
$C = 600(0) + 500(\$1.25) + 150(0)$
   $= \$625$

Point 7
$V_F = 0, V_P = 0, L_w = 0$
$V_B = \$1.00, L_c = -\$.50$
Not a feasible solution, $L_c < 0$

Point 8
$V_B = 0, V_P = 0, L_c = 0$
$V_F = \$.83, L_w = -\$.17$
Not a feasible solution, $L_w < 0$

■ ■ ■ ■ ■ ■
[2] The *net* opportunity cost is the cost incurred by the firm from producing a particular product because the opportunity cost of the fixed resources used up is greater than the profit contribution of the product.
[3] The number of possible solution points is obtained by finding the number of possible combinations of five things taken three at a time, since there are five variables (three of which must be zero at any solution point). The formula for the number of possible combinations of five things taken three at a time is

$$C_3^5 = \frac{5!}{3!2!} = \frac{5 \cdot 4 \cdot 3 \cdot 2 \cdot 1}{3 \cdot 2 \cdot 1 \cdot 2 \cdot 1} = 10.$$

Point 9

$V_B = 0$, $V_P = 0$, $L_w = 0$

$V_F = \$1.00$, $L_c = \$.50$

$C = 600(\$1.00) + 500(0) + 150(0)$
  $= \$600$

Point 10

$V_F = 0$, $V_B = 0$, $V_P = 0$

$L_c = -\$2.50$, $L_w = -\$1.00$

Not a feasible solution, as L_c
  and L_w are negative

By examining the solution values at the ten points, we find that the opportunity cost for the firm is minimized at point 3, where $V_F = \$.50$, $V_B = \$.50$, $V_P = 0$, $L_c = 0$, $L_w = 0$, and $C = \$550$. Moreover, as we interpret the meaning of these values and relate them to the primal solution, it will become obvious that, given the primal solution, we could have immediately picked point 3 as the optimal solution to the dual program.

First, L_c and L_w being equal to zero means that for both champagne and wine, the sum of the opportunity cost valuations placed on the resources necessary to produce one unit of each product is just equal to the respective unit profit contributions of both wine and champagne, and both products will therefore be produced. That V_P is zero indicates that the opportunity cost of using the fixed champagne purifying resources is zero, which means that at the optimal point, there is excess or slack champagne purifying capacity. Thus, since we knew from the primal that at the optimal point, Q_c and Q_w were positive, we then knew that at the optimal point for the dual program, L_c and L_w must be zero. We also knew from the primal program solution that there was excess champagne purifying capacity, so that V_P must be equal to zero.

The value of V_F indicates the marginal effect the fixed fermenting input has on the level of profits for the firm. Thus another unit of the fixed fermenting resource would add $\$.50$ to the total profit of the firm. A similar interpretation of V_B holds for the fixed bottling resource. If the market price of a unit of these resources is below $\$.50$, the firm may wish to make plans to increase its fermenting and/or bottling capacity in the future. It may also wish to reduce its champagne purifying capacity. Note also that the minimum value of C (equal to $\$550$) is equal to the maximum πC, which is as it should be, since it states that the opportunity cost valuation of the fixed resources is equal to their contribution to the firm's profit at the optimal point.

In the next section, we construct and solve the dual program for the primal cost minimization problem discussed earlier in the chapter.

Dual Maximization Problem

In this section we shall discuss the dual to the cost minimization problem presented earlier. The original objective was to minimize

$$C = \$500Q_1 + \$400Q_2,$$

where C was total advertising cost, Q_1 was the number of advertisements in Magazine 1, and Q_2 was the number of advertisements in Magazine 2. The firm wished to minimize C subject to the following constraints:

Age	$20{,}000Q_1 + 30{,}000Q_2 \geq 600{,}000,$
Income	$15{,}000Q_1 + 5{,}000Q_2 \geq 180{,}000,$ and
Stereo ownership	$10{,}000Q_1 + 10{,}000Q_2 \geq 260{,}000.$

These three constraints state that the firm wishes the advertisements to reach at least 600,000 people under 50 years of age, at least 180,000 people with incomes of $40,000 or greater, and at least 260,000 people who already own stereo systems.

For the dual program, the objective now becomes to maximize

$$Z = 600{,}000V_A + 180{,}000V_I + 260{,}000V_O$$

subject to the constraints that

$$20{,}000V_A + 15{,}000V_I + 10{,}000V_O \leq \$500 \qquad \text{(Magazine 1)},$$

and

$$30{,}000V_A + 5{,}000V_I + 10{,}000V_O \leq \$400 \qquad \text{(Magazine 2)}.$$

In this case Z represents an imputed value or cost to the firm of the three age, income, and ownership constraints in the primal program, which is obtained by finding an imputed value that is really the *marginal cost* to the firm of changing each individual constraint. The first constraint for the dual program states that the marginal cost to the firm of the age constraint times 20,000 (the number of people under age 50 that an advertisement in Magazine 1 reaches) plus the marginal cost to the firm of the income constraint times 15,000 (the number of people with annual incomes of at least $40,000 that one advertisement in Magazine 1 reaches) plus the marginal cost to the firm of the stereo ownership constraint times 10,000 (the number of people who own stereo systems who are reached by an advertisement in Magazine 1) must be less than or equal to $500 (the cost of placing one advertisement in Magazine 1). A similar interpretation holds for the second constraint. Basically, the constraints state that the imputed value or marginal cost of each of the primal constraints times the number of people in each category reached by an advertisement in a particular magazine must be less than or equal to the cost of such an ad.

If we transform the constraints into equalities, we obtain

$$20{,}000V_A + 15{,}000V_I + 10{,}000V_O + L_1 = 500,$$

and

$$30,000V_A + 5,000V_I + 10,000V_O + L_2 = 400.$$

The two variables L_1 and L_2 represent the net opportunity cost or relative inefficiency of using Magazine 1 and Magazine 2, respectively, as advertising media. If neither magazine is relatively inefficient, L_1 and L_2 will both be zero and the firm will advertise in both magazines.

At the optimal primal solution, we found $C = \$10,900$, $Q_1 = 5$, $Q_2 = 21$, $S_A = 130,000$, $S_I = 0$, and $S_O = 0$. Since Q_1 and Q_2 are positive, we know that L_1 and L_2 must be zero at the optimal primal solution; that is, both magazines are relatively efficient advertising media. As before, since S_A is positive, there is an excess over the minimum required number of people under age 50 being reached at the optimal point; therefore, the marginal cost of increasing the age constraint, V_A, must be zero at that point. Following a similar line of reasoning, we can also conclude that at the optimal point, V_O and V_I must be positive. Thus we can conclude that the optimal point for the dual program will be found where L_1, L_2, and V_A equal 0.

Substituting these values into the dual constraint equations, we get

$$15,000V_I + 10,000V_O = \$500,$$

and

$$5,000V_I + 10,000V_O = \$400.$$

Subtracting the second equation from the first, we obtain $10,000V_I = \$100$, or $V_I = \$.01$. Substituting $V_I = \$.01$ in the second equation, we find that $V_O = \$.035$. We can now find that optimal $Z = 600,000(0) + 180,000(\$.01) + 260,000(\$.035) = \$10,900$, the minimum value we found for C in the primal program.

To utilize the values obtained for V_I and V_O, the firm must have a reliable estimate of the actual value or marginal benefit to the firm (in terms of increased profit contribution) obtained by increasing the income and stereo ownership constraints, respectively. For example, if the marginal benefit from increasing the income constraint is greater than $\$.01$, the firm should consider increasing this constraint. On the other hand, if the marginal benefit is less than $\$.01$, the firm should consider reducing the minimum number of people it reaches who have annual incomes of at least $\$40,000$. A similar analysis would apply for the stereo ownership constraint.

Summary of How to Construct the Dual Program
In this section we summarize the steps for setting up the dual program from the primal.

1. The dual objective function will be obtained by assigning a valuation variable to each of the primal constraints and summing the values of these variables multiplied by the numbers which represent the maximum or minimum values of their respective primal constraints. If the primal objective function is to be maximized, the dual objective function should be minimized, and vice versa.
2. The dual constraint inequalities are obtained by finding the sum of each *valuation variable* in the dual objective function multiplied by the *coefficient* of the corresponding *primal objective function* variable in the corresponding primal constraint. There will be one dual program constraint for each primal decision (objective function) variable. Also, the direction of the dual program constraint inequalities will be the reverse of those in the primal program constraints.

We present two general examples of the relationships between the primal and the dual linear programs, as follows:

■ Example 1

Primal

Maximize $\pi = \pi_1X_1 + \pi_2X_2$

Subject to $a_1X_1 + b_1X_2 \leq Y_1$,

$\qquad a_2X_1 + b_2X_2 \leq Y_2$,

$\qquad a_3X_1 + b_3X_2 \leq Y_3$,

$\qquad$ and $X_1, X_2 \geq 0$.

Dual

Minimize $C = Y_1V_1 + Y_2V_2 + Y_3V_3$

Subject to $a_1V_1 + a_2V_2 + a_3V_3 \geq \pi_1$,

$\qquad b_1V_1 + b_2V_2 + b_3V_3 \geq \pi_2$,

$\qquad$ and $V_1, V_2, V_3 \geq 0$.

■ Example 2

Primal

Minimize $C = C_1X_1 + C_2X_2$

Subject to $a_1X_1 + b_1X_2 \geq Y_1$,

$\qquad a_2X_1 + b_2X_2 \geq Y_2$,

$\qquad a_3X_1 + b_3X_2 \geq Y_3$,

$\qquad$ and $X_1, X_2 \geq 0$.

Dual

Maximize $Z = Y_1V_1 + Y_2V_2 + Y_3V_3$

Subject to $a_1V_1 + a_2V_2 + a_3V_3 \leq C_1$,

$\qquad b_1V_1 + b_2V_2 + b_3V_3 \leq C_2$,

$\qquad$ and $V_1, V_2, V_3 \geq 0$.

ACTIVITY ANALYSIS: ONE PRODUCT

In this final section of the chapter, we discuss another kind of decision problem for which linear programming is useful. This is a situation where, given fixed amounts of certain inputs, a firm wishes to determine the optimal combination of processes that it should use to produce the greatest quantity possible of a single product. A type of activity analysis is needed in this case, where each of the processes may be considered to be an activity.

For example, suppose a firm can produce a product using any one of three different processes. Using process A, the firm needs three units of capital and one unit of labor to produce one unit of the final product. Using the second process, process B, the firm needs two units of capital and two units of labor to produce one unit of output. If the firm uses process C, it requires one unit of capital and four units of labor to produce one unit of the product. In Figure 7–7 we have drawn three rays, each of which represents a different process. Points A_1, A_2, A_3, and A_4 represent the inputs needed to produce one, two, three, and four units of output, respectively, using process A. A similar interpretation holds for B_1, B_2, B_3, and B_4 and for C_1, C_2, C_3, and C_4. We have also drawn *isoquants* for levels of *output* equal to one, two, three, and four units, where the segment of an isoquant between two production process rays implies that a *combination* of the two processes is being used to produce that particular level of output.

Figure 7–7   Three Production Process Rays and Isoquant Curves for Four Levels of Output

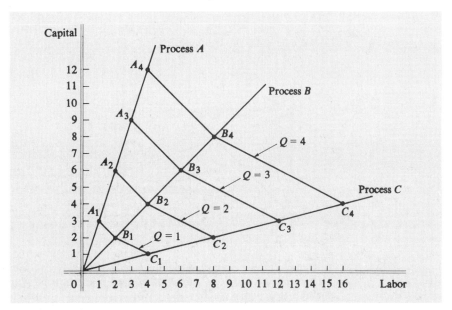

Using process A, the firm needs three units of capital and one unit of labor to produce one unit of the final product. Using process B, the firm needs two units of capital and two units of labor to produce one unit of the final product. Using process C, it needs one unit of capital and four units of labor for each unit of output.

If the firm wishes to find the production process that would minimize the cost of producing a particular level of output, say three units, it can use an isocost and isoquant analysis similar to that presented in Chapter 4. As before, the firm would wish to be on the lowest isocost line possible and still achieve the desired level of production.[4]

In Figure 7–8 we have drawn three isocost lines for cost levels of $90, $126, and $144, respectively, assuming the price of a unit of capital is $18 and the price of a unit of labor is $6. We have also drawn the isoquant curve for $Q = 3$. In this case we see that the least-cost process for producing three units of output is process C, where the quantity used of capital is three units, the quantity used of labor is twelve units, and total cost is $126.

However, suppose the goal of the firm is to produce the maximum level of output possible, given that it has available only four units of capital and ten units of the skilled labor necessary to manufacture this product. In Figure 7–9 we have drawn the three production process rays; the isoquant curves for the production of one, two, and three units of

Figure 7–8   The Least Cost Process for Producing Three Units of Output

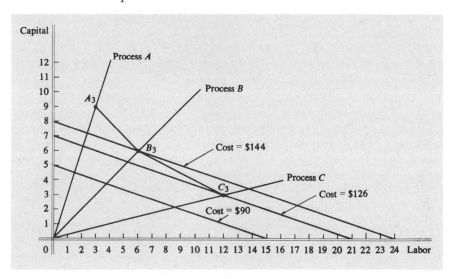

Three isocost lines, for $90, $126, and $144, respectively, are shown here. $A_3B_3C_3$ is the isoquant for three units of output. The least cost combination of inputs for three units of output is at C_3 with a cost of $126.

■ ■ ■ ■ ■ ■

[4] At the optimal point, however, the marginal rate of substitution of labor for capital would not necessarily equal (minus-one times) the ratio of the price of labor to the price of capital. In Figure 7–8 the slope of the isocost line is not equal to the slope of the isoquant at the optimal input combination.

Figure 7–9   Optimal Production Processes, Given Input Constraints

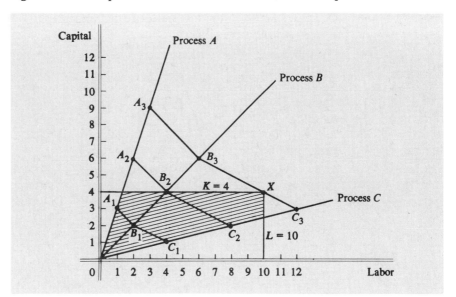

The production process rays are the same as in Figures 7–7 and 7–8. In this case, however, only four units of capital and ten units of labor are available. The feasible region is now indicated by the diagonal lines.

output; and the input constraints. We have also shaded in the feasible region of production.

It is obvious from Figure 7–9 that, given these input constraints, the greatest level of output that this firm can produce is three units, using the combination of process B and process C represented by point X. We can find the number of units to be produced by each process by drawing a line parallel to the process C ray beginning at point X and continuing toward the origin until it touches the process B ray, which it does at B_1 in Figure 7–10. The fact that this line intersects the process B ray at B_1 indicates that one unit of output should be produced using process B and that the remainder, two units in this case, should be produced using process C.

We could also easily solve for the optimal quantity to be produced by each production process using an algebraic method. We can express the objective of the firm as to maximize

$$Q_A + Q_B + Q_C,$$

where

Q_A is the quantity of output produced by process A,
Q_B is the quantity produced by process B, and
Q_C is the quantity produced by process C.

Figure 7–10   Finding the Optimal Production Process Combination

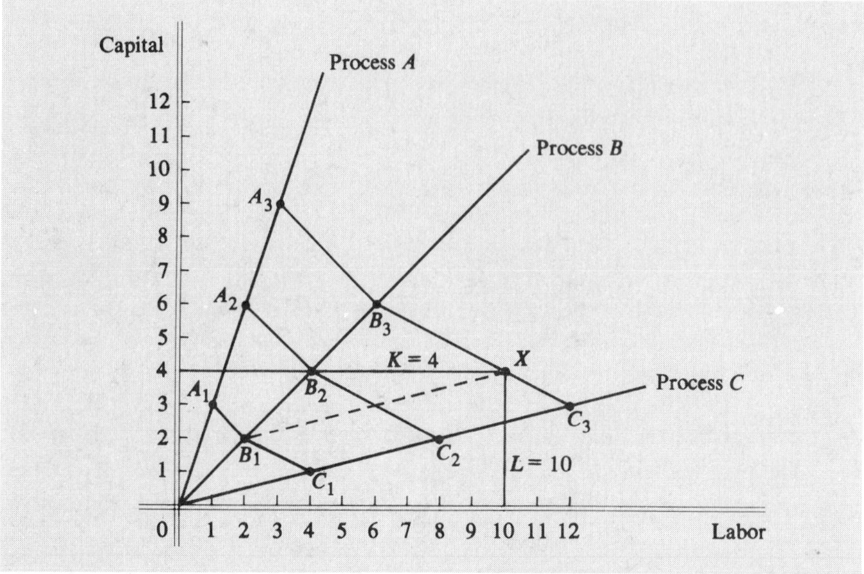

The maximum amount of output that can be produced with four units of capital and ten units of labor is three using a combination of processes B and C (point X). Line segment B_1X indicates that one unit should be produced using process B and two units using process C.

The input constraints will be

Capital $3Q_A + 2Q_B + (1)Q_C \leq 4$, and

Labor $(1)Q_A + 2Q_B + 4Q_C \leq 10$.

The first constraint indicates that the number of units of capital it takes to produce one unit of output using process A times Q_A *plus* the units of capital necessary to produce one unit of output using process B times Q_B *plus* the units of capital necessary to produce one unit of output using process C times Q_C must be less than or equal to four units—the total amount of capital available. A similar interpretation can be given to the labor constraint.

If we add a slack variable for capital in the first equation and a slack variable for labor in the second equation, we get

$$3Q_A + 2Q_B + Q_C + S_K = 4,$$

and

$$Q_A + 2Q_B + 4Q_C + S_L = 10.$$

We know from Figure 7–9 that at the optimal point S_K, S_L, and Q_A equal zero. Substituting these values into the above equations, we obtain

$$2Q_B + \quad Q_C = \quad 4,$$

and

$$2Q_B + 4Q_C = 10,$$

and subtracting the second equation from the first, $-3Q_C = -6$ or $Q_C = 2$. We then can find $Q_B = 1$, which gives us the same solution as we found graphically. A combination of graphical and algebraic methods, where feasible, may offer the easiest and most precise solution.

■ ■ ■ ■ ■ ■ ■ ■   **SUMMARY**

Linear Programming as an Optimizing Tool

In this chapter we have discussed linear programming, a mathematical decision-making tool particularly useful when a firm faces an optimizing problem that can be specified in terms of a linear objective function and linear constraints in the form of inequalities. The primal program directly specifies the objective of the firm in terms of the decision variables, whereas the dual program gives information regarding various opportunity costs connected with the problem. However, as we demonstrated, it is possible to find the optimal values of the decision variables using either the primal or the dual program.

In this chapter we have demonstrated only the simplest algebraic and graphical methods of solving linear programs in order to give some examples of how this tool can be used by business without being too complex. In many real-world situations with more variables than those in our examples, decision makers are likely to utilize more sophisticated algebraic techniques, such as the simplex method, as well as the computer. Moreover, linear programming is only one of a class of mathematical tools called mathematical programming. These other techniques, including nonlinear programming and dynamic programming, are beyond the scope of this book, but the interested reader can learn more about them from the sources in the list of references at the end of this chapter.

■ ■ ■ ■ ■ ■ ■ ■ ■ ■ ■ ■   **Questions**   ■ ■ ■ ■ ■ ■ ■ ■ ■ ■ ■ ■

1. Compare the techniques of linear programming and calculus. For what types of decision problems is calculus more useful? For what types of decision problems is linear programming more useful?

2. Give some examples of specific business decisions where linear programming could be useful.
3. Why is maximizing the *total profit contribution* of the firm's inputs equivalent to maximizing its total profit in the short run?
4. What type of information does one get by solving the dual program that one does not obtain by solving the primal program? Give an example.
5. Why may the dual problem be easier to solve than the primal problem? How can the optimal values of the primal problem be found from those of the dual? Give an example.

■ ■ ■ ■ ■ ■ ■ ■ ■ ■ ■ ■ ■ ■   **Problems**   ■ ■ ■ ■ ■ ■ ■ ■ ■ ■ ■ ■ ■

1. Polynesian Pineapples, Inc., is a company that imports raw pineapples. It markets two products, canned pineapple slices and raw pineapples. Polynesian has capacity limitations in three areas: warehouse space, canning facilities, and crating facilities. A raw pineapple requires .6 of a unit of warehouse space before it is shipped, .2 of a unit of crating facilities, and no canning facilities. One can of pineapple slices requires .3 of a unit of warehouse space, .2 of a unit of crating facilities, and .1 of a unit of canning facilities.

   The total available monthly amount of warehouse space is 1,200,000 units; of crating facilities, 600,000 units; and of canning facilities, 250,000 units. The profit contribution is $.20 per raw pineapple and $.25 per can of slices.
   a. Find the monthly profit-maximizing quantities of raw and canned pineapple, respectively, for Polynesian Pineapple.
   b. What is the total monthly profit contribution from pineapples in part a?

2. Holiday on Wheels (HOW) manufactures two types of recreational vehicles. One is a trailer that is towed behind a car or pickup, and the other is a motorized vehicle that moves under its own power. HOW is trying to determine the optimal combination of trailers and motor homes to produce per day, given that three of the inputs (power train assembly, paint and trim line, and body assembly) needed to produce these products are available in limited amounts. Manufacture of one motor home requires 2.0 hours of power train assembly capacity, 2.5 hours of paint and trim capacity, and 3.0 hours of body assembly capacity, whereas the production of one trailer requires only 2.0 hours of paint and trim capacity and 2.0 hours of body assembly capacity.

   HOW has available on a daily basis 300 hours of power train assembly capacity, 500 hours of paint and trim capacity, and 540 hours of body assembly capacity. The profit contribution of a motor home is $4,000, while that of a trailer is $3,000.

a. Using both algebraic and graphical solution methods, find the profit-maximizing combination of motor homes and travel trailers that HOW should produce daily.

b. What is HOW's daily contribution to profit at the optimal point?

3. Set up the dual program for Holiday on Wheels in Problem 2.

a. What useful information would Holiday on Wheels obtain by solving the dual program? Explain.

b. What is the optimal solution to this dual program?

c. State the economic significance of the values of each of the dual variables at the optimal point.

4. Hill Country Concrete, Inc. (HCC) does asphalt and concrete paving. HCC is now trying to make a short-run decision on the optimal mix of asphalt and concrete paving, given capacity constraints involving road grader, roller, and power trowel time. The maximum number of hours of road grader time available per month is 640; of roller time, 1,500; of power trowel time, 150. It takes 2 hours of road grader time and 5 hours of roller time for each 1,000 square feet of asphalt paving; and each 1,000 square feet of concrete paving requires 2 hours of road grader time, 3 hours of roller time, and .5 hour of power trowel time. The profit contribution for 1,000 square feet of asphalt paving is $200; for 1,000 square feet of concrete paving it is $300.

a. How many square feet of concrete paving and of asphalt paving should HCC do per month to maximize profit? Why? Use both graphical and algebraic solution methods.

b. What is the total monthly profit contribution from paving for Hill Country Concrete?

5. Set up the dual program for Hill Country Concrete in Problem 4.

a. What economic interpretation can be given to each of the dual decision variables, the objective function, and the constraints?

b. At the optimal point, what is the opportunity cost associated with using the road grader? The roller? The power trowel?

c. At the optimal point, what is the net opportunity cost to HCC of doing asphalt paving? Of doing concrete paving? Why?

6. A firm that manufactures and retails a variety of women's clothes from the moderately priced department store lines to the more expensive boutique styles is expanding its market and, accordingly, is trying to determine how many stores of each type it will lease. The firm wishes to lease its department store space in large shopping areas, such as larger malls. On the other hand, the boutique stores that the firm wishes to lease are in small, elite shopping centers in very high income areas of cities. The choice department stores lease for $10,000 per month, and boutique stores in good locations lease for $2,000 per month.

Given its product mix, the firm wishes to be in locations such that *at least* 10,500 customers under 45 years of age and at least 1,150 customers with annual household incomes over $50,000 will, on the average, visit its stores daily. Moreover, the firm believes that 420 people less than 45 years of age and 5 people with incomes over $50,000 will visit each of the department stores daily, while an average of 20 people less than 45 years of age and 10 people with annual incomes over $50,000 will visit each of its boutique stores daily.

  a. Given the above information, how many of each type of store should the firm lease if it wishes to minimize leasing costs?
  b. What is the total cost to the firm of leasing these stores at its optimal point?
  c. What is the marginal cost to the firm of increasing the age constraint? The income constraint?
  d. Given your answers in part c, do you think the firm should consider changing the income or age constraints and/or other alternatives to leasing stores? Why or why not?

7. A firm can manufacture its product using any one or a combination of three processes. Production of 1 unit of output per month using process A requires 10 units of capital and 2 units of labor, whereas production of 1 unit of output using process B requires 5 units of capital and 5 units of labor, and production of 1 unit of output using process C requires 3 units of capital and 10 units of labor. Since this product is classified top secret by the government and all inputs must receive a security clearance, there are fixed amounts of capital and of labor available to the firm in the short run. In fact, at this point in time, the firm has available on a monthly basis 24 units of labor and 40 units of capital.

  a. Find the maximum quantity of output that this firm can produce per month under these constraints.
  b. How much of this output is produced using each of the three available processes?

8. A commercial feedlot operation, Best-Fed Beef, Inc. (BFB) is trying to determine the least cost combination of two types of feed that will meet the nutritional requirements of its cattle. The first kind of feed is a grain mixture, and each ton of grain contains, on the average, 200 pounds of protein, 1,000 pounds of carbohydrates, and 300 pounds of roughage plus 500 pounds of miscellaneous minerals, vitamins, fats, and water. The second feed is a type of silage, and an average ton of silage contains 40 pounds of protein, 400 pounds of carbohydrates, and 600 pounds of roughage, as well as a substantial amount of water and some minerals, fats, and vitamins.

  BFB believes that its cattle need a minimum of 1,200 pounds of protein, 8,000 pounds of carbohydrates, and 3,600 pounds of roughage daily. The grain mixture costs $80 per ton, and the silage costs $30 per ton.

  a. Find the least cost combination of grain and silage that will meet the daily nutritional requirements of BFB's cattle.

b. What is the total cost of the optimal combination of feeds found in part a?

c. Set up the dual program, find its optimal solution, and explain the economic significance of the values you found for the dual decision variables.

d. How would the information that you found in part c be useful to BFB? Why?

9. Malibu Motor Company is trying to decide the optimal number of two automobile models to maintain in inventory. Model 1 is a mid-sized car, and Model 2 is a luxury sports car. The company has a showroom and lot space constraint, a financing constraint, and a constraint on the number of Model 2 cars that the manufacturer will allow it to keep in inventory. One car of Model 1 type takes up 600 square feet of showroom or lot space, and 1 car of Model 2 type takes up 450 square feet of space. The firm would need $3,200 financing for each car of Model 1 and $6,400 for each car of Model 2. Moreover, Malibu can keep a maximum number of 40 Model 2 cars on hand in inventory. The maximum total amount of showroom and lot space available is 60,000 square feet, while the maximum total amount of financing available is $400,000. The profit contribution is $1,000 per Model 1 car and $3,000 per Model 2 car.

a. Using *both* algebraic and graphical solution methods, find the optimal combination of Model 1 and Model 2 cars for Malibu Motors.

b. What is the total profit contribution at the point you found in part a? What are the values of all slack variables?

c. What is the marginal value to the firm of one more square foot of showroom or lot space? Of one more dollar of financing?

10. Intergalactic Products, Inc., manufactures two different products, surgical gloves and toy balloons. It has capacity limitations on three inputs in the production process: latex heating, injection molding, and sterile packaging. Specifically, it has 780 units of latex heating capacity, 630 units of injection molding capacity, and 180 units of sterile packaging capacity available per day. Both surgical gloves and balloons are sold to distributors in boxes of 500. For IPI, profit contribution per box of gloves is $100, while that per box of balloons is $40. Production of one box of surgical gloves requires 2.4 units of latex heating, 2.8 units of injection molding, and one unit of sterile packaging. Production of one box of balloons requires 4 units of latex heating, 2 units of injection molding, and no sterile packaging.

a. Using both algebraic and graphical solution methods, find the optimal combination of surgical gloves and toy balloons that IPI must produce to maximize its total profit. What are the values of the slack variables at this point?

b. What is the total profit contribution for IPI at the point you found in part a?

c. How much would the per unit profit contribution of surgical gloves have to decrease to change the optimal combination of surgical gloves and toy balloons?

This problem can be solved with Decision Assistant

11. Abe Jackson learned the cabinetmaking business from his father, as his father did before him. Because pride is built into every cabinet Abe and his crew make, demand always seems to exceed supply. In addition, the business expands slowly because Abe himself carefully selects each worker. Abe often says he would rather lose a sale than produce a cabinet that his grandfather could not be proud of. The summer of this year has proved to be no exception with regard to demand.

Abe's son, Robert, who has been away at college, is working in the shop as he has in summers past. However, this year Robert brings more to his summer job than just his skills in cabinetmaking. Having just completed a college course in linear programming, Robert knows he can assist his father even more this year. In previous years, production scheduling and determination of the product mix has been completed by Abe, who relied on his past experiences and intuition. This year Abe has decided to produce equal quantities (5 per day) of each type of cabinet. Robert thinks he can do better, although it would be no easy task to convince his father there might be a "better way."

Before setting out to convince his father, Robert gathers the following data about the shop's operation:

■ Two basic styles of cabinets are being produced: standard and designer. Standard cabinets are cut, sanded, stained, and varnished in the shop. Designer cabinets are produced the same as standard cabinets with the addition of an extra step of applying antiquing. The standard cabinet has a profit contribution of $12 while the designer cabinet contributes $9 in profit.

■ All cutting and sanding is done in the preparation department. It takes 1 hour to cut either type of cabinet. A total of 10 hours per day could be devoted to the cutting and sanding of cabinets.

■ Staining and finishing is done in the finishing department where a total of 32 hours per day are available for these activities. It takes 4 hours to stain and finish each standard cabinet and 2 hours to stain and finish each designer cabinet. (Designer cabinets actually take less stain since they will be antiqued.)

■ Between the staining and finishing steps in the finishing department, each designer cabinet goes to the antiquing department where skilled craftspeople apply a special antiquing. A total of 21 hours per day are available in the antiquing department. It requires 3 hours for each designer cabinet to go through this step.

Armed with this data, Robert feels confident he can improve upon the shop's performance. Do you agree? Use the linear programming (graphical method) tool in the *Managerial Economics Decision Assistant* to help you answer the following questions:

a. How many cabinets of each type will Robert recommend be produced?

b. How much profit will the shop make under Abe's plan (calculate manually) and under Robert's plan?

c. Under Robert's proposed solution, how many "extra" hours (if any) will be available in each of the three departments: preparation, finishing, and antiquing?

Use the linear programming (simplex method) tool in the *Managerial Economics Decision Assistant* to assist you with working the dual program to answer the following questions (you will need to restate your constraints and objective function):

d. If the business were to expand, which department(s) would need to be expanded?

e. How much should Abe be willing to pay to expand each department?

■ ■ ■ ■ ■ ■ ■ ■ ■ ■ **Selected References** ■ ■ ■ ■ ■ ■ ■ ■ ■ ■

Chiang, Alpha C. *Fundamental Methods of Mathematical Economics*, 3d ed. New York: McGraw-Hill, 1984, Chapters 19–21.

Childress, Robert L. *Mathematics for Managerial Decisions.* Englewood Cliffs, N.J.: Prentice-Hall, 1974, Chapters 5–8.

Dorfman, Robert. "Mathematical, or Linear, Programming," *American Economic Review*, XLIII (December 1953), pp. 797–825.

Garvin, W. W., H. W. Crandall, J. B. John, and R. A. Spellman. "Applications of Linear Programming in the Oil Industry," *Management Science* III (July 1957), pp. 407–430.

Kamien, Morton I., and Nancy L. Schwartz. *Dynamic Optimization: The Calculus of Variations and Optimal Control in Economics and Management.* New York: North Holland, 1981.

Silberberg, Eugene. *The Structure of Economic Analysis*, 2d. ed. New York: McGraw-Hill, 1990, Chapter 14.

Takayama, Akira. *Mathematical Economics.* Hinsdale, Ill.: Dryden Press, 1974, Chapter 1.

Integrating Case 2A

Frontier Concrete Products Company[1]

Frontier Concrete Products Company is planning to open a new concrete plant in another city. The owner-manager of the company is currently trying to determine the optimal size plant to build, given the estimated cost and revenue data presented in Table 1.

The data in Table 1 show that Frontier Concrete Company has determined that there are at least 4 different combinations of plant size and labor that would enable the firm to produce a given level of output. Since the company believes that its optimal level of output will be between 30 and 60 cubic yards of concrete per hour, it is considering only 12 different plant sizes.

In Table 1 the company has prepared the input figures in terms of standardized units of capital and standardized units of labor. A unit of capital is estimated to increase the expenses (depreciation, repairs and maintenance, interest expense, and utilities) of the firm by $18,000 per year, based on a year consisting of 260 eight-hour working days. The estimated cost to the firm for one unit of labor is $7.00 per hour. Other costs—for raw materials and delivery, which were not included in Table 1—are estimated to be as follows (*per cubic yard* of concrete produced):

Aggregate (rock)	$3.34
Cement	$7.50
Delivery costs	$4.00

The company has also estimated the demand for its product, and these figures are presented in Table 2.

■■■■■■

[1] This case is based on production and cost information from an antitrust case in the ready-mix concrete industry.

Table 1   Various Combinations of Capital and Labor Needed to Produce 30, 45, and 60 Cubic Yards of Concrete per Hour

Q = 30 Cubic Yards per Hour

Plant 1	Plant 2	Plant 3	Plant 4
K = 4	K = 3	K = 2	K = 1
L = 1	L = 2	L = 5	L = 10

Q = 45 Cubic Yards per Hour

Plant 5	Plant 6	Plant 7	Plant 8
K = 6	K = 4.5	K = 3	K = 1.5
L = 1.5	L = 3	L = 7.5	L = 15

Q = 60 Cubic Yards per Hour

Plant 9	Plant 10	Plant 11	Plant 12
K = 8	K = 6	K = 4	K = 2
L = 2	L = 4	L = 10	L = 20

Table 2   Estimated Demand for Frontier Concrete Produced by the New Plant

Cubic Yards Per Hour	Price Per Cubic Yard
20	$24.00
30	22.34
40	21.26
50	20.40
60	19.66
70	19.00
80	18.38

■ ■ ■ ■ ■ ■ ■ ■ ■ ■ ■ ■ ■ ■ **Questions** ■ ■ ■ ■ ■ ■ ■ ■ ■ ■ ■ ■ ■ ■

1. How do Frontier's total manufacturing costs (exclusive of raw materials and delivery costs) vary for each of the four capital-labor combinations given, as output is increased from 30, to 45, to 60 cubic yards per hour? Does it appear that this production function has increasing, decreasing, or constant returns to scale?

2. What are the total costs, including raw materials and delivery costs, for each of the capital-labor combinations in Question 1?

3. Which capital-labor combination is a least-cost combination of inputs for each of the three levels of output?

4. Frontier's owner has plotted a curve showing how the minimum total delivered cost for each output varies when all inputs—including capital, labor, raw materials, and delivery costs—are variable. What should this curve be called? Given the above data, what does it look like?

5. What are the long-run average cost figures and the long-run marginal cost figures that correspond to the curve drawn in question 4?

6. What are the firm's total revenue schedules and marginal revenue schedules, given the information presented in Table 2?

7. Suppose that Frontier had decided to build Plant 10. Suppose also that of the $108,000 annual capital expenses connected with the plant, $96,000 were fixed costs and the remainder were variable. If all labor costs are assumed to be variable and a yard of concrete includes the average variable raw material and delivery costs stated previously, what is the break-even point for this plant, assuming the price of concrete is $20 per cubic yard?

8. Based on the values computed in question 7, what is the profit-maximizing level of output per hour for Frontier Concrete's new plant?

9. Based on the values computed in questions 5 and 6, what is the profit-maximizing level of output per hour for Frontier Concrete if all inputs are variable? (Assume $LAC = \$16.17$ for any level of output per hour.)

10. If the cost figures presented here are *accounting costs*, what *types* of adjustments do you think would be needed to transform them into *economic cost* figures?

Integrating Case 2B

Shanghai Magnificent Harmony
Foundry I

Mr. X. C. Fei is in charge of export sales analysis for a large firm in the People's Republic of China, Shanghai Magnificent Harmony Foundry (SMHF). Most of the foundry's cast-iron output has been destined for the domestic market, principally the locomotive, rail-car, and machinery industries. It has been suggested to Mr. Fei that he investigate the overseas market for manhole covers, a product that is simple to manufacture and for which there seems to be endless demand. The target market he has chosen is the United States. Mr Fei's research assistant has found that India is currently the main source of cast-iron manhole covers that are imported into the United States and that many small Indian foundries make the product. Further, competition is always forthcoming from other less-developed countries, since the United States has a favorable trade policy for such producers.

It is evident to Mr. Fei that SMHF will have to meet the world market price for the covers. In addition, he believes that the amount of output he wishes to sell can be marketed in the United States without cutting price below the world level. Currently, the covers are selling for $0.48 per pound, landed at U.S. West Coast ports. The tariff on such castings is $.02 per lb., but less-developed country producers can qualify for trade preferences that will reduce the tariff to zero. India and certain other producers have successfully qualified for the reduction.

A further consideration that has troubled Mr. Fei is the price of iron ore, which China imports. He expects that while some of his foreign competitors that do not import iron ore will not experience a change in production costs in the near future, his company may have to pay higher ore prices, which could increase the raw materials cost of cast manhole covers by as much as 20 percent.

The central management committee of SMHF has told Mr. Fei that 6,500 short tons per year (one short ton = 2,000 lbs.) of casting capacity can be utilized for the manhole cover exports but that this type of production will have to carry allocated fixed overhead in the amount of 1,500,000 Renminbi Yuan (RY) annually. The plant must sell all dollar proceeds from its exports to the Chinese government at an official fixed rate of 4.8 RY to the U.S. dollar. The government is not expected to change this rate for at least three years.

The committee has requested that Mr. Fei prepare a report on the manhole cover exports and has directed that he specifically analyze three cases. First, the best-case scenario, which conforms to (a) obtaining U.S. trade preferences and paying no tariff and (b) not being faced with the 20 percent materials cost increase; second, a case in which the trade preferences are *not* granted, but materials costs remain at their current level; and third, the worst-case scenario, in which the firm does not obtain the trade preferences and also faces a 20 percent increase in raw materials cost.

Fei has been instructed to render the analysis in U.S. dollars, since materials, freight, and the final product are normally priced in dollars in the international market. For the best-case scenario, he has estimated the following unit costs per pound:

Direct materials	$0.10
Fuel	0.11
Direct labor	0.08
Variable selling expenses	0.03

Mr. Fei knows that the average U.S. manhole cover weighs 160 pounds and will use this figure to determine how many he can export. Currently, he believes he will be able to sell all of the covers he can make to U.S. buyers, and he foresees no new investment in plant and equipment to produce the output. He has checked into ocean freight rates and figures the transport cost per pound of finished product will be 10 U.S. cents.

■ ■ ■ ■ ■ ■ ■ ■ ■ ■ ■ ■ ■ ■   **Questions**   ■ ■ ■ ■ ■ ■ ■ ■ ■ ■ ■ ■ ■ ■

1. Complete the best-case scenario for Mr. Fei's report.
2. Explain how the results would change if materials costs were to remain constant but SMHF could not obtain the U.S. trade preference to eliminate the $.02 per lb. tariff. (Assume SHMF "absorbs" the tariff in its selling price to keep the landed U.S. price at the $0.48 level.)
3. Complete the worst-case scenario, assuming that the tariff must be paid *and* that materials costs rise by 20 percent.

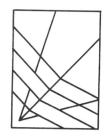

Markets and the Behavior of the Firm

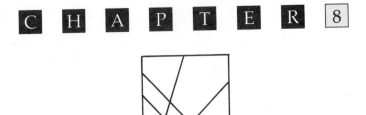

Perfect Competition and Monopoly: The Limiting Cases

To determine its revenue and therefore its profit-maximizing level of output and product price, the individual business firm must develop some notion of the demand for its product. Certain basic demand propositions were reviewed in Chapter 2 and reintroduced in Chapter 6 in connection with our discussion of the conditions for profit maximization. The present chapter deals exclusively with two theoretical market models that represent the opposite ends of a very broad spectrum of possible market situations in which a given firm might find itself.

The first limiting case is *perfect competition,* a market structure where the firm takes market price as given and therefore needs only to determine what cost/output combination maximizes its net revenue or profit. Our second limiting case is *monopoly,* where there is only one seller of a particular product and the *market* demand curve of consumers is the *firm's* demand curve. Most firms in the real world have to deal with market conditions that lie between the two extremes of perfect competition and monopoly, but we shall leave these other market structures until Chapters 9 and 10. In this chapter we shall concentrate on gaining some insights into how firms in the two extreme situations should act to maximize profits, so that it will be easier to understand how firms that are between the two extremes behave.

■ ■ ■ ■ ■ ■ ■ ■ ■ PERFECT COMPETITION AND ITS SETTING

We have noted that the perfectly competitive firm is a *price taker* in the sense that it views market price as a given upon which it can have no

Under **perfect competition**, there are many small firms, and the individual firm takes the market price as a given.

effect. We must now take a closer look, from the viewpoint of the firm, at the market situation that produces such an outcome. Normally, **perfect competition** is described as a product market structure characterized by the following set of conditions:

1. There is a very *large number of buyers and sellers* in the market.
2. The *product* of each seller is identical to that of every other seller *(homogeneous product)*.
3. There are *no artificial interferences* with the activities of the buyers and sellers (for example, government price controls).
4. All buyers and sellers *have perfect knowledge* of market conditions and of any changes in market conditions that occur.
5. Over the long run (the period of time in which it is possible to build or get rid of a plant), there is *freedom of entry* into or *exit* from the industry.

These conditions have some very important implications as far as the operation of the perfectly competitive model is concerned. For example, the existence of a very large number of buyers and sellers in the market (condition 1) and the situation that products of all firms are identical (condition 2) are the basis for the proposition that the individual firm takes market price as given. If a firm knows (condition 4) that there are many other sellers of a product identical to its own and that there is nothing it or anyone else can do to interfere with the activities of such sellers (condition 3), it will conclude that if it raises price, it will lose all its customers to the other firms, since there is no reason to assume that other firms will also raise price. (There are too many firms to be able to get together and effectively agree on restricting quantity supplied and raising price, as many national farm organizations have discovered.) On the other hand, because there are many buyers in the market willing to pay the going price, the firm has no reason to *lower* price either. In a very important sense, the assumption of perfect competition makes the individual firm insignificant with respect to the total market for its product, and that is why it must take price as given.

In a market that is characterized by **free entry**, profit serves the function of drawing new firms into the industry when greater than normal and causing some firms to leave when less than normal.

Our assumptions also ensure one other result: that firms will enter or leave the perfectly competitive industry over the long run depending on the level of profit in that industry. If there are no artificial barriers to entry and there is perfect knowledge of market conditions, there will be incentives for new firms to be established when the industry is more profitable than other industries. When profit is less than in other industries, some firms will leave the industry. We identify the level of profit necessary to keep the number of firms in the industry constant as "normal profit." If there is **free entry** in *any market structure*, greater than normal profit will lead to entry, and less than normal profit will cause firms to leave. The result, of course, is that industries characterized by freedom of entry will tend toward only normal profit over the long run, which we can think of as a rate of return on investment similar to that attainable in closely related industries. Finally, as stated in Chapter 5, we shall consider normal profit to be a *cost of production*, since over the long run, there would be no output produced if the firm's owners did not receive at least a normal return on investment. Thus all of our cost curves for the firm will include normal profit as an opportunity cost.

What we have said thus far allows us to easily paint a verbal picture of the perfectly competitive model. It is a market structure where individual firms, each of which is insignificant with respect to the total market, go about maximizing profit based on a fixed market price and tend over the long run to attain only normal profit. We can, however, supply a good deal more detail regarding how all of this comes about, and we shall do so in the sections that follow.

Market Demand versus Firm Demand

The demand curve for the homogeneous product of a perfectly competitive *industry* (i.e., all of the firms that produce the same product) is determined by the preferences of consumers. At any given point in time, if this demand curve is "normal" in the economic sense, it will be characterized by an inverse relationship between the going market price for the product and the quantity consumers are willing to purchase per unit of time (that is, price must be lowered to entice consumers to buy a larger quantity). The demand curve in Figure 8–1, D_i, conforms to such a case. The supply curve of the industry, S_i, shows the amounts that producers are willing to place on the market at various prices. In the short run, we expect such a curve to exhibit a direct relationship between price and the quantity supplied, since production cost per unit (particularly marginal cost, as we saw in Chapter 5) rises as the firms in the industry near their physical capacity per month. An equilibrium price, P_e, is established where the amount of output that producers are willing to put on the market per month is exactly equal to that which consumers are willing to buy.

It is obvious in Figure 8–1 that price P_e is the only price at which the quantity that producers are willing to place on the market is equal to that which consumers are willing to buy. Further, we can explain a tendency for this price to be established and hold as the "going price" by considering what would happen if some other price were temporarily in effect. At P_2, for example, producers would want to put Q_s per month on the market, while consumers would be willing to buy only Q_d. There would be a surplus of $Q_s - Q_d$ units of output in the market, producers' inventories would pile up, and producers would cut price in order to sell more product. This would be the case for any price above P_e. It can easily be verified that for prices *lower* than P_e, the quantity consumers would want to buy in the market would exceed the quantity producers would wish to

Figure 8–1   Industry Demand and Supply

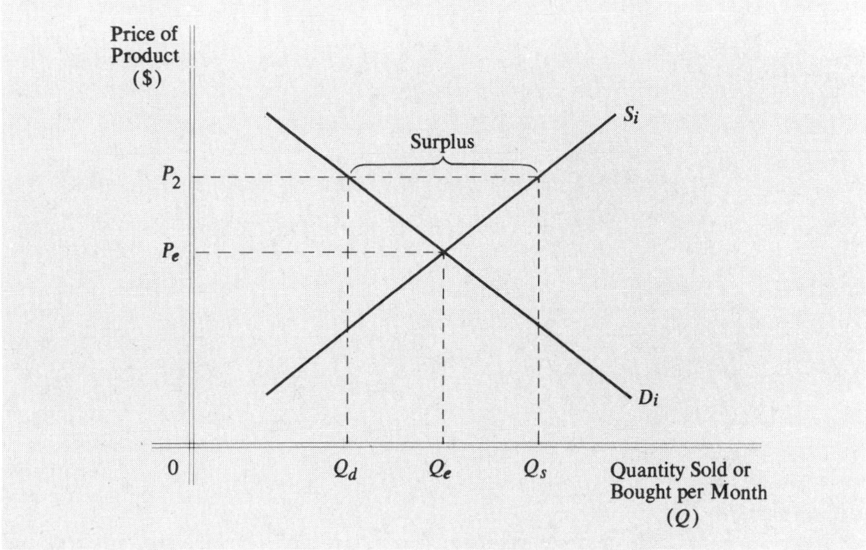

Equilibrium in this market occurs at P_e, Q_e. Any price higher than P_e will result in a surplus and lead to price reductions. Prices below P_e will result in shortages and price increases.

supply. Consequently, buying activity would reduce producers' inventories and lead to rising prices as consumers bid for the insufficient quantity of output coming into the market. (Use Figure 8–1 to illustrate this situation by drawing a horizontal line over to the S_i and D_i curves for some price lower than P_e. Identify for yourself the shortage in quantity supplied that exists for the lower price.)

An **equilibrium price** is one that equates quantity demanded in the market with quantity supplied so that there is no surplus or shortage of the product being traded.

It is clear that the **equilibrium price,** P_e, is the only price that can exist for any length of time when market conditions are such as those given by demand curve D_i and supply curve S_i.

It is important to note that D_i, the demand curve of the perfectly competitive industry in Figure 8–1, is *not* the demand curve facing an individual firm in that industry. Remember, we established early in this chapter that the individual competitive firm takes the market price, P_e, as given and believes it cannot by itself have any effect on this price. Figure 8–2 illustrates the relationship of the market demand curve to that of the individual firm. In panel (b) we see the same market situation that was depicted in Figure 8–1. Panel (a), however, shows the demand curve for the product as it is perceived by the individual perfectly competitive firm. Since the firm takes the market price as given, the horizontal line P_eD_f in panel (a) is its demand curve. Note that the Q axis of panel (a) measures the firm's output in *units* of output per month, whereas the Q axis of

Figure 8–2   Relation of Perfectly Competitive Firm's Demand Curve to the Industry

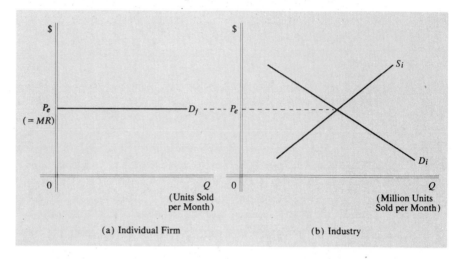

(a) Individual Firm   (b) Industry

The perfectly competitive firm views its demand curve as horizontal at the market price of its product.

panel (b) measures market quantities sold and bought in *millions* of units per month. The point is that movements along P_eD_f in panel (a) are so insignificant that they do not materially affect the equilibrium price and quantity of panel (b). This is a realistic notion as long as the output of the firm is very small with respect to the total market for the product.

From the standpoint of profit maximization, the situation depicted in panel (a) has some further implications for the perfectly competitive firm. First of all, as we know from Chapter 2, the horizontal line P_eD_f is both the marginal and the average revenue curve for the firm, since revenue per unit never changes as output is increased.[1] Finally, since MR is the

---

[1] More formally, we know

$$TR = P \cdot Q$$

$$MR = \frac{dTR}{dQ} = P + Q\frac{dP}{dQ},$$

where

$$P \text{ is constant,}$$

$$\frac{dP}{dQ} = 0, \text{ and}$$

$$MR = P.$$

Also, $AR = \frac{TR}{Q} = \frac{P(Q)}{Q} = P$, the same constant.

rate of change of TR, the TR curve must be a straight line emanating from the origin, as in break-even analysis.

Profit Maximization Under Perfect Competition

If a perfectly competitive firm has short-run cost curves similar to those depicted in Chapter 5 and is incurring greater than normal profit, we can easily illustrate its profit-maximizing output using either marginal and average cost and revenue curves or total cost and total revenue curves. In Figure 8–3, panel (a), we see the firm's total cost and total revenue curves along with a net revenue or profit curve, $T\pi = TR - TC$. The firm maximizes profit at Q_e, where the $T\pi$ curve has its peak and where the slope of the TR curve, MR, equals that of the TC curve, SMC, as we learned in Chapter 6. In panel (b) the Q axis is identical to that of panel (a), but the $ axis measures per unit cost and revenue rather than total cost and total revenue. At Q in panel (b), $SMC = MR$ and economic profit per unit is $(P_e - C)$. Total profit may be calculated by taking the per-unit profit $(P_e - C)$ times the number of units sold ($0Q_e$ or CC') and is, therefore, equal to the area of rectangle $CP_eP'C'$. No output greater or less than Q_e will yield a profit as large as the one that exists at Q_e when the market price is P_e.

The firm in Figure 8–3 has profit greater than normal at Q_e, since $T\pi > 0$. This is a feasible result for a perfectly competitive firm in the *short run*, since the number of firms in the industry remains constant and the entry of new producers cannot drive price downward. However, market conditions could easily produce three other possible results for the perfectly competitive firm:

1. normal profit,
2. operating loss, or
3. cessation of operations (temporary shutdown).

Panels (a) and (b) of Figure 8–4 provide total and average or per-unit curves for a firm with only normal profit in the short run. Panels (c) and (d) do the same for a firm operating at a loss. Note that in each diagram, the condition $SMC = MR$ holds at the equilibrium output, Q_e. *In panels (a) and (b), $T\pi = 0$, $C = P_e$, and there is only normal profit. In panels (c) and (d), $T\pi < 0$, $C > P_e$, and there is a loss equal to $0L$ in the upper diagram or to the area $CP_eP'C'$ in the lower diagram.*

An important point in this latter case is that the operating loss at output Q_e, $0L$ in panel (c), is less than fixed cost, $0F$. Since fixed cost is $0F$ even when output is zero, the firm should shut down only when $0L$ exceeds $0F$ (or $0F'$), as we learned in Chapter 6. You should be able to verify that the firm in Figure 8–5 will minimize its losses by temporarily shutting down.

In the short run, the firm that is a loss minimizer as well as a profit maximizer will not produce when price is below AVC but will produce at

Figure 8–3   Perfectly Competitive Firm with Profit Greater than Normal

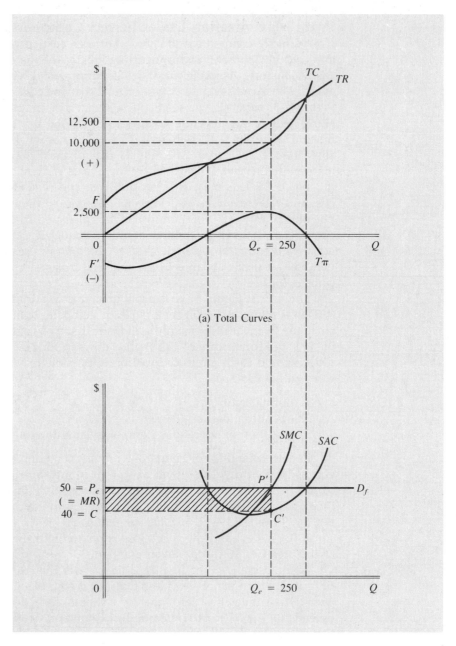

(a) Total Curves

The firm maximizes profit where $SMC = MR$, which corresponds to the peak of the $T\pi$ curve in panel (a). In panel (b) profit is equal to the area of the shaded rectangle, or $(P - SAC)$ multiplied by Q_e.

Figure 8–4   Normal Profit and Operating Loss Under Perfect Competition

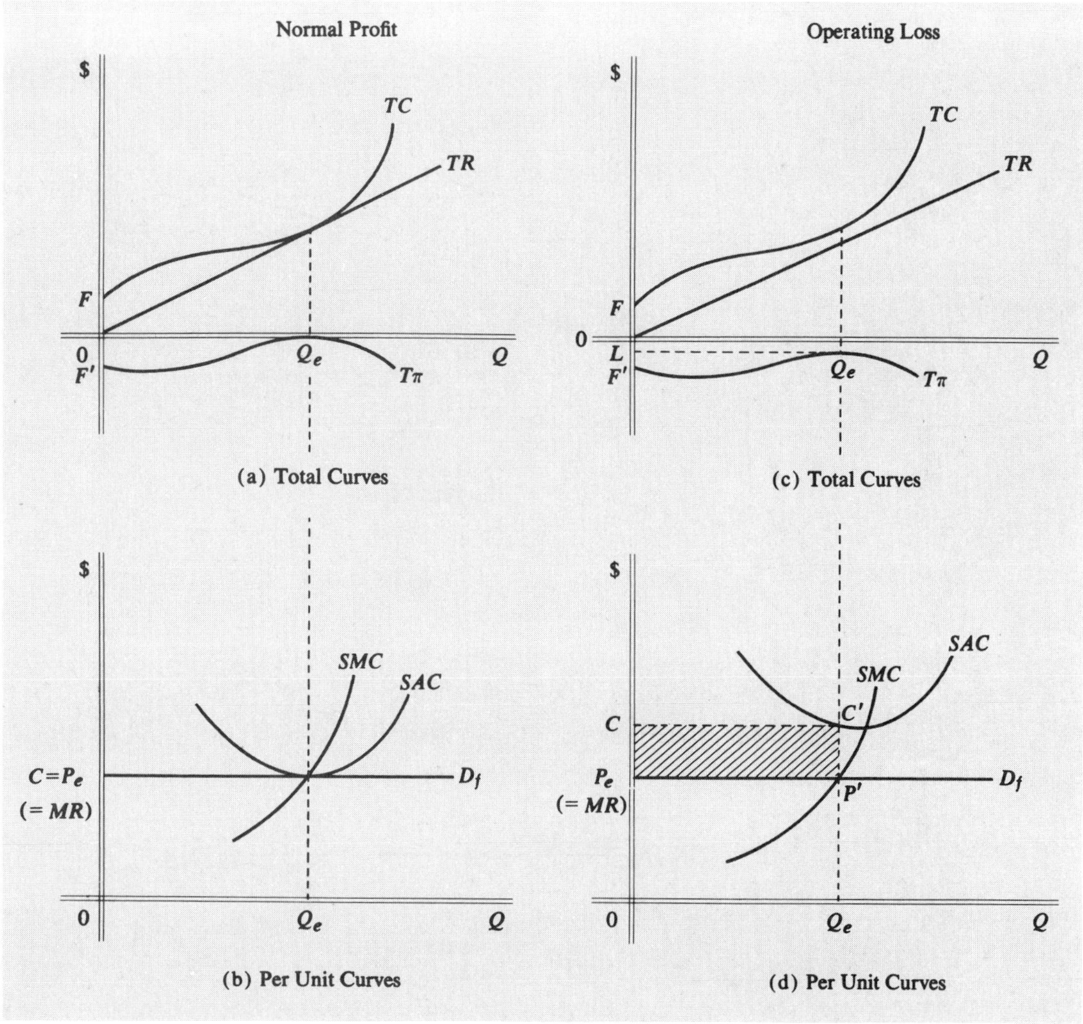

(a) Total Curves

(b) Per Unit Curves

(c) Total Curves

(d) Per Unit Curves

In panels (a) and (b), $T\pi = 0$, since $TC = TR$ and $P = SAC$ at Q_e. In panels (c) and (d), the firm has a loss at Q_e but should operate, since the loss is less than total fixed cost.

$SMC = MR = P_e$ when price is above AVC. It follows from this profit-maximizing principle that the *short-run supply curve* of a perfectly competitive firm is that portion of its marginal cost curve (SMC) which lies above AVC. Note in Figure 8–6 that as price (and MR) moves upward from P_1 to P_2 to P_3 in response to shifting market demand, the firm's equilibrium output increases from Q_1 to Q_2 to Q_3. Because the firm's SMC (above minimum AVC) gives the relationship between price and the quantity

Figure 8–5   Shutdown Conditions Under Perfect Competition

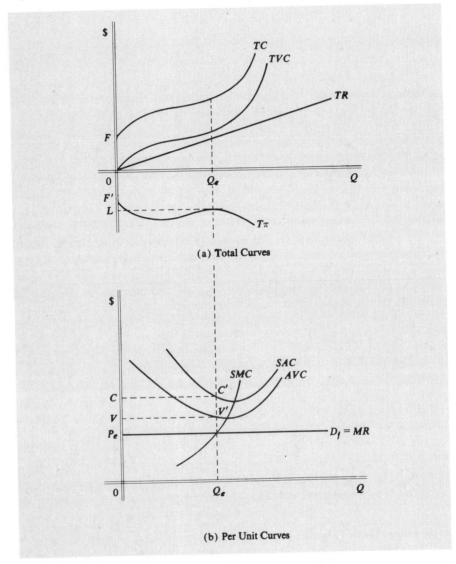

(a) Total Curves

(b) Per Unit Curves

The firm in these diagrams should temporarily shut down, since its operating loss at Q_e would exceed total fixed cost.

supplied by the firm, the short-run industry supply curve, S_i in panel (b), which is the sum of the firms' short-run supply curves, is also the sum of the $SMCs$ of all firms in the industry. In other words, for each price, we sum the quantities of output supplied by the various firms (sometimes called a "horizontal" sum). It follows that S_i or ΣS_f will shift outward in

Figure 8–6   Short-Run Supply Under Perfect Competition

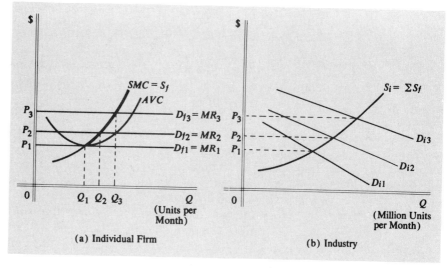

(a) Individual Firm

(b) Industry

The perfectly competitive firm's short-run supply curve is its *SMC* curve for the range where *SMC* is above *AVC*. The industry supply curve is the horizontal sum of all the firms' *SMC* curves over the same range.

the long run if firms enter the industry and inward if firms leave the industry.

The Long Run Under Perfect Competition

In the long run, the firm will maximize profit by equating long-run marginal cost to the going market price and its constant marginal revenue ($LMC = P_e = MR$). As we indicated in Chapter 6, this involves adjusting plant size to that plant that has a short-run average cost just equal to long-run average cost at the long-run, profit-maximizing output ($LAC = SAC$). This occurs where the *SAC* curve is tangent to *LAC* and also where $SMC = LMC = P_e = MR$. Under perfect competition in the long run, there will be only normal profit for the typical firm in the industry. If profit is greater than normal, new firms will enter the industry, thereby increasing industry supply and reducing market price. Entry will continue to take place as long as profit is greater than normal.

In terms of the short- and long-run average cost curves of the individual firm, the long-run equilibrium position is shown in Figure 8–7, panel (a). The industry adjustment to the equilibrium price, P_e, is shown in panel (b). If the short-run industry supply curve is initially at S_i and price is P', the typical firm will have greater than normal profit. (In panel (a), P' would intersect *SMC* well above the minimum point on the *SAC* curve.) The entry of new firms attracted by the greater than normal profit shifts the industry supply curve rightward to S_i', where it intersects the market

Numerical Example: Perfect Competition and Sunk Costs in Farming

Pansy Witherspoon grows natural cabbage (no chemical fertilizers or pesticides used). She has an 800-acre farm. While her planting and cultivating costs per acre are sunk (have been incurred and cannot be reduced) at $10 per acre, her harvesting costs are still variable. Pansy's land is of uneven quality, and the yield per acre drops as she incorporates less and less productive land into her cabbage production. She has 150 acres that will yield 20 bushels per acre, 150 that will yield 18 bushels per acre, 200 that will yield 16 bushels per acre, 150 that will yield 14 bushels per acre, and another 150 that will yield only 10 bushels per acre.

Pansy figures the harvesting costs for the cabbage are $30 per acre. Assuming she plants the entire acreage, how much of it should she harvest if when the cabbage is mature the going market price that she can obtain is $2.75 per bushel?

Answer. Pansy should harvest all but that grown on the lowest-yielding land (the 150 acres that yield only 10 bushels per acre). We have a sunk cost problem here, because the planting and cultivating costs are already expended by harvest time. Thus, the relevant marginal cost for decision making is the marginal cost per bushel for harvesting. For each class of land, this is the acre cost divided by the yield per acre, the figure that appears in the right-hand column below:

Acres	Yield	$30/yield = MC per Bu. to Harvest
150	20	1.50
150	18	1.67
200	16	1.88
150	14	2.14
150	10	3.00

Since Pansy's marginal revenue is $2.75 (assume perfect competition), the lowest-yielding land will not be worth harvesting, and the plants should just be left to decay and then ploughed under when ploughing time comes. Pansy will have a profit contribution of $10,750 on the 650 acres she harvests, assuming all variable costs are accounted for in the harvesting costs stated earlier. (At this point, the planting and cultivating costs are sunk costs and must be treated like fixed costs as Pansy makes her decision with regard to how many acres to harvest.)

Figure 8–7   The Long Run Under Perfect Competition

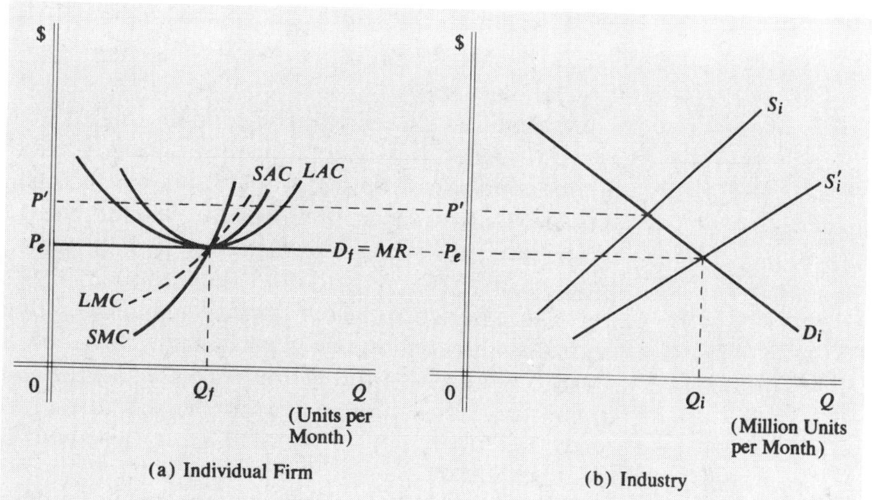

In the long run under perfect competition, profit will tend toward normal (zero economic profit), since firms will enter whenever profit exceeds normal and leave whenever profits are below normal.

demand curve at a price consistent with attainment of only normal profit by the typical firm. This price must be P_e in Figure 8–7, since minimum long-run average cost is equal to P_e. At any price higher than P_e, the typical firm would still have greater than normal profit, and entry would continue. If S_i were to shift out further than S_i', price would fall below P_e. In this instance some firms would leave the industry, and S_i would shift leftward until P_e was established.

As long as there are no changes in input prices or technology, the industry long-run equilibrium price will be P_e. This is the long-run equilibrium price because Q_f is the only level of output at which P ($= MR$) = LMC, so the firm's profit maximization rule is met, and $P = LAC$, so there are no economic profits. Of course, if industry expansion is accompanied by rising input prices, P_e will rise over time. Falling long-run input prices or improvements in technology, on the other hand, could lead to decreases in P_e as the industry expands. Whatever the result in terms of long-run price, firms will tend toward operation at the bottom of the LAC curve, with price equal to average cost, and they will tend to settle on the size of plant that has its minimum SAC tangent to the lowest point on LAC.

Overview of Perfect Competition

We can now summarize the perfectly competitive model and relate it to behavior of firms in the real world. First, the model assumes that the firm has no market power—in the sense that it can obtain no price higher than

Managerial Perspective: The Cocoa Industry and the Competitive Model

It is frequently argued that the model of perfect competition would apply reasonably well to agriculture if there were no government intervention such as price support and acreage restriction programs. It is also argued that certain world commodity markets would conform closely to perfect competition, if there were no international commodity agreements to help stabilize them.

Alas, poor cocoa. After many years of operating with price support from the London-based ICCO, an international organization set up to buy surplus production of cocoa and resell it during periods of shortage, the industry in 1990 was in a shambles. The price of cocoa had plummeted from a 1977 high of about $5,500 per ton to less than $1,300 per ton, and, for producers, there seemed to be no relief in sight. At the bottom of the trouble was the shortage of 1977, which not only brought on the $5,000-plus price level and huge industry profits but also prompted many new growers in tropical countries to plant vast tracts of seedling trees. As the trees matured, the cocoa supply curve shifted to the right, and prices fell markedly.

It would be easy to get the idea that cocoa production takes place on a few huge plantations owned by the descendants of foreign adventurers who went to the tropics a century or more ago to exploit the land. However, while there are no doubt some very wealthy third- or fourth-generation planters, there are also many, many smaller growers. In its poverty-stricken Northeast, Brazil alone counts more than 20,000 small cocoa growers, and small planters are also found in West Africa and Malaysia.

As noted earlier, the profits reaped by growers in the late 1970s led to entry. As the new cocoa plants matured, prices began their downward trend. In 1988, the bottom fell out, with cocoa prices dropping from almost $2,000 a ton to about $1,600 in three months. The ICCO throughout the period of declining prices had been intervening in the market to lessen the rate of fall. However, in February 1988, that organization reached the limit of its buying authorization and was powerless to continue supporting the price. There were simply too many new producers bringing too much output to market, and efforts by both the ICCO and the governments of producer nations failed to stem the flow.

In 1988, one expert was predicting that cocoa prices would firm up and settle at about $2,100 per ton, but he did not explain why. Two years later the price was still $700 below that. Meanwhile, big chocolate makers such as Hershey were savoring the low prices of their raw material but would not comment on whether they would pass any of the savings on to consumers.

■ ■ ■ ■

References: "Commodities Futures Prices," *The Wall Street Journal*, May 8, 1990, p. C14, and "Bitter Times for Cocoa Growers," *Business Week* (April 4, 1988), p. 83. For another example of the effects of entry, see "Dentists Step Up Services and Marketing As Competition Increases in Crowded Field," *The Wall Street Journal*, November 20, 1987, p. 29.

the going price for its output and that price cutting is made unnecessary by its ability to sell all it wishes at the going price. In the short run, the firm takes the fixed market price as its marginal revenue curve and maximizes its profit at the output where $SMC = MR = P$. It may operate with normal profit, greater than normal profit, or less than normal profit, but it will temporarily shut down only if market price is less than average variable cost.

In the long run, firms in the perfectly competitive industry will tend to have only normal profit, since entry will occur when profit is greater than normal, whereas less than normal profit will cause some firms to leave. The typical firm will adjust its plant size over the long run to a size that is consistent with minimum long-run average cost, since higher cost plants will not be able to achieve normal profit. Productive efficiency in terms of the least possible cost per unit of output is thus assured in the perfectly competitive industry, and this result is one reason why perfect competition is frequently used as a norm or standard against which to assess other types of market structures and their consequences.

Many firms, particularly small firms, face some of the conditions of the perfectly competitive model in their everyday operations. However, it is rare that all of the perfectly competitive assumptions prevail. After all, the U.S. economy and industrial economies in general are characterized by the corporate form of business organization, where certain lines of production are dominated by a few very large enterprises. In many of these industries, entry of new firms is extremely difficult, similar products are differentiated from one another by superficial changes and heavy advertising, and the activities of one firm have very substantial effects on others.

It is significant, though, that small firms often cannot block entry into their markets or differentiate their products sufficiently to have much effect on their competitors. In a large city, Hank's Garage may try to develop a reputation for fair prices and good service, but Hank is unlikely to be able to charge prices that are much different from other garages, and he can do little or nothing to keep Rosa Alonso from opening a new garage in his market area. If Hank is an efficient operator, however, he will be able to run his business at a normal level of profit. Many other small businesses are in much the same position. In such a setting they may have greater than normal profit for some short period of time, but this is the exception and not the rule. The small-business person who "makes a killing" is generally one who was in the right place at the right time and thus was able to cash in on *temporarily* greater than normal profits.

■ ■ ■ ■ ■ ■ ■ ■ MONOPOLY AND ITS SETTING

Monopoly, in its purest form, is the case of a single seller. The market demand for its product is the only constraint on the firm's pricing policies. Barriers to entry prevent new firms from coming into the industry.

Monopoly is the name applied to the extreme case in which there is only *one* seller of a given product. In a sense it lies at the opposite end of the product market spectrum from perfect competition, and we shall see later that the monopoly model provides the basic analytical framework for virtually all less than perfectly competitive product market structures.

The monopoly structure's key requirement of a single seller with a product not duplicated by other firms leads directly to two results:

1. The market demand curve is the firm's demand curve.
2. Entry is blocked over the long run.

Of course, if the firm is a monopolist, it can hardly be unaware that it is the only seller in the market for its product; therefore it must know that to the extent that it can estimate market demand, it has estimated the demand curve it faces. To remain a monopolist, the firm must be in a setting where entry is effectively blocked. This is possible if the firm controls the sole source of a mineral, for example, or if it has a patent or license that prohibits others from producing its product or selling a similar product within a given geographical area.

We expect the monopolist to have a downward-sloping demand curve that will be elastic over some range. In spite of the fact that a firm is the sole seller, it will be able to raise the price sufficiently to cause a proportionately large reduction in the number of buyers who will want to or be able to purchase its product. Since the monopolistic firm knows it faces such a demand curve, it is aware that the quantity of output it can sell will depend on the price it sets.

Profit Maximization Under Monopoly

If the monopoly firm's demand curve is linear, we can expect its profit-maximizing short-run equilibrium to look like Figure 8–8 whenever it is fortunate enough to have greater than normal profit. Note that where $SMC = MR$ and the $T\pi$ curve is at its peak, *both* the *market price* and the *quantity produced* are determined. If one compares Figure 8–8 to Figure 8–3, it is apparent that the differences between the graphical analyses of monopoly and perfect competition stem from their respective assumptions concerning the demand curve of the firm. *TR* in Figure 8–3 is a straight

Figure 8–8   Monopoly in the Short Run with Profit Greater than
Normal

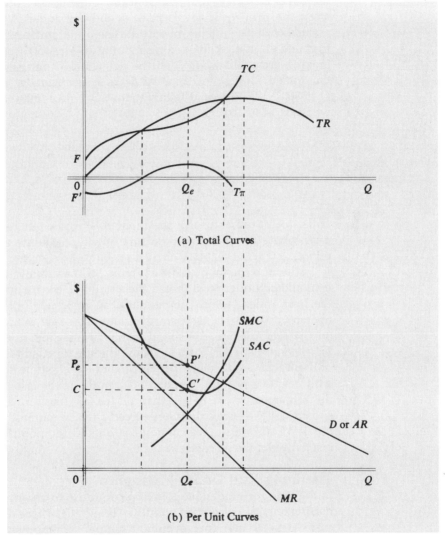

In panel (a), profit is maximized at Q_e, where the $T\pi$ curve has its peak. In panel (b), $SMC =$
MR at Q_e and profit equals $(P_e - C)$ multiplied by Q_e.

line from the origin because D_f is a horizontal line, meaning price is
constant and equal to marginal revenue. In Figure 8–8, TR is a curve with
a maximum because the demand curve, D, is a downward-sloping line.
In addition, MR lies below D or AR in the lower panel of Figure 8–8
because price must be lowered on *all* units sold to sell larger levels of
output, as was explained in Chapter 2.

The profit-maximizing monopoly must determine its equilibrium (profit-maximizing) output where $MR = MC$ or where $M\pi = 0$, subject to the usual condition that $M\pi$ is negative for greater output levels. Thereafter, the firm must set its price at the demand curve point that corresponds with its equilibrium output. The firm depicted in Figure 8–8 would first find Q_e, the profit-maximizing output. The corresponding profit-maximizing price, P_e, would then be determined. Suppose, for purposes of illustration, that $Q_e = 200$. *If the firm's demand curve is given by the equation* $Q = 800 - 2P$, it would follow that at Q_e, $200 = 800 - 2P$. Solving for P, we find:

$$2P = 800 - 200 = 600,$$

and

$$P = 300 = P_e.$$

Thus, to maximize profit, the monopoly would set its price at $300 per unit, where consumers would buy exactly 200 units of output per time period.

Although the monopolist of Figure 8–8 has greater than normal profit, it should be understood that in the short run, the monopoly firm (just like the firm under perfect competition) can also have only normal profit, *or* operate at a loss, *or* temporarily choose to cease production, depending on the relationship of demand to the firm's short-run cost structure. In Figure 8–9, panels (a) and (b) show the monopolistic firm operating with only normal profit, while panels (c) and (d) illustrate short-run operation with negative profit. Operation at Q_e in the latter case is rational, since in the upper panel, $0L$ is less than $0F$ (or $0F'$), and in the lower panel, P_e exceeds AVC. If price does not exceed average variable cost at the $SMC = MR$ level of output, the monopolist should temporarily shut down and lose only the fixed costs.

The Long Run Under Monopoly

In the long run, the monopoly firm continues to determine both its profit-maximizing rate of output and its selling price where (long-run) marginal cost is equal to marginal revenue. As in pure competition, if a monopolistic firm has predicted its optimal long-run output correctly, it can produce that output with the optimal combination of inputs; therefore its long-run cost curves are appropriate for determining its profit-maximizing output. As in the short run, the firm may or may not have greater than normal profit. However, in the event that profit *is* greater than normal, entry will not occur, since other firms are not free to come into the industry. It follows that greater than normal profit can exist indefinitely. Figure 8–10 depicts such a case. Note that Figure 8–10 differs from panel (b) of Figure 8–8 only by the inclusion of the firm's long-run average and marginal cost curves.

Figure 8–9 Monopoly in the Short Run: Normal Profit and Operating Loss Cases

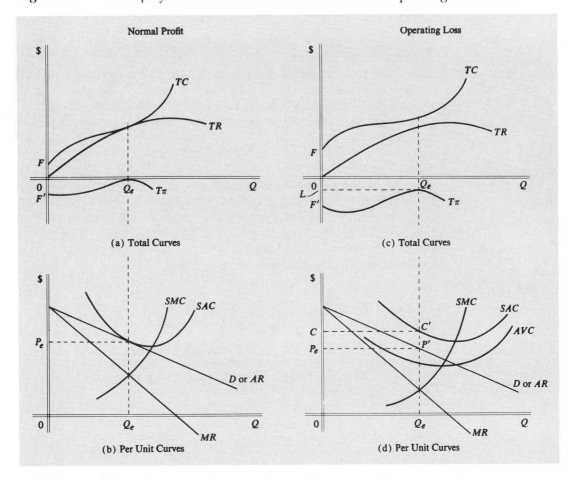

The monopoly in panels (a) and (b) has $T\pi = 0$, since at Q_e, $TC = TR$ and $P = SAC$. In panels (c) and (d), the firm has a loss, since at Q_e, $TR < TC$ and $P < SAC$. However, it should operate, since its operating loss is less than total fixed cost.

If Q_e is a long-run profit-maximizing output, then it must be true that both SMC for the appropriate-sized plant and LMC are equal to MR. The long-run equilibrium of Figure 8–10 differs from that of the perfectly competitive firm in Figure 8–7 not only by the existence of a greater than normal profit, but also by the operation of the firm at a level of output where LAC is falling, which means that even the least cost plant for producing Q_e produces it at an average cost higher than the long-run optimum plant under perfect competition. (The appropriate plant under perfect competition is the one whose SAC is tangent to LAC at its minimum point and is both larger and has a lower per-unit cost associated with it than that in monopoly.) In fact, under monopoly we can draw no special

Numerical Example: The Pricing of Water in a New Housing Development

Artie Fender, a developer in Saugus, California has opened a new housing tract just outside of town where he also owns the water system. Artie figures that, based on average home size, the demand for water in the development is expressed in the following equation:

$$Q_w = 80,000 - 2000P_w,$$

where Q_w is the number of thousands of gallons of water consumed per month and P_w is the price per 1,000 gallons. If Artie's marginal cost of producing the water is constant at $5 per 1,000 gallons, what price should he charge for the water? If the average home consumes 10,000 gallons per month, what will be the household's water bill? (Assume Artie's company faces no regulation.)

Answer. Since Artie is a pure monopolist, he should just set his marginal cost equal to the marginal revenue from the preceding demand curve. Transposing the demand equation yields

$$P_w = 40 - .0005Q_w$$

$$MR_w = 40 - .001Q_w.$$

Setting $MR = MC$,

$$40 - .001Q_w = 5$$
$$.001Q_w = 35$$
$$Q_w = \underline{35,000}.$$

Substituting,

$$P_w = 40 - .0005(35,000) = \underline{\$22.50}.$$

If the average household uses 10,000 gallons per month, it will pay a water bill of $225 per month.

conclusion regarding plant size in the long run when profit is greater than normal, since the long-run equilibrium output for a monopoly in this case may be to the left, right, or at the output level where minimum LAC can be achieved.

When profit is only normal, however, the monopolist must be producing a level of output where the LAC is falling, since normal profit requires that the two appropriate average cost curves (SAC and LAC) be tangent to the downward-sloping demand curve (P must equal SAC and

Figure 8–10   Monopoly in the Long Run with Greater than Normal Profit

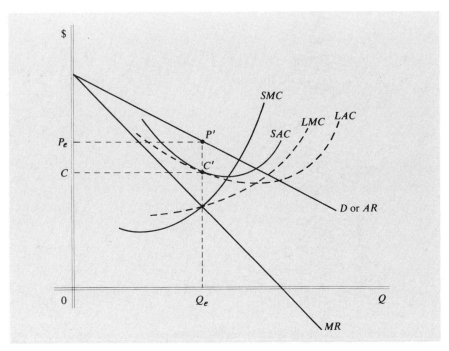

Since there is no entry in the long run under monopoly, the firm can have greater than normal profit indefinitely. In this case profit is equal to $(P_e - C)$ multiplied by Q_e.

LAC). Figure 8–11 illustrates the case of a monopolist with only normal profit in the long run.

Since, as we have shown, monopoly firms can indefinitely sustain greater than normal long-run profit, the government has undertaken the regulation of monopoly in many cases. There are two basic tools utilized by public agencies in the regulation of monopolies: taxes and price regulation. When taxes are used, the monopolist's costs are increased and profit is reduced. If the tax is a variable cost, output will also be reduced. When price regulation is used, the regulatory authority must determine whether the firm can cover costs with the price that is set. If it cannot, subsidization will be required to keep the firm from going out of business. We shall investigate these topics further in Chapter 16.

Overview of Monopoly

Briefly, we can summarize the monopoly case as that of a firm that is the sole seller of some product and maximizes profit in both the short and long run by equating marginal cost to marginal revenue, having derived marginal revenue from the market demand curve for the product. In determining its equilibrium output, the firm also determines the price of

Managerial Perspective: Love your Local Cable TV Monopoly?

In the Orwellian year of 1984, Big Brother decided to deregulate the cable TV industry. At the time, Congress thought such an action would stimulate the growth of the industry and encourage both entry and competition. Well, the industry certainly has grown, and some of the participants in it are extremely profitable firms. Revenue growth has been outstanding—from about $8 billion in 1984 to an estimated $17 billion in 1990. Advertising revenue for 1990 was about $2 billion; the rest came mainly from subscribers' monthly bills.

The average cable bill in 1984 was about $18 per month. By 1990 it had climbed to $25 per month. Most of this increase came from the basic rate, which in 1984 was about $9.50 but reached $17 in 1990. This occurred during a period of time when the overall inflation rate in the United States was very low.

While there has been substantial entry into the cable industry at the national level, where a number of large firms are slugging it out, consumers usually deal with only *one* company at the local level. Some of these companies are quite small when compared with the national cable networks like ESPN, CNN, TBS, or USA. However, the 1984 decision of Congress covered these companies too, thereby approving of deregulated monopoly at the local level. Since there is no entry possible at that level, where a single firm generally has a franchise let by local government, the firms are free to set a profit-maximizing price that moves upward as cable demand increases while there is no corresponding increase in supply. Thus the local cable operators can enjoy returns that are greater than normal with a perfect barrier to entry, the franchise.

In cases where profits *are* greater than normal, if entry occurred, it would lead to lower prices and therefore more households served. That is not what is happening in local cable markets. In the New York City area, for example, where cable prices rose from 44 percent to as much as 74 percent from 1986 to 1990, some consumers are simply deciding to do without. Meanwhile, members of Congress are getting some pretty hot letters from their constituents. Says Albert Gore of Tennessee, "Deregulation has allowed too many cable companies to gouge consumers and left too many consumers as unprotected victims." Says Donald Wagner, a retiree in Elk Grove, Illinois, "Frankly, we're getting raped for the money, . . . but if you want to watch TV, you gotta pay it."

■ ■ ■ ■

References: "Tune In, Turn On, Sort Out," *Time* (May 29, 1989), p. 68; and "Untangling the Debate Over Cable TV," *The Wall Street Journal*, March 19, 1990, pp. B1, B6.

Figure 8–11   Monopoly in the Long Run with only Normal Profit

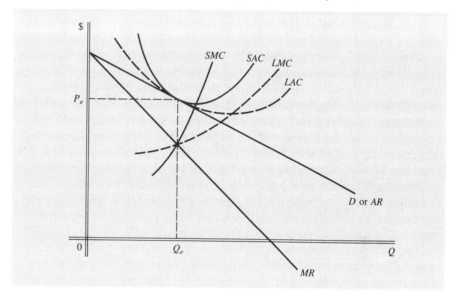

Normal profit is a possibility under monopoly. However, as this diagram shows, the monopoly firm with $P = SAC$ and $T\pi = 0$ will operate in a plant that lies on the falling portion of LAC.

its product, since both price and marginal revenue depend on the amount sold. This can easily be seen from the firm's downward-sloping demand and marginal revenue curves. The monopoly firm may have greater than normal profit, normal profit, or losses in the short run, depending on the relation between its costs and the market demand. If it remains in business over the long run, it can be expected to have at least normal profit.

We should note that the analysis of any firm that perceives or estimates a downward-sloping demand curve is graphically identical to that of monopoly, except that the firm's demand (or AR) curve is not the market demand curve for the product when there is more than one seller in the market. In the chapters that follow, therefore, we shall see a good deal more of the downward-sloping demand and marginal revenue curves. However, in contrast to monopoly, the market situations to be examined next generally assume that a number of firms are engaged in the production and sale of identical, or at least similar, products.

■ ■ ■ ■ ■ ■ ■ ■ ■ **SUMMARY**

Competition, Monopoly, and Analysis of the Firm

In this chapter we provided a brief review of the two limiting cases in the microeconomic analysis of the firm: perfect competition and monopoly.

The discussion was in large part theoretical, since we believe that few real-world firms exactly fit the assumptions of either case. However, the point was made that there are many real-world firms that face situations characterized by such attributes of perfect competition as a market with many buyers and sellers, similar costs from firm to firm, and relatively free entry in the long run. In addition, it was argued that a large number of firms in modern industrial economies depart from the perfectly competitive situation and, in fact, must be viewed in an entirely different light. For such firms the pure monopoly case holds some analytical keys that will be useful in the chapters that follow.

Our review of perfect competition extended the profit analysis of Chapter 6 to the setting of a firm too small to have any effect on its own price and situated in an industry characterized by long-run freedom of entry. In the short run, the firm acted as a price taker, and management's task was simply to determine the rate of output that would maximize profit or minimize loss. It was seen that the firm could do any of the following in the short run: operate with a greater than normal profit; operate with only normal profit; operate with a loss less than total fixed costs; or temporarily shut down, losing only fixed costs. In the long run, however, it was argued that the firm would have only normal profit because of freedom of entry into the industry. Thus any occurrence of temporarily greater than normal profits would be followed by entry of new firms and an increase in industry supply, which would depress the market price and eliminate the abnormal profits of older firms. Below normal profits would occur only temporarily, since they would provide an incentive to leave the industry in search of higher returns. In this chapter the long-run equilibrium of the perfectly competitive market was shown to result not only in normal levels of profit but also in economic efficiency, since all firms tended toward operation at the minimum point of the long-run average cost curve.

The discussion of monopoly noted that although the monopoly firm determines not only its profit-maximizing output, but also the appropriate price to charge for its product, it is still somewhat at the mercy of its demand curve. By this we mean that the monopoly firm's demand curve, which is the market demand curve for the product, might not provide the firm with any opportunities for greater than normal profit. In fact (as we showed previously) in regard to profit, the monopoly firm in the short run has all the same possible outcomes as the perfectly competitive firm, including normal profit, operating loss, and temporary shutdown. In the long run, however, the monopoly firm may reap greater than normal profit indefinitely, since entry into the industry is effectively blocked. The lack of entry that characterizes monopolistic market situations may also lead to inefficiency in production, since there is no assurance that the monopoly firm's profit-maximizing output will occur in an optimum-sized plant. Because of the profit and efficiency problems, monopolies are usually subject to rather strict regulation by government. The nature of such regulation is discussed in Chapter 16.

Many firms that are not monopolies operate under market conditions that approximate monopoly much more closely than they do perfect competition. The giant industrial enterprises of the United States and Europe are cases in point. The issue of government regulation of such firms is controversial and centers around the question of antitrust law. This subject will also be taken up in Chapter 16. Meanwhile, the next few chapters will further extend our analysis of managerial decision making to market situations notably more complex than the two limiting cases that we have reviewed here.

■ ■ ■ ■ ■ ■ ■ ■ ■ ■ ■ ■ ■ ■ **Questions** ■ ■ ■ ■ ■ ■ ■ ■ ■ ■ ■ ■ ■ ■

1. Under what conditions can we expect to find a perfectly competitive firm with greater than normal profit?
2. What is the profit expectation for a perfectly competitive firm in the long run? Why?
3. How is the short-run supply curve of a perfectly competitive *industry* derived? Is there anything that would ensure that such a curve would slope upward and to the right?
4. What control does the individual perfectly competitive firm have over the price it charges for its product? Explain.
5. The agricultural sector of the U.S. economy is often said to approximate a perfectly competitive market situation. Do you think this characterization is appropriate? What would you predict about the chances for success of farmers' strikes and protest marches (tractor parades), as well as of farm organizations bent on securing higher prices, given what you know about the perfectly competitive model?
6. What kind of market demand situation can we expect a monopolistic firm to face? Why?
7. Must monopoly firms always have greater than normal profits in the short run? Why or why not?
8. Under what conditions would a monopoly firm have only normal profit in the long run? (Assume no regulation.)
9. Why can an unregulated monopoly firm have greater than normal profit indefinitely over the long run?
10. If an unregulated monopoly firm has only normal profit in the long run, will it be operating at the minimum point of its long-run average cost curve? Why or why not?

■ ■ ■ ■ ■ ■ ■ ■ ■ ■ ■ ■ ■ ■ **Problems** ■ ■ ■ ■ ■ ■ ■ ■ ■ ■ ■ ■ ■ ■

1. Diagram the following situations using both total and per-unit (average, marginal) cost and revenue curves.
   a. A perfectly competitive firm producing output but minimizing its short-run loss.
   b. A monopoly producing its long-run profit-maximizing output with only normal profit.
   c. A perfectly competitive firm in the short run with greater than normal profit.
   d. A monopoly operating but minimizing loss in the short run.
2. Suppose a firm has the following short-run cost data:

SMC	MP_b	Output of X	Input of b	AP_b	AVC	STC
		0	0	—	—	
		100	2		0.40	240
		250	4			
		350	6			
		425	8			
		475	10			
		500	12			

Assume that b is the only variable input and that its price is fixed.
   a. Complete the table.
   b. Find its best short-run output if it has no choice but to sell its product at the prevailing market price of $0.78.
3. Determine whether the following perfectly competitive firm should produce output in the short run or temporarily shut down. Given

$$P = MR = \$60$$

$$TC = 4{,}000 + 204Q - 3Q^2 + 0.02Q^3$$

$$SMC = 204 - 6Q + 0.06Q^2$$

where

$$Q \text{ is units produced per month.}$$

If the firm does not operate, it will lose its $4,000 of fixed costs. What profit or loss will it have if it operates where $SMC = MR$?

4. Suppose a firm is operating under highly competitive market conditions and the going price for its product is $P_x = \$260$. If the firm's short-run total cost function is

$$TC = 1{,}000 + 80Q_x - 6Q_x^2 + 0.2Q_x^3,$$

and therefore marginal cost is

$$MC = 80 - 12Q_x + 0.6Q_x^2,$$

what is the firm's profit-maximizing output? (Show work.) How much profit will the firm have? (Assume all data pertain to monthly operations.)

5. Examine the following diagrams.

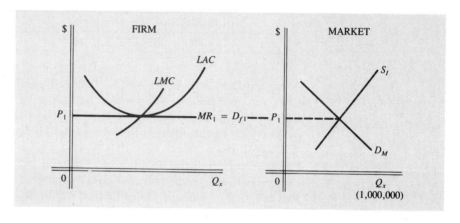

The industry is perfectly competitive. *Explain* and *illustrate* what would happen if market demand increased. That is, what adjustments would occur in the *long run?* (Assume the cost curves do not shift in any way.)

6. The following data pertain to a monopoly firm's demand and costs per quarter.

Q (quantity sold)	P (unit price)	TVC (total variable cost)
0	$20	0
5,000	18	$100,000
10,000	16	120,000
15,000	14	180,000
20,000	12	250,000
25,000	10	330,000
30,000	8	420,000
35,000	6	520,000
40,000	4	640,000

If total fixed costs are $10,000 per quarter, what will be the firm's maximum profit output? How much will profit be at this output level?

7. Complete the following table, assuming that the firm is in the short run and L is the only variable input.

TC	AFC	AVC	AP_L	Input of L	$TP_L =$ Output	MP_L	SMC
—	—	—	—	0	0		
						10	
960.00	90.00	6		1	10		
						18	3.33
		4.29		2	28		
		3.75		3	48		
		4.29	14.0	4			
						4	
	15.00			5	60		
						3	20.00
	14.29	5.71	10.5	6			

Assuming the firm operates in a perfectly competitive market and faces a market price of $12 per unit for its product, answer the following:

a. At which of the outputs in the table will it have the greatest profit (lowest loss)?

b. How much will the above profit (loss) be?

8. Complete the revenue and cost data in the following table, assuming that the firm, Calabasa Consolidated Cable, is a monopoly that has been allowed to set its own price for home TV cable service in the very small town of Calabasa, Wisconsin. (Q refers to number of subscribers, and the revenue and cost data are per month.)

MR	P	Q	TR	STC	AVC	TVC	MC
	110		1100			600	
	100	20		1500	35.00		
							20
		30	2700	1700		900	
							30
	80	40		2000			
	70		3500		32.00		
							50
		60	3600				
	50	70		3500		2700	

a. What output and price will Calabasa Cable choose? Explain why, relating your answer to the general condition for a profit maximum.

b. How much total profit will Calabasa have at the maximum?

c. In the table, $300 per month of the Cable Company's total fixed cost is a franchise fee paid to the city. If no other data change, but the city raises the franchise fee to $500 per month, what will be the effect on the company's output, price, and total profit? *Explain.*

The following problems require calculus.

9. Suppose the typical firm in a perfectly competitive industry has the following long-run total cost function:

$$LTC = 240Q_x - 6Q_x^2 + 0.08Q_x^3$$

If this function remains stable, what will be the long-run going price for Product x?

10. Assume a perfectly competitive firm has the following total cost function for the short run:

$$STC = 700 + 90Q - 4.5Q^2 + (1/3)Q^3$$

a. Determine its profit-maximizing or loss-minimizing output for the short run, given that the market price of its product is $180 per unit.

b. What will be the firm's short-run profit or loss?

11. A monopoly firm has the following demand curve:

$$Q = 2000 - 25P,$$

where Q is its monthy output. If its monthly short-run total cost is described by the function

$$STC = 500 + 8Q + .035Q^2,$$

answer the following questions.

a. What will be its profit-maximizing price and output?

b. How much profit will it have at the output above?

12. The following is a demand curve that has been estimated for a monopoly firm:

$$Q_x = 4,000 - 20P_x,$$

where Q_x is the quantity of Product x sold per month, and P_x is the price charged by the firm.

If its marginal cost is constant at $20 per unit, at what price and quantity will it maximize profit?

13. a. Solve problem 12 for a monopoly firm with the same demand curve but the following short-run total cost function:

$$TC = 8{,}750 + 176Q_x - 2.93Q_x^2 + 0.02Q_x^3$$

b. Indicate the dollar amount of profit for the firm at the preceding output per month.

This problem can be solved with Decision Assistant.

14. The Herridge family has been actively involved in growing oranges in the family orchard for four generations. Over that period many factors have contributed to periods of profit and loss. Next year is shaping up to be "one of those years." A mild winter in Texas and Florida translated to bumper crops and lower prices for the Herridge's oranges.

Jack Herridge is trying to predict next year's profit potential and is reviewing a recent trade-publication article that predicts a price of $10 per bushel for the variety of oranges Jack's family grows.

Although the price of oranges has fluctuated widely over the years, the cost of producing oranges has been fairly constant as given by the following total cost function:

$$TC = 5{,}000 + 4Q + .001Q^2,$$

where Q is the quantity in bushels of oranges grown and sold on the Herridge orchard.

Jack is now ready to project the profit (or loss) for the family business. (*Hint: TR* is P * Q or *TR* = 10Q.)

Use the Max/Min tool in the *Managerial Economics Decision Assistant* to complete the following:

a. Determine the quantity of oranges Jack's orchard should grow and send to market.

b. Suppose the price of oranges fluctuates to $12 per bushel. What will be the new quantity of oranges grown and sent to market?

c. Suppose the price of oranges fluctuates to $9 per bushel. What will be the new quantity of oranges grown and sent to market?

■ ■ ■ ■ ■ ■ ■ ■ ■ ■ **Selected References** ■ ■ ■ ■ ■ ■ ■ ■ ■ ■

Douglas, Evan. *Microeconomic Analysis: Theory and Applications.* Englewood Cliffs, N.J.: Prentice-Hall, 1982, Chapters 9 and 10.

Lipsey, Richard G., Peter O. Steiner, Douglas D. Purvis, and Paul N. Courant. *Economics.* New York: Harper & Row, 1990, Chapters 12 and 13.

Maurice, S. Charles, Owen R. Phillips, and C. E. Ferguson. *Economic Analysis.* Homewood, Ill.: Irwin, 1982, Chapters 8 and 9.

McConnell, Campbell R., and Stanley L. Brue. *Economics.* New York: McGraw-Hill Publishing Co., 1990, Chapters 25 and 26.

Nicholson, Walter. *Microeconomic Theory: Basic Principles and Extensions.* Chicago: The Dryden Press, 1985, Chapters 10–12.

Truett, Dale B., and Lila J. Truett. *Economics.* St. Louis: Times Mirror/ Mosby College Publishing, 1987, Chapters 21 and 22.

Monopolistic Competition, Oligopoly, and Rivalrous Market Structures

In the preceding chapter, our examinations of perfectly competitive and monopolistic firms demonstrated that such firms had two important points in common: (1) neither type of firm was motivated to differentiate its product from that of other sellers through advertising or other means and (2) neither type of firm needed to be concerned about the effects of rival firms' activities on its own operations or reactions by such firms to its decisions. However, most real-world firms are vitally concerned with one or both of the foregoing considerations. They know that what they do affects firms that are their rivals in the marketplace, and they are aware that they can capture a certain share of the market by convincing buyers that their product or service is superior to that of other sellers. (Thus Wendy's, Inc. goes to a lot of trouble trying to convince the world that its hamburgers are better than McDonald's; and likewise, the amount and kind of advertising done by McDonald's is often a function of the activities of its rivals.) What businesses attempt to do when they whittle away a certain portion of the market for themselves is to create a sort of mini-monopoly position for their individual firm. This is why monopoly analysis, rather than the perfectly competitive model, provides a suitable point of departure for examination of market structures where sellers are few enough in number that they are likely to be aware of the problem of rivalry among themselves.

Oligopoly is a market structure characterized by few sellers and interfirm rivalry.

Economists have settled on the term **oligopoly** to describe product market situations that are characterized by relatively few sellers (few enough so that nothing that approaches perfect competition will exist). More recently, the terms *rivalrous competition* and *rivalrous market structures* have been used to describe a broad range of oligopoly situations that lie somewhere between the extremes of monopoly and perfect competition. These market structures range from cases in which the number of sellers is very few and the product is homogeneous to cases in which there are relatively large numbers of sellers with products that vary markedly. In fact, efforts to differentiate the firm's product from similar goods produced by rival firms is an important strategy tool in many rivalrous markets. Such **product differentiation** may take the form of actual physical changes in the product or just advertising that makes people think the product is somehow superior to that produced by rivals. Oligopoly analysis is difficult because it tries to deal with some of the most complex interfirm relationships encountered in the real world, and many of these structures are characterized by *uncertainty*. In some cases, therefore, we are able to predict an outcome with respect to price and quantity sold only if certain rather heroic assumptions are allowed to hold. In others the best we can do is describe a range in which the solution will be found.

Product differentiation refers to a wide variety of activities, such as design changes and advertising, that rival firms employ to attract consumers to their products.

■ ■ ■ ■ ■ ■ ■ ■ ## MONOPOLISTIC COMPETITION: A CASE OF MANY FIRMS

Monopolistic competition is the name applied to a market structure with numerous firms that sell slightly differentiated products.

One market structure that is less than perfectly competitive and, as a result, draws on the tools of monopoly analysis is the case called **monopolistic competition.** The theory of monopolistic competition, developed by Harvard economist E. H. Chamberlin in the 1930s, occupies an in-between area in the analysis of market structures because it is not really an explanation of oligopoly or rivalrous competition but does allow for the element of product differentiation. Consequently, individual firms do have some control over price. We can describe monopolistic competition as a situation characterized by a relatively large number of sellers of somewhat differentiated products where each seller firm is not particularly concerned about the relationship between its individual actions and those of other firms in the industry. Each firm attempts to retain or increase its market share by differentiating its product from the output of other firms, either by making the product physically different, by advertising, or by combining both methods.

The individual firm thus perceives the relevant portion of its demand curve to be highly elastic (similar to the demand curve under perfect competition), but *not* perfectly so. In this setting very small price changes cause large changes in quantity demanded; and once the firm locates its

Managerial Perspective: Oligopoly Advertising and The Pickup Truck Wars

One characteristic frequently found in oligopolistic markets is product differentiation so fierce that it takes the form of negative advertising—commercial presentations that literally run down the product of a rival firm. For example, a maker of frozen pizzas in 1987 ran TV ads informing consumers that the main ingredient in its competitors' artificial cheese was casein, the same substance used to make *glue*. Similarly, some fast-food hamburger chains have attacked the nutritional value of rivals' food in TV advertising; and the negative advertising of political opponents in election campaigns reflects the same sort of strategy for gaining customers (in this case, voters).

A classic oligopoly advertising battle raged between General Motors (GM) and Ford in the pickup truck market from 1988 to 1990. It started when GM's Chevrolet division embarked on an all-out effort to bump Ford from its number-one position in that market, a position Ford had held for over a decade. Chevrolet's marketing gurus whipped up a slate of macho ads that supposedly pit the full-size Chevy pickup against similar Fords and proved the latter to be puny by comparison. In one ad, the four-wheel-drive version of the Ford was left bogged down in the "ditch of doom," while a Chevy cruised on by. In another a Ford loses a tug of war with a Chevy and plunges into a "crater of fire."

In 1988, when the ads first ran, Ford's marketing experts said there was "no value" in such negative advertising, but in 1989, Ford retaliated with similar comparison ads. Finally, in the spring of 1990, Ford announced a new advertising campaign that would emphasize the quality of some of its new and redesigned products in the light truck market. Spokespersons for the company stated flatly that their new ads would not mention any other firms' trucks by name, but they did say the program could be restructured to retaliate if the Chevy ad attack resurfaced at a later date. Ford marketing experts said they surveyed consumers to find out what they thought about the ad war. The public, they say, thought it was "a bunch of baloney" from both the Ford and Chevy sides. In any event, at the midpoint of the 1990 model year, Ford's pickup sales exceeded those of Chevrolet by about 20 percent more than in the previous year. But no one was saying whether either firm had obtained any *net* benefits from the marketing war.

■ ■ ■ ■

References: "Chevy Turns to Negative Ads in an Effort to Topple Ford as Pickup-Truck Leader," *The Wall Street Journal*, December 12, 1988, p. B1; and "Ford Calls a Truce in Battle With GM With New Ad Campaign for Its Trucks," *The Wall Street Journal*, April 12, 1990, p. B4.

profit-maximizing output and price, it tends not to tamper further with price adjustments but rather to focus its attention on product differentiation as a market weapon. It could, through this choice, increase its sales and profit at or near the existing price by enticing customers away from other firms.

Short-Run and Long-Run Equilibria Under Monopolistic Competition

Although firms do not explicitly recognize the interdependence of their prices under monopolistic competition, prices of the differentiated versions of the product do tend to move together. This occurs because the market has many buyers and sellers and will tend toward an equilibrium in a manner similar to that described for perfect competition.

Analysis of profit maximization by the individual monopolistically competitive firm requires that we not only consider the highly elastic demand curve (perceived or estimated by the firm on the assumption that it can adjust its price independently of other firms), but also a curve that shows what will happen if all firms' prices change together. This latter curve is called the firm's **market share curve**. In Figure 9–1, *d* is the demand curve perceived by the firm, and *M*, which looks like a less-elastic demand curve, is the individual firm's market share curve. Points on *M* show the

> The **market share curve** describes the amounts the firm can actually sell at various prices as all firms in the industry adjust price together.

Figure 9–1   Demand Curve, Market Share Curve, and Marginal Revenue Curve of the firm Under Monopolisic Competition

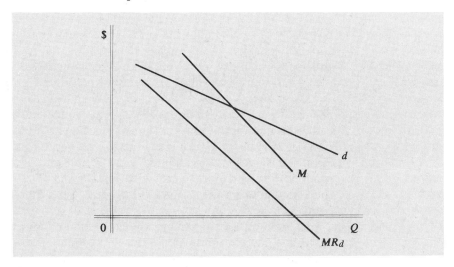

The monopolistically competitive firm ignores its rivals and estimates demand curve *d* and the marginal revenue curve, MR_d. The market share curve, *M*, shows how price and this firm's quantity demanded will be related when all firms' prices tend to move together.

quantities of output the firm can sell at various prices if (1) all firms' prices change together and (2) the firm neither increases nor decreases its share of the total market. The marginal revenue curve, MR_d, is based on the d curve, since that curve reflects the firm's view of demand.

Because of the tendency for firms' prices to reach a level consistent with a market-wide equilibrium, the individual firm in equilibrium will always be at the intersection of its d curve with its M curve. In other words, it will be selling the quantity consistent with its current price and market share and it will believe that it can do just that. If its belief is not consistent with its market share, it will adjust its price or differentiate its product (or both) until it reaches an intersection of d with M that is consistent with the profit-maximizing condition, $SMC = MR_d$.

The adjustment process could involve *both* revision of its estimate of d and the actual shifting of M as product differentiation alters its market share. With all firms in the industry practicing product differentiation, it is likely that they will just counteract one another's efforts. In this instance, M would hold still, and the path to profit maximization would entail shifting only the d curve.

Suppose a monopolistically competitive industry is in a period of falling costs and reductions in price by all firms. As adjustment takes place, an individual firm may find itself in a position such as that shown in panel (a) of Figure 9–2. At price P_a, the firm expected to maximize profit by selling Q_a but finds it can only sell Q_b. Why? Because its market share, shown by the M curve, is not sufficient to sell Q_a, at price P_a. The firm must therefore adjust its estimate of d. It may also adjust its price in order to find the profit maximum. Once it has done this, its solution will look like that in panel (b) of Figure 9–2, where its new estimated demand curve, d_2 and M intersect at the output consistent with $MR_{d2} = SMC$. In this example, the equilibrium price, P_e, is lower than the original one, P_a, and the quantity, Q_e, is higher than Q_b but lower than the previously anticipated quantity, Q_a. We have posited no change in market share, so the M curve in panel (b) is the same as the original one in panel (a).

The question arises as to whether, when all is said and done, the firm will regard segment BE of the M curve as its demand curve. This will not be the case, since the firm continues to believe that other firms will ignore its price changes and that demand will be very elastic, as shown by d_2. Since it believes it has attained a profit maximum relative to d_2 at Q_b, product differentiation (increase in market share) is viewed as the only route to higher profits. Successful product differentiation will move both d and M to the right.

In the long run under monopolistic competition, there is freedom of entry, and therefore firms will tend to have only normal profit. However, the long-run profit-maximizing position of the monopolistically competitive firm differs from that of the perfectly competitive firm because the firm's demand curve, d, has some downward slope. The negative slope

Figure 9–2   Adjustment to Short-Run Profit-Maximizing Output
Under Monopolisic Competition

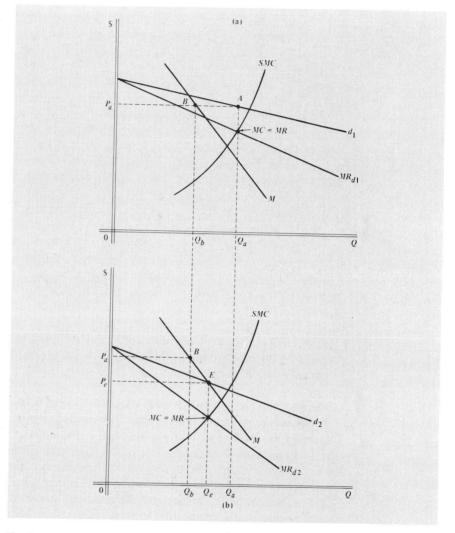

The firm is not in equilibrium in panel (a), since it cannot sell its estimated quantity, Q_a, but only amount Q_b, which is consistent with its market share. In panel (b) equilibrium and profit maximizaiton occur at Q_e and P_e, a combination of output and price that lies on both d_2 and the firm's market share curve, M.

of d ensures that the normal-profit, long-run position of the firm will occur at a level of output where the LAC is falling and, therefore, that the firm will utilize a somewhat smaller plant than it would have under perfect competition. In Figure 9–3, the tangency of d to LAC at Q_e shows that the

Figure 9–3   Long-Run Equilibrium Under Monopolistic Competition

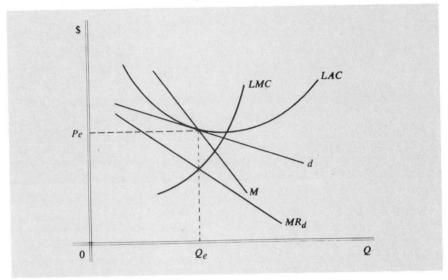

With free entry the long-run result under monopolistic competition is that $T\pi = 0$ and $P_e = LAC$ at Q_e. However, the firm does not produce at minimum LAC.

firm believes it can obtain only normal profit, while the intersection of d and M at this same point indicates that P_e, Q_e, is consistent with the market share of the firm.

Monopolistic Competition and the World of Business

When we look at the real world for examples of the monopolistically competitive market structure, a number of industries stand out as reasonable candidates. Certainly, most of the elements of monopolistic competition are found in independent retail trade in large metropolitan areas. In any given metropolitan market area, businesses such as boutiques, hairstyling salons, bars, and men's furnishings stores abound. Each has a slightly differentiated product in terms of location, brand names handled, atmosphere, or a combination of these characteristics. To the extent that one is more profitable than another, product differentiation will often be the key. However, extraordinary profits are unlikely to persist for any given firm unless it can block entry in the sense of keeping other firms from securing as good a location, array of merchandise, or atmosphere.

Obviously, the manager of a firm in this kind of industry will be more successful over the long run to the extent that the firm's operations are adjusted in terms of product differentiation in a way that will provide the firm with at least temporary periods of greater than normal profit. If location or some other factor allows the firm to operate with greater than

Numerical Example: Monopolistic Competition

Bonnie's Brake Shop is an independent auto repair facility that specializes in quick-service brake jobs. It is one of many similar firms operating in a large metropolitan area. Bonnie currently averages 80 brake jobs per month on American cars at her standard price of $190. Bonnie is about to embark on a new advertising campaign that she believes will increase her market share to the point where she will be able to sell 110 of the brake jobs per month at the same price.

a. If Bonnie's market share curve can be described by the equation $Q_m = 185 - 0.5P$ after the advertising campaign is in place, will she be able to sell 110 brake jobs per month? (Q is monthly output and P is price.)

b. Suppose Bonnie's marginal cost at her new output is $100. If her estimated demand curve is $Q = 280 - P$, will she be maximizing profit? (Assume AVC is covered.)

Answer. a. Bonnie will only be able to sell 90 brake jobs, since her market share at $P = \$190$ is

$$Q_m = 185 - 0.5(190) = 185 - 95 = \underline{90}.$$

b. Bonnie will be maximizing profit if $MC = \$100$, since for her estimated demand curve, $Q = 280 - P$,

$$P = 280 - Q, \text{ and } MR = 280 - 2Q.$$

Therefore

$$MR = 280 - 180 = \$100.$$

Thus

$$MR = MC.$$

normal profit on a regular basis, then one would have to conclude that the firm is not monopolistically competitive but rather has succeeded in redefining its own market structure as something closer to differentiated oligopoly (oligopoly with differentiated product) or monopoly.

■ ■ ■ ■ ■ ■ ■ ■ ## DUOPOLY: AN OLIGOPOLY WITH TWO FIRMS

As we noted earlier in this chapter, many conceivable oligopoly situations can be analyzed using tools developed in the monopoly case. Even nineteenth-century economists recognized this relationship, and some tried to extend monopoly by asking what would happen if there were just *two* sellers of a specific product—a case known as *duopoly*.

Cournot's Model

A Frenchman, Augustin Cournot, examined the case of a costless monopolist whose market was entered by a second firm. He argued that if a monopolist selling spring water that was produced at zero cost encountered a rival with a spring yielding the same water at no cost, the two would end up supplying a combined quantity equal to two-thirds of the quantity that would be taken by consumers at a price of zero. Cournot's case is illustrated in Figure 9–4.

Cournot assumed that each of the two firms would profit maximize based on the belief that the other would keep its *output* constant. In panel (a) of Figure 9–4, we see Firm 1, the costless monopolist, facing market demand curve D. Q_2 is the amount of spring water consumers would take if it were given away free ($P = 0$). The monopoly firm maximizes profit by selling $Q_1 = 1/2Q_2$ and charging P_1. With $MC = 0$, total profit is maximized where total revenue is maximized, or where $MR = 0$. With a straight-line demand curve, $MR = 0$ at Q_1, which is exactly 1/2 the output level where $P = 0$, or Q_2.

When the rival firm appears on the scene, it assumes that the first seller will keep output at Q_1 and then profit maximizes on the remaining market Q_1Q_2. Its demand curve is segment AD of the market demand curve, considering Q_1 as the origin, and from this relationship it derives MR'. It will profit maximize by selling quantity Q_1Q' or $1/2Q_1Q_2$, which is $1/4Q_2$. The two firms together are now supplying $1/2 + 1/4 = 3/4$ of the zero-price output. However, if Firm 1 tries to maintain price P_1, it will likely lose some of its customers to Firm 2. If Firm 1 assumes Firm 2 will keep its output constant at $1/4Q_2$, it will readjust to maximize profit based on the remaining 3/4 of the market. In Figure 9–4, panel (b), we see Firm 1 profit maximizing at $3/8Q_2$ by allowing $1/4Q_2$ for Firm 2 and setting price P_3 based on 1/2 of the remaining $3/4Q_2$ (in other words, $1/2 \times 3/4Q_2 = 3/8Q_2$). Now, the $3/8Q_2$ of Firm 1 plus 1/4 or $2/8Q_2$ allowed Firm 2 places the total quantity on the market at $5/8Q_2$ but Firm 2 will now react. It will assume that Firm 1 keeps output constant at $3/8Q_2$ and will maximize profit on the remaining $5/8Q_2$. This means that Firm 2 will increase its output to $5/16Q_2$. In Table 9–1 we summarize our results.

Note that if Firm 1 has an output of $1/3Q_2$ and Firm 2 maximizes profit on the remaining $2/3Q_2$, Firm 2 will sell 1/2 of $2/3Q_2 = 1/3Q_2$, which leaves $2/3Q_2$ not taken by Firm 2. Firm 1 now will maximize profit by producing $1/2 (2/3Q_2)$, leaving $2/3Q_2$ for Firm 2. The situation is stable. Each firm finds the other settling on $1/3Q_2$, and together they cover 2/3 of the zero-price output.

Figure 9–4   Cournot's Case of the Costless Duopoly

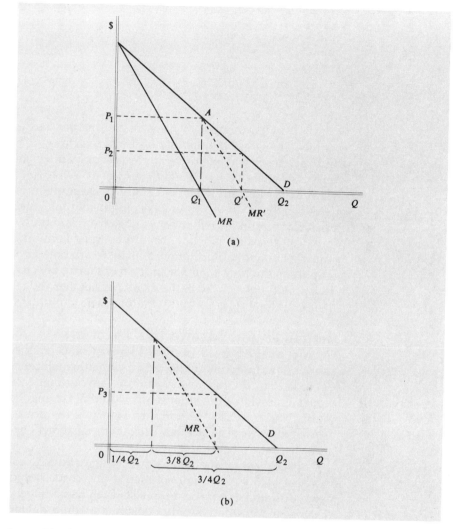

(a)

(b)

In panel (a) the second firm, believing the first will remain at Q_1, views its demand curve as segment AD. The second firm will, therefore, maximize profit at Q'. In panel (b) the first firm assumes the second will continue supplying $\frac{1}{4}Q_2$ and maximizes profit by selling $\frac{3}{8}Q_2$.

Cournot showed that for costless producers with a straight-line market demand curve, the general production solution is

$$\frac{n}{n+1}(Q_2),$$

Table 9–1 Behavior of Firms Under Cournot Assumptions

	Round 1	Round 2	Round 3	Final Round
Firm 1	$\frac{1}{2}Q_2$	$\frac{3}{8}Q_2$	$\frac{11}{32}Q_2$	$\frac{1}{3}Q_2$
Firm 2	$\frac{1}{4}Q_2$	$\frac{5}{16}Q_2$	$\frac{21}{64}Q_2$	$\frac{1}{3}Q_2$
Total Market	$\frac{3}{4}Q_2$	$\frac{11}{16}Q_2$	$\frac{43}{64}Q_2$	$\frac{2}{3}Q_2$
or,	$(0.750Q_2)$	$(0.688Q_2)$	$(0.672Q_2)$ ..	$(0.667Q_2)$

where n is the number of firms in the market and Q_2 is the zero-price output. The larger the number of firms, the closer $n/(n + 1)$ approaches 1 and the closer we get to the perfectly competitive solution, which with zero-cost would be $P = 0$ and $Q = Q_2$.

It would be hard to justify Cournot's assumption that each firm makes decisions based on the other's keeping its output constant, for there is no particular reason for either firm to believe this. Surely after one complete round of decisions is made, each firm must know the other will indeed adjust its quantity. Furthermore, if there are only two firms, we can ask why they don't get together and set the price and total market quantity back at P_1, Q_1, which, with the given market demand curve, will maximize their joint total revenue and therefore their joint total profit.

Bertrand's and Edgeworth's Theories

Cournot was criticized even in his own time for the constant quantity assumption. Joseph Bertrand, a French mathematician and economist who wrote later in the nineteenth century, argued that each of the duopolists would assume that the other's *price* would not change, paying no attention to the rival's quantity. In Bertrand's analysis the price simply falls to zero as each duopolist tries to steal the other's customers by cutting price again and again.

At the close of the nineteenth century, British economist F. Y. Edgeworth argued still another solution to the costless duopoly problem. Edgeworth stated that if the duopolists each had limited productive capacity with respect to the quantity consumers would demand at zero price, a lower limit would be established below which price would not fall. However, Edgeworth showed that this price would not be stable, for once it is reached, one firm will assume that the other will stay at the price where it reaches its capacity limit and perceive that under these circumstances (1) the rival firm can sell no more because it is at capacity, and (2) an increase in price will increase profit. Accordingly, one of the firms will now raise price to the level that will give it maximum profit on the remaining market. The other will follow suit but will raise price only to a level slightly *below* the one established by the first. The reaction of the first firm will be to cut price, and, with successive rounds of cutting, the price will fall back to the lower limit. This restores the opportunity for one of the two to gain by raising price, and the price moves back up. This goes on *ad infinitum*, as long as each assumes the other will not follow a price change.

Chamberlin and Duopoly Theory

Of course, the Cournot, Bertrand, and Edgeworth analyses are all based on assumptions of extreme naivete on the part of the two firms. E. H. Chamberlin, who developed the monopolistic competition analysis we surveyed earlier in this chapter, stated in 1933 that "When a move by one seller evidently forces the other to make a countermove, he is very stupidly refusing to look further than his nose if he proceeds on the assumption that it will not."[1] Chamberlin argued that the duopolists would recognize their interdependence and settle on a price that conformed to the monopoly price, splitting the profits between them. An agreement was not required, he stated, because the firms would realize quickly that any other strategy would be disastrous over the long run.

Chamberlin's approach to the problem of duopoly and certain of the notions he developed in his study of monopolistic competition represent a clear improvement over the older assumptions of naive behavior on the part of the individual firm or its managers. The key to Chamberlin's approach is what he called the recognition of *mutual interdependence* among oligopolistic firms. By this he meant that a firm in an oligopolistic situation will realize that its decisions affect other firms and that decisions made by other firms affect it. Some ideas about what constitutes rational behavior, from a profit-maximizing standpoint, are bound to emerge from this kind of setting.

The most obvious solution to the management problem of competing or rivalrous oligopolists is to get together (collude) to formulate a strategy that is at least satisfactory to all the parties. The problem with this approach is that in the United States and many other countries, such action would be viewed as a conspiracy in restraint of trade and therefore a violation of antitrust laws. Another possible solution is to merge the firms into a single unit, but such mergers are also prohibited when not clearly in the public interest. What, then, are we left with when oligopolistic firms recognize their mutual interdependence? The answer, of course, is what Chamberlin suggested. The firms' managers will have to analyze their environment carefully and try to adjust their operations in a manner that signals to other firms in their group the desire to be profitable without being destructively rivalrous. After all, a price war, even in an industry with a fairly large number of firms, might leave many firms in a position similar to that of Bertrand's poor duopolists—out of business! Moreover,

■ ■ ■ ■ ■ ■
[1] E. H. Chamberlin, *The Theory of Monopolistic Competition* (Cambridge: Harvard University Press, 1933), p. 46. Chamberlin's book includes an exhaustive bibliography in which the original references for the Cournot, Bertrand, and Edgeworth theories can be found.

in a setting where one firm is much larger and perhaps more efficient than its rivals, any attempt to crowd out the smaller firms is likely to meet with antitrust action. (The role of government in preventing business behavior that is not in the public interest or that is unfair to rival firms will be discussed in Chapter 16.) We turn now to several oligopoly situations in which some standard tools of analysis can be applied to determine the appropriate strategy for managers of an individual firm.

Managerial Perspective: Soda Pop Wars and Duopoly Theory

While Coca Cola Company and Pepsico are not the only players in the soft drink market, they are certainly the dominant ones. The two combined had almost 60 percent of the U.S. market for soft drinks in 1988. There is, of course, a tremendous amount of marketing hype pumped out by both companies. Both hire athletes and rock stars to push their products, and both jockey for market position by introducing product changes. Sometimes the latter backfire, as was the case with Coca Cola's introduction of "New Coke" in 1985.

Although attention in the business press seems frequently to be focused on market share and promotional strategies, the two firms battle it out on the price front as well. It is easy to observe this at the local grocery store, where one or the other (Coke products or Pepsi products) is on sale most of the time. Occasionally one finds *both* on sale at the same time in the same store.

Coke vs. Pepsi has the basic elements of a duopoly case, since neither is worried to any great extent about what some third party will do in response to a strategy change. If we compare the pricing pattern described here with the duopoly models discussed in this chapter, it seems that it has elements of both the Bertrand and the Edgeworth approaches. Certainly there is price cutting, as Bertrand described. However, as in Edgeworth's analysis, a point is reached after which prices begin to rise and may do so for some time.

Edgeworth attributed the eventual increase in prices to one firm's having run out of production capacity, thereby making it "safe" for the second one to raise price. In the cola market, while this *could* happen with respect to independent bottlers in a local market, most analysts do not believe the price oscillations can be traced to such a cause. Rather, they argue that Coke and Pepsi both have focused on enlarging market share as a major corporate goal. Much of their advertising, as well as the price cutting, is aimed at getting buyers to "switch" from one brand of drink to the other. It seems the firms believe that, over the long run, greater market share will be synonymous with a higher value of the firm. If investors concur, this will be reflected quickly in the relative stock prices of the two firms. However, long and frequent price wars may cost both firms more than either can hope to gain in market share. Industry research shows that about half of all soft-drink consumers are habitual brand switchers and are not likely to stay with a given brand when its price rises relative to that of a substitute. As one executive of a smaller beverage producer put it: "It is a battle between two very powerful companies that borders on a battle for bragging rights. . . . It's ego."

■ ■ ■ ■

References: "Coke and Pepsi Step Up Bitter Price War," *The Wall Street Journal*, October 10, 1988, p. B1; "Coca Cola Starts Drive to Pull Diet Coke Ahead of Pepsi," *The Wall Street Journal*, January 24, 1989, p. B1; and "The Soda War Fizzes Up," *Newsweek* (March 19, 1990), p. 38.

■ ■ ■ ■ ■ ■ ■ ■   THE KINKED OLIGOPOLY DEMAND CURVE: PRICE RIGIDITY WITHOUT COLLUSION

The two demand curves used by Chamberlin in his analysis of monopolistic competition have also been applied to the case of price rigidity in *noncollusive oligopolies* (oligopoly situations where firms do not make any agreement among themselves regarding price, market share, or other conditions).[2] By *price rigidity* we mean the tendency for all firms in an industry to charge approximately the same price for a specific product over long periods of time. Such a phenomenon can be an indication that prices are being administered by collusive agreements in the industry, but it can also mean simply that each firm, acting independently, has determined that it cannot gain by departing from the prevailing price.

In Figure 9–5 we redraw Chamberlin's d and M curves (as in monopolistic competition), but we now use them to describe the situation faced by an oligopolistic firm where mutual interdependence is recognized but firms do not collude. Unlike the monopolistically competitive firm, which always believed that some d curve was its actual demand curve, the oligopolistic firm is aware of the existence of both d and M. It knows that d shows what will happen if it changes price but no one else follows suit and that M shows what will happen if all firms change price together. However, the firm believes that if it raises price, no one else will (quantity will react along d) and customers will be lost to other firms. If it lowers

■ ■ ■ ■ ■ ■

[2] The kinked demand curve was first used by Paul Sweezy in a 1939 article, "Demand Under Conditions of Oligopoly," *Journal of Political Economy* (August 1939), pp. 568—573.

Figure 9–5   The Kinked Oligopoly Demand Curve

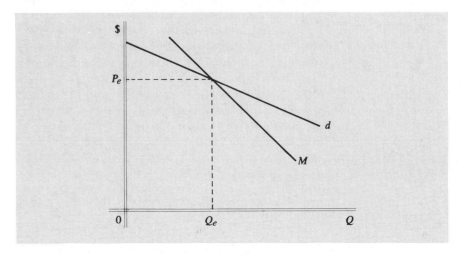

With a kinked demand curve, the firm believes that the d curve will apply for prices higher than P_e but that the M curve will apply for prices lower than P_e.

price, everyone will follow suit (there will be a price war, and quantity will react along M) and few new customers will be acquired. In either case profit is likely to fall, since d is highly elastic and M is relatively inelastic. The firm thus takes the view that the demand curve consists of d to the left of Q_e, and M to the right of Q_e. It has a kink in it at P_eQ_e; and price will, under most circumstances, remain at this kink. The reason for the inflexibility of price is that management will usually determine that no other attainable price-quantity combination will yield more profit than the one that exists at P_eQ_e.

The preceding point is examined further in Figure 9–6, where the marginal revenue curve relevant to the kinked demand curve is introduced. Note that at Q_e there is a gap in the MR curve. To the left of Q_e, the MR curve is derived from the elastic portion of the demand curve (a segment of d). As the firm's output moves through Q_e, MR falls from a relatively high level to a relatively low level and is now derived from the inelastic portion of the demand curve. Finally, SMC_1 represents the lowest short-run marginal cost curve that would result in profit maximization at Q_e. We know profit will be maximized at this quantity, since to the left of Q_e, $MR > SMC_1$ and to the right of Q_e, $MR < SMC_1$. However, notice that this relationship also holds for SMC_2 and SMC_3. Thus the firm could have a wide range of marginal cost curves, and management still would have to conclude that Q_e and P_e would be the profit-maximizing output and price, respectively. We should note also that shifts in demand and related changes in the quantity sold might not change the profit-maximizing price,

Figure 9–6   Kinked Demand Curve Related to Marginal Revenue and Various Marginal Cost Curves

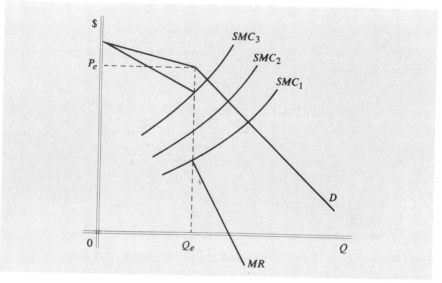

Since the kinked demand curve results in a gap in the *MR* curve, various marginal cost curves yield an equilibrium at Q_e and P_e.

since the kink still might occur at price P_e. (Imagine the demand curve in Figure 9–6 shifting outward so that the kink is at a greater Q_e but is at the same P_e—a quite conceivable result.) Returning again to the question of managerial strategy, we note that all of the preceding simply suggests that where the firm expects rivals to match a price cut but ignore a price increase, it is unlikely that profit can be increased by altering price.

Nevertheless, in the inflationary environment that has become characteristic of western economies in recent years, an oligopoly firm operating under conditions described by the kinked demand curve could easily find itself temporarily in a position where a price increase would make sense whether or not other firms followed suit. In Figure 9–7, the demand curve that management has estimated is *dCM*. The firm initially has marginal cost curve MC_1 and maximizes profit at P_1Q_1. If rising input prices push marginal cost upward to MC_2, the firm should not wait to see whether other firms raise price, since over the short run it will profit maximize at P_2Q_2 (which corresponds to point *B* on the elastic portion of *dCM*). If other firms follow suit (inflation would ensure this result), the first firm will adjust to point *F* on *M*, thereby increasing its quantity sold at price P_2 to Q_3. Ultimately, management would adjust its view of the market so that the kinked demand curve would be *dFM* and the firm would again be profit maximizing at the kink.

Figure 9–7 Adjustment of Product Price and Quantity Under Kinked Demand Curve Oligopoly After an Increase in Production Cost

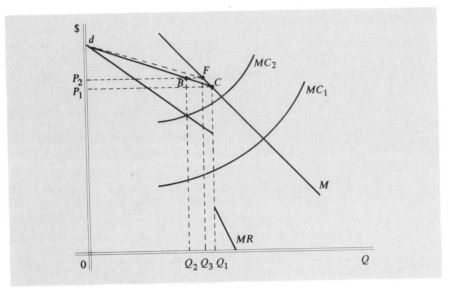

With inflation this firm's *SMC* curve (MC_2) intersects the upper segment of *MR*. Thus, it should raise price to P_2. If all firms' costs rise, a new kink will develop at point *F*.

The Kinked Demand Curve Applied

When managers of a firm believe they face a market situation characterized by a kinked demand curve, it will be necessary for them to determine whether or not they can maximize profit at about the same price charged by their rivals. Further, they may wish to look into the prospects for increasing market share (moving the *M* curve to the right) through product differentiation.

It is unlikely that a given firm will be able to maximize profit by pricing to the right of the kink in the demand curve, since this would require either extremely low or even negative marginal cost (an impossibility). However, when the industry is characterized by high rates of profit, some high-cost firms might well price to the left of the kink in their demand curves.

Suppose a firm selling electronic minicalculators of the type commonly sold in drugstores is operating in a market where management believes that price cutting will lead to retaliation by other firms but that other firms are unlikely to follow a price increase. (Industry profits are high at the going price.) The firm is currently pricing its machine at $10, but its marketing consultants have just come up with a new estimate of demand.

Specifically, they state that if all firms change price equally, the monthly demand curve will be $Q_M = 1,500 - 50P$. However, if the firm can change its price independently of rival reactions, the monthly demand curve will be $Q_d = 3,000 - 200P$. The firm's total cost function is $TC = 1,500 + 3Q + .0025Q^2$.

In Figure 9–8 we see the marketing consultant's plot of the two demand curves for the firm's calculators. By solving for the intersection of the two curves ($Q = Q_d = Q_M$ and $P = P_d = P_M$), we obtain the maximum quantity the firm can sell without encountering a precipitous drop in MR. (MR will not always be negative for outputs greater than that at the intersection of d and M.) This occurs at $Q = 1,000$, $P = \$10$, or where

$$3,000 - 200P = 1,500 - 50P,$$

$$1,500 = 150P,$$

Figure 9–8   Kinked Demand Curve Analysis for a Firm Selling Electronic Minicalculators

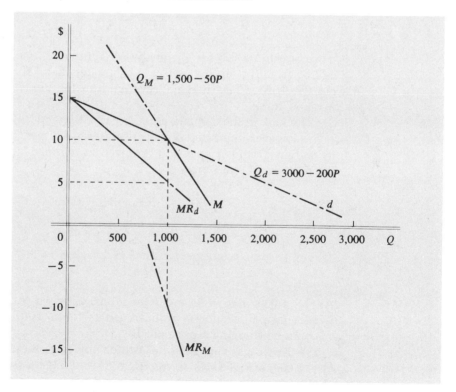

For this firm the gap in MR occurs at $Q = 1,000$, where $MR_d = \$5$. As long as SMC is less than $\$5$ at this output, the firm should charge $\$10$ per unit for its calculators.

and

$$P = \$10.$$

Using the d demand function ($Q_d = 3{,}000 - 200P$), we can solve for P and obtain $P = 15 - .005\, Q_d$. In this case

$$TR_d = P \cdot Q_d = 15Q_d - .005Q_d^2,$$

and

$$MR_d = \frac{dTR_d}{dQ_d} = 15 - .01Q_d.$$

Using the market share demand function ($Q_M = 1{,}500 - 50P$), we obtain $P = 30 - .02Q_M$. For this demand function,

$$TR_M = P \cdot Q_M = 30Q_M - .02Q_M^2$$

and

$$MR_M = 30 - .04Q_M.$$

If we substitute 750 for Q_M in the MR_M function, we can see that MR_M will be negative for any level of Q_M greater than 750. However, MR_M is not the firm's *actual* marginal revenue function until *after* the kink in the demand curve.

The kink in the demand curve occurs at $P = \$10$, $Q = 1{,}000$, and $MR_d = 5$. However, the firm should only charge $10 per unit if at $Q = 1{,}000$ its marginal cost is $5 per unit or lower. Given management's estimate of the firm's total cost function,

$$TC = 1{,}500 + 3Q + .0025Q^2,$$

and

$$SMC = \frac{dTC}{dQ} = 3 + .005Q.$$

At $Q = 1{,}000$, $SMC = \$8$ and $TC = \$7{,}000$. Since $TR = 1{,}000(\$10)$, the firm would have an economic profit of ($\$10{,}000 - \$7{,}000$) $= \$3{,}000$ if it were to continue charging a price of $10.

If the firm's managers are astute, however, they will notice that at $Q = 1{,}000$, $MR < SMC$, since $MR_d = \$5$ and $SMC = \$8$. In Figure 9–9 we show the marketing consultant's demand curves along with management's marginal cost curve. Obviously, $MR_d = SMC$ at an output *lower* than 1,000 units per month. Specifically, where $MR_d = SMC$,

Figure 9–9   Profit-Maximizing Output and Price for the Minicalculator Firm

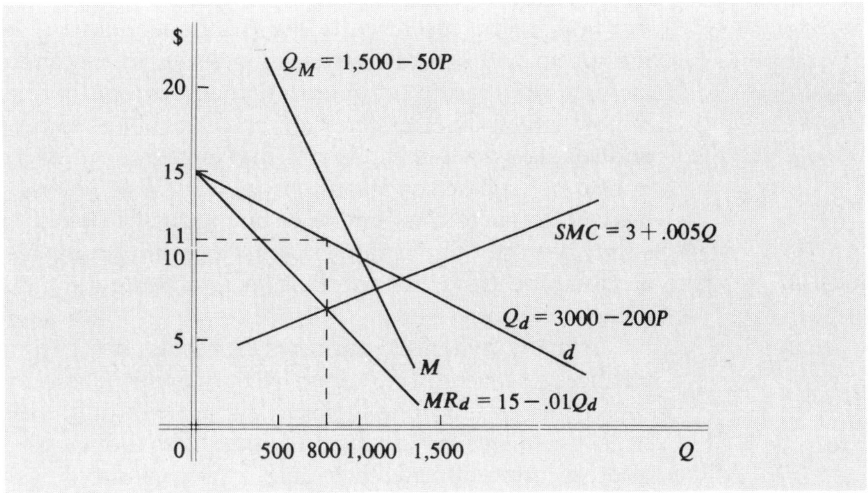

Since the firm's SMC curve intersects MR_d at $Q = 800$, a price of $11 per calculator should be charged, even though the kink in the demand curve occurs at $P = \$10$.

$$15 - .01Q = 3 + .005Q,$$

$$12 = .015Q,$$

and

$$Q = 800.$$

Along demand curve d, $P = \$11$ when $Q_d = 800$. If the firm charges $11 and sells 800 units, TR will be $8,800, TC will be $5,500, and economic profit will be ($8,800 − $5,500) = $3,300 per month. Since this profit is greater than the $3,000 per month economic profit at $P = \$10$, the price should be adjusted to $11 per unit, even though management does not expect rival firms to follow a price increase.

■ ■ ■ ■ ■ ■ ■ ■ TACIT COLLUSION AND PRICE LEADERSHIP

It should not be assumed from the analysis of the kinked demand curve that oligopolistic firms always determine their market strategy in the absence of interfirm negotiation or unwritten agreements. At the local level of operation, the existence of trade associations (the local homebuilders' association, for example) provides ample opportunity for exchange of information and tacit live-and-let-live agreements, even for relatively small and numerous firms.

In manufacturing industries characterized by large firms that are few in number, the incentive to avoid independent behavior detrimental to the group will be quite strong. However, in the United States, virtually any kind of specific communication agreement that has an effect (even a remote effect) on interstate commerce is subject to prosecution under the antitrust laws. Thus local firms that engage in price fixing in a given city but do not sell across state lines may still face federal prosecution if they have out-of-state competitors or buy inputs supplied from out of state. In short, it is only under rare circumstances that collusive business practices are immune from the antitrust laws, although some illegal practices do escape detection.

In many instances consumers are the only ones damaged by unfair business practices, and generally they are able to mount organized local campaigns against oligopolistic lawbreakers only when harm has been widespread and the identity of wrongdoers is obvious. Given the difficulty of prosecution of firms that utilize tacitly collusive business practices, it is not surprising that rather specific pricing patterns have developed in many oligopolistic industries. One of the best known patterns is that of **price leadership.** Usually, when the firm that is the leader changes its price, other members of the group shortly follow suit. In the United States such leadership has prevailed in the steel, automobile, rubber, and petroleum industries, although in any given industry the identity of the leader may have changed from time to time. Two market situations in which there is a clear reason for the price leader's identity are the *efficient firm case* and the *dominant firm case.*

Price leadership occurs when specific firms in an oligopolistic group (perhaps even one firm) sets a price that subsequently determines what other members of the group will charge.

Figure 9–10 depicts price leadership by an efficient firm where the market structure is duopoly. Here, Firm A is the efficient firm because of its lower marginal and average costs. The market demand curve is D, and if the two firms agree to split the market equally, each firm faces demand curve D'. (D' shows one-half as much quantity as does D for each price.) Price will be P_a, and quantity Q_a will be sold by each firm. Note that this is the price-quantity combination that maximizes profit for Firm A but that Firm B's managers would rather sell a smaller quantity (Q_b) at a higher price. However, Firm B will have to be content with price P_a, since if it charged P_b, it would at least temporarily lose customers to Firm A. If Firm B persisted in charging P_b, it would get customers only to the extent that they were unaware of Firm A's price or that Firm A's output was depleted. At the latter point, something would have to give, but that something might be that Firm A would expand or duplicate its plant, thereby putting Firm B out of business. The conclusion can be generalized to an oligopoly of many more firms: Inefficient firms will have to follow the pricing decisions of efficient firms in order to survive, even if such action means lower than desired rates of profit for the followers. Of course, if following

Figure 9–10   Price Leadership by an Efficient Firm

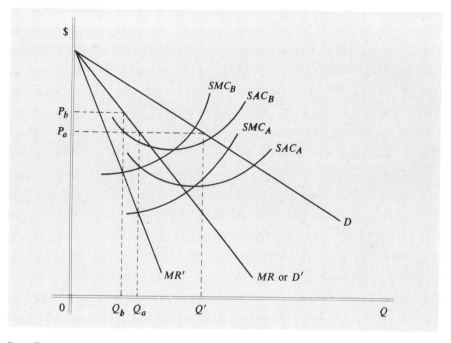

Since Firm *A* has the lowest *MC* curve, it will establish price P_a and Firm *B* will be forced to follow.

the price leader still produces normal or greater than normal profits for the less efficient firm and if other alternatives are risky, then followership may indeed be management's best strategy.

The dominant firm case of price leadership is usually described as one in which a single large firm is the price leader and smaller firms in the industry simply take its price as the going price, maximizing profit on this assumption. The problem for the dominant firm's management is to determine how much of the market small firms will absorb at each possible price and, based on this information, to choose the specific price that will maximize the profit of the dominant firm. In Figure 9–11 the dominant firm's estimate of market demand and the supply curve of the small firms is shown in the right-hand quadrant. Since the small firms take the leader's price as given, for them $P_e = MR_s$. Each small firm will equate its *MC* to MR_s; therefore the sum of the small firms' marginal cost curves, ΣMC_s, will be their supply curve, S_s. If the dominant firm were to set price at P_h, the small firms would absorb the entire market, selling the output at which S_s intersects D_M.

In the left-hand quadrant of Figure 9–11, we see the demand, marginal revenue, and marginal cost curves of the dominant firm. The demand

Figure 9–11   Price Leadership by a Dominant Firm

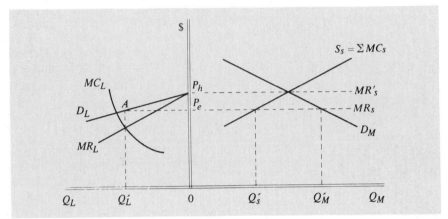

The dominant firm's demand curve, D_L is obtained by subtracting the quantity supplied by the small firms from the market quantity demanded at each possible price. The dominant firm then sets price P_e at quantity Q'_L which corresponds to the intersection of MC_L with MR_L.

curve D_L is derived by determining for each possible price the difference between the total quantity demanded and the quantity that would be supplied by the small firms. Since the small firms would absorb the entire market at price P_h, D_L intersects the vertical axis at this price. At price P_e we see in the right-hand quadrant that small firms will supply quantity Q'_s, the quantity consistent with $MR_s = \Sigma MC_s$, leaving $Q'_M - Q'_s$ of the quantity demanded for the dominant firm. Point A on D_L is plotted a distance of $Q'_M - Q'_s = OQ'_L$ to the left of the vertical axis at price P_e.

If P_e is the profit-maximizing price for the dominant firm, it must be true that at P_e, Q'_L we find $MC_L = MR_L$. This is true in Figure 9–11, so we can conclude that P_e is the price that will be set by the firm's management. The dominant firm would locate P_e by deriving its marginal revenue curve, MR_L, and finding the level of output at which $MR_L = MC_L$.

Of course, the dominant firm may be sufficiently powerful in terms of its ability (1) to sustain losses for a period of time, (2) to drive the smaller rival firms from the market, and (3) to establish a monopoly price based on the market demand curve, D_M. In the United States, the management of such a dominant firm would probably not take such a step because of the provision against *predatory price cutting* (cutting price to an unreasonably low level in order to eliminate competition) in the antitrust laws.

U.S. Steel: The Dominant Firm Case Applied

In September 1985, it was reported that domestic steelmaking firms, "following U.S. Steel Corp.'s pricing action," would raise selling prices of sheet steel products some 3 to 4 percent.[3] At the time, this move amounted to an increase of approximately $18 per ton on cold-rolled sheet steel, the type used in the manufacture of automobile bodies. For many years, United States Steel Corporation (hereafter USS, although today its legal name is USX Corporation) has been the dominant firm in its industry.[4] Over the past 20 years, the development of minimills that use scrap as their primary input has led to an increase in the number of small firms selling certain products alongside this giant firm. The small firms generally put out price signals when they believe a price increase is in order; but more often than not, they politely wait for USS to make its move.

A particularly interesting case of price leadership in cold-rolled sheet steel took place in 1976. In April of that year, William Verity, chairman of Armco Steel Corporation, stated at his company's shareholders' meeting that there was a "desperate need for adequate price relief [increases] for the flat-rolled carbon steels, which continue to bear a disproportionate burden in the fight against inflation."[5] However, *The Wall Street Journal* reported that when questioned further, Armco's officers said they would not *initiate* such a price increase.

In mid-August 1976, USS announced that it would increase the base prices of its flat-rolled products an average of 4.5 percent. The price of one of the major items in this category, a Class I cold-rolled sheet, would be raised from $296 a ton to $309 a ton.[6]

The Wall Street Journal reported that some of the other firms in the industry were not happy with USS's decision to raise prices by only $13 a ton on cold-rolled sheet. However, it is quite possible that a larger price change would not have been in USS's interest. We can use the dominant firm model to investigate the *type* of situation USS faced, even though we do not have the firm's actual data.

Suppose that USS estimates the supply curve of the smaller firms in the industry over the relevant range to be

$$Q_s = 0.9P + 150,$$

where Q_s is the quantity of cold-rolled sheet that small firms will put on the market (measured in thousands of tons of product per month), P is the market price, and industry demand for the product is (in thousand tons per month)

$$Q_M = 1,403 - 2.6P.$$

■ ■ ■ ■ ■ ■
[3] "Big Steelmakers Raising Prices to Fight Slump," *The Wall Street Journal,* September 26, 1985, p. 5.
[4] The name of the firm was changed to USX Corporation in 1986.
[5] "Bethlehem Steel Joins Price Rises on Certain Items," *The Wall Street Journal,* April 26, 1976, p. 8.
[6] "U.S. Steel Pricing Likely to Prompt Industry Boosts," *The Wall Street Journal,* August 16, 1976, p. 6.

Figure 9–12 illustrates these two curves in the \$200–\$400 per ton price range. USS would know that at a price of \$358 per ton, $Q_s = Q_M$ and the smaller firms would produce enough cold-rolled sheet to supply the entire market.

By subtracting the supply curve of the small firms from the market demand curve, the demand curve for USS (Q_L) can be obtained. Thus

$$Q_L = 1,403 - 2.6P - (0.9P + 150)$$
$$= 1,253 - 3.5P.$$

From the preceding, it follows that

$$P_L = 358Q_L - 0.2857Q_L,$$

$$TR_L = 358Q_L - 0.2857Q_L^2,$$

and

$$MR_L = 358 - 0.5714Q_L,$$

where TR_L and MR_L are USS's total and marginal revenue, respectively.

Suppose now that over the relevant range of production for the problem in question, USS estimates its marginal cost for cold-rolled sheet to be constant at \$260. At the existing price of \$296 per ton, the above demand curve shows that $Q_L = 1,253 - 3.5(296) = 217$. Accordingly, $MR_L = 358 - (0.5714)(217) = \$234$. Since marginal revenue is less than marginal cost (\$234 < \$260), a price increase and reduction in quantity sold are warranted. USS should adjust its output to the point where $MR_L = \$260 = MC_L$ and charge the corresponding price. We can easily see that the above condition is met where

$$MR_L = 358 - 0.5714Q_L = 260,$$

or where

$$Q_L = 171.5 \text{ thousand tons per month}$$

and

$$P_L = 358 - (0.2857)(171.5) = \$309 \text{ per ton.}$$

In panel (b) of Figure 9–12, we illustrate the outcome of USS's pricing decision. At the \$309 price, total quantity demanded will be 599,600 tons per month. USS will supply 171,500 tons per month, and the other firms in the industry will supply 428,100 tons per month. If USS's capacity is such that it can increase output substantially at a constant marginal cost of \$260, then other firms cannot successfully charge a price higher than \$309, since they will simply lose customers to USS. Of course, USS will

Figure 9–12   Demand Curve for Cold-Rolled Sheet and Solution to
U.S. Steel Price Leadership Problem

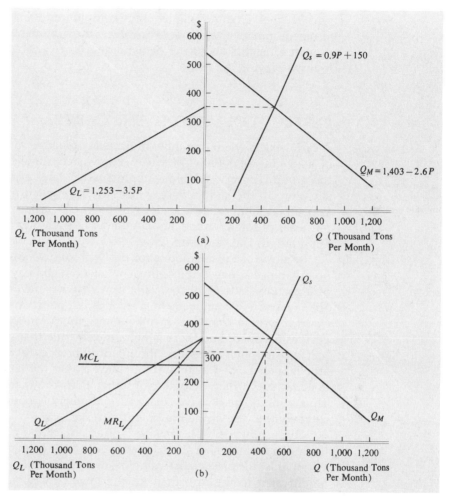

In panel (a), Q_L is equal to ($Q_M - Q_s$). In panel (b), the leader's price is established at \$309, since this price corresponds with the output where $MR_L = MC_L$. The small firms accept the \$309 price.

be quite happy to take their customers at $MR = \$309$, since this is a great deal more than the firm's \$260 marginal cost.

The preceding example has used a combination of actual and hypothetical data to illustrate how a dominant firm might determine a market price it wishes to establish for a single product. In reality the steel industry is characterized by a much more complex pricing system in which other firms frequently play the role of leader. However, it is clear that if another firm takes the lead and sets a price unfavorable to USS, the giant firm will react by undercutting the price leader. (This happened in August, 1975, when Armco played the role of leader and was undercut by USS.)[7]

What comes through from the real-world example of steel is that the price leadership game is much more complicated than the simple solution of our dominant firm model. However, the dominant firm case certainly provides insights about the demand and cost variables that are relevant to firms playing the game.

■ ■ ■ ■ ■ ■ ■ ■ ## PERFECT COLLUSION—THE CARTEL

A **cartel** is a group of firms that have joined together to make agreements on pricing and market strategy.

A **cartel** exists when a number of firms get together and agree on a policy of managing operations in a way that will maximize the joint profits of the group. *Perfect collusion* is simply another label applied to this market situation. In the United States, firms are prohibited from forming cartels for purposes of domestic trade. However, U.S. firms can form cartels for purposes of foreign trade, and a number of such organizations have been important in U.S. industry.

In terms of the conditions for profit maximization, there is absolutely no difference between the optimal managerial strategy of a cartel and that of a monopolistic or oligopolistic firm that has several different plants. Still, the cartel's management does face the additional problem of *distribution* of profits among its members once the profit-maximizing price has been established, and there is no particular rule that must be followed in that distribution. Moreover, the main difference between the cartel and an oligopolistic firm with several plants is that the latter must estimate a demand curve that is something other than the market demand curve. Thus it should be clear that there are a number of good reasons to examine carefully the case of the multiple-firm cartel.

To maximize profit, managers of a cartel must allocate *production* to the individual member firms based on the "rule of marginal cost." Simply stated, this rule dictates that marginal or incremental output should always be allocated to the firm that has the lowest marginal cost. Thus, if the cartel consists of two firms, Firm A and Firm B, and management is adjusting output in a situation where $MC_B < MC_A$, then additional output should be allocated to Firm B. Presumably, as Firm B's output is increased, its marginal cost will increase. When marginal cost reaches a level equal to that in Firm A, additional output may be allocated to Firm A. In fact, at any time that $MC_A \neq MC_B$, the cartel can gain by switching output from the firm with higher marginal cost to the one with lower marginal cost. Thus, where profit is maximized, it must be true that $MC_A = MC_B = MR$.

■ ■ ■ ■ ■ ■

[7] "U.S. Steel Pricing Likely to Prompt Industry Boosts," *The Wall Street Journal*, August 16, 1976, p. 6. For further discussion of price leadership in the steel industry, see Leonard W. Weiss, *Case Studies in American Industry* (New York: John Wiley and Sons, 1967), Chapter 4.

This condition can be generalized to a cartel consisting of any number of firms. For example, a graphical solution for a cartel consisting of three firms is shown in Figure 9–13. Management determines the cartel's total output and price at Q_T, P_e, in the quadrant to the extreme right. This quantity-price combination corresponds to the intersection of ΣSMC (the horizontal sum of SMC_A, SMC_B, and SMC_C) with MR. MR_e, the level of MR consistent with P_e, is projected to the cost curve diagrams for Firms A, B, and C, and each firm is allocated the output at which its $SMC = MR_e$. The cartel's total profit is the sum of the areas of the profit rectangles for the three firms, or $(P_e - SAC_A)Q_A + (P_e - SAC_B)Q_B + (P_e - SAC_C)Q_C$.

The cartel agreement might prescribe that each firm keep the amount of profit it produces, or it might provide for some other division of the total. For example, some of the profits of high cost firms might be redistributed to the lower cost firm (Firm C in Figure 9–13) as an incentive for the lower cost firm to cooperate with the cartel. Otherwise, it might try to break away and increase its market share by lowering price.

Usually the managers of a cartel place high priority on strategies that will keep the cartel from breaking up, since under rivalrous competition both group and individual firm profits are likely to be smaller in the long run. Nonetheless, bickering among cartel members over output and pricing decisions certainly can occur. The oil cartel, OPEC, represents such a case, where failure to agree on economic strategy led in 1990 to the Iraqi invasion of Kuwait and subsequent disasters.

The possibility of cartel breakup explains why managers might depart from the optimal solution of Figure 9–13 to some lower profit (for the short run) strategy that has a higher probability of keeping the organization intact. For example, where the cartel's markets are geographically widespread, the managers might decide only to divide markets, allowing

Figure 9–13   Allocation of Production by a Centralized Cartel

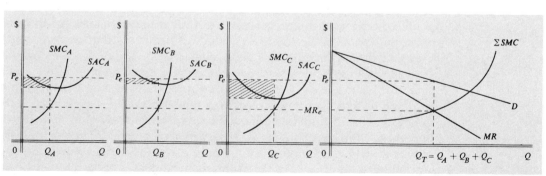

The marginal cost curves of Firms A, B, and C are summed horizontally to obtain the ΣMC curve. The cartel's price is established in keeping with $\Sigma MC = MR$, and output is allocated to each firm at the quantity where its $SMC = MR_e$.

prices to settle around a level so that price differentials are so small that it is not profitable for intermediaries to attempt to buy from one cartel member and sell in another member's territory. This approach might allow a higher cost producer to charge a somewhat higher price, particularly if that producer's territory is somewhat removed from those of other producers. Thus, while the perfect collusion approach to cartel management provides a point of departure for cartel strategy, it is easy to see that the decisions made by cartel management experts in any given case may differ significantly from the theoretically optimal solution.

■ ■ ■ ■ ■ ■ ■ ■ ■ SUMMARY

Oligopoly Analysis and Business Behavior

In this chapter we have taken an important step from the rather simplistic analyses of the perfectly competitive and monopolistic market structures to the more complex world of monopolistic competition and oligopoly. The importance of this chapter lies in the fact that the situations we have discussed encompass many additional elements with which a majority of U.S. firms must deal in the development of their managerial strategy. These elements (product differentiation, rival reactions, price leadership, and collusion) may be significant in the decision process any time a seller's market is not characterized by perfect competition or monopoly.

We have stated that a firm in an industry structure characterized by monopolistic competition maximizes profit at a level of output where its perceived demand curve intersects its market share demand curve and $MR_d = SMC$. In the long run, a monopolistically competitive firm can expect to make only a *normal* profit because of entry of other firms.

In the case of an oligopolistic market structure, however, there are substantial barriers to entry, and long-run economic profits are possible. Early in this chapter we discussed the duopoly theories of Cournot, Bertrand, and Edgeworth in which a firm makes naive assumptions regarding the behavior of the other firm, in spite of contradictory experiences. (Cournot indicates that each firm believes the other firm will not change its level of output, whereas Bertrand and Edgeworth assume that each firm believes the other firm will hold price constant.)

Later in this chapter, we discussed more realistic theories of oligopolistic firm behavior, each of them based to some extent on Chamberlin's assumption that such firms recognize their *mutual interdependence*. Such theories included the kinked demand curve, price leadership, and cartel hypotheses. We have shown that what actually happens in an oligopolistic market structure is influenced to a large extent by its legal environment and by the extent to which the firms in an industry cooperate with one another.

We have only scratched the surface of the number of conceivable oligopoly situations, but we hope to have demonstrated that it is possible

Numerical Example: Cartel Output Allocation

Producers in three countries, Irun, Uran, and Sheraq have formed a cartel to sell highly prized desert oasis water in the world market. They have negotiated a set price with world consuming nations of $3.00 per gallon for the water, f.o.b. Mideast oasis. There are three oases, one in each country, and marginal costs are as follows, where Q refers to gallons per day produced.

$$\text{Irun:} \quad MC_i = .25 + .00125Q_i$$

$$\text{Uran:} \quad MC_u = .50 + .002Q_u$$

$$\text{Sheraq:} \quad MC_s = .15 + .0015Q_s$$

To maximize profit, given the fixed world price, how much production should the cartel managers allocate to each country?

Answer. Set each marginal cost equal to the fixed $P = MR$ of $3 for the following results:

Irun: $\quad MC_i = .25 + .00125Q_i = 3$
$.00125Q_i = 2.75;$ $\qquad\qquad Q_i = \underline{2,200}.$

Uran: $\quad MC_u = .50 + .002Q_u = 3$
$.002Q_u = 2.50;$ $\qquad\qquad Q_u = \underline{1,250}.$

Sheraq: $\quad MC_s = .15 + .0015Q_s = 3$
$.0015Q_s = 2.85$ $\qquad\qquad Q_s = \underline{1,900}.$

to apply the tools developed in preceding chapters to management's decision problems in a wide variety of oligopolistic settings. (An additional analytical device, game theory, is discussed in the appendix to this chapter.) In Chapter 10, we will continue to apply now-familiar approaches to realistic situations, analyzing a number of specific pricing problems that firms in monopolistically competitive or oligopolistic markets are likely to face.

■ ■ ■ ■ ■ ■ ■ ■ ■ ■ ■ ■ ■ **Questions** ■ ■ ■ ■ ■ ■ ■ ■ ■ ■ ■ ■ ■

1. What is the significance of product differentiation in a market characterized by monopolistic competition?

2. How is the kinked oligopoly demand curve related to the demand curve faced by a monopolistically competitive firm? How does the oligopolistic firm's perception of the inelastic portion of its demand curve differ from the perception of the monopolistically competitive firm regarding its demand?

3. Give some examples of product markets in your community that can be identified as monopolistically competitive. Why do you believe they fit the case?

4. Why do the nineteenth-century oligopoly models generate different conclusions about duopoly? Can you see any relationship between Chamberlin's critique of the duopoly models and the cases of price leadership discussed in this chapter?

5. Under what conditions would an oligopolistic firm facing a kinked demand curve charge a price different from the one that occurs at the kink?

6. Although General Motors is not always the price leader in the U.S. automobile industry, do you think it can be characterized as the dominant firm? Why or why not?

7. Can you state simply the rule by which a cartel should allocate output among its members to maximize profit? Why might a cartel choose to do otherwise?

8. Why can we expect that monopolistically competitive firms will tend to have only normal profits in the long run, whereas oligopolistic firms may well have greater than normal profits?

9. Gasoline stations have often been used to describe kinked demand curve oligopoly. Why do they appear to fit the case?

10. Briefly explain how a large and dominant firm's demand curve may be related to the market demand curve for its product under the assumption that smaller firms will follow its price leadership.

■ ■ ■ ■ ■ ■ ■ ■ ■ ■ ■ ■ ■ ■ **Problems** ■ ■ ■ ■ ■ ■ ■ ■ ■ ■ ■ ■ ■ ■

1. The firm in the diagram is in the short run in a monopolistically competitive market.
   a. Derive the firm's marginal revenue curve.
   b. Indicate its short-run profit-maximizing output, supplying an appropriate *SMC* curve in the diagram.
   c. Add a short-run average cost curve such that the firm has greater than normal profit.

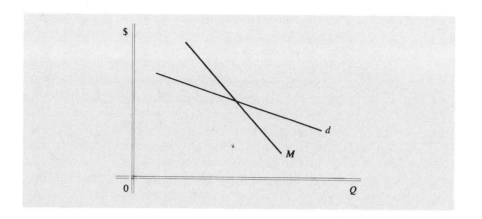

2. The monopolistically competitive firm in the following diagram is not in a long-run profit-maximizing position. Why not? What changes would have to occur for it to get to such a position? (*Hint:* Compare this diagram with Figure 9–3 in this chapter.)

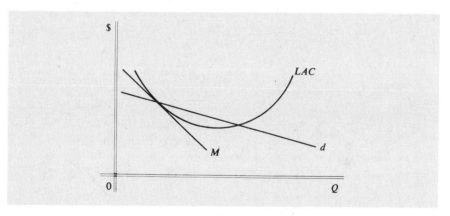

3. Suppose your favorite charity is participating in a fund-raising carnival that will run for three nights. You have been put in charge of managing the kissing booth. All labor at the carnival is voluntary, including that of the kissers, so you believe that you have a costless monopoly. Given your estimate of the nightly demand for kisses,

$$Q_k = 5,000 - 25,000P_k$$

a. What price will yield the most revenue for your charity?

b. If another charity opens a kissing booth adjacent to yours but demand remains as above (assume the product is undifferentiated), what price will prevail and how much revenue will each booth generate under the Cournot assumption?

   c. Could you improve the situation in part b through collusion? If not, why not? If so, how, and what would be the result in terms of revenue?

4. The diagram shows a case of price leadership by a dominant firm. SMC_L is the marginal cost curve of the dominant firm, S_s is the sum of the marginal cost curves of the "follower" firms, and D_M is the market demand for the product. Find graphically the following information:

   a. The demand and marginal revenue curves of the price leader.

   b. The price that will be set.

   c. The quantity sold by (i) the leader and (ii) the follower firms.

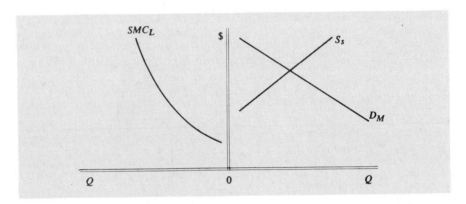

5. Suppose a large firm that is a price leader in an industry characterized also by many small, competing firms estimates the market demand for its product to be

$$Q_M = 81,000 - 200P,$$

and that it expects small firms in the industry to supply output according to the following function:

$$Q_S = 1,000 + 50P.$$

The large firm's marginal cost function is

$$MC_L = 100 + .014Q_L.$$

   a. What price will the large firm set?

   b. How much will the large firm sell?

   c. What quantity will the small firms sell?

6. The two firms in the following diagram decide to form a cartel. Find graphically the following information:

   a. The market price of their output.

b. The quantity each firm will sell.

c. The total profits of the cartel.

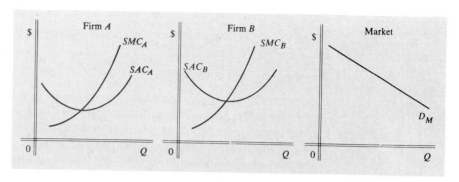

7. Because of a world shortage of resources, a cartel has negotiated a fixed world price of $25 per barrel for its product, which will be maintained for two years. Further, any quantity produced can be sold for the negotiated price. Suppose there are three firms in the cartel with the following respective marginal cost functions:

$$MC_1 = 2 + .001Q_1,$$

$$MC_2 = 1.9 + .0012Q_2,$$

and

$$MC_3 = 1.6 + .002Q_3.$$

How much output should be allocated to each cartel member? (Assume that Q_i is yearly output in barrels and that MC_i is marginal cost per barrel.)

8. Suppose an oligopolistic firm has the following cost and revenue data.

MR	Q	P	TR	TVC	AVC	AFC	SMC
	0	120	0	0	—	—	
	10		1150	600		60	
	20		2200		40		
	30	105	3150	900			
	40	100		1120			
	50	95			30		
	60		5400		40		
	70		5950		50	8.57	
	80		6400	4800		7.50	
	90	75		7200		6.67	

a. Fill in the blank spaces in the table.
b. What output should the firm produce? Why?
c. What price should the firm charge, and what will be its economic profit?

The following problems require calculus:

9. Gnoma Pest Control Company specializes in pest control services for single-family homes. Entry is easy in the local market, and a large number of local firms offer similar services. The typical contract provides whole-house service, including one interior spraying per month and a yearly foundation spray. The cost to the company can be regarded as a constant amount per unit at

$$AVC = \$5 \text{ per month per home.}$$

Advertising and image are important to pest control firms in the local market, since this method is about the only way they can differentiate what is otherwise a fairly homogeneous output. Gnoma's management advertised heavily to get the firm established but has recently cut the firm's advertising by one-half. Management now estimates the firm's demand curve for household service to be

$$Q = 25{,}000 - 2{,}000P$$

where Q is the quantity of homes under service contract and P is the *monthly* service charge.

a. Based on management's estimate of demand, at what price and quantity sold should Gnoma be able to maximize profit?
b. If monthly fixed costs are $12,000, what will monthly profit be?
After the reduction in advertising, Gnoma's sales fell to 5,250 homes under monthly contract. A market analyst states that this drop occurred because Gnoma's market share fell when advertising expenditures were cut. The analyst further states that under conditions of the current advertising level, Gnoma should estimate its demand curve as

$$Q' = 22{,}000 - 2{,}000P$$

The analyst states that Gnoma can either maximize profit subject to the preceding demand curve (Q') or spend an additional $5,000 per month on advertising and move back to the originally estimated demand curve, recovering its market share.

c. If Gnoma's management maximizes profit subject to

$$Q' = 22,000 - 2,000P$$

what is the firm's optimal output and price?

d. Is the preceding profit greater or less than the profit that would be obtained by spending the $5,000 per month on advertising and returning to

$$Q = 25,000 - 2,000P?$$

e. What should Gnoma do?

10. A firm's research department has estimated that if other firms in the industry are indifferent to changes in the price of its product, its demand curve will be

$$Q = 700 - 50P.$$

However, if other firms always charge the same price it does, the firm's demand curve will be

$$Q' = 200 - 10P$$

a. If the firm's marginal cost equals $8.00, what output and price will maximize profit? (Assume that the other firms will not follow a price rise above $12.50 but that they will follow a price cut below $12.50.)

b. If the firm's marginal cost equals $11.50, what output and price will maximize profit?

11. The following is a demand curve that has been estimated for an oligopolistic firm:

$$AR = P_x = 160 - (1/2)Q_x$$

where Q_x is the quantity of Product x sold per month, and P_x is its price per unit.

If the firm's total cost function is

$$TC_x = 500 + 40Q_x - 1.5Q_x^2 + (1/3)Q_x^3,$$

a. Determine the quantity produced (sold) that will maximize profit.

b. Indicate the dollar amount of profit for the firm at the above output per month.

12. Phunny Phaucet Corporation of America (PPCA) operates in a non-collusive oligopolistic market where firms tend to base their strategies

on fear of their rivals. PPCA believes that at its current price its demand curve will be $Q = 400 - 4P$ if it raises price, since it expects that other firms will not follow a price increase. For price cuts, however, it believes its demand curve is $Q = 250 - 2P$, since other firms are expected to follow a reduction in price.

a. With the above assumptions, what are PPCA's current price and quantity sold?

b. Suppose PPCA's total cost function is

$$STC = 50 + 20Q + 0.1Q^2.$$

Is PPCA maximizing its profit at the quantity and price you found in a? Explain why or why not.

c. Now suppose that PPCA has made an error in the estimate of its total cost function so that the actual total cost is:

$$STC = 60 + 30Q + 0.25Q^2$$

With this revised total cost function, what is the firm's best output and price?

13. Aqualor Corporation is a very large producer of swimming pool electronic control valves. Aqualor typically charges a standard price for a valve that fits many different brands of swimming pool equipment. Aqualor's management realizes that smaller firms in its industry will always charge exactly the price that Aqualor sets and currently estimates the market demand curve for the valves to be

$$Q_M = 7,520 - 75P.$$

Aqualor's total cost function can be represented by the equation $TC = 85,000 + 8Q + .001Q^2$. In addition, it has estimated that the smaller firms' supply curve can be represented by the equation $Q_s = 120 + 25P$.

a. What price will Aqualor charge for its valves, and how many will it sell?

b. How many valves will the smaller firms supply?

c. What will be the total profit or loss of Aqualor Corporation?

These problems can be solved with Decision Assistant.

14. CAM Automotive, Inc., is in a highly interactive market for its remote-controlled toy vehicle, the Cyclone. CAM knows if it raises the price of the Cyclone, no other manufacturers will follow, and CAM will receive a relatively larger loss of sales in proportion to the price in-

crease. Conversely, if CAM lowers the Cyclone's price, the interacting competitors will do the same.

Sarah Burg, vice president of marketing at CAM, is reviewing sales projections for next year's Cyclone. Her marketing research department has estimated if CAM raises the price of the Cyclone, the appropriate demand function is given by the following equation:

$$Q_1 = 85 - P_1,$$

where Q is the quantity (in thousands) of Cyclones demanded per month and P is the price. Likewise, the marketing department has estimated if CAM lowers the Cyclone's price, the demand function is given by the following equation:

$$Q_2 = 32.5 - .25P_2,$$

where Q is the quantity (in thousands) of Cyclones demanded per month and P is the price.

After meeting with the production department, Sarah has determined the following equation describes the Cyclone's total cost function:

$$TC = 375 + 25Q + .6Q^2,$$

where Q is the quantity (in thousands) of Cyclones produced per month.

Use the Oligopoly-Kinked tool in the *Managerial Economics Decision Assistant* to complete the following:

a. Given the preceding information, determine the selling price and the quantity of Cyclones that CAM should produce per month.
b. Sarah knew the estimate of the Cyclone's total cost function from the production department would be critical in determining the proper quantity of Cyclones to produce. Accordingly, she has asked for two additional total cost functions to be provided: one based on slightly less optimistic cost data (resulting in a demand function with higher total manufacturing costs) and one based on an optimistic prediction that CAM would be able to successfully negotiate lower prices with four of its major suppliers. The total cost functions are, respectively,

$$TC_2 = 375 + 40Q + .6Q^2,$$

and

$$TC_3 = 375 + 2.9Q + .1Q^2,$$

where Q is the quantity (in thousands) of Cyclones produced per month.

Determine the selling prices and quantities of Cyclones CAM should produce and sell each month under each of these two equations.

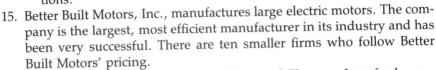

15. Better Built Motors, Inc., manufactures large electric motors. The company is the largest, most efficient manufacturer in its industry and has been very successful. There are ten smaller firms who follow Better Built Motors' pricing.

A new model year is approaching and Florence Langford, marketing manager for Better Built Motors, Inc., is reviewing pricing practices. Better Built Motors has always allowed the smaller competing firms to sell all they wish at the price it established. This year, Florence projects the total market demand for large electric motors to be

$$Q_M = 40,000 - 20P,$$

where Q_M is the market quantity demanded and P is the price in dollars.

Better Built Motors' expected marginal cost function for large motors is

$$MC_{BBM} = 200 + .02Q_{BBM}.$$

Florence has further estimated that the supply function of the ten smaller firms is

$$Q_S = 10,000 + 5P.$$

Use the Oligopoly–Price Leadership tool in the *Managerial Economics Decision Assistant* to assist Florence in determining the following:
a. Her firm's profit-maximizing output and price, assuming that Better Built Motors will again act as the dominant firm in the industry.
b. The output for the combined smaller firms.

■ ■ ■ ■ ■ ■ ■ ■ ■ ■ **Selected References** ■ ■ ■ ■ ■ ■ ■ ■ ■ ■

Chamberlin, Edward H. *The Theory of Monopolistic Competition.* Cambridge, Mass.: Harvard University Press, 1933.

DeSerpa, Allan C. *Microeconomic Theory.* Boston: Allyn and Bacon, 1988, Chapters 12, 13.

Lipsey, Richard G., Peter O. Steiner, Douglas D. Purvis, and Paul N. Courant. *Economics*. New York: Harper & Row, 1990, Chapter 14.

Maurice, S. Charles, Owen R. Phillips, and C. E. Ferguson. *Economic Analysis*. Homewood, Ill.: Irwin, 1982, Chapter 10.

McCloskey, Donald N. *The Applied Theory of Price*. New York: Macmillan, 1985, Chapters 20 and 21.

Truett, Dale B., and Lila J. Truett. *Economics*. St. Louis: Times Mirror/ Mosby College Publishing, 1987, Chapter 23.

Appendix 9

Game Theory in Oligopoly Analysis

Emphasized in Chapter 9 as an important characteristic of certain oligopoly situations is the recognition by managers that their individual firms' success or failure may well depend on a strategy decision made by a rival firm. In some of the market situations we surveyed, rather restrictive assumptions were made regarding the behavior of a firm's rivals. From a strictly theoretical point of view, the horizon for describing alternative decision strategies based on various modes of rival reaction was much expanded by pioneering work in *game theory* during the period since 1944.[1] However, interest in the subject outside the academic world has waned since the 1960s, largely because the new technique and applications failed to provide concrete solutions to many oligopoly problems using real-world data. Nonetheless, some degree of familiarity with the approach broadens one's perspective of the problems faced by oligopolistic firms.

In theoretical jargon a "game" is a situation involving a payoff for a specified number of players, each of whom knows that the strategies chosen by other players will affect each individual player's success. A strategy consists of a well-defined course of action a player will take, given each possible contingency of the game. The game can be as simple as tic-tac-toe or as complicated as chess, military strategy, or a firm's marketing decisions. Many conceivable games are indeterminate; that is, their outcomes cannot be predicted. A very simple form of game can be used to show the potential usefulness of the approach in the decision analysis of the business firm. This form is the two-person, zero-sum game.

A two-person game, as its name implies, has only two players. If the game is zero-sum, this means that the sum of the gains and losses equals zero, or that one player's gains are the other's losses. It has been shown in theory that a two-person, zero-sum game will have a determinate

---

[1] The pioneer effort in this field was John von Neumann and Oskar Morgenstern, *Theory of Games and Economic Behavior* 3d ed. (Princeton, N.J.: Princeton University Press, 1953).

solution as long as a specific rule, known as the *minimax principle*, holds and mixed strategies are permitted.[2] The minimax principle is simply an assumption that each player believes the opposition will counter a given strategy with one that will leave the first player with the worst possible result. One assumes, then, that for each strategy one chooses, the other side will choose a strategy that maximizes its share of the payoff. Therefore one chooses a strategy that minimizes the opponent's maximum gain. This can be stated alternatively as a strategy that maximizes one's own minimum gain (*maximin*).

A suitable example can be drawn from a situation in which two rival firms are contemplating advertising or product differentiation strategies that will have predictable effects on the share of the total market obtained by each. It is a zero-sum game, since if Firm A gets 30 percent of the market, that would be 30 percent not obtained by Firm B. There is only 100 percent to be had, and one firm's gains are the other's losses. Hypothetical data for such a market share game are presented in Table 9A–1, which shows the outcomes in terms of Firm A's percentage of total sales in the market where it has three possible marketing strategies (A_1, A_2, and A_3), each of which maybe countered by one of three different strategies of Firm B (B_1, B_2, and B_3).

In the setting of Table 9A–1, Firm A will adopt a maximin strategy—that is, one that maximizes the firm's minimum gain. It does so by examining the possible outcomes for each one of its own strategy options and determining the worst possible result. For example, strategy A_1 will yield Firm A 90 percent of the market if Firm B counters with strategy B_1, 65 percent of the market if firm B counters with strategy B_2, and 40 percent of the market if Firm B counters with strategy B_3. Since strategy combination A_1,B_3 yields the worst result for Firm A, its managers will expect this to be the outcome from their own choice of A. This follows from their

Table 9A–1   Payoff Matrix for a Two-Firm, Zero-Sum Game (Outcomes in Terms of Firm A's Percentage share of Market)

A's Strategy	B's Strategy		
	B_1	B_2	B_3
A_1	90#	65	*40
A_2	75	70#	*60#
A_3	*20	30	50

■ ■ ■ ■ ■ ■

[2] Mixed strategies allow for the assignment of statistical probabilities to the payoffs accompanying each alternative strategy. Because the introduction of such strategies complicates the analysis, we will not concern ourselves with them here. The zero-sum game example to follow will produce a solution without our having to consider mixed strategies.

assumption that Firm B will always counter with whatever is worst for Firm A. We place an asterisk (*) in the upper right-hand box in Table 9A–1 to indicate Firm A's expected result when strategy A_1, is chosen.

When strategies A_2 and A_3 are examined, we find that the worst possible result under A_2 is A_2,B_3, which leaves Firm A with 60 percent of the market, while under A_3 the worst result for Firm A is A_3,B_1, which yields it only 20 percent of the market. We have placed asterisks in boxes A_2,B_3 and A_3,B_1 to indicate that these outcomes are expected by Firm A's managers under strategy options A_2 and A_3, respectively. Since strategy A_2 yields the maximum of the three minimum gains, Firm A's managers will choose this strategy.

Under the conditions of Table 9A–1, Firm B will choose a *minimax* strategy; that is, it will choose the Firm B strategy that minimizes Firm A's maximum gain. For example, Firm B's managers believe that if they choose strategy B_1, Firm A will counter with A_1, to maximize its share of the market. We have placed a crosshatch (#) in the upper left-hand corner of Table 9A–1 to indicate the outcome expected by Firm B. Similarly, if Firm B chooses strategy B_2, its managers will expect Firm A to counter with A_2; and for strategy B_3, Firm A is expected to counter with A_2 once again. We have placed crosshatches in boxes B_2,A_2 and B_3,A_2 to indicate Firm B's expected outcomes under strategy options B_2 and B_3, respectively. Firm B's managers will choose strategy B_3, since this is the strategy that yields the least maximum gain for their rival, Firm A.

Note that in Table 9A–1, only the box A_2, B_3 contains both an asterisk and a crosshatch. This is so because it represents the solution to the game, as we have shown by the preceding logic. In theoretical jargon the game we have examined is "strictly determined"; that is, the strategy chosen by Firm A produced the expected countermove from Firm B, and vice versa. However, if the game had not been strictly determined or the firms had not been assumed to play by the complementary maximin-minimax strategies, things could have become much more complicated—perhaps even to the point that no solution could be found.

More advanced forms of game theory and decision theory generally introduce even greater information requirements than were required for the preceding game. For example, the probability of occurrence of each outcome must be known by the players. The introduction of probability into the analysis is very appealing intellectually, since it broadens the range of solvable game situations. For example, two-person, zero-sum games that are not strictly determined can be solved when the various outcomes are weighted by their *known* probabilities. However, as one economic theorist noted some years ago, in the more difficult and interesting games, " . . . the probability that the probabilities are known is negligible."[3]

■ ■ ■ ■ ■ ■
[3] C. E. Ferguson, *Microeconomic Theory* 3d ed. (Homewood, Ill.: Irwin, 1972), p. 348.

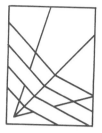

Selected Topics in Pricing and Profit Strategy

In preceding chapters our analysis of the firm and its markets has included only situations in which the firm produces and sells a single product in one market and charges a uniform price on all units sold. We have always assumed that the objective of the firm's managers is to maximize net or economic profit in both the short run and the long run. The main objective of the present chapter is to expand our analysis to take into account situations in which the firm produces more than one product, sells a product in more than one market, or considers the level of profit to be only a secondary goal. First, however, we will look at the practice of marking up merchandise by specific proportions (percentages) to show how this simple approach to pricing is related to the economics of profit maximization.

■ ■ ■ ■ ■ ■ ■ ■ ■ MARKUP PRICING

In **markup pricing** a percentage of cost or price is added to obtain market price.

Markup pricing is a pricing technique whereby a certain percentage of cost of goods sold or of price is added to the cost of goods sold in order to obtain the market price. In many industries or lines of merchandise, the experienced manager will be familiar with rules of thumb concerning the typical markup on goods sold. However, the term *markup* is understood by different people to mean different things. What some would call a 50 percent markup others would define as a 100 percent markup. For example, suppose an item costs $50 to produce and is sold for $100. In some industries this would be known as a 50 percent markup, whereas in others it would be considered a markup of 100 percent. The difference, of course, is that in the first instance the margin is a *markup on price* (the proportion of the *selling price* that represents an amount added to the cost of goods sold), whereas in the second case the markup is a *markup on cost* (the proportion of *cost of goods sold* that is added on to that figure to arrive at the selling price). In the material that follows, we shall use the *markup-on-cost* approach. To avoid confusion, we recommend that when analyzing any particular industry, one begins by determining the conventional use of the term "markup" in that industry.[1]

Markup pricing has long been a traditional way of doing business for large U.S. manufacturing companies. Firms tried to set price at a level that would allow them to achieve a certain long-run target rate of return at a particular volume of production. Price cutting in periods of short-term declines in demand was not looked on with much favor. (However, especially with the availability of computer technology, which allows a firm to do market research and to maintain sophisticated cost controls more easily, target pricing is currently not being used as rigidly as it has been in the past.[2])

When a manager decides on a given markup for a product, the manager anticipates some specific result over the planning period in terms of quantity sold and sales revenue. To the extent that such a decision maximizes profit, the manager will have correctly estimated the elasticity of demand for the product. Alternatively, a correct estimation of the elasticity of demand for the product will allow management to determine the appropriate markup.

We can demonstrate this point by examining the general relationship between marginal revenue and price elasticity of demand. We know from Chapter 2 that

$$MR = P \left(1 + \frac{1}{e_p}\right),$$

and from Chapter 6 that

$$MR = MC$$

where profit is maximized.[3] If incremental costs of production are relatively constant and average variable selling and administrative costs are immaterial, MC is approximately equal to AVC. (If the firm is a manufacturing firm, fixed manufacturing overhead per unit must also be immaterial.)

■ ■ ■ ■ ■ ■
[1] In the garment industry, for example, the term *keystoning* is used to mean pricing an item at twice its wholesale cost. However, in the trade, this practice is also called a "markup of 50 percent."
[2] "Flexible Pricing," *Business Week* (December 12, 1977), pp. 78–88.
[3] See Chapter 2, footnote 20. Also, Chapter 6, section on profit maximization.

Thus, at the profit-maximizing output and price,

$$P\left(1 + \frac{1}{e_p}\right) = MC = AVC,$$

and

$$P = \frac{AVC}{1 + \frac{1}{e_p}}.$$

We can simplify the right-hand side of this equation by first writing the denominator as one fraction and then inverting and multiplying as follows:

$$\frac{AVC}{1 + \frac{1}{e_p}} = \frac{AVC}{\frac{e_p + 1}{e_p}} = AVC\left(\frac{e_p}{e_p + 1}\right)$$

We can break this last term into two terms in the following manner:

$$AVC\left(\frac{e_p}{e_p + 1}\right) = AVC\left(\frac{e_p + 1 - 1}{e_p + 1}\right)$$

$$= AVC + AVC\left(\frac{-1}{e_p + 1}\right)$$

$$= AVC + mAVC,$$

where m is the proportion of markup on *cost*. Of course,

$$m = \frac{-1}{e_p + 1},$$

so the estimation of a profit-maximizing output and price is tantamount to estimating the elasticity of demand, e_p. Note that as long as e_p (which is nearly always negative) has an absolute value larger than one (as we showed in Chapter 2 will be the case when MR is positive), m will be *positive*. Moreover, if one knows P^*, Q^*, and e_p at point Q^*, a linear equation approximating the demand curve around that point can be found.[4]

■ ■ ■ ■ ■ ■
[4] For example, if $P^* = 2$, $Q^* = 10$, and $e_p = (dQ/dP) \cdot P^*/Q^* = -2.0$ then $-2.0 = 2/10 \cdot dQ/dP$, or $dQ/dP = -10$. Since dQ/dP is the slope (b) of the linear demand curve, $Q_d = a + bP$, we know that $Q_d = a - 10P$ is the equation for a linear demand curve, given the above information. We can find the intercept term a by substituting $Q^* = 10$ and $P^* = 2$ in that equation, so $10 = a - 10(2)$, or $a = 30$. Thus, $Q_d = 30 - 10P$ is a linear approximation of the demand function at the point $Q^* = 10$, $P^* = 2$.

Naturally, in a small business, management might not recognize the technical side of what is taking place when it determines the appropriate markup. However, the foregoing analysis certainly makes it clear that the manager who correctly chooses the profit-maximizing markup, given the unit variable costs, either has a good feel for demand conditions in the market or has made a lucky guess.

▪ ▪ ▪ ▪ ▪ ▪ ▪ ▪ ▪ ## DECISIONS INVOLVING MULTIPLE PRODUCTS

Given both the large number of technologically related products sharing today's consumer markets and the trends toward merger and acquisition in the modern business world, multiproduct firms presently outnumber single-product firms in the United States and other industrialized countries. A major task of management in a multiproduct enterprise is to analyze carefully the profitability of the various final and intermediate products that compete internally for a share of the firm's resources. For example, in the mid-1980s one of America's corporate giants, General Electric Company, was reshuffling its product mix in an effort to improve its future profitability. Specifically, it had left the small-appliance field and sold off its subsidiaries that produced minerals and oil, choosing to enter markets in microcircuits, computer graphics, and radio and television broadcasting; in addition it had moved to increase its market share in major home appliances.[5]

The Gillette Company provides another good example of a firm that faces many decisions involving multiple products. Gillette's U.S. production includes razors, blades, and many other consumer items; its European subsidiary, Braun, makes more than 400 products, most of which are in the electrical appliance line. Prior to 1977, Braun's output consisted of more than 600 products; but in order to improve its profit picture, Gillette's management dictated that about one-third of the products be eliminated.[6]

Like Braun, many of today's multiproduct firms are subsidiaries or divisions of very large companies. Moreover, the affiliation between such productive units often occurs in a setting where one of the entities responsible to a firm's top management must either *supply inputs to* an affiliate or *obtain inputs* from an affiliate. Thus the multiple product question has two major dimensions: (1) the determination of the optimal output combination for jointly produced products, and (2) the establishment of an appropriate price (known as the *transfer price*) for a product sold by one division of a firm to another division of the (same) firm. We shall consider the joint product question first.

▪ ▪ ▪ ▪ ▪ ▪

[5] "Can Jack Welch Reinvent GE?," *Business Week* (June 30, 1986), pp. 62–67.

[6] "Gillette after the Diversification that Failed," *Business Week* (February 28, 1977), pp. 58–62.

The Joint Product Problem

A multiproduct firm that has separate production facilities for each product will maximize its short-run profit by producing each product at the level of output where $MC = MR$, subject, of course, to the condition that MC is higher than MR at greater levels of output. Over the long run, the firm should move resources out of less profitable product lines and into more profitable ones. However, if the products are produced in the same plant and they are joint products or co-products in the sense that one cannot be produced without getting some of the other (in this case one of the products might be called a by-product), the firm will face a very special kind of problem in determining the profit-maximizing price and output combination for each product. When joint products are produced in fixed proportions, the analysis is relatively simple, but it becomes more complex when proportions can be varied.

In the former case (that is, joint products produced in fixed proportions), each increment of output, Q, consists of a certain amount of each jointly produced product. For example, if there are two products, A and B, one unit of Q might consist of one unit of Product A and one unit of Product B. Marginal revenue would in this case consist of $MR_A + MR_B = MR_J$. Marginal cost would be the increase in total cost as Q increases, and profit would be maximized where $MR_J = MC$, *provided that neither MR_A nor MR_B is negative*. The necessity for this latter qualification can be made clear by considering Figure 10–1.

In Figure 10–1 the demand and marginal revenue curves for Products A and B are shown, and the two MR curves are vertically summed (add $MR_A + MR_B$ at each level of output) between the origin and Q^* to obtain MR_J. The firm should never sell more than Q^* of Product B, since for larger outputs, MR_B is negative. The relevant marginal revenue curve for the firm is MR_J between the origin and Q^* and MR_A to the right of Q^*. If the firm's marginal cost curve were SMC, management's profit-maximizing strategy would be to sell Q_e of each product. On the other hand, it should be clear that if the firm's marginal cost curve is SMC', Q'_e of Product A should be sold, but only Q^* of Product B should be put on the market. An amount of Product B equal to $Q'_e - Q^*$ should be withheld from the market, even though the firm has to produce it. If storage costs are not too great and demand is expected to increase, the excess output may be stored until market conditions for Product B are such that it is rational to sell more. Alternatively, if Product B is a perishable product or if its cost of storage is high, it may be rational for the firm to destroy the excess output.

One would not have to search very far in the real world to find cases that conform to the situation just described. In Canada producers of natural gas obtain sulphur as a co-product in the process of scrubbing poisonous gases from the fuel. During the early 1970s, sulphur markets became so weak relative to world supply that the Canadian producers'

Figure 10–1   Profit-Maximizing Output Rates for Two Joint Products
Produced in Fixed Proportions

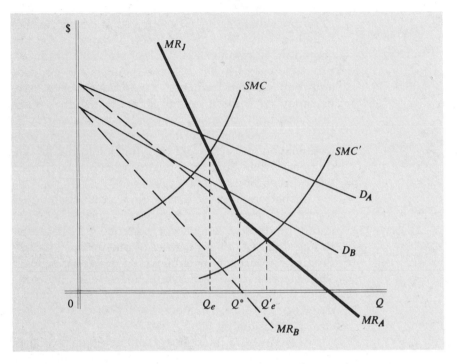

The relevant *MR* curve is *MR$_J$* for quantities less than *Q** and is *MR$_A$* for quantities greater
than *Q**. If the marginal cost curve is *SMC*, *Q$_e$* of both products should be sold. However, if
the marginal cost curve is *SMC'*, an amount equal to (*Q'$_e$* − *Q**) of Product *B* should be
withheld from sale.

stockpiles reached 10 million tons, enough to supply all U.S. industry for
an entire year. The Canadian firms could not sell their natural gas without
obtaining the sulphur, and there was no way to destroy the excess output.
Hence the sulphur just piled up on the ground and became an environmental problem in western Canada.[7] Processors of foodstuffs face similar
problems with joint products, although disposal of excess output is usually
possible. For example, pineapple packers in many instances obtain more
juice than they can feasibly market, and orange juice producers are bound
to wind up with a lot more rind than is likely to be marketable as a spice.

In cases where it is possible to vary the proportions in which joint
products are produced, management must determine the output combi-

■ ■ ■ ■ ■ ■
    [7] See testimony of D. B. Truett before the United States Tariff Commission in hearings
entitled, "Elemental Sulphur from Canada," Antidumping Investigation No. AA1921-127,
1973.

Numerical Example: Joint Products in Fixed Proportions

Pacific Porchposts produces fine ornamental wood columns in standard eight-foot lengths. For every column it produces, it obtains one pound of wood chips that can be sold as a byproduct. The demand for columns is estimated to be $Q_n = 1,400 - 20P_n$, while that for wood chips is $Q_w = 800 - 1,000P_w$. If its marginal cost of production for the two joint products is constant at \$18, will it be able to sell all of the wood chips profitably?

Answer: The company will not be able to sell all of the wood chips. This can be determined easily by noting that for wood chips, $P_w = 0.8 - .001Q_w$ and $MR_w = 0.8 - .002Q_w$. The latter equals zero when $Q = 400$. However, if $Q = 400$, since $P_n = 70 - .05Q_n$ and $MR_n = 70 - .1Q_n$, $MR_n = 70 - 40 = \$30$. Since this is greater than MC of \$18, the firm will wish to produce beyond the output where $MR_w = 0$. Thus it will obtain more wood chips than it can sell profitably. (If you carry this example further, you will find that $Q = 520$ is the profit-maximizing production level.)

nation that maximizes profit. The easiest approach to this problem is to determine the various possible outputs *for each level of total cost* and identify the output that yields maximum total revenue (at least one for every level of cost). The set of profit-maximizing cost-output combinations can be determined, and the highest of these would define the firm's optimal strategy. We can employ a set of *product transformation curves* (production possibilities curves) to describe the cost-output combinations.

In Figure 10–2, panel (a), the contour $A_1 B_1$ is a product transformation curve representing the possible output combinations the firm can produce with a given total cost. It is concave toward the origin because resources cannot be perfectly transferred from the production of Product A to the production of Product B. If the market prices of Products A and B are given (for example, if there is perfect competition), isorevenue lines such as TR_1 and TR_2 will show the various combinations of Products A and B that will yield a specific total revenue. With a total cost of \$50, the firm could attain a total revenue of \$55 by producing at R or S or at a point inside the product transformation curve on segment RS. However, if it produces at D, where the transformation curve is tangent to TR_2, the firm will attain a total revenue of \$60 and thus maximize profit for the \$50 level of total cost.

In panel (b) of Figure 10–2, we depict transformation curves for the $50, $60, and $100 levels of total cost. The situation is similar to one in which management would have to decide whether to operate a plant on one, two, or three shifts, given that both costs and the possible output combinations increase as we move from (transformation) curve A_1B_1 to curve A_2B_2 to Curve A_3B_3. Assuming that the market prices of Products A and B remain given, the profit-maximizing output combinations for the three transformation curves are D, E, and F, respectively. Management would choose combination E as the best of these three, since here $\pi = TR_2 - TC_2 = \$15$, which is the greatest profit attainable. At point D profit is only $10, and at point F it is −$5.

The foregoing analysis seems to require that the firm's managers obtain a great deal of information in order to ascertain the exact nature of the transformation and isorevenue curves. However, in any given case, management might be able to perform a perfectly satisfactory analysis by identifying only a few feasible output combinations at each cost level, rather than trying to describe completely the product transformation curve. (Indeed, smooth transformation curves, such as those of Figure 10–2, may not even exist for the firm.) In Figure 10–3 we show a transformation "curve" for a firm in which management believes it is technologically feasible to produce Product A exclusively, Product B exclusively, or a combination consisting of 25 percent A and 75 percent B. In this case the transformation curve consists only of the points C, D, and F, and the combinations represented along the dashed lines connecting these points cannot be produced. If Product B is relatively low priced (as expressed by isorevenue line TR), the firm will produce only Product A, operating at point C. If the slope of the isorevenue line is identical to that of line segment CD, the firm will attain its maximum total revenue at either C or D. As the isorevenue line becomes steeper than CD, D will become the revenue-maximizing output combination. When its slope is equal to that of segment DF, both D and F will yield the same total revenue; if steeper than DF, the firm's best output will occur at F. Thus, in the setting of Figure 10–3, it will be relatively easy for managers to compile a complete description of the alternatives and their profit outcomes, making an output decision based on the maximum profit attainable.

Finally, if we return to the problem of choosing whether to employ one, two, or three shifts with the kind of product transformation limitations illustrated in Figure 10–3, a complete description of the alternatives and their outcomes might be given by a table such as Table 10–1. Here it would take an analysis of nine possible outcomes to make a decision on the best strategy in production and sale of the joint products. Under current market conditions, management would determine that profit will be maximized when two shifts are used to produce only Product A.

Figure 10–2 Product Transformation Curves and Profit-Maximizing Output Combinations for Joint Products Produced in Variable Proportions

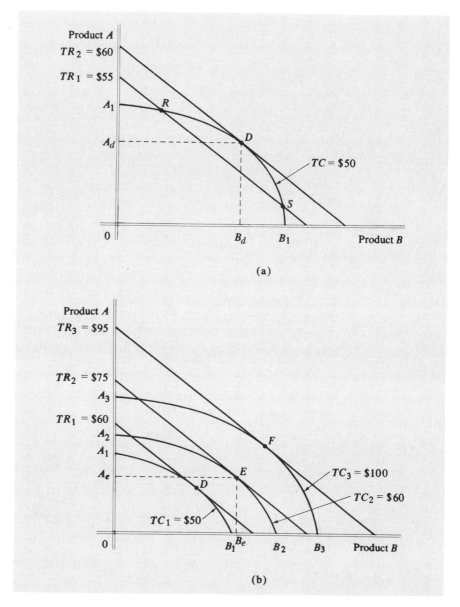

In panel (a) profit is maximized at point D, where combination A_d, B_d of the two products is produced and sold. In panel (b) the firm chooses to operate with two shifts at point E, since this strategy provides the highest profit.

Figure 10–3 Product Transformation Curve When Only One Joint Output Combination Exists

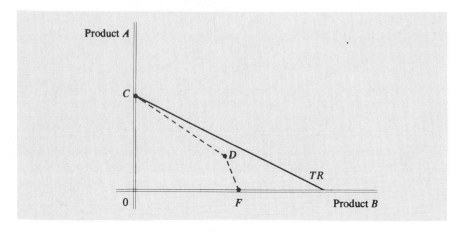

With transformation curve *CDF* and isorevenue curve *TR*, the firm would produce Product *A* only. It would produce both products when the isorevenue curve is less steep than *DF* but steeper than *CD*.

The Transfer Product Problem

Many large firms are vertically integrated, which means that at least one division of the firm produces a good that is an *input* for the product of another division. When a vertically integrated firm's top management sets

Table 10–1 Revenue, Cost, and Profit Outcomes with Two Products and Three Shifts

	Output Combinations		
No. of Shifts	*100%* *Product A*	*25% Prod. A* *75% Prod. B*	*100%* *Product B*
1	$TR = 50$ $TC = \underline{45}$ $\pi = \ \ 5$	$TR = 45$ $TC = \underline{45}$ $\pi = \ \ 0$	$TR = \ \ \ \ 30$ $TC = \ \ \ \ \underline{45}$ $\pi = \ -15$
2	$TR = 80$ $TC = \underline{65}$ $\pi = 15$	$TR = 70$ $TC = \underline{65}$ $\pi = \ \ 5$	$TR = \ \ \ \ 65$ $TC = \ \ \ \ \underline{65}$ $\pi = \ \ \ \ \ 0$
3	$TR = 95$ $TC = \underline{85}$ $\pi = 10$	$TR = 92$ $TC = \underline{85}$ $\pi = \ \ 7$	$TR = \ \ \ \ 80$ $TC = \ \ \ \ \underline{85}$ $\pi = \ \ -5$

Managerial Perspective: Cows and Farmers Mad at Good Ol' Jack Daniel

It seems the famous Jack Daniel Distillery in Lynchburg, Tennessee, produces not only sippin' whiskey, but also an interesting byproduct called "thick slop," which is used as a fortifier for cattle feed. Around Lynchburg, a feedlot industry burgeoned for decades. The cows reportedly just loved the slop-laced feed; one farmer said they would ". . . stick their snoots in all the way up beyond their eyes."

Jack Daniel at first gave the slop away to farmers who would pick it up in tank trucks. Eventually, it began to charge for the stuff, first $2 a thousand gallons, later $4. When the cattle industry grew so much that manure was polluting local streams, Daniel announced it would continue to sell slop only to farmers who invested in pollution control. However, in 1984 Jack Daniel decided to switch to the "dry house" method of handling slop, which allowed the firm to recover from it grain that could be sold for $10 per ton. The remaining thin slop did not have many nutrients, and farmers argued they could not afford to buy grain to replace what Jack Daniel had removed. Eventually, they sued Jack Daniel's parent company, Brown-Forman Distillers, arguing that Jack Daniel was requiring them to invest in pollution control at the same time it was planning to do away with thick slop. Meanwhile, the cattle industry in the area has declined significantly.

■ ■ ■ ■

Reference: "Tennessee Cattlemen Are Suin' Jack Daniel Instead of Sippin It," *The Wall Street Journal*, February 12, 1986, pp. 1, 19.

out to maximize profit, it must ensure that the divisions of the firm that supply inputs produce such goods in a quantity that is consistent with profit maximization for the entire firm. The appropriate quantity, as we shall see, may be less than, equal to, or greater than the needs of the division of the firm to which the inputs are transferred, depending on the state of the external market for the transferred input. To maximize firm profit, the price of the transfer product will be determined internally by the firm's management if there is no external market for the transfer product, and by the market if there is a perfectly competitive external market for the transfer product. In the event that the external market is not perfectly competitive, different internal and external prices will exist for the transfer product.

To simplify our discussion, we shall use throughout as an example the case of a firm having just two divisions—a final product division and a transfer product division. Further, we shall consider only cases in which one unit of the transfer product is required per unit of final product output.

Where there is no external market for the transfer product, the final product division can be viewed as either a distribution division for the transfer product or a division that combines the transfer product with other inputs to produce a different final good. The marginal cost of the entire firm, MC_e (marginal cost of the enterprise), will be the sum of MC_F (the marginal cost of the final product division excluding the transfer price finally assigned to the transferred product) and MC_T (the marginal cost of the transfer product division), which is shown as follows:

$$MC_e = MC_F + MC_T.$$

The firm generates external revenue solely from the sale of the final good. If D_F is a downward-sloping demand curve for the final good and MR_F is the marginal revenue curve derived from it, the firm will maximize profit where

$$MC_e = MR_F.$$

This is shown in Figure 10–4, panel (a), at E—where Q_e is the profit-maximizing output of both the final product and the transfer product. Since $MC_e = MC_F + MC_T$, we can restate the profit-maximizing condition as follows:

$$MR_F = MC_F + MC_T.$$

Subtracting MC_F from both sides of the equation, we get

$$MR_F - MC_F = MC_T.$$

Now, for the firm as a whole, the left-hand term above is the **net marginal revenue** (NMR_F) obtained from selling the final product after deduction of all incremental costs except that of the transfer product. The net marginal cost (NMC_F) of the *final product* is MC_T (the difference between the marginal cost of the entire enterprise, MC_e, and MC_F, the marginal cost of the final division):

$$MC_T = MC_e - MC_F = NMC_F.$$

We can restate the profit-maximizing condition as

$$NMR_F = MR_T = MC_T = NMC_F$$

Figure 10–4   Optimal Production of Final and Transfer Product with
No External Market for the Transfer Product

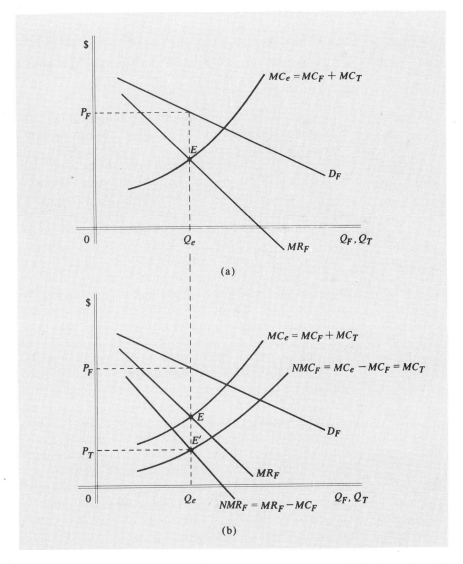

(a)

(b)

In panel (a) the firm maximizes profit at Q_e, where $MC_e = MR_F$. Panel (b) shows that with
no external market for the transfer product, profit maximization is consistent with the
condition $NMR_F = MC_T$.

In panel (b) of Figure 10–4, the preceding condition is met at E'. E' must
occur directly below E, since NMC_F is MC_e reduced by MC_F and NMR_F is
MR_F reduced by the same amount.

Given the preceding profit-maximizing conditions, management must develop a strategy that will ensure the following two results:

1. That the transfer product division will supply Q_e of the transfer product
2. That the final product division will demand Q_e of the transfer product

These results can be accomplished by either of two strategies. First, management might decide to let the final product division fix the price of the transfer product, giving precise information on the marginal cost curve of the division producing the transferred product and instructing the division to set the transfer price of the transfer product equal to the marginal cost of the transfer product at the optimal level of output. The final product division would then know that the price it sets will constitute the MR curve of the transfer product division, since like a perfectly competitive firm facing a fixed price, the latter will regard its situation as one in which $P = MR$. The transfer product division will profit maximize where $P_T = MR_T = MC_T$, and the final product division will have set the transfer price equal to MC_T at Q_e, the output that maximizes the firm's profit. In terms of Figure 10–4, the price would be P_T, determined by the intersection of NMC_F with NMR_F. Note that $NMC_F = MC_T$, since after accounting for all variable costs of the final product division, the remaining marginal costs will consist of those attributable to the transfer product division.

The second strategy that management might follow to ensure that Q_e of the transfer product is produced and that P_T is established as the transfer price would involve letting the transfer product division set P_T based on the final product division's *demand curve* for Product T. Since NMR_F in Figure 10–4, panel (b), shows the amount of Product T that the final product division would purchase when it equates a given P_T to NMR_F, it is the final product division's demand curve for Product T. With this information available, the transfer product division would be instructed to expand output up to the point at which the price that the final product division is willing to pay is exactly equal to MC_T. Again, this will occur at E' in Figure 10–4, panel (b).

Where there is a perfectly competitive external market for the transfer product, the final product division should not pay the transfer product division a price in excess of that at which the transfer product can be obtained from outside suppliers. Likewise, the transfer product division should not sell to the final product division at a price that is *less* than it can obtain in the external market. All of this leads to the conclusion that the appropriate transfer price will be the prevailing, perfectly competitive, external market price. This being the case, there is no assurance that the transfer product division will produce an amount of Product T equal to that demanded by the final product division when profits are maximized for the firm.

Figure 10–5 presents two situations in which there is a perfectly competitive external market for the transfer product and the output of the

Figure 10–5   Optimal Production of Final Product and Transfer Product

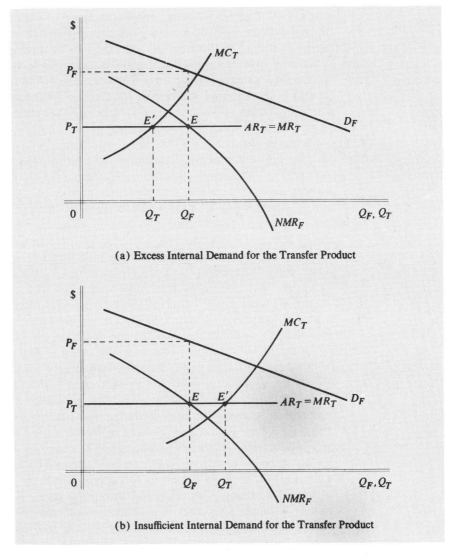

(a) Excess Internal Demand for the Transfer Product

(b) Insufficient Internal Demand for the Transfer Product

In panel (a) the final product division produces Q_F and obtains $(Q_F - Q_T)$ of the transfer product from outside suppliers. In panel (b) the transfer product division sells $(Q_T - Q_F)$ to outside purchasers.

transfer product division is not equal to the quantity demanded by the final product division when firm profits are maximized. In panel (a) the demand curve facing the transfer product division is $AR_T = MR_T$ since the price of the product, P_T, is determined in the perfectly competitive market. At the final product equilibrium quantity, P_T is also equal to NMR_F. NMR_F is obtained by subtracting MC_F from MR_F.

The final product division maximizes profit at Q_F, P_F, since this is consistent with the intersection of NMR_F with AR_T at E. In this case P_T, given by AR_T, *represents the appropriate marginal cost of the transfer product to the final division.* MC_T no longer gives the appropriate marginal cost of the transfer product to the final division because where $MC_T < P_T$, the firm incurs an opportunity cost if it sells the transfer product to the final product division at a price less than P_T. That is because the transfer product could be sold in the external market for P_T. On the other hand, if $MC_T > P_T$, it would not be economically sound to produce the transfer product and sell it to the final product division at a price greater than P_T, since that division could always purchase the transfer product externally at a price of P_T.

The profit-maximizing condition for the transfer product division is met at E', where $MR_T = P_T = MC_T$. Thus only Q_T is produced by the transfer product division, and the final product division must purchase $Q_F - Q_T$ of the transfer product in the external market. Since the transfer product division cannot produce units of output beyond Q_T at a marginal cost as low as the external price, P_T, the final product division should not force the transfer product division to supply the additional amount needed to maximize firm profit.

Figure 10–5, panel (b), illustrates a situation in which firm profits are maximized when the transfer product division produces *more* output than is needed by the final product division when the latter is maximizing profit from the sale of the final good. In this instance the quantity $Q_T - Q_F$ of the transfer product should be sold in the external market for P_T per unit— the prevailing market price. Such activity clearly adds to the total profit of the firm, since $MC_T < MR_T = P_T$ between Q_F and Q_T.

It is obvious that the transfer pricing problem is one that must be confronted by many firms and that it has numerous dimensions. The foregoing discussion only scratches the surface of the issue. For example, the analysis becomes more complex when the transfer product can be sold in a less than perfectly competitive external market and the external price is not a given. (See the appendix to this chapter.)

Transfer pricing is an especially important issue in international business. If a transfer product is sold across international boundaries by a multinational corporation, management must take into account the tax consequences of accruing divisional profits in one location rather than another. In this setting, transfer prices may be manipulated to move profits out of divisions located in countries with high taxes or restrictions on capital flows and accumulate them in divisions located in lower tax areas

Numerical Example: Transfer Pricing

Camgo Company makes inexpensive, fixed-focus 35mm cameras. Its subsidiary, Focrude, Inc., makes the lenses for the cameras. The market for such lenses is highly competitive, and they can be either bought or sold at the equilibrium market price of $2. Camgo estimates the demand for its cameras to be $Q_c = 12,000 - 400P_c$, so that $MR_c = 30 - .005Q_c$. The marginal cost of manufacturing the cameras, *not* including the lenses, is constant and equal to $5. The marginal cost of the Focrude division for making the lenses is given by the equation $MC_f = .30 + .0004Q_f$. Each camera requires one lens. Will Focrude be able to both supply Camgo's required number of lenses and sell profitably in the outside market?

Answer. To find out how many cameras Camgo should sell to maximize profit, set net marginal revenue from camera sales equal to the price of the transfer product:

$$\text{Definition: } NMR_c = MR_c - MC_c = 30 - 0.005Q_c - 5$$
$$= 25 - 0.005Q_c$$

Because of the external competitive market, $NMC_c = 2$. Thus

$$25 - .005Q_c = 2; \quad \text{and} \quad Q_c = 4,600.$$

The Focrude division will maximize profit where its marginal cost equals the marginal revenue of $2 from sales both inside and external to the firm. So

$$.30 + 0004(Q_f) = 2,$$
$$.0004(Q_f) = 1.70;$$

and

$$Q_f = 4,250.$$

Focrude will be unable to supply Camgo with enough lenses to meet its requirements, and Camgo will buy 350 of them on the external market.

with freer movement of capital. Some very large multinational corporations have established divisional "profit centers" to which profits from certain designated geographical areas are transferred.[8] Needless to say, such practices may have noticeable effects on the economies of countries in which the multinational corporations operate, and many nations have taken steps to curb the use of transfer pricing as a mechanism for changing the locus of profits.

■ ■ ■ ■ ■ ■ ■ ■ ■ **DECISION STRATEGY WITH MULTIPLE MARKETS**

We return now to the setting of the single-product firm to examine managerial strategy in situations where it is possible to identify more than one *market* for the product. Such a situation is a relatively common phenomenon encountered by firms that are oligopolistic or monopolistic. The separation of buyers into distinct markets characterized by different prices is known as **price discrimination** or **market segmentation**. It is a practice that is legal under certain circumstances and illegal under others. Briefly, in the United States, price discrimination is prohibited in interstate commerce when its effect is to lessen competition substantially or when it tends to create a monopoly. It is permitted when it can be justified on the basis of differences in grade, quality, or quantity sold; differences in transportation costs; or the lowering of price in good faith to meet competition. The prohibition against price discrimination applies only to products that will be resold; it does not apply to sales to the final consumer.[9]

Price discrimination allows different prices for the same product in different markets.

Firms in many different lines of business take advantage of opportunities to increase profits by selling what is essentially the same product to different groups of consumers at different prices. Persons attending conventions get lower hotel room rates than are regularly charged. Theaters charge afternoon moviegoers a lower price than is paid by those who see the same films at night. So-called commercial rates abound in everything from electric power to rental cars. Many of the discriminations in price that occur daily in the United States have not been tested in the courts, but such testing would undoubtedly prove a large proportion of them to be justifiable. The individual firm must seek competent legal guidance in the question of pricing for multiple markets, but it must also be prepared to recognize opportunities to increase profit through acceptable forms of market segmentation.

The mechanics of increasing profit through the separation of markets are easily understood. We shall use convention rates at hotels to illustrate the steps taken by management in the multiple price-setting decision. First, management must determine whether it is actually better off to establish a convention rate and a regular rate, rather than charge the same

■ ■ ■ ■ ■ ■

[8] For a good discussion of transfer pricing in multinational business, see David K. Eiteman and Arthur I. Stonehill, *Multinational Business Finance* 5th ed. (Reading, Mass.: Addison-Wesley, 1989) pp. 555–561.

[9] Lawrence S. Clark and Peter D. Kinder, *Law and Business: The Regulatory Environment* 3d ed. (New York: McGraw-Hill, 1991), pp. 912–915.

rate to all occupants of rooms of a given quality. This latter question will depend upon the *elasticity* of demand for rooms in the general market as opposed to that in the convention market. (Our definition of the "general market" is that in which rooms are rented singly or in small quantities, and the "convention market" is that in which rooms are blocked in large quantity and subsequently rented to members of a special group.) We shall see that if the elasticity of demand in the general market is lower than that in the convention market, management should establish a general market room rate that is higher than the rate it charges in the convention market.

Let us say that we are looking at the multiple rate question from the standpoint of a big-city hotel that can expect to do a considerable amount of convention trade at all times during the year. Management wishes to maximize daily profit from combined general market trade and convention market trade. The hotel has 1,600 rooms of equal quality that it expects to rent in the $60 to $90 per day category. Based on studies of the general and convention markets for hotel rooms in the city in which it is located and management's experience in other large cities, the demand curves for rooms in the two markets have been estimated to conform to the following equations:

$$\textit{General market} \qquad R_g = 1,400 - 10P_g,$$

where R_g is the number of rooms rented per day and P_g is the room rate for the general market.

$$\textit{Convention market} \qquad R_c = 2,400 - 20P_c,$$

where R_c is the number of rooms rented per day and P_c is the room rate for the convention market. These two demand curves are plotted, along with their respective marginal revenue curves, in panels (a) and (b) of Figure 10–6. The curves are drawn with solid lines only in the $60 to $90 range, where management expects to establish prices.

Now, suppose that management has estimated the total cost function for the hotel to be

$$TC = 18,200 + 30R_g + 30R_c$$

where R_g *and* R_c are, respectively, the number of general rate and convention rate rooms rented per day and daily fixed cost is $18,200. It should be clear from the preceding formula that the marginal cost of a room, whether rented to an occupant in the convention market or the regular market, is $30. Short-run average cost, however, will fall as the daily fixed cost is divided by an increasing quantity of rooms rented.

Figure 10–6 Hotel Pricing Analysis with and without Discrimination Between Convention and General Markets

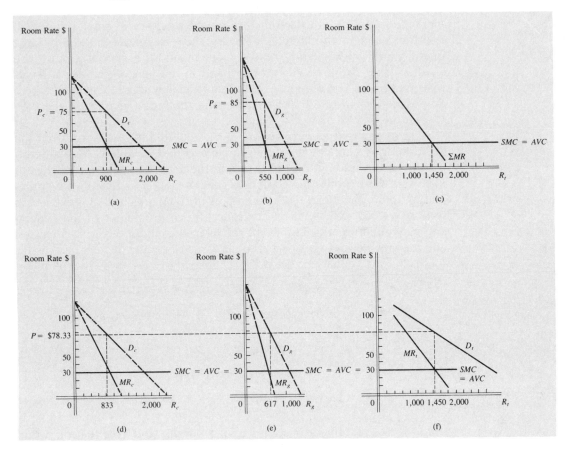

Panels (a), (b), and (c) show the hotel practicing price discrimination and charging a $75 convention rate but an $85 general rate. In panels (d), (e), and (f), there is no discrimination and both groups of consumers are charged $78.33.

The average variable cost and marginal cost curves appear in panel (c) of Figure 10–6. The ΣMR curve in panel (c) is derived by summing the quantities that correspond to each MR level in panels (a) and (b). For example, at the $30 level of MR, MR_c corresponds to 900 rooms rented in the convention market, and MR_g corresponds to 550 rooms rented in the general market. Thus we show the sum of these, 1,450 rooms, as the total quantity that can be rented (along ΣMR) when $MR = \$30$.

The profit-maximizing condition when selling in two markets is that marginal cost is equal to marginal revenue in both markets, or (in terms of our hotel)

$$MR_g = MR_c = SMC.$$

To understand why this must be so, consider any situation where $MR_g \neq MR_c$. For example, if $MR_g > MR_c$, the hotel can increase total revenue simply by renting one less room in the convention market and one more in the general market. As in other profit-maximizing problems, output should be increased as long as marginal cost is less than MR_g and MR_c, or up to the point where $SMC = \Sigma MR$ in panel (c) of Figure 10–6. This locates the optimum output, which for the hotel is 1,450 rooms rented per day. We satisfy the condition $MR_g = MR_c = SMC$ in panels (a) and (b) by projecting $\Sigma MR = SMC = \$30$ back to each MR curve. The price and quantity relevant to each market can then be determined as those corresponding to the intersection of $\Sigma MR = SMC = \$30$ with the individual market MR curves. For the general market, the profit-maximizing quantity is 550 rooms per day and the rate per room is $85. For the convention market, the optimum quantity is 900 rooms per day and the rate per room is $75. Mathematically, this information is expressed as follows:

(10–1)
$$P_g = 140 - .1R_g$$
$$TR_g = 140R_g - .1R_g^2$$
$$MR_g = 140 - .2R_g$$

(10–2)
$$P_c = 120 - .05R_c$$
$$TR_c = 120R_c - .05R_c^2$$
$$MR_c = 120 - .1R_c$$

Since SMC is constant at $30, when profit is maximized,

(10–3)
$$30 = MR_g = MR_c$$

(10–4)
$$30 = 140 - .2R_g$$
$$R_g = 550$$

(10–5)
$$30 = 120 - .1R_c$$
$$R_c = 900$$

From equations 10–1 and 10–2, we can then obtain $P_g = \$85$ and $P_c = \$75$. Profit is calculated as follows:

$$
\begin{aligned}
\pi &= TR - TC \\
&= R_g(P_g) + R_c\,(P_c) - 18{,}200 - 30R_g - 30R_c \\
&= 550(85) + 900(75) - 18{,}200 - 30(550) - 30(900) \\
&= \$52{,}550 \text{ per day.}
\end{aligned}
$$

It can be shown that no single price could produce as much profit for the hotel as the two previous prices, given the two demand curves in panels (a) and (b) of Figure 10–6. The mathematics of this situation are somewhat complicated; however, we present a simple graphical explanation in panels (d), (e), and (f) of Figure 10–6. Panels (d) and (e) contain the same demand and MR curves represented in panels (a) and (b). In panel (f), instead of summing the MR quantities from each market, we sum the quantities demanded at each price to obtain an aggregate demand curve, D_t. This curve expresses the total amount sold at various prices subject to the condition that $P_g = P_c$. The curve MR_t in panel (f) is the marginal revenue curve relevant to D_t. Where $SMC = \$30$ intersects MR_t, we establish the optimum quantity, 1,450 rooms, and the price, \$78.33. Note, however, that when this price is applied to the demand curves in panels (d) and (e), quantities are obtained that do not correspond to the intersection of $SMC = 30$ with MR_g and MR_c. In fact, we can see that at a price of \$78.33, $MR_g < SMC$ *and* $MR_c > SMC$. In terms of profit, the hotel is worse off, since

$$\pi = 1{,}450(78.33) - 18{,}200 - 30(1{,}450)$$
$$= \$51{,}879 \text{ per day.}$$

Clearly, if the law permits discrimination between the two markets, the hotel's management should establish a higher rate for general market customers than for convention market customers.

Earlier we noted that when markets are segmented, the market with the lowest (in absolute value) elasticity of demand would have the highest price when profit is maximized. This can be established from the general relationship between marginal revenue and elasticity of demand, which was introduced in Chapter 2 and is expressed as follows:

$$MR = P\left(1 + \frac{1}{e_P}\right) = P\left(1 - \frac{1}{|e_P|}\right), \quad \text{since } e_p < 0.$$

Recall that in the two market case, $MR_g = MR_c$ when profit is maximized. Therefore, it must also follow that

$$P_g\left(1 - \frac{1}{|e_g|}\right) = P_c\left(1 - \frac{1}{|e_c|}\right).$$

From the preceding equation, we can see that when $P_g > P_c$ it must be true that $|e_g| < |e_c|$, or, in the case of our hotel, the elasticity of demand for rooms is higher in the convention market than in the general market.

Of course, there are numerous cases in which management may be faced with a multiple-market pricing decision. We can expect the possi-

Managerial Perspective: Computers and Price Discrimination

Price discrimination is becoming increasingly common in two large U.S. service industries, hotels and airlines. Travelers who use the airlines regularly are quite aware of the term "limited seat availability" that almost always appears in the fine-print footnote to air carriers' ads that trumpet special discount fares. This qualification allows the companies to switch seats from the discount market to the full-fare market when demand on a given route heats up. The discount fares are based on a specific demand estimate for each class of travel (discount, full coach, first class, etc.). With computer booking now pervasive in the industry, it is easy to track changes in demand and reduce the availability of discount seats if higher marginal revenue can be obtained from sales of nondiscounted seats. The hotels have learned from the airlines, and now the big chains that have computerized booking also reduce the availability of advertised discount rooms when demand in the nondiscount market increases. Some state attorneys general have eyed the practice warily, fearing that consumers will be treated unfairly if sufficient numbers of the advertised rooms are not made available.

■ ■ ■ ■

References: "No Cheap Room? Blame Yield Management," *The Wall Street Journal*, January 4, 1988, p. 8; and "Computers Permit Airlines to Use Scalpel to Cut Fares," *The Wall Street Journal*, February 2, 1987, p. 25.

bility of profit maximization through price discrimination or market segmentation to exist any time that distinct groups of consumers purchase a product in different quantities, at different times of the year, or of slightly different attributes (first class vs. tourist transportation, for example). In many cases such discrimination in pricing will be justifiable. Thus the competent manager must be able to recognize such possibilities if the firm is to be guided to maximum profit.

■ ■ ■ ■ ■ ■ ■ ■ ALTERNATIVES TO PROFIT MAXIMIZATION

All of the situations discussed thus far in this chapter—and indeed, throughout this book—have focused on the managerial goal of profit maximization. Although it seems reasonable to accept profit maximization as at least the long-run goal of a firm's managers, there are good reasons to question this assumption. One of the well-recognized characteristics of business in the United States today is *separation of ownership and control.*

Since modern corporations are owned by shareholders but controlled by managers who may or may not have the shareholders' interest as their prime concern, there is a possibility that profit maximization, even when desired by shareholders, will not be the objective of the firms' managers. For example, a corporation manager whose goal is personal success, measured in terms of both income and job prestige, might perceive that personal rewards are more closely tied to the *size of the firm* than to profitability. In this setting, the manager might wish to expand sales beyond the point of profit maximization in order to capture a larger share of the market or to give the illusion of rapid growth. The firm might then be led to operate where *sales* are maximized, subject to the constraint that profit is sufficient to keep shareholders satisfied.[10]

The preceding situation is described in Figure 10–7, where instead of operating at Q_e, the firm operates at Q^*. At output level Q^*, sales revenue

Figure 10–7   Maximization of Sales Revenue Compared with Profit Maximization

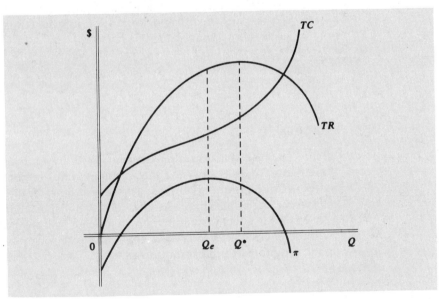

If the firm chooses to maximize sales revenue, it will operate at Q^*, even though maximum profit would be obtained at Q_e, a lower output.

■ ■ ■ ■ ■ ■
[10] See "GE's Wizards Turning from the Bottom Line to Share of the Market," *The Wall Street Journal,* July 12, 1982, pp. 1, 14; and "Position Wanted: Corporate Strategists Giving New Emphasis to Market Share, Rank," *The Wall Street Journal,* February 3, 1978, pp. 1, 23.

is maximized but profit is less than at Q_e. Presumably, shareholders will not complain because profit at Q^* is still greater than normal. Of course, for certain firms appreciation of stock prices may, during one time period or another, be more closely correlated with growth than with profits. In such a setting both shareholders and management might be more interested in sales increases than in maximum profit.

Although profit maximization and the conditions necessary to attain it are bound to be of importance to every manager, it is clear that the question of objectives of the firm includes a number of other considerations. Survival is not the least of these, and in a world characterized by oligopoly, risk aversion on the part of management could easily take precedence over profit maximization. In fact, in the game-theory model we presented in the appendix to Chapter 9, the firm was seen to choose a strategy that would maximize its *minimum* market share (the least market share it could obtain given rival reactions to its various possible strategies). Finally, we must note that most profit-maximizing rules based on market demand tend to be utilized where rather short-run views of the market are estimated. As the time horizon pertinent to a management decision becomes longer, the difficulty in estimating demand increases, since more variables are likely to become relevant. Further, the possibility exists that short-run profit maximization may not be consistent with long-run profit maximization. A firm might choose in the short run to have lower profit and higher sales because over the long run or in subsequent periods, the consequences of early market penetration may have a very positive effect on profit. In other words, capturing additional markets today at rather low rates of profit may mean greatly increased profits in the future. To some extent the capital budgeting approach to long-run planning of the firm takes into account the effects of strategies that produce differential profit outcomes over time. This approach, which is an extension of the profit-maximizing analyses we have been using all along, will be discussed in Chapter 13.

■ ■ ■ ■ ■ ■ ■ ■   SUMMARY

Multiple Products, Segmented Markets, and the Firm

In this chapter we have discussed pricing and output decisions of the firm in more complex situations than those assumed to exist in previous chapters. At the beginning of the chapter, we examined markup pricing and found that it is not inconsistent with the conditions for profit maximization. More complex pricing problems were then discussed, beginning with the profit-maximizing behavior of firms that produce multiple products. The first case considered was that where two products can or must be produced jointly. If the two products *must* be produced in fixed proportions, the firm will maximize profit if it produces where the joint marginal revenue of the two products is equal to their joint marginal cost. (If the marginal revenue of one of the products becomes negative before this point is reached, some of the output of this product should be either destroyed or stored.) We also demonstrated that the situation is much more complex if the products can be produced in variable proportions.

Next we directed our attention to the case in which one division of a firm produces a product, called the *transfer product*, that is also used as an intermediate product in making the product of another division of the firm, the *final product* division. We discussed how the firm would determine the profit-maximizing quantities of the final division product and the transfer product and the appropriate price that should be charged the final product division for the transfer product. We saw that the determination of the optimal transfer price and quantities of both products differed, depending on whether or not the transfer product could be sold in an external market.

We then considered the situation in which the firm sells the *same product in two separate markets* and can legally charge a different price (price discriminate) in each market. As we saw, for price discrimination to be economically sound, customers in the two markets must have different elasticities of demand, and the firm must be able to prevent customers in the higher priced market from buying the product in the lower priced market. The general profit-maximizing rule for the firm in this situation is that the firm should produce and sell in each market until marginal revenue in each market is equal to firm marginal cost.

Finally, we discussed alternative goals to profit maximization, such as sales maximization. It may be that firm *managers* are more likely to have goals other than profit maximization if they are not also the firm's *owners*.

In the next chapter we turn to the issue of economic forecasting. Economic forecasting refers to the process of analyzing available information regarding economic variables and relationships and then predicting the future value of certain variables of interest to the business firm or to economic policymakers. Then, in Chapter 12, we return to the simpler case of the firm producing one product for one market and discuss how the firm can determine the short-run, profit-maximizing quantity of a variable input to be employed, assuming that all other inputs are fixed.

■ ■ ■ ■ ■ ■ ■ ■ ■ ■ ■ ■ ■ ■ ■ **Questions** ■ ■ ■ ■ ■ ■ ■ ■ ■ ■ ■ ■ ■ ■ ■

1. Under what set of circumstances would a firm that produces two joint products in fixed proportions be forced to withhold a portion of one product from the market?

2. How can a product transformation curve be employed to illustrate profit maximization with joint products produced in variable proportions? How is revenue represented in such a setting?

3. What is a transfer product? Under what circumstances might such a product be sold externally, as well as transferred?
4. State in two different ways the necessary condition for optimal production of a transfer product in the case of no external market for the transfer product.
5. What is meant by market segmentation or price discrimination? Where a firm is selling in two separate markets, what is the condition that must be fulfilled in order to maximize the firm's profit?
6. Under what circumstances would it be useless (although not illegal) to charge different prices in two separate markets?
7. Why might a firm's management choose to operate at a rate of output greater than the rate that maximizes profit? How can such behavior be reconciled with the profit maximization norm?
8. Why is transfer pricing an important issue in international business?
9. Under what circumstances is price discrimination legal in the United States?
10. Name some industries in your community in which firms legally and overtly practice price discrimination.
11. What is meant by markup pricing? Has it been used by firms as a long-run or a short-run pricing strategy? Explain.

■ ■ ■ ■ ■ ■ ■ ■ ■ ■ ■ ■ ■ ■ **Problems** ■ ■ ■ ■ ■ ■ ■ ■ ■ ■ ■ ■ ■ ■

1. Given the following product transformation curve, indicate the amount of X and Y that will maximize profit for the firm if the selling price per unit of X is 1/2 the price per unit of Y

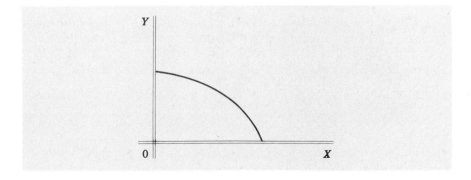

2. Sketch a product transformation curve for a firm that produces two joint products (X and Y) but has only the following input-output production possibilities:
   a. 100 percent X
   b. 75 percent X and 25 percent Y

  c. 50 percent *X* and 50 percent *Y*
  d. 25 percent *X* and 75 percent *Y*
  e. 100 percent *Y*
  Note: Assume that resources cannot be perfectly transferred from the
  production of *X* to the production of *Y*.

3. Suppose Randy Corporation is selling its product both in the United
    States and overseas and faces the two demand curves illustrated here.
    If the company's marginal cost is constant at $7.50 per unit of output,
    determine from the graphs what price it will charge in each market.
    (The United States has a large tariff on the product.)

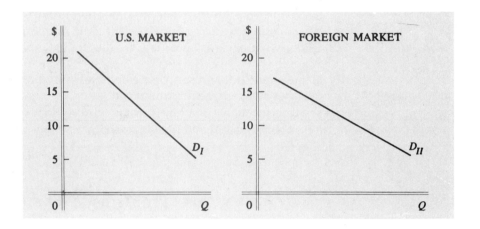

4. Suppose a company produces two products, *A* and *B*, and the pro-
    duction process is such that one unit of *A* is always obtained with one
    unit of *B*. If the demand curves for *A* and *B* are estimated to be:

    $Q_A = 100 - P_A$ (so that $MR_A = 100 - 2Q_A$)

    $Q_B = 120 - 0.8P_B$ (so that $MR_B = 150 - 2.5Q_B$),

    and the marginal cost of production is $MC = 4 + 1.5Q_J$, where Q_J
    consists of one unit of each product, how much of each product should
    the firm sell in order to maximize profit?

5. A company that produces plastic products by using injection molding
    machines has the following production and revenue alternatives for
    three products (*A*, *B*, and *C*) that are feasible to produce with the
    existing plant and equipment:

Product Combinations

No. of Shifts	100% A	50% A 50% B	100% B	75% A 25% B
1	TR = 200	TR = 225	TR = 275	TR = 200
2	TR = 380	TR = 410	TR = 500	TR = 400
3	TR = 490	TR = 575	TR = 575	TR = 600

TR is in thousands of dollars per month. *Total* cost for the first shift is $125,000 per month—of which $80,000 is labor, $40,000 is other variable costs, and $5,000 is fixed cost. As the number of shifts is increased, fixed cost remains at $5,000 per month while variable costs other than labor remain the same *per shift*. For the second shift, labor must be paid 1.25 times the amount paid in the first shift; for the third shift, labor must be paid 1.50 times what it receives in the first shift.

a. Determine total cost for the two-shift and three-shift alternatives.

b. Indicate the product combination and shift level that maximizes profit.

6. The Maxton Company produces a number of household appliances, including an electric coffee pot. The final product division of the company manufactures the metal pot and all plastic parts and then assembles, packages, and distributes the product. The electrical components unit of the coffee pot (consisting of a heating element, a thermocouple, and related wiring items) are produced by a separate electrical parts division of the firm.

   The electrical parts division could sell the coffee pot components unit in the open market to a number of assemblers at a standard price of $2.80. There is vigorous competition in the electrical components industry, and it is unlikely that any but the going price can be obtained.

   Management has determined that the demand curve for quantity sold per month of the final product is

$$Q_f = 3,000 - 125P_f \quad \text{(so that } MR_f = 24 - .016Q_f \text{),}$$

while the marginal cost of the final product, *excluding* the cost of the electrical components unit, is

$$MC_f = .004Q_f.$$

In addition, management has determined that the marginal cost of the transfer product division is

$$MC_t = .008Q_t,$$

where Q_t is the quantity of the transfer product produced.

a. At what final product price and rate of output will the firm maximize profit?

b. How much of the transfer product should be produced?

c. Should the final product division obtain *all* of its electrical components units for the coffee pot from its own components division? Why or why not?

d. Construct a diagram corresponding to the above situation. Show the equilibrium output for each division.

7. The management of Castle's Fried Chicken is planning a pricing policy based on market segmentation. M. J. Pyronic, the firm's sales manager, argues that the eat-in customer can be differentiated from the carry-out customer because the latter will generally purchase a large quantity of chicken to serve a group of people at home. Pyronic estimates that carry-out demand is more elastic than eat-in demand and states that carry-out buckets should be priced at a lower rate per serving of chicken (one wing, one drumstick, and one thigh) than the price per serving for eat-in customers.

Pyronic's estimate of carry-out demand is

$$Q_c = 10,000 - 2,000P_c \qquad \text{(so that } MR_c = 5 - .001Q_c),$$

where Q_c, is the number of carry-out orders sold per week and P_c is the price per carry-out serving. She estimates the eat-in demand per week to be

$$Q_j = 6,000 - 1,000P_j \qquad \text{(so that } MR_j = 6 - .002Q_j),$$

where P_j is the price per eat-in serving. Marginal cost per serving is constant at $1.20.

a. Should the price per serving for the carry-out market be lower than that for the eat-in market?

b. How many servings per week should be sold in each market to maximize profit?

c. What price or prices should be charged?

d. Diagram the case showing the profit-maximizing rates of output and the average revenue.

8. Salmagam Corporation purchases video camcorder batteries from a manufacturer in Hong Kong and distributes them to retail stores throughout the United States. Salmagam's management has estimated that within the range of feasible prices for the batteries, the elasticity of demand of the retail stores for them is -3.5. If Salmagam can obtain any quantity of the batteries from the manufacturer for a fixed price of $18, answer the following:

a. What will be its profit-maximizing markup percentage?

b. What price should it charge for the batteries?

The following problems require calculus:

9. Schmooker Chemical Company produces bubble bath powder using a process that yields a joint product of one unit of deadly Z41 pesticide for each unit of bubble bath produced. Schmooker's demand curve for bubble bath is $Q_b = 3,800 - P_b$. Its demand curve for Z41 has the equation $Q_z = 6,000 - 5P_z$. Schmooker's total cost function for the two joint products is $TC = 500 + 20Q + .095Q^2$. Answer the following:
    a. How much of each product should Schmooker sell?
    b. What price should it charge for each product?
    c. Should it withhold any of either product from the market? If so, which one (and how much) should it keep off the market?

10. Taipei Electronics makes compact disc players under license from CRA Corporation. One of Taipei's subsidiaries, Lenscan Corporation, makes the optical stylus for the players. The total dollar cost of production of the stylus by Lenscan is

$$TC_s = 12,000 + 2Q_s + .0001Q_s^2$$

Taipei's marginal cost (in dollars) for the final production of the disc players (not including the cost of the stylus) is $MC_d = 10 + .003Q_d$. The demand curve for the disc player is:

$$Q_d = 70,000 - 400P_d, \qquad \text{where } P_d \text{ is in dollars.}$$

If the optical stylus can be bought or sold in the open market at a fixed price of $5 per unit, determine the following:
    a. The number of disc players Taipei should sell.
    b. The price that should be charged for the players.
    c. The number of optical styli the Lenscan subsidiary should produce.
    d. The price that Lenscan should charge for the stylus.

11. Down Under Products is an Australian firm that produces wine for sale to manufacturers of wine coolers. Due to spoilage in the production process, it also sells a co-product, wine vinegar. The ratio of vinegar to wine it produces is constant and equal to one case of vinegar for each case of wine produced. Down Under's current estimate of wine demand is represented by the following equation:

$$Q_w = 12,000 - 100P_w,$$

where Q_w is the number of cases of wine sold per month and P_w is the price obtained per case of wine.

Respectively, the demand curve for wine vinegar and the firm's total cost function are the following:

$$Q_v = 6,000 - 200P_v,$$

where Q_v is the number of cases of vinegar sold per month and P_v is the price per case; and

$$TC = \$100,000 + 4.16Q + 0.006Q^2,$$

where $\$100,000$ is monthly fixed cost and Q represents the number of case equivalents of the two products it produces.

Down Under's present strategy is to maximize profit from the sales of the two products, given that there is no disposal cost for any excess product. Find the profit-maximizing quantities sold of the two products, their prices, the amount of excess product not sold, if any, and Down Under's total profit from sales of the two joint products.

12. Gongalong Company makes grandfather's clocks. One of its subsidiaries, Boing, Inc., makes the mainsprings for the clocks. The market for such springs (which have many other novel uses) is highly competitive, and the going market price for them is $\$28.00$ per unit. Gongalong estimates the demand for its clocks to be $Q_c = 14,000 - 20P_c$. The marginal cost of manufacturing the clocks, *not* including the mainsprings, is given by the function $MC_c = 23 + .12Q_c$. The marginal cost of the Boing division for making the mainsprings is $MC_s = 4 + .005Q_s$. There is one mainspring in each clock. Answer the following:
   a. How many clocks should Gongalong produce, and what price should it charge per clock?
   b. How many mainsprings should Boing Inc. produce, and what price should it charge Gongalong per spring?
   c. Will Gongalong have to buy any mainsprings from suppliers other than Boing? If not, why not? If so, how many?

Problem 13 requires both partial differentiation and constrained maximization. It should be attempted only if you have covered the material in the Appendix that follows Chapter 4.

13. The Chilidome Regency Hotel is planning to use price discrimination between convention and general room rates. For a standard double room, its estimated demand curve for the general market is

$$Q_g = 4,344 - 20P_g.$$

For the convention market, its estimated demand curve is

$$Q_c = 5,800 - 50P_c.$$

In both equations, Q represents weekly quantity of rooms and P represents price per night. The hotel's weekly total cost is

$$TC = 112,000 + 40Q + .01Q^2,$$

where Q is weekly total number of rooms rented ($Q_g + Q_c$).

a. With price discrimination, how many rooms will be rented in each market?

b. What price will the hotel charge in each market?

c. What will be the hotel's weekly profit?

d. Compare the results above, in terms of both price and profit, with what the firm could obtain if it did not practice price discrimination.

This problem can be solved with Decision Assistant

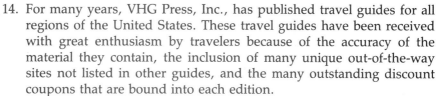

14. For many years, VHG Press, Inc., has published travel guides for all regions of the United States. These travel guides have been received with great enthusiasm by travelers because of the accuracy of the material they contain, the inclusion of many unique out-of-the-way sites not listed in other guides, and the many outstanding discount coupons that are bound into each edition.

   The president of VHG Press, Victor Garrett, has been watching the recent trends of increasing visits to the United States by English-speaking Europeans. Victor knows this trend presents a unique opportunity to VHG Press—the possible marketing of the company's existing guides through various large European outlets. The opportunity is unique in two ways: no additional fixed costs would be incurred, as the current English edition could be used, and VHG Press could possibly charge a different price in its European market.

   The marketing department has provided the following information:

$$\text{Domestic Demand} \qquad Q_d = 30 - P_d,$$

where Q_d is the quantity demanded (in thousands) in the domestic market and P_d is the domestic price, and

$$\text{International Demand} \qquad Q_i = 22 - P_i,$$

where Q_i is the quantity demanded (in thousands) in the international market, and P_i is the international price.

   The production department has provided the total cost function for the production of travel guides as being

$$TC = 2Q_t + .1Q_t^2,$$

where TC is total costs and Q_t is the total quantity printed (in both markets).

   Use the Price Discrimination tool in the *Managerial Economics Decision Assistant* to assist Victor in preparing a report on the feasibility of this new venture. The report should include the following information:

a. The price currently charged and the quantity being sold in the domestic market.

b. The proposed price in the international market along with the estimated quantity to be sold in the international market.

c. The profit–maximizing price and quantity in the domestic market with the proposal.

■ ■ ■ ■ ■ ■ ■ ■ ■ ■ **Selected References** ■ ■ ■ ■ ■ ■ ■ ■ ■ ■

Adams, Walter (ed.). *The Structure of American Industry*, 6th ed. New York: Macmillan, 1982.

Koch, James V. *Industrial Organization and Prices*, 2d ed. Englewood Cliffs, N.J.: Prentice-Hall, 1980.

Lanzillotti, Robert F. "Pricing Objectives in Large Companies," *American Economic Review* (December 1958), pp. 921–940.

Mansfield, Edwin. *Microeconomics: Theory and Applications*, 7th ed. New York: Norton, 1991, especially pp. 274–280.

Plott, Charles R. "Industrial Organization Theory and Experimental Economics," *Journal of Economic Literature* (December 1982), pp. 1485–1527.

Scherer, F. M. *Industrial Market Structure and Economic Performance*, 3d ed. Boston: Houghton Mifflin, 1990.

Appendix 10A

Transfer Pricing With a Less-Than-Perfectly Competitive Market for the Intermediate Product

In this appendix we analyze the transfer pricing problem facing managers of a two-division, two-product firm when the transferred product can be sold externally in a market that is less than perfectly competitive. The relationship of the transfer product division to the final product division remains unchanged from the examples covered in this chapter; that is, the transfer product division knows it must price its output at marginal cost when selling to the final product division. Presumably, with an oligopolistic external market for the transfer product, T, the final product division cannot be supplied its T inputs from rival firms at a price as low as the level of the marginal cost of Product T when profit for the firm is maximized. However, if the T division has the opportunity to sell its product in such an external market, management will need to determine the combination of final and transfer product outputs that maximizes profit, as well as the profit-maximizing prices of each of the products.

In this situation, the firm's profit will be maximized when MC_T, the marginal cost of product T, is equal to the net marginal revenue of the entire enterprise, NMR_e. In the chapter, NMR_F was identified as $MR_F - MC_F$, the marginal revenue remaining after all marginal costs except that of Product T are subtracted from the marginal revenue resulting from the sale of the final product. However, with an external market for T that is less than perfectly competitive, the T division finds itself selling in what is essentially a two-market setting (internal and external) or a situation similar to the case of two market price discrimination (also discussed within Chapter 10). From management's point of view, then, the NMR_e will consist not only of $MR_F - MC_F$, but also of MR_T—the marginal revenue obtainable from sales of T in the external market.

The firm as a whole will be able to increase profit by switching output of T from the internal market to the external market whenever $MR_T > (MR_F - MC_F)$. Note, however, that this can be accomplished only by also varying the amount produced and sold of the final product, as well as the price of the final product. Such a result follows because the amount of T supplied to the final product division cannot be reduced without also reducing the output of the final product itself.

Figure 10A–1 provides a graphical solution to the profit-maximizing problem that exists when management knows it can sell some amount of T in an oligopolistic external market. As in previous examples in Chapter 10, we depict a situation in which there is a fixed amount of T used in the manufacture of one unit of the final product. Thus the Q axis of panel (a) will measure both production of the final product, F, and utilization of T by the final product division. In panel (a) the curve $MR_F - MC_F$ is derived from D_F in the usual manner. The external market for Product T is illustrated in panel (b), where MR_T is derived from the external demand curve D_T. Finally, in panel (c) the two curves $MR_F - MC_F$ and MR_T are summed horizontally (quantities added for each level of MR) to obtain NMR_e—the net marginal revenue of the enterprise.

Profit maximization occurs in Figure 10A–1 where $NMR_e = MC_T$. By projecting the profit-maximizing level of MC_T (that is, MC_T^*) leftward to panels (b) and (a), we find the quantities of T sold to the final product division (Q_e) and the external market for the transfer product Q_{T_x}', such that $MC_T^* = MR_T = MR_F - MC_F$. The equality of $MR_F - MC_F$ with MR_T ensures that the firm cannot gain by switching output from the internal market to the external market, or vice versa. Since the transfer product division is instructed to set a transfer price equal to MC_T, $P_{T_i} = MC_T^*$ will

Figure 10A–1   Transfer Pricing With a Less-Than-Perfectly Competitive Market for the Transferred Product

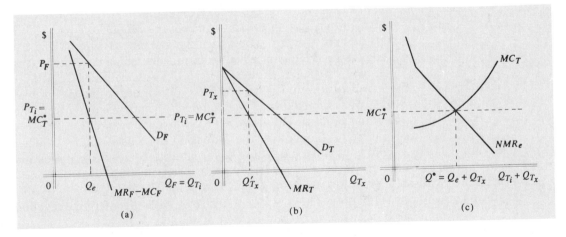

(a)   (b)   (c)

be the price charged the final product division for its inputs of T. However, in the external market, a price of P_{T_x} will be charged [panel (b)]. Back in panel (a), the final product division can be seen to produce Q_e, of final product F and charge a price of P_F.

The situation depicted in Figure 10A–1 is illustrative of the kind of analysis that must be done in order for managers to maximize profit where a transfer pricing decision must be made and the external market for the transfer product is not perfectly competitive. It should be clear from the preceding that sales of the transfer product to purchasers outside the firm may contribute importantly to the firm's total revenue and profit. Another way to examine this issue is to ask what would happen if the external demand for the transfer product were to increase (D_T and MR_T shift to the right). In terms of Figure 10A–1, we can verify that NMR_e would also shift toward the right, thereby intersecting MC_T at a level higher than MC^*_T. This would undoubtedly lead to increased sales in the external market for the T product, but what would happen to Q_F? If final product demand has not changed, then Q_e must fall and P_F must rise when the profit-maximizing level of MC_T rises above MC^*_T. Thus the firm would actually be best off to reduce sales of its final product and increase the final product's price in order to be able to market more of Product T externally.

The lesson to be learned from the preceding analysis is that a change in one of the markets faced by a multiple-product, multiple-market firm can have pervasive effects on several aspects of the firm's operations. However, these effects may be predictable to some degree if the firm has sufficient information on demand and costs. Another example that could be illustrated by making some changes in Figure 10A–1 is a situation in which demand for the final product has increased [D_F shifts rightward in panel (a)] but D_T has not. The reader should be able to verify that in this setting, less of T should be sold externally and P_{T_x} should be increased.

Appendix 10B

Mathematics of Price Discrimination*

The model of two-market price discrimination discussed in Chapter 10 was developed only for the case of constant marginal cost, since the mathematics of the situation is somewhat complex if marginal cost is variable. To illustrate why, we will return to the example of hotel pricing used in the chapter and use the same demand data found there with a total cost function characterized by increasing marginal cost. The demand curves given for the hotel example were the following

$$\text{General market:} \quad P_g = 140 - 0.1R_g.$$

$$\text{Convention market:} \quad P_c = 120 - 0.05R_c.$$

P_g and P_c are the prices charged in the two markets, respectively, while the R terms denote the quantity of rooms demanded in each market per day.

Whereas the original example was developed with a constant marginal cost of \$30 per additional room rented, we will now suppose that the hotel has the following total and marginal cost functions:

$$TC = 18{,}200 + 4R + 0.02R^2$$

$$MC = 4 + 0.04R$$

---

* This material utilizes both partial differentiation and the Lagrangian multiplier approach to constrained maximization. It is highly recommended for students who have sufficient mathematical preparation to have been introduced to these techniques in the appendix to Chapter 4.

In these two expressions, R is the number of rooms rented in *both* markets. From the example in the chapter, it might appear that profit could be maximized by just setting the above MC equal to the marginal revenue equation for each market. However, this will not yield the correct answer, since the renting of an additional room in *one* of the two markets changes the marginal cost of the next room rented in *either* market.

■ ■ ■ ■ ■ ■ ■ ■ ■ **SOLUTION PROCEDURE IF DISCRIMINATION IS PERMITTED**

The usual approach to solving the price discrimination problem when marginal cost is variable is to set up a profit function where both revenue and cost depend on two independent variables, the quantities sold in each market. From the demand equations, it follows that the total revenue function for sales in both markets is

$$TR = 140R_g - 0.1R_g^2 + 120R_c - 0.05R_c^2$$

The profit function results when the total cost function stated earlier is subtracted from this total revenue equation. However, we restate the "R" term in the cost function as $(R_g + R_c)$.

$$\pi = 140R_g - 0.1R_g^2 + 120R_c - 0.05R_c^2 - 18{,}200 - 4R_g - 4R_c$$
$$- 0.02R_g^2 - 0.04R_cR_g - 0.02R_c^2,$$

or, collecting terms,

$$\pi = 136R_g - 0.12R_g^2 + 116R_c - 0.07R_c^2 - 0.04R_gR_c - 18{,}200.$$

To solve for the profit-maximizing quantities of R_g and R_c, we now take the two partial derivatives of the profit function and set each equal to zero. This will satisfy the necessary conditions for a maximum.[1]

$$\frac{\partial \pi}{R_g} = 136 - 0.24R_g - 0.04R_c = 0$$

$$\frac{\partial \pi}{R_c} = 116 - 0.04R_g - 0.14R_c = 0$$

■ ■ ■ ■ ■ ■

[1] We will deal only with first order conditions here. Second order conditions are discussed in the mathematical appendix at the end of the book.

These two partials can be solved easily by multiplying the second equation by -6 and adding it to the first, an operation that yields

$$-560 + 0.80R_c = 0,$$
$$R_c = 700,$$

and substituting 700 for R_c in either partial,

$$R_g = 450.$$

Thus the hotel should rent 1,150 rooms, 700 in the convention market and 450 in the general market. From the demand equations for each market, it follows that the prices will be

$$P_g = 140 - 0.1(450) = \$95,$$
$$P_c = 120 - 0.05(700) = \$85.$$

The total daily profit of the hotel with price discrimination will be

$$95(450) + 85(700) - 18,200 - 4(1,150) - 0.02(1,150)^2 = \$53,000.$$

No other combination of prices and quantities sold in the two markets will yield a higher profit.

■ ■ ■ ■ ■ ■ ■ ■ ■ **SOLUTION PROCEDURE IF DISCRIMINATION IS NOT PERMITTED**

Using calculus, it is possible also to show that profit with price discrimination is greater than it would be if the firm were to charge a uniform price in both markets. In effect, this is a constrained maximization problem where the constraint is that the price in one of the two markets must be equal to that in the other. For the preceding case, this would mean that $P_g = P_c$, or

$$140 - 0.1R_g = 120 - 0.05R_c,$$

which can be rewritten as

$$20 - 0.1R_g + 0.05R_c = 0$$

To solve for the quantities that will maximize profit subject to this constraint, we form the Lagrangian function as follows.

$$L\pi = 136R_g - 0.12R_g^2 + 116R_c - 0.07R_c^2 - 0.04R_gR_c - 18,200$$
$$+ \lambda(20 - 0.1R_g + 0.05R_c).$$

To solve for the profit-maximizing quantities of R_g and R_c, we now take three partial derivatives of the Lagrangian function and set each equal to zero. This will satisfy the necessary conditions for a maximum.

$$\frac{\partial L\pi}{\partial R_g} = 136 - 0.24R_g - 0.04R_c - 0.1\lambda = 0.$$

$$\frac{\partial L\pi}{\partial R_c} = 116 - 0.04R_g - 0.14R_c + 0.05\lambda = 0.$$

$$\frac{\partial L\pi}{\partial \lambda} = 20 - 0.1R_g + 0.05R_c = 0.$$

The Lagrangian multiplier, λ, can be eliminated from the first two expressions by multiplying the second equation by 2 and adding it to the first one. This yields the following:

$$368 - 0.32R_g - 0.32R_c = 0.$$

Finally, R_g, can be eliminated by multiplying the partial derivative with respect to λ by -3.2 and adding it to the preceding expression. This results in

$$304 = 0.48R_c, \quad \text{and} \quad R_c = 633.33$$

Substituting the preceding value of R_c into the constraint equation, we find that $R_g = 516.67$. Thus, to the nearest room, the profit-maximizing quantities are 633 rooms in the convention market and 517 rooms in the general market.

If this answer is correct, we should expect to find that the room rate charged is the same for both markets. To demonstrate this, we return to the unrounded values of R_g and R_c. From the demand curve equations initially given,

$$P_g = 140 - 0.1(516.67) = \$88.33,$$

and

$$P_c = 120 - 0.05(633.33) = \$88.33.$$

Thus the room rate should be set at $88.33. Note that this price is between the two prices that were charged with discrimination and that quantity has increased in the general market but decreased in the convention market. However, the total quantity of rooms rented is still 1,150 per day. Quantity will always be the same as under discrimination, since what happens when discrimination takes place is that rooms with low marginal revenue (general market) are switched for rooms with higher marginal revenue (convention market) until both of the marginal revenues are equal to marginal cost.

As we stated earlier, profit will be less with a uniform price than it was with discrimination. Recall that with discrimination profit was calculated to be $53,000. Without discrimination it is

$$\$88.33(1,150) - 18,200 - 4(1,150) - 0.02(1,150)^2$$
$$= 101,579.50 - 49,250 = \$52,329.50$$

Thus the hotel makes $670.50 per day more with price discrimination than without. Note that total cost is the same in either case, but that price discrimination increases total revenue. This will always be the case.

■ ■ ■ ■ ■ ■ ■ ■ ■ ■ ■ ■ ■ **Problem** ■ ■ ■ ■ ■ ■ ■ ■ ■ ■ ■ ■ ■

Trenchwich Corporation manufactures power trenching machines in the United States. It also sells them in the international market. The company spends a lot of money on lobbying and has been successful in obtaining a high tariff on competing foreign output. The annual domestic demand for its product is given by

$$Q_{US} = 30,000 - 2P_{US}.$$

Annual foreign demand for the same machine is given by the equation

$$Q_f = 50,000 - 4P_f.$$

Trenchwich's total cost function is

$$TC = 200,000 + 2,000Q + .5Q^2.$$

a. Assuming the firm practices price discrimination, what will be its price per unit in each of the two markets, and how many machines will it sell in each market?
b. Calculate the firm's total profit under the preceding conditions.
c. Find the firm's profit-maximizing price, sales quantity in each market, and total profit under the assumption that it does not discriminate in pricing.

International Capsule II

Markets and Pricing Strategy in International Trade

As Chapters 8 through 10 have shown, an important problem facing the firm is the *structure* of the market or markets in which it sells its product. By this we mean the nature of both consumer demand and competition from other firms. Although we cannot cover all of the possible market structures encountered in international trade in this brief capsule, a number of the situations discussed here are frequently faced by firms that deal outside their own national boundaries, and an introductory review of them will provide some food for thought regarding both the opportunities and difficulties associated with pricing strategies in world markets. We will begin with a strategy that is frequently employed by firms, that of market segmentation.

MARKET SEGMENTATION IN INTERNATIONAL TRADE

Chapter 10 showed that firms often have opportunities to employ price discrimination or market segmentation to increase their sales revenues from markets that are physically separated and characterized by different elasticities of demand. Of course,

this concept carries over to the international market, as does another important maxim, the rule that it pays to sell incremental output as long as the price of that output exceeds its average variable cost.

Low-Priced Foreign Sales

Any firm that sells both at home and in a foreign market must make some determination regarding whether to charge different prices in the two outlets. How can it make the choice?

Our discussions of the determinants of demand (Chapter 2) and the impact of various market structures (Chapters 8 and 9) lead to the conclusion that the price elasticity of demand for any product is likely to be greater the larger the number of substitute goods available. Thus, if a firm sells in a largely unfettered world market where there are many substitute products, it may well maximize profit by selling at a *lower* price in the international market than at home. For many products, the world market is vastly larger and more competitive than any one country's internal market. Therefore the foreign elasticity of demand may be the greater of the two. As the hotel pricing example in Chapter 10 showed, in the case of two-market price discrimination, profit maximization dictates that the market with the higher elasticity of demand be the one that will be charged the lower price.

There are other reasons a firm may choose to sell outside its national boundaries at a price below that charged domestic consumers. First, as noted earlier, in incremental analysis it is argued that incremental sales add to profit as long as price exceeds average variable cost. A firm that has already covered all of its fixed costs from profit contribution on home country sales would be rational to sell outside the country at *any* price that is above its average variable cost. When foreign sales are viewed strictly as an incremental decision, the firm may choose to sell in the foreign market at prices that are so far below the home price that they *appear* to be unprofitable. However, such sales likely are actually adding to profit, as Figure II–1 shows. Here it is as-

sumed that the world market is perfectly competitive with a prevailing price of P_w, that marginal cost is rising in straight-line fashion, that $P_w > AVC$ at E_f, and that the home market is insulated from foreign sellers (perhaps by a nontariff barrier). In panel (a), the firm maximizes profit on home country sales at the output where $MC = MR_h$ and charges price P_h to domestic consumers. However, in panel (b) it sells an additional amount, $0Q_w$, to foreign purchasers at the world market price. The addition to its profit from the foreign sales is triangle P_wZE_f, which measures the difference between MR and MC on the $0Q_w$ units sold. (Note that this is a price discrimination problem that differs from those discussed in Chapter 10 in that the firm itself sets only one of the two prices, and the firm has not obtained the maximum possible profit, since $MR_w > MR_h$ at Q_h. Thus the firm would be better off to switch output from

Figure II–1   One Rationale for a Low Foreign Price

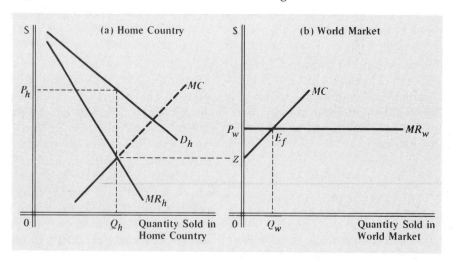

This firm maximizes profit in the home market and then sells an additional amount, $0Q_w$, in the world market until $MC = MR_w$. While this strategy adds to profit, the firm is not maximizing profit since $MR_w > MR_h$. To maximize profit, it must sell less at home and more in the world market.

home to foreign sales until it reaches a combination where $MR_h = MR_w$.)

Thus far we have seen that both price discrimination and incremental analysis support the possibility that a firm might charge a lower price internationally than at home for the same product. There is another reason, also related to the discussion of Chapter 10, that could account for selling at a low price to foreign purchasers. Suppose a firm produces two joint products. If there is limited domestic demand for one of them, foreign sales might provide an outlet that is cheaper than paying for disposal of unwanted product at home. In fact, if a firm bases its production quantity of two joint products strictly on the domestic demand for them, and one product is produced in excess quantity, it will be rational to sell an amount in the foreign market equal to the excess *plus* any amount of domestic sales for which domestic marginal revenue is below foreign marginal revenue. Here again, there may be a strong incentive to sell outside the home market at a very low price.

High-Priced Foreign Sales

While we have emphasized foreign market prices that are below home market prices, we should realize that firms also have opportunities to maximize profit by charging *higher* prices in the foreign market than at home. After all, price discrimination just says that the higher price should be charged where demand is least elastic; it does not say home demand is always less elastic than foreign. What kinds of situations might conform to a lower foreign demand elasticity than at home? Again, our earlier observation about market size gives a hint. If the foreign market is small in comparison with the home market, it may pay to charge a higher price on foreign sales. This may be the case for luxury goods that are in common use in the market of a highly developed country such as the United States but would be purchased by only a small proportion of consumers in many less-developed countries. Keeping in mind·that demand is a "willing and able" concept, we note that in some countries many consumers are willing but *not* many are able to buy certain types of goods. Within the markets of those countries, goods exported from the industrialized countries may command very high prices, and the demand of the small consuming group for such goods will likely be less elastic than that found in the industrialized countries. In addition, less developed countries are characterized by both limited and uncertain domestic production of many types of manufactured goods, and these characteristics on the supply side of such markets can also lead to higher prices than those found elsewhere.

THE PROBLEM OF DUMPING

The term "dumping" has a very specific meaning in international trade. It refers to the practice of selling in a foreign market at a price that is lower than the home market price.[1] Since we have seen that there are a good number of reasons for a firm to charge foreigners a low price, it should be no surprise that dumping often occurs. In some cases, the main result of dumping is just that some consumers get a bargain price on foreign goods. However, there are laws regulating dumping that can cause serious difficulties for a firm, particularly if its managers are unaware of how a foreign

■ ■ ■ ■ ■ ■
[1] Some of the laws that regulate dumping state that it occurs when the foreign price is below the home cost of production. These laws usually are difficult to administer, since precise data on home cost are not easily obtained and definitions of cost vary. Note that if the definition of cost is average variable cost, a·firm that is dumping is doing so for negative incremental profit.

government may react. If consumers in the country where goods are dumped get them at bargain prices, what is the issue? The problem is that producers in the same country may view dumping as a form of unfair competition. After all, to remain in business they must generate sufficient revenues to cover both variable and fixed costs. The firm that is dumping in a foreign market probably has already covered its fixed costs from home sales and, as we have already noted, can sell profitably to foreigners at any price above average variable cost.

To keep foreign firms from damaging domestic firms through dumping, national governments have enacted antidumping laws that may deal rather harshly with foreign firms. The United States has one of the most actively used antidumping laws in the world—the Antidumping Act of 1921. Under this act, as modified by later legislation, the U.S. Treasury Department is required to initiate an investigation whenever a United States firm or group of firms files a complaint alleging that it is being "injured" by competition from foreign goods dumped in the U.S. market. If Treasury investigators do find dumping, the next step is hearings before the United States International Trade Commission (ITC), which must make a determination regarding the question of injury. In the event the ITC does find injury, antidumping duties may be assessed against the U.S. firms that *purchased* the dumped merchandise, and the foreign exporters' shipments may be subject to surveillance for several years. Although antidumping duties may be substantial, in many cases the litigation costs of defending an antidumping charge far exceed the penalties.

A U.S. firm that exports its goods to a foreign country may find that it faces a similar situation to that faced by foreign firms that dump in the United States. Dumping

in the foreign market could not only disrupt its export activities but also lead to substantial foreign legal expenses.[2]

WEBB-POMERENE AND EXPORT TRADING COMPANIES

In 1918, largely as a response to German cartels that were set up before World War I, the U.S. Congress passed the Webb-Pomerene Act, which allows U.S. firms to form export trade associations to market their products abroad. In effect, it permits for export trade purposes a number of practices—such as price fixing and division of markets—that in domestic trade are in violation of the antitrust laws (see Chapter 16). What this means for U.S. firms is that they need not compete in the international market and have the alternative of taking a cartel approach to pricing and division of markets in foreign trade.

Historically, the U.S. export trade associations have been most important in certain natural-resource-based industries such as minerals and forest products. The associations have had a checkered past, since they have at times engaged in anticompetitive practices that may have had an adverse impact on the domestic market in the United States as well as on foreign markets. For example, in the 1930s the Sulphur Ex-

■ ■ ■ ■ ■ ■

[2] We should note also that in the United States the antidumping law has sometimes served as a nontariff trade barrier. By this we mean that U.S. firms that are *not* in danger of significant injury from imports file antidumping complaints simply to discourage foreign competition of any kind. Part of the job of the International Trade Commission is to fend off groundless complaints so that the U.S. market will not be unduly restricted. Antitrust authorities from the Federal Trade Commission frequently attend the ITC hearings and give testimony when they believe a U.S. industry is using the antidumping law as a market weapon to restrict competition.

port Corporation suppressed a newly dis-covered Norwegian process for sulphur production by purchasing a patent to en-sure that no one outside Norway would ever be able to employ it without their con-sent.[3] Further, throughout the Great Depression, U.S. domestic prices of sulphur were quite stable and differed from the ex-port price by only $2 per ton. In the 1960s the Phosphate Export Corporation sold phosphate rock to Korea for an export price substantially above the U.S. domestic price. It was later discovered that the phosphate was purchased with U.S. aid money and that the U.S. government (and its taxpay-ers) had been charged the foreign price.

Despite the less than satisfactory results of the Webb-Pomerene Act, there has been much interest in the establishment and pro-motion of new U.S. export trading compa-nies. The reason for this development is the great success of Japanese export trading companies in world markets. These com-panies have specialized in representing broadly based consortia of corporations, in league with banking interests, to market a very large number of different products. In 1982, the U.S. Congress passed the Export Trading Companies Act (PL 97-290), which amended the Webb-Pomerene Act and pro-vided for active government promotion of export trading companies. The new law al-lowed a variety of financial institutions to invest in export trading companies and au-thorized the Export–Import Bank (a govern-ment institution) to provide loan guarantees to trading companies. With regard to the antitrust laws, it clarified the position of U.S. firms that formed trading companies and set up a certification procedure for es-tablishing limited antitrust immunity.

■ ■ ■ ■ ■ ■
[3] U.S. Federal Trade Commission, *Report of the Fed-eral Trade Commission on the Sulphur Industry and Inter-national Cartels* (Washington, D.C., 1947), p. 56.

Although there has not been a rush to take advantage of the new law, the appa-ratus is now in place to allow U.S. firms to harmonize their international pricing through the trading company approach. This could have far-reaching consequences in the future.

THE EFFECTS OF TRADE RESTRICTIONS ON PRICES

As indicated in our first international cap-sule, tariffs and other trade restrictions may be important considerations affecting a firm's prospects for selling abroad. Clearly, if the tariff wall surrounding a given foreign market is so high as to be totally prohibi-tive, export sales to that market will not be pos-sible. However, we should ask what hap-pens when a new tariff that is not prohibi-tive is levied on an export product of a firm. In general, economic theory shows that the foreign market price will rise by *less* than the amount of the tariff if the foreign supply elasticity is not infinite. In other words, if the country imposing the tariff is large enough that its purchases will impact the world market price, its domestic price will rise by less than the amount of the tariff. This happens because there is a drop in the quantity of foreign goods purchased after imposition of the tariff, which means sellers will move down their supply curves and thereby absorb some of the tariff in a lower supply price.

We can illustrate this for a two-country case as follows. Suppose the exporting in-dustry is in the United States and the amount its producers are willing to supply abroad is represented by the export supply curve SX_{US} in Figure II–2. S is the supply curve of producers in the foreign country, and SS is the horizontal sum of the two supply curves. SS is the curve that will de-fine equilibrium in the country's internal

Figure II–2   Price Effect of a Per-Unit Import Tariff

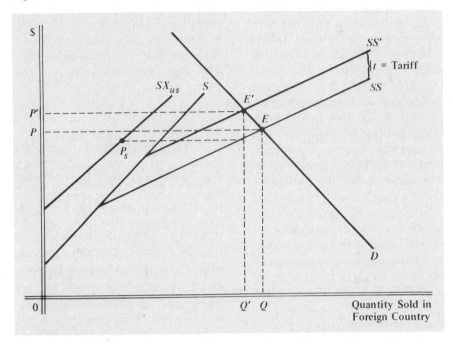

Imposition of a per-unit tariff equal to t (the vertical distance between SS and SS') causes price to rise to P' in the foreign country, while quantity sold falls. The price increase $(P' - P)$ is less than the amount of the tariff, as one can see along the vertical line $Q'E'$. The price received by producers after the tariff as shown by P_s.

market when both imported and internally produced output are available. Imposition of a per-unit import tariff equal to t will shift SS to SS' and move the importing country's equilibrium point from E to E', raising its internal price from P to P'. However, note that the amount of the price increase is less than t, since t is the vertical distance between the old supply curve and the new one and is larger than $(P' - P)$. Thus the price U.S. producers receive for their exports will fall (to level P_s on the supply curve). Any U.S. firm that is exporting this product can expect to sell less *and* realize a lower price after the tariff is imposed.

Of course, import tariffs are not the only type of trade restriction that may affect prices or sales volume in foreign markets. Import quotas and other types of quantitative restrictions will have similar effects. This is true because any reduction in quantity of exports sold will be accompanied by a fall in price if the supply curve of those exports is upward sloping. While the type of analysis we have been employing here does not give an exporting firm a way to predict *when* trade restrictions will be imposed, it does help to show what the effects of such restrictions will be when and if they are imposed. Given that trade restrictions are a fact of life in many foreign markets (particularly in less-developed countries, where they are used to promote industrialization), it is useful to have some idea of how to analyze their impact on a firm's exports and the prices it receives for them.

INTERNATIONAL TRANSFER PRICING

Our final topic in this brief survey is transfer pricing, a subject that is significantly more complicated in the international marketplace than in a single country. As Chapter 10 showed, the optimal transfer price within divisions of a firm that do not trade across international boundaries is argued to be a price equal to the marginal cost of the transfer product. While a situation *could* exist in international trade where a transfer product is exchanged between two units of the same firm at a price equal to its marginal cost, a number of factors make this unlikely.

When products are transferred internationally, they move from one country with one set of laws, regulations, and financial institutions to another country with different laws, regulations, and financial institutions. Thus the transfer prices may be employed as a device to obtain a wide variety of results, given the objectives of the firm. For example, suppose a firm has a subsidiary in a developing country where the government places restrictions on remitting profits to foreign investors. This would mean that the subsidiary is limited in the amount of profit it can send to the parent company. To keep profits from piling up in the subsidiary, the parent may decide to charge very high prices for goods transferred to the subsidiary, thereby switching profits from the latter to the parent.[4]

The firm may use transfer pricing for a variety of other purposes. For example, it may choose to use a low transfer price when shipping goods to a subsidiary located in a country with high duties on those goods. Another strategy relates to income tax minimization and calls for arranging transfer prices to shift profits to units of the firm located in low-tax countries. Finally, transfer pricing may be used to "dress up" financial statements by reporting high profits for units located in countries where borrowing and other financing are likely to take place.

■ ■ Questions and Problems ■ ■

1. Explain how each of the following strategies discussed in earlier chapters is related to pricing problems firms frequently encounter in international trade.
   a. Incremental profit analysis
   b. Price discrimination
   c. Pricing of joint products
2. Discuss the problem of dumping in international trade. Under what circumstances might a firm be likely to have legal problems if it dumped in a foreign market?
3. What is an export trading company? How is it related to recent U.S. interest in more permissive laws regulating business?
4. Suppose a firm sells in only two markets, its home market and one foreign market. Its total cost function is $TC = 200,000 + 120Q$. Suppose its home demand curve has the equation $Q_h = 10,000 - 20P_h$ and the foreign market demand curve has the equation $Q_f = 7,500 - 12.5P_f$.
   a. Will the prices in the two markets be the same, assuming no trade barriers in the foreign market? Explain, and calculate the price(s) the firm will charge as well as its profit from sales in the two markets.
   b. If the importing country imposes an import tariff of $10 per unit, what

---

■ ■ ■ ■ ■ ■
[4] It is not surprising that many countries have enacted laws regulating transfer pricing in an attempt to thwart such activity.

price will be charged in that country after the tariff? Calculate the firm's profit after the tariff.

5. How does transfer pricing in international business differ from that in firms that do not operate across national boundaries?

■ ■ ■ Selected References ■ ■ ■

Cateora, Phillip R. *International Marketing,* 6th ed. Homewood, Ill.: Irwin, 1987, especially Chapter 16.

"EEC Acts on Japanese Dumping," *Business Europe* (January 25, 1985), p. 31.

Exporter's Encyclopedia. Dunn & Bradstreet, Inc., New York (annual).

Grennes, Thomas. *International Economics.* Englewood Cliffs, N.J.: Prentice-Hall, 1984, especially Chapters 6 and 7.

Kistler, Robert. "Export Pricing in Today's Market, *Business America* (July 9, 1984), p. 21.

Robock, Stefan H., and Kenneth Simmonds. *International Business and Multinational Enterprises*, 3d ed. Homewood, Ill.: Irwin, 1983.

C H A P T E R 11

Economic Forecasting

In Chapters 2, 3, 5, and 6, the importance of accurate revenue and cost data to a profit-maximizing firm was stressed. In Chapter 5, several techniques for estimating a firm's cost function were described; and in Chapter 3 and its appendix, various procedures for estimating a firm's demand function were examined.

Forecasting is the process of analyzing available data on economic variables and relationships and predicting future values of certain economic variables.

In this chapter we turn specifically to the issue of forecasting. **Forecasting** refers to the process of analyzing available information regarding economic variables and relationships and then predicting the future values of certain variables of interest to the firm or economic policymakers. As we shall see later, economic forecasting is one of the fastest growing industries in the United States.

■ ■ ■ ■ ■ ■ ■ ■ ■   ## TYPES OF ECONOMIC FORECASTS

Forecasts are made regarding a great variety of economic variables. For example, on an *aggregate* (national economy or macroeconomic) level, forecasts are made regarding future levels of the gross national product, investment spending, consumption spending, government expenditures, and net exports.

Gross national product for a country is the market value of all final goods and services produced in the country during some particular time period, usually one year.

Gross national product (GNP) is the final market value of goods and services produced in a country during some time period. In the United States, the time period under consideration is usually one year. The gross national product is measured by the *final* market value of newly produced goods and services in order to avoid double counting. For example, a ton of iron ore may pass through several stages and forms (such as sheet metal) before it finally becomes part of an automobile. Nevertheless, the

413

Investment spending includes all purchases of capital goods, including buildings, equipment, and inventories by private businesses and nonprofit institutions. It also includes all expenditures for residential housing.

Consumption spending is the market value of purchases of newly produced goods and services by individuals and nonprofit organizations and the value of goods and services received by them as income in kind. It includes the value of owner-occupied houses but does not include the purchase of dwellings, which are considered to be capital goods.

Government expenditures are expenditures for newly produced goods and services, including government investment expenditures, by all levels of government.

Net exports are equal to the purchases of new goods and services produced in the home country by foreigners (*exports*), less the purchases of new foreign-produced goods and services by the residents of the home country (*imports*).

value of all of the work that takes place on the iron ore and steel will eventually be reflected in the price of the automobile when it is sold to a consumer.

It is important also to note that GNP refers to the value of goods and services *produced* during the time period in question. For example, if you sold your old car to a friend, the price of your car to your friend would not be included in GNP, since the car was not newly produced. (However, the *profits* of used-car dealers are included because the dealers do perform a productive service.)

Investment spending refers to the purchases of new plant, equipment, and inventories by businesses. It also includes purchases of new residential housing by individuals. Inventory investment varies to a greater degree than the other two types of investment spending when the level of GNP changes.

Consumption spending refers to expenditures by individuals and nonprofit organizations on newly produced goods and services (except for housing). Consumption spending is frequently broken down into three categories: nondurable goods, durable goods, and services. Nondurable goods are consumption goods with an expected useful life of less than three years. Accordingly, durable goods have an expected useful life of at least three years.[1] By contrast, services cannot be stored but must be consumed at the point of production. Consumer expenditures on durable goods are most affected by changes in GNP.

Government expenditures are expenditures for goods and services by state and local governments and the federal government. These expenditures include such items as national defense goods and wages for fire fighters and teachers. Government expenditures do not include such things as welfare payments. These are considered to be transfers of income, not payment for goods and services.

Finally, **net exports** is the term denoting the value of newly produced U.S. goods and services purchased by foreigners (exports) less the value of newly produced foreign goods purchased by the United States (imports). Net exports make an allowance for the excess of goods produced in the United States but purchased by foreigners over the value of goods produced abroad but purchased by U.S. citizens.

In addition to the aggregate levels of gross national product, investment spending, consumption spending, government expenditures, and net exports, forecasts are made regarding the regional (such as southwestern United States or northern Florida) or local (such as Kansas City, Missouri) values of these variables. Forecasts are also made for individual components of each type of production and spending—for example, fed-

■ ■ ■ ■ ■ ■
[1] See U.S. Department of Commerce, Bureau of the Census, *Historical Statistics of the United States, Colonial Times to 1970*, Bicentennial Edition, Part 1, p. 218.

eral government spending on defense equipment, business expenditures on new plants, and consumer expenditures on durable goods. Forecasts are also made at the industry, the firm, and the individual product levels—for example, the annual sales of the automobile industry, of General Motors Corporation, and of Chevrolet Caprices, respectively.

Forecasts can be short run or long run. In many cases a business needs to forecast its quarterly, monthly, or even weekly sales. A bakery will try to predict accurately its *daily* sales. However, when a firm makes decisions regarding long-term investment projects, it is important for the firm to obtain accurate forecasts of sales and costs perhaps five, ten, or even twenty years in the future. As we know from Chapter 4, some inputs are *not* variable in the short run. Consequently, a firm manager finds making decisions about investment in plant and equipment to be a hopeless task without forecasts. The recent difficulties of some firms in the automobile, airline, and steel industries are just a few examples of the need for accurate forecasting.

■ ■ ■ ■ ■ ■ ■ ■   TWO MAJOR KINDS OF DATA

Time series data are observations of a particular variable over a number of time periods.

The two general types of data that are used by forecasters are time series data and cross-section data. **Time series data** are observations regarding a specific variable over a number of time periods. For example, data giving the sales of Ford Motor Company over the last ten years would be time series data. **Cross-section data** are observations regarding a particular variable at a single point in time. For example, the sales of each of the U.S. automobile manufacturers in 1984 would be cross-sectional data.

Cross-section data are observations of a variable at a specific point in time.

■ ■ ■ ■ ■ ■ ■ ■   FACTORS AFFECTING ECONOMIC VARIABLES

The types of factors that affect the values of economic variables are often classified into four general categories: trend, seasonal, cyclical, and other.

Trend Factors

Trend factors are related to movements in economic variables over time.

Trend factors are those that reflect movements in economic variables over time. One example of a trend factor that would affect the demand for automobiles is the average annual rate of growth of real GNP over several years. (*Real GNP* is the value of gross national product adjusted for inflation so that it better reflects changes in the production of goods and services that have occurred over the period in question.) Another relevant trend factor would be the population growth rate. A third trend factor would be a change in consumer tastes that occurs progressively over time.

Seasonal Factors

Seasonal factors are those related to a specific season of the year (spring, summer, fall, or winter) that affect the economic variable or variables in question. For example, more bathing suits are generally sold during the spring than during the fall. More construction activity is usually carried on during the summer than during the winter. More snowmobiles and sleds are sold during the winter than during the summer.

Cyclical Factors

Cyclical factors are those related to fluctuations in the general level of economic activity. Economists often use the term *business cycle* to refer to these fluctuations.

A business cycle consists of four parts—a peak, a contraction, a trough, and an expansion, as shown in Figure 11–1. At the peak, economic activity has reached its greatest positive deviation from the long-term trend index of business activity. During a contractionary period, real GNP is falling and unemployment is rising. At the trough, economic activity has reached its greatest (in absolute value) negative deviation from the trend. During an expansionary period, aggregate real GNP is rising and unemployment is falling.

Figure 11–1   A Business Cycle

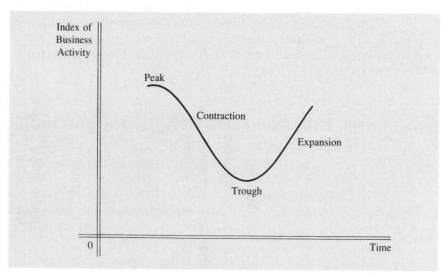

A business cycle consists of four parts—a peak, a contraction, a trough, and an expansion. At the peak, economic activity has reached its greatest positive deviation from the long-term trend index of business activity. At the trough, economic activity has reached its greatest (in absolute value) negative deviation from the trend.

Other Factors

This category includes all other factors that affect the values of an economic variable. Changes in consumer tastes or preferences not specifically related to the passage of time would be one example of an "other" factor. The level of advertising by a firm's competitors could also be an "other" factor.

It is frequently rather difficult in practice to separate the effects of trend, seasonal, cyclical, and other factors. Linear regression analysis is one means of breaking down the effects of various factors. This procedure was discussed in the appendix to Chapter 3. Other techniques for dealing with this problem involve less sophisticated and less formal procedures.

Some of the general types of forecasting techniques will be discussed in the next section.

■ ■ ■ ■ ■ ■ ■ ■ ■   FORECASTING METHODS

Six different types of forecasting techniques are discussed in this chapter: trend analysis, ARIMA models, barometric forecasting, surveys, econometric models, and input-output analysis. Each procedure has its advantages and its disadvantages; thus, in a given situation, a firm may find it worthwhile to use more than one of the procedures.

Trend Analysis

Trend analysis is a forecasting technique that relies primarily on historical data to predict the future.

Trend analysis relies primarily on historical data to predict the future. The more naive models emphasize the manipulation of historical data in order to discern a long-run trend (rate of change over time) and treat as less important the understanding of the underlying causal relationships.

Probably the simplest form of forecasting using trend analysis is the projection into the future of the current value of an economic variable. For example, we might forecast that $Y_{t+1} = Y_t$, where Y_{t+1} is the dollar value of a firm's sales during the coming year and Y_t is the dollar value of sales for the year just completed.

A slightly more sophisticated model would predict that next year's dollar sales would be a function of this year's sales and the change in dollar sales between this year and last year. For example, a marketing department might predict that $Y_{t+1} = Y_t + \gamma(Y_t - Y_{t-1})$, where $(Y_t - Y_{t-1})$ is the increase in dollar sales this year over last year. The forecasters might estimate a value for γ based on casual observation or through linear regression analysis (discussed in Chapter 3) using time series data.

A forecaster using trend analysis might also predict the dollar value of future sales by sketching a line which appears to "best fit" the historical data, plotted with Y (dollar sales) on the vertical axis and time (t) on the horizontal axis, as shown in Figure 11-2. Finally, linear regression analysis could be used to determine the straight line that would best represent the historical data. In this case the forecaster would use those techniques to

Figure 11–2   Forecasting by Sketching a "Best Fit" Line

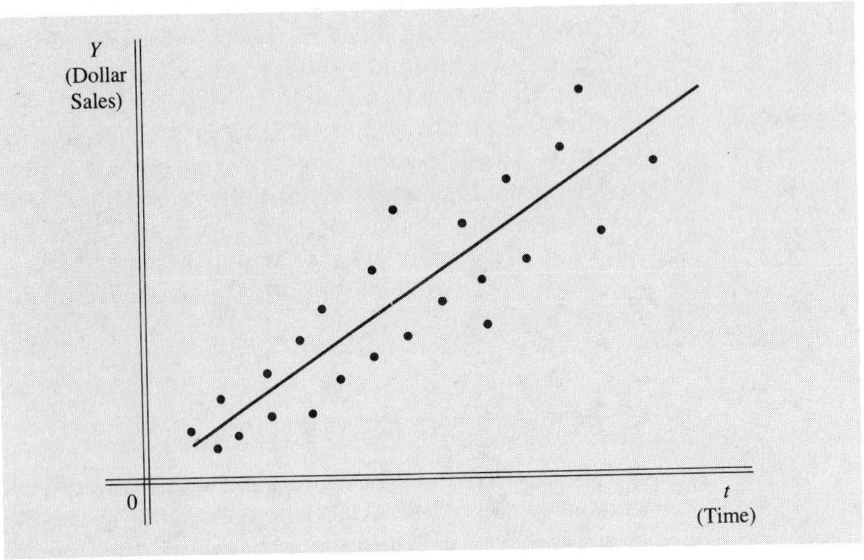

Using this method, a forecaster predicts the dollar value of future sales by sketching a line that appears to "best fit" the historical data.

estimate α and β in an equation of the form $Y_{t+1} = \alpha + \beta t$, where t represents the number of time periods that have passed since some base period.

Far more sophisticated models than those discussed here may be used in trend analysis, and they may be quite useful in making long-run forecasts. However, regardless of their sophistication, models that consider *only* trend factors will probably not be as useful, at least for short-run forecasts, as will models which attempt to incorporate causal relationships that include adjustments for seasonal, cyclical, and other factors. Seasonal factors will be quite important when forecasting the monthly sales of items such as bathing suits, boats, snowblowers, snow and water skis, air conditioners, and coats, for example. Cyclical factors will be important in forecasting the sales of products like automobiles, new houses, and automatic dishwashers, since the level of consumer income is an important determinant of consumer spending on such items.

ARIMA Models[2]

Autoregressive integrated moving average (ARIMA) models are a general class of models used often in forecasting time series. These models are

■ ■ ■ ■ ■ ■
[2] This section may be omitted without loss of continuity. It will be helpful to students to be familiar with the appendix to Chapter 3 on linear regression analysis before they read this section.

based on the hypothesis that adequate forecasts of future values of a time series can be obtained from past values of the series. In general, ARIMA models are linear functions of the sample data, and the sample data must generally constitute a stationary series.[3] The assumption of stationarity is important because the ARIMA models by their nature, based solely on past observations of the series to be forecasted, assert that there is some regularity to the process that is generating the series. Such a situation will not occur, for example, if a value of a series is constantly growing over time. In addition, these models are most useful for nonseasonal data or data from which the seasonality aspect has been removed.[4] ARIMA models are frequently utilized by forecasters because they yield adequate representation of the time series under investigation with relatively few parameters. This attempt to find efficiently parameterized models is known as the *principle of parsimony.* Some of the special subclasses of the general ARIMA models are discussed next.

Autoregressive Models   Autoregressive models are based on the assumption that future values of a series are a function of the past values of the series. For example, a first-order autoregressive model is of the form

$$X_t = A + \phi_1 X_{t-1} + \epsilon_t,$$

where A is a constant, ϕ is the autoregressive parameter, and ϵ is an error term. The assumptions regarding ϵ are similar to those involving the error term in linear regression analysis discussed in the appendix to Chapter 3: it is assumed that (1) ϵ is a random variable with zero mean and constant

■ ■ ■ ■ ■ ■

[3] A *stationary* time series is one that has both a constant mean and a constant variance over time. We state these conditions more formally as follows.

A time series, X_t, is weakly stationary if the following three conditions are satisfied:

1. The mean, μ, is constant at all points in time:

$$E(X_t) = \mu \quad \text{for all } t.$$

2. The variance, σ_x^2, of the series is the same over time:

$$\text{Var }(X_t) = E[(X_t - \mu)^2] = \sigma_t^2 \text{ for all } t.$$

3. The covariance between any two values of the series depends only on the number of time periods between them, not on their absolute location in time:

$$\text{Cov }(X_t, X_{t-k}) = E[(X_t - \mu)(X_{t-k} - \mu)] = \gamma_k$$

for all t, where γ is the covariance between any two values separated by k time periods.

[4] More advanced ARIMA models can be constructed to deal with seasonal data. See Paul Newbold and Theodore Bos, *Introductory Business Forecasting* (Cincinnati: South-Western, 1990), pp. 271–299.

variance over all time periods, and (2) the ϵ_t are not autocorrelated, so there is no correlation between ϵ_t and the error in any other time period.[5] A more general form of the autoregressive model of order p, denoted by $AR(p)$, is given by

$$X_t = A + \phi_1 X_{t-1} + \phi_2 X_{t-2} + \cdots + \phi_p X_{t-p} + \epsilon_t.$$

Some statistical programs estimate this model in a slightly different form where the constant term, A, is omitted and the mean, μ, of the series is subtracted from each value of X:

$$\dot{X}_t = \phi_1 \dot{X}_{t-1} + \phi_2 \dot{X}_{t-2} + \cdots + \phi_p \dot{X}_{t-p} + \epsilon_t,$$

where $\dot{X}_t = X_t - \mu$.

Moving Average Models   Moving average models express a time series as a function of past and present values of the ϵ terms, where the ϵ_t series exhibits all of the properties discussed above and is said to be generated by a white noise process. A first-order moving average model is of the form

$$X_t - \mu = \dot{X}_t = \epsilon_t + \Theta_1 \epsilon_{t-1},$$

where Θ is a fixed parameter and ϵ_t is white noise. A more general moving average model of order q, denoted by $MA(q)$, has the following form:

$$X_t - \mu = \dot{X}_t = \epsilon_t + \Theta_1 \epsilon_{t-1} + \Theta_2 \epsilon_{t-2} + \cdots + \Theta_q \epsilon_{t-q},$$

where $\Theta_1, \Theta_2, \ldots \Theta_q$ are moving average parameters.

Autoregressive Moving Average Models   Autoregressive moving average (ARMA) models are a combination of an autoregressive and a moving average model. An autoregressive moving average model of order (p,q), denoted by ARMA(p,q) is of the form

$$X_t = \phi_1 \dot{X}_{t-1} + \ldots + \phi_p \dot{X}_{t-p} + \epsilon_t + \Theta_1 \epsilon_{t-1} + \ldots + \Theta_q \epsilon_{t-q},$$

where $\dot{X}_t = X_t - \mu$ and ϵ_t is white noise. For example, a first order autoregressive moving average ARMA(1,1) model is

$$X_t = \phi_1 \dot{X}_{t-1} + \epsilon_t + \Theta_1 \epsilon_{t-1}.$$

■ ■ ■ ■ ■ ■
[5] A series formed by $X_t = \epsilon_t$, where ϵ_t has a zero mean, constant variance, and the correlation $(\epsilon_t, \epsilon_s) = 0$, where $t \neq s$ is often said to be generated by a *white noise* process.

Pure autoregressive models and pure moving average models are special subclasses of the more general ARMA models. The advantage of this more general model is that it can at times provide an acceptable representation of the behavior of a series using fewer parameters than would be necessary using only a pure autoregressive model or a pure moving average model.

Integrated Moving Average Models   We stated earlier that the models discussed above could be used when a series is stationary. However, many times business and economic data cannot be represented by a stationary series. Such would be the case, for example, when the series grows over time. Series of GNP data, consumption, and investment spending for the United States over time would be nonstationary series. A nonstationary series can frequently be transformed into a stationary series by taking the *first differences* of the series. The first differences of the series X_t are given by $X_t - X_{t-1}$. An autoregressive moving average model is then fitted to the series of first differences. In some cases *second differencing*, or differencing of the first differences, may be necessary to achieve stationarity. A process for which differencing is necessary to achieve stationarity is called an *integrated process*, and autoregressive moving average models applied to such data are called *autoregressive integrated moving average (ARIMA)* models. General autoregressive integrated moving average models are denoted by ARIMA (p,d,q), where p is the order of the autoregressive process, d is the degree of differencing, and q is the number of moving average terms in the model. Two simple models that are special cases of ARIMA models are the random walk model and a simple exponential smoothing model.

The *random walk* model is of the form

$$X_t - X_{t-1} = \epsilon_t.$$

It is denoted by ARIMA $(0,1,0)$. It states that the change in the series from one period to the next is generated by a random process. Some investigators have found such a model to provide an adequate description of the behavior of prices in speculative markets, such as the stock market and foreign currency markets.

A simple *exponential smoothing* model is of the form

$$X_t - X_{t-1} = \epsilon_t - (1-\alpha)\epsilon_{t-1},$$

where α is a smoothing parameter. Such a process is an ARIMA $(0,1,1)$ model, which means that the first differences of the series follow a first-order moving average process.

Simple exponential smoothing models like the one above are relatively easy to estimate and are frequently used when forecasts of a large number of time series are required on a regular basis. For example, such models can be utilized by a firm with a number of mature product lines when the firm wishes to estimate the monthly sales of each one.

An alternative specification of an exponential smoothing model that can be used for forecasting nonseasonal time series with a constant mean is

$$X_t = \alpha X_{t-1} + \alpha(1-\alpha)X_{t-2} + \alpha(1-\alpha)^2 X_{t-3} + \ldots + \epsilon_t,$$

where α is the smoothing constant. This is in the form of an autoregressive equation with $\phi_j = \alpha(1-\alpha)^{j-1}$, $j = 1, 2, 3 \ldots$. However, for small values of α, a large number of the autoregressive terms may be needed to obtain adequate forecasts. In this case, the above model can be easily transformed into the ARIMA(0,1,1) exponential smoothing model discussed above.

Such exponential smoothing models use a weighted average of past values of a series to forecast a future value. It would be possible to use a simple arithmetic average of the past values of the series to forecast the future. Such a procedure results in each past value of the series being given equal weight in the forecasted value, although in many cases it may seem appropriate to give greater weight to values in the more recent past. The other extreme would be to consider only the value in the most recent past to forecast the future. Exponential smoothing models are a compromise between these two positions in that they consider data over a number of periods but the weights attached to each value decrease as the values fall further in the past.

Box and Jenkins have developed a procedure for estimating ARIMA models. Basically, this methodology involves an iterative procedure with three steps. The first task is to select a specific model from the general class of ARIMA models. This means that the autoregressive order p, the degree of differencing parameter d, and the moving average order q must be specified. These decisions are made based on statistics calculated from the sample data. The second step is to estimate the parameters of the chosen model, and the third step is to check the estimated model to see if it adequately represents the series. A number of computer programs written for personal as well as mainframe computers are available for the Box-Jenkins procedure.[6]

Barometric forecasting uses current values of certain variables, called indicators, to predict future values of other economic variables.

Barometric Forecasting

Barometric forecasting involves the use of current values of certain economic variables called *indicators* to predict the future values of other economic variables.

■ ■ ■ ■ ■ ■
[6] See G. E. P. Box and G. M. Jenkins, *Time-Series Analysis, Forecasting and Control* (San Francisco: Holden-Day, 1970).

The philosophy behind barometric forecasting is that if researchers can find a set of economic variables whose fluctuations in value consistently *precede* similar fluctuations in other economic variables, then the first set of variables—called *leading indicators*—can be used to predict future values of the second set of variables. Much of the current barometric forecasting, at least on a macroeconomic level, is based on work done at the National Bureau of Economic Research by Arthur Burns, Geoffrey Moore, Julius Shiskin, and Wesley C. Mitchell.[7]

As we have stated, variables whose current changes give an indication of future changes in other variables are called leading indicators. Variables whose changes roughly coincide with changes in other economic variables are called *coincident indicators*. Finally, variables whose changes typically follow changes in other economic variables are called *lagging indicators*.[8]

The Department of Commerce publishes data on more than 100 leading, coincident, lagging, and unclassified indicators in *Business Conditions Digest*, a monthly publication. These indicators are subdivided according to the aspect of the economy being described and their timing at business cycle peaks and troughs. The seven general classification headings are employment and unemployment; production and income; consumption, trade, orders, and deliveries; fixed capital investment; inventories and inventory investment; prices, costs, and profits; and money and credit.

The Department of Commerce also publishes a shorter list of 21 indicator variables, shown in Table 11–1. These variables were selected on the basis of six characteristics—economic significance, statistical adequacy, consistency of timing at business peaks and troughs, conformity to business expansions and contractions, smoothness, and prompt availability. Of the 21 superior indicators, 11 are leading indicators, 4 are coincident indicators, and 6 are lagging indicators.

Each group of indicators (leading, coincident, or lagging) is then used to calculate a *composite*, or overall, indicator for the group.[9] Since they give diversified economic coverage based on a superior set of indicators, the composite indexes tend to give more reliable signals than do the individual indicators. The relationship of the values of these variables to the value of gross national product from 1979 to 1988 is illustrated in Table 11–2.

Ideally, to be good predictors, changes in leading indicators would consistently precede changes in the values of other variables which the

■ ■ ■ ■ ■ ■

[7] See, for example, A. F. Burns and W. C. Mitchell, *Measuring Business Cycles* (New York: National Bureau of Economic Research, 1946); W. C. Mitchell and A. F. Burns, *Statistical Indicators of Cyclical Revivals*, Occasional Paper 69 (New York: National Bureau of Economic Research, 1938); and G. H. Moore and J. Shiskin, *Indicators of Business Expansions and Contractions* (New York: National Bureau of Economic Research, 1967).

[8] The values of coincident and lagging indicators may be used to confirm short-run trends in the economy previously indicated by the leading indicators.

[9] See Geoffrey H. Moore (ed.) for the National Bureau of Economic Research, *Business Cycle Indicators, Volume 1: Contributions to the Analysis of Current Business Conditions* (Princeton, N.J.: Princeton University Press, 1961), Chapter 3, especially p. 72.

Table 11-1 Short List of Economic Indicators

	Median Lead (−) or Lag (+) in Months
Leading indicators (12 series)	
Average workweek, production workers, manufacturing	− 4.5
Initial claims, unemployment insurance	− 5.5
Index of net business formation	− 4.5
New orders, manufacturing, consumer goods and materials, 1982 dollars	− 4.5
Contracts and orders, plant and equipment, 1982 dollars	− 3.5
New building permits, private housing units	− 9.5
Change in inventories on hand and on order, 1982 dollars	− 5.5
Percent change in sensitive prices	− 5.5
Stock prices, 500 common stocks, Index	− 5.5
Change in credit outstanding	− 7.0
Percent vendor companies reporting slower deliveries	− 6.0
Money supply (M_2) in 1982 dollars	−10.0
Roughly coincident indicators (4 series)	
Employees in nonagricultural establishments	0
Industrial production Index	0
Personal income less transfer payments, 1982 dollars	0
Manufacturing and trade sales, 1982 dollars	− 1.5
Lagging indicators (6 series)	
Average duration of unemployment	+ 3.5
Ratio, consumer installment debt to personal income	+ 6.0
Labor cost per unit of output, manufacturing	+10.0
Commercial and industrial loans outstanding, 1982 dollars	+ 4.5
Average prime rate charged by banks	+ 5.5
Ratio, inventories to sales, manufacturing and trade, 1982 dollars	+10.0

Source: U.S. Department of Commerce, Bureau of Economic Analysis, *Handbook of Cyclical Indicators* (1984), pp. 172–173.

researchers are trying to predict. Moreover, these changes should not only always precede changes in the other variables, but also consistently precede them by a certain length of time, such as one month or six months.

Unfortunately, the leading indicator variables are not always that reliable. As a result, the notion of a diffusion index has been developed. *A diffusion index* indicates what percentages of values of the leading indicators are rising (with half of the unchanged components considered rising). Thus, if the values of all of the leading indicators are rising, the diffusion index is equal to 100. If all of the values are falling, the diffusion index is

Table 11-2 Index of Cyclical Indicators and Rate of Growth of Real GNP

	1979	1980	1981	1982	1983	1984	1985	1986	1987	1988
Rate of Growth of Real GNP	2.5	−0.2	1.9	−2.5	3.6	6.8	3.4	2.7	3.7	4.4
LEADING INDICATORS										
Composite index, 1982 = 100	**103.6**	**99.2**	**101.2**	**100.0**	**116.2**	**121.8**	**124.0**	**132.1**	**139.6**	**142.5**
Indexes:										
Building permits.[1] 1967 = 100	123.6	96.7	80.0	80.7	131.1	134.8	138.1	141	122.9	116.0
Common stock prices.[2] 1941–43 = 10	103.0	118.8	128.0	119.7	160.4	160.5	186.8	236.3	286.8	265.8
Percent:										
Change in sensitive materials prices[3,4]	1.3	.4	−.1	−.9	1.1	.2	−.8	.3	1.1	.4
Vendor companies reporting slower deliveries	58	41	46	43	57	57	48	51	57	58
Initial claims, unemployment insurance (1,000)	379	480	446	578	426	366	383	373	320	305
Avg. workweek, manufacturing[5] (hours)	40.2	39.7	39.8	38.9	40.1	40.7	40.5	40.7	41.0	41.1
Plant and equip. contracts and orders (1982 dols.) (bil. dol.)	407	361	352	310	317	380	410	407	464	537
New orders, manufacturing, consumer goods and materials (1982 dols.) (bil. dol.)	1,004	891	888	810	901	965	955	968	1,015	1,046
Money supply (M2) (1982 dols.) (bil. dol.)	1,929	1,835	1,819	1,874	2,043	2,113	2,224	2,363	2,430	2,454
Consumer expectations index, 1966 = 100	52.8	⁻56.8	65.0	62.7	84.7	92.7	86.5	85.8	81.2	85.2
Change in manufacturers' unfilled orders, durable goods (1982 dol.) (bil. dol.)[4]	33	−13	−13	−28	14	28	—	−1	16	22
COINCIDENT INDICATORS										
Composite index, 1982 = 100	**110.8**	**107.2**	**107.3**	**100.0**	**101.9**	**112.2**	**116.0**	**118.8**	**122.7**	**128.6**
Industrial production index, 1977 = 100	110.7	108.6	111.0	103.1	109.2	121.4	123.7	125.1	129.8	137.2
Employees, nonagric. payrolls (mil.)	89.8	90.4	91.2	89.6	90.2	94.5	97.5	99.5	102.2	105.6
Personal income less transfer payments (1982 dols.) (bil. dol.)	2,253	2,233	2,275	2,261	2,301	2,454	2,540	2,632	2,704	2,792
Sales, mfg and trade (1982 dols.) (bil. dol.)	4,456	4,341	4,358	4,183	4,360	4,721	4,863	5,033	5,235	5,427
LAGGING INDICATORS										
Composite index, 1982 = 100	**102.8**	**105.5**	**102.8**	**100.0**	**91.4**	**100.7**	**107.7**	**111.7**	**111.6**	**115.9**
Percent:										
Change in labor cost per unit of output, manufacturing[4]	9.2	10.5	6.4	7.0	−5.9	.6	2.0	1.1	−1.2	1.0
Ratio, consumer installment credit to personal income	13.9	13.3	12.1	11.9	12.1	13.2	14.5	15.6	15.6	15.7
Average prime rate charged by banks[4,8]	12.7	15.3	18.9	14.9	10.8	12.0	9.9	8.3	8.2	9.3
Change in CPI for services[4,8]	12.1	15.2	14.0	6.8	3.1	5.6	5.0	4.7	4.2	4.7
Average duration of unemployment, Weeks	10.8	11.9	13.8	15.6	19.9	18.1	15.6	15.1	14.5	13.5
Ratio inventories to sales, mfg. and trade (1982 dols.) (bil. dol.)	1.6	1.6	1.6	1.7	1.6	1.6	1.6	1.5	1.5	1.5
Commercial and industrial loans outstanding (1982 dols.) (bil. dol.)[7]	219	225	233	268	261	296	329	349	354	365

— Represents zero. [1] New private housing units authorized. [2] Standard and Poor's 500 stocks. [3] Producer prices of selected crude and intermediate materials and spot market prices of selected raw industrial materials. [4] Smoothed by an autoregressive-moving-average filter developed by Statistics Canada. [5] Production workers. [6] Copyrighted by the University of Michigan's Survey Research Center. [7] Includes commercial paper issued by nonfinancial companies. [8] Consumer price index.

Source: U.S. Bureau of Economic Analysis, *Business Conditions Digest*, monthly.

equal to zero. Moore found that the diffusion index is usually above 50 percent during business cycle expansions and below 50 percent during business cycle contractions.[10]

Barometric techniques are frequently used to forecast turning points in the level of general economic activity in a country. They may also be useful in forecasting the direction of change in the values of other economic variables. However, these forecasting methods are not as useful in predicting the *magnitude* (size) of such changes.

Surveys

The use of surveys by firms in estimating the demand for their products was discussed in Chapter 3. However, surveys are also used to predict future levels of general economic activity.

Surveys can be quite useful in indicating the plans of businesses to purchase new plants and equipment. Such investment spending can have a relatively large impact on the economy-wide demand for goods and services.

Several agencies regularly conduct surveys of business investment in plant and equipment. For example, McGraw-Hill conducts a survey twice a year of such plans and publishes the results in *Business Week* in November and April. This survey covers all large corporations and a great number of medium-sized firms. A joint quarterly survey is conducted by the Department of Commerce and the Securities and Exchange Commission and published in the third month of each quarter in the *Survey of Current Business*. The National Industrial Conference Board surveys capital expenditures commitments made by the boards of directors of 1,000 manufacturing firms. The results of these surveys are also published in the *Survey of Current Business*.

Consumer spending has an important effect on the aggregate level of income (GNP) through its impact on aggregate demand. Both the Bureau of the Census and the Survey Research Center at the University of Michigan conduct surveys regarding consumer intentions to purchase specific products. The information gathered by the Census Bureau is published quarterly in "Consumer Buying Indicators," *Current Population Reports* (Series P-65). The Survey Research Center surveys consumer attitudes and buying plans, and an index of general attitudes is calculated. The results of these surveys are reported annually in the *Survey of Consumer Finances*, published by the Survey Research Center.

Surveys regarding business expectations of future sales and business plans for inventories are also conducted by the Department of Commerce and the Securities and Exchange Commission. These results are published quarterly in the *Survey of Current Business*.

■ ■ ■ ■ ■ ■
[10] Ibid.

Managerial Perspective: The Economic Indicators: Astronomy, Astrology, or Gambling?

In the spring of 1990, Alan Greenspan, chairman of the Federal Reserve Board, told Congress that there was only a 20 percent chance of a recession in 1990, compared with a 30 percent chance predicted a year earlier. He went on to say, moreover, that the National Bureau of Economic Research's monthly Experimental Recession Index indicated that the risk of an economic slowdown was even lower—only a 10 percent chance. Of course, that prediction was made before Iraq invaded Kuwait in August of that year and oil prices skyrocketed.

While we cannot expect Mr. Greenspan to have been able to predict the actions of Iraqui President Saddam Hussein, the predictions of the Federal Reserve Board and other economic soothsayers have not always been accurate in the past even in the absence of unanticipated international crises. Among other things, the Federal Reserve's predictions are based on an analysis of the Department of Commerce's leading economic indicators. Unfortunately, these indicators have had only a 64 percent accuracy record for predicting recessions over the last 40 years. The NBER forecasters give less weight to manufacturing performance than does the Commerce Department. The NBER also excludes stock prices from the data used in preparing its forecasts.

Some economic forecasting skeptics assert that Greenspan's predictions would be as nearly accurate (or no more inaccurate) if he used the "Hemline Index" or the "Super Bowl Index." During the 1940s, 1950s, and 1960s, it appeared that there was a relationship between the length of women's dresses and the economy: when hemlines rose, the economy tended to grow; when hemlines fell, the economy declined. Another interesting predictor variable is the winner of the Super Bowl, which so far has a 91.3 percent accuracy rate. In 21 of the 23 years since Super Bowl I, a National Football Conference team winning the Super Bowl was followed by rising stock prices and a booming economy. On the other hand, an American Conference team winner was followed by falling stock prices. Although an NFC team won the 1990 Super Bowl, the economy grew only slightly in real (inflation-adjusted) terms in 1990.

Some economists contend that the reason forecasts based on the leading indicator series sometimes do not pan out is that some of the variables that make up this series are no longer as relevant as they should be. For example, Professor Paul Samuelson has stated that the indicators do not properly consider inflation. Others argue that there is a problem with how the Commerce Department constructs its series on contracts and orders for plant and equipment because it does not reflect orders placed with foreign firms. In addition, it has been suggested that the service sector is not adequately represented by the indicator series. Other recommended additions to the series include a Dow Jones price index for 20 corporate bonds, a measure of the number of operating businesses, the rate of worker layoffs, and the rate at which workers quit their jobs. Recognizing the difficulties facing economic forecasters, David Hale, chief economist for Kemper Financial Services, stated: "I have more in common with seismologists than with meteorologists."

■ ■ ■ ■

References: "Laying Odds on a Recession: How the Game is Played," *Newsweek* (February 12, 1990), p. 43; "A Mess of Misleading Indicators," *Time* (June 13, 1988), p. 49; and "Shaky Statistics Pose Peril for Forecasters," *The Wall Street Journal*, May 9, 1988, p. 1.

Econometric Models

Econometric models are a fourth way of forecasting in the field of economics. These models range from simple, linear demand functions for the product of a firm to very large models containing hundreds of equations, designed to describe many of the economic relationships in an entire nation. Both models describing firm or industry level relationships and models describing relationships involving economic aggregate variables (covering large sectors of or an entire national economy) can be quite useful to firm managers.

For example, we have already explained how important it is for a firm to know the nature of the demand function for its product. Given estimates of consumer incomes, competitors' prices, advertising expenditures, and the price it plans to charge, a firm can make a prediction about the future sales of its product. However, the larger econometric models can be quite valuable to a firm in developing forecasts of general business conditions in the economy and, consequently, what consumer incomes and competitors' prices will be in the future. This information, in turn, is necessary in making forecasts regarding the sales of the individual firm. The procedure for estimating the demand function for an individual firm was discussed at length in the appendix to Chapter 3. In this chapter, therefore, we will concentrate on explaining the nature of larger econometric models.

One of the first mathematical models describing the workings of an entire economy was developed in 1939 by the Dutch Nobel prize-winning economist, Jan Tinbergen. However, this model was not sufficiently well specified to be very useful for forecasting. Since that time, however, many advances have been made in the areas of mathematical economics, statistics, and the development of computers and computer programs. Three of the largest current econometric models are those of Wharton Econometric Forecasting Associates (headed by Nobel prizewinner Lawrence Klein); Data Resources, Incorporated; and Chase Econometrics.

All econometric models have two types of equations—behavioral equations and identities. *Behavioral equations* describe how the values of one or more economic variables are related to the behavior of economic units and, therefore, the value of another economic variable. *Identities* are equations that must be true by definition—for example, $4/2 \equiv 2$. The sign $\equiv$ means "identically equal to."

The workings of a macroeconomic econometric model can be illustrated by the simple one described below. Suppose that aggregate consumption spending, C, is a function of aggregate income or GNP last period, Y_{t-1}, plus the change in income during this time period, ΔY_t. We can write one version of this relationship as follows:

$$C_t = \alpha + \beta_1 Y_{t-1} + \beta_2 \Delta Y_t + \epsilon_t.$$

The subscript t refers to values for the current period, and $t-1$ refers to values for the last period. As discussed earlier in this chapter and in the appendix to Chapter 3, the term ϵ_t is a term reflecting random errors, with an expected value of zero. Furthermore, let us hypothesize that aggregate investment spending (new plant and equipment, residential housing, and inventories) will be a value determined by factors outside our model. Thus $I_t = I_t^*$.

Finally, if there were no government expenditures or foreign trade, as we shall assume is true in our simple model, the aggregate level of income in an economy must, by definition, be equal to the sum of consumption and investment spending. Therefore

$$Y_t \equiv C_t + I_t.$$

In other words, everything that is produced in an economy during period t must be demanded by some economic unit—consumers or businesses. (However, businesses might find that some of their investment spending has gone for inventories in excess of desired levels.)

Our simple model, therefore, consists of the following three relationships:

(11–1)
$$C_t = \alpha + \beta_1 Y_{t-1} + \beta_2(Y_t - Y_{t-1}) + \epsilon_t,$$

(11–2)
$$I_t = I_t^*,$$

and

(11–3)
$$Y_t \equiv C_t + I_t.$$

Equations 11–1 and 11–2 are behavioral relationships because they indicate something about the behavior of consumption and investment spending, respectively. Equation 11–3 is an identity. The variables C_t and Y_t are called *endogenous* variables because their values will be determined within the framework of our model.

Investment, I_t^*, is an *exogenous* variable because its value is determined by factors outside this model. In this case Y_{t-1} is a *predetermined* variable—its value has already been determined by the time we are ready to try to predict C_t and Y_t. The remaining terms—α, β_1, and β_2—are called parameters. Although their values may change from time to time, they represent numerical constants that describe the behavior of economic units (consumers, in this case). They are not thought to vary as much as the values of the endogenous variables.

If we substitute equations 11–1 and 11–2 into 11–3 for C_t and I_t, respectively, we can obtain the following equation for Y_t, which involves only predetermined or exogenous variables and parameters, except for Y_t itself:

$$Y_t = \alpha + \beta_1 Y_{t-1} + \beta_2 (Y_t - Y_{t-1}) + I_t^* + \epsilon_t.$$

Subtracting $\beta_2 Y_t$ from both sides, we obtain

$$Y_t - \beta_2 Y_t = \alpha + \beta_1 Y_{t-1} - \beta_2 Y_{t-1} + I_t^* + \epsilon_t.$$

Factoring out $(1 - \beta_2)$ on the left-hand side, we get

$$Y_t(1 - \beta_2) = \alpha + \beta_1 Y_{t-1} - \beta_2 Y_{t-1} + I_t^* + \epsilon_t.$$

Finally, dividing by $1 - \beta_2$, we obtain

$$Y_t = \frac{\alpha}{1 - \beta_2} + \frac{\beta_1}{(1 - \beta_2)} Y_{t-1} - \frac{\beta_2}{(1 - \beta_2)} Y_{t-1} + \left(\frac{1}{1 - \beta_2}\right) I_t^* + \left(\frac{1}{1 - \beta_2}\right) \epsilon_t,$$

or

(11–4)
$$Y_t = \frac{\alpha}{(1 - \beta_2)} + \frac{(\beta_1 - \beta_2)}{(1 - \beta_2)} Y_{t-1} + \left(\frac{1}{1 - \beta_2}\right) I_t^* + \left(\frac{1}{1 - \beta_2}\right) \epsilon_t.$$

Now, substituting for Y_t from equation 11-4 into equation 11-1, we find

$$C_t = \alpha + \beta_1 Y_{t-1} + \beta_2 \left[\frac{\alpha}{1 - \beta_2} + \left(\frac{\beta_1 - \beta_2}{1 - \beta_2} \right) Y_{t-2} \right.$$

$$\left. + \left(\frac{1}{1 - \beta_2} \right) I_t^* + \left(\frac{1}{1 - \beta_2} \right) \epsilon_t - Y_{t-1} \right] + \epsilon_t,$$

or

$$C_t = \alpha + \beta_1 Y_{t-1} + \beta_2 \left[\frac{\alpha}{(1 - \beta_2)} + \left(\frac{\beta_1 - \beta_2}{1 - \beta_2} - 1 \right) Y_{t-1} \right.$$

$$\left. + \left(\frac{1}{1 - \beta_2} \right) I_t^* + \left(\frac{1}{1 - \beta_2} \right) \epsilon_t \right] + \epsilon_t.$$

Simplifying, we get

$$C_t = \alpha + \frac{\alpha \beta_2}{(1 - \beta_2)} + \left[\frac{\beta_2(\beta_1 - \beta_2)}{(1 - \beta_2)} - \beta_2 + \beta_1 \right] Y_{t-1}$$

$$+ \left(\frac{\beta_2}{1 - \beta_2} \right) I_t^* + \left(\frac{\beta_2}{1 - \beta_2} \right) \epsilon_t + \epsilon_t,$$

$$C_t = \frac{\alpha - \alpha \beta_2 + \alpha \beta_2}{1 - \beta_2} + \left[\frac{\beta_2 \beta_1 - \beta_2^2 - \beta_2 + \beta_2^2 + \beta_1 - \beta_2 \beta_1}{1 - \beta_2} \right] Y_{t-1}$$

$$+ \left[\frac{\beta_2}{1 - \beta_2} \right] I_t^* + \left[\frac{\beta_2 + 1 - \beta_2}{1 - \beta_2} \right] \epsilon_t,$$

and

(11–5)

$$C_t = \frac{\alpha}{1 - \beta_2} + \left(\frac{\beta_1 - \beta_2}{1 - \beta_2} \right) Y_{t-1} + \left(\frac{\beta_2}{1 - \beta_2} \right) I_t^* + \left(\frac{1}{1 - \beta_2} \right) \epsilon_t.$$

Equations 11–4 and 11–5 are said to be in *reduced form* because they express the relationships for Y_t and C_t, respectively, in terms of only exogenous and predetermined variables and the parameters.

Using historical data and regression analysis techniques, an econometrician could now statistically estimate the values for $[\alpha/(1 - \beta_2)]$, $[(\beta_1 - \beta_2)/(1 - \beta_2)]$, and $[1/(1 - \beta_2)]$ in equation 11–4. The same procedure could also be used to estimate the constant term and the coefficients of Y_{t-1} and I_t^* in equation 11–5. Once these relationships are statistically estimated, the current value of Y_t and the expected value of I_{t+1}^* could be used to forecast Y_{t+1} and C_{t+1}.[11]

■ ■ ■ ■ ■ ■
[11] Other methods of statistically estimating relationships involving simultaneous equations may be desirable. See J. Johnston, *Econometric Methods*, 3d ed. (New York: McGraw-Hill, 1984), Chapter 11.

In recent years, econometric models have been developed for use on personal computers. At least one of these programs, the FAIRMODEL, has been performing quite favorably compared with the larger models. The personal computer versions of the models are much cheaper to use than the big models, and economists anticipate that these smaller models will be quite helpful to business persons in forecasting the future path of economic activity.[12]

Input-Output Analysis

Input-output analysis is concerned with the connection between the demand for final output and the productive efforts required of individual industries and their interrelationships. For example, an increase in the quantity demanded of automobiles by consumers will require an increase in the quantity of steel, aluminum, tires, and glass produced. It will also require an increase in the quantity produced of brake drums, engines, transmissions, and drive shafts. Some of these items will be totally or partially produced by industries other than the automobile industry, while some will be produced by the automakers themselves. As may be obvious already, these relationships can get quite complicated. Input-output tables are one method of organizing and depicting them.

If we classify the gross national product by type of spending, it can be divided into four categories: investment spending, consumption spending, government expenditures, and net exports (all defined previously). GNP can also be divided into the types of income that were created when the gross national product was produced. These categories of income include wages, rent, profit, interest, a capital consumption allowance (basically depreciation), and certain indirect business taxes and net surpluses of government businesses.

The division of the gross national product into expenditure categories and into income categories in an input-output framework is shown in Table 11–3. The top line of the table shows the expenditure categories, and the first column of the table shows the income categories. Note that rent, interest, profit, and the capital consumption allowance are combined into one type of income. It should also be pointed out that income taxes are *not* included in the government sector. They are included in the other two sectors as a part of wages and "profit-type" incomes. Indirect business taxes are taxes (such as sales taxes) that are not directly related to the level of a firm's profits.

Table 11–3 shows only the final demand for the products produced and the categories of income that their production creates. In this case both the items in the top *row* of the table and the items in the first *column* of the table sum to GNP. Table 11–4 is an expanded version of Table

■ ■ ■ ■ ■ ■
[12] "How Personal Computers Are Changing the Forecaster's Job," *Business Week* (October 1, 1984), pp. 123–124.

Table 11–3   The Gross National Product in Input-Output Format

	Persons	Investors	Foreigners	Government	Gross national product
Producers	Personal consumption expenditures	Gross private domestic investment	Net exports of goods and services	Government purchases of goods and services	Gross national product
Employees					
Employee compensation					
Owners of business and capital					
Profit-type income and capital consumption allowances					
Government					
Indirect business taxes and current surplus of government enterprises, etc.					
Gross national product					

Source: U.S. Department of Commerce, Bureau of the Census, *Historical Statistics of the United States: Colonial Times to 1970* (Washington: U.S. Government Printing Office, 1975), p. 268.

Table 11–4 Input-Output Flow

		Producers								Final markets			
		Agri-culture	Mining	Con-struction	Manufac-turing	Trade	Transpor-tation	Services	Other	Persons	Investors	Foreigners	Govern-ment
Producers	Agriculture									Personal consumption expenditures	Gross private domestic investment	Net exports of goods and services	Government purchases of goods and services
	Mining												
	Construction												
	Manufacturing												
	Trade												
	Transportation												
	Services												
	Other												
Value added	Employees	Employee compensation											
	Owners of business and capital	Profit-type income and capital consumption allowances											
	Government	Indirect business taxes and current surplus of government enterprises, etc.											

Gross national product

Source: U.S. Department of Commerce, Bureau of the Census, *Historical Statistics of the United States: Colonial Times to 1970* (Washington: U.S. Government Printing Office, 1975), p. 269.

11–3 that includes the interindustry relationships among the producers. Now, the top row of the table indicates both the final markets for agricultural products plus the *purchases of agricultural products by other industries.* This type of input-output table showing the flow of goods and services and incomes among the various sectors of an economy is called an *input-output flow table.*

Table 11–5 shows a portion of an actual input-output flow table for the United States economy for 1967. It was prepared by the Bureau of Economic Analysis (BEA) of the Department of Commerce. The BEA periodically constructs such tables, some far more detailed than that shown here. The value of the total output produced in the United States can be computed by summing the column totals for the four final markets. For example, $490,660 + 120,477 + 5,132 + 179,119 = $795,388 million, the value of GNP in producers' prices for 1967. The value of GNP can also be found by reading the value in the *total output column* corresponding to the *value-added row.* Each *row* of Table 11–5 shows the *distribution* of an industry's *output.* Each *column* shows the *inputs used* in producing each industry's output.

A *direct requirements table* is a form of input-output table that is quite useful for economic forecasters. A direct requirements table indicates the fraction of each dollar of an industry's *output* that is made up of inputs from each other industry. The direct requirements table is constructed by dividing each input item in a column in the input-output flow table by the corresponding column value for total inputs in that table.

Table 11–6 is a direct requirements table corresponding to Table 11–5. It indicates that 18,542/63,097 (or 29.4 cents) of each dollar of final output produced by the agricultural industry consists of intermediate products produced by the agricultural industry itself. Table 11–6 also shows that 2,451/63,097 (or 3.9 cents) of each dollar of final output of the agricultural industry is made up of products from the chemical industry. Similar computations can be made between the products of all of the other industries.

A third input-output table that is very important for economic forecasting is the *total requirements table.* A total requirements table indicates the value of the total inputs (direct and indirect) required per dollar of an industry's product produced for final demand. The total requirements table must take into account all of the interrelationships among the inputs and products of the various industries.

The total requirements table can be constructed from the direct requirements table (Table 11–6) in the following manner. By looking at the column for the metal-mining industry, we can see that each dollar of final mining products produced requires an input of 9.5 cents of metal-mining industry products. Thus the metal-mining industry must produce $1.095 of output for each dollar of final output produced. Hence the production of $100 of final output for the mining industry requires the production of $109.50 worth of metal-mining products. This production, in turn, will

Table 11–5 Value of Input-Output Transactions Among Industries in the U.S. Economy: 1967 (in millions of dollars at producers' prices)

Industry No.	Producing industry \ Consuming industry	Agriculture, forestry, and fisheries	Metal mining	Petroleum and natural gas mining	Other mining	Construction	Food, feed, and tobacco products	Textile products and apparel	Wood products and furniture	Paper, printing and publishing
	1967									
1	Agriculture, forestry, and fisheries	18,542	–	–	–	263	28,505	1,603	1,125	
2	Metal mining	–	320	–	9	–	–	–	–	–
3	Petroleum and natural gas mining	–	–	374	1	–	–	–	–	–
4	Other mining	138	17	(Z)	535	930	53	20	8	154
5	Construction	603	46	476	50	30	264	91	94	224
6	Food, feed, and tobacco products	3,762	–	–	–	–	16,493	47	6	135
7	Textile products and apparel	201	2	5	31	279	145	18,954	511	352
8	Wood products and furniture	123	14	(Z)	23	5,528	124	28	4,683	1,212
9	Paper, printing, and publishing	161	1	2	26	295	3,225	402	216	11,213
10	Chemicals and chemical products	2,451	78	173	125	1,477	874	3,298	379	1,477
11	Petroleum and coal products	1,113	10	33	112	2,024	220	51	118	172
12	Rubber, plastics, and leather	216	23	34	64	749	739	324	404	434
13	Stone, clay, and glass products	33	4	83	131	7,128	1,002	99	198	34
14	Primary and fabricated metals	192	101	230	201	15,192	2,438	81	1,203	614
15	Machinery, except electrical	322	118	276	222	1,842	250	169	137	200
16	Electrical equipment and supplies	55	3	171	17	2,509	6	19	35	2
17	Transport equipment and ordnance	38	8	–	1	5	4	4	45	6
18	Other manufacturing	12	2	16	3	535	84	448	97	341
19	Transportation and trade	4,144	214	321	203	10,839	5,970	1,960	1,374	2,293
20	Electric, gas, and sanitary services	304	89	172	187	74	645	331	180	514
21	Other services	5,235	318	2,886	606	7,824	5,730	1,795	991	3,794
22	Government enterprises	9	3	6	5	66	94	76	20	301
23	Scrap and secondhand goods	–	14	86	21	14	1	39	–	239
DI	Directly allocated imports	36			–	101	1,318	62	2	3
TrI	Transferred imports	1,025	858	1,076	203	–	1,355	825	791	1,387
I	Intermediate inputs, total	38,716	2,244	6,420	2,776	57,705	69,539	30,727	12,616	25,127
VA	Value added	24,382	1,117	8,611	3,762	45,575	27,852	15,638	8,584	19,402
T	Total inputs	63,097	3,362	15,031	6,538	103,280	97,391	46,365	21,200	44,529
Tr	Transfers	1,189	1,024	1,298	365	–	2,922	1,358	1,443	2,003

Sources: "The Input-Output Structure of the U.S. Economy: 1967," *Survey of Current Business*, Vol. 54 (February, 1974), pp. 24–56; and U.S. Department of Commerce, Bureau of the Census, *Historical Statistics of the United States: Colonial Times to 1970* (Washington: U.S. Government Printing Office, 1975), pp. 272–273.

require $109.50 × .00497 = $.54 worth of products from other mining industries, $109.50 × .01359 = $1.49 worth of products from the construction industry, $109.50 × .00062 = $.07 worth of products from the textile industry, and so on. Each of these industries will need products from other industries to produce the required increases in their products, and the circle continues.

The calculations necessary to construct a total requirements table for the U.S. economy would be quite laborious if done by hand. However, such calculations can be done quickly by a computer. A total requirements table has been calculated by the Bureau of Economic Analysis for a more detailed level of industry classification than that shown in Table 11–6.

Intermediate markets—Con.						Final markets						
Other manu-facturing	Trans-porta-tion and trade	Electric, gas, and sanitary services	Other services	Govern-ment enter-prises	Scrap and second-hand goods	Personal con-sump-tion expendi-tures	Gross private domestic invest-ment [1]	Net exports [2]	Govern-ment pur-chases [3]	Total output	Trans-fers [4]	Industry No.
												1967
21	196	–	3,014	392	–	6,152	1,162	3,301	−1,314	63,097	4,006	1
3	1	1	14	–	–	–	38	158	60	3,362	25	2
–	25	2,521	165	–	–	–	257	82	–	15,031	1,138	3
9	16	896	89	145	–	128	145	538	47	6,538	366	4
62	1,833	1,137	9,191	1,771	–	–	54,338	15	31,231	103,280	–	5
31	1,067	2	3,797	121	10	66,244	1,089	2,507	1,131	97,391	4,397	6
358	433	17	434	25	72	20,227	640	583	645	46,365	605	7
199	252	1	54	–	–	4,293	2,017	413	528	21,200	467	8
2,694	2,103	44	11,395	75	129	5,694	564	924	1,442	44,529	12,410	9
693	679	58	2,628	165	–	7,867	607	2,863	2,656	44,999	1,609	10
43	3,374	275	1,644	141	12	10,194	541	765	1,370	26,975	2,509	11
618	1,042	23	1,434	43	14	5,928	187	385	589	19,069	913	12
136	340	1	456	7	–	562	166	322	111	14,808	562	13
1,883	1,134	78	2,163	25	588	1,232	2,636	2,253	983	87,906	3,834	14
262	746	39	2,020	33	108	812	22,108	5,249	2,648	53,593	3,242	15
809	554	74	1,723	24	96	8,566	7,312	1,989	7,964	46,759	3,537	16
179	1,022	3	1,545	18	168	17,271	16,828	4,300	20,221	82,831	3,258	17
1,422	959	31	3,492	29	35	6,047	2,919	1,222	2,181	22,288	2,032	18
998	11,447	765	14,285	1,440	58	120,763	8,108	6,506	6,091	216,165	10,201	19
101	2,757	6,888	3,242	1,268	–	13,935	–	74	1,942	37,321	188	20
1,601	30,671	1,002	51,351	1,392	11	178,786	3,142	1,599	12,459	335,588	132	21
35	3,931	5,610	3,660	23	–	2,148	–	106	819	17,337	9,768	22
–	16	–	40	(Z)	–	1,286	−3,042	580	554	1,991	–	23
182	942	–	290	341	–	9,870	558	−18,221	3,967	–	–	DI
870	1,363	145	376	–	689	–	–	−20,807	–	–	20,807	TrI
13,210	66,904	19,609	118,502	7,480	1,991	−2,047	122,320	2,908	−861	–	–	I
9,078	149,261	17,712	217,087	9,857	–	4,701	−1,843	4,517	81,654	795,388	–	VA
22,288	216,165	37,321	335,588	17,337	1,991	490,660	120,477	5,132	179,119	–	–	T
4,283	8,466	5,947	28,062	–	1,991	–	–	–	–	–	–	Tr

Sometimes an *output distribution* table is also constructed. This table is obtained by dividing each item of a row of the input-output flow table by the value of the total output for that row. For example, the first entry in the output distribution table would show that 18,542/63,097 = .294 or 29.4 percent of the output of the agriculture industry is used by the agriculture industry itself. The first entry in each of the next three columns would have zero values. The first entry of the construction column would show that 263/63,097 = .0042 or .42% of the output of the agriculture industry is distributed to the *construction* industry.

Input-output analysis can be quite useful to forecasters in tracing the interindustry effects of a change in the final demand for some product or group of products. It can be used by government policymakers, industry associations, or firm managers to spot potential bottlenecks in the supply of certain inputs. It also can be used by firm managers as one tool in

Table 11–6   Direct Requirements per Dollar of Gross Output: 1967 (in dollars, producers' prices)

Industry No. / Producing industry	Agriculture, forestry, and fisheries	Metal mining	Petroleum and natural gas mining	Other mining	Construction	Food, feed, and tobacco products
1967						
1 Agriculture, forestry, and fisheries	.29386	–	–	–	.00254	.29268
2 Metal mining	–	.09527	–	.00136	–	–
3 Petroleum and natural gas mining	–	–	.02487	.00017	–	–
4 Other mining	.00219	.00497	.00002	.08189	.00901	.00055
5 Construction	.00956	.01359	.03168	.00760	.00029	.00271
6 Food, feed, and tobacco products	.05962	–	–	–	–	.16935
7 Textile products and apparel	.00319	.00062	.00032	.00477	.00270	.00148
8 Wood products and furniture	.00194	.00428	(Z)	.00352	.05353	.00127
9 Paper, printing, and publishing	.00255	.00033	.00011	.00396	.00286	.03311
10 Chemicals and chemical products	.03885	.02317	.01149	.01918	.01430	.00898
11 Petroleum and coal products	.01764	.00289	.00220	.01708	.01960	.00226
12 Rubber, plastics, and leather	.00343	.00687	.00227	.00982	.00725	.00759
13 Stone, clay, and glass products	.00052	.00110	.00552	.01999	.06902	.01028
14 Primary and fabricated metals	.00304	.03019	.01534	.03077	.14709	.02503
15 Machinery, except electrical	.00510	.03507	.01839	.03394	.01784	.00257
16 Electrical equipment and supplies	.00088	.00104	.01136	.00255	.02429	.00007
17 Transport equipment and ordnance	.00060	.00235	–	.00011	.00005	.00004
18 Other manufacturing	.00018	.00074	.00105	.00054	.00518	.00087
19 Transportation and trade	.06568	.06371	.02134	.03105	.10495	.06130
20 Electric, gas, and sanitary services	.00482	.02659	.01145	.02854	.00071	.00662
21 Other services	.08297	.09468	.19198	.09275	.07576	.05883
22 Government enterprises	.00014	.00080	.00042	.00076	.00064	.00097
23 Scrap and secondhand goods	–	.00422	.00573	.00315	.00014	.00001
DI Directly allocated imports	.00058	–	–	–	.00098	.01353
TrI Transferred imports	.01624	.25512	.07159	.03108	–	.01391
VA Value added	.38641	.33237	.57287	.57542	.44128	.28598
T Total inputs	1.00000	1.00000	1.00000	1.00000	1.00000	1.00000

Source: U.S. Department of Commerce, Bureau of the Census, *Historical Statistics of the United States: Colonial Times to 1970* (Washington: U.S. Government Printing Office, 1975), pp. 278–279.

forecasting the demand for their products. Less aggregated versions of Tables 11–5 and 11–6 would be more useful at the firm level.

However, some assumptions implicit in the construction of input-output tables should be kept in mind. First of all, these tables are valid only as long as the relative prices of the various inputs and products remain the same. Constant prices were assumed when the tables were constructed. Second, it is assumed that the same production relationships hold over all output levels. For example, it is assumed that $1 worth of metal-mining products always requires 2.3 cents worth of chemical products (see Table 11–6). Finally, the usefulness of the input-output tables to forecasters will depend on the accuracy of the predicted changes in the final demand for the various products. An inaccurate forecast of the final demand for these goods and services will certainly reduce the usefulness of input-output tables.

Stone, clay, and glass products	Primary and fabricated metals	Machinery except electrical	Electrical equipment and supplies	Transport equipment and ordnance	Other manufacturing	Transportation and trade	Electric, gas, and sanitary services	Other services	Government enterprises	Scrap and second-hand goods	Industry No.
											1967
–	–	–	–	–	.00094	.00091	–	.00898	.02262	–	1
00149	.02971	–	.00017	–	.00012	(Z)	.00003	.00004	–	–	2
–	–	–	–	–	–	.00012	.06756	.00049	–	–	3
.06365	.00878	.00024	.00020	.00027	.00041	.00008	.02400	.00027	.00836	–	4
.00881	.00543	.00308	.00304	.00260	.00276	.00848	.03047	.02739	.10216	–	5
.00041	.00012	.00014	–	–	.00141	.00494	.00005	.01131	.00696	.00502	6
.00571	.00120	.00113	.00144	.01061	.01607	.00200	.00045	.00129	.00147	.03631	7
.00597	.00424	.00256	.00789	.00691	.00895	.00116	.00003	.00016	–	–	8
.03329	.00729	.00495	.01159	.00276	.12089	.00973	.00118	.03395	.00435	.06493	9
.02606	.01441	.00283	.01429	.00725	.03110	.00314	.00156	.00783	.00949	–	10
.00750	.00299	.00394	.00213	.00245	.00195	.01561	.00737	.00490	.00812	.00583	11
.01467	.00463	.01061	.01629	.01465	.02771	.00482	.00061	.00427	.00248	.00718	12
.10276	.00411	.00718	.01489	.00684	.00609	.00157	.00002	.00136	.00042	–	13
.02187	.29260	.16884	.11176	.14788	.08449	.00525	.00210	.00645	.00145	.29533	14
.01619	.03243	.12591	.02720	.05127	.01175	.00345	.00105	.00602	.00189	.05409	15
.00329	.01006	.06476	.16299	.03270	.03628	.00256	.00198	.00514	.00140	.04801	16
.00101	.00794	.01835	.01608	.22469	.00804	.00473	.00008	.00460	.00106	.08422	17
.00500	.00362	.00597	.01117	.00992	.06381	.00444	.00083	.01041	.00168	.01778	18
.07871	.05823	.04325	.03943	.03583	.04480	.05295	.02049	.04257	.08305	.02938	19
.03334	.01787	.00582	.00664	.00485	.00452	.01276	.18456	.00966	.07313	–	20
.06800	.04600	.06558	.07156	.05232	.07183	.14189	.02684	.15302	.08028	.00567	21
.00154	.00077	.00107	.00131	.00115	.00158	.01819	.15031	.01091	.00134	–	22
.00068	.02003	.00112	.00005	.00257		.00007	–	.00012	.00001	–	23
.00005	.00072	.00055	.00185	.00096	.00818	.00436	–	.00087	.01970	–	DI
.01829	.04403	.02545	.02527	.01189	.03903	.00631	.00389	.00112	–	.34626	TrI
.48171	.38281	.43670	.45275	.36964	.40729	.69050	.47458	.64688	.56858	–	VA
.00000	1.00000	1.00000	1.00000	1.00000	1.00000	1.00000	1.00000	1.00000	1.00000	1.00000	T

■ ■ ■ ■ ■ ■ ■ ■   ACCURACY OF FORECASTS

As we have indicated, forecasts may be either long run or short run in nature. Businesses use short-run forecasts, for example, to plan short-run production schedules and inventory holdings. Long-term forecasts are essential for decisions regarding investment in plant and equipment. Many of the best-known macroeconomic forecasts are short run (that is, they cover not more than two years in the future), and we shall discuss their reliability next.

Short-Run Forecasts

The American Statistical Association and the National Bureau of Economic Research have collected the short-run forecasting records of over 50 separate forecasting operations since 1968. These organizations then put together a *median* (middle value) forecast based on the figures.[13] Several studies have now been made of these forecasts.

According to an investigation by Su and Su, the root-mean-square errors in terms of 1958 dollars of the median forecasts for the period from late 1968 to mid-1973 were $3.0 billion and $6.1 billion for quarterly and annual nominal (current dollar) predictions of GNP and $3.4 billion and $7.0 billion for forecasts of real GNP.[14] There is also evidence to indicate that the forecasting errors were larger during the first half of the 1970s than during the earlier (but partly overlapping) period.[15] The errors usually amounted to approximately one-fourth of the *change* for nominal quarterly forecasts but only about one-eighth of the change for nominal annual forecasts. The corresponding figures for forecasts of real GNP are one-half and one-third, respectively.[16] Annual forecasts tend to be more nearly accurate than quarterly forecasts because the impact of short-run events (such as strikes, production bottlenecks, and inventory adjustments) is less significant over an entire year.

Approximately 60 percent of the forecasts whose predictions are compiled by the American Statistical Association and the National Bureau of Economic Research used a judgmental approach, basing forecasts on the forecaster's judgment and exogenous variables. About 20 percent used primarily econometric models, whereas 10 percent used a leading indicators approach. According to one source, the differences between the forecasting errors resulting from the use of judgmental methods and those resulting from the use of econometric models have been relatively small— with the judgmental forecasts tending to be more nearly accurate. However, the accuracy of the econometric models was improved when their use was combined with a judgmental approach with respect to such things as the future values of exogenous variables. The record of those forecasters using the indicators approach reflected greater errors than did the other

■ ■ ■ ■ ■ ■

[13] The American Statistical Association and the National Bureau of Economic Research (NBER) publish the median (middle value) forecasts in the *American Statistician* and *Explorations in Economic Research,* published by the NBER.

[14] See Vincent Su and Josephine Su, "An Evaluation of ASA/NBER Business Outlook Survey Forecasts," *Explorations in Economic Research* 2 (Fall 1975), pp. 588–618, especially p. 600. The root-mean-square error is equal to

$$\left[\frac{\sum_{t=1}^{n} (GNP_t - G\hat{N}P_t)^2}{n} \right]^{1/2},$$

where GNP_t is the actual value of GNP, $G\hat{N}P_t$ is the predicted value of GNP, and n is the number of time periods.

[15] See Stephen K. McNees, "How Accurate are Economic Forecasts?" *New England Economic Review* (November/December 1974), pp. 2–19; and Stephen K. McNees, "An Evaluation of Economic Forecasts," *New England Economic Review* (November/December 1975), pp. 3–39.

[16] William Ascher, *Forecasting: An Appraisal for Policy-Makers and Planners* (Baltimore: Johns Hopkins University Press, 1978), p. 74.

two approaches with respect to nominal GNP and greater errors than did the judgmental approach with respect to real GNP.[17]

In a recent study, Professor Geoffrey Moore found that since the 1950s business executives have generally outperformed economists in forecasting inflation rates for the coming year. There was hardly any relationship between the previous year's inflation rate and the business people's predictions; however, economists' forecasts were highly correlated to past inflation rates.[18] Thus these results further reinforce the conclusion that the performance of forecasters using econometric techniques could be improved if they would also use a judgmental approach in analyzing the results from the models.

Stephen McNees, of the Boston Federal Reserve Bank, compared the record of seven forecasters using econometric models with a naive prediction that the future growth rate of GNP would be equal to the latest observed growth rate. These forecasts were also compared to those from a simple forecasting rule espoused by economist Milton Friedman that GNP in one quarter would be proportional to the average level of the money supply two quarters *earlier*. McNees summarizes his findings this way:

> Clearly, the naive same-change rule is far inferior to the monetarist [Friedman's] forecasting procedure. All of the economic [econometric model] forecasters, on the other hand, were more successful than the monetarist rule. The margin of superiority varies widely: the Fair model's forecasting errors were, on average, about 10 percent smaller than the monetarist technique while the most successful GNP forecasters' errors are only a little more than half as large as the monetarist formula.[19]

Long-Run Forecasts

Five well-known organizations that make long-term economic forecasts include the National Planning Association, the Joint Economic Committee of the U.S. Congress, McGraw Hill, the Committee for Economic Development, and the Organization for Economic Cooperation and Development. Short-term factors, such as temporarily high interest rates or a temporary change in government spending, have a less significant effect on long-run forecasts than on short-run forecasts. Still, since many of these forecasts rely on estimates of the long-run productive capacity of

■ ■ ■ ■ ■ ■
[17] Ibid., pp. 75–76, 81.
[18] See "Executives Make the Best Inflation Forecasters," *Business Week* (June 9, 1986), p. 24.
[19] Stephen K. McNees, "How Accurate Are Economic Forecasts?" *New England Economic Review* (November/December 1974), p. 19. The FAIRMODEL is relatively judgment free.

the economy and give less consideration to demand factors, they tend to be overly optimistic with regard to their projections of GNP growth.[20]

The Current Prognosis

Economic forecasters continue to have problems with the accuracy of their forecasts. In fact, a 1980 *Business Week* article argued:

> Not only have the economists missed the intensity and timing of each of the seven postwar recessions, but their forecasts seem to be getting worse, even as their acceptance by policymakers and businessmen rises.[21]

The difficulties of the forecasters, especially those using econometric models, can at least partly be explained by changes in the structure of the economy since the 1960s. For example, during the 1970s and early 1980s, inflation was a far more important factor than it had been in the 1950s and 1960s. Supply shortages of some basic materials developed, and the structure of the international oil market changed. Further, the impact of international product and money markets on the domestic economy has expanded, and there have been some significant shifts in consumer behavior. Finally, economic forecasters have not always correctly anticipated the monetary and fiscal policies that were implemented over the last 15 years.

When structural factors in the economy change, the parameters in large econometric models estimated using historical data may no longer be valid. Robert Solow, an economist at the Massachusetts Institute of Technology, summarized the problem this way:

> One advantage the physicist has over the economist is that the velocity of light has not changed over the past thousands of years, while what was in the 1950s and 1960s a good wage and price equation is no longer so.[22]

Nevertheless, econometrics is one of the fastest-growing industries in the United States. Its annual revenues were estimated to be over $100 million in the early 1980s; and its customers included most major corporations, as well as large governmental departments.[23]

More and more corporations are beginning to use *consensus forecasting*, a technique that involves making a composite forecast based on the predictions of many other forecasters. Chrysler Corporation maintains that this technique has worked successfully with regard to forecasts of GNP

■ ■ ■ ■ ■ ■

[20] William Ascher, *Forecasting: An Appraisal for Policy-Makers and Planners* (Baltimore: Johns Hopkins University Press, 1978), p. 92.

[21] 1980: The Year the Forecasters Really Blew It," *Business Week* (July 14, 1980), p. 88.

[22] "Theory Deserts the Forecasters," *Business Week* (June 29, 1974), p. 53.

[23] "Where the Big Econometric Models Go Wrong," *Business Week* (March 30, 1981), p. 70.

and inflation, though not so well for interest rates.[24] Another study of the *Blue Chip Economic Indicators* consensus forecast computed from those of 50 leading economists found that the consensus forecasts performed best with respect to October forecasts of the growth of real GNP for the next year. The forecasts of inflation for the next year were not quite as accurate as those for real GNP. However, forecasts of quarterly growth rates had average errors more than twice that of the other predictions.[25]

In any event it seems apparent that despite the problems associated with economic forecasting, corporate managers still believe that an attempt must be made to predict the economic future. After all, it is on the basis of such projections that many managers must bet the life—or at least the good health—of their firms.

■ ■ ■ ■ ■ ■ ■ ■ **SUMMARY**

Economic Forecasting and the Firm

Economic forecasts can be made regarding a great variety of economic variables. On an aggregate level, for example, forecasts are made regarding future levels of the gross national product, investment spending, consumption spending, government expenditures, and net exports. On a microeconomic level, forecasts are made regarding such variables as sales of a firm and its competitors and the level of input prices. Forecasts may be either long run or short run in nature.

There are two major types of data used by forecasters in studying the nature of economic relationships—time series data and cross-section data. *Time series data* are observations of a specific variable over a number of time periods. *Cross-section data* are observations of a particular variable at a single point in time.

The types of factors that affect the values of economic variables are often classified into four general categories: trend, seasonal, cyclical, and other. *Trend factors* are those that reflect long-term movements in economic variables. *Seasonal factors* are related to a specific season of the year. *Cyclical factors* are related to fluctuations in the general level of economic activity. Other factors include such things as changes in consumer tastes not specifically related to the passage of time.

We discussed six forecasting methods—trend analysis, ARIMA models, barometric techniques, surveys, econometric models, and input-output analysis. *Trend analysis* relies primarily on historical data to predict the

■ ■ ■ ■ ■ ■

[24] John Koten, "They Say No Two Economists Ever Agree, So Chrysler Tries Averaging Their Opinions," *The Wall Street Journal*, November 3, 1981, p. 29.

[25] See Jim Eggert, "Consensus Forecasting—A Ten-Year Report Card," *Challenge* (July-August 1987), pp. 59–62.

future. These techniques range from rather simple projections of past data to more sophisticated methods.

Autoregressive integrated moving average (ARIMA) models are a general class of models used in forecasting time series based on the hypothesis that adequate forecasts of future values of a time series can be obtained based solely on past information of the series. In general, ARIMA models are linear functions of the sample data, and the sample data must generally constitute a nonseasonal, stationary series. Autoregressive models and moving average models are subsets of the more general ARIMA model class. The random walk model and an exponential smoothing model are two relatively simple ARIMA models that are sometimes used in economic forecasting.

Barometric forecasting involves the use of current values of certain economic variables called *indicators* to predict the future value of other economic variables. The indicator variables are divided into three categories: leading, coincident, and lagging. *Leading indicators* are variables whose current changes give an indication of future changes in other economic variables. *Coincident indicators* are variables whose changes roughly coincide with changes in other economic variables. *Lagging indicators* are variables whose changes typically follow changes in other economic variables.

The use of *surveys* by firms in estimating the demand for their products was discussed in Chapter 3. Surveys are also conducted by various governmental agencies and private firms regarding business investment and consumer spending plans and expected sales and inventory changes.

Econometric models are a fifth method of economic forecasting. These models range from simple, linear demand functions for the product of a firm to very large models containing hundreds of equations, designed to describe many of the economic relationships in an entire nation. Econometric models have two types of equations—behavioral equations and identities. *Behavioral equations* describe how the changes in certain economic variables are related to changes in another economic variable. *Identities* give relationships that are true by definition.

Input-output analysis is concerned with the connection between the demand for final output and the productive efforts required of individual industries and their interrelationships. An input-output table showing the flow of goods and services and incomes among the various sectors of an economy is called an *input-output flow table*. A *total requirements table* indicates the value of the total inputs (direct and indirect) required per dollar of an industry's product produced for final demand. Such tables are prepared periodically for the United States by the Bureau of Economic Analysis of the Department of Commerce.

Unfortunately, none of the forecasting methods discussed in this chapter yields completely accurate forecasts. Nevertheless, economic forecasting, particularly econometrics, is one of the fastest-growing industries in the United States. Its customers include major corporations as well as large governmental departments.

■ ■ ■ ■ ■ ■ ■ ■ ■ ■ ■ ■ ■ Questions ■ ■ ■ ■ ■ ■ ■ ■ ■ ■ ■ ■ ■

1. What is the difference between time series data and cross-section data?
2. Explain how barometric forecasting is done. What are indicator variables?
3. What is trend analysis? How does it work?
4. What is an econometric model? Can you construct a simple one?
5. What are input-output tables? How are they utilized in forecasting? Give an example using only two products.
6. List and explain four general categories of factors that may affect the quantity demanded of a product. Give an example.
7. Explain how forecasts involving aggregate economic (macroeconomic) variables can be useful to a business person. Give some examples.
8. What are two sources of survey information regarding planned business investment and planned consumer spending?
9. Discuss the accuracy of economic forecasts in recent years. What factors have led to problems in making forecasts? How might forecasters improve their accuracy?

■ ■ ■ ■ ■ ■ ■ ■ ■ ■ ■ Selected References ■ ■ ■ ■ ■ ■ ■ ■ ■ ■

Burns, Arthur F. *The Business Cycle in a Changing World.* New York: National Bureau of Economic Research, 1969. Distributed by Columbia University Press, New York.

Granger, C. W. J. *Forecasting In Business and Economics,* 2d ed. Boston: Academic Press, 1989.

Henry, William R., and W. Warren Haynes. *Managerial Economics: Analysis and Cases,* 4th ed. Dallas: Business Publications, Inc., 1978, Chapters 4 and 5.

Johnston, J. *Econometric Methods,* 3d ed. New York: McGraw-Hill, 1984.

Lansing, John B., and James N. Morgan. *Economic Survey Methods.* Ann Arbor, Michigan: Institute for Social Research, The University of Michigan, 1971.

McGuigan, James R., and R. Charles Moyer. *Managerial Economics,* 5th ed. St. Paul: West, 1989, Chapters 8, 9, and 10.

Newbold, Paul, and Theodore Bos. *Introductory Business Forecasting,* Cincinnati: South-Western, 1990, especially Chapter 7.

Simon, Julian L. "Great and Almost-Great Magnitudes in Economics," *Journal of Economic Perspectives* IV (Winter 1990), pp. 149–156.

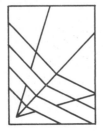

Factor Markets and Profit-Maximizing Employment of Variable Inputs

In the first edition of this book, we stated that two major newsworthy events affecting productive inputs were wage rate *increases* negotiated by the United Auto Workers (UAW) and OPEC hikes in the price of oil. In recent years news headlines have proclaimed wage rate *concessions* made by the UAW and *decreases* in the price of oil.[1]

In our earlier editions, we predicted that the wage rate increases by the UAW would tend to encourage the automobile manufacturers to become more capital intensive—and that prediction was accurate. High wage rates and competition from foreign automobile manufacturers provided the incentives for U.S. automakers to begin significantly increasing their use of robots.[2] The increasing use of robots and the recession of the early 1980s (with its corresponding effects on the demand for automobiles and

■ ■ ■ ■ ■ ■

[1] See "Labor Draws an Empty Gun," *Time* (March 26, 1990), pp. 56–59; "OPEC Agrees on Higher Output Ceiling," *The Wall Street Journal*, June 8, 1989, p. A2; The GM Settlement Is a Milestone for Both Sides," *Business Week* (October 8, 1984), pp. 160–162; "2001: A Union Odyssey," *Newsweek* (August 5, 1985), pp. 40–42; "Oil-Price Drop Spurs Many Firms to Switch from Using Gas, Coal," *The Wall Street Journal*, April 7, 1986, pp. 1, 10; "Slowing the Decline in the Auto Work Force," *Business Week* (October 25, 1976), pp. 114–118; "How OPEC's High Prices Strangle World Growth," *Business Week* (December 20, 1976), pp. 44–50; and "Detroit's New Balance of Power," *Business Week* (March 1, 1982), p. 90.

[2] "High Tech to the Rescue," *Business Week* (June 16, 1986), pp. 100–108; and "Detroit Area Is Becoming Home to Robotics," *The Wall Street Journal*, April 10, 1985, p. 6.

the employment of auto workers) prompted the UAW to make virtually unheard-of wage concessions.[3]

The earlier increase in the price of oil resulted in higher energy prices, which tended to reduce the usage of capital equipment because the cost of operating such machinery increased. However, the primary impact of the price increases seemed to be the encouragement of industry to develop more fuel-efficient equipment. As a result of increased fuel efficiency (and also a recession), oil suppliers in the early 1980s found themselves saddled with huge surpluses; thus crude oil prices began to fall. As we shall discover later in this chapter, the net result of all these events on the capital intensity of firms will depend on the marginal productivity of labor relative to its marginal cost, as compared with the marginal productivity of capital relative to its marginal cost with the new prices.[4]

Some of the most critical decisions a firm manager must make concern the employment of factors of production by the firm; such factors account for a large portion of the firm's *costs*. The firm with a goal of profit maximization wishes to produce at its optimal level of output and to do so at the lowest possible cost, given the market structures within which it operates. To accomplish this goal, the firm manager must make economic judgments with regard to how much of each input to use and, often, corresponding decisions with regard to the prices paid for inputs or for their services. We shall begin this chapter with a discussion of how the profit-maximizing quantity of a variable input is determined, and then relate this analysis to the determination of the demand curve for an input and the equilibrium price and quantity of the input.

As we stated in Chapter 4, the least cost combination of inputs *a* and *b* associated with a given level of output requires that

$$\frac{MP_a}{P_a} = \frac{MP_b}{P_b}$$

as long as the firm cannot affect P_a and P_b. However, we also stated that in the short run, the firm may not be able to achieve the least cost combination of inputs for its optimal level of output because the amounts of some of its inputs may be fixed. The relevant question in such a situation becomes this: *How can the firm maximize profits in the short run by utilizing the inputs that are variable?*

■ ■ ■ ■ ■ ■

[3] Although robots have been used and are still being introduced in a number of manufacturing plants in a variety of industries, their use has not always been as profitable as managers anticipated. See "Limping Along in Robot Land," *Time* (July 13, 1987), pp. 46–47; "Factory of the Future Becomes a Vision of the Past," *The Wall Street Journal*, September 1, 1988, p. 1; and "GM Bets an Arm and a Leg On a People-Free Plant," *Business Week* (September 12, 1988), pp. 72–73.

[4] The least cost condition for inputs capital, K, and labor, L, requires that $(MP_K/P_K) = (MP_L/P_L)$. As we shall see later, this rule applies only if the firm considers P_K and P_L to be "given." The net result of higher oil prices on total employment is a matter of controversy because of possible declining employment in capital goods industries and slower economic growth. See "Commentary/Economics," *Business Week* (September 12, 1977), pp. 134, 138.

■ ■ ■ ■ ■ ■ ■ ■ ■ # PROFIT-MAXIMIZING EMPLOYMENT OF ONE VARIABLE INPUT

Consider the plight of a local soda-pop bottler. It has $1 million worth of capital equipment and another $1 million invested in the building and land. The equipment, building, and land are relatively fixed in the short run. The only decisions the firm's management needs to make regarding them are in the nature of long-range planning decisions. What management must determine now is how much labor (of various types) should be employed and what level of output should be produced to maximize profits, *given* the plant and equipment.

Directly related to the managerial decisions involving the bottler's labor force and level of output will be decisions regarding raw materials and intermediate goods, such as concentrated soda mix, aluminum for cans, and empty bottles. Certainly, in the real world, the amounts of raw material and intermediate products could vary widely per unit of output produced (and sold), as workers are more or less careless (and drink more or less of the product) while on the job. However, we shall assume for the sake of simplicity that such inputs are used in fixed proportions to the level of output produced. We shall also assume that when the firm decides on the level of its labor force and, correspondingly, its level of output, it will have automatically decided on the required amounts of the raw materials and intermediate-good inputs. How does the bottler determine the optimal labor force and level of production in the short run? To some extent the minimum number of workers necessary to operate the plant will influence its decision. However, the plant could operate and function well with many different quantities of labor above the minimum required. So how is the profit-maximizing quantity determined?

Managerial Perspective: Profit and Chocoholic Cows

Farmer McGregor is feeding Hershey bars to dairy cows and increasing profits. As a result, the cows are happy and so is McGregor.

Feeding chocolate bars to cows may seem hardly a profitable way to run a dairy business, but it is apparently more profitable than giving them only things that would seem to be more nutritious—like hay and corn, for example. As most human chocoholics who are concerned about their weight know, a chocolate bar has a plentiful supply of carbohydrates and fat, which translates into calories. In humans, eating chocolate bars may merely result in unwanted pounds. Dairy cows do not gain weight from the bars, but the butterfat content of their milk rises, which means that the price the farmer can receive for the milk increases. More specifically, the basic butterfat standard for whole milk is 3.5 percent. For every .1 percent of butterfat above the 3.5 standard, a farmer received an increase in price of 1.28 cents per gallon.

The situation is almost too good to be true—very rare in the business world, where typically every move to increase productivity has its price. In the case of the chocoholic cows, feeding chocolate both lowers costs and raises revenue. The farmers in Maryland, New Jersey, and Pennsylvania obtained damaged chocolate bars from Hershey Foods Corporation in Hershey, Pennsylvania, at $60 a ton, while the price of corn was $85 a ton. Even better, the energy content of a candy bar is about twice that of an ear of corn.

The chocoholic cows on these farms get an average of four to eight pounds of chocolate a day mixed in with their hay and grain. One farmer, Stephen Mason, calculated that adding chocolate to his cows' diet raised the fat content of their milk to 3.9 percent. That translated to a higher price of 5.12 cents per gallon.

There are not many situations in business where a firm can so painlessly reduce cost while simultaneously increasing output and revenue. In fact, as more farmers discover the profit possibilities in feeding chocolate to dairy cows, the price of damaged chocolate bars may increase to the point where the tradeoff between chocolate and corn becomes closer to what economists would expect to see given the least cost combination of inputs condition. In the meantime, profit-maximizing employment of inputs for dairy farmers means that they should continue to feed chocolate bars to their cows up to the point where the marginal revenue received from another chocolate bar is just equal to its marginal cost. Apparently this strategy makes for both happy farmers and *very* happy cows.

■ ■ ■ ■

Reference: "Now the Question Is: How Do You Get Rid of a Cow's Pimples?" *The Wall Street Journal*, June 1, 1988, p. 25.

To employ one variable factor of production (labor, in this case) in a manner so that profits will be maximized, the firm should follow the same type of marginal rule as it does with respect to output: *Continue using additional units of the input until the last unit just pays for itself.* (That is, continue employment of additional units of a factor of production until the additional revenue resulting from employment of one more unit of the input is just equal to the amount the input adds to the costs of the firm.) If we (the authors) have done our job well, such a decision rule should seem obvious at this point. We emphasize again that the situation we are considering is one in which the firm has the problem of trying to decide how much of one particular variable input to use, *given* certain fixed inputs and a fixed quantity of raw materials and intermediate goods required for each unit of output.

To phrase our rule—*continue to employ an input until the last unit just pays for itself*—in the language of economists, we state that the firm should continue to employ an input until its marginal revenue product is equal to the input's marginal cost. Thus the manager of the bottling company should employ labor until the marginal revenue product of the last person hired is just equal to that person's marginal cost—both with respect to some specific time period, of course, such as per hour, day, or week.

We have already defined marginal revenue product of an input in Chapter 4, but we shall do so in greater depth here to ensure that its meaning is understood. The *arc* **marginal revenue product of input *a*** (MRP_a) is defined as the arc net marginal revenue the firm can obtain by selling an additional unit of output produced by input *a* multiplied by the number of additional units of output produced per additional unit of input *a*. (As we stated in Chapter 4, input *a*'s **marginal product,** MP_a, equals $\Delta Q/\Delta a$.) The *arc* **net marginal revenue** (NMR_a) the firm can get from selling one more unit of output produced by input *a* is the addition to total revenue that the sale of one more unit of output will bring in—or arc marginal revenue of the output ($\Delta TR/\Delta Q$)—*less* the cost of raw materials and the intermediate goods required for each additional unit of output.[5] Obviously, we cannot consider *all* of the additional revenue going to the bottler as a result of the sale of another case of soda produced by the last person hired as being solely the result of that person's efforts, as the firm still had to contribute additional raw materials for the soda and the packaging materials. Thus, if the sale of an additional case of soda would bring in additional revenue of $2 and the additional mix and other materials needed cost $.50 per case, the arc net marginal revenue, NMR, would be equal to $1.50 per case of soda.

However, we need a little more information to find the arc marginal revenue *product* of input *a*. The arc net marginal revenue of input *a* and its arc marginal revenue product are usually *not* equal because an additional unit of input *a* frequently does not produce *exactly* one additional unit of output during the time frame of reference the firm is using. For example, suppose the last worker hired enabled the firm to produce four more cases of soda per hour. The arc marginal revenue product, or the additional revenue per hour that *the worker* would bring in for the firm, would be the arc net marginal revenue of $1.50 per case *multiplied by* the four cases per hour added to production, or $6.00.

At last we are in a position to restate our profit-maximizing rule for employing input *a*: Employ input *a* until its arc marginal revenue product equals its arc marginal cost, or until MRP_a (or $NMR \times MP_a$) = MC_a. MC_a

---

The marginal revenue product of input *a* is equal to the net marginal revenue of input *a* multiplied by the marginal product of input *a*:

$MRP_a =$
$\quad NMR_a \times MP_a.$

The marginal product of input *a* is the additional output that the firm can produce by adding one more unit of input *a*:

$MP_a = (\Delta Q/\Delta a).$

The net marginal revenue of input *a* is equal to the marginal revenue received from selling one more unit of output less the cost of raw materials and intermediate products required for it:

$NMR_a =$
$\quad MR - MC_M,$

where MC_M is the marginal cost of materials and component parts per unit of output.

■ ■ ■ ■ ■ ■
[5] In calculus terms, the marginal revenue product of input *a* equals net marginal revenue times the marginal product of *a*, or

$$MRP_a = NMR \cdot MP_a = \left(\frac{dTR}{dQ} - \frac{d\,Materials\,Cost}{dQ}\right) \cdot \frac{\partial Q}{2a}.$$

The **marginal cost of an input** is the increase in the firm's total cost from employing one more unit of the input:

$MC_a = (\Delta TC/\Delta a)$.

If the price of an input is constant, the marginal cost of the input is equal to its price.

is the change in a firm's total costs as a result of using another unit of input a ($\Delta TC/\Delta a$).[6] If the price of input a is *constant*, the **marginal cost of an input** is equal to its price. In our soda-pop bottling company worker example, if the arc marginal revenue product of the *last* person hired was

■ ■ ■ ■ ■ ■

[6] We can mathematically derive this decision rule in the following way. If $TR = P \cdot Q$ where $P = f(Q)$, the production function is given by $Q = Q(a, b)$, and the total cost is given by $TC = (P_a \cdot a) + (P_b \cdot b)$, then the total profit function is

$$T\pi = [P \cdot Q(a, b)] - (P_a \cdot a) - (P_b \cdot b).$$

A firm manager who wishes to find the quantities of inputs a and b that will maximize profits must find the first partial derivatives of $T\pi$ with respect to inputs a and b and set them equal to zero, so that

(12–1)
$$\frac{\partial T\pi}{\partial a} = P \cdot \frac{\partial Q}{\partial a} + Q \frac{dP}{dQ} \frac{\partial Q}{\partial a} - P_a - \frac{dP_a}{da} \cdot a$$

$$= \left(P + Q\frac{dP}{dQ}\right) \frac{\partial Q}{\partial a} - \left(P_a + \frac{dP_a}{da} \cdot a\right) = 0,$$

and

(12–2)
$$\frac{\partial T\pi}{\partial b} = P \cdot \frac{\partial Q}{\partial b} + Q \frac{dP}{dQ} \frac{\partial Q}{\partial b} - P_b - \frac{dP_b}{db} \cdot b$$

$$= \left(P + Q\frac{dP}{dQ}\right) \frac{\partial Q}{\partial b} - \left(P_b + \frac{dP_b}{db} \cdot b\right) = 0,$$

The term $[P + Q(dP/dQ)]$ is the marginal revenue of the firm from selling the output, and $[P + Q(dP/dQ)](\partial Q/\partial a)$ and $[P + Q(dP/dQ)](\partial Q/\partial b)$ are the marginal revenue products of inputs a and b, respectively, if there are *no* marginal materials costs. If there *are* marginal materials costs ($= MC_M$), these must be subtracted from $[P + Q(dP/dQ)]$ to get *net* marginal revenue, so

$$NMR = P + Q(dP/dQ) - MC_M,$$
$$MRP_a = [P + Q(dP/dQ) - MC_M]\, \partial Q/\partial a,$$

and

$$MRP_b = [P + Q(dP/dQ) - MC_M]\, \partial Q/\partial b.$$

Notice that as long as dP/dQ is negative and/or MC_M is positive, NMR is less than P.

The terms $[P_a + (dP_a/da) \cdot a]$ in equation 12–1 and $P_b + (dP_b/db) \cdot b$ in equation 12–2 measure the marginal costs of inputs a and b, respectively. Thus equations 12–1 and 12–2 state that for profit maximization of inputs a and b,

(12–3)
$$MRP_a - MC_a = 0$$

and

(12–4)
$$MRP_b - MC_b = 0.$$

We could rewrite equations 12–3 and 12–4 as

(12–5)
$$MRP_a = MC_a$$

and

(12–6)
$$MRP_b = MC_b.$$

If both inputs are variable, *both* equations 12–5 and 12–6 must be satisfied.   (continued)

$6.00 per hour and the additional worker *cost* the firm $6.00 per hour, the bottler would maximize profit by holding its employment of labor at that level. If the worker cost the firm $7.00 per hour, that person should be let go (a gentle phrase for "fired"). If the worker cost the firm only $5.00, the firm manager should consider hiring another worker, as the additional worker might bring in additional profit after all additional costs were subtracted from additional revenue. (In this case, the last person hired would have added $1 per hour to the total profit of the firm.)

The **profit-maximizing rule for employment of a variable input,** say input *a*, is to employ that input until its marginal revenue product is equal to the marginal cost of the input; that is, to where

$$MRP_a = MC_a,$$

and at higher levels of output $MRP_a < MC_a$.

Unfortunately, the process of finding the optimal amount of an input is usually a bit more complicated in the real world than we have made it appear up to this point. One reason is that the marginal product of an input usually does not stay constant as more units of the input are added (remember the law of diminishing returns). A second reason is that marginal revenue may also change—usually in a downward direction, since many firms have to lower price to sell larger quantities of output.

Moreover, once we acknowledge the fact that the marginal product of an input may first increase and then decrease, we must recognize the possibility that the *MRP* of an input may also first rise and then fall. In this case we must add another condition to our profit-maximizing rule for employing a variable input: Employ the input up to the point where its *MRP* is equal to its marginal cost, *as long as the marginal cost of the input*

■ ■ ■ ■ ■ ■
[6] (concluded)   We can find a more general condition for obtaining the least cost combination of inputs than that developed in Chapter 4 by dividing equation 12–5 by equation 12–6 and rearranging terms

(12–7)
$$\frac{MRP_a}{MRP_b} = \frac{MC_a}{MC_b},$$

and

(12–8)
$$\frac{MRP_a}{MC_a} = \frac{MRP_b}{MC_b}.$$

If the firm cannot significantly affect P_a or P_b by using more or less of input *a* or input *b*, dP_a/da and $dP_b/db = 0$, $MC_a = P_a$, $MC_b = P_b$, and equation 12–8 becomes

(12–9)
$$\frac{MRP_a}{P_a} = \frac{MRP_b}{P_b}.$$

Dividing both sides of this equation by *NMR*, which is equal to $(P + Q(dP/dQ) - MC_M)$, we obtain our previous rule for the least cost combination of inputs, which is as follows:

$$\frac{MP_a}{P_a} = \frac{MP_b}{P_b}.$$

In this case equations 12–5 and 12–6 become

(12–10)
$$MRP_a = P_a$$

and

(12–11)
$$MRP_a = P_a.$$

Numerical Example: Profit-Maximizing Input Use

Complete the following table and find the profit-maximizing level of use of input L. Assume that L is the only variable input, that its price (P_L) is \$110 per unit, that there are no components costs, and that total fixed cost (TFC) is \$350.

Arc MP_L	L	Q	P	TR	Arc MR	Arc MRP_L
10	0	0	22	0		
	2		20	400	20	200
	4	60	16	960	14	
15	6	90	13	1,170	7	
	8	110	11	1,210	2	
6	10		10	1,220	0.8	4.80

Answer. The missing MP_L values are 20 and 10, each obtained by calculating $\Delta Q/\Delta L$. The missing Q values are 20 and 122, each obtained by multiplying the relevant MP by ΔL and adding on the ΔQ to the preceding Q value. The missing MRP_L values are 280, 105, and 20, each calculated as $MR(MP_L)$.

Profit is maximized where, $P_L \leq MRP_L$ but for an increase in L, $P_L > MRP_L$. This occurs at $L = \underline{4}$, since increasing L to 6 would result in $P_L = 110$, but $MRP_L = 105$. Profit is $TR - TC = 960 - L(P_L) - TFC = \$960 - 440 - 350 = \underline{\$170}$.

would be at least equal to or above the MRP of the input for a greater quantity of the input. Thus, if the last soda-pop bottler hired had an MRP of \$6.00 and a marginal cost of \$6.00, but the *next* person to be hired would have an MRP of \$7.00 and a marginal cost also of \$6.00, then the firm should continue to hire workers until there are no further opportunities to hire a worker whose MRP is above marginal cost. This is another way of saying employ the input until the last unit just pays for itself, but additional units of the input will cost more than the additional revenue they would bring to the firm.

For example, in Table 12–1 we give revenue and labor productivity data for the manufacturer of a black-and-white portable television. Arc marginal revenue is obtained by finding $\Delta TR/\Delta Q$, and NMR_L is obtained

Table 12-1 Revenue, Labor Productivity, and Cost Data for a Manufacturer of Black-and-White Televisions

Quantity Produced per Hour	Price (P)	Total Revenue (TR = P·Q)	Arc Marginal Revenue (MR = ΔTR/ΔQ)	Components Cost (per Unit)	Arc Net Marginal Revenue of Labor (NMR_L = MR − Marginal Components Cost)	Quantity of Labor (L)	Arc Marginal Product of Labor (MP_L = ΔQ/ΔL)	Arc Marginal Revenue Product of Labor (MRP_L = NMR_L·MP_L)	Hourly Wage Rate	Arc Marginal Cost of Labor (MC_L = ΔTC/ΔL)
0	$240	$ 0		$20		0			$9.00	$9.00
			$230		210		.5	$105.00		
5	230	1,150		20		10			9.00	9.00
			200		180		1.0	180.00		
15	210	3,150		20		20			9.00	9.00
			150		130		1.5	195.00		
30	180	5,400		20		30			9.00	9.00
			100		80		1.0	80.00		
40	160	6,400		20		40			9.00	9.00
			64		44		.8	35.20		
48	144	6,912		20		50			9.00	9.00
			38		18		.5	9.00		
53	134	7,102		20		60			9.00	9.00
			24		4		.2	.80		
55	130	7,150				70			9.00	9.00

by subtracting the $20 components cost from MR at each level of output. The arc marginal product of labor is obtained by finding $\Delta Q/\Delta L$. The MRP_L is then found by multiplying NMR_L by MP_L. If the wage rate is fixed at $9.00, then the price of labor also equals the MC_L, and the firm maximizes profits (assuming labor is the only variable input besides the components) where *output* is between 48 and 53 television sets per hour and the firm's *labor force* is between 50 and 60 people. Between 48 and 53 units of output, the MRP_L = $9.00 and MC_L = $9.00. Between 53 and 55 units of output, the MRP_L = $.80 and MC_L = $9.00. Thus 70 workers would clearly be too many to employ in order to maximize profits, since workers 61 through 70 would each bring in an average of $.80 net revenue per hour but would each cost $9.00 per hour.

Finally, if more than one input is variable, changes in the quantity utilized of one will affect the productivity of the other inputs *if* the inputs are *related*, thereby changing their optimal levels. The resulting changes in those inputs will, in turn, affect the optimal level of the first input. In this kind of situation, we define related inputs as being either substitutes or complements. Two inputs are *substitutes* if utilizing more of one *decreases* the marginal product of the other. Two inputs are *complementary* if utilizing more of one *increases* the marginal product of the other. Two inputs could be substitutes or complements, depending on the situation. For example, the use of a paint sprayer by a painter would probably reduce the marginal product of a paint roller. However, the use of a computer by a research institution might well increase the marginal product of an employee engaged in research. In the first example, the paint sprayer and the paint roller are substitutes. The paint sprayer might also be a substitute for an additional painter with a brush. In the second example, the computer and the employee are complements. We shall leave further consideration of related inputs to a more advanced text. It is sufficient at this point to be aware of the possibility (and probability) of relatedness among inputs and to take that possibility into account when determining the optimal levels of variable factors of production for the firm.

■ ■ ■ ■ ■ ■ ■ ■ ■ DETERMINATION OF EQUILIBRIUM PRICES FOR INPUTS: PERFECT COMPETITION IN THE INPUT MARKET

As in the output market, if perfect competition exists in the market for an input, there are many buyers and sellers of that input, and an individual firm considers the price of the *input* to be "given." Since the amount demanded of an input by an individual firm is too small relative to the total market demand and supply of the input to influence its price significantly, the marginal cost of a unit of the input is constant and equal to its price. When we considered the case of a firm *selling its output* in a perfectly competitive market, we said (1) that the firm considered the price it received for its *output* to be given, (2) that the *demand curve* for its product was a horizontal line, and (3) that *output price was equal to marginal revenue*. On the other hand, when a firm is *buying an input* in a perfectly competitive market, it accepts (1) that the input price is given, (2) that the *supply curve* of the input *to the firm* is horizontal, and (3) that the *input price equals the input's marginal cost* (as was the case in the example in Table 12–1).

In this case, therefore, the firm's profit-maximizing condition for utilizing input *a* is to employ input *a* up to the point where the *marginal revenue product of* a *is equal to its price*, which (as we have just said) is equal to its marginal cost.[7] In this case, the firm should employ input *a* up to the point where $MRP_a = P_a$ (as long as MRP_a is decreasing). Thus the firm's *demand curve* for input *a* is given by the portion of the marginal revenue product curve for input *a* where MRP_a is decreasing. This part of the MRP_a curve is the demand curve for input *a* because it indicates the quantity of input *a* the profit-maximizing firm will employ at each price.[8]

■ ■ ■ ■ ■ ■
[7] If the firm also *sells* its *output* in a perfectly competitive market, marginal revenue equals price and NMR_a = price minus marginal materials cost. In this case economists also call MRP_a the *value of the marginal product of a*, or VMP_a.

[8] However, the output price must also be sufficiently high to cover AVC, or the firm will at least temporarily shut down. With *more than one* variable input, a change in the amount used of one input, say input *a*, may affect the MRP(s) of the other variable input(s), which will change the profit-maximizing quantity(ies) of the other input(s). A change in the quantity(ies) utilized of that input (those inputs) will cause the MRP_a to shift because the MP_a will change. Whether the MRP_a shifts rightward or leftward will depend on whether input *a* is being increased or decreased in the first step. For example, if the inputs are substitutes, then the use of more of input *a* will decrease the marginal product of the other variable input(s) and the quantity used of it (them) will decrease. This decrease, in turn, will cause the MP_a to *increase*, shifting the MRP_a curve to the right. If the inputs are complements, then an increase in the use of input *a* will increase the marginal product of the other input(s) and the quantity used of it (them) will increase. This increase will also cause the MP_a to *increase*, again shifting the MP_a curve to the right. The demand curve will consist of points where $MRP_a = P_a$, but each point will be on a different MRP curve, as shown below:

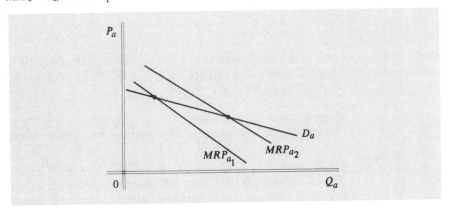

In Figure 12–1 we have shown the firm's demand curve for input a, the supply curve for input a, and the profit-maximizing quantity of a (Q_a^*) for the firm to employ. In the case of the television manufacturer discussed in the previous section, Q_L is approximately equal to 55 and $P_L = \$9.00$ (see Figure 12–2). We say that Q_L is approximately equal to 55 because we are using arc values for MRP_L, which gives an *average* value for a particular interval (such as $L = 50$ to $L = 60$). We must plot such figures at the midpoint of the interval.

We now understand the process by which a firm manager determines how much of an input the firm should employ to maximize its profit, *given the price of the input*. However, how is the price of the input determined? The answer is that in perfectly competitive input markets, the input price is determined by the total market demand for and supply of the input. A rough approximation to the *market demand* for the input is obtained by summing the quantity of the input that each firm which utilizes the input will demand at each price.[9] Thus we obtain the market *demand* curve for an *input* in a perfectly competitive input market much as we determined

Figure 12–1   Optimal Employment of an Input in a Perfectly Competitive Input Market

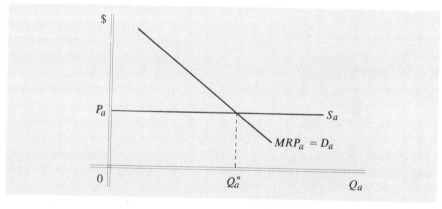

The marginal revenue product curve for input a, MRP_a, is the firm's demand curve for input a. The supply curve of the input to the firm is a horizontal line, S_a, at the market-determined price of P_a. The firm will maximize profit by employing Q_a^* units of input a at price P_a.

▪ ▪ ▪ ▪ ▪ ▪

[9] This horizontal summation of firm demand curves for inputs is only an approximation to the market demand curve for an input because as all firms in an industry expand, the market price and marginal revenue for a firm's product may fall more than is indicated by an individual firm's demand and marginal revenue curve. For example, the horizontal demand curve of a perfectly competitive firm is drawn under the assumption that only the individual firm is changing its level of output and therefore that price will not be affected. The market demand curve for an input must take into account the effects on the price and marginal revenue of the firm's product caused by factors external to the firm.

Figure 12–2   Demand and Supply Curves of Labor for a Television Manufacturer

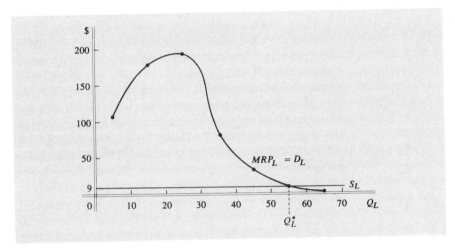

In this case the supply curve of workers to a television manufacturer is a horizontal line at $9 per hour. The firm will employ workers up to the point where the MRP_L = $9, at Q_L^* = 55, approximately.

the market *supply* curve in a perfectly competitive *output* market. The market supply curve of the *input* merely reflects the quantity of the input that will be supplied at each price. We shall assume, as is generally realistic, that the market supply curve for an input is upward sloping, which means that more of the input will be supplied at higher prices.

We have drawn the market demand and supply curves for input *a* in Figure 12–3, panel (a), and a firm's demand and supply curves for input *a* in Figure 12–3, panel (b). Note that the horizontal axis of panel (a) is in *thousands* of units per time period, whereas that of panel (b) is in single units per time period. The equilibrium price and total quantity of input *a* utilized are determined in panel (a) to be P^* and Q_T^*. The individual firm considers P^* to be fixed and employs Q_F^* of input *a*.

The determination of the price of an input when the market for its services is imperfectly competitive is a little more complicated, as we shall now see.

■ ■ ■ ■ ■ ■ ■ ■ ■ ■ **DETERMINATION OF EQUILIBRIUM PRICES FOR INPUTS: MONOPSONY IN THE INPUT MARKET**

A **monopsony** is a market with one buyer.

Monopsony is the label we attach to a market structure that is characterized by one *buyer* of some particular product or service. In this case we shall use monopsony to refer to the situation where there is one firm that

Figure 12–3   Demand and Supply Curves for Input *a*

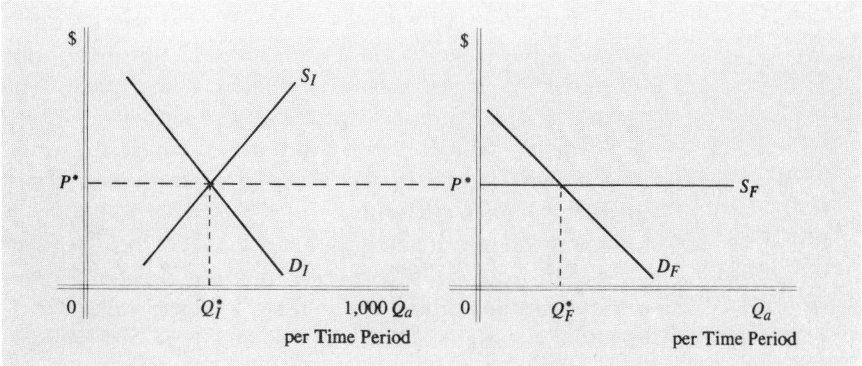

In panel *(a)* the industry supply and demand curves for input *a* determine the input's price, P^*, and the total quantity sold of input *a*, Q_I^*. In panel *(b)* an individual firm accepts the price of input *a*, P^*, as given (S_F is horizontal). The firm employs Q_F^* units of input *a* at a price of P^*, where D_F intersects S_F.

An **oligopsony** is a market with a few buyers, or a few dominant buyers.

A market characterized by **monopsonistic competition** has many buyers of a differentiated product.

demands the services of an input. You will recall that we used the term *monopoly* to describe the situation where there is only one firm that *supplies* a product, *oligopoly* where there are a few suppliers of a product, and *monopolistic competition* where there are many suppliers of a differentiated product. In a similar fashion we also use the terms **oligopsony** to describe the market structure where there are a few *buyers* of a product and **monopsonistic competition** where there are many buyers of a differentiated product. We shall discuss only the case of monopsony in the input market in this book, but the profit-maximizing decision rule discussed here applies to oligopsony and monopsonistic competition as well. In this section we shall further assume that the *suppliers* of the input are perfectly competitive in the sense that they do not organize and attempt to affect the price received for the services of the input.

In a monopsonistic input market, the firm *buying* the input knows that the price of the input will be determined by the quantity of the input that it purchases. In this case, changes in the quantity of an input demanded by the firm will appreciably affect the input's price because we have assumed that the market supply curve of the input is upward sloping, meaning that a greater quantity of the input will be supplied only at a higher price. Since there is only one buyer of that input, changes in the quantity demanded of the input by that buyer will noticeably affect the input's price.

In this situation, the profit-maximizing firm that is utilizing the input will still follow the decision rule stated earlier in this chapter: *Employ the input until its marginal revenue product is equal to its marginal cost.* Unlike the case of perfect competition in the input market, however, for the monopsonistic firm the price of an input is (theoretically, at least) *not* equal to its marginal cost. The marginal cost of another unit of an input is greater than its price because it is assumed that the monopsonistic firm has to pay a higher price to get an additional unit of the input per time period. Moreover, it is also assumed that if a firm pays a higher price for one more unit of the input, it must pay the same price for *all units* of the input.

Consider the following situation, which the only garage in a small town might face if it wishes to hire another mechanic. The garage has three mechanics currently working for it at $10.00 an hour and can hire a fourth mechanic for $12.00 an hour. If it hires the fourth mechanic for $12.00 an hour, the firm will find that the first three mechanics will be unhappy unless their wage rates are also raised to $12.00 per hour. In fact, their dissatisfaction may cause their productivity to decline unless their salaries are raised. In this case the marginal cost of the fourth mechanic is $18.00 per hour, which is $12.00 for the fourth mechanic's wage plus $2.00 per hour for each of the other three mechanics. The supply and marginal cost schedules of mechanics to the garage are given in Table 12–2, and the corresponding curves are drawn in Figure 12–4.

The profit-maximizing garage should now follow the decision rule stated at the beginning of this chapter: Employ an input up to the point where its marginal revenue product is equal to its marginal cost. Therefore the *profit-maximizing rule for employment of a variable input in a monopsonistic input market* is to employ that input until its marginal revenue product is equal to its marginal cost. In this case, the price of the input will be less than its marginal cost.

In Figure 12–4, the *MRP* of mechanics is just equal to the marginal cost of mechanics when the garage hires four mechanics. Note that whereas the marginal cost of the fourth mechanic is $18.00 per hour, all of the mechanics are actually being paid only $12.00 per hour. Since the garage is the only buyer of this input, the number of mechanics it employs to maximize profits will determine both the total number of mechanics employed in this town and their wage rate. Thus $12.00 per hour is the market wage rate, at least in this limited market for mechanics.

Table 12–2   Supply and Marginal Cost Schedules of Mechanics to a Garage

Number of Mechanics	Hourly Wage Rate	Marginal Cost of Labor (MC_L)
0	$ 4.00	
		$ 6.00
1	6.00	
		10.00
2	8.00	
		14.00
3	10.00	
		18.00
4	12.00	
		22.00
5	14.00	

Figure 12–4   Supply and Marginal Cost of Mechanics to a Garage

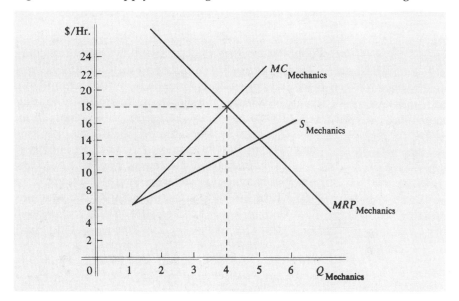

Here, the supply curve of mechanics to a garage is upward sloping, which means that the marginal cost of another mechanic to the firm, given by $MC_{Mechanics}$, also increases as the number of mechanics employed increases. In this case the firm will employ mechanics up to the point where the $MRP_{Mechanics} = MC_{Mechanics}$, at 4 mechanics and an hourly wage of $12.00.

In the next section, we shall discuss a third extreme case involving an input market—the situation of bilateral monopoly in which there is only one buyer and *one seller* of an input.

■ ■ ■ ■ ■ ■ ■ ■   **DETERMINATION OF EQUILIBRIUM PRICES FOR INPUTS: BILATERAL MONOPOLY IN THE INPUT MARKET**

Bilateral monopoly in the input market means that there is one buyer and one seller of the input.

Bilateral monopoly in the input market means that there is only *one buyer* and *one seller* of an input. Admittedly, we are talking about an extreme case, but bilateral monopoly may more nearly approximate the market structure between "big business" and "big labor" in industries such as automobiles and steel than does any of the other cases we have described.

Since both the seller of the input and the buyer of the input are the sole businesses involved on their respective sides of the market, the *seller* of the input may wish to behave as a monopolist and the *buyer* may wish to behave as a monopsonist. Suppose all of the potential mechanics in the small town in the example earlier in the chapter form a union and bargain as a group with the owner of the garage. In Figure 12–5 we have redrawn

Managerial Perspective: The Age of Agrimation

Robots in the factory are now an everyday fact of life, but the use of robots in agriculture has been much less prevalent. If researchers at a number of universities and countries around the world are successful, however, the age of agrimation is not far away.

Through automation, the direct labor cost of most items manufactured by mass-production methods has been reduced to 5 to 15 percent of their selling price. However, direct labor costs may be as much as 30 percent of the selling price of agricultural products, and proponents of agrimation contend that robots could reduce costs significantly in the production of agricultural goods. Take fruit, for example. These researchers state that a worker hired to harvest fruit could pick approximately 1,000 pieces of fruit per hour during six- to eight-hour working days. However, one-armed robots have already been developed that can pick fruit almost as quickly as a person, and two-armed robots are under consideration. In one laboratory test, a one-armed robot picked 15 oranges per minute, while an experienced human picker did 20 oranges per minute. France is developing an apple picker that technicians believe will be able to pick 30 apples a minute, more than double that of a skilled apple picker. Moreover, these machines would be willing to put in 24-hour days, so that fruit could be picked at the optimal time. The new robots also handle the fruit far more gently than the old mechanical pickers, which shook the trees or blasted them with air to force the fruit to fall to the ground, often bruising it in the process. The researchers figure that even if the robots cost as much as $100,000, they will pay for themselves in three seasons.

Even European milkmaids may soon feel competition from their steel-collared counterparts. Vicon, a Netherlands-based company is spending $3 million to develop a "cowbot," that will feed dairy cows, hook them up to the milking machines, and later clean the equipment. Such a helper could save dairy farmers more than four hours each day. Vicon estimates that if the robot costs less than $100,000 the machine would pay for itself in four years.

Clearly, if these new robots are successfully developed, farmers will have to consider the productivity and cost of human labor compared with that of robots. In turn, farm workers may be forced to consider ways to increase their productivity, working for lower wages, or new careers.

■ ■ ■ ■

References: "Robots Head for the Farm," *Business Week* (September 8, 1986), pp. 66–67; and "Moo! Those Hands Are Cold!" *Business Week* (September 8, 1986), p. 67.

Figure 12–5   A Case of Bilateral Monopoly

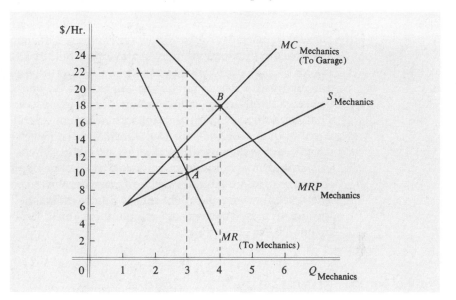

This figure describes a case of bilateral monopoly. Both the mechanics selling their services and the firm buying their services have some monopoly power. As in Figure 12–4, the marginal cost of mechanics increases as the quantity of mechanics employed increases, and $MC_{Mechanics}$ is above $S_{Mechanics}$. The marginal revenue to mechanics from selling their services is given by $MR_{(To\ Mechanics)}$. The firm will wish to employ 4 mechanics at a wage rate of $12 per hour, where $MRP_{Mechanics} = MC_{Mechanics}$. Mechanics will wish to offer their services up to the point where $MR_{Mechanics} = S_{Mechanics}$, at an hourly wage of $22 for 3 workers. The final result will depend on the relative bargaining strength of the firm and of the mechanics.

Figure 12–4 and added one more curve, which indicates the marginal revenue to the *supplier* from selling another unit of the *input* under the assumption that the buyer could be forced to pay a wage rate equal to the marginal revenue product of the input.

In this situation the old supply curve of mechanics is now not really their supply curve *if* their union behaves as a profit-maximizing monopolist. It merely indicates what quantities they would be willing to supply at each wage rate *if* they thought they had to accept whatever wage rate the garage offered them *or* not work as mechanics. If their old supply curve in some sense measures their marginal cost of supplying labor, the mechanics will maximize their group profit by selling their services up to the point where the marginal cost *to themselves* of their services is equal to the marginal revenue brought in by those services. At point *A* the marginal revenue brought in by the mechanics' services is just equal to the marginal cost to the mechanics of supplying their services, and the mechanics' union would like to have three people employed at a wage rate of $22.00.

However, it would be quite a feat for the mechanics' union to get three people hired at a wage rate of $22.00, because when a seller gets a buyer to pay the *maximum* price the buyer would be willing to pay for that particular quantity of the product (or input) in question, the buyer usually assumes any monopsony power previously held has been lost in bargaining for a lower price. Such a case should not occur here. The garage should perceive that it has some monopsonistic power, and it would like (as we indicated in Figure 12–4), to employ four workers at a wage rate of $12.00. That is because at point B the marginal revenue product of mechanics is equal to their marginal cost to the firm, at least if we consider $S_{Mechanics}$ the supply curve of mechanics. In this situation where bilateral monopoly exists, presumably the mechanics and the garage owner will bargain, and the wage rate agreed upon will be somewhere between $12.00 and $22.00. The level at which the wage rate is finally established will depend upon the relative persuasiveness of the mechanics' union and the garage owner.[10]

■ ■ ■ ■ ■ ■ ■ ■ ## SUMMARY

Profit Maximization and Employment of Inputs

In this chapter we have discussed the decision rule that a firm must follow in order to determine the *quantity* of a variable input that it should utilize to maximize profit: Employ a variable input, input a, up to the point where the $MRP_a = MC_a$. If P_a is constant for all levels of input a employed by the firm, $MC_a = P_a$, and the firm should utilize the input until $MRP_a = P_a$.

We have also discussed input *price* determination under three types of market structures: (1) where both the firms buying the input and the suppliers of the input are perfectly competitive, (2) where there is only one buyer of the input (monopsony) but the suppliers view the market as perfectly competitive, and (3) where there is only *one* buyer and *one* seller of the input (bilateral monopoly). In the case of a perfectly competitive

■ ■ ■ ■ ■ ■

[10] An alternative theory regarding this situation is based on a joint profit maximization model, which yields a determinate level of employment of the input and a corresponding determinate level of final product output and price. See A. L. Bowley, "Bilateral Monopoly," *The Economic Journal* (December 1928), pp. 651–659; and Roger D. Blair, David L. Kaserman, and Richard E. Romano, "A Pedagogical Treatment of Bilateral Monopoly," *Southern Economic Journal* 55, no. 4, pp. 831–841. The limiting cases of the input price described in the Blair, Kaserman, and Romano model depend, however, on the assumption that the dominant firm can force the other firm to purchase (or sell) a quantity of the input that is not consistent with the usual marginal profit requirements for profit maximization. However, an equilibrium input price would exist at the joint profit-maximizing quantity where the *MRP* of the input is equal to the marginal cost of supplying it.

market for an input, the market price and equilibrium quantity are determined by market demand and supply. In the case of a monopsonistic input market, the market price and equilibrium quantity are determined by the quantity of the input utilized by the one buyer of the input. This firm employs an input (for example, input a) until $MRP_a = MC_a$. Finally, in the case of bilateral monopoly, the market price and equilibrium quantity of an input are determined through a bargaining process.

It is fairly easy to find an approximation to a perfectly competitive (buyer and seller) type of market structure for an input—the market for unskilled, nonunion labor in a large metropolitan area is one example. It is somewhat more difficult to find an example of a monopsonistic firm that is faced with quite the situation we described earlier; that is, facing a perfectly competitive market on the supply side for an input. Recall that such a firm was forced to pay a higher price for *all* units of that input that it employed in order to obtain additional units of the variable input. Consider the case of the finance department in a university where the university is the only institution of higher education in a given area. The university will probably find that to get an *additional* finance professor, it may have to pay *that professor* more than the salary paid to comparable professors already working for the institution. However, to the extent that the university has monopsony power in the area in regard to the employment of finance professors, it may not have to *increase* the salaries of the professors it is currently employing but has hired previously. We have observed such a phenomenon first-hand numerous times in economics departments. Only when faculty members who were hired earlier are *willing* and *able* to accept jobs elsewhere in lieu of a raise at their present university must the university also raise the pay of the current employees to correspond to that of the new employee in order to keep the department intact. To have any clout with the university, the current employees must have alternative job opportunities elsewhere that they have convinced the university they are willing to accept—a situation that means that the firm really was not a monopsonist after all. (However, the market for these professors is still imperfectly competitive.) It is illegal to price discriminate purely on the basis of race or sex, but it is not illegal to price discriminate solely on the basis of when someone was hired. To the extent that a firm can do such discriminating in regard to wages paid employees, the marginal cost of another employee will still be that employee's *wage rate*, even though that wage rate is greater than the wage rate of employees hired previously.

Finally, concerning bilateral monopoly, we suggest that in the case of big labor and big business—for example, the UAW and the automakers—our wage-determination model may be somewhat inappropriate to the extent that the labor union involved does not behave as a profit-maximizing monopolist. The union must be concerned about the level of employment of its members, *as well as* their wage rate(s); thus the assumption that the goal of a union is profit maximization may be neither meaningful nor realistic. The bilateral monopoly model might be realistic in a situation where the United States government was purchasing some classified military equipment from a firm that had the sole patent for the product. Even in this situation, however, we would have to assume that the Department of Defense behaved as a profit-maximizing monopsonist.

Still, none of the above comments alters our basic decision rule for a firm interested in employing the profit-maximizing quantity of a variable input: *Employ the input until its marginal revenue product equals its marginal cost.*

■ ■ ■ ■ ■ ■ ■ ■ ■ ■ ■ ■ ■ ■ **Questions** ■ ■ ■ ■ ■ ■ ■ ■ ■ ■ ■ ■ ■ ■

1. What is meant by profit-maximizing employment of one variable input?
2. What is the general decision rule for determining the profit-maximizing employment of one variable input?
3. Compare the general decision rule for determining the profit-maximizing employment of one variable input when its price is fixed and when its price is variable.
4. How are the market price and equilibrium quantity of a variable input determined when the input is sold in a perfectly competitive market?
5. How are the market price and equilibrium quantity of a variable input determined when the input is sold in a monopsonistic market?
6. How would your answer to question 5 change if the input were sold in a market characterized by bilateral monopoly?
7. Compare the decision rule for the least cost combination of inputs and that for profit-maximizing employment of one variable input. What does each tell the firm? How are they different? Under what circumstances should each be used?

■ ■ ■ ■ ■ ■ ■ ■ ■ ■ ■ ■ ■ ■ **Problems** ■ ■ ■ ■ ■ ■ ■ ■ ■ ■ ■ ■ ■ ■

1. The following table shows worker, quantity of output, and output price information for a sweatshirt manufacturer. The cost of materials used in each sweatshirt is $.50.
   a. Complete the table shown at the top of the next page.
   b. How many sweatshirts should the company produce to maximize profits if the wage rate is $4.50 per hour? Why?

Workers per (Hour)	Quantity (Total Product) per Hour	Price of Output	Total Revenue	Arc Marginal Revenue	Arc Net Marginal Revenue of Labor	Arc Marginal Product of Labor	Arc Marginal Revenue Product of Labor
0	0	$2					
1	10	2					
2	25	2					
3	45	2					
4	60	2					
5	70	2					
6	77	2					
7	81	2					
8	84	2					
9	85	2					

2. A tire company has the relationship between the number of workers per hour and the total product per hour shown in the following table. The relationship between output produced per hour and the price at which it can be sold is also given. Assume that the cost of materials in tires is $6.50.

Number of Workers	Quantity (Total Product) per Hour	Price of Output	Total Revenue	Arc Marginal Revenue	Arc Net Marginal Revenue of Labor	Arc Marginal Product of Labor	Arc Marginal Revenue Product of Labor
0	0	$50.00					
10	200	40.00					
20	300	35.00					
30	350	32.50					
40	380	31.00					
50	400	30.00					
60	410	29.50					

    a. Complete the table.

    b. If the wage rate is $5 per hour, how many workers should this firm hire to maximize profits? Why?

3. Suppose the workers in question 2 organize, form a union, and succeed in bargaining the wage rate up to $9.50 per hour. How many workers should the tire company employ now? Does your answer to this question indicate a reason why a labor union would not necessarily want to bargain for the highest wage rate it might achieve? Why or why not?

4. Wizard, Incorporated, produces electronic business calculators. Revenue and labor productivity data are given in the following table. The components cost for one calculator is $20. The wage rate is constant and equal to $7.00 per hour.

Price of Output	Number of Calculators per Hour	Quantity of Labor	Total Revenue	Arc Marginal Revenue	Arc Net Marginal Revenue of Labor	Arc Marginal Product of Labor	Arc Marginal Revenue Product of Labor
$100.00	0	0					
						1.0	
95.00	10	10					
						2.0	
85.00		20					
						1.5	
77.50		30					
						1.0	
72.50		40					
						.5	
70.00		50					
						.2	
69.00	62	60					

    a. Complete the table.

    b. How many workers should Wizard employ? Why?

    c. How much output per hour should Wizard produce and what price should it charge?

    d. What is the marginal cost of a calculator at this point? (You should be able to determine this figure using relationships discussed in Chapter 5.)

5. The bar in a small town is faced with the situation depicted in the table on page 469 in regard to revenue per night from the sale of drinks, the number of bartenders working per evening, and the wage rate paid the bartenders. The average cost of ingredients in one drink is $.50. The average price of one drink varies with the number of customers because more people patronize the bar as more "specials" are offered on various drinks.

    a. How many bartenders should this bar employ and what should be the average price of drinks in order to maximize profit? Why?

    b. What is the equilibrium wage rate?

Table for Problem 5

Number of Drinks Sold per Hour	Number of Bartenders	Average Price of One Drink	Total Revenue per Hour	Arc Marginal Revenue	Arc Net Marginal Revenue	Arc Marginal Product of Bartenders	Arc Marginal Revenue Product	Hourly Wage Rate	Arc MC of Bartenders
0	0	$5.00						—	
20	1	4.00						$4.00	
50	2	3.40						5.00	
70	3	3.00						6.00	
85	4	2.70						7.00	
95	5	2.50						7.75	
100	6	2.40						8.50	

6. Vinox Company makes portable copying machines. Demand and labor productivity data per month are given in the table below. The components cost per machine is $200. The average monthly cost of labor is $1,800.

Quantity of Labor	Quantity of Copiers	Price	Total Revenue	Arc Marginal Revenue	Arc NMR_L	Arc MP_L	Arc MRP_L
0	0	$1,000					
10	100	900					
15	200	800					
25	300	700					
45	400	600					
70	500	500					

a. Complete the table.
b. What is the profit-maximizing number of copiers to be produced monthly, price, and number of workers for Vinox? Why?
c. If Vinox tried to produce and sell 100 more copiers than it does at the profit maximum you identified above, what will be the arc marginal cost per copier over this range? Explain how the profit-maximizing number of copiers that you found in part b is consistent with the $MR = MC$ condition for copiers.

The following problems require calculus.

7. Suppose the total product (per hour) of labor for a restaurant is given by $TP_L = 38L - 2L^2$.
   a. Find the MP_L function.
   b. How many workers should the restaurant employ if the wage rate is $4, the average price of a meal is $6, and the average cost per meal of the food ingredients is $2? Why?
8. In Problem 15 of Chapter 4, a firm was said to have the following short-run total product curve:

$$TP_L = Q = 48L + 4L^2 - (1/3)L^3,$$

where labor, L, is the only variable input and TP_L is the total output produced per day. Suppose the firm faces a fixed price of $2 per unit for its output.
   a. If the firm must pay a market-determined wage rate of $78 per day for each unit of labor hired, how much labor should it employ?

b. If the firm's daily fixed costs total $250, what will be its total profit per day?

■ ■ ■ ■ ■ ■ ■ ■ ■ ■ ■   **Selected References**   ■ ■ ■ ■ ■ ■ ■ ■ ■ ■

Bilas, Richard A. *Microeconomic Theory*, 2d ed. New York: McGraw-Hill, 1971, Chapter 11.

Lyons, Ivory L., and Manuel Zymelman. *Economic Analysis of the Firm: Theory and Practice*. New York: Pitman, 1966, Chapters 15 and 16.

Mansfield, Edwin. *Microeconomics: Theory and Applications*, 7th ed. New York: Norton, 1991, Chapters 12 and 13.

McCloskey, Donald N. *The Applied Theory of Price*, 2d ed. New York: Macmillan, 1985, Chapters 22–26.

Integrating Case 3A

German-American Metals Corporation

German-American Metals Corporation (GAMC) is an affiliate of a Stuttgart firm that uses a patented process to recover lead and other nonferrous metals from very fine-sized mixed metallic scrap. The process used by GAMC is based on thermal separation of metals in a smelter. The smelting plant consists of a drying system, a lead-smelting separator, separating equipment for other nonferrous metals, and an exhaust purification system with related utility devices. GAMC uses natural-gas-fired burners to generate heat for the smelter, and it currently has a long-term contract guaranteeing it natural gas at $4 per 1,000 cubic feet for the next two years.

GAMC's overall production is dependent on the lead segment of its operations, since its source material contains predominantly lead scrap. The company has two primary outlets for the lead it recovers. First, there is the general market for lead ingots, an oligopolistic market in which GAMC must follow the price leadership of a large, established domestic firm. Its second outlet is sales to one of its own U.S. subsidiaries, Southern Electrical Devices, Incorporated, a producer of lead battery plates for large industrial batteries.

A forecast prepared by GAMC's planning department indicates that the lead component of its scrap purchases next year will cost $0.15 per pound. On the surface this appears to management to be a favorable development, since lead ingot is expected to sell for $520 per short ton (2,000 lbs.). GAMC has been studying its recovery plant data to come up with reasonably accurate cost projections in the light of high but stable energy prices. The firm's engineers have indicated that, given the quality

■ ■ ■ ■ ■ ■

This case is based on research conducted in Germany in 1982. We wish to thank the officers and management of Texas Shredder Parts, Inc., as well as their German counterparts, for their help in making it possible for us to carry out our investigation.

of scrap available, 20,000 cubic feet of gas must be burned to recover a short ton of lead. Fixed overhead and fixed labor costs comprise most of the remaining costs of lead recovery. However, because of pollution control expenses, marginal cost is expected to rise by $.02 per ton of lead recovered up to GAMC's capacity of 8,500 tons per year.

GAMC's subsidiary, Southern Electrical Devices (SED), may choose to purchase lead ingot either from GAMC or from other outside suppliers. Not including the expected price of lead ingot for next year, SED's total cost function for the production of battery plates has been estimated to be the following:

$$TC_B = 4,000,000 + 80Q_B + 0.1Q_B^2,$$

where total cost (TC_B) is in dollars, and Q_B is the number of tons of battery plates produced. The SED plant makes efficient use of all the lead it purchases, so that one ton of ingot yields one ton of battery plates. SED's management is not certain whether to plan to purchase lead from outside suppliers next year or to restrict its production of battery plates to those it can make from GAMC's total lead output. Its marketing department has estimated a statistical demand function for the battery plates such that

$$Q_B = 131,720.0 - 80.0P_B + 255.5P_n + 0.5I,$$

where Q_B is the number of tons of battery plates produced, P_B is the sales price per ton of plates, P_n is an index number of regional industrial production, and I is regional per-capital income. SED has contracted with an economic forecasting firm that regularly supplies it with forecasts of a large set of economic variables relating to output, prices, and income levels. For next year the forecasters have estimated that the average value of the regional production index will be 210 and that regional per-capita income will average $13,250.

■ ■ ■ ■ ■ ■ ■ ■ ■ ■ ■ ■ ■ ■ **Questions** ■ ■ ■ ■ ■ ■ ■ ■ ■ ■ ■ ■ ■ ■

Given the foregoing data, answer the following questions.

1. What strategy will maximize the joint profits of GAMC and its SED subsidiary?
2. For the two products (lead and battery plates), what will be the prices and outputs consistent with a profit-maximizing strategy during the coming year?
3. For next year should SED plan to restrict its output to that which can be produced from the ingot output of GAMC? Why or why not?

Integrating Case 3B

Bonco, Incorporated: A Firm in Transition

Bonco, Incorporated, produces a patented surgical device known as the incis-a-matic. The device has been sold successfully in the U.S. market, but it has been produced in two of the company's outdated plants, in Columbus, Ohio, and in Cincinnati, Ohio.

Barry Cosgrove, a young economist hired to assist management in making decisions regarding the future of incis-a-matic production and marketing strategies, has been developing cost and revenue data relevant to next year's operations.

His boss, Mary Thompson, has argued that for next year, the company should plan to duplicate this year's annual output of 2,400 units and raise price from $10,000 to $12,000 per unit. Thompson's reasoning is that the company plans to build a new plant that will begin operating year after next and has arranged to dispose of its two old plants. She believes they should simply "mark time" as far as output is concerned (in the old facilities) but raise price to cover some anticipated overall inflation in the economy.

Cosgrove's data for the two plants are as follows:

Columbus Plant		Cincinnati Plant	
Output per Month	Arc MC	Output per Month	Arc MC
0		0	
100	$ 4,000	100	$ 3,000
200	7,000	200	5,000
300	9,000	300	7,200
400	11,000	400	9,200
500	13,000	500	11,000

From the company's chief accountant, Cosgrove has learned that total fixed costs per month will be $700,000 in the Columbus plant and $600,000 in the Cincinnati plant. He has discovered that no one in the company has ever attempted to estimate a demand curve for the incis-a-matic and that Thompson has always based her pricing and output recommendations on her general impressions about the state of the economy. In order to estimate the demand for the incis-a-matic, Cosgrove performed a survey of hospital administrators and department chiefs. The result was the following demand schedule:

Price per Unit	Quantity Sold per Month
$16,000	0
14,000	100
12,000	200
10,000	300
8,000	400
6,000	500
4,000	600

■ ■ ■ ■ ■ ■ ■ ■ ■ ■ ■ ■ ■ **Questions** ■ ■ ■ ■ ■ ■ ■ ■ ■ ■ ■ ■ ■

Given Cosgrove's demand data, answer the following questions.

1. What should Cosgrove recommend regarding next year's total output and price per unit of the incis-a-matic?
2. How should next year's total output be allocated between the two plants? Why?
3. What will be next year's profit from sales of the incis-a-matic if Cosgrove's data are accurate and his recommendations are followed?
4. How does the Cosgrove recommendation compare with Thompson's strategy in terms of profit?

Beginning year after next, Bonco will be operating in its new plant, where a constant marginal cost of $5,000 per unit can be achieved over the 200- to 1,200-unit-per-month output range. Cosgrove has been asked to study the prospects for both U.S. and foreign sales of the incis-a-matic once the new plant is operational. For two years from now, based on analysis of surgical data for foreign hospitals and projections of U.S. demand, Cosgrove has estimated the following demand curves:

$$AR_f = 20,000 - 15Q_f$$

$$AR_{us} = 21,000 - 20Q_{us},$$

where

AR_f = average revenue from foreign sales,
Q_f = quantity sold per month in the foreign market,
AR_{us} = average revenue from sales in the U.S. market, and
Q_{us} = quantity sold per month in the U.S. market.

In addition, preliminary data on the new plant indicate that in the first year of operation, total fixed costs will be $800,000 per month.

Given the data on costs and on U.S. and foreign demand, answer the following questions for the first year of operations in the new plant:

5. What price should be charged in the U.S. market?
6. What price should be charged in the foreign market?
7. What will be the amount sold in each market if the preceding prices are charged?
8. What will be the maximum profit obtainable from incis-a-matic sales for the year?

Integrating Case 3C

A Hare-Raising Decision

On January 24,1983, the AP news wire reported that a West Lafayette, Indiana, firm, Rex Rabbit, Incorporated, was launching a fast-food business specializing in rabbit dinners. Rex Rabbit had 42 ranches in the area that raised rabbits for the fur trade. The restaurant venture was initiated to develop a market for byproduct rabbit meat. The following case was suggested by the Rex Rabbit undertaking, but all of the data are hypothetical and not intended to be an exact representation of any firm hopping or dead.[1]

Wonder Bunny, Incorporated, raises rabbits and sells their pelts to manufacturers of fur hats and accessories. For the past 10 years, it has also sold a by-product, unprocessed rabbit meat, to packinghouses that use it as an ingredient in canned pet foods. Chico Saltar, a production manager for Wonder, has noted that the company has recently encountered disposal problems with the rabbit meat, due to a tapering off in packinghouse demand for the product. As a result, Wonder has had to pay a waste disposal firm to haul away and destroy the excess meat. Currently, disposal costs are running $0.30 per unit on all unsold meat (production of one rabbit pelt yields one unit of meat). For the foreseeable future, Chico does not expect a recovery in packinghouse demand for the meat.

His current estimate of this demand is represented by the following equation:

$$Q_m = 12{,}000 - 5{,}000P_m,$$

where Q_m is the number of units of meat sold per quarter and P_m is the price obtained per unit of meat. Respectively, he has estimated the demand

[1] "Firm Hopping into Fast-Food Bunny Trade," *San Antonio Express*, January 24, 1983, p. 3-D.

function for pelts and the firm's total cost of production to be

$$Q_f = 3,600 - 4,000P_f + 1,000P_s + 1.8I,$$

where Q_f is the number of rabbit pelts sold per quarter, P_f is the price per rabbit pelt, P_s is the price of squirrel pelts, and I is household income; and

$$TC = \$38,000 + 1.8Q + 0.0001Q^2,$$

where $38,000 is quarterly fixed cost and Q represents the number of rabbits processed or production of one pelt *and* one unit of the by-product meat. Wonder's present strategy is to maximize profit from the sales of the two products, given the disposal cost per unit applicable to any amount of excess meat.

Mariel Hutch, a financial consultant for Wonder, has come to the company with a proposal that it stop selling rabbit meat to packing houses and process the meat for sale to a new market, fast food restaurants specializing in rabbit dinners. She has estimated that Wonder's demand curve for sales in this market is given by the equation

$$Q_r = 18,500 - 5,000P_r,$$

where Q_r is the number of units of meat sold per quarter and P_r is the price charged for a unit of meat. (The unit of meat remains the amount obtained with the production of one pelt.) While this demand clearly exceeds Chico's current estimate of demand in the packinghouse market, the changeover would require an increase in fixed costs of $14,000 per quarter as well as additional marginal costs of $0.28 per rabbit to process the meat to specifications of the new market. The cost increases will be applicable to all production of pelts and meat, because of once-over changes that will have to be made in the processing line. In other words, the new costs cannot be allocated to meat production alone. Moreover, it would not be feasible for Wonder to sell in both the restaurant market and the packing house market, since the decision to interrupt sales to the latter would likely cause a permanent loss of customers there. In the event that all of the meat cannot be sold in the restaurant market it will still be possible to use the waste disposal alternative described above.

Wonder must make a decision regarding the two by-product market possibilities within the next few weeks. As far as the pelt market is concerned, the company believes that the demand function variables other than the rabbit pelt price will remain constant. The current price of squirrel pelts is $3.20, and household income is $18,000. Given this additional information, what should Wonder do?

Hint: It is rational for Wonder to accept negative marginal revenue from meat sales as long as the negative MR per unit is less than the disposal cost per unit.

Integrating Case 3D

Omega Distributing Company II

(Note: This case is a continuation of the analysis done in Integrating Case 1B, Omega Distributing Company I, which is found at the end of Part I. A review of that case would be helpful for understanding this one.)

Duncan Haynes, a member of the team that developed a demand function for Omega Distributing Company's Blast fabric softener, has been assigned the task of determining whether the price of the product should be changed. (Duncan had earlier suggested changing price, since the results of a regression analysis of demand indicated that the company had been pricing the product in the inelastic range of its demand curve.) The demand function for Blast from the earlier analysis is

$$Q = -820 - 689P_b + 1{,}972P_c + 18A.$$

Q is denominated in hundreds in the equation and refers to the number of hundreds of units of Blast sold per week.

Duncan has decided that the pricing decision can best be analyzed by assuming that the price of the competing brand of softener, Cloud (P_c in the preceding equation) remains at its average recent value, $1.42 per unit, and that his own company cuts its advertising expenditure on Blast (A in the equation, denominated in ten thousands) to $20,000 per week ($A$ = 2.0). This leaves only P_b, the price per unit of Blast, as an unknown in the preceding equation.

Duncan knows that Omega pays the manufacturer of Blast $0.875 and that Omega's unit variable cost for the product is equal to 112 percent of the amount it pays the manufacturer. Given that the price of Blast and that of Cloud in the estimated demand function are denominated in dollars, what sales price per unit should Duncan recommend? What impact on profit would these changes in price and advertising have as compared to the profit Blast would generate with the average price and advertising levels determined in Integrating Case 1B (P_b = $1.37, P_c = $1.42, and A = 3.86)? Should Omega be cautious about instituting the price increase that Duncan's demand curve calls for? Why or why not?

Analysis of Project Decisions

Fundamentals of Project Evaluation

In many of the preceding chapters, our primary concern was the way a firm's managers identify a profit-maximizing rate of output and its corresponding price under various types of market situations. Over the short run, as we defined it, a significant proportion of the firms' inputs were envisioned as fixed (plant and equipment, for example), and the issue of investment in new capacity did not arise. Generally, when we considered the long run, the firm remained in a given industry or product line, even though it might change the size of its plant. Moreover, product differentiation or an adjustment in the share of output of joint products did not constitute a change in the type of activity undertaken by the firm.

In the present chapter, we change our emphasis to the question of management's analysis of investment opportunities, which include wholly new undertakings of the firm. Such ventures range all the way from the expansion of capacity in a given line of activity to entry into a new and different industry. It is a characteristic of today's industrial society that firms typically have many investment opportunities before them; and as the firms grow, their managers must be prepared to determine not only how and when to expand existing operations but also whether to steer the firm toward new types of activities in which profitable investments can be made. The large U.S. and European business conglomerates are an obvious case in point. Many of these giant corporations, such as Eastman Kodak, Gulf + Western Industries, and Textron, are characterized by divisions that produce totally unrelated types of output. The managers of these large firms must constantly review the expansion alternatives before them; and in a given firm, viable alternatives may range from developmental expenditures in space technology to the introduction of a new pastry snack into the consumer market.

A recent example of a firm faced with vexing investment alternatives is USX Corporation, which until 1986 was called United States Steel Corporation. During the 1980s, much of management's efforts were expended on evaluating alternative investments and acquisitions designed to move the company out of the declining steel industry and into more promising economic activities. As a result, USX invested heavily in oil and gas ventures and in the chemical industry, while its chief executive, David M. Roderick, chose to limit new capital projects in steel to only four of the company's eleven existing plants.[1]

Firms in the food industry have also been involved with major investment decisions. In 1980, Kraft merged with Dart. In 1985, Philip Morris purchased General Foods and three years later bought Kraft as well. The 1980s' biggest deal was Kohlberg Kravis Roberts's acquisition of RJR Nabisco in 1989. Kohlberg Kravis Roberts had purchased Beatrice Company in 1986.[2]

Smaller, less-diversified firms also must face important decisions regarding new product development. For example, the Ball Corporation—an old-line manufacturer of glass bottles, mason jars for home canning, and metal containers—has in recent years added copper-zinc penny blanks, small satellites, and aircraft instruments to its product mix. Although it was reported in 1982 that Ball's traditional products still contributed 80 percent of the firm's profits, growth in the canning and packaging industry was slow. Thus a 24 percent increase in Ball's 1981 profits was attributed to "an upturn in its small industrial products operation." Richard M. Ringoen, Ball's president and chief executive officer at the time, was pursuing a strategy of expansion in high-technology aerospace products, which he believed would attain greater earnings growth in the future.[3]

A major factor on the recent business scene has been the emergence of what are virtually stateless corporations. These firms represent a further evolution of multinational businesses that once were based primarily in one country, such as the United States, with subsidiary operations in other parts of the world. Frequently, these foreign appendages produced goods designed and developed in the home country. As *Business Week* puts it,

■ ■ ■ ■ ■ ■

[1] "Why USX Isn't Afraid of the Bogeyman," *Business Week* (May 14, 1990), p. 112; "It's USX Vs. Everybody," *Business Week* (October 6, 1986), pp. 26–27; and "The Toughest Job in Business," *Business Week* (February 25, 1985), pp. 50–56.

[2] "The Best and Worst Deals of the '80s," *Business Week* (January 15, 1990), pp. 52–57; and "LBOs: The Stars, the Strugglers, the Flops," *Business Week* (January 15, 1990), pp. 58–62.

[3] "Ball: Reaching Beyond Mason Jars to Satellites and High Technology," *Business Week* (August 16, 1982), pp. 76–77.

"The chain of command and nationality of the company were clear."[4] Today, however, the national identities of these corporations are becoming much less clear. *Business Week* continues:

> With the U.S. no longer dominating the world economy or holding a monopoly on innovation, new technologies, capital, and talents flow in many different directions. The most sophisticated manufacturing companies are making breakthroughs in foreign labs, seeking to place shares with foreign investors and putting foreigners on the fast track to the top. A wave of mergers, acquisitions, and strategic alliances has further clouded the question of national control.[5]

As a result of the new world market environment, managerial decision making, particularly with regard to new investment, has become far more complex than it was in the past. A company can no longer afford to ignore the impact of the international business community on the firm's operations, including its proposed capital projects.

■ ■ ■ ■ ■ ■ ■ ■ CAPITAL BUDGETING AND PROJECT ANALYSIS

Capital budgeting is the analysis of alternative investment opportunities by a firm.

The analysis of alternative investment opportunities is the focus of a subject area known as **capital budgeting,** which encompasses both economics and finance. Generally, we can view capital budgeting as the process by which a firm's managers determine how to allocate investment expenditures among alternative projects. The projects that are the subject of analysis usually include only those that will yield dollar returns to the firm for periods longer than one year. *Capital project analysis* is a major part of the capital budgeting process, since it provides managers with the raw materials, in terms of data, that are necessary to carry out capital budgeting decisions. Accordingly, we will first consider the analysis of a single undertaking (investment project) and later turn to the question of deciding which of a number of alternative investment projects should be accepted.

■ ■ ■ ■ ■ ■ ■ ■ COSTS IN NEW UNDERTAKINGS

From our earlier analysis of the firm, we know that any operation of a given size (plant) normally has both fixed and variable costs of production. Thus, to analyze a specific capital project, it is necessary to determine such costs and compare them with the revenues the project will generate. However, a *new* undertaking has one-time costs associated with obtaining and organizing the resources necessary to bring it into existence, and

---

■ ■ ■ ■ ■ ■
[4] "The Stateless Corporation," *Business Week* (May 14, 1990), p. 98.
[5] Ibid.

project analysis must also take these costs into account. For convenience we will call this latter set of costs the *price* or *initial cost outlay* of the project. A capital project's price includes initial outlays for land, buildings, and equipment, as well as developmental costs both for the undertaking itself and for the product it is intended to produce. Another item that should be included in a project's price is the cost to the firm of any increase in working capital requirements attributable to the project. Finally, if the project involves replacement of existing capital goods, the after-tax salvage value of the old equipment should be deducted from the project's price.

Capital budgeting puts managers into an accept-or-reject framework with respect to the individual capital project. The following general rule for acceptance of a single project is exceedingly simple:

> A project should be accepted as long as the *present value* of the expected *net receipts* it generates *equals or exceeds its price* (the net outlay required).

In other words, worthy investments are those that yield returns at least equal to their costs, where the costs include a normal or target rate of return on invested capital. *Returns* from the project are defined as the present value of net receipts, or a discounted stream of *net cash flows.* Such a concept will be familiar to students who have had a course in finance, but others should give it particular attention. The following section provides a summary of how to calculate the discounted stream of net receipts. More detailed information on the use of discounting and compounding methodologies appears in the appendix to this chapter.

■ ■ ■ ■ ■ ■ ■ ■ STREAM OF RECEIPTS OR RETURNS

In general, capital projects have a finite life, even though it is not always clear to the project analyst how long a given venture might be expected to yield net operating returns to the firm. Even if the life of a particular project were viewed as indefinitely long or infinite, it would be possible to calculate just what one would be willing to pay today in order to obtain an infinite stream of annual receipts of a given amount per year. In approaching this problem, we would quickly find out that we would not be willing to pay very much for an amount that is not to be received until many, many years in the future. To understand this point, ask yourself what you would be willing to pay for a piece of paper that guarantees you will receive $50 thirty years from today. Not much! The exact answer, assuming no inflation, would depend on the interest rate.[6]

■ ■ ■ ■ ■ ■

[6] We use the term "interest rate" very loosely at this point. In general, when we employ the term, we are referring to the rate of return expected from alternative uses   (continued)

To examine the effect of interest rate considerations on management's evaluation of net receipts from a capital project, let us suppose a firm's project analysts are reasonably certain that a given project will generate net receipts for the firm for the next ten years. Specifically, let us suppose that in terms of today's prices (this means that inflation is adjusted out of all calculations), $100,000 will be generated each year. We shall assume that the first annual receipts of the project are received at the end of one year's time from completion of the project and shall treat the project's net outlay as a current value (paid immediately, at time-period zero). Thus the first $100,000 is received at the end of year one, the second $100,000 at the end of year two, and so forth.

The value at the time of project completion of $100,000 of receipts that will be earned at the end of, say, year three is not $100,000, but rather something less. In particular it is the amount of money that would *accumulate to* $100,000 at the end of year three if it were invested today at some specific rate of interest per year. This is so because the firm at project completion and initiation of production is in the same position as the person who is promised a given sum of money at some future time. The current value, or **present value,** of that promised amount is something less than the future amount itself. If the interest rate is 6 percent, the present value of $100,000 received at the end of year three is $83,961.93. Alternatively, if we receive $83,961.93 *now* and put it into an account paying 6 percent interest per year, at the end of this year we will have ($83,961.93)(1.06) = $88,999.64. If we do not remove any of the funds from the account, at the end of year two we will have ($88,999.64)(1.06) = $94,339.62; and at the end of year three we will have ($94,339.62)(1.06) = $100,000.00. Thus we can say that if the interest rate is 6 percent, $83,961.93 in our hands today is *equivalent* to $100,000 received at the end of year three. Similarly, both of the foregoing are equivalent to $94,339.62 received at the end of year two. The process by which we have determined the amount or **future value** that the $83,961.93 will accumulate to is called **compounding.** In the foregoing example, 6 percent interest was compounded at the end of each year. This means that at the end of each year, the interest for that period is added to the amount that was in the account at the beginning of the year. Therefore the 6 percent interest is paid on a larger amount the next year.

The proposition that discounted future amounts are equal to a certain present amount is known as the *concept of equivalency.* The process by which we determine the present value of an amount to be received at

The **present value** of a future payment or series of payments represents the amount received today that would be equivalent in value to the future payment or payments.

The **future value** of a sum of money held today is the amount that would be accumulated at some future date if we invested that sum of money now at a particular rate of interest.

Compounding is the process of computing the value of a current sum of money at some future date.

■ ■ ■ ■ ■ ■

[6] (concluded) of funds. If we are certain that the funds paid out for the guarantee of receiving $50 thirty years from now can be placed in a risk-free account paying 6 percent interest compounded annually, we could ascertain that $8.71 placed in such an account would reach a value of $50 in thirty years. Therefore we would not want to pay more than $8.71 for the paper guaranteeing $50 at the end of thirty years.

Discounting is the process of computing the present value of sums of money to be received in the future.

some time in the future is called **discounting,** and the interest rate we use in the determination of the present value is called the **discount rate.**

Clearly, the farther out in time a future amount is received, the lower its present value. Returning to the previous project with a $100,000 annual net receipts figure, for year ten the present value of $100,000 is only $55,839.47 if a discount rate of 6 percent is applied. Such a present value is found by the formula

(13–1)
$$PV = \frac{FV_n}{(1 + r)^n}$$

The **discount rate** is the rate of interest used to compute present values.

where

PV = present value,
FV_n = future value at the end of year n,
r = applicable discount rate,

and

n = number of periods (years) until the amount is received.

In the preceding case, n would be 10 and r would be 0.06. We can derive the present value formula by further examining the concept of equivalency discussed above. We have already seen that when r = 0.06, $100,000 received at the end of year three is equal to a present value of $83,961.93. Note that the $100,000 received at the end of year three is equal to an initial amount of $83,961.93 increased by 6 percent at the end of year one to $88,999.64, compounded at 6 percent again at the end of year two to $94,339.62, and compounded at 6 percent at the end of year three to $100,000.00. So we have the following:

Amount at the end of
year one: ($83,961.93)(1.06) = $88,999.64
year two: ($83,961.93)(1.06)(1.06) = $94,339.62
                                    = ($83,961.93)(1.06)^2
year three: ($83,961.93)(1.06)(1.06)(1.06) = $100,000.00
                                    = ($83,961.93)(1.06)^3

or for each year,

(13–2)
$$FV_n = PV(1.06)^n,$$

where FV is received at the end of n periods in the future. If we divide both sides of the preceding expression by $(1.06)^n$, we get

(13–3)
$$PV = \frac{FV_n}{(1 + .06)^n} \; .$$

Since 0.06 is the discount rate, r, we have

(13–4)
$$PV = \frac{FV_n}{(1 + r)^n},$$

which is identical to equation 13-1.

We can also state equation 13-4 as

(13–5)
$$PV = FV_n(PVF\ r,\ n),$$

where $(PVF\ r,\ n) = 1/(1 + r)^n$ is the *present value factor*. Tables have been developed for the value of the *PVF* (also known as the present value of $1) for given rates of interest and numbers of periods in the future. In Appendix B at the end of the text, Table B–3 gives the values of the *PVF*. To find the present value of $100,000 received at the end of the third year for the preceding project, we simply multiply $100,000 times the present value factor from the table, which for $n = 3$ and $r = 0.06$ is 0.8396. (Read down the 6 percent column of Table B–3 to $n = 3$.) Thus

$$\$100,000(PVF\ 6\%,\ 3) = \$100,000(0.8396) = \$83,960,$$

which corresponds closely to the $83,961.93 in the previous example. The slight difference in the result is due to the rounding of the *PVF*, which is more precisely given by 0.83962.

To evaluate our example of $100,000 per year stream of annual net receipts for ten years, we construct Table 13–1, using the 6 percent present

Table 13–1 Present Value of $100,000 per Year Stream of Net Receipts Discounted at 6 Percent per Year

Period (n)	FV = Future Value (At End of Period)	PV Factor (PVF 6%, n)	Present Value (FV × PVF)
1	$100,000	0.9434	$ 94,340
2	100,000	0.8900	89,000
3	100,000	0.8396	83,960
4	100,000	0.7921	79,210
5	100,000	0.7473	74,730
6	100,000	0.7050	70,500
7	100,000	0.6651	66,510
8	100,000	0.6274	62,740
9	100,000	0.5919	59,190
10	100,000	0.5584	55,840
		PV of 10-year stream	$736,020

value factors from Table B–3. Each of the ten annual $100,000 amounts is multiplied by its respective 6 percent present value factor, and the present values in the fourth column are then summed to obtain the present value of the entire ten-year stream of receipts. From Table 13–1, we can see that the present value of the ten-year flow of $100,000 in net receipts per year is $736,020—the sum of the *discounted* future values where the applicable discount rate is 6 percent.

However, this result can be obtained more easily by multiplying $100,000 times the present value factor for an annuity (PVF_a) of ten years discounted at 6 percent. Defined briefly, an *annuity* is a constant amount payable at the end of each year for a specified number of years. In the case of our current example, if we let $A = $100,000$, then PV_a (the present value of the ten-year stream of $100,000 per year) is

(13–6)
$$PV_a = \frac{A}{(1 + r)^1} + \frac{A}{(1 + r)^2} + \cdots + \frac{A}{(1 + r)^n} \text{ ,}$$

where $n = 10$. Restating, we obtain

(13–7)
$$PV_a = A \left[\frac{1}{(1 + r)^1} + \frac{1}{(1 + r)^2} + \cdots + \frac{1}{(1 + r)^n} \right].$$

The present value factor for the annuity is the term in brackets in the preceding equation, or

(13–8)
$$PVF_a = \left[\frac{1}{(1 + r)^1} + \frac{1}{(1 + r)^2} + \cdots + \frac{1}{(1 + r)^n} \right],$$

so that we can state $PV_a = A(PVF_a\ r, n)$. A table of present value of annuity factors also appears in Appendix B. For a discount rate of 6 percent and 10 periods (PVF_a 6%, 10), the present value factor is 7.3601. Thus, in the case of our example, we have

$$PV_a = $100,000(PVF_a\ 6\%, 10) = $100,000(7.3601) = $736,010.$$

The **net present value (NPV)** of an investment is the present value of its net cash inflows minus the present value of its cost outlays. An investment project is acceptable if its *NPV* is greater than or equal to zero.

In round numbers, then, we have determined that the present value of the profit or the net receipts stream anticipated from our example project is $736,000. This assumes, of course, that management has determined that 6 percent per year is an appropriate rate of discount to apply.

According to the general rule stated in the preceding section, the project should be accepted as long as its price is not more than $736,000. Another way of stating this requirement is to say that the **net present value (NPV)** of the project must be *nonnegative* (zero or greater). The net present value of a project is the difference between the discounted stream of expected net cash flows from the project and the project's price, or

(13–9)

$$NPV = \sum_{i=1}^{n} \frac{(TR_i - TC_i)(1 - T) + D_i}{(1 + r)^i} - C_p,$$

The **net cash flow** of a project is equal to any increase in revenues brought about by the project less any increase in operating expenses and depreciation, multiplied by $(1 - T)$, where T is the firm's marginal income tax rate. The incremental depreciation associated with the project is then added to the above sum.

where TR is total revenue, TC is total operating cost (short run and including depreciation for the project), T is the firm's marginal income tax rate, D is depreciation, and C_p is the price or net outlay for the project. Equation 13–9 indicates that we should determine the *net* receipts for each time period (i) and discount such receipts at the rate r for all time periods for one through n; then, we should sum them (the Greek letter Σ, sigma, indicates that we should sum all items with an i subscript from $i = 1$ to $i = n$) and subtract the price of the project to obtain the NPV.

Managerial Perspective: The Saturn: A Product Made in Heaven?

"All-new aluminum engine, fail-safe sophisticated marketing research and highly automated assembly technique . . . a revolutionary change from a company and industry that heretofore have stressed slow, evolutionary change." These words could have been used to describe General Motors' Saturn, a new small car introduced in the fall of 1990, but here *The Wall Street Journal* was quoting them from J. Patrick Wright's 1979 book, *On A Clear Day You Can See General Motors*. And where did Wright pick them up? From General Motors' claims for the Vega, a car introduced in 1970.

An indication of the Vega's success, or lack thereof, can be gleaned from a comment by Mr. Richard LeFauve, the boss at General Motors' Saturn subsidiary, who admits: "We've had many letters from people saying, 'Don't let this be another Vega.'"

Work on the Saturn began in 1983, and since that time General Motors has spent $3.5 billion on the project. The Saturn is supposed to be a top-quality small car that will be more technologically advanced than competing Japanese cars. The Spring Hill, Tennessee, plant that is manufacturing the new cars cost $1.9 billion, and it will have a capacity of 240,000 cars a year. However, Thomas G. Manoff, Saturn's vice-president of finance, calculates that plant capacity will have to double if Saturn is to become profitable.

General Motors began the Saturn project by attempting to design a plant that would be so automated that very little human labor would be required. Later, however, the company had to modify that plan because comparable equipment in other General Motors facilities was not performing as well as had been hoped.

In contrast, Honda began developing a United States plant in 1982 in Marysville, Ohio, at a cost of about $2 billion. Initially, the degree of automation at the plant was relatively low, but Honda gradually added sophisticated equipment as workers became more adept at using it. The company also added capacity as demand for the car expanded. Although the plant began by building an existing model of the Accord, by 1985 it had introduced a new Accord model. For approximately the same cost as General Motors' Saturn project, Honda got two assembly plants with a total annual capacity of 510,000 cars as well as a factory capable of building nearly all of the engines, transmissions, and related parts needed by its auto assembly plants plus a motorcycle plant.

The Saturn is approximately the size of a Toyota Corolla, which has a base price of $9,000 to $13,000. The Saturn's projected price range is $10,000 to $13,000. GM hopes that the Saturn will get 80 percent of its sales from competing cars made by other companies: the Honda Civic, for example, and Mazda MX6 Coupe, as well as the Toyota Corolla.

As a result of a limited capital budget and capital rationing decisions, the allocation of funds to develop the Saturn caused a delay in the development of a new line of four-door, mid-sized cars to compete with Ford Motor Company's Taurus and Sable. That delay allegedly contributed to a decline in GM's U.S. market share from 44 percent in 1983 to 35.7 percent in 1990. Even Saturn's management believes that it will be at least another five years before the company will know if Saturn will become a profitable project for General Motors.

■ ■ ■ ■

Reference: "GM's Plan for Saturn, To Beat Small Imports, Trails Original Goals," *The Wall Street Journal*, July 9, 1990, pp. A1, A12.

The internal rate of return (IRR) of a project is the discount rate that will result in a net present value of zero for the project.

If the *NPV* in equation 13–9 turns out to be zero, the project will yield a return identical to the return that would be received if an amount equal to C_p were put into an account paying $(r \times 100)$ percent interest compounded annually. Where *NPV* is greater than zero, the project yield will exceed the discount rate, *r*.

In fact, it is possible to determine the net annual percentage yield of a project (its **internal rate of return**) when its price and annual dollar receipts are known by setting *NPV* equal to C_p and solving for *r* in equation 13–9. Thus we find *r* such that

$$\sum_{i=1}^{n} \frac{(TR_i - TC_i)(1 - T) + D_i}{(1 + r)^i} = C_p.$$

The *r* value can be found by trial and error or by interpolation. There is no simple formula for finding it, and not all financial calculators have this capability. However, there are computer programs available for determination of the internal rate of return.[7] Later in this chapter, an example of trial and error determination of a project's internal rate of return will be introduced.

■ ■ ■ ■ ■ ■ ■ ■ ■   A SIMPLE CAPITAL PROJECT ANALYSIS

Any investor, whether a large corporation or an individual, must go through an analysis similar to that outlined previously in order to make an appropriate accept-or-reject decision on a capital project. For the large enterprise contemplating a major undertaking, the process of enumerating project costs and returns may be very tedious and expensive. For an individual or a small business, however, the procedure may be relatively simple.

Let us consider as an example the case of a small firm, Clickwash, Incorporated, that operates a chain of coin laundries in a given area. The firm's managers are quite experienced in the construction and operation of such facilities but are now considering opening a coin-operated car wash in a location that appears to be desirable. A car wash franchising company owns the site and has offered Clickwash an attractive ground lease in exchange for a franchise fee of 30 percent of sales revenue.

According to our prior discussion of project analysis, Clickwash's management will have to determine the following:

1. The price or net outlay of the project
2. Anticipated annual sales revenues from the project
3. Operating costs of the project
4. A salvage value at the end of the project's life

■ ■ ■ ■ ■ ■

[7] As long as the project cash flows follow the pattern of negative cash flows in the first few periods and positive cash flows thereafter, there will usually be only one positive-valued solution for the *IRR* (the others are negative or imaginary). However, if there is a mixture of positive and negative cash flows during future periods, it is possible to have more than one positive-valued solution for the *IRR*. In such cases one reverts back to the *NPV* method to determine the acceptability of the project in question.

Based on its experience with coin laundries, management has determined that five years is an appropriate project life, since the machinery receives rather rough use and leases on suitable locations can seldom be negotiated for a term greater than five years. The car wash will have seven bays made of structural steel and aluminum siding. The bays and washing equipment can be dismantled and sold or moved at termination of the project; however, driveway pavement, the concrete slab on which the bays rest, and plumbing placed in the slab will all be abandoned when the project is over. The initial cost of the bays and washing equipment is $159,000. They can be sold at the end of the project for $66,500. The paving, slab, nonsalvageable plumbing, and plant installation cost an additional $20,000. The management of Clickwash thus knows that the price or net outlay of the project will be $C_p = \$179,000$.

The next step for management is to calculate the annual net receipts from the project and determine the present value of the five-year receipts stream. Suppose they have the following information:

1. The car wash will operate an average of 360 days a year.
2. An average of 36 car washes per day will occur at each of the seven bays.
3. The average receipts for a single wash are $0.875. This result is based on an assumption that the average wash will yield $1.25 in revenues (some people will spend four quarters per wash and others six) but that 30 percent of that amount belongs to the franchising company ($0.375).
4. Variable costs per wash are as follows:

Utilities and water	$ 0.08
Soap and supplies	0.04
Maintenance of machinery	0.02

5. Fixed costs per month are as follows:

Rent	$750.00
Utilities (fixed portion)	90.00
Site maintenance	80.00
Labor	190.00
Administrative Expense	100.00

6. Depreciation is $22,500 per year.
7. The company is in the 34 percent income tax bracket.

From 1, 2, and 3, it can be determined that annual receipts from sales will be

7 bays x 36 washes x 360 days x $0.875 = $79,380.

Based on the preceding cost information, management can determine the annual cost of the car wash project as in Table 13–2. Our format in Table

Table 13–2   Annual Operating Cost of Car Wash Project

Variable Costs:		
Utilities and Water (0.08 × 90,720 washes per year)	$7,258	
Maintenance of Machines (0.02 × 90,720 washes per year)	1,814	
Soap and Supplies (0.04 × 90,720 washes per year)	3,629	
		$12,701
Fixed Costs:		
Utilities (fixed portion, $90 per month)	$1,080	
Rent ($750 per month)	9,000	
Site Maintenance ($80 per month)	960	
Labor ($190 per month)	2,280	
Administrative Expense ($100 per month)	$1,200	
		14,520
Depreciation		22,500
Total Annual Operating Cost of Project		$49,721

13–2 is a hybrid of the economic and accounting costs discussed in Chapter 5. At this point we do not take into account the opportunity cost to the firm of using its own funds for the project. However, the discount rate applied to the future net receipts and the criterion that the present value of such receipts be greater than the price of the project do account for the opportunity cost of investing the funds in another way.

Table 13–3 is a worksheet for the project itself. Here, the anticipated receipts from sales are reduced by the annual cost of operations from Table 13–2 and by federal income taxes, which are 34 percent of net income before taxes. In order to obtain the annual net inflow of cash from the project, the firm's managers must add back the yearly depreciation figure, since depreciation is charged against current receipts but not paid to anyone else outside the firm.[8] As Table 13–3 shows, after this adjustment the annual net inflow from the project is $42,075. Then management applies a discount rate of 10 percent to analyze the project. (The question of choosing the appropriate discount rate will be discussed later in this chapter.)

The present value of a cash inflow of $42,075 for five years when discounted at 10 percent is $159,498, a figure substantially lower than C_p,

■ ■ ■ ■ ■ ■

[8] Depreciation expense is an accounting concept employed to reflect the using up of certain fixed assets (that is, having them wear out or become obsolete) in the production process of the firm. On the firm's income statement, depreciation is an expense, but no cash is paid out. Because of this the firm's *net flow of cash benefits* will exceed net income. Therefore we must add the depreciation back to the net income to account for its contribution to the benefits stream.

Table 13–3   Worksheet for Car Wash Project *NPV* Analysis

Annual Receipts from Sales		$ 79,380
Less:		
Annual Cost of Operations	$49,721	
Net Income Before Taxes		29,659
Less:		
Income Tax	10,084	
Net Income		19,575
Plus:		
Depreciation	22,500	
Annual Net Inflow from Project		$ 42,075
PV of Five-Year Net Inflow[1]		$159,498
Salvage Value of Equipment		
$66,500		
PV of Salvage Value[2]	41,290	
GPV of Project		200,788
Price of Project (C_p)		(179,000)
NPV of Project		$ 21,788

[1]This amount is $42,075(PVF_a \ 10\%, \ 5) = \$42,075(3.7908)$. See the discussion of PVF_a earlier in the chapter, and consult Table B–4 in Appendix B.
[2]This amount is $66,500(PVF \ 10\%, \ 5) = \$66,500(0.6209)$. See Table B–3 for PVF.

the price of the car wash project ($179,000). However, we must recall that management estimates the equipment to have a salvage value of $66,500 at the end of the five-year project life, and the present value of that salvage amount (discounted at 10 percent) is $41,290.[9] This gives a gross present value (*GPV*) figure for the project of $159,498 + $41,290 = $200,788. Since C_p is only $179,000, the project is acceptable. Alternatively, it is shown in Table 13–3 that the net present value of the project is $21,788. Since the net present value is greater than zero, the project meets the general rule for acceptability.

■ ■ ■ ■ ■ ■ ■ ■ ■ **PROJECT YIELD OR RATE OF RETURN**

It will also be of interest to management to know the return that is generated by the project in terms of a percentage yield or rate of return on the $179,000 of invested capital. Logically, the project has a return of

■ ■ ■ ■ ■ ■

[9] In this example, the salvage value is exactly equal to the book value of the equipment at the end of five years. If these two values were not equal, the income tax due (saved) on the gain (loss) as a result of the sale of the equipment would have to be considered.

more than 10 percent per year, since its *NPV* is greater than zero. If the *NPV* were just zero, the net inflows from the project discounted at 10 percent per year would exactly equal $179,000. In financial analysis the *internal rate of return* (*IRR*) of a project is its yield. As explained earlier in the chapter, the *IRR* can be defined as the discount rate that will just equate the present value of the stream of net receipts with the price of the project. To estimate the *IRR* in the context of our car wash project, we would want to find a discount rate such that the five-year stream of $42,075 in net receipts per year plus the present value of the salvage amount (*PV* of $66,500) is just equal, in present value terms, to C_p, or

$$\$42,075(PVF_a\ IRR\%,\ 5) + \$66,500(PVF\ IRR\%,\ 5) = \$179,000.$$

Mathematically, solving for the *IRR* is a difficult process. However, it is quite easy to estimate a project's *IRR* using an ordinary financial calculator or a set of present value tables and employing a trial-and-error method. In the preceding case, we know that the *IRR* is greater than 10 percent. We can calculate the present value of the stream of annual receipts plus the salvage amount at discount rates of 12 and 14 percent and see that which most closely approximates $179,000. The following are the *PV*s of the five-year stream of $42,075 per year plus the salvage value for the above rates of discount.

Discount Rate (IRR)	PV of $42,075/yr. + $66,500 (n = 5)
12%	$189,404
14%	$178,987

The *PV* for 12 percent is too high, indicating that the *IRR* exceeds 12 percent. In fact, the *IRR* must be about 14 percent. For 14 percent, if we calculate the *PV* of an annual net inflow of $42,085 for five years plus the *PV* of the $66,500 salvage value, we get $178,987, which is very close to the project price. Thus we can conclude that Clickwash's management will enjoy a yield of approximately 14 percent on its investment in the car wash project. Since this yield is greater than the 10 percent discount rate, the project should be undertaken. This provides a new and slightly different statement of the accept-reject rule: An individual project is acceptable if its *IRR* equals or exceeds the discount rate.[10]

■ ■ ■ ■ ■ ■

[10] Some exceptions to this rule exist, particularly when there are multiple positive-valued solutions for the IRR. For more information on this topic see J. Fred Weston and Thomas E. Copeland, *Managerial Finance*, 8th ed. (Chicago: The Dryden Press, 1989), Chapter 6.

■ ■ ■ ■ ■ ■ ■ ■ ■ ## PROJECT RANKING IN CAPITAL BUDGETING ANALYSIS

We have shown how to determine whether a single given project is acceptable from an investment standpoint. However, we have not yet developed any rules for ranking alternative projects in terms of their relative acceptability. In the context of our hypothetical firm, Clickwash, this issue would emerge if management had to decide not only whether a car wash would be an acceptable investment but also whether such an investment would be *better* than several other alternatives that have the same initial price and project life.

For example, Clickwash might be faced with whether it should build the car wash, take over an existing pizzeria, build a donut shop, add another laundromat to its chain, or build an automobile muffler shop—each of which would entail an outlay (project price) of $179,000 and have a planned project life of five years. Under these circumstances there is little difficulty choosing the most desirable project. In this case, the appropriate procedure for choosing among the projects is simply to go through the *NPV* analysis for each of the five projects and select the one with the highest *NPV*. Further, if the firm had enough funds to undertake four of the five projects, management could decide which one to reject by determining which had the lowest *NPV*.

If the projects were of different size (price) but the same planned life, the *NPV* approach to ranking them could be applied, but management would have to take into account the possibility that various *combinations* of projects might generate different aggregate *NPV*s. Thus management would end up ranking various feasible *packages* of projects, rather than each project individually. Returning to the example of Clickwash, suppose that the five projects previously stated are analyzed and the following results are obtained:

Project	*Price*	*NPV*
Car wash	$179,000	$21,788
Pizzeria	100,000	15,200
Donut shop	70,000	10,150
Coin laundry	80,000	10,800
Muffler shop	181,000	18,100

All of the projects meet the general rule for acceptability, since each has an *NPV* greater than zero. Suppose that the firm has only $360,000 to allocate for new investments. Management will then have to devise a plan for *capital rationing;* that is, deciding which of the numerous projects to undertake, given the limited capital budget of $360,000. Management's objective should be to select the combination of projects that provides the greatest aggregate *NPV* for an outlay of $360,000 or less.

Our first step is to rank-order the projects by price, as in Table 13–4. This provides a way to determine both the minimum and maximum number of projects that can be accepted. From Table 13–4 we can see that the minimum number of projects is two (Projects 1 and 2, which exhaust the $360,000). Further, all combinations of two projects require $360,000 or less and thus could be undertaken. However, it is easy to see that no two-project combination will yield as much as the combination 1,2. We illustrate this with a complete enumeration of the possible two-project combinations in Table 13–5. Since none of the two-project combinations has an *NPV* greater than combination 1,2 or greater than $39,888, we can drop all two-project combinations other than 1,2 from consideration.

Mathematics would indicate that there are also ten possible three-project combinations from the list of Table 13–4, since

$$c_b^a = \frac{a!}{b!(a-b)!}$$

Table 13–4   Clickwash, Inc. Project Array in Rank Order by Price

Project	Price	NPV
1. Muffler Shop	$181,000	$18,100
2. Car Wash	179,000	21,788
3. Pizzeria	100,000	15,200
4. Coin Laundry	80,000	10,800
5. Donut Shop	70,000	10,150

Table 13–5   Clickwash, Inc. Analysis of Possible Two-Project Investment Combinations

Project Combination	Price	NPV
1,2	$360,000	$39,888
1,3	281,000	33,300
1,4	261,000	28,900
1,5	251,000	28,250
2,3	279,000	36,988
2,4	259,000	32,588
2,5	249,000	31,938
3,4	180,000	26,000
3,5	170,000	25,350
4,5	150,000	20,950

is the formula for the number of combinations of *a* things taken *b* at a time. In Table 13–6 we enumerate all three-project combinations, showing their respective aggregate *NPV*s and prices. Note that only six three-project combinations fall within the capital budget constraint of $360,000. Of these, combination 2,3,4 has the greatest aggregate *NPV*—$47,788. This particular combination of projects has a total *NPV* that exceeds that of the best two-project combination—combination 1,2 (aggregate *NPV* of only $39,888). The conclusion is that combination 2,3,4 (the car wash, the pizzeria, and the coin laundry) should be undertaken.

In the preceding analysis, the alternative projects all had the same planned project life (five years). Obviously, firms can be faced with making accept-reject decisions on capital undertakings of unequal project life. There are a number of ways to handle the problem of unequal project life in capital budgeting analysis. One way is to set up "replacement chains," which would extend the capital budgeting analysis to the number of years divisible by the respective project lives. For example, if we are comparing two projects—one that has a life of two years and one that has a life of three years—we could use six years as our period for comparison, assuming that we would repeat the first project three times over the period and the second project twice over the period. This would be a reasonable approach to use in a case such as the evaluation of two machines, one of which is more durable than the other. Employing such an approach, management could decide whether to use a less durable machine that would be replaced every two years or a more durable one that would be replaced every three years.

We should also note that where alternative projects have rather long lives (30 to 40 years or more), it might be reasonable to compare them using some arbitrary point (say, 30 years), which is set as the "life" of each alternative. This is so because as the flow of project returns is ex-

Table 13–6 Clickwash, Inc. Analysis of Possible Three-Project Capital Budgeting Combinations

Project Combination	Price	NPV
1,2,3	$460,000	$55,088
1,2,4	440,000	50,688
1,2,5	430,000	50,038
1,3,4	361,000	44,100
1,3,5	351,000	43,450
1,4,5	331,000	39,050
2,3,4	359,000	47,788
2,3,5	349,000	47,138
2,4,5	329,000	42,738
3,4,5	250,000	36,150

tended into the more distant future, not only does the present value of far-off receipts fall, but also the uncertainty of their occurrence increases.[11]

■ ■ ■ ■ ■ ■ ■ ■ ■ ## COST OF CAPITAL AND THE DISCOUNT RATE

The **marginal cost of capital** (*MCC*) is the discount rate which represents the marginal cost of investment funds to the firm. It is calculated as a weighted average of the after-tax cost of funds from each source.

As our example of Clickwash, Incorporated, has shown, the discount rate is an extremely important item in conducting a capital project analysis. Thus far we have not discussed how a firm goes about determining the discount rate used to calculate the present value of project cash flows. In its most basic form, this rate represents the cost to the firm of obtaining new funds to invest. It is called the **marginal cost of capital.**

Generally, firms have two principal sources of investment funds—debt and equity. In other words they can obtain new financing either by borrowing or by using owner-supplied funds (the latter can be internally generated or raised by issuing new stock). Since interest paid on borrowed funds is tax deductible, it is the after-tax cost of debt that is relevant to estimating the effect of debt on the firm's overall marginal cost of capital. Its marginal cost of capital at any point in time will then be the weighted average of its cost of debt and cost of equity.

To illustrate, let's assume that the interest rate on new bonds issued by the firm is 12 percent and that the firm's owners expect a return of 14 percent on funds that they invest. Further, assume that the best capital structure for the firm is 60 percent debt and 40 percent equity.[12] If the corporate income tax rate (*T*) is 34 percent, the firm's marginal cost of debt will be the interest rate on borrowed funds (*bond rate*) multiplied by the quantity $(1 - T)$, or $0.12(1 - 0.34) = 0.0792$. Its marginal cost of capital will be this rate multiplied by the proportion of debt in its capital structure *plus* the expected rate of return on equity (14 percent) multiplied by the proportion of owner-supplied funds in the capital structure. For the preceding numbers, the marginal cost of capital (*k*) is calculated as follows:

$$k = 0.0792(0.6) + 0.14(0.4) = 0.0475 + 0.056 = 0.1035.$$

Ordinarily, as a firm expands the amount of its new investment at any point in time, the marginal cost of capital will rise. This occurs because

■ ■ ■ ■ ■ ■

[11] Another technique that is used to evaluate projects with unequal lives is that of the equivalent annual annuity approach, which essentially assumes that the replacement chains extend to infinity for each project. For more information on comparing projects with unequal lives see Eugene F. Brigham and Louis C. Gapenski, *Financial Management*, 6th ed. (Chicago: The Dryden Press, 1991), pp. 369–372.

[12] By *best* or *optimal capital structure* we mean the combination of debt and equity that will minimize the weighted average cost of capital for the firm, all other factors remaining the same. For a more thorough discussion of this issue see Eugene F. Brigham and Louis C. Gapenski, *Financial Management*, 6th ed. Chicago: The Dryden Press, 1991, Chapters 8, 12.

the firm must turn to more and more expensive means of financing as the total amount of investment funds to be raised is increased. Thus a curve relating the marginal cost of capital to the size of the capital budget will look something like the *MCC* curve in Figure 13–1. Similarly, one can construct a curve that relates the internal rates of return of available investment alternatives to the amount of investment undertaken. This is done by rank-ordering capital projects in decreasing order of internal rate of return. The *IRR* curve of Figure 13–1 reflects the decrease of the internal rate of return as less and less profitable projects are undertaken.

Figure 13–1   Determination of the Firm's Capital Budget and Marginal Cost of Capital

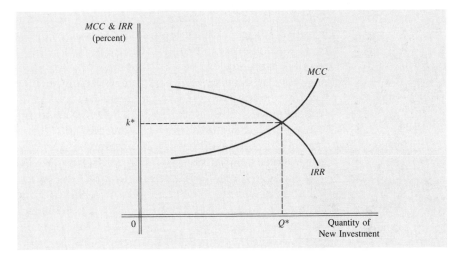

As the quantity of new investment undertaken increases, the firm's marginal cost of capital rises. However, the internal rate of return falls because less and less attractive new investments are undertaken. At *k**, where *MCC* = *IRR*, the optimal size capital budget and the firm's *MCC* are determined.

If we recall the rule that states that a project is acceptable as long as its internal rate of return exceeds the firm's discount rate, we can find both the equilibrium size of the capital budget and the firm's *MCC* in Figure 13–1. This occurs where the rising *MCC* curve intersects the falling IRR curve. Beyond *Q**, the return on additional projects is less than the firm's marginal cost of capital, so these projects will not be undertaken. Thus *k** is the firm's marginal cost of capital for the given *MCC* and *IRR* curves.

Of course, firms generally have to choose among investment alternatives that not only are risky but also vary in riskiness. Therefore it is

Managerial Perspective: The Leverage Roller Coaster

In the world of corporate finance, the 1980s were known as the decade of the leveraged buyout (LBO)—the purchase of a company typically by management primarily through the use of borrowed money. By the end of 1989, $1.3 trillion had been spent on mergers and acquisitions and leveraged buyouts; between 1982 and 1988, nonfinancial companies doubled their debt from $.9 to $1.8 trillion. The biggest deals of the decade included Philip Morris's purchase of Kraft for $12.6 billion and Kohlberg Kravis Roberts's leveraged buyout of RJR Nabisco for $24.7 billion.

Borrowed money became a popular means of financing corporate takeovers because *if* a company is highly profitable, the after-tax cost of debt is typically cheaper than the cost of equity financing. For example, if a corporation is in the 34 percent income tax bracket and borrows money at a 12 percent annual rate of interest, the after-tax cost of debt is $(1 - .34) \times 12\% = 7.92\%$. The return that stockholders will require to keep their money invested in the firm will depend on the level of interest rates in the economy and the risk associated with a particular company's stock, together with the riskiness of the stock market as a whole. The rate of return on a long-term U.S. government bond, considered virtually risk-free in terms of default risk, has been around 9 percent on an annual basis. The added-on amount, called the market risk premium, associated with general market riskiness, has historically ranged from 4 percent to 7 percent per year. If an individual company's stock is perceived to be riskier than the market as a whole, an additional risk premium will be required as well. Thus, since it is not tax deductible, the cost of equity capital can easily exceed 15 percent on an annual basis.

Although debt may be a relatively inexpensive source of funds for a firm, it may increase the risk of bankruptcy. If a company's stock does not yield the rate of return required by the stockholders, the price of the stock will very likely fall, but this situation does not force a firm into bankruptcy. On the other hand, if a company cannot meet the required payments for its debt, holders of the firm's debt can force it to resort to a declaration of bankruptcy.

One measure of the amount of corporate leverage is the ratio of debt to the market value of equity. This ratio reached its highest value, 106 percent, in 1974, as a result of generally low prices for stocks. As a result of rapidly increasing stock prices in the 1980s, this ratio fell to 75 percent in spite of the increased amount of corporate borrowing. Moreover, this ratio is about twice as large for similar foreign companies. Nevertheless, the increases in leverage for some U.S. companies do appear to be impacting the bankruptcy statistics: in 1984, 54 large companies defaulted on $11 billion of debt, whereas in 1987, 87 companies defaulted on $21.4 billion of debt. Some note-worthy LBOs that eventually led to Chapter 11 bankruptcy protection filings included that of Revco, Hillsborough Holdings (involving an LBO of Jim Walter Corporation), and Dart Drug Stores.

On the other hand, an increase in the percentage of a firm's financing from debt may have positive effects in addition to its lower component cost. Obligations for the repayment of debt and interest payments place pressure on firm management to control cost and carefully plan corporate strategy; the margin for error diminishes as leverage increases. A company may become more innovative and more profitable as a result. In fact, some LBOs, including Allegheny Ludlum, Metromedia, and Wilson Sporting Goods were quite prof-itable.

Thus, while a high amount of corporate leverage may result in a lower cost of capital and substantially higher earnings per share for stockholders, it frequently also means "betting the company." A successful future for a highly leveraged company requires astute management at the very minimum.

■ ■ ■ ■

References: "All That Leverage Comes Home to Roost," *Business Week* (September 10, 1990), pp. 76–77; "The Best and Worst Deals of the '80s," *Business Week* (January 15, 1990), pp. 52–62; "Learning to Live With Leverage," *Business Week* (November 7, 1988), pp. 138–143; and "What does Equity Financing Really Cost?" *Business Week* (November 7, 1988), pp. 146, 148. The risk premium attached to the stock of an individual company will increase as the percent of the value of the company financed by debt increases, all other factors remaining the same.

necessary to modify capital project analyses to take explicit account of the problem of risk. In the following chapter, several approaches to handling the problem of decision making under risk will be discussed.

■ ■ ■ ■ ■ ■ ■ ■ ## SUMMARY

Project Analysis and Capital Budgeting

In this chapter we have examined the application of interest and discount rate methodologies to managerial decisions concerning capital projects or new investments. We defined *capital budgeting* as the process by which a firm's managers determine how to allocate investment expenditures among alternative projects. The evaluation of individual investment undertakings, or *capital project analysis,* was shown to be a major part of the capital budgeting process.

The concept of *equivalency* was introduced to show that a present amount of money is equal in value to a discounted future amount. The present value of an amount received *n* years in the future, we saw, can be found by the formula

$$PV = \frac{FV_n}{(1 + r)^n},$$

where *r* is the applicable discount rate (a target yield or rate of return on similar alternative investments). Tables of *present value factors* were introduced to simplify the mathematics of the discounting process.

Application of the preceding concepts led us to the conclusion that the present value of an anticipated stream of net receipts generated by a capital project is something less than the additive amount of such receipts. In particular the present value is the discounted value of the stream. We argued that a given capital project is *acceptable* when adjustments are made for depreciation and salvage value as long as such a *discounted stream of net cash flows is at least equal to the price of the project.* The *net present value* (*NPV*) of the project (*PV* of net receipts minus project price) would thus be equal to or greater than zero. This criterion was related to an alternative statement: namely, that the yield on the project's price, or its *internal rate of return* (*IRR*), should be at least equal to the marginal cost of capital for the firm. A simple capital project analysis involving a coin-operated car wash (Clickwash, Inc.) was introduced as an example of the steps management must go through to make an accept-or-reject decision on a new undertaking.

Later in the chapter, we discussed the *capital rationing* aspect of the capital budgeting process. Here, we examined the special problem of allocating a limited amount of investment dollars to various feasible combinations of capital projects. The net present value approach was extended to this setting, and a methodology for identifying the combination of projects producing the greatest aggregate *NPV* was developed. The simple methodology we employed is usable for projects with different prices and equal planned project lives but must be modified somewhat if projects with unequal lives are being analyzed.

Finally, we introduced the notion of the firm's *marginal cost of capital* and its marginal cost of capital curve. The equilibrium quantity of investment and marginal cost of capital was defined by the intersection of the firm's *MCC* curve with its *IRR* curve.

This chapter did not deal with the problem of differences in the risk associated with dissimilar capital projects. For example, in the case of our hypothetical firm, Clickwash, we treated the flows of returns from investments in endeavors (muffler shop, pizzeria, donut shop) unfamiliar to the firm as being either risk free or equal in risk to undertakings (an additional laundromat) that are thoroughly covered by management's prior experience. It is unlikely that such a view would be taken by managers in real-world capital budgeting situations. Generally, managers will attempt to take into account differences in the risks associated with alternative capital projects. In Chapter 14, we will examine some methodologies that allow for comparison of projects with unequal risk.

▪ ▪ ▪ ▪ ▪ ▪ ▪ ▪ ▪ ▪ ▪ ▪ ▪ **Questions** ▪ ▪ ▪ ▪ ▪ ▪ ▪ ▪ ▪ ▪ ▪ ▪ ▪

1. From an economist's point of view, would you characterize capital budgeting decisions as long- or short-run decisions? Why?
2. Which of the following would you include as part of the price of a capital project undertaken to expand a company's production of minicomputers? (For each item you *exclude*, give a brief explanation of why it should not be considered a part of the project price.)
   a. Production labor for minicomputers
   b. Product development costs
   c. Interest on construction loan for new building to house project
   d. Components for assembly of minicomputers
   e. Architectural fees for new building
   f. Present value of expanded working capital requirements
   g. Cost of fuel to heat new building
   h. New machine tools for manufacture of minicomputer parts.
3. What is the definition of the net present value (*NPV*) of a capital project? What *NPV* rule should be followed in classifying capital projects as acceptable or unacceptable?
4. How would you define the internal rate of return of a capital project?
5. A certain capital project has anticipated net cash receipts of $180,000 per year for ten years and a salvage value of $20,000. What is the maximum price a firm should pay for this project if the appropriate discount rate is 12 percent?
6. If a capital project has estimated net receipts of $8,000 per year and a life of 15 years with no salvage value, what would be its *NPV* if its price were $54,487 and the applicable discount rate were 9 percent?
7. What is the IRR (internal rate of return) of the preceding project?
8. Briefly explain how a firm's managers can use the *NPV* approach to allocate a limited capital budget among a number of acceptable capital projects, each having the same life and price.
9. Suppose a firm has a given-size capital budget. Explain how the best combination of a number of acceptable capital projects with *different* prices but the *same* lives can be determined using the *NPV* approach.

■ ■ ■ ■ ■ ■ ■ ■ ■ ■ ■ ■ ■ ■ **Problems** ■ ■ ■ ■ ■ ■ ■ ■ ■ ■ ■ ■ ■ ■

1. A project has an anticipated stream of annual net receipts of $23,500. Its life is 12 years. No salvage value is expected at the end of the 12 years. Compute the net present value of the project if its price is $130,000 and the applicable discount rate is each of the following:
   a. 6 percent
   b. 9 percent
   c. 12 percent

2. Gretna Corporation is about to sell some used equipment to Allied Leasing. Allied has offered the following two payment schemes:
   a. $100,000 now and $250,000 at the end of five years.
   b. $100,000 now, $50,000 at the end of two years, and $215,000 at the end of eight years.

   If the appropriate discount rate for either transaction is 6 percent, which would be the better of the two alternatives for Gretna? Why? Show your work.

3. In the preceding problem, what would you advise Gretna's management to ask for if it desired to settle the transaction this year for a single cash payment?

4. Jayne Corporation has decided to undertake a capital project that has a life of eight years and estimated annual net inflows of $27,460. At a discount rate of 6 percent, what is the present value of the eight-year receipts stream?

5. Hamstrung, Incorporated, is contemplating an investment in a new food processing plant. Management's best estimate of the project's price is $620,000. The plant will have an indefinite life, but management expects to divest it at the end of 12 years at an estimated after-tax salvage value of $273,000. Annual net inflows from operations are expected to be $60,000. Is the project acceptable at a discount rate of 9 percent? Why or why not? What would happen if a discount rate of 6 percent were applied to the project?

6. Pickadilly Peppers is trying to decide whether to invest in a new cannery, to set up a wholesaling operation that would eliminate intermediaries currently selling its product, or to computerize several older plants. All three alternatives are viewed as having the same project life of 15 years. However, different project prices are applicable to each, and each has a different expected stream of annual net inflows. The firm's managers believe that a discount rate of 6 percent is appropriate for evaluating the alternatives. Data are as follows:

Project	Price	Annual Net Inflows
(a) New Cannery	$190,000	$20,000
(b) Wholesale Operation	168,000	18,000
(c) Plant Computerization	159,000	17,000

After examining the project prices, management finds it has a sufficient capital budget to undertake two of the projects. Assuming that the cash flows from the projects are independent of one another (i.e., that undertaking one of the projects will have no effect on the returns from another), which two projects should be undertaken?

7. All of the following projects have an initial cost (project price) of $87,500. Which are acceptable at a discount rate of 9 percent?

   a. Purchase of a vintage car that can be sold for $120,000 at the end of five years.

   b. Investment in a restaurant partnership that will return you a net inflow of $5,000 per year for 10 years and will provide a buy-out of your share for $100,000 at the end of ten years.

   c. Purchase of a piece of machinery that will generate net inflows of $18,000 per year for eight years and have an after-tax salvage value of $7,000 at the end of the period.

8. The following is a list of four projects that Capital Corp. must choose from for the coming year:

Project	Project Price	Annual Net Inflows	Internal Rate of Return
A	$700,000	$118,861	11%
B	670,000	109,039	10%
C	184,000	32,549	12%
D	273,000	48,305	12%

John Smart, a junior vice-president of the company, has argued that Projects A, C, and D should be accepted, since they all have higher internal rates of return than Project B and their prices sum to less than the capital budgeting constraint of $1,700,000. Jane Cranston, a consultant to the company, politely suggests that Smart is not so smart and that Projects A, B, and D should be undertaken. If the appropriate rate of discount for all four projects is 9 percent and each has a life of ten years, who is right—Smart or Cranston? (Assume no salvage values.)

9. The managers of Zeron Corporation have determined that their firm's optimal capital structure is 40 percent debt financing and 60 percent equity. The current interest rate is 14 percent for borrowers like Zeron, and the company's shareholders expect a return on equity of 16 percent. The company's corporate income tax rate is 40 percent, and interest is a deductible expense.

   a. What is Zeron Corp's marginal cost of capital?

   b. If Zeron is considering an investment project with a life of ten years, an annual net flow of benefits of $470,000, a project cost of $2,500,000, and no salvage value, what advice would you give to management?

10. Lagrange Chicken Farm is considering the installation of new auto-mated chicken feeders. The feeders are more efficient and will reduce wastage of chicken feed. The new feeders will cost $160,000 and will have an expected life of five years with a salvage value of $10,000. They are expected to result in a cost savings of $30,000 a year. The old feeders were purchased five years ago at a cost of $65,000 and have been depreciated on a straight line basis with an expected life of ten years and a salvage value of $5,000. Their current market value is $40,000. The firm's marginal cost of capital is 12 percent, and its marginal tax rate is 40 percent. The firm will also be able to get an investment tax credit equal to 5 percent of the cost of the new feeders. (Do not adjust the cost basis of the feeders to reflect the tax credit when calculating depreciation.)

a. What is the initial cash outlay required for the new machine?
b. What are the annual after-tax cash flows from the new feeders in years one through four?
c. Should the company purchase the new feeders? Why or why not?
d. Suppose that the cost saving on the new feeders will be $30,000 the first year but will increase by 10 percent a year each year for the next four years. What is the *NPV* of the new feeders now?

The following problem can be solved with Decision Assistant.

11. SA Service Bureau, Incorporated, is a small data processing service bureau that has experienced rapid but sound growth over the past ten years. SA Service Bureau has just signed a new major customer with such a large volume of payroll transactions that SA would be required to expand its data processing facilities. The new contract is expected to produce incremental billings (revenues) of $50,000 per year for the next five years.

   Bill Lane, chief financial officer for SA, has asked the purchasing department and the data processing department to work together to determine several different approaches to meeting the new processing requirements. Helen Trask, a financial analyst working for Bill Lane, has been provided with all the information generated by the purchasing and data processing departments. The data follows:

   Expansion Plan 1: This plan represents a "modular" approach to the problem of the expansion. A new minicomputer, completely compat-ible with the existing hardware and software, would be purchased and dedicated to processing the new client's data. Data for this plan are

Initial cash outlay:	$135,000
Estimated annual costs:	15,000
Estimated project life:	5 years

Expansion Plan 2: This plan utilizes the existing minicomputer and upgrades it (more memory, storage capacity, etc.) to perform the increased workload. Additional personnel will also be hired to run a second shift. Data associated with this plan are

Initial cash outlay:	$75,000
Estimated annual costs:	25,000
Estimated project life:	5 years

Use the Net Present Value, Future Value, IRR tool in the *Managerial Economics Decision Assistant* to complete the following.

a. Assume you are helping Helen Trask and prepare an analysis of the two projects from an economic and financial point of view (calculate the Net Present Value and the Internal Rate of Return). SA Service Bureau uses a 10 percent discount rate. (Do not consider data processing strategy, as this will be discussed and decided on by Mr. Lane.)
b. Using a 12 percent discount rate, recalculate the Net Present Value for the two projects.
c. Using an 8 percent discount rate, recalculate the Net Present Value for the two projects.

■ ■ ■ ■ ■ ■ ■ ■ ■ ■ ■ **Selected References** ■ ■ ■ ■ ■ ■ ■ ■ ■ ■ ■

Engler, George N. *Business Financial Management.* Dallas: Business Publications, Inc., 1975, Chapters 5 and 6.

Gitman, Lawrence J. *Principles of Managerial Finance,* 6th ed. New York: Harper and Row, 1991, Chapters 9, 11, and 12.

Grant, Eugene L., and W. Grant Ireson. *Principles of Engineering Economy,* 4th ed. New York: The Ronald Press, 1964, Chapters 3–9.

Mao, James C. T. *Corporate Financial Decisions.* Palo Alto, Cal.: Pavan, 1976, Chapters 7 and 8.

Moyer, R. Charles, James R. McGuigan, and William J. Kretlow. *Contemporary Financial Management,* 4th ed. St. Paul: West, 1990, Chapters 9, 10, 12, and 13.

Neveu, Raymond R. *Fundamentals of Managerial Finance,* 3d ed. Cincinnati: South-Western, 1989, Chapters 9, 10, and 14.

Rao, Ramesh K. S. *Fundamentals of Financial Management.* New York: Macmillan, 1989, Chapters 10 and 11.

Ross, Marc. "Capital Budgeting Practices of Twelve Large Manufacturers." *Financial Management* 15, no. 4 (Winter 1986), pp. 15–22.

Taylor, George A. *Managerial and Engineering Economy.* New York: D. Van Nostrand, 1980, Chapters 7–9.

Weston, J. Fred, and Eugene F. Brigham. *Essentials of Managerial Finance.* Chicago: The Dryden Press, 1990, Chapters 15–17.

Appendix 13

Compounding and Discounting

COMPOUND INTEREST

The process of determining the amount to which a given sum will accumulate over a specified number of periods of time at a stated rate of interest per period is known as *compounding*. An example of a compound interest problem would be the determination of the amount to which a $1,000 savings deposit will accumulate in ten years if 6 percent interest is added to the account at the end of each year. We can analyze this problem as follows:

		Account Balance	*Interest Earned = .06 × Previous Account Balance*
Initial Deposit:		$1,000.00	
Amount at End of Year:	1	1,060.00	$ 60.00
	2	1,123.60	63.60
	3	1,191.02	67.42
	4	1,262.48	71.46
	5	1,338.23	75.75
	6	1,418.52	80.29
	7	1,503.63	85.11
	8	1,593.85	90.22
	9	1,689.48	95.63
	10	1,790.85	101.37

If the account is left untouched and each year's interest is compounded on the previous year's ending balance (including interest), the ten-year result will be $1,790.85. Each entry in the "Interest Earned" column is .06 times the previous year-end balance; for example, year 5 will yield $75.75 —.06 × $1,262.48, the ending balance for year 4.

It is easy to derive a formula for the amount that the $1,000.00 will accumulate to at the end of year 10. Denote FV (future value) as the account balance at the end of a given period. For the end of year 1, we have

$$FV_1 = PV(1.06),$$

where PV is the initial deposit (a present value). At the end of year 2, FV will be increased by 6 percent so that

$$FV_2 = FV_1(1.06) = [PV(1.06)](1.06) = PV(1.06)^2.$$

At the end of year 3, we will have

$$FV_3 = FV_2(1.06) = [PV(1.06)^2](1.06) = PV(1.06)^3.$$

For each period that we compound the interest, the exponent of the above expression will rise one digit. Thus for ten years we have

$$FV_{10} = PV(1.06)^{10},$$

or

$$FV_{10} = \$1,000(1.06)^{10} = \$1,000(1.7909) = \$1,790.90,$$

a rounded-off version of the answer we obtained in the preceding calculations.

Compound interest tables are commonly used to determine future values, as stated previously. Such tables contain the values of the term $(1 + r)^n$ where r is the rate of interest and n is the number of periods the interest is compounded. In the preceding example, $(1 + r)^n = (1 + .06)^{10} = 1.7909$. The number 1.7909 is called a compound interest factor, CIF, and it is the amount to which one dollar will accumulate in ten years with interest annually compounded at 6 percent. To find the future value of $1,000.00 compounded at 6 percent for ten years, we simply multiply the CIF for a 6 percent interest rate and ten-year term (CIF 6%, 10) times the present amount ($PV = \$1,000$):

$$
\begin{aligned}
FV_{10} &= PV(CIF\ 6\%,\ 10) \\
&= \$1,000(1.7909) = \$1,790.90.
\end{aligned}
$$

Table B–1 in the Interest Factor Tables at the end of the book provides compound interest factors. To use the table, simply look up the CIF for the number of periods that interest will be compounded and multiply the factor times the principal or present value. The result will be the future amount. Thus, if we wished to determine the future value of $25,000 compounded at 9 percent annually for 18 years, we would find

$$FV_{18} = \$25,000(CIF\ 9\%,\ 18)$$
$$= \$25,000(4.7171) = \$117,927.50.$$

■ ■ ■ ■ ■ ■ ■ ■ PRESENT VALUE AND DISCOUNTING

The present value of some amount to be received at a specific future date is equal to the present amount that would accumulate to the future amount by the date in question at some appropriate rate of interest. The rate of interest applied to such calculations is called the *discount rate*, since the present value will be smaller than the future value by a specific percentage per year.

Discounting, then, is the reverse of compounding. To understand this, ask how much you would be willing to give for $1,790.90 received ten years from now if you expect you can easily make 6 percent interest per year on any present amount you have on hand. From our above discussion of compounding, it is clear that $1,000 will accumulate to the sum of $1,790.90 in ten years if 6 percent interest is compounded annually. Thus the discounted value of $1,790.90 received ten years from now is $1,000.00, and 6 percent is the discount rate.

Alternatively, from our formula for compounding, we know

$$FV_{10} = PV(1 + r)^{10}.$$

Therefore

$$PV = \frac{FV_{10}}{(1 + r)^{10}} = FV_{10}\left[\frac{1}{(1 + r)^{10}}\right].$$

The term in brackets is the *present value factor, PVF*. For the preceding problem, we can write

$$PV = FV_{10}(PVF\ 6\%,\ 10),$$

where, for the term in brackets, $r = .06$ and $n = 10$. This factor appears in Table B–3 in the Interest Factor Tables and its value is 0.5584. Thus, for a future value of $1,790.90, we have

$$PV = \$1,790.90(0.5584) = \$1,000.04 \approx \$1,000.$$

The slight error is due to the rounding of the present value factor, which is more accurately 0.558394.

The notion of present value is extremely important in managerial economics and finance, since project decisions generally involve evaluations of benefits or receipts that are generated at some future date or over some period of years in the future. For further discussion of this point, see the relevant sections within this chapter.

■ ■ ■ ■ ■ ■ ■ ■ ■   ANNUITIES

An annuity is a fixed sum received at the end of each period for some specified number of periods in the future. The *compound* value of an annuity is the amount to which such period-end payments would accumulate if each payment were left in an account at a specified rate of interest compounded annually. For example, if you are to receive an annuity of $1,000 for ten years and you leave all of the payments in an account with 6 percent interest compounded annually, at the end of the tenth year you will have $13,180.80. The compound value is determined as follows, where A is the amount of each period-end payment and n is the number of periods:

Year 1	Year 2	Year 3	Year 10
$FV_a = A$	$A + A(1 + r)$	$A + [A + A(1 + r)](1 + r)$	
or	or	or	$A[(1 + r)^0 + (1 + r)^1$
$FV_a = A(1 + r)^0$	$A[(1 + r)^0 + (1 + r)^1]$	$A[(1 + r)^0 + (1 + r)^1 + (1 + r)^2]$	$+ \cdots + (1 + r)^9]$

Therefore the general formula is

$$FV_{a_n} = A[(1 + r)^0 + (1 + r)^1 + \cdots + (1 + r)^{n-1}].$$

Again, tables have been developed for the term in brackets, which is the compound value factor for an annuity, CVF_a. For 6 percent and ten years, CVF_a 6%, 10 equals 13.181 (see Appendix B, Table B–2). For our $1,000 annuity, we can write

$$FV_{a_{10}} = \$1,000(CVF_a \text{ 6\%, 10})$$
$$= \$1,000(13.181) = \$13,181.$$

The *present value of an annuity* is the amount that, if received today, would accumulate to the same amount as an annuity received for a specified number of periods with interest compounded at the end of each period. With a 6 percent interest rate, the present value of the $1,000 per-year annuity discussed previously is $7,360.27, which is its future compound value, $13,181, discounted at the given rate of interest. From our formula for the compound value of an annuity, we derive the formula for the present value of an annuity, PV_a, in the following way.

We know that the present value of the annuity is the same as the PV of $13,181 received ten years from now, or

$$PV_a = \frac{FV_a}{(1 + r)^n} = \frac{A[(1 + r)^0 + (1 + r)^1 + \cdots + (1 + r)^{n-1}]}{(1 + r)^n}$$

$$= A\left[\frac{(1 + r)^0}{(1 + r)^{10}} + \frac{(1 + r)^1}{(1 + r)^{10}} + \cdots + \frac{(1 + r)^9}{(1 + r)^{10}}\right]$$

$$= A\left[\frac{1}{(1 + r)^{10}} + \frac{1}{(1 + r)^9} + \cdots + \frac{1}{(1 + r)}\right].$$

The term in brackets in the last expression is the present value factor for an annuity, and its general formula is

$$PVF_a = \left[\frac{1}{(1 + r)^n} + \frac{1}{(1 + r)^{n-1}} + \cdots + \frac{1}{(1 + r)}\right].$$

Table B–4 in the Interest Factor Tables contains such factors for up to 60 payment periods. For the present problem, we have PVF_a (6%, 10) = 7.3601. Therefore PV_a = $1,000 ($PVF_a$ 6% 10) = $7,360.10, which is the same (except for rounding) as the present value of $13,181 received ten years in the future where the discount rate is 6 percent.

In capital project analysis, the present value of an annuity approach can be used to determine the present value of project benefits or inflows when a certain fixed dollar return per period is expected to be generated by the project for a specified number of periods in the future. For a direct application of this method, review the case of Clickwash, Incorporated, in Chapter 13.

■ ■ ■ ■ ■ ■ ■ ■ ■ ■ ■ ■ ■   **Problems**   ■ ■ ■ ■ ■ ■ ■ ■ ■ ■ ■ ■ ■

1. To what amount will $20,000 left untouched in an account accumulate at the end of 13 years if 9 percent interest is added to the account at the end of each year?
2. What is the present value of a single payment of $187,000 received eight years in the future if the discount rate is 12 percent?
3. Suppose your company puts $2,000 per year into an annuity for you at the end of each year and you are guaranteed to receive 6 percent per annum interest on all funds left in your annuity account. How much

will your account balance be at the end of six years if you are not permitted to make any withdrawals?

4. A retiring executive of Pygmalion Enterprises has offered to sell her 20-year annuity back to the company for cash. She or her survivors were to receive $18,000 per year at year-end over the 20-year period. If the company normally applies a 6 percent discount rate to such transactions, how much will it be willing to pay for the annuity?

5. Barclay Concrete Company owes its supplier, Ace Cement, $172,000 for trade credit extended to Barclay's account for cement purchases. Barclay has had cash flow problems and cannot pay off the account with current revenues. Ace's management has offered to convert the account to a long-term debt, extending a ten-year balloon note at 9 percent compound interest per year. If the principal and interest are not due until the end of the ten years, how much will Barclay have to pay Ace when the note comes due?

6. A given investment project is expected to yield $10,000 in net receipts per year for each of ten years following its undertaking. If the discount rate is 12 percent, what is the present value of the net receipts stream?

7. You are offered a risk-free investment that you can sell at the end of three years for $14,000. You know that you can easily and safely earn 6 percent interest on your funds. What is the maximum amount you would be willing to pay for the investment?

Risk in Project Analysis

Chapter 13 introduced some tools for the analysis of capital projects or alternative investment possibilities. Throughout that chapter we assumed that the decision maker was certain about the outcome of each project that was evaluated. Combinations of projects were also compared without considering the possibility that the success of an individual undertaking might depend on whether the undertaking was combined with a related project.

Our task in the present chapter is to analyze the problem of risk in capital projects or investments in general and to describe a workable approach to decision making under risk. We begin with discussions of the nature of risk and the application of both economic theory and statistical methods to the evaluation of risky situations. A practical example from real estate development is used to introduce the notion that risk can be viewed as the variance of a probability distribution of uncertain outcomes. The chapter moves from a two-project, single-payoff analysis toward situations that are more complex in terms of cash flows over time and interrelationships between projects. Finally, we discuss a practical approach to decision making under risk.

■ ■ ■ ■ ■ ■ ■ ■ CERTAINTY VERSUS RISK

A situation is certain when there is absolutely no doubt as to its outcome. Most people would regard the purchase of a certificate of deposit (CD) at a bank as an investment characterized by certainty. It is clear to the decision maker who has made the purchase that a given return will be received if the CD is held to maturity. A situation is characterized as *risky* when there is some doubt regarding the occurrence of its expected outcome. Thus a person who invests in a restaurant may expect to receive a given return from the investment if the restaurant is successful in attracting enough customers and if costs of operation do not change. Clearly, this type of investment is something different from the purchase of a CD. It is a risky alternative, since the decision maker is faced with some doubt about the outcome of the decision.

Fundamentally, the analysis of risk has to do with the comparison of alternatives having outcomes that are certain with alternatives having outcomes about which there is doubt. Differences in the degree of riskiness of various alternatives can be analyzed using statistical methods. The statistical approach will be outlined after we discuss what economic theory has to say about risk and human behavior.

■ ■ ■ ■ ■ ■ ■ ■ RISK IN ECONOMIC ANALYSIS

A **risk-averse** investor is one that given a choice between two investments with the same expected return will always prefer the less risky one.

To analyze risk from an economic point of view, we must first make a behavioral assumption about the decision maker who is confronted with alternatives of unequal risk. In project analysis the assumption usually made is that the decision maker is **risk averse.** Simply stated, this means that the decision maker will prefer a situation that promises a guaranteed or certain return of a given amount of money to a situation in which the receipt of the same amount of money is less certain. From our preceding example, a risk averter would choose to invest, say, $5,000 in a certificate of deposit rather than in a restaurant if both investments were expected to yield a net return of $2,000 at the end of five years. That is because the return from the CD is certain and the return from the restaurant is not. Whenever the amount invested, the term of the investment (the time elapsed to maturity or final receipt of returns), and the expected amount of return are identical, the risk averter will choose the certain investment over the risky investment.

A **risk seeker** is an investor that given a choice between two investments with the same expected return will prefer the riskier one.

A **risk-neutral** investor is indifferent between two investments with the same expected return, regardless of their risk.

Economic theory also recognizes the possibility that a decision maker may be a risk seeker or have a neutral attitude toward risk. If the decision maker in the previous example were a **risk seeker,** the restaurant investment would be chosen, even though the money return expected from it was the same as that for the CD. A **risk-neutral** decision maker would be indifferent between the two alternatives. It has been argued that very wealthy decision makers (individuals *or* firms) will be risk neutral when confronted with investment alternatives involving amounts of money that are small in comparison with their wealth. This would follow from the notion that the differences in the outcomes that are attributable to riskiness are virtually inconsequential to the wealthy decision maker. In the discussion that follows, we focus mainly on the risk-averse decision maker, since risk seeking is viewed as a relatively uncommon attitude in project analysis and since risk analysis is unnecessary if the decision maker is risk neutral.

■ ■ ■ ■ ■ ■ ■ ■ RISK-RETURN INDIFFERENCE CURVES

A risk-return indifference curve shows combinations of risk and return that are equally attractive to a given investor. Figure 14–1 illustrates two risk-return indifference curves. We assume that risk is measurable and that it increases along the vertical axis. (The question of how risk can be measured is taken up in a later section.) For the moment we will use the numbers 1, 2, 3, and 4 to indicate increasing levels of risk. The horizontal axis of the diagram shows money returns expected by the investor. A single risk-return indifference curve traces out combinations of risk and expected money return that will make the investor equally happy. Consider curve I_5 in Figure 14–1, for example. It indicates that the investor would be indifferent between combination A (which consists of zero risk and a return of $1,000) and combination B (which consists of a risky return of $1,750). The risk-return indifference curve slopes upward to the right because the risk-averse investor will be indifferent toward higher risk only if he or she expects a greater return to be associated with it. The curvature of the indifference curve reflects one further assumption—that as risk increases, progressively larger increments in expected return will be re-

Figure 14–1   The Risk-Return Indifference Curve Concept

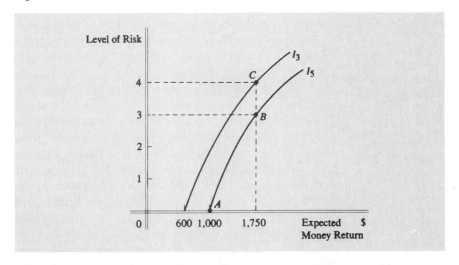

Risk-return indifference curve I_3 is less desirable to the investor than I_5, since each combination of risk and return on I_3 is equal to a certain return of only $600, which is much less than the certain return of $1,000 associated with I_5 combinations.

quired to offset given increments in risk (in order to keep the investor equally happy).

In Figure 14–1, combinations of risk and return that lie on risk-return indifference curve I_3 are less satisfying to the investor than those that lie on I_5. Why? Clearly, it is because the former all involve either higher risk for any given return or a lower return for any given level of risk. For example, point C, which corresponds to a return of $1,750, is less satisfying to the investor than is point B. This is because the return associated with C is the same as with B, but B is on a lower level of risk.

In general, for a risk-return indifference curve diagram such as Figure 14–1, we view the quadrant as being filled with indifference curves such as I_5 and I_3, all of which are nonintersecting. Return decreases and risk increases as we move toward the northwest area of the quadrant, so that less desirable indifference curves lie to the northwest of any given point (risk-return combination), while more desirable indifference curves lie to the southeast. The risk-return indifference curve is a concept similar to the equal-product isoquants employed in production analysis (Chapter 4). However, risk-return indifference curves are concave toward the X or "return" axis, since at the margin the decision maker's willingness to accept additional risk for an additional dollar's worth of return diminishes.

If we consider a whole family of risk-return indifference curves for a given investment decision maker, we can conclude that for any amount of expected money return, the risk averter will be less happy the greater the level of risk. This is shown in Figure 14–2. Note that the investor regards point A on I_5 as a risk-return combination equivalent to a certain return of $1,000. If, however, we consider a combination involving more risk than level 4 for a $1,300 return, the investor is seen to be on a lower risk-return indifference curve (the *certain return*, which is viewed as equally desirable to the risky return, *falls*). Thus, points B, C, and D represent successively less desirable risk-return combinations for an expected money return of $1,300.

If we retain the assumption of risk aversion, then, we can conclude that the economic nature of risk is that its presence *lessens the desirability* of a given undertaking or investment project. Further, the more risky a given undertaking, the less desirable it will be in comparison to other alternatives having the same expected money outcome. At this point, however, we cannot go further until we have a way to measure risk or to differentiate among risky undertakings those that are more risky and those that are less so. It is to this matter that we now turn.

■ ■ ■ ■ ■ ■ ■ ■ ■ **PROBABILITY AND UNCERTAINTY**

To measure risk in a meaningful way, we must apply the tools of statistics known as *probability analysis*. In probability analysis the term *event* is used

Figure 14–2   A Family of Risk-Return Indifference Curves

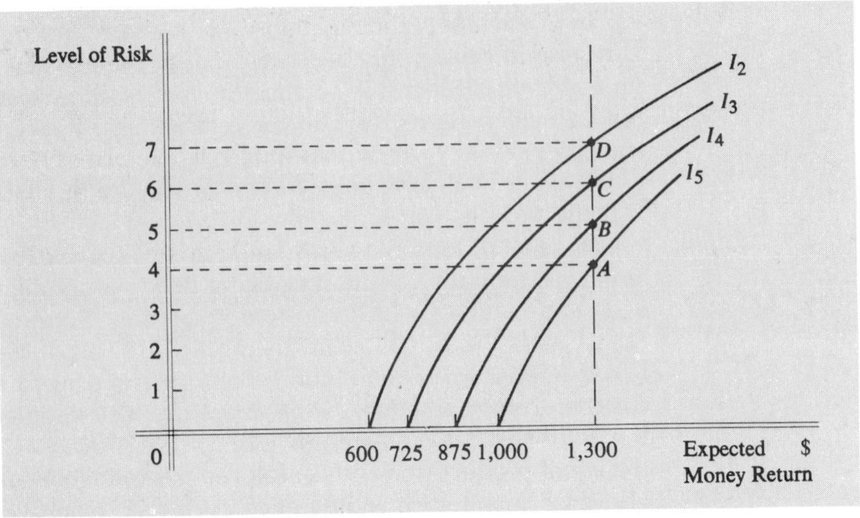

Assuming the investor is risk averse, higher risk levels associated with a given expected return yield less and less satisfaction. Thus, for an expected return of $1,300, the investor's satisfaction decreases progressively from point *A* through points *B*, *C*, and *D*.

to designate an outcome. The probability of a particular event is a numerical value measuring the uncertainty that the event will occur. More specifically it is the proportion of times under identical circumstances that the event can be expected to occur, or

$$P(E) = \frac{\text{number of times event occurs}}{\text{number of times situation is repeated}}.$$

If an event is certain to occur, its probability is one. If it can never occur, its probability is zero. An event's probability can be viewed as the *odds* that the event will occur or the percentage of times it will take place when a given set of circumstances is repeated many times. Running an experiment where a situation is repeated many times is a way to determine empirically the probability of a specific event. However, it is also possible to determine an event's probability deductively if enough information is available. For this, we need a few more definitions.

Each event in a listing of all the possible outcomes of a given situation is called an *elementary event*. For example, in picking a card from a deck of 52 cards, each card is an elementary event. A *composite event* consists of a number of elementary events, and an *event set* consists of all the elementary events that satisfy a particular outcome. Thus we can restate our formula for the probability of an event as

$$P(E) = \frac{\text{number of elementary events in event set}}{\text{number of equally likely elementary events}}.$$

From the preceding, we can see that the probability of picking a two of spades from a deck of 52 cards is 1/52, but the probability of picking a deuce is 4/52, since the event set includes the four elementary events: two of spades, two of hearts, two of diamonds, and two of clubs. For a deck of 52 cards, the sum of the probabilities of all the cards (elementary events) is one (there are 52 elementary events, each having a probability of 1/52). In general, any time a listing of all possible events includes every conceivable outcome—one of which *must* occur—the sum of the probabilities of all the elementary events will be one.

There are many situations in which probabilities can be ascertained empirically or through experimentation. The card-picking examples are cases in point. For the composite event, "pick a deuce," a deck of cards can be shuffled and a card picked. This can be repeated a very large number of times, and the more the experiment is run, the closer the ratio of deuces picked to the total number of cards picked will approach 4/52. It is also true that in many cases probabilities can be ascertained logically. Again, card picking suffices as an example. Since we know there are 52 possible elementary events, four of which constitute the event set "pick a deuce," the odds (or probability) of picking a deuce equal 4/52.

When the probability of events in an uncertain situation cannot be ascertained either empirically or logically, we enter the realm of *subjective probability*. A subjective probability is simply a probability value *assigned* to an event by an investigator. It is a judgmental estimate, rather than strictly an empirical one. Subjective probability is used in the analysis of investment projects, since decision makers frequently must rely on expert opinion (their own personal judgment, perhaps) regarding the likelihood of any particular event. For example, the decision maker may be able to estimate how successful in terms of dollar return a project will be, *given* various rates of growth in personal income for a particular region or state; but there may be a great deal of uncertainty about the occurrence of each possible rate of growth in income. An approach that employs the subjective probabilities of the possible rates of growth in income may be used to determine both a weighted average outcome for the project and a measure of its riskiness. In the following section, we provide an example of the probability approach to project analysis under risk.

■ ■ ■ ■ ■ ■ ■ ■ ■   APPLICATION OF PROBABILITY ANALYSIS TO RISK

Statistical analysis of risk becomes quite complicated when the time horizon for a payoff or return from an investment is long or when alternatives consisting of multiple-project combinations are being considered. However, we can gain considerable insight into the application of probability to risk situations from a simple example involving a choice between two investments—each of which has a single cash payoff that is received one year in the future. To illustrate, we choose an example from real estate investment.

Suppose the Texland Corporation has obtained similar tracts of land in Houston and Dallas at identical cost and is considering subdivision and marketing alternatives for next year. Management has information indicating that the cost of subdividing and marketing the land will be the same in each city and that under even the most pessimistic assumptions, either project will yield a positive net present value. However, the firm's financial condition and resource base are such that it cannot develop both tracts in the coming year.

From past experience Texland's managers are confident that the returns from either project will depend on the rate of growth of personal income in Texas during the year. Their estimates of the cash inflow generated by each alternative appear in Table 14–1. Texland's managers do not believe that the rate of income growth in the state will fall below 6 percent or exceed 14 percent, but they are uncertain about the probabilities of occurrence of various growth rates within this range. As the table shows, the potentially higher payoffs associated with the Dallas project are attractive, but it is clear from the payoff estimates that the Dallas alternative will yield less than the Houston alternative if the rate of growth of personal income is relatively low.

To help analyze the growth rate problem, Texland has employed an economist from Austin Commerce College who has provided the following subjective probabilities for the growth rates in Table 14–1.

Rate of Growth in State Personal Income	Probability of Occurrence
6%	0.15
8%	0.20
10%	0.30
12%	0.20
14%	0.15

Texland's management then used the preceding probabilities to construct the payoff tables shown in Table 14–2.

The expected value of an investment is found by multiplying each possible outcome by the probability that it will occur, then summing these values.

For each project an **expected value** is calculated. The expected value is a weighted average of the possible outcomes, and it is obtained by multiplying each outcome by the probability associated with it and then summing the individual outcome values (sum of the fourth column of each payoff table). In effect, each payoff is associated with an event (rate of growth in personal income) that has a subjective probability. Weighting the payoffs by their respective associated probabilities and summing the weighted values, one obtains the expected value of the project. It is this

Table 14–1   Cash Flow Estimates for Two Land Development Projects

Percentage Rate of Growth in State Personal Income	Estimated Cash Inflow	
	Dallas Project ($1,000)	Houston Project ($1,000)
6	$ 600	$770
8	700	790
10	800	800
12	900	810
14	1,000	830

Table 14–2   Payoff Tables for Land Development Projects

(a) Dallas Project

Percentage Rate of Growth in State Personal Income (Event)	Subjective Probability (P_i)	Cash Flow Payoff (X_i) ($1,000)	X_iP_i ($1,000)
6	0.15	$ 600	$ 90
8	0.20	700	140
10	0.30	800	240
12	0.20	900	180
14	0.15	1,000	150
		$\overline{X}$ = Expected Value = ΣX_iP_i =	$800

(b) Houston Project

Percentage Rate of Growth in State Personal Income (Event)	Subjective Probability (P_i)	Cash Flow Payoff (X_i) ($1,000)	X_iP_i ($1,000)
6	0.15	$ 770	$115.5
8	0.20	790	158.0
10	0.30	800	240.0
12	0.20	810	162.0
14	0.15	830	124.5
		$\overline{X}$ = Expected Value = ΣX_iP_i =	$800.0

kind of weighted average that appears on the "return" axis of the indifference curve diagrams in Figures 14–1 and 14–2.

As Table 14–2 shows, Texland found that the expected values of the two alternatives were exactly the same. We shall see, however, that this does not mean that there is no basis for choosing one project over the other. To complete the analysis, we must consider the risk of each alternative; and, in fact, the information of Table 14–2 does provide a means for quantifying risk and differentiating between the two projects.

An acceptable way to measure risk is to examine the *probability distribution* of the possible outcomes of a given situation. A probability distribution may be represented by a rod graph relating the probability of each growth rate (event) to its outcome in terms of cash inflow. For the data of Table 14–2, probability distributions are constructed in Figure 14–3. In each panel of Figure 14–3, the payoffs associated with each possible growth rate appear on the horizontal axis, and the probability value associated with each payoff appears on the vertical axis.

Figure 14–3   Rod Graphs of Probability Distributions of Returns from Two Land Development Alternatives

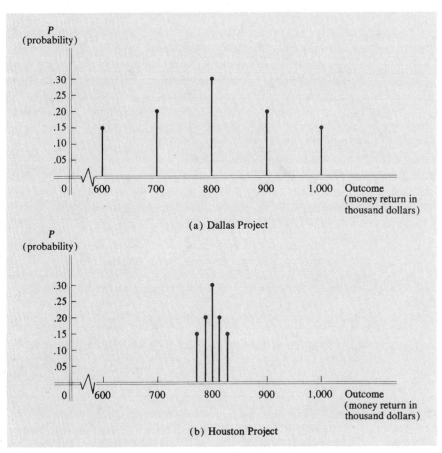

(a) Dallas Project

(b) Houston Project

The rod graphs above show that the Dallas project is riskier than the Houston project, since the expected money outcomes associated with the Dallas project display greater dispersion.

The probability distributions of Figure 14–3 are called *discrete* probability distributions because they do not include information on the probabilities associated with payoffs that might occur at growth rates in between those of Table 14–2. (For example, we do not have any information on the probability of a growth rate between 8 and 10 percent.) A *continuous* probability distribution would be represented by a line rather than a bar graph and would contain information on the probability values associated with a wide range of possible payoffs. It might look like Figure 14–4. If we added up all of the probability values associated with the outcomes in Figure 14–4 (i.e., in calculus terms, if we "integrated the area under the probability distribution"), we would get a value of one for their *cumulative* probability. In other words, we would say that it is certain that one of the outcomes will occur. Similarly, we could ascertain the probability of obtaining a result between *a* and *b* by integrating the area under the curve between these two values. A particularly useful continuous probability distribution is the *normal* distribution, which is symmetrically shaped about its *mean* or expected value (the value at point *a* in Figure 14–4). We shall use such a distribution here to help interpret the results of the risk analysis of Texland's Dallas and Houston projects.

Returning to Figure 14–3, note that the distribution of outcomes along the horizontal axis is much wider for the Dallas project than for the Houston project. In statistical terms we would say that the *range* of the Dallas outcomes is greater or that there is more *dispersion* of the possible

Figure 14–4   A Continuous Probability Distribution

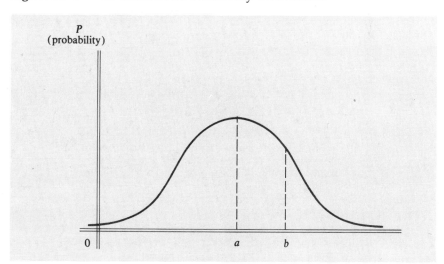

A continuous probability distribution that is normal will plot as a bell-shaped curve. The cumulative probability of obtaining a result between *a* and *b* above is equal to the area under the curve between *a* and *b*.

The **variance** of the possible returns of a project is found by subtracting the expected value of the project from each possible outcome, squaring each of these values, multiplying each squared deviation by the probability of each respective outcome, and summing the resulting products. The variance, a measure of the dispersion of possible project outcomes, is one indicator of risk.

outcomes about the mean (expected) value, $800,000. The **variance** of a given set of data is a statistic that measures the dispersion about the mean of the set of probable outcomes or payoffs. It is calculated by squaring the difference between each probable outcome and the weighted average (mean or expected value) of the outcomes, multiplying each such squared value by its associated probability, and summing these multiplied values. In other words we have

$$\text{variance} = \sigma^2 = \sum_{i=1}^{n} (X_i - \overline{X})^2 P_i,$$

where σ^2, a standard notation for variance, is read "sigma squared"; the X_i are the outcomes; $\overline{X}$ is the expected value; and the P_i are the respective probabilities associated with the outcomes.

In project analysis the variance of the distribution of probable returns (payoffs or cash inflows) is often employed as a measure of risk. Generally, the higher the variance of the distribution, the greater the risk. In Table 14–3, variance calculations are shown for the Dallas and Houston tract

Table 14–3 Variance Calculations for Two Land Development Projects

(a) Dallas Project

Percentage Rate of Growth in State Personal Income	P_i	$(X_i - \overline{X})$ ($1,000)	$(X_i - \overline{X})^2$ ($1,000)	$(X_i - \overline{X})^2 P_i$ ($1,000)
6	0.15	$-200	$40,000,000	$ 6,000,000
8	0.20	-100	10,000,000	2,000,000
10	0.30	0	0	0
12	0.20	100	10,000,000	2,000,000
14	0.15	200	40,000,000	6,000,000

Variance = σ^2 = $16,000,000
Standard Deviation = σ = $126,490

(b) Houston Project

Percentage Rate of Growth in State Personal Income	P_i	$(X_i - \overline{X})$ ($1,000)	$(X_i - \overline{X})^2$ ($1,000)	$(X_i - \overline{X})^2 P_i$ ($1,000)
6	0.15	$- 30	$ 900,000	$ 135,000
8	0.20	- 10	100,000	20,000
10	0.30	0	0	0
12	0.20	10	100,000	20,000
14	0.15	30	900,000	135,000

Variance = σ^2 = $ 310,000
Standard Deviation = σ = $17,610

Managerial Perspective: A Gamble on Tigers, Dolphins, and a Volcano

What do tigers, dolphins, a volcano, and beds have in common? They are all part of the recently opened Mirage casino and hotel in Las Vegas. The hotel, brainchild of Stephen Wynn, is estimated to have an initial cost of from $620 million to over $700 million. Its features include a five-story volcano that erupts with gray smoke every five minutes, a lobby displaying white tigers behind a glass wall and several sharks in a 20,000-gallon aquarium, dolphins in a tank near the pool, and a $37-million golf course containing 10,000 transplanted pine trees. Moreover, the annual hotel operating costs will include such things as $11.5 million for magicians.

The Mirage will be the largest hotel in Las Vegas, with 3,056 rooms. Still, industry analysts estimate that the Mirage will have to generate $1 million *per day* to break even; Wynn himself puts the daily break-even revenue at $800,000. Of all the casino-hotels in Las Vegas, only Caesar's Palace does that kind of volume.

Mr. Wynn owns 31 percent of the equity in Golden Nugget, Incorporated. Since construction began on the Mirage, Golden Nugget's debt has increased to over $900 million, so that equity makes up only 12 percent of the firm's capital. In 1988, Golden Nugget lost $7.6 million, and in the first nine months of 1989 it lost $11.4 million. Still, the revenue picture could change dramatically for the better once the Mirage opens; of course, operating costs will increase as well.

The Mirage's competing Las Vegas hotels are preparing for the new entry by adding new rooms and casino space and refurbishing their old ones. All of these factors should have been taken into account by Mr. Wynn and the other investors when the discounted value of the future cash flows of the project were estimated and compared with its purchase price. Whether these forecasts were accurate remains to be determined.

▪ ▪ ▪ ▪

Reference: "Tigers, A Volcano, Dolphins, and Steve Wynn," *Business Week* (November 20, 1989), pp. 70–71.

---

development projects of Texland Corporation. The variance is frequently an extremely large number, since it expresses dispersion in terms of original units (dollars, in this case) squared. For the Dallas project, we obtain a variance of $16,000,000,000, whereas the variance for Houston is only $310,000,000.

It is sometimes quite useful to calculate the square root of the variance,

$$\sqrt{\sigma^2} = \sigma = \sqrt{\sum_{i=1}^{n} (X_i - \overline{X})^2 P_i,}$$

The **standard deviation,** another measure of risk, is the square root of the variance.

which is called the **standard deviation** of the probable outcomes (payoffs). The standard deviation is also used as a measure of risk. For the Dallas project, $\sigma = \$126{,}490$; whereas for the Houston project, it is $\$17{,}610$.

Whether the variance or the standard deviation is used as a measure of risk, it is clear from the preceding calculations that the Dallas project is riskier than the Houston project, since both statistics are higher for Dallas than for Houston. Using the standard deviation as a risk measure, we can carry the analysis one step further if we are willing to assume that the distribution of probable returns in each case is normal or forms a symmetrical, bell-shaped curve (such as that in Figure 14–4) around the expected value. This assumption may be acceptable if the outcomes constitute values of a continuous random variable, which means a variable that is measured on a continuous scale (dollars, heights, weights, etc.), and the outcomes have values determined by chance only after the experiment (project) is over.

Statistics tells us that for a normal distribution, approximately 68 percent of the distribution (its *area*) lies within plus or minus *one* standard deviation about the mean, and that approximately 95 percent of the distribution lies within *two* standard deviations of the mean. In the case of the Dallas project, this would mean that we expect only a 5 percent probability that we would get a cash inflow outside the range

$$\$800{,}000 \pm 2(\$126{,}490),$$

or that there is a 95 percent probability of a cash inflow between $\$547{,}020$ and $\$1{,}052{,}980$. However, with the Houston project, our 95 percent probability is between $\$764{,}780$ and $\$835{,}220$. If Texland's managers are risk averters, they will choose the Houston project.

Now we can return to the concept of risk-return indifference curves to complete our analysis of the Texland decision. Figure 14–5 is very similar to Figure 14–1. As we noted in our earlier discussion, the assumption of a risk-averse decision maker assures a preference structure in which less desirable combinations of risk and expected money return lie on indifference curves that are, in general, successively further toward the northwest area of the indifference curve map. Alternatively, indifference curves representing less and less desirable combinations of risk and return will have successively lower and lower intercepts on the expected-money-return axis (the intercept being the risk-free equivalent dollar value of the risky returns that lie on a given indifference curve).

Figure 14–5   Risk-Return Combinations for Two Land Development
Projects

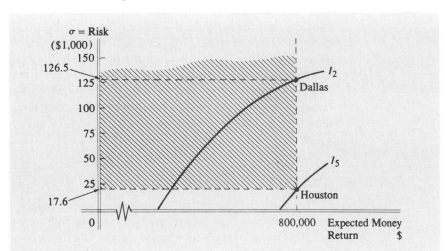

Risk-return indifference curves for the Dallas and Houston land development projects show
that the Dallas project is less desirable, since both projects have an expected return of $800,000
and the standard deviation of the return is much higher for Dallas.

As Figure 14–5 shows, the risk-return combination for the Dallas project must correspond to a lower risk-free return and lie on a less desirable
indifference curve than the Houston combination, since both have the
same expected value and the Dallas combination has higher risk (a larger
σ). Again, we must conclude that if Texland's managers are risk averters,
they will choose the Houston project.

One final observation can be made about Figure 14–5 as it applies to
decisions involving more than two projects. Even if we do not know the
shape of I_5, the Houston project will be preferred over all other projects
that have any of the following: (1) a lower expected money return but an
identical σ; (2) a higher σ but an identical expected money return; or (3)
a lower expected money return *and* a higher σ. Thus graphically we can
say that the Houston project is preferred not only to the Dallas project
but also to any project that falls in the shaded area of the indifference
curve diagram. In more advanced analysis of decision making under risk,
this notion (which is called *dominance*) provides a means of defining an
efficient set of risk-return alternatives.

An **efficient portfo-
lio** is a project or a
combination of in-
vestments that will
involve the least
risk for a given rate
of return.

An **efficient portfolio** is a project or a combination of projects or
investments that have the lowest risk for a given rate of return. In other
words, there is no other investment that has the same expected return
but lower risk. A risk averse investor would prefer such a portfolio to any

other portfolio with the same expected return and higher risk. The **efficient
set** is the set of all efficient portfolios.

Thus many portfolios (and projects) can be systematically rejected
because they lie outside the efficient set. In Figure 14–6 we provide an
example. Here, points *A*, *D*, and *E* dominate points *B*, *C*, and *F*, respectively. Therefore, points *B*, *C*, and *F* lie outside the efficient set. However,
among points *A*, *D*, and *E*, none clearly dominates any of the others. The
optimal portfolio (or project) among those in the efficient set is determined
for each investor by his or her preferences regarding risk and expected
return.

■ ■ ■ ■ ■ ■ ■ ■ ■ EVALUATING RISKY STREAMS OF RECEIPTS

Unlike the preceding Texland example, many project analyses deal with
more than one expected return per project. Where an individual project
has a number of periodic returns, such as a flow of annual receipts over
a number of years, there will be a probability distribution of payoffs for
each year. In such cases the standard deviation of the entire stream of
discounted receipts must be calculated in order to measure the project's
risk.

The procedure for determining the expected present value of a stream
of risky returns is summarized in the following formula:

$$E(PV) = \sum_{t=1}^{n} \frac{\overline{X}_t}{(1 + r)^t} \, ,$$

where

$\overline{X}_t$ = expected value of net receipts in period *t*,
r = the appropriate discount rate, and
t = time period.

The formula simply says to sum up the discounted expected values of the
future net cash inflows.

If the future cash flows are independent of one another (that is, if the
cash flow outcome in time period one has no effect on the cash inflows
in subsequent periods), then for *each period*, the standard deviation is:

$$\sigma_t = \sqrt{\sum_{i=1}^{m} (X_{it} - \overline{X}_t)^2 P_i},$$

where P_i is the probability associated with the *i*th net cash inflow. For the
entire project, the standard deviation is as follows:

$$\sigma = \sqrt{\sum_{t=1}^{n} \frac{\sigma_t^2}{(1 + r)^{2t}}}$$

Figure 14–6   The Concept of Dominance in Risk Analysis

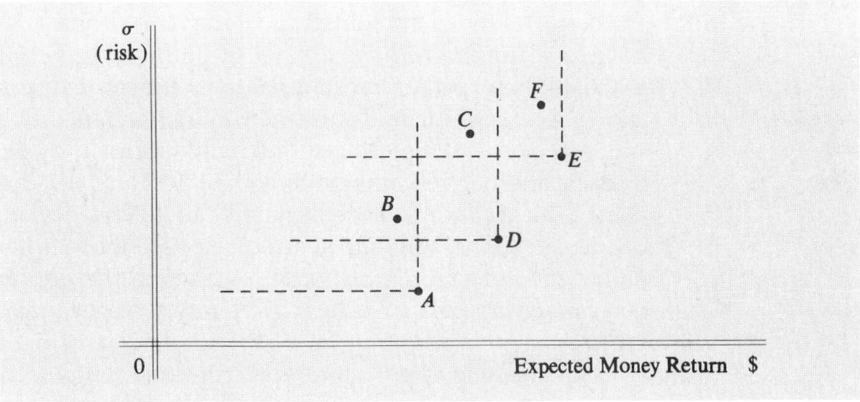

A risk-return combination will dominate other combinations of either equal risk and lower return *or* greater risk and the same return. Thus, combination *A* dominates *B*, combination *D* dominates *B* and *C*, and combination *E* dominates *C* and *F*. Among combinations *A*, *D*, and *E*, none dominates.

Although derivation of the preceding three formulas is beyond the scope of this text, some of the selected references at the end of this chapter provide more detail for the interested student.

If cash flows are *inter*dependent (in other words, if the net cash flow in one time period has some relationship to that in another time period), the calculation of expected value and variance for the stream of receipts becomes more complicated. In such a case (and many projects will necessarily fit this case), the *covariances* of the probable returns must also be taken into account. Defined briefly, the covariance of one probable return with respect to another is a measure that reflects the degree to which the first return is correlated with the second. To the extent that two returns are positively correlated, when a high value occurs for the first, a high value will also occur for the second. In general, the greater the degree of correlation between a project's cash flows, the greater the standard deviation of the expected present value of the project. Thus it is important to recognize the existence of interdependence between individual period cash flows in the stream of receipts.

■ ■ ■ ■ ■ ■ ■ ■ ■ PROBABILITY APPROACH TO MULTIPLE PROJECT ALTERNATIVES

The analysis of our previous chapter culminated with a discussion of methodologies for selecting the optimal combination of projects under conditions of certainty. As we have indicated, the probability approach to risky investment alternatives can be extended to encompass the evaluation of alternative combinations (*portfolios*) of projects. For each portfolio, such a procedure involves an analysis of the degree of interdependence of cash flows over time. Thus the analyst of alternative portfolios would have to calculate the expected present value or expected return of each portfolio, taking into account not only the interdependence of cash flows in each single project but also the interdependence of cash flows *between projects* in each alternative combination of projects. Once the expected present value of each portfolio is determined and its variance or standard deviation is calculated, the dominance approach described earlier can be applied to define the efficient set of portfolios. Again, the optimal portfolio will be determined by the investor's preferences regarding risk and expected return.

The portfolio approach to multiple-project alternatives is usually modified when it is applied to capital budgeting situations for a variety of reasons. First, the approach was developed for application to the question of analyzing portfolios of securities, primarily common stock.[1] It is possible to divide a common stock portfolio into almost any combination of available stocks. However, the share of a total capital budget that is allocated to a given physical capital undertaking often is not divisible. Such projects must be either accepted or rejected in total, and the possibility of undertaking, say, one-half of one project and one-fourth of two others just does not exist. In addition the covariances and correlation coefficients that are needed to analyze interdependent projects are much more difficult to obtain for capital projects than for common stocks. Finally, there is the problem of identifying the risk-return preferences of a firm. For any given firm, management may consist of a group of decision makers, each group member having his or her own preference set (set of risk-return indifference curves); furthermore, the preferences of managers, either singly or in the aggregate, may not reflect the wishes of the owners (shareholders) of the firm.

■■■■■■■■ ACCEPTABLE SHORTCUTS TO RISK ANALYSIS

Although the portfolio approach outlined in the preceding section is generally viewed as a theoretically correct approach to risk evaluation and project selection problems, some shorter methodologies that directly ad-

---
■■■■■■

[1] One interesting result obtained from portfolio theory supports the old adage about not putting all of one's eggs in the same basket. In particular it can be shown that adding new projects to a portfolio can reduce its overall risk (standard deviation) as long as the projects are not perfectly positively correlated. In the literature of finance, such risk reduction through diversification of investments is known as the *portfolio effect*.

just present values for perceived differences in project riskiness are widely used. These methodologies are (1) the risk-adjusted discount rate approach and (2) the certainty equivalent approach.

Risk-Adjusted Discount Rate

The risk-adjusted discount rate approach simply alters the standard present value formula by substituting a higher discount rate, k, for the risk-free rate, r, that was employed in Chapter 13. Thus we would have

$$k = r + \rho,$$

where ρ (the Greek letter *rho*) is called the *risk premium*. The present value formula would then be

$$PV|k = \sum_{t=1}^{n} \frac{\overline{X}_t}{(1 + k)^t}.$$

Since k is larger than r, the effect of the risk-adjusted discount rate is to lower the value of PV for a risky future return. The higher the risk premium, the more risky the project and the lower the risk-adjusted PV for each future cash inflow.

For two projects of equal size (cost), equal lives, and approximately equal subjective risk, the selection procedure is simply to choose the one with the higher risk-adjusted net present value. If the risks of the two projects differ, then it is appropriate to apply a higher discount rate to the project judged to be riskier. The selection of the discount rate may be a subjective matter, a point that will be discussed further in the following section.

If we were to apply the preceding methodology to the Texland example, management would evaluate the Dallas project using a higher discount rate than the one applied to the Houston project. Suppose that instead of one-year lives, the land development alternatives were expected to have four-year net cash inflows of $200,000 per year and that each alternative had a price of $550,000. If management chose to apply a 12 percent discount rate to the Dallas project and a 9 percent rate to the Houston project, the result would be as follows:

Dallas Project
$NPV|k_D = \$200{,}000\ (PVF_a\ 12\%,\ 4) - \$550{,}000 = \$57{,}460$

and

Houston Project
$NPV|k_H = \$200{,}000\ (PVF_a\ 9\%,\ 4) - \$550{,}000 = \$97{,}940.$

Clearly, the Houston project would be the best choice.

Certainty Equivalent Approach

Remaining for the moment with the question of evaluating two mutually exclusive projects with uncertain cash flows, we turn now to the certainty equivalent approach. This approach relates closely to the risk-return indifference curve trade-off we discussed in connection with the portfolio approach. It adjusts the present value of an uncertain return through the numerator of the present value formula as follows:

$$PV|\alpha_t = \sum_{t=1}^{n} \frac{\alpha_t \overline{X}_t}{(1 + r)^t} ,$$

where α_t is a "certainty equivalent adjustment factor" and r is the risk-free discount rate. For all but completely certain returns, $0 < \alpha_t < 1$. Thus $\alpha_t = 1$ would indicate that the tth return (X_t) was certain, whereas $\alpha_t = 0$ would indicate that the probability of the tth return was zero. Thus very risky projects will have low α_ts whereas less risky ones will have α_ts closer to one.

The certainty equivalent adjustment factor, in theory, is derived from the decision maker's risk-return preferences, as indicated in a set of risk-return indifference curves. In Figure 14–7 we illustrate two risk-return indifference curves and the expected money returns and risk levels (α_i) of two projects, A and B. The risk-return indifference curves show that the certain return equivalent to the expected money value of Project A is $500,

Figure 14–7 Relation of Risk-Return Indifference Curves to Certainty Equivalent Adjustment Factor

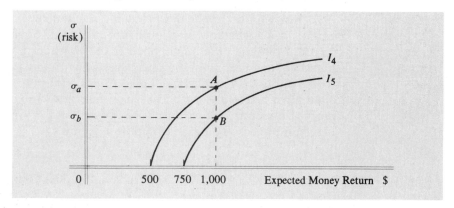

The certainty equivalent adjustment factor is equal to the ratio of the certain return (indifference curve intercept on the return axis) to a given equivalent risky return. Thus, the certainty equivalent adjustment factor for risk-return combination A is 0.5, while that for combination B is 0.75.

while that equivalent to Project B is $750. For either project the certainty equivalent adjustment factor is

$$\alpha_i = \frac{\text{certain return}}{\text{equivalent risky return}}.$$

Thus we have for Project A

$$\alpha_a = \frac{500}{1,000} = 0.5,$$

and for Project B

$$\alpha_b = \frac{750}{1,000} = 0.75.$$

In the analysis of any given project, the certainty equivalent adjustment factor can be different for each future return. Thus, if a project is believed to become less risky as time passes, higher αs can be applied to the cash flows for more distant periods. Returning again to our land development alternatives, Texland may be virtually certain it can sell all of either tract at its desired prices by the end of four years, but management may believe that the cash flows early in the projects' lives are less certain. For example, management might choose to apply the following α_ts to the two projects:

Year	α_t Dallas	α_t Houston
1	0.78	0.85
2	0.84	0.85
3	0.90	0.90
4	0.90	0.95

Given a risk-free discount rate of 8 percent, our earlier projected annual inflows of $200,000, and project prices of $550,000, we have for the Dallas project

$$NPV|\alpha_t = \frac{0.78(\$200,000)}{(1.08)^1} + \frac{0.84(\$200,000)}{(1.08)^2} + \frac{0.90(\$200,000)}{(1.08)^3}$$

$$+ \frac{0.90(\$200,000)}{(1.08)^4} - \$550,000$$

$$= \$13,672.81,$$

and for the Houston project

$$NPV|\alpha_t = \frac{0.85(\$200,000)}{(1.08)^1} + \frac{0.85(\$200,000)}{(1.08)^2} + \frac{0.90(\$200,000)}{(1.08)^3}$$
$$+ \frac{0.95(\$200,000)}{(1.08)^4} - \$550,000$$
$$= \$35,700.68,$$

Again the Houston project would be judged the better alternative on the basis of its adjusted *NPV*. The difference in the two *NPV*s reflects both the generally lower α_ts of the Dallas project and the higher certainty equivalents of the Houston inflows *early* in the life of the project.

It is argued that the certainty equivalent approach is superior to the risk-adjusted discount rate approach when project returns do not become increasingly risky over time. Still, the risk-adjusted discount rate approach is more frequently used because (1) it is easier to calculate *NPV* and (2) the two approaches, it can be shown, will yield the same result whenever $\alpha_t = (1 + r)^t/(1 + k)^t$—that is, whenever the certainty equivalent adjustment factor for each future period equals the ratio of the present value factor (including a risk premium) to the risk-free present value factor. It follows that if far-off returns are viewed as increasingly less certain, the risk-adjusted discount rate approach will frequently be chosen.

■ ■ ■ ■ ■ ■ ■ ■ RISK ADJUSTMENT IN PRACTICE

With the exception of the risk-adjusted discount rate, most of the approaches to the problem of risk that were described in the previous sections are the result of systematic examination of risk problems by financial and economic experts during the period since 1960. Corporations—and to some extent, public sector agencies—have applied these tools selectively, but many of them are not in common use by practical decision makers. This is particularly true of the probability approach, since the probabilities can be ascertained only roughly and the entire procedure becomes quite cumbersome when future cash flows are interdependent.[2]

■ ■ ■ ■ ■ ■

[2] We note at this point that an extension of the probability approach in decision theory, the decision tree methodology, has become popular with some analysts although it relies on probabilities that are unlikely to be known. (See the game theory discussion in the appendix to Chapter 9.) Decision trees are usually covered in quantitative management courses, so we omit the discussion of them here. For a managerial economics text that makes primary use of the decision tree approach, see Julian Simon's *Applied Managerial Economics*, listed in the selected references at the end of this chapter. The probability approach also is at the foundation of the *capital asset pricing model* (*CAPM*), a method of calculating risk-adjusted discount rates that is sometimes used by large firms.

While much of the literature on project analysis published in economics and finance journals is highly theoretical, academicians do occasionally conduct survey research on how risk analysis is employed by corporate financial planners. Three well-known surveys were conducted during the 1970s. James C. T. Mao[3] interviewed executives of several medium- and large-sized corporations and concluded from their responses that (1) the executives tended to characterize risk as not meeting a target rate of return, especially in the case of small investments, and (2) there was a tendency to emphasize downside risk, so that in the case of large projects the danger of insolvency was carefully considered.

Mao found that the executives frequently employed the risk-adjusted discount rate approach when evaluating capital projects. However, this rate seemed to be quite high in relation to the return realized on common stock or a rate that would reflect a typical company's cost of capital (roughly, the rate at which new funds can be obtained). He attributed the tendency to choose high rates of discount to a desire to offset overly optimistic projections of returns or cover for items of project cost that might be overlooked (federal regulations requiring special facilities for handicapped workers, for example).

In 1977 and 1978, the results of surveys conducted by several other academic researchers were published.[4] These surveys indicated that corporate decision makers still relied heavily on risk-adjusted discount rates and that subjective methods were used to estimate the rates. One of the studies reported that 56 percent of the sample firms attempted to assess risk subjectively, while another 4 percent did not assess risk at all. However, this study also found that of the 40 percent that did attempt formal analysis of risk, the probability distribution approach was the most widely employed method. Another study published in 1986 revealed that certain large firms did not ordinarily perform thorough financial analysis of small-sized capital projects, but instead penalized them by subjecting them to excessively high rates of discount.[5]

It is evident from the available surveys that most financial executives do attempt to make some adjustment for risk in the analysis of capital projects. It seems likely that the outpouring of theoretical literature on risk analysis, the increased exposure of business students to that literature, and the availability of computer programs to simulate the possible outcomes of risky investment projects will lead to more widespread applica-

■ ■ ■ ■ ■ ■

[3] James C. T. Mao, "Survey of Capital Budgeting: Theory and Practice," *Journal of Finance,* XXV (May 1970), pp. 349–360.

[4] Lawrence D. Schall, Gary L. Sundem, and William R. Geijsbeek, Jr., "Survey and Analysis of Capital Budgeting Methods," *Journal of Finance* XXIII (March 1978), pp. 281–287; and Lawrence J. Gitman and John R. Forrester, Jr., "A Survey of Capital Budgeting Techniques Used by Major U.S. Firms," *Financial Management* 6 (Fall 1977), pp. 66–71.

[5] Marc Ross, "Capital Budgeting Practices of Twelve Large Manufacturers," *Financial Management,* 15, No. 4 (Winter 1986), pp. 15–22.

Managerial Perspective: Risk, Capital Budgeting, and Kevlar

In the early 1960s a group of chemists at Du Pont's experimental lab in Wilmington, Delaware, began work on developing a material made of carbon molecules that would be extraordinarily strong. Initially known as Fiber B, the cloth-like material that was eventually developed was named Kevlar. The development process took place over a 25-year period and entailed $700 million in capital costs together with an additional $200 million in operating losses. By 1987, its annual sales had finally reached $300 million, and Du Pont estimated that these revenues would grow by 10 percent a year over the next five years.

Unfortunately, the early sales projections for Kevlar were too optimistic. By 1980, more than half of the Kevlar produced by Du Pont was being used in automobile tires, and some people expected that eventually Kevlar would be the only material used in tires. As a result Du Pont invested in its first commercial Kevlar plant, capable of making 45 million pounds each year. Soon after Du Pont began construction on the $500 million plant, the tire manufacturers chose steel instead of Kevlar for tires, arguing that Kevlar was too expensive and that customers were more attracted to steel-belted tires. At that point, the new plant appeared to be an investment with little chance of becoming profitable.

Kevlar was used in race cars and trucks, where its added durability made it worth its higher price. In addition, Du Pont asked the U.S. Army to consider Kevlar as a replacement for nylon in flak jackets, because nylon did not protect soldiers from shrapnel. Kevlar then went through seven years of testing by the Army and further development to meet the Army's specifications. The Army was finally satisfied when 100 goats were covered with half-inch-thick blankets of Kevlar and shot with .38-caliber pistol bullets and sustained only minor bruises from the experience. Bulletproof vests made of Kevlar also were demanded by other law enforcement entities. Still, the specialty tire market and the bulletproof-vest market were not sufficiently large to make Du Pont's investment profitable.

As a result, Du Pont began to look for people who would be willing to devote their careers to finding new markets for Kevlar. The company decided to change its marketing strategy so that rather than trying to think of new uses for Kevlar on its own, it would try to discover customer needs that might be appropriate for the material, and then to further develop Kevlar so that it would meet those needs.

As a result, Kevlar has become one of the materials specified by aerospace engineers in their plans, a substitute for asbestos, and an insulator of fiber optic cable. Kevlar is now also used to make gloves, and Du Pont is considering using it to reinforce the heels and toes of socks to keep them from wearing out. Sam Walton, chairman of Wal-Mart Stores, Incorporated, has suggested that Kevlar booties be designed to protect the feet of hunting dogs.

Not all of the Kevlar products developed by Du Pont initially performed as anticipated. Cables designed for off-shore drilling platforms for Exxon snapped when they were tightened. Kevlar sails also initially tore in the wind. However, both products have been redesigned, and it appears that these problems have been corrected.

By 1987, Du Pont reported that Kevlar had generated operating profits for the last two years. Although the intrinsic value of Kevlar was no longer doubted, some industry analysts questioned whether the investment would eventually turn out to be profitable, particularly since Du Pont's basic patents on the material would begin expiring in 1990 and other competing fibers were becoming available.

The saga of the development of Kevlar illustrates that even a large company such as Du Pont cannot develop a new product without risk. Clearly, a careful analysis of potential markets, corresponding revenues, and costs in such a situation combined with an estimate of the risk involved is extremely important.

■ ■ ■ ■

Reference: "Du Pont's Difficulties in Selling Kevlar Show Hurdles of Innovation," *The Wall Street Journal* (September 29, 1987), pp. 1, 20.

tion of formal risk assessment techniques by firms of all sizes. However, one must keep in mind that any sophisticated technique is only as good as the information it is used to analyze.

Given the realities of investment project evaluation, one might ask whether there is a feasible shortcut approach to the identification of an optimal combination of projects when a limited capital budget is available. For example, without too much difficulty could we expand the *NPV* approach of Chapter 13 to encompass risky investments? The answer is yes, and the methodology would be simply to evaluate each project using a risk-adjusted discount rate and thereafter select from the possible combinations the one that yields the highest aggregate adjusted *NPV*. The main caution to observe in this procedure relates to what we have learned about the interdependence of cash flows. The project combination yielding the highest *NPV* might well be carefully reviewed alongside those having *NPV*s that are not greatly different, since a subjective evaluation of the correlation between the projects in each combination might lead to some revision of *NPV*s based on the effect of such correlation on the standard deviation or risk of the project combinations.

■ ■ ■ ■ ■ ■ ■ ■ ■ **EXTERNALITIES AND THEIR NATURE**

The cautious attitude of executives toward new capital projects and their tendency to apply what might seem to be excessive risk-adjusted discount rates to project inflows may in many cases be a sign of prudence rather than of paranoia. A hint about the problems underlying such behavior is found in the preceding assertion that certain elements of cost, such as federal requirements concerning facilities for the handicapped, may have been overlooked by project analysts. There is a tendency in project evaluation to analyze first and foremost the estimated revenue and operating cost components of the flow of annual benefits and to compare the discounted net amount of those two figures with project price. However, the operating cost item directs attention to nuts-and-bolts aspects of annual cost, which are very much *internal* to the firm. In other words the emphasis is on those cost items over which the firm has direct control through management's ability to plan and organize the process of production.

For any given project, there are likely to be elements of cost markedly affected by changes in data that are *externally* determined—that is, over which management has no control. Changes in input prices are perhaps the most obvious of such external factors. A firm may be faced with rising input prices because it is in an industrial sector where many rapidly expanding firms are bidding against one another for relatively scarce resources. Thus costs may rise for an individual firm even though no changes have occurred in its production function. Such externalities, which economists have called *pecuniary externalities*, are occasionally overlooked by project evaluators. More likely to be overlooked are certain other types of externalities, particularly those associated with what have come to be known as *public goods*.

A public good is a good that is jointly consumed by many people and, once it is made available, the marginal cost of increased consumption is zero. A highway bridge provides a good example. Once the bridge has been built, it can handle any amount of traffic up to the capacity per unit of time of the roadway. If it is being used at one-half its capacity, and an additional user wishes to cross it, the additional user will be able to do so at zero addition to the cost of the bridge. Theoretically, no price should be charged for using the bridge, since marginal cost equals zero; therefore the perfectly competitive $P = MC$ market solution is price equals zero. The users of public goods who benefit from but do not pay for them through market transactions enjoy what are known as *third-party benefits*.

The cost of operation of an investment undertaking in the private sector is seldom affected by such public goods as a bridge, although we could certainly imagine circumstances where it might be. (In an under-developed country or region, the roads, the bridges, and the electric power plants often are externalities upon which successful private capital projects ultimately depend.) However, over the past few decades we have come to the realization that clean air, clean water, the preservation of wildlife, and a relatively quiet environment are public goods that have often been neglected in our economic calculus. This neglect has provided the business sector an array of public-good externalities, such as free water, zero-cost dumping of pollutants, and the prerogative to increase noise and temperature levels at will.

The recent awakening of both the general public and governmental authorities to the fact that much private sector output is produced in a setting where external costs are imposed on third parties has caused business decision makers to be wary about regulatory changes and penalties that might well *internalize* such costs.

▪ ▪ ▪ ▪ ▪ ▪ ▪ ▪ AN EXAMPLE OF INTERNALIZATION

On January 6, 1978, *The Wall Street Journal* reported that Foothills Pipe Lines, Ltd., a Canadian corporation organized for the purpose of constructing and operating a 2,000-mile stretch of the Alaska Highway Natural Gas Pipeline, had been informed by the Canadian government that it would have to bear all operating costs of a new government agency established to monitor the pipeline.[6] In addition, Foothills was told that it would be assessed penalties of up to $10,000 per day if it failed to comply with any order of the agency.

According to the *Journal,* Foothills had not planned on paying the costs of the monitoring agency, and such costs apparently were not included in its original estimate of project price or annual cost. Obviously, the Canadian government's move caused the costs of pipeline monitoring (which were at first presumed to be external to the firm) to be *internalized* by the firm. For the firm to continue to have a feasible project, it would be necessary to ensure that the future revenue stream would be sufficient to yield the desired return on investment, given the required alterations in project price and annual cost of operations. If provisions were not made to increase the annual cash inflows to Foothills, the entire project could become unattractive. In terms of standard capital project analysis where

$$NPV = \sum_{i=1}^{n} \frac{X_i}{(1 + k)^i} - C_p,$$

▪ ▪ ▪ ▪ ▪ ▪

[6] "Foothills Must Pay for Agency to Monitor Pipeline Construction," *The Wall Street Journal,* January 6, 1978, p. 2.

the initial costs of the monitoring agency would increase C_p, while its annual costs after the pipeline is completed would reduce the X_i. Further, if k is a risk-adjusted discount rate, uncertainty regarding *changes* in the regulatory picture might warrant reevaluating the project with a higher k.

Fortunately for Foothills Pipe Lines, the Canadian government made an adjustment in the tariffs charged for gas transported through the line, thereby allowing for an adequate return on investment while transferring most of the burden of financing the monitoring agency to natural gas consumers in the United States.[7]

The preceding example calls attention to the fact that externalities do have to be anticipated by project evaluators, particularly because of their effects on project price and annual costs. Government has many ways in which it can cause third-party costs attributable to a firm to become internal. Among these are legislation of standards and penalties, user charges, taxes, and assignment of property rights. However, many private capital projects also create external *benefits* as well as costs, and project evaluators must be aware of the prospects for internalization of such flows.

One of the best recent examples of an attempt to internalize the potential third-party benefits of a capital project is Walt Disney World in Florida.[8] When Walt Disney Productions constructed the original Disneyland in California, only enough land was purchased by the Disney interests to provide for the amusement park and a few related activities. The result was that the project supplied tremendous external benefits to owners and users of surrounding property in the development boom that the area experienced after Disneyland opened. In planning the Florida Disney World project, the corporation ensured its own capture (internalization) of many of the potential external benefits that it would create by purchasing 6,000 acres of land, thereby assuring control over nearby related activities. There were still some spillover benefits to third parties who owned land or set up businesses on the perimeter of the Disney World tract, but the distance of these sites from the park itself much reduced external benefits and enhanced the long-run profitability of the Disney project. The moral is clear: Successful investors take into account opportunities to internalize project-related external benefits. If at first they do not, they will indeed *learn* to do so!

■ ■ ■ ■ ■ ■

[7] Since the increase in tariff would probably cause a reduction in quantity sold, some of the burden would still be borne by Foothills.

[8] This example has been used previously elsewhere. See Richard B. McKenzie, *Economics* (Boston: Houghton Mifflin, 1986), p. 689. Recently, it has been argued that Disney World has resulted in external costs to the citizens of Florida as the result of the increased demand for public services that has resulted from its existence. See "A Sweet Deal for Disney Is Souring Its Neighbors," *Business Week* (August 8, 1988), pp. 48–49.

■ ■ ■ ■ ■ ■ ■ ■   **SUMMARY**

Risk and Risk Adjustment in Capital Projects

In this chapter we extended our analysis of capital projects to include situations involving risk. Our basic behavioral assumption throughout the chapter was that the decision maker is a *risk averter*. This means that the decision maker will be willing to accept a risky project over one that is less risky but involves the same initial outlay (project price) *only if* the risky alternative yields a sufficiently greater net present value to more than offset its added risk. To illustrate this point, the concept of risk-return indifference curves was introduced and eventually related to a probability approach to risk analysis.

We showed in this chapter that the riskiness of various investment alternatives can be evaluated by examining the probability distribution of payoffs of each alternative. For each alternative, a weighted average or expected value is calculated, and this is used, along with the distribution of probable outcomes, to obtain two measures of riskiness—the *variance* and the *standard deviation* of net project returns. For projects with equal prices, lives, and expected values, we showed that a risk-averse decision maker will choose the alternative with the lowest variance. In addition the *normal distribution* was utilized to make some inferences about the probability of payoffs outside a specified range.

One result of applying the probability approach to project analysis is the attention it directs toward the question of interdependence of cash inflows. In particular we noted that the cash flow in a given time period might in some way be correlated with that in another time period. Thus a thorough analysis of a project's risk using the probability approach would have to take into account the covariance between project inflows. This increases the information requirements of the approach and complicates the calculation of variance. When combinations or portfolios of projects are evaluated, it becomes necessary to consider not only the interdependence of cash flows within each individual project but also the problem of interdependence of cash flows *between* projects.

In the last part of this chapter, some shortcuts to risk analysis were described and evaluated. Specifically, we examined the *risk-adjusted discount* rate concept and its application. Use of the risk-adjusted discount rate is viewed as a practical and acceptable approach as long as its shortcomings are understood by the project analyst. Its primary shortcoming, the fact that it treats project cash flows as becoming increasingly risky over time, can be offset by using a related method, the *certainty equivalent approach*, in which each future cash flow is separately adjusted for risk, and a risk-free discount rate is applied to the present value calculation.

The chapter closed with discussions of the views of corporation executives on the matter of risk and the treatment of risk and externalities in project evaluation. We concluded that it would be reasonable to evaluate risky alternatives using the risk-adjusted discount rate approach examined in the light of what is known about interdependence of project cash flows. In addition, we implied that it would be wise for capital project analysts to review carefully the external costs and benefits related to each project and to assess the probable consequences of internalization of such costs and benefits.

This chapter has dealt almost entirely with the more obvious quantitative aspects of project evaluation under risk. However, many capital projects have both inflows of benefits and elements of cost or price that might easily escape analysis if a strictly private or internal point of view is taken by the firm's managers or project evaluators. In the next chapter, we extend our discussion not only to such externalities and, in some cases, nonquantitative considerations, but also to the question of project evaluation in the public sector.

■ ■ ■ ■ ■ ■ ■ ■ ■ ■ ■ ■ ■ ■ **Questions** ■ ■ ■ ■ ■ ■ ■ ■ ■ ■ ■ ■ ■

1. What is the economic nature of risk? How can risk be described using a trade-off concept?
2. What is meant by the term *expected return*?
3. What is the usual assumption regarding the risk attitude of decision makers in economic theory? What other kinds of attitudes toward risk exist? Describe each attitude in terms of the behavior of the decision maker in a risk situation.
4. What is a probability distribution of returns? How can it be related to the risk associated with a given capital project?
5. Suppose two projects have the same lives and prices but that one of them (Project A) has an expected value that is greater than that of the other (Project B). Can you determine from this which project should be selected? Why or why not?
6. Explain how the concept of the standard deviation of probable returns from a capital project relates to that of risk-return indifference curves.
7. What problem in project analysis arises from the possible interdependence of cash flows in a project or a portfolio of projects?
8. What is a risk-adjusted discount rate? Explain how it is used, and discuss the problems inherent in its application to project analysis.
9. What is a certainty equivalent adjustment factor? Why do some experts argue that use of the certainty equivalent adjustment factor is a better approach than is the risk-adjusted discount rate method?
10. There is evidence that executives of medium- and large-sized corporations tend to rely on a variant of the risk-adjusted discount rate approach when evaluating capital projects. Explain how the variant

described in this chapter differs from the ordinary risk-adjusted discount rate approach. Why do you think the corporation executives prefer this method?

■ ■ ■ ■ ■ ■ ■ ■ ■ ■ ■ ■ ■ **Problems** ■ ■ ■ ■ ■ ■ ■ ■ ■ ■ ■ ■ ■

1. Using a set of risk-return indifference curves for a single decision maker, describe a case in which the decision maker would prefer a risky investment returning an expected $1,500 to a less risky one with an expected return of $1,000. Explain how an increase in the perceived riskiness of the project with the $1,500 expected return might cause the decision maker to reject it and to choose the less risky project with the $1,000 expected return instead.

2. Suppose a one-year project has the following probable returns in relation to the percentage growth in population for a given region:

Percent Growth in Population	Net Cash Inflow of Project
1.0	$150,000
1.5	185,000
2.0	210,000
2.5	275,000

The following are the subjective probabilities of occurrence of the preceding population growth rates:

Percent Growth in Population	Subjective Probability (P_i)
1.0	0.25
1.5	0.50
2.0	0.20
2.5	0.05

What is the *expected value* of the cash inflow from the project?

3. Construct a rod graph showing a discrete probability distribution of the cash inflows from the project in Question 2, and then determine the variance and standard deviation of the inflows. What could be said about the relation of the standard deviation to the expected value of the cash inflow if the true probability distribution of the cash inflows were normal?

4. Given the following data on two one-period capital projects, calculate (1) the expected value of each project's cash flows and (2) the standard

deviation of probable cash flows from each project. Indicate which of the two projects would be chosen by a risk-averse decision maker if their prices were the same and they had similar lives.

Net Cash Flows		Subjective Probability
Project A	Project B	(P_i)
200	190	0.05
240	250	0.25
250	260	0.40
290	270	0.25
300	290	0.05

5. Belco Corporation has been evaluating two possible alternative locations for a small oil refinery. One of the locations is in the United States, whereas the other is in a nearby Latin American republic. The cost will be $22 million if the project is built in the United States, but because of lower land and labor costs it will be only $19 million if the project is built in the Latin American country.

Recent uncertainties in the oil and gas industry have convinced Belco's managers that the lives of such projects should not be treated as longer than seven years. Management doubts that the project will have any salvage value if it is undertaken in Latin America, but it is willing to attach a $7 million after-tax salvage value to the U.S. alternative.

The estimated net annual cash inflows, which are believed to be independent, are $5 million per year if the project is located in the U.S. and $5.2 million per year if it is located in Latin America. Due to the inherent risk of changes in government regulations in the Latin American republic, Belco's managers have decided to apply a risk-adjusted discount rate of 22 percent to the inflows from the foreign alternative, while their risk-adjusted discount rate for the U.S. project will be 16 percent. Which project will they choose? (Note: PVF_a 22%, 7 = 3.4155; PVF_a 16%, 7 = 4.0386.)

6. Develop a set of certainty equivalent adjustment factors from the following information on a decision maker's preferences:

Certain Return	Equivalent Risky Return
$120,000	$160,000
170,000	210,000
250,000	300,000
325,000	400,000
500,000	625,000

7. Given the following set of risk-return indifference curves, calculate the certainty equivalent adjustment factors for an expected return of $1,400,000.

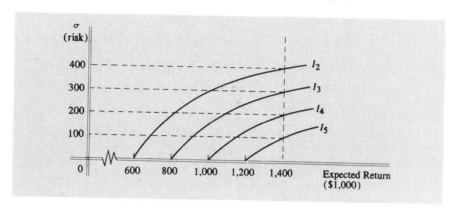

8. International Cosmographics, a small corporation in the printing industry, is considering expanding into the greeting card market. Its managers have hired two consultants to evaluate an investment project that involves both an addition to factory space and the purchase of new printing equipment. Consultant A has suggested that the company adjust its expected annual cash inflows using a risk-adjusted discount rate approach. Consultant B argues that such an approach is inappropriate and that what should be used is a certainty equivalent approach that takes into account the fact that after the first two years risk will decline because a market share will have been established.

   Consultant B has estimated that the following certainty equivalent adjustment factors should be applied to the cash inflows from the project, assuming a risk-free discount rate of 6 percent.

Year	Certainty Equivalent Adjustment Factor
1	0.9464
2	0.8957
3	0.9197
4	0.8944
5	0.8698
6	0.8458
7	0.8225
8	0.7999

Consultant A argues that the risk-adjusted discount rate approach is simpler and equally applicable, since a risk-adjusted discount rate of

12 percent for the first two years of project life should be applied and 9 percent should be used for the remaining 6 years. The annual inflows (before risk adjustment) follow. They should be treated as being independent.

Year	Net Cash Inflow
1	$100,000
2	175,000
3	200,000
4	200,000
5	200,000
6	200,000
7	200,000
8	200,000

If both risk-adjustment methodologies are applied to the preceding inflows, what difference in present value will the two approaches yield? Explain the difference you find.

9. Using a set of risk-return indifference curves, explain how the concept of dominance makes it possible in theory to eliminate certain risk-return combinations from the "efficient set" of project portfolios.

10. American Astrotronics Corporation is evaluating two new investment projects for possible undertaking next fiscal year. One is the short-term operation of a cleaning franchise that will yield a net after-tax cash flow of $42,000 per year for the next three years. The second is short-term operation of a parking lot that will yield net after-tax cash flows of $36,000 for each of two years and $56,000 for the third and final year of operation. Neither project has a salvage value, and either can be acquired for a present outlay of $90,000.

   a. Evaluate the two projects using a risk-adjusted discount rate of 18 percent per year.

   b. If the company can undertake only one of the two projects, which should it choose? Why?

11. Garfield just won $2 million in the California lottery. Since he knows that many long-lost cat relatives will want to share in his good fortune, Garfield is trying to find the optimal place to invest his funds. At the present time, he is considering two options. The first is a real estate investment trust that is purchasing repossessed property in Texas. The second is a well-diversified mutual fund whose return closely approximates that of the market. The possible returns on the real estate investment trust, R_T, the market, R_M, and their associated probabilities, P_i, are given in the table. The risk-free rate of return, R_F, is .06.

% Growth in Real GNP	P_i	R_{T_i}	R_{M_i}
-1%	.05	-.40	-.10
1%	.3	.30	.10
2%	.5	.30	.20
3%	.15	.40	.30

a. Calculate the expected rate of return for the real estate trust and for the market.

b. Calculate the standard deviation of the returns for the real estate trust and for the market.

c. With no other information regarding alternative investment opportunities, how would Garfield choose whether to invest in the real estate investment trust, the mutual fund, or a risk-free asset?

■ ■ ■ ■ ■ ■ ■ ■ ■ ■ **Selected References** ■ ■ ■ ■ ■ ■ ■ ■ ■ ■

Brightman, Harvey J. *Statistics in Plain English*, Cincinnati: South-Western, 1986, Chapters 2 and 3.

Engler, George N. *Business Financial Management*. Dallas: Business Publications, 1975, Chapter 7 and appendices to Chapter 7.

Gitman, Lawrence J. *Principles of Managerial Finance*, 6th ed., New York: Harper and Row, 1991, Chapter 10.

Mansfield, Edwin. *Statistics for Business and Economics*. New York: Norton, 1980, Chapter 3.

Mao, James C. T. *Corporate Financial Decisions*. Palo Alto, Cal.: Pavan, 1976, Chapters 7 and 8.

Moyer, R. Charles, James R. McGuigan, and William J. Kretlow. *Contemporary Financial Management*, 4th ed. St. Paul: West, 1990, Chapter 11.

Naylor, Thomas H., and John M. Vernon. *Microeconomics and Decision Models of the Firm*. New York: Harcourt, Brace and World, 1969, Chapter 16. (Chapter is written by E. T. Byrne, Jr.)

Neveu, Raymond R. *Fundamentals of Managerial Finance*, 3d ed. Cincinnati: South-Western, 1989, Chapter 12.

Simon, Julian. *Applied Managerial Economics*. Englewood Cliffs, N.J.: Prentice-Hall, 1975, Chapters 3, 6, 11, and 17.

Weston, J. Fred, and Eugene F. Brigham. *Essentials of Managerial Finance*, 9th ed. Hinsdale, Ill.: The Dryden Press, 1990, Chapter 16.

International Capsule III

Project Analysis in a Multinational Setting

Chapters 13 and 14 provided a brief introduction to the subject of capital projects and their evaluation. There the emphasis was on comparison of alternative investment opportunities available to the firm over the long run. As we saw, the procedures normally followed in project evaluation take into account the price tags attached to various undertakings and the stream of benefits the firm expects to receive from each of them. The methodology of determining the net present value (*NPV*) of the alternatives is fairly straightforward and involves the use of pro-forma income statements based on discounted future revenues and costs for some specified project life. But a number of complexities enter the analysis when capital budgeting techniques are applied to international projects.

INTERNATIONAL DIMENSIONS OF PROJECT ANALYSIS

Today, the most common setting for international capital budgeting decisions is one in which a large firm is evaluating whether or not to set up a subsidiary in a foreign country, or, perhaps, whether or not to add

to the fixed assets of an existing foreign subsidiary. In multinational finance, the country where a foreign subsidiary is located is commonly called the "host country," the firm that owns the subsidiary the "parent firm," and the country where the parent firm is located the "home country." The basic framework for analysis of foreign capital projects is the same as that used for domestic projects. However, in the case of international projects, the evaluation is complicated by a number of factors that do not enter the picture in home country capital project analysis. Some of the more important considerations follow.

1. Should the capital budgeting analysis be conducted from the viewpoint of the parent company, that of the foreign subsidiary, or both?
2. Will remittances of profits from the foreign operation be restricted by the host country of the subsidiary?
3. What will be the income tax treatment of subsidiary earnings by the host government and parent company income by its home government?
4. Will there be differential rates of inflation between the home country

and the host country of the subsidiary?

5. How will net flows of income to the parent company be affected by changes in foreign exchange rates between its currency and that of the subsidiary?

6. What are the political risks associated with investment in the host country?

7. What additional factors will affect the cost of capital and therefore the discount rate applicable to the project?

From this list, it should be apparent that many of the differences between domestic and international capital projects call for quantitative adjustments that will affect either the discounted cash flows or the rate of discount for any given international investment undertaking. In addition, a firm planning a significant foreign investment project will have to ascertain whether or not there are unusual elements that may increase or decrease the initial amount of investment (project price). For example, a government may require that a firm undertake certain ancillary investments (worker housing, medical clinics, etc.) along with its investment in plant facilities, or it may provide subsidies to foreign firms that invest in certain types of activities deemed essential for economic growth.

Parent vs. Subsidiary

While a thorough analysis of a foreign capital project might include a capital budgeting analysis from the point of view of the subsidiary as an independent firm operating in the foreign country, it is widely argued by financial experts that the overriding consideration in analyzing a foreign capital project is whether or not the project is acceptable when analyzed from the viewpoint of the parent company. The two viewpoints may produce different results because of

limitations on the amount of profits that can be transferred to the parent and because of the tax treatment of such flows. If the objective of the firm is to maximize shareholder wealth, then it is the cash flows to the parent that are available to pay dividends and use for reinvestment purposes that will determine whether or not a foreign project is acceptable.[1]

Adjustment of Project Cash Flows

Cash flows into a projected foreign subsidiary are estimated as in any capital budgeting analysis on the basis of anticipated annual sales revenues, operating costs, and depreciation, as well as the salvage value that may occur from disposition of fixed assets at the end of the project. These calculations usually are made in the currency of the country where the subsidiary is located (local currency).

If the subsidiary is destined to sell only in the local market, an analysis of local demand will be required for the revenue estimates. This may not be an easy matter for the parent company, since the determinants of local demand may differ from those used to analyze demand in the home country. Operating costs may differ in the foreign country for a variety of reasons ranging from labor union practices to such cost items as those associated with locally pur-

■ ■ ■ ■ ■ ■

[1] Contemporary research on international capital budgeting shows that many firms do use the subsidiary's point of view rather than that of the parent. This is partially explained by the historical evidence that remittances are seldom permanently blocked and that firms can use transfer pricing and other techniques to get around restrictions on remittances of earnings. See, for example, Vinod B. Bashevi, "Capital Budgeting Practices at Multinationals," *Management Accounting* (August 1981), pp. 32–35; and Marjorie Stanley and Stanley Block, "An Empirical Study of Management and Financial Variables Influencing Capital Budgeting Decisions for Multinational Corporations in the 1980s," *Management International Review* 23, no. 3 (1983), pp. 61–71.

chased materials and parts and local charges for insurance, utilities, and government-provided services. Moreover, both cost and revenue estimates may have to be adjusted for anticipated inflation. Finally, the net cash flow of the subsidiary will depend also on the host country's laws regarding income taxes and allowable depreciation.

Once the net cash inflow to the subsidiary is determined, a number of additional adjustments must be made in order to arrive at the net inflow to be received by the parent company. First, the funds remitted annually by the subsidiary must be converted into the currency of the parent. This is not a simple matter, since the exchange rate applicable to one time period may differ substantially from that applicable to another. While forecasting exchange rates is difficult, any tendency for a rate to move in a predictable direction should be taken into account. With the flows to the parent now expressed in its own currency, the next adjustment would be for income taxes owed by the parent to the home country. In general the United States tax laws have provided that a parent company may credit any foreign income taxes paid against the U.S. tax liability on remittances. Thus the tax on earnings transferred annually to the parent from the subsidiary is reduced by the amount of foreign income taxes already paid. There may be a final inflow to the parent due to transfer of funds from the sale of the entire project or some of its assets at the end of the project's life. A home country tax liability may be incurred, depending on the relation between the sale price and book value of the assets sold.

Risk and the Discount Rate

It is widely recognized that risk in foreign capital projects may differ from risk in home country capital projects. Besides exchange rate risk, there are important elements of political risk that can affect anticipated project inflows. For example, if the host country has an unstable government, flows into the subsidiary may be interrupted by economic or social disorder. There is also the possibility that the host country may expropriate or confiscate foreign businesses. Clearly, the evaluation of a foreign capital project must take these additional types of risk into account.

There is a temptation to argue that the firm can allow for the additional risks associated with foreign projects by applying a higher discount rate than that used in home country analyses. In fact, many firms do take this approach.[2] However, it is argued that doing so is too simplistic and overlooks such possibilities as the fact that a fall in the value of the foreign currency, for example, may either decrease or increase the net inflows, depending on where output is sold and the sources of inputs. A high discount rate may also penalize early inflows excessively and not penalize distant inflows enough.

Because of these complications, many analysts argue that, wherever possible, adjustment for the foreign risks of a project should be handled by adjusting its forecasted cash flows. Then, when the cash flows to the parent are determined, they are discounted at a rate that reflects only overall business and financial risk. In effect this is the same rate used for home country projects. However, if the firm's presence in a country with extremely high foreign risk (such as Libya in the 1980s) increases its overall risk of bankruptcy, this would likely drive up its cost of obtaining funds and thus also the discount rate.

■ ■ ■ ■ ■ ■

[2] See David K. Eiteman and Arthur I. Stonehill, *Multinational Business Finance*, 5th ed. (Reading, Mass.: Addison-Wesley, 1989), p. 524.

EXAMPLE OF A FOREIGN PROJECT

Perhaps the best way to understand how foreign capital project analysis differs from analysis done for investments at home is to consider an example of such a project. In our example we will follow the pattern used for the capital project study in Chapter 13 (Clickwash), indicating where specific steps are taken to adjust for foreign operations. The name of our parent firm will be MacWash, Incorporated, and its product line will be washing machines. MacWash is considering an investment in a plant in a developing country, Lavaria, where the sales of modern laundry detergents have been growing rapidly. The company has developed a hand-operated washing machine that takes advantage of the new detergents and can be used in areas where electricity is not widely available. It believes Lavarians will respond dramatically to the introduction of this product, especially if it is produced in their country.

MacWash will have to set up a subsidiary that is incorporated in Lavaria. The initial investment (project price) will be $4,800,000. Studies indicate that the subsidiary can be expected to have annual gross sales receipts amounting to 12,000,000 units of local currency. In Lavaria, the local currency is the Elsie, abbreviated $L\mathcal{C}$. Annual operating costs including depreciation are estimated to be $L\mathcal{C}7,200,000$. The income tax rate in Lavaria is 25 percent, and the subsidiary will have allowable straight-line depreciation of $L\mathcal{C}800,000$ per year. The Elsie is a stable currency and is expected to remain at $L\mathcal{C}1 = \$0.30$ throughout the life of the project, which MacWash knows will be six years. At the end of the six years, the Lavarian Development Bank will pay MacWash $L\mathcal{C}11,200,000$ (the book value of the project) and take over the plant. The

U.S. tax rate is 34 percent. MacWash has decided to use a risk-adjusted discount rate of 14 percent for the project, even though it currently uses only a 12 percent rate on domestic investments. Finally, Lavaria does not restrict remittances or assess additional taxes against them.

Table III-1 is a worksheet for the MacWash project. The top portion of the table shows the project's net cash inflows in local currency. This is what the subsidiary in Lavaria would receive as a firm incorporated there. The bottom half of the sheet continues the analysis to determine the net present value (NPV) of the project from the viewpoint of the parent. Here the annual net cash inflows to the parent are converted to U.S. dollars, and the additional U.S. tax liability is deducted. The present value of the net after-tax inflows for the six-year period is then added to that of the net after-tax inflow from the development bank payment occurring at the end of the six years to obtain the present value (PV) of the net cash inflows to the parent. Finally, the NPV of the project is obtained by subtracting its price from the PV of the net cash inflows. Since the NPV is positive, the project should be accepted.

Although our MacWash example is greatly simplified, it does call attention to three of the important foreign variables that must be considered in any analysis of this type—taxes, exchange rates, and political risk. A different tax treatment of income or remittances by Lavaria or of foreign source income by the United States might possibly yield a negative NPV for the project. This is one reason why it would not be prudent to evaluate the project from the standpoint of the subsidiary alone. A weakening of the Elsie would present additional problems, since the $L\mathcal{C}$ earnings of the subsidiary might not translate into a sufficient net cash inflow to the parent to make the project

Table III–1   Worksheet for MacWash Foreign Capital Project

Annual Gross Receipts from Sales		LC̷12,000,000
Less:		
Annual Cost of Operations	LC̷7,200,000	
Net Income Before Taxes		LC̷4,800,000
Less:		
Income Tax (Lavaria, 0.25)	LC̷1,200,000	
Net Income		LC̷3,600,000
Plus:		
Depreciation	LC̷800,000	
Annual Net Inflow from Project		LC̷4,400,000
Annual Net Inflow to Parent (LC̷ = $0.30)		$1,320,000
Less:		
U.S. Income Tax	$489,600[a]	
Credit Local Tax	(360,000)	
	$ 129,600	
Parent Net Annual Inflow After Taxes		$1,190,400
PV of 6-Year Net Inflow [PVF_a (14%, 6) = 3.8887]		$4,629,108
PV of Development Bank Purchase		
Payment [LC̷11,200,000 × .30] = $3,360,000		
Times PVF (14%, 6) =	$1,530,816	
PV of Net Inflow to Parent		$6,159,924
Project Price		($4,800,000)
NPV of Project		$1,359,924

[a][.34 × LC̷4,800,000 × .30 = .34 × $1,440,000]

feasible. Finally, this project is acceptable with the end payment from the Lavarian development bank but would not be acceptable without it. If the Lavarians were to delay this payment very much, its PV would fall and likely make the project unacceptable.

In practice, capital budgeting analyses of projects such as this one can become extremely complex. Since a project of this type is often fraught with uncertainties, it is not uncommon to simulate a number of scenarios, including a worst-case possibility, before making a final decision on it. However, despite the difficulties involved and the additional risks that confront a firm when it operates on foreign turf, the widespread success of multinational corporations suggests that the rewards are often well worth the effort.

■ ■ Questions and Problems ■ ■

1. How is foreign capital project analysis similar to home country project analysis? How is it different? Identify specific considerations the firm must take into account in foreign project analysis that do not exist in home country analysis.

2. Do firms ever employ a higher risk-adjusted discount rate for foreign than for domestic capital budgeting? Why or why not? Discuss the use of such a rate as opposed to the adjustment of project flows as an approach to foreign capital project analysis.

3. Reevaluate the MacWash project of Table III-1 on the assumption that the Lavarian Elsie will have the following values over the life of the project:

Year	Dollar Value of One Elsie
1	$0.30
2	0.34
3	0.32
4	0.28
5	0.28
6	0.28

4. Garibaldi Pizza Machine Corporation (a U.S. firm) is evaluating an investment project in Blutonia. The government of Blutonia is anxious to establish a capital goods industry and believes pizza machines would be a good place to start, since Blutonians prefer high-calorie foods. The plan calls for Garibaldi to set up a subsidiary in Blutonia at an initial outlay cost of $5.2 million (U.S.). It will be allowed to operate the subsidiary for four years and return all the profits to the United States each year. At the end of the four years, the subsidiary must be turned over to the Blutonian government, which will sell it to local private investors and retain all proceeds from the sale.

The local currency is the Bluto. At the inception of the project, the value of one Bluto is $0.50 U.S. It is projected that the before-tax earnings of the subsidiary will be:

Year	Earnings Before Taxes (Blutos)
1	2,000,000
2	4,000,000
3	6,000,000
4	6,000,000

The subsidiary will have a cash inflow from allowable depreciation of 200,000 Blutos per year. The Bluto is expected to remain stable. The corporate income tax rate in Blutonia is 20 percent, while in the United States it is 38 percent. Garibaldi currently uses a risk-adjusted discount rate of 12 percent for international projects.

a. What will be the estimated after-tax net cash inflows to the parent?

b. Should Garibaldi accept the project?

■ ■ ■ **Selected References** ■ ■ ■

Booth, Laurence D. "Capital Budgeting Frameworks for the Multinational Corporation," *Journal of International Business Studies* (Fall 1982), pp. 114–23.

Eiteman, David K., and Arthur I. Stonehill. *Multinational Business Finance*, 5th ed. Reading, Mass.: Addison-Wesley, 1989, especially Chapters 16–18.

Lessard, Donald R. "Evaluating Foreign Projects: An Adjusted Present Value Approach." In *International Financial Management*, ed. D. R. Lessard. New York: Wiley, 1985.

Madura, Jeff. *International Financial Management*, 2d ed. St. Paul: West, 1989, especially Chapters 15–16.

Weston, J. Fred, and Bart W. Sorge. *Guide to International Financial Management*. New York: McGraw-Hill, 1977.

Integrating Case 4A

A "Guaranteed" Foreign Investment

Western Consolidated Industries, a diversified manufacturing firm, has been negotiating with the government of a large Latin American country regarding a proposal to install and operate a packaging equipment plant in a new industrial park located outside the nation's capital city. The foreign government's current offer would allow Western Consolidated to operate the plant for a period of six years and to transfer its after-tax profits to the United States each year. The foreign tax rate on profits would be equal to that in the United States (46 percent), so that under U.S. tax laws no U.S. income tax would be due. Presently there are two variations of the project that would be acceptable to the foreign government.

PROPOSAL I

Western Consolidated would install a plant with facilities for manufacturing two types of packaging machines: Type *A*, a light-duty machine commonly used by small packaging firms, and Type *B*, a heavy-duty machine capable of handling larger jobs and faster rates of output. The government would guarantee the following quantities sold and prices for the six years that Western Consolidated is permitted to operate the plant:

	TYPE A		TYPE B	
Year	Price	Quantity Sold	Price	Quantity Sold
1	$12,000	50	$22,000	20
2	13,000	50	24,000	20
3	14,000	60	26,000	40
4	16,000	60	28,000	40
5	18,000	60	30,000	60
6	20,000	60	32,000	60

At the end of the six years of operation, the government would buy the plant from Western Consolidated at U.S. book value, thereby returning the remainder of invested capital to the company with no gain on the sale and therefore no U.S. tax due.

Western Consolidated's management estimates that the initial outlay to install the plant will be $1,200,000 and that the book value of the plant to be returned at the end of the sixth year will be $960,000. Annual fixed costs, including depreciation, will be $200,000 for the first year of operation and will increase 10 percent each year over the remaining five years. For any one year, the average variable cost of each type of unit is expected to be constant, but AVC will have to be adjusted upward for rising input prices. The AVC estimates by year for the two types of machines are as follows:

Year	AVC_A	AVC_B
1	$ 9,600	$15,500
2	10,400	17,100
3	11,200	17,940
4	12,000	19,320
5	14,400	20,250
6	16,000	21,500

The Latin American government has agreed to make all guaranteed payments in U.S. dollars, so that Western Consolidated will run no exchange-rate risk. Management normally uses a discount rate of 12 percent for its U.S. investments, and it has been argued that the same rate should be applied to this foreign project, since the government guarantees will minimize risk.

■ ■ ■ ■ ■ ■ ■ ■ ■ **PROPOSAL II**

Under this alternative, Western Consolidated would install a somewhat less flexible plant with facilities for producing only the Type B packaging machine. The initial outlay on the plant installation would be only $960,000, but the book value that would be returned at the end of six years would also be less: $768,000. Annual total fixed costs for this type of plant will be only $180,000 in the first year of operation but will increase by 10 percent each year. The prices guaranteed for the Type B machine would be the same as those stated for each year in Proposal I. In addition the above data on AVC for the Type B machine would continue to be applicable. However, the guaranteed quantity sold of the Type B machine when it is the only kind produced would be as follows:

Year	Quantity Sold of Type B
1	50
2	60
3	60
4	80
5	100
6	100

The tax rate of 46 percent on profits will apply as in Proposal I, and the purchase of the plant at book value will ensure that no capital gains taxes will be due on the amount received when the government takes over the operation at the end of six years. Finally, the company's management will use a 12 percent discount rate in the evaluation of this alternative, again because of the low level of risk assured by government guarantees.

■ ■ ■ ■ ■ ■ ■ ■ ■ ■ ■ ■ ■ **Questions** ■ ■ ■ ■ ■ ■ ■ ■ ■ ■ ■ ■ ■

(Hint: When evaluating project inflows, be sure to reduce annual gross profits by the amount of foreign profits taxes paid.)

1. Is Proposal I an acceptable capital project? Why or why not?
2. Is Proposal II an acceptable capital project? Why or why not?
3. If the discount rate is raised to 14 percent, would either proposal be acceptable?
4. What kinds of information about the projects or the environment of the country might lead to a decision to employ an even higher discount rate to evaluate inflows?

Integrating Case 4B

Shanghai Magnificent Harmony Foundry II

Happy Mr. Fei! His manhole cover project (Case 2B, "Shanghai Magnificent Harmony Foundry I," following Chapter 7) has been deemed a smashing success, since he was able to obtain U.S. trade preference status and iron ore prices did not increase. The Central Management Committee is so impressed with Fei's handling of the matter that they now want him to search out other types of simple cast-iron products that could be exported to the United States.

On a trip to the United States, Mr. Fei discovered that the health and fitness boom has created dramatic increases in demand for all types of exercise equipment. Cast-iron weights for body-building programs at fitness centers and gyms seemed to be selling very well in the U.S. market. Mr. Fei realized that it would be a simple matter for Shanghai Magnificent Harmony Foundry (SMHF) to cast the circular weights used on lifting bars, but producing the bars themselves would present an additional problem.

To be competitive with other producers of weight-lifting equipment, Mr. Fei will have to provide lifting bars to the U.S. firms that would distribute the cast-iron weights. These bars must be of forged metal, and they are normally machined and chromium-plated to improve their appearance and deter rust. While SMHF has sufficient idle capacity in forging to manufacture the bars, it has no facilities for machining and chrome plating and will have to invest in both types of equipment to realize the new project. The cost of the equipment is estimated to be 960,000 Renminbi Yuan, or 200,000 U.S. dollars at the official exchange rate applicable to both offshore sales and valuation of capital investments.

Because of a slowdown in China's shipbuilding industry, SMHF will be able to release some casting capacity to Mr. Fei for export-oriented production of the weights. This is estimated to be 500 short tons per year (2,000 lbs. = one short ton) over the next five years.

Mr. Fei has been told that the weight-lifting equipment undertaking must be evaluated with a five-year project life, since management expects it will have to reallocate the casting capacity to parts for shipbuilding as demand recovers in that sector. If casting capacity increases due to government allocation of investment funds, exports of the new product would be continued, but there is certainly no guarantee of this.

Given the success of his previous project, Mr. Fei is certain that no tariff will have to be paid on the weight-lifting equipment. For every pound of weights sold, 0.25 lb. of lifting bars (straight bars, curling bars, and dumbbell bars) will be sold. The simple cast-iron weights will have to be sold at the world market price of cast iron, which comes to $0.48 per lb. delivered to U.S. West Coast ports. His net price for both weights and bars will have to be reduced by $0.06 per lb. for freight. The landed price of the bars will be double that of the weights. Mr. Fei estimates that the forging, machining, and chrome plating processes will increase the cost of the bars by 75 percent in comparison with ordinary cast-iron products. Further, he believes that all of the 500-ton output can be sold each year.

Mr. Fei has been instructed to evaluate the weight-lifting equipment project over the five-year time horizon using a risk-adjusted discount rate of 18 percent per year. The Central Management Committee has chosen not to require this project to carry any allocated fixed costs. Variable cost per pound of product will be the same as for manhole covers (see SMHF I), with appropriate adjustment for the production of the lifting bars. The bars and weights must sum to the available capacity allocated to the project. Mr. Fei has been told not to assume any salvage value for the equipment. Assume that the project will not be assessed income taxes, and therefore that Mr. Fei will not be able to achieve any tax savings from depreciation of the new equipment.

■ ■ ■ ■ ■ ■ ■ ■ ■ ■ ■ ■ ■ ■ **Questions** ■ ■ ■ ■ ■ ■ ■ ■ ■ ■ ■ ■ ■

1. From the data given in this case, will the project be acceptable given the investment that must be made to do the plating of the bars?
2. Calculate the impact that the following would have on the project:
   a. A reduction in the risk-adjusted discount rate to 15 percent per year.
   b. A shortening of the project life to four years, given the original (18 percent per year) risk-adjusted discount rate.

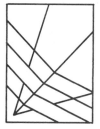

The Firm and the Public Sector

15
Economics of Public Sector Decisions

16
Legal and Regulatory Environment of the·Firm

17
The Firm and the Future

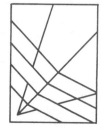

Economics of Public Sector Decisions

In this chapter and the two that follow, we direct attention to the economic interrelationships between business firms and government. We begin at an operational level, adapting the optimizing decision rules discussed in previous chapters to problems of public sector decision making. We shall find that many of the economic principles developed in the context of the profit-maximizing firm can be carried over to certain types of public managerial problems. However, the nature of much of the public sector's product is such that some new tools of analysis must also be developed.

This chapter deals primarily with managerial decisions concerning the supply of goods and services by the public sector. In Chapter 16 we address the matter of the effects of one of the public sector's products, laws and regulations, on private firms and their managers. Finally, Chapter 17 is devoted to an overview of recent developments in the sphere of government-business relationships and an attempt to identify trends that will define the environment of business firms and managerial decision makers in the not-too-distant future.

■ ■ ■ ■ ■ ■ ■ ■ MICRO- VERSUS MACROECONOMICS IN PUBLIC SECTOR ANALYSIS

In the United States, public sector purchases of goods and services amount to about 20 percent of GNP. Much of our national economic policy focuses on the *macroeconomic* variables (aggregate consumption expenditures, gross private domestic investment, total government expenditures, taxes, and the money supply) that determine the level of employment and activity in the economy. In a very broad and general sense, the GNP is an indicator of the well-being of the nation's citizens, and increases in real GNP (i.e., GNP adjusted for changes in the purchasing power of the dollar) can be interpreted as improvements in the overall standard of living, as long as they are not outstripped by population increases and the picture is not distorted by shifts in the distribution of income among individuals or groups. Of course, the way in which resources are utilized by government is another important factor affecting the well-being of a society.

The federal government through its budgetary processes and its management of monetary policy, attempts to make the decisions necessary to move toward the attainment of an overall goal of full employment and relatively stable prices. However, in the process of managing the federal budget and the activities subsumed under it, literally thousands of *microeconomic* decisions must be made each day in the agencies and the bureaus that are responsible for the particular uses to which government-obtained resources are put. As some well-known public expenditure experts have stated:

> The evaluation of aggregate expenditure and taxation levels is an important ingredient in establishing national goals and priorities. However, expenditures are not made in the aggregate, but rather for specific goods and services. Whether the aggregate level is ideal in part depends on whether these specific expenditures can be justified on an individual basis.[1]

Administrators working in public bureaus and agencies (whether local, state, or federal) frequently occupy slots not unlike those held by business managers. Therefore the decision analyses developed for profit-maximizing firms can prove very useful to such administrators, even if the objective of their agency seems remote from the notion of economic profit. To apply managerial economics to the problems of public sector microeconomic decisions, we must first take a close look at the nature of public sector output and the objectives its production is meant to fulfill. We then emphasize in the balance of this chapter the techniques used in making public sector decisions relating to governmental output of specific goods and services.

■ ■ ■ ■ ■

[1] Gary Fromm and Paul Taubman, *Public Economic Theory and Policy* (New York: The Macmillan Company, 1973), p. 28.

■ ■ ■ ■ ■ ■ ■ ■ ■ **THE PUBLIC SECTOR'S PRODUCT**

The public sector (for our purposes, federal, state, and local government) produces an output of goods and services that consists mainly of public goods and *mixed goods* (goods that are partly public). In Chapter 14 we noted that an essential characteristic of a public good is that it provides benefits to parties who do not engage in a market transaction to obtain it. We also called these benefits *external benefits* or *third-party benefits*.

Perhaps the most obvious example of a public good is national defense. The benefits to all members of our society as a result of "consuming" national defense are generally considered to be significant. However, we do not individually engage in market transactions to purchase national defense, and the amount any given consumer would be willing to pay for defense would probably be zero if the consumer thought that the defense would be supplied whether or not he or she paid anything for it.

A **pure public good** is a product or service that is indivisible and nonexcludable.

Economists say that a good is a **pure public good** if it is *indivisible* (if one person cannot consume a unit of it apart from other units) and *nonexcludable* (if it is difficult or impossible to keep it from consumers who do not pay for it). Aside from national defense, other examples of public goods are scenic views, lakes and rivers, food and drug regulation, criminal justice, and "free" radio and television. Clearly, not all public goods are produced by the public sector—God or NBC may be the supplier of some of them.

The public sector also produces a large quantity of mixed goods that provide third-party benefits, as well as private benefits, to users who pay (perhaps not the full cost) for the privilege of using them. Postal service, public housing projects, state and federal parks, and toll roads are all examples.

Finally, the public sector does produce certain goods that are almost purely private. For example, the Tennessee Valley Authority (TVA), which was set up primarily to control floods and provide rural electricity, produces fertilizer that is sold to farmers in the marketplace alongside similar products made by private industry. However, in this case it can be argued that an important reason for the production by the public sector of such a divisible and excludable good as fertilizer is that such production results in social benefits that exceed the private benefits to farmers from their use of the product. For example, excess or off-peak generating capacity can be used in fertilizer production rather than left idle, and the TVA is able to conduct research on the production and use of fertilizer in depressed agricultural areas. Thus, even when an element of the public sector's output takes on the appearance of a private good, its character can be expected to be mixed because of external benefits related to its production.

Although we have so far characterized public and mixed goods by focusing on external benefits that accompany their production, it should be noted that the production of many goods (including public, mixed, and private goods) also entails external costs. As we shall see in the following section, both external costs and external benefits raise serious problems regarding the extent to which a free market system can achieve an economically efficient allocation of resources.

■ ■ ■ ■ ■ ■ ■ ■ ■ **RESOURCE ALLOCATION AND THE SUPPLY OF PUBLIC GOODS**

If government undertakes to supply a particular good or service, it must withdraw resources from the private sector, usually by purchasing them in the market. Since a reallocation of resources and a change in the economy's output follow, it is important that government decision makers ascertain whether these products result in an increase in the general well-being of the citizenry as a whole. There are really two parts to this question. First, will the government activity result in a more efficient allocation of resources? And second, will the distribution of income be altered in a way that is likely to improve the general well-being? The second question is necessary, since the provision of certain types of public sector output may involve taking income from one group of citizens and transferring it to another. At this point, however, we will concentrate on answering only the first of the two questions.

The resource allocation question applies both to privately produced goods and to public sector output. In theory the amount of any good that should be supplied at a point in time is the quantity that *equates the marginal social cost of the good with its marginal social benefit.* We need a few definitions to understand this concept.

The **marginal social cost** of a good is equal to the marginal private cost of producing it plus any marginal external costs imposed on third parties by its production. The marginal social cost of a good reflects the value of resources used in its production.

First, the marginal *private* economic cost of a good includes all explicit and implicit costs of its production that are borne by the producer. A product's **marginal social cost** differs from its marginal private cost by the amount of external costs (third-party costs) that accompany the production of an incremental unit of output. This cost includes the value to consumers of any alternative product or products whose production is reduced or eliminated. If there are no external costs, marginal social cost and marginal private cost will be identical at each level of output.

The **marginal social benefit** of a good is equal to the marginal private benefits the good provides plus any additional external or third-party benefits.

In similar fashion we can define **marginal social benefit** as the sum of marginal private benefits and marginal external or third-party benefits. The private benefits accrue to those who directly pay a price for the good, while the external benefits are enjoyed by either the purchaser and/or nonpurchasers but are not accounted for in the product's market price. Of course, where there are no external benefits, marginal social benefit and marginal private benefit will be identical at each level of output.

If we argue that all sorts of benefits and costs can be given a dollar value, we can proceed very straightforwardly to the rationale behind the assertion that a good should be provided up to the quantity where marginal social cost equals marginal social benefit. Actually, this principle is a simple extension of the profit-maximizing decision rule for a firm: that the firm should produce up to the point where its marginal revenue equals its marginal cost. Where the decision-making unit is a governmental unit rather than a firm, we merely substitute "social benefit" for revenue and "social cost" for private cost:

The **net social benefit** of a good is equal to its total social benefit less its total social cost.

To maximize the **net social benefit** received from a good or service, it should be produced up to the point where its marginal social benefit is equal to its marginal social cost. The net social benefit of a good is equal to its total social benefit less its total social cost.

In Figure 15–1, we illustrate a total social benefit curve and a total social cost curve, both of which are increasing functions of the quantity of public good x. Net benefits are maximized at Q_x^*, where marginal social cost equals marginal social benefit. In the lower panel, the marginal social cost curve intersects the marginal social benefit curve at Q_x^*, and the slopes of the two curves ensure that for levels of output greater than Q_x^*, additions to social cost will exceed additions to social benefit. Thus Q_x^* is the amount of output that will maximize society's net benefit from production of this good.

A theoretically optimal allocation of society's resources exists when for all goods the condition that $MSB = MSC$ is attained. We can further examine this principle by looking at a two-good case, where x and y are the goods, where both costs and benefits are measured in dollars, and where initially we have

(15–1)
$$MSB_x = MSC_x = 20,$$

and

$$MSB_y = MSC_y = 40.$$

Thus the social cost of producing the marginal or last unit of x is \$20, while that of producing the marginal unit of y is \$40. Obviously, it is also true that

(15–2)
$$\frac{MSB_x}{MSC_x} = \frac{MSB_y}{MSC_y} = 1.$$

Now assume that the following conditions exist:

1. All resources are fully employed.
2. Marginal social benefit *falls* as the quantity of each good produced is increased.

Figure 15–1   Maximization of Net Social Benefits

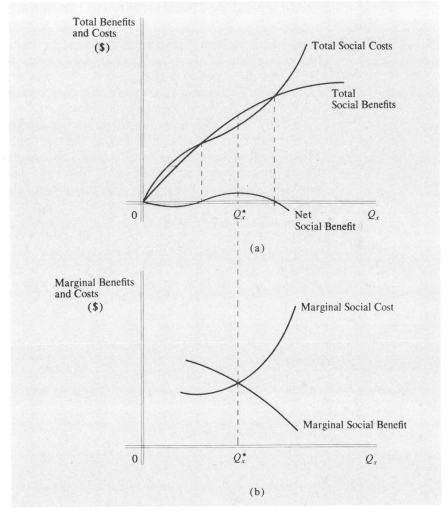

The optimal quantity of a public good is produced where the marginal social benefit of the good equals its marginal social cost. At Q_x^*, net social benefit—the difference between total social benefit and total social cost—is maximized. Production beyond Q_x^* would add more to social cost than to social benefit.

3. Marginal social cost is constant at $20 per unit of x and $40 per unit of y.

What would happen to equation 15–2 if one more unit of y is produced? First of all, a marginal social cost of $40 will be incurred; this means *two* units of x production must be forgone. Since MSB_x will *rise* as the quantity

> ## Managerial Perspective: The $5 Billion Mistake
>
> Long Island Lighting Company had a problem on its hands—a $5.3 billion problem. Its Shoreham nuclear plant, completed at the end of 1983, had not received a license to operate and was not likely to receive one. The reason was that nearby communities were not satisfied with LILCO's emergency evacuation plan.
>
> Finally, New York Governor Mario Cuomo decided that the plant must not start up. After a great deal of negotiation, the state of New York agreed to take the plant off LILCO's hands for $1. However, the $1 price included an agreement to dismantle the plant and haul away the pieces, at least when someone can come up with a safe way to dispose of the radioactive core. Moreover, the state will guarantee LILCO annual rate increases of 5% for at least three years and perhaps as long as 10 years. As a result, LILCO customers will be forced to pay for part of LILCO's expensive white elephant.
>
> ■ ■ ■ ■
>
> Reference: "The $5 Billion Nuclear Waste," *Time* (June 6, 1988), p. 55.

of x is reduced, and MSB_y will *fall* as the quantity of y is increased, the result must be

(15–3)
$$\frac{MSB_x}{MSC_x} > 1 > \frac{MSB_y}{MSC_y}.$$

For example, we might have

(15–4)
$$\frac{22}{20} > 1 > \frac{38}{40}.$$

What are these ratios saying? The answer is much the same as the one we derived in the theory of production with regard to the substitution of inputs in the long run. In particular, for the new output combination, the social *benefit gained* from a *dollar's worth of expenditure* on Product x is $22/20 = 1.10$, whereas the social *loss* from spending a *dollar less* on resources to produce y is $38/40 = 0.95$. Clearly, resources are *misallocated* in the new position (equation 15–4). The production of y should be reduced and that of x increased until the original position is again attained and $MSB_x/MSC_x = MSB_y/MSC_y = 1$.

Finally, we should note that marginal social *cost* is likely to *increase* as production of a good increases and decrease as production falls. This more realistic assumption would not change the directions of the inequalities in

The **incremental benefit-cost ratio** (*MSB/MSC*) of a project is equal to the marginal social benefit divided by the marginal social cost of an incremental unit of the project. The net benefit obtained from a project or activity will be maximized by increasing the size of the project or scope of the activity up to the point where the incremental benefit-cost ratio, *MSB/MSC*, is equal to 1.

equations 15–3 and 15–4, since MSC_x would be less than 20 and MSC_y would be greater than 40. Our case would simply be reinforced by having both marginal social benefits *decrease* and marginal social costs *increase* as the output of a good expands.

We can now summarize the implications of the preceding discussion. First, for a given income distribution, efficient resource allocation will take place when, for *n* goods,

$$\frac{MSB_a}{MSC_a} = \frac{MSB_b}{MSC_b} = \cdots = \frac{MSB_n}{MSC_n} = 1 \qquad \text{(15–5)}$$

This condition simply means that a dollar's worth of social benefit is received for an additional dollar spent on the production of each good. Any deviation from this condition would result in a situation where too much of some good (or goods) and too little of some other good (or goods) is produced.

Furthermore, we can make the following important statement:

No incremental activity (j) should be undertaken where $MSC_j > MSB_j$.

Where the production of public goods is concerned, therefore, it is justifiable to increase output only where $MSB_j/MSC_j \geq 1$—that is, when the incremental social benefit exceeds or equals the incremental social cost of the activity.

The **benefit-cost ratio** (*B/C*) for an activity or project is equal to the present value of its benefits divided by the present value of its cost. A project is acceptable from a social welfare point of view if and only if its *B/C* is greater than or equal to 1.

The fraction *MSB/MSC* is called the **incremental benefit-cost ratio**; and, in cost-benefit analysis, it is employed to determine the optimal *size* of a given public sector activity or project. In the following section, we will contrast this ratio with the ratio of *total* benefits to *total* costs, *B/C*, a concept frequently utilized to identify worthwhile projects and to rank-order them. The ratio *B/C* is often called the **average benefit-cost ratio,** or simply the **benefit-cost ratio.**

■ ■ ■ ■ ■ ■ ■ ■   ## COST-BENEFIT ANALYSIS: A PROCEDURAL OUTLINE

Cost-benefit analysis is an extension of capital project analysis to public sector project decisions that attempts to take into account the economic criteria for an optimal allocation of society's resources.

Cost-benefit analysis is simply the extension of capital project analysis, described earlier in Chapters 13 and 14, to public sector microeconomic decisions. It proceeds from the notion that the aggregate output of government or any subsector thereof consists of an array of alternative projects, each having costs and benefits and each of which can be undertaken at various sizes or operated at various levels of output. To the extent that each of these is carefully screened, their aggregate is likely to have the most beneficial effect on national well-being.

The steps usually taken in the construction of a cost-benefit analysis for a government undertaking are as follows:

1. Specify objectives and identify constraints.
2. Formulate alternative means of meeting objectives.
3. Estimate costs of each alternative.
4. Estimate benefits attributable to each alternative.
5. Select the best alternative.

Every item in the preceding list poses a substantial problem or set of problems for the decision maker. First, the objectives of a public expenditure project are often easy to state in general terms but are difficult to quantify. If, for example, our objective is to improve mass transit services in a given metropolitan area, how can we state it specifically? Do we just want to move a given number of people in less time? Should *more* service be available to a broader range of potential users? What kind of service should we offer (buses, streetcars, subway)? What about passenger comfort? Will the project impose environmental costs or perhaps reduce them?

Some of the preceding questions will be unanswerable until the study is completed, since each of the possible outputs will have a social cost that might exceed its social benefit. In addition, the constraint structure will help to identify feasible characteristics of the preliminary planning objectives. For example, it might be clear at the outset that the metropolitan government can afford to consider only projects with an initial capital outlay of $24 million or less. Thus no combination of services requiring a larger outlay could be considered. There may also be technological constraints. (For example, if the city is located near sea level, a subway might be an impossibility.) Finally, there may be political or institutional constraints or barriers that limit the way in which the undertaking can be designed. For example, if a separately incorporated area that is opposed to a metropolitan transit system lies in the way of one possible alternative route, then the route may not be feasible.

Once the objectives and the constraints are well understood, alternative proposals for the undertaking can be formulated. The next step is to delineate the costs and benefits for each alternative. Then a dollar value estimate must be obtained for each item of cost and benefit. This is not a simple procedure, since a correct analysis of the alternatives must consider *all* economic costs and benefits attributable to each.

In the calculation of costs and benefits, items are usually categorized as *direct* or *indirect* costs or benefits. **Direct costs** of an undertaking include research and planning outlays, initial capital outlay, and maintenance and operating expenses over the project's life. Some items of direct cost will be difficult to estimate because they are implicit. For example, the cost of using government-owned resources (perhaps land) in the project would be estimated using an opportunity cost approach. In the case of land, the cost would be estimated by ascertaining its present value in its next best use.

The **direct costs** of a project or activity are the costs directly associated with the project or activity.

Indirect costs of a project are generally those costs related to externalities that are outputs of the project not accounted for in outlays of the government for project components. For example, if streets must be dug up to construct a subway, the resulting disruption of traffic and business activity will have real costs to society. These kinds of costs are always difficult to estimate because of their partly nonmarket nature. Nonetheless, they must enter into the analysis; and, indeed, a good part of the literature on cost-benefit analysis is directed precisely toward issues of measurement. The one maxim that is universally mentioned by writers on the subject is that such costs should be estimated using the closest possible approximation to the market value of their negative effects. For example, one might use the average value of a working motorist's time to estimate the cost of disruption caused by public works construction.

The **direct benefits** of a project or activity are the benefits obtained by the users of the project or activity.

On the benefits side, **direct benefits** generally accrue to *users* of the project's facilities or primary outputs. In passenger transportation, for example, the main direct benefits accrue to riders of the transportation system. Direct benefits may also accrue to persons employed in the construction and/or operation of the facilities if such persons were previously unemployed. Otherwise, employment associated with the project may simply reflect changes in the distribution of employment, which may produce little or no net social gain.

The **indirect benefits and costs** associated with a project or activity are external, or third-party, benefits and costs.

Much like indirect costs, **indirect benefits** stem mainly from externalities. Thus a system of public mass transit may eliminate congestion for nonusers of the system, and it may enhance the environment by reducing exhaust fumes. A roundabout means of estimation may be necessary to come up with a figure for the dollar value of such benefits. Indeed, the elusiveness of indirect benefits, and especially of their estimation, is one of the major dangers in cost-benefit analysis. This point will be discussed further in a following section.

Since some costs and virtually all benefits will be flows occurring over time, it will be necessary to discount the dollar value of such streams. In the final analysis, the evaluation of each alternative undertaking will rest on the trade-off between the present value of project cost and the present value of benefits. For the field of public investment, the matter of the appropriate discount rate (the *social* rate of discount) has been the subject of much controversy. At this point, it is sufficient for us to note that it is generally a lower rate than that used in the private sector, since government can usually borrow at low rates of interest (for example, the low rates usually paid on municipal bonds). In a subsequent discussion, we will provide an example of the effect of changes in the discount rate on project acceptability.

In capital project analysis in Chapter 13 we saw that a project was acceptable as long as its net present value was greater than or equal to zero. Similarly, a public project or activity is acceptable as long as its net

Managerial Perspective: Valuing a Sea Otter, Asthma Attacks, and Fishing Trips

We have stated that valuing intangibles has presented public officials and economists involved in cost-benefit studies with estimation problems. However, recently natural resource economists have been increasingly in demand to do just that with respect to the environment. In the past, for example, cost-benefit studies of air pollution controls have usually included reduced medical costs among the benefits. Now a recent study has shown that people might be willing to pay as much as $10 per day to avoid the discomfort of coughing and eye irritation caused by pollution.

When the New Bedford Harbor in Massachusetts was found to be polluted by PCBs, the calculated damages included not only the loss to commercial lobster fishers, but also $11 million in damages to beachgoers. Similar calculations were done with respect to lost recreational opportunities as a result of contamination of the Eagle River in Colorado from mining operations. Exxon Corporation and the state of Alaska have both employed economists to estimate the damages to wildlife (such as sea otters) and recreational users as a result of the oil spill in Prince William Sound. In one recent case, a court ruling held that those responsible for dumping oil or toxic chemicals must either restore the environment to its original condition or pay compensation for the total value of the damages, included the loss of nonmarket benefits.

Many of these estimates of nonmarket damages involve asking people how much they would be willing to pay in higher taxes to maintain some natural resource. Some examples of values placed on intangibles in different areas include $73 per household per year for fishing trips on the Eagle River, for an aggregate annual value of $0.5 million; $10 per household per year for preserving the bald eagle in Wisconsin, for a total annual value of $30.0 million; and $25 per household for one less asthma attack per year, for an aggregate annual value of $175 million. Although such figures are still often disputed, it is becoming clear that these nonmarket or intangible costs of pollution are quite real to those who incur them.

■ ■ ■ ■

Reference: "How Much Is a Sea Otter Worth?" *Business Week* (August 21, 1989), pp. 59–62.

benefit is greater than or equal to zero or, equivalently, as long as its benefit-cost ratio is greater than or equal to one. Moreover, an increase in the size of a project or activity will increase the net benefit associated with the project as long as its incremental benefit-cost ratio (MSB/MSC) is greater than one. The net benefit of a project will therefore be maximized by increasing the project size until MSB/MSC is equal to 1. This condition implies that $MSB = MSC$ at the optimal point for the production of a project, the social welfare maximization rule discussed earlier in this chapter.

With the preceding general notions about benefit and cost estimation in mind, we now turn to an example of the application of cost-benefit analysis.

An Application to Urban Mass Transit

Perhaps the best way to illustrate steps taken in reaching a decision through the cost-benefit approach is to look at an application to a specific problem. Let us suppose that we are preparing a cost-benefit analysis of proposed improvements in the transportation system of one of the nation's 15 largest metropolitan areas. It is widely agreed that the current public transportation system, consisting solely of buses and airport limousines, is woefully inadequate. A county-wide metropolitan transit authority has been set up to deal with the problem.

The transit authority has engaged our firm to prepare a cost-benefit analysis of the metropolitan problem. A rough dollar constraint has been established for a number of possible improvement alternatives to be financed by a 20-year bond issue. The maximum amount of funds available for the improvements, which will be completed within 18 months of the sale of the bonds, will be $24 million. Throughout our analysis we will be able to use this figure (or a lower one) as the present value of the project price, even though as many as two years will be required to complete improvements to the system, since the metropolitan authority can earn interest on the unexpended portion of the funds raised at about the same rate as it pays bondholders.[2]

Project Design: The Alternatives

Obviously, in an urban mass transportation project, one of the main items that will determine the possible configurations of services is the demand of the users and potential users. In the present case, we know that existing bus service is considered to be inadequate and that some specific type of service between the airport and certain other points is warranted. Undoubtedly, the existing transit system will have records providing infor-

■ ■ ■ ■ ■ ■
[2] This is possible, since the bonds would be tax exempt and may therefore bear a rate of interest no higher than that on large-size time deposits.

mation on routes and passenger utilization of services. It may even have survey data on passenger opinions regarding new routes and types of service. If not, one of the tasks of the project analysts would be to conduct such surveys. In addition, nontransit objectives (such as pollution control, noise abatement, and general aesthetics) would be items of interest to both the community and the decision makers in the transit authority. To the extent that there are such secondary objectives of the project, they must be made as explicit as possible, and the effects of different alternative solutions on these objectives (the indirect costs and benefits of each alternative) must enter into the overall project calculations.

Let us suppose that in consultation with local authorities, a set of planning objectives is generated. Let us also suppose that based on these objectives and some preliminary estimates of passenger demand, the following alternatives are chosen for evaluation:

1. Modernize and expand the existing bus fleet and continue airport limousine service (initial capital outlay: $4,000,000).
2. Combine bus modernization with helicopter service to the airport and minibus service around the central shopping area (initial capital outlay: $6,000,000).
3. Modernize the existing bus fleet and utilize an existing railway right-of-way to provide commuter train service between the airport, nearby points, and the central business district (initial capital outlay: $11,000,000).
4. Modernize the bus fleet and construct a subway line linking the central business district with the airport and intermediate points (initial capital outlay: $17,000,000).
5. Modernize the bus fleet and construct a monorail train line from the airport and nearby points to the central business district (initial capital outlay: $22,000,000).

With the project alternatives thus set out, the next step is to determine the cost of each alternative. In the present case, each alternative will, in theory, have an optimal size. That size can be expressed in dollar terms as the level of cost that is consistent with provision of service up to the point where marginal social cost equals marginal social benefit. Thus, using alternative 1 as an example, we know there is a limit beyond which additions to the bus fleet and limousine service will likely increase social cost more than they will increase social benefits. However, this does not mean that a change to another type of service, such as the types described in alternatives 2, 3, 4, and 5, would have no potential for net additions to social benefit. We are merely establishing the level of operation of alternative 1 that will provide the maximum net benefit from its employment.

Since there is already a transit system in operation, the relevant cost of each of the improvement alternatives is the present value of the *differential* in cost between the alternative and operation of the existing system *without* modification. Such costs will consist primarily of the initial outlay (from the bond issue) on new capital equipment or modernization of old equipment, the present value of the difference in operating costs over the project life, and any indirect or external costs associated with undertaking and operating the new project—over and above those generated by continued operation of the existing system.

Measurement of the preceding cost items is relatively straightforward, except in the case of indirect or external costs. For example, if we consider alternative 4 or alternative 5, there will be external costs of disruption of traffic caused by the construction of subway or monorail facilities. Indeed, construction of such facilities may require some permanent adjustment in street routes (some may be blocked off by the rapid transit lines and become dead ends), which imposes external costs on motorists in a given area. These costs will by nature be more difficult to estimate than will direct capital costs or operating expenses.

Once the present value of the cost differential for each alternative has been estimated, the calculation of benefits begins. Again, the relevant measure is the differential between benefits generated by each new alternative and benefits that would occur if the existing system were continued over the time period identified as project life.

Turning our attention now to the question of benefits, we expect that most of the incremental benefits will accrue to passengers who use the transit system and pay a fare for the service. However, public transportation is a mixed good that in almost all circumstances generates external benefits. For example, we can expect that nonusers of the transit system will benefit from reduced congestion if the system attracts riders who formerly drove their cars to destinations served by mass transit. In addition, businesses may benefit from reduced expenditures on employee parking facilities or company-subsidized car pool arrangements. Obviously, in this and in almost all public investment projects, we are dealing with a *flow* of benefits over time. Thus the appropriate measure of benefits will be the present value of the differential benefits generated by each alternative.

In Table 15–1 we show an enumeration of the differential costs and benefits attributable to alternative 1. As mentioned previously, the direct cost items are generally the easiest to estimate. The indirect cost item, pollution and noise, is difficult but not impossible to estimate. One well-known procedure is to ascertain the effect of pollution and noise on land values and then use this figure as a proxy for external cost. Obviously, where diesel fumes become noxiously thick, land values are likely to suffer. Fortunately, data on the effect of pollution and environmental decay on land values can frequently be obtained.

In the benefits portion of Table 15–1, we see the estimation problem in a different light. To some extent the direct benefits can be estimated by ascertaining the price that users of the service would be willing to *pay* to ride the system at the optimal level of operation. In fact, this is the theoretically correct way to estimate private benefits to users. However, it

Table 15–1   Present Value of Differential Costs and Benefits of
Mass Transit Improvements: Alternative 1[1]

Differential Costs	
(a) Direct:	
1. Initial capital outlay	$ 4,000,000
2. *PV* of operating cost differential	2,900,000
(b) Indirect:	
1. *PV* of additional pollution and noise	600,000
Total Differential Costs (*PV*)	$ 7,500,000
Differential Benefits	
(a) Direct:	
1. *PV* of time saved by users	$ 2,500,000
2. *PV* of motor fuel saved by users	3,000,000
3. *PV* of other automobile-operating expenses saved	
by users	2,000,000
(b) Indirect:	
1. *PV* of reduced congestion to motorists	2,000,000
2. *PV* of parking and car pool savings of businesses	1,000,000
Total Differential Benefits (*PV*)	$10,500,000

[1]The project life is assumed to be 20 years, and the discount rate is 5 percent. The $3,500,000 *PV* of future differential costs is a discounted stream of $280,847 per year. The $10,500,000 *PV* of future differential benefits is a discounted stream of $842,541 per year.

may be somewhat difficult to estimate, *ex ante*, the fare that will yield the optimal level of use (the passenger volume consistent with $MSC = MSB$). Nevertheless, surveys can be used to determine approximately the number of people who would use the new service, given various prices.

As far as indirect benefits are concerned, the *PV* of reduced congestion to motorists can be estimated by calculating the amount of time that would be saved and then multiplying that figure by an appropriate dollar value per hour. The *PV* of savings to businesses from reduced expenditures on parking facilities and car pool arrangements can be estimated from data supplied by firms.

Once estimation problems have been surmounted, an enumeration such as Table 15–1 is prepared for each alternative. From these enumerations of costs and benefits, data for selecting the best alternative are calculated. Note that from Table 15–1, we have for alternative 1 a ratio of total differential benefits to total differential cost of $10,500,000/$7,500,000 = 1.40. Since the differential benefits exceed the differential costs, or the average benefit-cost ratio is greater than one, alternative 1 is an acceptable project. In fact, any alternative that has an average benefit-cost ratio greater than one is acceptable, since it generates *net* social benefits.

Table 15–1 has been prepared using a discount rate of 5 percent to calculate the present values of future costs and benefits (operating costs, indirect costs, and all of the differential benefits). At this point we provide no rationale for the use of the 5 percent rate and proceed as though the rate itself were not an issue, but the effect of changing the discount rate will be examined later in this chapter.

In Table 15–2 we present summary data on the five alternative projects. Using the average benefit-cost ratio as an accept-reject criterion, we see that all five of the projects are acceptable, since $B/C > 1$ for each one of them.

In Table 15–2 the projects have been listed in order of *ascending cost*. This is a convenient format for our next step—the selection of the optimal project. What we need to know in order to select the best alternative is whether the additional costs incurred when going from a smaller project to a larger one are offset or more than offset by the additional benefits attributable to the larger project. The *incremental benefit-cost ratio*, $\Delta B/\Delta C$, answers this question. A move from a smaller undertaking to a larger one (in terms of total differential costs) is warranted as long as $\Delta B/\Delta C > 1$. Thus, according to Table 15–2, alternative 2 should be selected, since it yields net benefits above alternatives 1 and 3, whereas selecting either alternative 5 or alternative 4 over alternative 2 would add more to differential costs than to differential benefits.[3]

The preceding procedure is simply a way to approximate the condition $MSB = MSC$ where data are discrete or "lumpy" rather than continuous and smooth. From our earlier discussion of profit maximization and its relation to benefit-cost analysis, it should be evident that net benefits will be maximized when the project selected is the largest one for which $\Delta B/\Delta C > 1$. Indeed, the last column of Table 15–2 substantiates this result, since net differential benefits are largest for alternative 2.

■ ■ ■ ■ ■ ■ ■ ■ ■ ## PUBLIC INVESTMENT AND THE DISCOUNT RATE

Although the discount rate was assumed not to be an issue in the foregoing example, it has been the subject of much concern in public investment projects for two reasons. First, there has been a long debate among economists on how to determine the appropriate discount rate for public capital projects. Second, the choice of the discount rate in many cases affects the

---

■ ■ ■ ■ ■ ■

[3] The student should note that if alternative 3 had yielded an incremental cost-benefit ratio less than one, it would have been appropriate to compare alternative 2 with alternative 1, rather than with alternative 3. For example, if the PV of differential costs for alternative 3 had been $15,500,000 instead of $12,000,000, its $\Delta B/\Delta C$ would have been $7,000,000/$8,000,000 = 0.88. We would then check $\Delta B/\Delta C$ between alternative 1 and alternative 2. We would find for this increment that $\Delta B/\Delta C = $13,500,000/$10,000,000 = 1.35. Accordingly, our rule should be that when projects are listed in ascending order of costs, each successively larger project should be compared with the last project for which $\Delta B/\Delta C > 1$ to determine whether or not it should be undertaken. To test your understanding, show that alternative 5 would be the best choice if the PVs of differential costs for alternatives 3 and 2 were $15,500,000 and $21,500,000, respectively.

Table 15–2 Cost-Benefit Comparison of Five Alternative Metropolitan Mass Transit Projects[1]

Alternative No.	PV of Differential Costs (C)	PV of Differential Benefits (B)	B/C	$\dfrac{\Delta B}{\Delta C}$	Net Differential Benefits (B-C)
1	$ 7,500,000	$10,500,000	1.40		$3,000,000
				1.56	
3	12,000,000	17,500,000	1.46		5,500,000
				1.18	
2	17,500,000	24,000,000	1.37		6,500,000
				0.74	
5	27,000,000	31,000,000	1.15		4,000,000
				0.71	
4	34,000,000	36,000,000	1.06		2,000,000

[1]All future differential costs and benefits are discounted at a rate of 5 percent per annum for 20 years. See Table 15–3 for division of costs between capital outlay and discounted future flows, as well as annual benefit inflows.

decision as to which of several alternative projects is optimal. In fact, we shall see below that our decision in the urban transit example will be altered if a sufficiently higher discount rate is applied to the future streams of benefits and costs. Before we examine the effects of various discount rates on project selection, however, it would be useful for us to consider the question of the *theoretically* correct rate.

The "Appropriate" Discount Rate

The social rate of discount is the discount rate appropriate for evaluating public sector projects.

The rate of discount that, in theory, should be applied to public investment projects is called the **social rate of discount** by economists. Since public investment usually involves a reallocation of resources from private to public sector use, many economists argue that the opportunity cost, in terms of rate of return, for the private sectors from which the public undertaking would draw its resources constitutes the appropriate rate of discount. Returns from public sector activities are not taxed; therefore, the before-tax rate of return for the foregone private output should be used as the discount rate. Finally, analysts would also want to take into account the full social costs and benefits of the forgone private output when calculating the rate of return, since this is the procedure they would normally use in estimating the costs and benefits associated with the alternative public use of the resources.[4]

■ ■ ■ ■ ■ ■
[4] See David F. Bradford, "The Choice of Discount Rate for Government Investments," in Robert H. Haveman and Julius Margolis (eds.), *Public Expenditure and Policy Analysis*, 3d ed. (Boston: Houghton Mifflin, 1983), Chapter 6.

Where *neither externalities nor risk* are viewed as materially affecting the opportunity-cost rate of return, the social rate of discount can be viewed as the riskless market rate of return, adjusted for federal income taxes. Thus, if a business can place its funds in riskless government bonds yielding 6 percent interest tax-free, and if the tax rate on its corporate income is 46 percent, its required before-tax rate of return on a riskless project that will generate taxable income will be

$$\frac{.06}{1 - .46} = 11.11\%.$$

If a business were to place $10,000 in a 6 percent, tax-free bond, at the end of the year it would receive a return of $600 = $10,000(.06). However, at the 46 percent income tax rate, we can see that an 11.11 percent taxable return would yield the same after-tax income, since

$$\$10,000(.1111) = \$1,111$$
$$\$ 1,111(-.46) = \underline{\ -511}$$
$$\text{Net Yield} = \$ \ \ 600$$

In practice, analysts of public sector capital projects have seldom attempted to estimate a social rate of discount that reflects the opportunity cost of resources withdrawn from private use. Historically, many federally funded projects have been evaluated using a very low discount rate (4.875 percent during the late 1960s) that was thought to be appropriate because it approximated the cost to the Treasury of borrowing funds.

In a 1967 study of federal budgeting practices, it was discovered that 13 agencies of the government used no discount analysis at all when evaluating expenditure projects. The same study showed that the discount rates used by the 10 agencies that *did* use them to evaluate their 1969 programs ranged from zero to 12 percent.[5] Typically, the rates employed by project analysts at the federal level have been prescribed before the fact and have had little or nothing to do with the opportunity cost of resources.

After more than two decades of criticism of government use of discount rates that in most cases were too low, there has emerged a fairly broad consensus both inside and outside the public sector that rates more realistically reflecting opportunity costs should be used. Accordingly, in recent years the Office of Management and Budget of the federal govern-

■ ■ ■ ■ ■ ■
[5] See Elmer B. Staats, "Survey of Use by Federal Agencies of the Discounting Technique in Evaluating Future Programs," in Harley H. Hinrichs and Graeme M. Taylor (eds.), *Program Budgeting and Benefit-Cost Analysis* (Pacific Palisades, Cal.: Goodyear, 1969), pp. 212–228.

ment has frowned on the use of discount rates lower than 10 percent per year for the evaluation of public programs.[6]

In the final analysis, the best estimate of the appropriate social rate of discount may be the discount rate that reflects the cost of funds for a project of similar length and riskiness in the private sector. Public projects do take resources from the private sector, and the fact that a government may be able to borrow money more cheaply than a private firm because of the tax laws seems irrelevant when one is attempting to value these resources. Therefore it seems reasonable to argue that the private sector cost of funds reflects the opportunity cost of funds used by the public sector for a similar project.

Effect of Changing the Discount Rate

In the preceding discussion, we asserted that changes in the discount rate can markedly affect the outcome of a capital project evaluation. Clearly, the *higher* the discount rate, the *lower* the value of a project's net inflow of benefits, since most of these occur over long periods of time. Moreover, different projects will likely have different ratios of present costs to future costs. Where a project's costs are in large part *future* costs, the present value of total cost may fall dramatically as the discount rate is increased. We can return to our urban transit alternatives to demonstrate how project choice may be affected by higher discount rates.

In Table 15–3 the five mass transit projects described earlier in this chapter are reviewed, and their future costs and benefits are discounted at rates of 5, 7, and 9 percent per year. The 5 percent result is identical to that in Table 15–2, from which we determined that alternative 2 would be optimal. Note the difference in the average and incremental benefit-cost ratios for the higher rates of discount. At a discount rate of 7 percent, alternative 2 is still the project to select, since the incremental benefit-cost ratio between it and the next smallest project is 1.02. Also, its net benefits of $3,876,000 are the highest that can be obtained from any of the alternatives when the discount rate is 7 percent. If the discount rate is increased to 9 percent, alternative 2 is no longer the best choice, since the incremental benefit-cost ratio between it and the next smallest project (alternative 3) falls to 0.89. Given the 9 percent discount rate, however, *alternative 3* has an incremental benefit-cost ratio of 1.34 in comparison with alternative 1, so alternative 3 is the best choice. Note that at the 9 percent discount rate, the net differential benefits of $2,423,000 for alternative 3 are the highest for any of the projects.

From the preceding illustration, we certainly can conclude that the choice of the discount rate is important in project selection. However, our

■ ■ ■ ■ ■ ■
[6] Steven H. Hanke and Richard A. Walker, "Benefit-Cost Analysis Reconsidered: An Evaluation of the Mid-State Project," in Robert H. Haveman and Julius Margolis (eds.), *Public Expenditure and Policy Analysis*, 3d ed. (Boston: Houghton Mifflin, 1983), Chapter 14, especially p. 332.

Table 15–3   Effect of Different Discount Rates on Cost-Benefit Comparison of Five Alternative Metropolitan Mass Transit Projects[1]

Alternative	Discount Rate (r)	Initial Capital Outlay	PV of Future Differential Costs	PV of Total Differential Costs (C)	PV of Total Differential Benefits (B)	B/C	ΔB/ΔC r = 5%	ΔB/ΔC r = 7%	ΔB/ΔC r = 9%	Net Differential Benefits (B-C)
1	5%	$ 4,000,000	$ 3,500,000	$ 7,500,000	$10,500,000	1.40				$3,000,000
	7%	4,000,000	2,975,000	6,975,000	8,926,000	1.28				1,951,000
	9%	4,000,000	2,564,000	6,564,000	7,691,000	1.17				1,127,000
3	5%	6,000,000	6,000,000	12,000,000	17,500,000	1.46	1.56			5,500,000
	7%	6,000,000	5,101,000	11,101,000	14,877,000	1.34		1.44		3,776,000
	9%	6,000,000	4,395,000	10,395,000	12,818,000	1.23			1.34	2,423,000
2	5%	11,000,000	6,500,000	17,500,000	24,000,000	1.37	1.18			6,500,000
	7%	11,000,000	5,526,000	16,526,000	20,402,000	1.23		1.02		3,876,000
	9%	11,000,000	4,761,000	15,761,000	17,579,000	1.12			0.89	1,818,000
5	5%	17,000,000	10,000,000	27,000,000	31,000,000	1.15	0.74			4,000,000
	7%	17,000,000	8,501,000	25,501,000	26,353,000	1.03		0.66		852,000
	9%	17,000,000	7,325,000	24,325,000	22,706,000	0.93			0.60	(1,619,000)
4	5%	22,000,000	12,000,000	34,000,000	36,000,000	1.06	0.71			2,000,000
	7%	22,000,000	10,201,000	32,201,000	30,603,000	0.95		0.63		(1,598,000)
	9%	22,000,000	8,790,000	30,790,000	26,368,000	0.86			0.57	(4,422,000)

[1]Assumes the following annual inflows and costs for a period of 20 years:

Alternative	Annual Inflow of Differential Benefits	Annual Differential Costs
1	$ 842,547	$280,849
3	1,404,245	481,456
2	1,925,822	521,577
5	2,487,520	802,426
4	2,888,733	962,911

mass transit example still gives no clue as to which discount rate we should choose. Obviously, proponents of alternative 2 will not want to accept the results of the analysis at 9 percent, even if we, as consultants, argue that the 9 percent discount rate is the appropriate one. The final decision is thus likely to be a political one, but it will at least be tempered by a realistic attempt to measure what the public is getting from the various alternatives.

■ ■ ■ ■ ■ ■ ■ ■ ■ **COST-BENEFIT ANALYSIS AND DIVERGENT PUBLIC OBJECTIVES**

We have focused thus far on the selection of an optimal project from an array of alternatives, each of which serves approximately the same objective. However, public funds often must be allocated among alternative programs or investments that have greatly different objectives. For example, a city commission may have to decide whether to allocate funds from a bond issue to mass transit improvements, expansion of hospital facilities, development of new parks and recreation facilities, or improvements of streets and sewers. In such a setting, cost-benefit analysis can again be useful.

Economists generally argue that more efficiency is obtained from public expenditures *the greater the benefit per dollar spent*. Benefit per dollar of expenditure is what we measure with the average benefit-cost ratio, *B/C*. Thus, where alternatives involve roughly the same outlay of public funds, those with the highest *B/C* ratios are viewed as the best choices.

In Table 15–4 we show a list of widely divergent public investment alternatives along with the *B/C* ratio for each. Assuming that approximately the same amount of funds is required for each alternative, their rank order in terms of efficiency is *D, A, C,* and *B*. That is, they are ranked such that the alternative with the highest *B/C* ratio is the most desirable, followed by that with the second highest ratio, and so forth.[7] Naturally, this is the point at which competing public agencies and citizens' interest groups are most likely to attack the results of a cost-benefit analysis. There is likely to be no shortage of persons who will argue that improved medical facilities are more important than better streets and sewers, regardless of what the benefit-cost ratios show.

Public outcry against the results of cost-benefit analyses and related types of economic impact analyses (environmental impact studies, for example) is not to be taken lightly. Indeed, the history of cost-benefit analyses in the United States is a very checkered one, and economists

■ ■ ■ ■ ■ ■

[7] If the required outlays for the various projects are *not* equal, the social welfare will be maximized if officials select that *group* of projects that yields the highest total net social benefit and still satisfies the budget constraint under which the governmental authority must operate.

Table 15–4   Average Benefit-Cost Ratios and Ranking of Widely
Divergent Public Investment Alternatives

Alternatives	Description	B/C (Average Benefit-Cost Ratio)	Project Rank
A	Mass Transit Improvements	1.17	2
B	Hospital Facilities Expansion	1.02	4
C	Development of Parks and Recreation Facilities	1.05	3
D	Improvement of Streets and Sewers	1.35	1

themselves disagree on issues of cost and benefit measurement, as well
as on the appropriate method of determining the social rate of discount.
We investigate these problems further in the following section.

■ ■ ■ ■ ■ ■ ■ ■ ■ ■ PITFALLS OF COST-BENEFIT ANALYSIS

The following passage from a contemporary study of cost-benefit analysis
and its use in federal water resources management exemplifies typical
problems of public investment analysis:

> The Bureau of Reclamation has traditionally been accused of using the
> tools of economic analysis to justify decisions that have been deter-
> mined politically. Economists have long been critical of the apparent
> manipulation of cost-benefit analysis in project planning and approval
> processes . . . studies conclude that the Bureau tends to overstate
> benefits and understate costs and that this policy enables projects to
> be built that would not be feasible if "proper" evaluation techniques
> were employed.[8]

Historically, the reputation of cost-benefit analysis as a policy tool has
been severely damaged by over-eager users of the approach who have
seldom failed to justify their pet projects in terms of stated economic
benefits and costs. The Bureau of Reclamation, cited in the previous paragraph, is certainly not alone in its questionable application of cost-benefit
analysis to project evaluation. The economics literature contains cases
too numerous to cite where such branches of government as the Army
Corps of Engineers, the Department of Agriculture, the Department of

■ ■ ■ ■ ■ ■
[8] Steven H. Hanke and Richard A. Walker, "Benefit-Cost Analysis Reconsidered: An
Evaluation of the Mid-State Project," in Robert Haveman and Julius Margolis (eds.), *Public
Expenditure and Policy Analysis,* 3d ed. (Boston: Houghton Mifflin, 1983), p. 324.

Labor, and many state and local authorities or their consultants have produced project studies involving unsound cost-benefit analyses that served
mainly to foster bureaucratic ends. The saving grace of some of these doc-
uments is that they also ignited the flames of public opinion against
both the projects and their sponsors. One example of such a case is the
Cross-Florida Barge Canal, a long-term pet project of the Army Corps
of Engineers.

The Corps of Engineers has one of the longest histories of use and
abuse of cost-benefit analysis in U.S. public works. The Corps has employed cost-benefit analysis to evaluate its waterways projects since 1900.[9]
The Cross-Florida Barge Canal was first proposed by President John
Quincy Adams, and nine studies of its feasibility were made by the government during the period from 1826 to 1930. Some digging was done in
1930, but the project was abandoned.

Congress authorized construction of the canal as a war measure in
1942, but it took another 20 years to appropriate any funds for the project.
The Corps resumed work on the canal in the early 1960s; by 1970 it had
completed roughly 25 miles of the waterway and had spent about $50
million in the process. The canal was finally scuttled by President Nixon
in 1971 after a successful campaign was waged against it by environmen-
talist groups.[10]

Throughout the period that the Cross-Florida Canal was under consideration, the Corps never failed to justify the project from a cost-benefit
standpoint. A 1965 article surveying how cost-benefit analysis has been
used compares a Corps of Engineers estimate of the canal's benefits with
that of the railroad lobby to show a glaring example of self-serving benefit-
cost studies. Whereas the Corps had come up with a benefit-cost ratio of
1.20 for the project, the railroad interests estimated the ratio to be 0.13.
The Corps attributed a large share of total benefits to transportation savings, an item that was much disputed by the railroads. In addition the
Corps included indirect benefits from flood control, recreational boating,
fishing, and enhancement of land values in its estimate. In the railroads'
study, each of these items was valued at zero! The authors of the survey
article concluded:

> To what extent the divergence is due to the facts that the Corps likes
> to build canals and that the consultants were retained by the railroads,
> and to what extent it is due to the intrinsic impossibility of making
> accurate estimates is left entirely to the reader to decide![11]

▪ ▪ ▪ ▪ ▪ ▪

[9] David N. Hyman, *The Economics of Governmental Activity* (New York: Holt, Rinehart, and
Winston, 1973), p. 136.

[10] See "Florida Sets Out to Restore Wetlands By Refilling a Canal Inadvisably Dug," *The
Wall Street Journal*, July 5, 1990, p. A10; and "The Environment: Blocking Florida's Big Ditch,"
Newsweek (February 1, 1971), p. 55.

[11] A. R. Prest and R. Turvey, "Cost-Benefit Analysis: A Survey," *The Economic Journal*
(December 1965), p. 718.

In 1984, environmentalists in Florida won another victory over the Corps of Engineers when the South Florida Water Management District initiated a project to fill in a part of the Kissimmee River Channel, a 20-year-old Corps project that had dried up vast areas of marshland and damaged the complex ecology of South Florida. It was reported that the Water Management District might spend as much as $65 million to undo the alleged damage caused by the channel.[12] However, the very next year, the Corps celebrated the completion of another southern dredging project, the Tennessee-Tombigbee Waterway. Bigger than the Panama Canal and with a price tag of $1.8 billion, this was widely recognized as the grand-daddy of pork-barrel projects. Shortly after its opening, it was reported that barge traffic on the waterway was running at only about 5 percent of the optimistic projections that had been prepared by its proponents.[13]

The use and misuse of cost-benefit analysis are not likely to go away. The possible pitfalls of cost-benefit analysis are summarized in the following three points:

1. *Estimation*, particularly of *indirect benefits*, is not governed by strict standards, so an analysis can be "cooked" to show what its sponsors wish to show.
2. The opportunity-cost approach to the *social rate of discount* may bias the analysis against many worthwhile public undertakings.
3. The sheer *cost* of performing a credible cost-benefit analysis makes the approach unfeasible for many public investment decisions.

A good deal of research has been done on the estimation problems in cost-benefit studies; and, in general, it suggests that the estimation of direct benefits can be adequately accomplished by careful application of the market value or opportunity-cost approaches. Extension of such valuation techniques to the estimation of indirect benefits is questionable and may be unnecessary in many cases. In fact the current trend seems to be toward leaving all but the most obvious indirect benefits out of cost-benefit calculations and including a discussion of their existence and probable extent in the nonquantitative part of project studies or reports. What is being recognized is that the opinions or values of public decision makers and their constituencies regarding nonmarket benefits (and costs) of a given public undertaking might best be expressed by the decision makers themselves rather than by professional economic analysts. Indeed, the nature of many indirect benefits is so elusive that the professional literature on them has taken to referring to them as "intangibles," "irreducibles," and "incommensurables." Thus, from the analyst's standpoint, the best prescription would seem to be to provide a very careful estimate of direct

■ ■ ■ ■ ■ ■

[12] "Now You See It, Now You Don't," *Time* (August 6, 1984), p. 56.
[13] "Rivaling Cleopatra, A Pork-Barrel King Rides the Tenn-Tom," *The Wall Street Journal*, May 31, 1985, pp. 1, 10.

and clearly measurable costs and benefits in public investment studies but to call intangibles by their proper name and make their existence clear to public decision makers.

Turning to the discount rate dilemma, we wish to make two points. First, it is clear from research on the issue that many studies have been made using questionably low rates of discount for future streams of benefits. Certainly, proponents of the opportunity-cost approach would argue as much. Second, and perhaps of more importance, is the question of whether public investment undertakings should be measured using the same criterion, in terms of the rate of return, as that used in the private sector. A minority of analysts and policymakers argue that such projects should not. As one member of Congress has put it, the view that the appropriate discount rate for evaluation of public investment is one that reflects the opportunity cost rate for resources withdrawn from the private sector leads to the conclusion that society would benefit more from a new gadget than from the construction of a new school or sewerage system because the financial return was 5.5 percent on the gadget and only 5 percent on the school or sewerage system.[14] Nevertheless, one could respond that an economic problem would not occur in such cases if the social benefits from each project were estimated with a reasonable degree of accuracy.

Finally, we are left with the pitfall of the *cost* of cost-benefit studies. Much was learned about this problem during the administration of President Lyndon B. Johnson, when the Bureau of the Budget (now called the Office of Management and Budget) implemented an approach to government expenditure analysis known as the Planning, Programming, and Budgeting System (PPBS). Under PPBS, agencies were expected to conduct a yearly review of all of their programs, using the cost-benefit technique. The idea was that the agencies would each rank their projects internally and that the Bureau of the Budget would oversee the process from above, making appropriate recommendations to the Executive Branch regarding interagency allocation of funds.

Although PPBS proved useful in the internal evaluation processes of the agencies, it failed as a *system*, since it proved to generate more information (in terms of sheer information volume) than the Budget Bureau could handle. Indeed, in 1969 it was reported to Congress that 1,145 positions were added to 21 agencies just to support PPBS activities.[15] Not only was PPBS costly, but Congress itself made little use of the output produced by the system and went about business as though PPBS scarcely existed. In any event the PPBS experience suggested that while cost-benefit

■ ■ ■ ■ ■ ■

[14] The statement was made by Senator William Proxmire and is cited in H. H. Liebhafsky, *American Government and Business* (New York: Wiley, 1971), p. 561.

[15] U.S. Congress, Joint Economics Committee, *Analysis and Evaluation of Public Expenditures: The PPB System*, Vol. 2 (Washington: U.S. Government Printing Office, 1969), p. 636.

Managerial Perspective: Toronto's $360 Million
SkyDome

The city of Toronto, Canada, has a new $360 million domed stadium
that city managers forecast will turn a profit. In fact, SkyDome officials expect the stadium to generate a cash flow of $20 million its first
year. In contrast, the Superdome in New Orleans, built for less than
$180 million 14 years ago, still has more than $6 million in annual
operating losses.

The SkyDome was designed as a multiple-use facility that includes a restaurant center, a hotel, and retail mall in the center of
Toronto. The SkyDome is also unique in that it is the first full-size
stadium to have a retractable roof. Including Toronto Blue Jays' home
games, the SkyDome is expected to be used at least 200 days a year
for sporting events, concerts, conventions, and trade shows.

Financing for the $360 million initial outlay came from a variety
of sources: bank loans, corporate investors, presold boxes and seats,
the Ontario government, metro-Toronto governments, a public stock
sale, and the sale of advertising rights. The stadium does have its
critics, however. Some have argued that too much was given to the
corporations in return for their investment. Moreover, visiting seagulls from Lake Ontario have presented the SkyDome with one
unforeseen problem, although one contractor offered to provide fal-
cons to keep the seagulls away for $100,000 a year. Still, as many as
20 retractable-roof stadiums may be built in Japan during the 1990s,
including a $1.6 billion project by Daiei, Incorporated.

■ ■ ■ ■

Reference: "After Skydome, Stadiums Will Never Be the Same," *Business Week* (March
20, 1989), pp. 136–138.

analysis could prove quite useful in the evaluation of individual projects,
its use would have to be tempered by consideration of the cost of the
studies themselves and the ability of the decision-making apparatus to
comprehend and absorb cost-benefit information.

■ ■ ■ ■ ■ ■ ■ ■ ## THE FUTURE OF COST-BENEFIT ANALYSIS

As a policy tool, cost-benefit analysis has been heavily sold by economists
in the past 15 years or so. There is no question that despite the demise of
PPBS, cost-benefit analysis has survived and will continue to be an important policy evaluation tool. From the material presented in this chapter,

the appropriate conclusion to draw is that judicious application of the approach is probably the closest economic analysis can get to a straightforward evaluation of the overall consequences of public investment decisions. In addition, cost-benefit analysis has had enough public exposure to make it a familiar tool to many public sector managers. Fortunately, such exposure has also bared its abuses and shortcomings, so the ability of unscrupulous users to misguide policymakers is somewhat limited. Certainly there are many public investment decisions that can be reviewed adequately using the cost-benefit approach if the pitfalls discussed here are avoided.

■ ■ ■ ■ ■ ■ ■ ■ SUMMARY

Managerial Decisions in the Public Sector

In this chapter we have attempted in a selective way to discuss some of the issues surrounding the application of managerial economics to micro-level decisions in the public sector. We noted that one of the primary characteristics of many goods and services supplied by the public sector is that *external benefits* accrue to persons or groups who do not pay a direct charge for what they receive. The same was also shown to be true for some private sector production. We also found that both types of output (public and private sector) might be accompanied by *external costs*. To the extent such costs and benefits could be measured, it was shown that the optimal allocation of a society's resources at a given point in time would occur if each product or service were supplied up to the point where its *marginal social benefit equaled its marginal social cost*.

The chapter also provided a survey of *cost-benefit analysis*, an approach for evaluating public capital projects that attempts to take into account the economic criteria for an optimal allocation of society's resources. We applied cost-benefit analysis to five alternative proposals for improving a metropolitan area's mass transit system and related the concepts of the *average benefit-cost ratio* (B/C) and the *incremental benefit cost ratio* ($\Delta B/\Delta C$) to the acceptability of projects and the determination of the optimal project size. Finally, our discussion turned to some of the problems associated with cost-benefit analysis, and we noted that application of the technique must be tempered in the light of *estimation difficulties, discount rate questions*, and the *expense* involved in preparing such studies.

We concluded that cost-benefit analysis is a tool that will likely be applied to public managerial questions in the future. In Chapter 17 we will offer some additional predictions about the future of managerial economics. First, however, in Chapter 16 we consider the interrelationships between the public and private sectors in matters of law and business regulation.

■ ■ ■ ■ ■ ■ ■ ■ ■ ■ ■ ■ ■ ■ **Questions** ■ ■ ■ ■ ■ ■ ■ ■ ■ ■ ■ ■ ■ ■

1. How can you distinguish between micro- and macroeconomic decisions of public sector managers? In what sense do some public sector managers occupy positions similar to those of managers of private firms?
2. What is the importance of externalities in the analysis of public goods? Do market prices of privately produced goods usually reflect externalities? Why or why not?
3. Theoretically, what principle determines the optimal amount supplied of a public good? Explain why this principle applies equally to privately produced output.
4. What are the procedural steps that are usually taken in the preparation of a cost-benefit analysis? How is the analysis similar to a private capital project evaluation? How is it different?
5. What is the importance of the *incremental* benefit-cost ratio in making a decision based on cost-benefit analysis? What is the importance of the *average* benefit-cost ratio? Are projects with high average benefit-cost ratios necessarily more desirable than those with lower ones? Explain.
6. Why is the discount rate a more complex issue in public managerial decision making than in private sector analysis? What problems have analysts found in the use of discount rates by federal agencies?
7. What are the main pitfalls of cost-benefit analyses? How can some of them be avoided?
8. Do you think cost-benefit analysis can prove useful in a setting where decision makers must choose between widely different projects? Why or why not? How might the average benefit-cost ratio be utilized in such a case?

■ ■ ■ ■ ■ ■ ■ ■ ■ ■ ■ ■ ■ ■ **Problems** ■ ■ ■ ■ ■ ■ ■ ■ ■ ■ ■ ■ ■ ■

1. Illustrate graphically how the socially optimal amount of a public good is determined in economic theory. Provide an appropriate verbal explanation for what you show, and discuss why the market is unlikely to provide an acceptable solution to the optimal amount problem.
2. City Councillor Foghorn has argued that a new sports stadium should be constructed, since it would provide the city annual lease receipts of $900,000 per year for the next 20 years. The capital outlay for the stadium is $15,000,000. Normally, the City Planning Department employs a discount rate of 6 percent per year in its evaluation of capital projects. It is expected that revenues from food and drink concessions will offset the city's annual operating and maintenance costs for the stadium. Given this information, do you agree with Councillor Foghorn? Why or why not?

3. Which of the following projects would be acceptable from a benefit-cost standpoint if the applicable discount rate is 9 percent per year?

Project	Project Life (Years)	Annual Differential Benefits	Annual Differential Costs	Capital Outlay
(A) Flood Control	20	$100,000	$30,000	$700,000
(B) Street Paving	15	40,000	5,000	250,000
(C) Playground Eqpt.	12	10,000	1,000	75,000
(D) Rat Control	5	30,000	20,000	40,000
(E) Street Lighting	20	20,000	7,000	100,000
(F) Alarm System	20	80,000	10,000	500,000

4. Although the projects in the preceding question are not comparable in size or scope, you have been asked to rank those that are acceptable. In what order would you rank the projects based solely on the given information? Explain why.

5. The Board of County Commissioners is attempting to choose one project from among the following drainage control alternatives:

Drainage Control District	Capital Outlay	Annual Differential Costs	Annual Differential Benefits
Northeast	$180,000	$17,000	$34,000
Northwest	160,000	20,000	33,000
Central	175,000	22,000	32,000
Southeast	150,000	16,000	33,000
Southwest	165,000	20,000	35,000

If the appropriate discount rate is 6 percent per year and such projects are normally viewed as having a 20-year life, which project should the commissioners choose?

6. How would your response to the preceding question change if the appropriate discount rate were 9 percent per year instead of 6 percent per year?

7. The City Parks and Recreation Department is considering the expansion alternatives shown in the following table for the next fiscal year. Projects A and D are located in high-crime areas. Therefore the City Council has instructed the Parks and Recreation Department to add a 10 percent premium to the annual differential benefits given for each of these projects. Evaluate the five alternatives based on the table, the Council's adjustment for Projects A and D, and a standard city policy of utilizing a life of 20 years and a discount rate of 6 percent for capital projects.

Project	Initial Capital Outlay	Annual Differential Operating Expense	Annual Differential Benefits
(A) Build New Swimming Facility at Royer Park	$110,000	$10,000	$20,000
(B) Improve J.F.K. Park Playground Area	70,000	4,000	8,500
(C) Build Tennis Center at G. W. Park	120,000	12,000	21,000
(D) Install Lighting at Thorp Track & Field Facility	80,000	5,000	13,000
(E) Add 2,000 Seats to Memorial Gym	105,000	6,000	17,000

This problem can be solved with Decision Assistant

8. The City of New Urbania is considering projects for its new fiscal year. The city's residents propose new projects for the city council's consideration. The city council tries to balance the benefits of each proposed project with the associated costs. The list of projects has been consolidated and analyzed. Below is the tentative list for consideration.

Sports facility—a project to construct a large domed stadium and sports facility. The project has been one of considerable interest to many of the city's citizens who are avid sports fans. It is anticipated that should the facility be completed, the city could attract major league football and baseball teams. It is anticipated the facility will require an initial capital outlay of $60 million. The project is expected to have a life of 20 years. In addition, it is expected to have differential costs of $20 million per year and differential benefits of $28 million per year.

Convention facility—a project to expand the city's convention facility. The city has enjoyed a history of tourism and conventionism based on its mild weather, excellent facilities, and central location. The additional facilities will require an initial capital outlay of $30 million. The project will have a life of 20 years with differential benefits of $15 million per year and differential costs of $10 million.

Flood control—a multifaceted approach to one of the city's oldest problems, poor flood control. This project includes a combination of dams, reservoirs, and drainage improvements. The Army Corps of Engineers has estimated the initial capital outlay will be $1.5 million. Differential benefits total $0.5 million per year with differential costs of $0.25 million per year. The project is expected to have a life of 20 years.

Street maintenance—a project to refurbish many of the older city streets. The project will have a life of 10 years. Initial capital outlay is estimated by the city to be $12.5 million. Differential costs are estimated at $10 million while differential benefits are projected to be $14 million.

Airport maintenance—a modernization project designed to bring the city's aging airport up to standards. Initial capital outlay is estimated to be $35 million. The project is expected to have a life of 15 years. Differential benefits are expected to be $6.5 million with differential costs of $2.5 million.

Park expansion—a project to purchase additional land for conversion into parks. The city has been the beneficiary of many beautification awards, partly due to the number of parks it provides for its citizens. Initial capital outlay is estimated to be $0.7 million. The project is expected to have a life of 10 years. Differential costs are projected to be $25,000 and differential benefits are estimated to be $150,000.

Biomedical industrial park—a project to acquire acreage for an industrial park engaged in biomedical research. The city has identified biomedical research as the next technological wave, and as such it should provide many jobs for the city. Initial capital outlay is expected to be $1 million. The project is expected to have a life of 25 years. Differential benefits are expected to be $0.85 million. Differential costs are projected to be $0.8 million.

a. Use the Net Present Value, Future Value, IRR tool in the *Managerial Economics Decision Assistant* to assist the city in evaluating the cost-benefit of each of these projects independently.
b. Write a report giving your recommendation regarding each project if the applicable discount rate is 9 percent. Be sure to include a cost-benefit ratio calculation for each project in your report.
   (*HINT*: Use the Present Value, Future Value, IRR tool by calculating the present value of differential costs—including the initial capital outlay at Period 0—*separately* from the present value of differential benefits. You can then use the Calculator tool to determine the cost-benefit ratio.)

■ ■ ■ ■ ■ ■ ■ ■ ■ ■   **Selected References**   ■ ■ ■ ■ ■ ■ ■ ■ ■ ■

Allen, Joan W., Keon S. Chi, Kevin A. Devlin, Mark Fall, Harry P. Hatry, and Wayne Masterman. *The Private Sector In State Service Delivery: Examples of Innovative Practices.* Washington, D.C.: The Urban Institute Press, 1989.

Baker, Samuel, and Catherine Elliott (eds.). *Readings in Public Sector Economics.* Lexington, Mass.: D. C. Heath, 1990.

Baumol, William J. "On the Discount Rate for Public Projects." In Robert H. Haveman and Julius Margolis (eds.). *Public Expenditure and Policy Analysis.* Chicago: Rand-McNally, 1977, pp. 161–179.

Boadway, Robin W., and David E. Wildasin. *Public Sector Economics,* 2d ed. Boston: Little, Brown, 1984.

Fisher, Ronald C. *State and Local Public Finance.* Glenview, Ill: Scott, Foresman, 1988.

Fromm, Gary, and Paul Taubman. *Public Economic Theory and Policy.* New York: Macmillan, 1973, especially Chapters 1–5.

Haveman, Robert H. and Julius Margolis, (eds.). *Public Expenditure and Policy Analysis,* 3d ed. Boston: Houghton Mifflin, 1983.

Hinrichs, Harley H. "Government Decision Making and the Theory of Benefit-Cost Analysis," In Harley H. Hinrichs, and Graeme M. Taylor (eds.). *Program Budgeting and Benefit-Cost Analysis.* Pacific Palisades, California: Goodyear, 1969, pp. 9–20.

Liebhafsky, H. H. *American Government and Business.* New York: Wiley, 1971, pp. 559–562.

Lynch, Thomas D. *Public Budgeting In America,* 3d ed. Englewood Cliffs, N.J.: Prentice Hall, 1990.

Palm, Thomas, and Abdul Quayum. *Private and Public Investment Analysis.* Cincinnati: South-Western, 1985.

Prest, A. R., and R. Turvey. "Cost-Benefit Analysis: A Survey." *The Economic Journal* (December 1965).

C H A P T E R 16

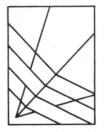

Legal and Regulatory Environment of the Firm

Businesses do not operate in a legal vacuum, and infractions of laws designed to regulate their activities can prove costly both to firms and to individual managers or officers of a firm. There is no shortage of examples to make this point. In 1986, the Supreme Court of the United States upheld an antitrust verdict against Kaiser Aluminum and Chemical Company (for monopolizing the market for aluminum drainage pipe) that cost the company $16.2 million in damages payments and interest.[1] Between 1983 and 1985, investigations of price-fixing conspiracies in the electrical contracting industry yielded jail sentences for at least 14 executives, and 33 companies paid fines, damages, and legal expenses totaling more than $20 million.[2] In 1989 Panasonic agreed to pay $16 million to consumers as well as $2 million in administrative costs to avoid charges that it fixed retail prices on electronics products sold during a six-month period in 1988. As part of the settlement, Panasonic agreed not to engage in the alleged activities for the next five years, although it refused to admit to any wrongdoing.[3]

■ ■ ■ ■ ■ ■

[1] "Top Court Lets Stand Antitrust Verdict Against Kaiser Aluminum in Pipe Case," *The Wall Street Journal*, June 24, 1986, p. 7.

[2] "Busting a Trust: Electrical Contractors Reel Under Charges They Rigged Bids," *The Wall Street Journal*, November 29, 1985, pp. 1, 5.

[3] "Panasonic to Pay Rebates to Avoid Antitrust Charges," *The Wall Street Journal*, January 19, 1989, pp. B1, B5.

While jail sentences are not common in cases involving violations of business practices or antitrust laws, over the past two decades some judges have argued that managers simply will not obey the law if they suffer no personal consequences for their actions. A significant number of judges now believe that fines and damages payments are insufficient deterrents to corporate lawbreaking, since some firms just view them as a cost of doing business.

The question of purposeful lawbreaking in business management has deep ethical dimensions. Some laws that adversely affect businesses are poorly designed and deserve to be challenged. Others are well designed to foster business competition and to protect consumers. Managers who break any law relating to their responsibilities within a firm are courting trouble, especially if the law involves well-established maxims of business behavior. Moreover, even in the case of bad or ill-conceived laws, civil disobedience can be viewed only as a measure of last resort.

Of course, many businesses find themselves in costly legal proceedings because of *mistakes* made by managers rather than because of intentional lawbreaking. Such mistakes are frequently the result of ignorance of the law on the part of a specific decision maker or group, but the old saying that "ignorance of the law is no excuse" can make legal mistakes very costly indeed. The typical manager is not a lawyer and cannot be expected to have a very complete knowledge of all the legal ramifications of business decision making. In general, the best that can be expected is that managers have a broad conception of the purview of business law and government regulations, so that they will know when to seek legal advice and thus avoid some of the pitfalls that laws and regulations hold for the firm. In addition, a competent manager should be able to recognize the possibility that a rival firm or group of firms might be damaging his or her firm through illegal business practices.

In this chapter we attempt to provide an overview of the legal and regulatory environment in which firms operate in the United States. We emphasize those areas of regulation that bear upon the economic decisions of managers whose objective is to maximize the firm's value over the long run. We look first at the nature of business law and the types of laws that apply to the firm, and then we turn to a very specific part of business regulation: the antitrust laws. The major facets of antitrust law are discussed, and this is followed by an examination of administrative agencies that both create and enforce laws affecting business. A later section deals with the specific problem of regulated industries, such as public transportation and utilities. Finally, we return to the question of the behavior of managers in the context of what we have said about the legal and regulatory environment in the United States and provide a general prescription for including legal and regulatory variables in the short- and long-run decision processes of the firm.

■ ■ ■ ■ ■ ■ ■ ■   MANAGERS AND THE LAW

In the preceding chapter, we noted that one of the most important "products" of the public sector is laws and regulations. Rules of the game are necessary to attain and secure both social and economic order. Indeed, countries and societies where rules of the game are ill defined or cast aside by an oligarchy are often plagued by civil strife. The need for a system of rules is obvious, but the extent to which economic regulations should supplant market-determined solutions to a society's problems of production and distribution of output has long been a burning issue.

From the standpoint of the manager of a business firm, government regulations are a very mixed bag. Much of the conventional wisdom of the private sector leans toward "that government is best that governs least," but it seems clear that if government did not regulate business, there would be many firms that could not survive. For example, small firms could easily be destroyed by predatory pricing strategies of large firms if government failed to make such practices illegal or failed to enforce sanctions against such activities. Thus, from the private point of view of the business firm, most managers today are sufficiently enlightened to realize that government regulations produce both costs and benefits; that is, some of the regulations have positive effects on the firm and others affect it adversely.

In the United States, private sector managers have only recently been made aware of an apparently new potential cost of decision making—that of *personal liability.* Historically, the corporate form of organization has caused penalties for breaking business rules and regulations to be exacted in the form of monetary payments (fines and/or damage settlements) from the firms that break the law. In cases where culpability could be traced to specific managers, their fines were usually paid from corporate coffers. As a result, the costs of lawbreaking in the business sector were viewed by many managers as just another business expense. The Department of Justice has taken a very dim view of this attitude and recently has begun to demand that judges mete out prison sentences to executives who knowingly break antitrust laws. The electrical contractors' case cited previously is one example.

■ ■ ■ ■ ■ ■ ■ ■   TYPES OF LAW AFFECTING THE FIRM

Setting aside for the moment the special areas of antitrust laws, business practices laws, and the regulations of administrative agencies, we may divide the laws affecting the firm into basically three types: criminal law, the law of torts, and the law of contracts. All three of these have their bases partly in English common law, civil law (Roman law), and statutory law (that law produced by local, state, or federal legislative bodies). In all three types of law, procedures are set up to determine who is a wrongdoer (person or corporation) and what should be done about a wrongful act. **Criminal law** deals with wrongful acts that are viewed as offenses against the state or government. **Tort law** has to do with injuries sustained by private parties because of a wrongful act involving the breach of a duty created by law. **Contract law,** of course, deals with the establishment of contractual obligations (agreements between parties) and wrongful acts in breach of contract. A single wrongful act can simultaneously be a crime, a tort, and a breach of contract. For example, suppose that a firm enters into a conspiracy to divide markets, which causes it to break a contractual agreement with one of its distributors and to interfere with contracts made between other suppliers and *their* distributors. In such a case the firm will have not only violated the antitrust laws (a crime) and broken a contract, but also intentionally interfered with contracts of a third party (a tort).

Criminal law pertains to acts that are viewed as offenses against a federal, state, or local government.

Tort law deals with injuries sustained by private parties as a result of nonperformance of a duty created by law.

Contract law pertains to the establishment of contractual obligations and to wrongful acts in breach of contract.

Business Crime

Criminal wrongdoing in business is seldom the result of a managerial mistake. Often it involves some willful wrong act such as receiving stolen goods, embezzlement, arson, false labeling, swindling, or obtaining goods through false pretenses. Mistakes are more likely to result in violations of state and federal antitrust laws or fair business practices laws, although in some cases such violations do constitute crimes. For example, many supplier firms in the franchise food business require franchisees to enter into tying agreements whereby all types of food inputs must be bought from the franchiser. Such contracts are often unwittingly drawn in a manner that places both parties in violation of federal antitrust laws. Although criminal penalties are not likely to be assessed against managers in such a case, the fact remains that the breaking of the federal antitrust sanction against such behavior is viewed as an offense against the state. We shall return to this problem in the section on antitrust violations.

Torts

In today's business environment the largest volume of tort cases occurs in the area of *negligence*. We can define negligence as failure to exercise reasonable care in performing a duty created by law. Underlying the whole negligence field is a concept known as the "duty of care," which is in its simplest terms the duty of a person or firm to act prudently or carefully so as not to harm other persons or things. The notion extends all the way from industrial accidents to product liability and rests on the idea of a "reasonable person" concept. That is, all steps that a reasonable person would take to avoid injuring other persons or things within his or her zone of influence should be adhered to. It is a variable standard that can be applied to all sorts of cases, and in any given case its precise definition rests with the jury.

In cases of negligence, there are generally three major determinations to be made: (1) Was the defendant negligent? (2) Was there contributory negligence on the part of the plaintiff or plaintiffs? and (3) What is the extent of injury to the plaintiff or plaintiffs? The injury phase of many legal proceedings can be both involved and costly, since expert analysis and testimony may be necessary. Frequently, parties on both sides of an injury case will hire expert witnesses (physicians, economists, engineers) to estimate damages and testify in court. The value of life itself becomes an issue when the tort involves a wrongful death.

Besides negligent acts or omissions that result in personal harm or damage to property, other common business torts are invasion of privacy; slander; trespassing upon land; interference with contracts between others; and infringement of copyrights, patents, or trademarks.

Contracts

A *contract* is a binding agreement between two or more parties (persons, corporations, partnerships, government entities), wherein one of the parties is obliged to do or refrain from doing a specific act and the obligation incurred is recognized or enforced by law. Most business activities involve a contract of one kind or another.

For example, a person or a firm agrees to sell something to another party for a specified amount, or a firm agrees to purchase raw materials from a supplier at a stated price. For a contract to exist, there must be an offer made by one party (the offeror) and an acceptance by another party (the offeree). A typical written contract will include the date of the agreement, the name and address of each party to the contract, a statement of the agreement or *promise* made by each party, the *consideration* received or to be received by each party as the price of the respective promise, and the signature of the parties.

Contracts can, of course, be very intricate, and our only purpose here is to make several important points about them and about contract law. Clearly, in the case of a large corporation, legal counsel will be available for the preparation of contractual agreements normally and regularly used, as well as for special types of contracts regarding capital projects, mergers, acquisitions, and so forth. Small businesses will also obtain legal expertise when entering into complex agreements or those involving large undertakings. However, there are many everyday transactions involving contracts that are not prepared by an attorney and, in some cases, may not be written down at all.

A good general rule regarding agreements intended to be contractual is that they should be *written*. Nonetheless, oral contracts can also be valid and enforceable; thus it is important to understand that an oral agreement may be a contract. Further, in every state, there are certain kinds of contracts that cannot be enforced unless they are evidenced by a writing. The Uniform Commercial Code (UCC), which has been adopted in whole or in part by all 50 states, provides that sales contracts for goods where the price is $500 or more are not enforceable (with certain exceptions) unless there is some writing sufficient to indicate that a contract for sale has been made between the parties and signed by the party against whom enforcement is sought or by a qualified agent or broker. Other agreements that generally must be evidenced by a writing (not necessarily a contract, but perhaps just a memorandum or a note) are those involving a duty that cannot be performed within one year of the date of contract, those involving the sale or transfer of real estate, and those involving a promise to pay the debt of another party.

Remedies for *breach of contract* (failure to keep the promise as originally stated) include the following: (1) rescinding the contract, (2) suing for specific performance, and (3) bringing an action for damages. The injured party may have the option to rescind the contract; that is, to treat it as discharged, provided the entire contract is rescinded and the party in breach is restored, as far as possible, to its original position (the one that existed before the contract). The rescinding party may still recover the value of any performance rendered or money paid. *Specific performance* (wherein the party in breach of contract is compelled by the court to carry out the terms of the contract) is generally available as a remedy to the injured party only in cases involving the purchase of real estate, the purchase of personal property having a unique value (works of art, old relics), or the purchase of stock essential for control of a closely held corporation.

When there is a breach of contract, the injured party is always entitled to sue for damages. The award of economic damages to the plaintiff is the most common remedy in cases involving breach of contract and, of course, may be a very costly occurrence for the party or the firm that is at fault. Ordinarily, the injured party can be compensated only for actual loss sustained as a result of the breach of contract and cannot be awarded *punitive damages* (excess damages sought in order to punish the wrong-doer). However, actual loss can include such items as the difference between a contract price and the price a purchaser had to pay to obtain goods not delivered due to breach of contract, interest expenses incurred because of a breach, and loss of *actual* and *future* profits attributable to a breach of contract. Where the future profits of an injured party are affected, damages can sometimes be quite substantial. In addition, the costs of litigation for a case involving such a claim often mount up, since it is likely that expert witnesses may be hired to estimate the damages. Estimation of damages suffered by injured parties can be a substantial portion of the litigation of cases involving violations of the antitrust laws, a subject to which we now turn.

■ ■ ■ ■ ■ ■ ■ ■ ■ ■ ## ANTITRUST AND BUSINESS PRACTICES LAWS

Both the federal government and the states have enacted laws to preserve competition and prevent concentration of economic power in one or a few firms (antitrust laws) and to prevent deceptive and otherwise unscrupulous business methods (business practices laws). Such laws have as their objectives both the protection of individual firms from wrongful acts of other firms and consumer protection from such evils as monopoly control of prices, price discrimination, deceptive advertising, and the sale of adulterated or otherwise unfit products.

With respect to such acts as monopolization, price fixing, tying agreements, boycotts or exclusive dealing, and price discrimination, the principal body of statutes in the United States is the federal **antitrust laws.** **Price fixing** is the practice of a group of firms agreeing to set the price of a product at a specific level. **Tying agreements** occur when a buyer of certain goods agrees to purchase certain other goods only from that same seller. **Exclusive dealing** refers to a situation where a firm buying or leasing the goods of one firm agrees not to deal with competing suppliers. As explained in Chapter 10, *price discrimination* is the practice of charging different buyers different prices for the same or similar products or services, where the price differentials cannot be justified by differences in the cost of supplying them.

The antitrust laws primarily include the Sherman Act of 1890, the Clayton and Federal Trade Commission Acts of 1914, and the Robinson-Patman Act of 1936. The original Sherman Act declared in very broad terms that contracts, combinations, and conspiracies in restraint of trade are illegal, and it provided criminal penalties for persons or firms guilty of the acts of "monopolizing, attempting to monopolize" and "combining or conspiring to monopolize." The act also provided for actions in equity (damage suits) on behalf of parties injured by such illegal acts. Under the act, as amended, injured parties are to be awarded *treble damages* (an amount paid by the wrongdoers to the injured parties that is three times the amount of the actual economic loss).

Because the Sherman Act lacked specificity regarding the types of business conduct to be regarded as illegal and because inadequate provision had been made for enforcement of its antitrust sanctions, Congress in 1914 passed the Clayton Act and the Federal Trade Commission Act. The primary effects of these two pieces of legislation were as follows: (1) to identify some specific wrongful acts that would be punishable as antitrust violations; (2) to embody the common law approach of trial, error, and precedent into the development of the rules of antitrust; and (3) to create a federal commission (the Federal Trade Commission) with far-reaching authority to regulate business practices.

With the growth of chain stores in the 1920s and the 1930s, the Federal Trade Commission (FTC) recommended to Congress that more precise prohibitions in the area of price discrimination were needed. The result

Antitrust laws are laws regulating any business practices and agreements that intensify monopoly power or otherwise restrict trade.

Price fixing is the practice of a group of firms agreeing to set the price of a final or intermediate product at a specific level.

A **tying agreement** occurs when a firm agrees that goods sold or leased will be used only with other goods of the seller or lessor.

Exclusive dealing refers to a situation where a firm buying or leasing the goods of one firm agrees not to deal with competing suppliers.

was the Robinson-Patman Act of 1936, which forbade price discrimination between buyers of like commodities purchased under like conditions and broadly prohibited price discrimination where its effect was to injure, destroy, or prevent competition. The broad nature of the act reaffirmed that the rules of antitrust would be developed on a case-by-case basis through the judicial process.

Today, the federal antitrust laws are developed to the point that it is clear that certain acts or practices will be viewed as wrongful "in and of themselves." In technical jargon such acts are called *per se violations* of the antitrust laws. The list of *per se* violations includes the following:

1. Price fixing
2. Division of markets
3. Group boycotts
4. Tying agreements

From a managerial point of view, any agreement that appears on its face or could be construed to be one or more of the preceding violations deserves careful scrutiny.

The fact that the preceding are *per se* violations of federal law does not mean that contracts between firms are unlikely to include any of them in their provisions. To the contrary, since state laws sometimes do not forbid the same acts or practices and since not all lawyers who prepare contracts are well versed in antitrust law, many contracts are written that are in violation of federal antitrust sanctions if an effect on interstate commerce can be shown. Further, the trend in the federal courts has been that an effect on interstate commerce is easily demonstrated.

As we mentioned in the introductory section of this chapter, penalties for violation of the antitrust laws can be quite severe—fines ranging up to $1,000,000 per violation for firms and fines and/or prison sentences for individuals. In addition the provisions that allow recovery of treble damages by injured parties further punish offenders and also constitute a strong incentive for aggrieved parties to file antitrust actions. The money damages paid by defendants often amount to many times the fines levied by the court. In 1985, for example, it was reported that MCI Communications Corporation had agreed to accept an offer by American Telephone & Telegraph to settle two antitrust suits for damages payments and other considerations valued at well above $113 million. In fact, MCI would not disclose the exact amount of the settlement, but it was publicly known that a jury had awarded $113 million in the first of the two suits. MCI's original claim was for $5.8 billion, and at one point a jury had awarded it $1.8 billion, but that decision was overturned in a new trial. The litigation between MCI and AT&T (including the regional Bell companies) went on for 11 years.[4] AT&T also had its problems with the Justice Department,

■ ■ ■ ■ ■ ■
[4] "MCI Says It Settled Two Antitrust Suits Against AT&T, Former Bell Companies," *The Wall Street Journal*, November 19, 1985, p. 2.

Managerial Perspective: Some Legal Aspects of Retail Pricing

Friction has frequently occurred between manufacturers of a product, company authorized retailers who do not discount the price of the product below the manufacturer's suggested retail price, and retailers who do offer the product at a lower price. Retailers who wish to sell at discounted prices believe that it should be their right to sell their products at any price at which they can make a profit. Those sellers who refuse to discount the price and would like to have other retailers prevented from doing so argue that the discounters are able to offer the products at a lower price because they do not provide the customer service that the nondiscounting firms do. For example, the list-price stores contend that potential customers visit their showrooms to learn about the features of the various products, using the services of their sales personnel, and then actually purchase the goods through a mail-order discount house or similar establishment that offers little or no customer service other than supplying the product ordered.

There have been a number of court decisions involving these issues during the twentieth century. In 1911, for example, the Supreme Court ruled that "agreements between manufacturers and independent retailers fixing the retail price of goods are so likely to be anticompetitive that they automatically violate antitrust law." In such a case, the existence of the agreement *in itself* would be a violation of the law, regardless of whether it could be shown to have been anticompetitive in nature or to have resulted in injury to another party. In later years, the courts have issued differing rulings in cases where there were agreements between manufacturers and retailers that could possibly affect prices but that were not direct price-fixing agreements.

In 1988, the Supreme Court reached a noteworthy decision on this issue involving Sharp Corporation and Business Electronics Corporation, a discounter in the Houston area. Sharp stopped supplying Business Electronics with its product after another firm complained about Business Electronics' low prices. The Court held that the fact that a company stops doing business with a discount retailer after receiving complaints from other full-price retailers does not in and of itself constitute a violation of the antitrust laws. Justice Antonin Scalia stated that manufacturers should be able to refuse to do business with discounters who take unfair advantage of the services offered by nondiscount stores. Thus the impact of the Court decision seemed to be that agreements between manufacturers and retailers were illegal only if they involved explicit efforts to fix prices.

In a more recent case, the Supreme Court held that a competing firm does not *automatically* have the right to sue a distributor or manufacturer for setting *maximum* retail prices, although setting maximum retail prices *may* violate the antitrust laws. Predatory pricing, or setting prices so low that they preclude making a profit and are designed to drive competitors out of business, are illegal. However, the Court decision indicated that for a competing firm to bring a successful suit in a situation where a manufacturer set a maximum retail price, it would be necessary to show that the firm was in fact damaged by prices that were sufficiently low to be predatory in nature. The decision did not prevent individual retailers of the merchandise or customers from bringing suits challenging the prices. (For example, dealers could argue that the maximum prices were so low that they could not offer adequate customer service, and customers could contend that the maximum prices were in fact a price-fixing scheme designed to limit competition.)

The history of these decisions by the Supreme Court shows that relationships between manufacturers and retailers and those between different retail firms may involve complex legal issues. A responsible business firm manager must be aware of potential problems in such dealings and be willing to seek legal advice.

■ ■ ■ ■

References: "Justices' Antitrust Ruling to Help Firms Crack Down on Retailers That Discount," *The Wall Street Journal* (May 3, 1988), p. 4; "A Red Flag for Red Tags," *Business Week* (May 16, 1988), p. 38; and "Supreme Court Hardens Stance on Pricing Suits," *The Wall Street Journal*, May 15, 1990, p. A3.

which spent six years trying to break up the company's telephone monopoly before a federal judge finally came up with a plan that did just that. The estimated costs of defending the suit over the six years were said to have been $350 to $500 million.[5] Even for small firms involved in private antitrust suits, litigation costs can be quite substantial. Moreover, if a defendant firm loses such a suit, its costs are further escalated by the requirement that it pay the plaintiff's costs of suit, including a reasonable attorney's fee.

■ ■ ■ ■ ■ ■

[5] "Antitrust Grows Unpopular," *Business Week* (January 12, 1981), pp. 90–93.

There are many cases involving a probable antitrust violation that do not end up in the federal courts. One reason is that most states have some form of antitrust legislation under which complaints can be pursued. Another is that once a federal court agrees to hear a case, it may never reach the trial stage because the plaintiff and defendant settle the damages issue in an out-of-court negotiation. Finally, minor violations that are in restraint of trade may be settled through the actions and authority of an administrative agency, such as the FTC, which is empowered to take regulatory steps to restrain persons or firms from using unfair methods of competition or deceptive or predatory practices.

Recent Developments in Antitrust

During the period from 1980 through 1988, under the administration of President Ronald Reagan, the federal government took a permissive attitude toward many business deals that in earlier years would probably have been viewed as questionable from an antitrust viewpoint. There was a rash of merger and acquisition activity that seemed to have the potential of substantially lessening competition in a number of important industries (airlines, food and beverages, radio and television communications). Further, Secretary of Commerce Malcolm Baldrige, himself the former head of a large conglomerate, was pushing to soften the provisions of the Clayton Act in regard to anticompetitive mergers and acquisitions.

In January 1986, the Reagan administration unveiled a legislative package that largely reflected Baldrige's views. However, this occurred at a time when many members of Congress believed the Justice Department and the Federal Trade Commission were becoming lax in enforcing the antitrust laws.[6] As a result, Congress took no action on the administration proposal, and no significant overhaul of the antitrust laws occurred before the 1988 elections, since even those lawmakers in league with the administration apparently wanted to avoid any perception that they were anticonsumer. Meanwhile, it seemed that evidence was piling up in favor of leaving the existing laws intact. For example, a Georgetown University study covering over 2,000 antitrust cases filed in federal courts during a ten-year period showed that most private suits were settled both quickly and inexpensively. Some experts were ready to argue that the existing system was working very well.[7]

Perhaps in response to a less active stance taken by the Justice Department, during the second half of the 1980s state attorneys general were becoming much more aggressive in enforcing state antitrust laws and consumer protection laws. In some cases, the attorneys general from several states combined forces to combat what they perceived were anti-

■ ■ ■ ■ ■ ■

[6] "New Era for Antitrust?" *Newsweek* (January 27, 1986), p. 46; and "Antitrust: The Pendulum is Swinging Back," *Business Week* (December 9, 1985), p. 38.

[7] "Antitrust: the Pendulum is Swinging Back," *Business Week* (December 9, 1985), p. 38.

trust violations.[8] Moreover, it appeared that the Bush administration would be more vigorous in its enforcement of the antitrust laws.[9]

■ ■ ■ ■ ■ ■ ■ ■ ■ ## ADMINISTRATIVE AGENCIES AND THE LAW

Today, it is well recognized in the United States that government administrative agencies have both legislative and judicial powers. In general, Congress and the courts have delegated such authority to the agencies because of the difficulty inherent in making judgments and setting up rules and regulations where the problems and information involved are of a highly technical nature. We have already mentioned the FTC, an agency that takes direct action outside the courts in matters involving competition and business practices. Other federal agencies that operate similarly in various fields of administration affecting business are the Interstate Commerce Commission, the Internal Revenue Service, the International Trade Commission, the Federal Maritime Commission, the Environmental Protection Agency, and the Federal Communications Commission.[10]

A **consent decree** is a statement of certain provisions agreed to by both the government and the defendant.

Typically, an administrative agency develops standards and rules, as well as means for dealing with violations of such regulations. The latter include fines, confiscation of property, informal settlements, and **consent decrees** (agreements by wrongdoers to adjust their behavior along lines specified by the agency), as well as procedures for investigating possible wrongful acts and providing a remedy. An action is usually initiated by a *complaint*, which may be filed by an alleged injured party or initiated by the agency itself. The complaint is served on the alleged wrongdoer, who is given time to answer it. The agency may then proceed with a hearing, and the administrator (generally a panel or a commission) makes a decision either dismissing the complaint or requiring the wrongdoer to take certain actions or refrain from doing certain things. The order of an administrative agency may not be self-enforcing, and the law generally provides that either the administrator may turn to the courts for enforcement or the wrongdoer may appeal the administrator's ruling through the courts. The phase involving investigation of the complaint may be quite detailed and may require that the alleged wrongdoer supply a great deal of business

■ ■ ■ ■ ■ ■

[8] "Attorneys General Flex Their Muscles," *The Wall Street Journal*, July 13, 1988, p. 21.

[9] "Psst! The Trustbusters Are Back in Town," *Business Week* (June 25, 1990), pp. 64–67; and "Putting the 'Anti' Back in the Antitrust Division," *Business Week* (June 19, 1989), pp. 64–70.

[10] We have mentioned only a few of the 120 or so federal government departments, bureaus, and agencies that implement regulatory programs. For further discussion see Juanita M. Kreps, "Why We Need a Regulatory Budget," *Business Week* (July 31, 1978), p. 14. (Dr. Kreps was Secretary of Commerce at the time of this article.)

information to federal or state investigators. In fact, the modern tendency is for prehearing investigations to become very long and involved.

As an example of the actual procedures of a regulatory agency and the effects of its activities on individual firms, we will review briefly a case that was heard by the U.S. Tariff Commission (now called the International Trade Commission) in 1973.[11] A complaint involving the sulphur industry was brought to the Treasury Department (Bureau of Customs) by U.S. sulphur producers. The U.S. firms alleged that producers of by-product sulphur located in Western Canada were selling sulphur in the United States at less-than-fair value, a practice that violated the Federal Anti-dumping Act of 1921. The act provided that imported goods could not be sold in the United States at prices below their adjusted home market price (fair value) if the effect of such sales was to injure competing U.S. producers.

The immediate effect of the complaint was to set off a Treasury Department investigation of the *fact* of less-than-fair-value sales (dumping) by the Canadians. Treasury Department investigators demanded to see the relevant records of no less than five Canadian firms, some of which were affiliates of U.S.-based multinational corporations. The firms were compelled to supply the data, since the Treasury could direct its customs officials to withhold shipments of Canadian sulphur at U.S. ports of entry in the event of noncompliance. After several months of investigation, the Treasury reported to the Tariff Commission that the fact of less-than-fair-value sales had been established, and it was determined that the Commission would hear the case.

The next step in the prehearing activities was to allow the parties time to prepare their cases. The issue at the hearing would be whether or not, or to what extent, the U.S. producers were damaged by the Canadian dumping. Thus both sides launched substantial research efforts to examine this point. The Canadians were permitted by their own antitrust authorities to mount a common defense to the charge that they had injured U.S. producers. They engaged several top Washington and New York law firms to work with their in-house attorneys and an economic consultant on the preparation of their defense.

The Commission had three options available to it on the injury question. First, it could decide, based on the evidence presented by both sides, that there had been no injury. In this case the Canadian defendants would be out their costs of litigation but would otherwise have to do nothing. A second possibility would be a finding that the U.S. producers had indeed suffered injury. In this instance antidumping duties would be assessed the *customers* of the Canadian firms, based on the amount of product they

---

■ ■ ■ ■ ■ ■
[11] This account is based on *Elemental Sulphur from Canada*, Hearings Before the United States Tariff Commission, Antidumping Investigation, No. AA1921–127, Washington, 1973.

had imported and the margin between the U.S. price and the less-than-fair-value price on each shipment. (Obviously, from the standpoint of the Canadian sellers, this was no way to win friends, and they would probably decide to reimburse the buyers to keep them as customers.) A final possibility for the Commission was to decide that a "likelihood of injury" existed, although actual injury could not be established. In this event, and this *was* the Commission's ultimate decision, antidumping duties would not be assessed, but the Canadians would be warned not to dump in the future and would be subject to Treasury Department monitoring of their shipments for a period of three years. Thus, although antidumping duties (which in this case would have amounted to about $225,000) were not assessed, the Canadian producers, by the end of the case, had probably spent a like sum on their defense.

It is clear from the preceding discussion that the power and reach of administrative agencies is strong and pervasive. Although parties adversely affected by their decisions do have appeal rights, the courts seldom rule against the agencies *if* they are willing to admit an appeal at all. In fact, the courts tend to reverse administrative agency decisions only when they are contrary to law or when it can be proved that the administrator's exercise of authority was "arbitrary or capricious." The latter charge is rarely argued successfully.

■ ■ ■ ■ ■ ■ ■ ■ ■   ## THE REGULATED INDUSTRIES

Some administrative agencies deal exclusively with specific industries that provide public services under conditions of monopoly or near monopoly. For example, electric and gas utilities are broadly subject to regulation by the Federal Power Commission, and their retail pricing within each state is usually governed by a state public utilities commission. Other economic sectors characterized by regulation of conditions of service and price are transportation and communications.

A **natural monopoly** is present where economies of scale are sufficiently large that if two or more firms were to be involved in the production of the industry output, unit cost would be higher than for a monopoly.

Firms in the preceding sectors are often described as **natural monopolies** for two primary reasons. First, it is a matter of public convenience that within a given market area, a large number of sellers of a public-utilities type of good are not allowed to operate. (Imagine what it would mean to have, for example, four competing natural gas retailers digging up the streets of a given town to install pipelines!) Second, the fixed capital investment of public utilities suppliers is usually very large, since there are economies of scale in the production of their output and since variations in demand between peak-load periods and slack periods require that they have a capacity far in excess of *average* output. The result is that although the marginal cost of output may be very low and may even fall as output increases, average costs (particularly AFC) will be very high when output is well below capacity. With too many firms in a given market area, each one would have a strong incentive to cut price and increase output. Only the largest and strongest would survive. In fact, the only way smaller firms could continue to exist would be through a policy of price regulation that would maintain the high prices necessary for them to cover their inordinately high fixed costs. The onerous consequences for consumers in such a setting are obvious.

Price Regulation in Theory

Government, having determined that monopoly or partial monopoly is inevitable in certain economic activities such as public utilities, has taken on the task of regulating the prices that such monopolies can charge. Economic theory has provided some guidelines on this problem, and we can summarize the theoretical case briefly with the help of Figure 16–1.

In Figure 16–1, we depict a monopoly firm that is assumed to be a public utility. Of course, one of government's options in such a situation is simply to allow the firm to make its own pricing decisions, in which case the firm would charge price P_a for each unit of its output and supply quantity Q_a to its customers. From a social point of view, this has two

Figure 16–1   Marginal Cost Vs. Average Cost Pricing for a Regulated Public Utility Firm

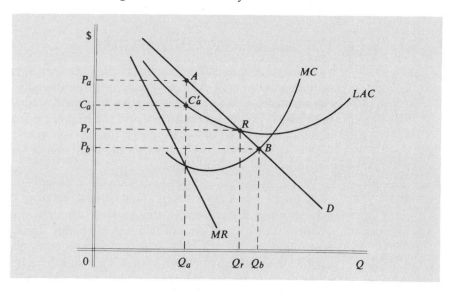

The unregulated profit-maximizing monopoly would produce where $MR = LMC$ (at Q_a) and charge a price of P_a. In this case economic profit is equal to $(P_a - C_a) \times Q_a$. If the government were to follow a marginal cost pricing policy and set a ceiling price of P_b (where LMC intersects demand curve D), the firm would produce Q_b units of output if it produced at all. However, the firm would be incurring an economic loss at Q_b, so it would leave the industry in the long run. If the government were to follow a policy of average cost pricing, it would set a ceiling price of P_r, where LAC intersects D. In this situation the firm would produce Q_r units of output and receive a normal profit.

undesirable consequences. First, the firm will have greater-than-normal profits (equal to the area of rectangle $C_aP_aAC'_a$), which can persist indefinitely, since no other firms can enter its market. Second, if price is regarded as a measure of the marginal social benefit of the output to consumers and the firm's marginal cost approximates marginal social cost, the socially optimal output is Q_b, which is consistent with marginal social benefit equaling marginal social cost.

From a resource allocation point of view, it has been argued that a policy of marginal cost pricing, in which the regulators establish price P_b and that price becomes the marginal revenue curve of the firm up to Q_b, would provide the socially optimal result. At Q_b, marginal social benefit would be equal to marginal social cost. Furthermore, the firm could do no better than to produce Q_b, since for smaller outputs, $P_b = MR > MC$. For larger outputs, the original marginal revenue curve once again depicts the correct marginal revenue value, and $MR < MC$.

Of course, the problem with price P_b is that it will not cover the firm's long-run average cost of production. For the firm to stay in business at Q_b, a subsidy will have to be provided. The lowest price on the given demand curve that *will* cover LAC is P_r, which occurs at the intersection of the firm's LAC curve with the market demand curve. Setting the regulated price at P_r is known as *average cost pricing;* and, as we shall see below, this approach is similar to the one that regulatory agencies pursue in practice. Although average cost pricing assures that profit will be only normal and increases the quantity of output (from Q_a to Q_r in Figure 16–1), it does not ensure that the socially optimal output will be produced.

Another alternative for the regulatory agency is to allow the utility to employ price discrimination in a way that increases the quantity of output and the firm's profit. In Figure 16–2, we show the same firm as in Figure 16–1. This time, however, the regulators have instructed the firm to use *price discrimination* or *block pricing* and to sell Q_r of output at price P_r and an additional amount, Q_rQ_b, at price P_b. (The firm can accomplish this by providing each customer with a reduced rate on consumption over and above a specified amount, a practice regularly followed by electric utilities.) On amount Q_r of the total quantity sold, $TR = TC = OP_rRQ_r$ and profit is only normal. On the additional quantity sold at P_b, amount Q_rQ_b, total revenue is equal to area $Q_rP'_bBQ_b$; however, the additional cost the firm incurs is equal to the shaded area under the marginal cost curve (an amount obtained by summing all the individual MCs of the units of output between Q_r and Q_b). Since the incremental cost of the output sold for P_b is less than the incremental revenue (by an amount equal to area ZP'_bB), the firm will be quite happy to oblige the regulators.

Price Regulation in Practice

Although economic analysis has provided some useful tools for studying regulatory pricing, it must be conceded that, in practice, price regulation employs the method of trial, error, and precedent in much the same

Figure 16–2 Use of Price Discrimination to Increase Output and Profits of a Regulated Utility

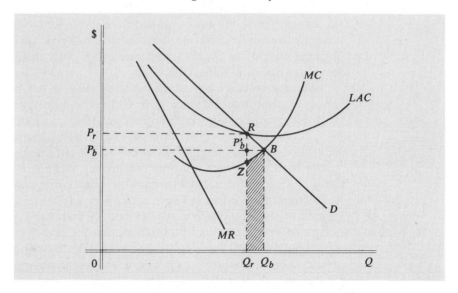

This graph illustrates government regulation with a combined average cost and marginal cost pricing policy. Here, the government sets a ceiling price of P_r on the first Q_r units of output (average cost pricing). Then, the regulators instruct the firm that it may practice price discrimination and charge a lower price, such as P_b, for additional units. If the firm establishes a price of P_b on incremental units beyond Q_r, it will sell an additional $Q_b - Q_r$ units. The firm would receive incremental revenue equal to the area $Q_r P_b' B Q_b$ on these units and incur an incremental cost given by the shaded area within $Q_r Z B Q_b$. The firm, therefore, would receive an incremental profit on these units equal to $Z P_b' B$, and the public would benefit from the opportunity to buy the additional units at the lower price.

fashion as is used in antitrust and other regulatory matters. Typically, the rates set by regulatory authorities are the result of hearings in which accounting data on costs, equity capital, and sales revenues substitute for the cost and revenue *functions* necessary for the solutions familiar to economic theorists. The result is that emphasis is placed on insuring the regulated firm a "fair rate of return" on its investment, subject to the provision of an acceptable level of service to consumers.

The notion of a fair rate of return is similar to the theoretical concept of average cost pricing. That is, if we define total costs in their economic sense as including a return to entrepreneurship or investment that is sufficient to keep industry output at or near the socially desirable level in the long run, then when price equals long-run average cost ($P = LAC$), such a return is assured. Of course, our model of Figures 16–1 and 16–2 showed that such a rate of return is not necessarily consistent with the $P = MC$ socially optimal level of output.

Accordingly, public utilities have been permitted to employ price discrimination to push output beyond the level that would likely be supplied with a single-rate approach. Discrimination has been of both the rate-block type, or "second degree discrimination" and the segmented-market type, or "third degree discrimination" (see Chapter 10 for an example). In the latter case, separate rates have been established for commercial, industrial, and residential users. Some studies have shown that the result of these practices in public utilities pricing has been to favor commercial and industrial users at the expense of the residential consumer.[12]

■ ■ ■ ■ ■ ■ ■ ■ ■ **WHOSE INTERESTS DO REGULATORS SERVE?**

From the preceding discussion, it should be clear that in the case of public utility rate setting, one of the jobs of regulators is to make sure that privately owned utility firms are profitable. Many analysts have suggested that in public utilities (and even more so in transportation, communications, and banking), the regulators have represented producer interests much better than they have those of the public in general. A study published in 1971 summed up the situation as follows:

> . . . the regulatory agencies have become the natural allies of the industries they are supposed to regulate. They conceive their primary task to be to protect insiders from new competition—in many cases from any competition.
>
> The Civil Aeronautics Board prevents qualified airlines from entering markets they desire to serve. The Interstate Commerce Commission keeps new motor carriers from competing with existing carriers. The Comptroller of the Currency and the Federal Reserve Board prohibit new banks from opening. In none of these fields is there any natural barrier to entry. There may be neither technical nor valid economic reasons for such decisions. Instead, the primary purpose often seems to be nothing more nor less than the protection of the "ins" from new competition by the "outs."[13]

As many writers have indicated, the trucking industry provides an outstanding example of the protection of established interests by government regulatory agencies. Trucking in interstate commerce is regulated by the Interstate Commerce Commission (ICC). The ICC was established in the nineteenth century to regulate the railroads, which had been engaging

■ ■ ■ ■ ■ ■

[12] See Paul W. MacAvoy, ed., *The Crisis of the Regulatory Commissions: An Introduction to a Current Issue of Public Policy* (New York: Norton, 1970); James Miller III and Bruce Yandle, eds., *Benefit/Cost Analysis of Social Regulation* (Washington, D.C.: American Enterprise Institute, 1979); and George C. Eads and Michael Fix, eds., *The Reagan Regulatory Strategy: An Assessment* (Washington, D.C.: Urban Institute, 1984).

[13] Morton Mintz and Jerry S. Cohen, *America, Inc.: Who Owns and Operates the United States?* (New York: Dial Press, 1971), p. 103.

in discriminatory rate wars that had proved detrimental to both themselves and their customers. As trucking developed in the twentieth century, the ICC first attempted to protect the railroads from the competing motor carriers. Eventually, its role changed to that of protector of large established trucking companies from the competition of smaller firms. The result was a maze of regulations that stifled competition and a licensing policy that blocked entry through elaborate and expensive procedural requirements.

For example, in his book *Economic Concentration: Structure, Behavior, and Public Policy*, John M. Blair cites the case of a small trucking firm in the mid-South that petitioned the ICC to obtain approval to extend its routes to two small Alabama towns not served by any large carrier. After more than *four years* of proceedings, the Commission granted the firm limited approval to serve only one of the two towns. Another writer reported in 1975 that ICC regulations caused a carrier to detour 800 miles out of its way and waste 160 gallons of fuel on a trip from Dallas to San Diego.[14] In 1978 *Newsweek* reported that independent trucking was about to die because of continued ICC restrictions on routes and "certificates of authority" (licenses).[15] However, a crack appeared in the facade of protection and restriction that the regulatory agencies had constructed over the years.

Alfred E. Kahn, a respected economist in the fields of regulation and antitrust who had been appointed Chairman of the Civil Aeronautics Board (CAB) by President Jimmy Carter, began to dismantle the system of fare regulation that for many decades had determined the prices charged by airlines. Kahn allowed the firms much freer rein in the area of price competition and permitted entry of firms into certain key markets where access had been restricted. The immediate result was a flurry of fare reductions and a tremendous increase in passenger traffic (an indication of highly elastic demand for the service).[16] Eventually, the CAB was eliminated from the roster of federal agencies, and its duties, which no longer included setting fares, were transferred to the Department of Transportation.

In the wake of air fare deregulation, the federal government took action to reduce legal restrictions and thus—it was hoped—increase competition in two other important economic sectors, banking and trucking. The Depository Institutions Deregulation and Monetary Control Act, passed by Congress in 1980, was designed to put savings banks and credit unions on a more-or-less equal footing with commercial banks, particularly

■ ■ ■ ■ ■ ■

[14] See John M. Blair, *Economic Concentration: Structure, Behavior, and Public Policy* (New York: Harcourt, Brace, Jovanovich, 1972), p. 397; and Mark Frazier, "Highway Robbery—Via the ICC," *Readers' Digest* (January 1975), p. 72.

[15] "The Joy of Truckin'," *Newsweek* (February 20, 1978), p. 68.

[16] "The Double Standard of CAB Enforcement," *Business Week* (August 14, 1978), p. 26.

Managerial Perspective: The Cost of Regulation Can Make a Hospital Sick

Most people know that government regulation imposes costs as well as benefits on society, but sometimes the magnitude of the cost is far greater than is generally recognized. Sequoia Hospital, a 430-bed nonprofit hospital in San Francisco, illustrates this point. The hospital estimates that the annual cost of dealing with various regulatory bodies and government mandated paperwork is about $7.8 million.

The current average daily census of patients in the hospital is the same—250 people—as it was in 1966, but the hospital staff is 75 percent larger (from 448 to 734 people). Part of this increase can be accounted for by a greater number of people treated on an outpatient basis as well as by a greater proportion of seriously ill inpatients.

Nevertheless, complying with the governmental requirements requires a staff of 140 full-time employees, plus many hours on the part of physicians as they cooperate with government mandated audits and utilization review programs. For example, four full-time and one part-time employee spend all their time reviewing patient records. Another nine or ten people investigate the appropriateness of hospitalization.

The Federal Peer Review Act requires that all government-reimbursed hospital care be reviewed by an independent agency employed by the Health Care Finance Administration. It takes 20 employees just to supply the information needed for these audits. In addition, to obtain Medicare funds, the hospital must also be audited by the Joint Commission on Accreditation of Health Care Organizations. The hospital has added four people to the medical staff office to assist physicians with completing paperwork. An additional three data processors are also required.

The point of this story is not that all government regulation is bad, but that it all costs society in terms of resources that could be used elsewhere. Thus the benefits and costs of each government regulation must be evaluated if the welfare of society is to be maximized.

Moreover, it is clear that a business firm cannot ignore the cost of government regulations in its long-term planning. To do so would substantially underestimate the firm's costs and could lead to unprofitable investment.

■ ■ ■ ■

Reference: "One Hospital Tells the Cost of Regulation," *The Wall Street Journal* (June 26, 1990), p. A18.

by relaxing restrictions on the types of loans that could be made and allowing widespread use of interest-bearing checking accounts. Although competition increased, so did the cost of borrowing. Thus the final impact on consumers was difficult to assess.

Steps toward deregulation of the trucking industry were spelled out in the Motor Carrier Act of 1980. Specifically, the Act made entry into the industry much easier and provided for the removal of numerous geographical and commodity restrictions that had plagued independent truckers. According to one report, 2,700 restriction-removal applications filed during the first five months of 1981 were approved by the ICC.[17] The same source noted that service seemed to be qualitatively better, while both shipping rates and profits had fallen off.

The Federal Communications Commission (FCC) is another agency that has taken numerous steps to reduce regulation in the past decade or so. The FCC is in charge of overseeing the telecommunications and broadcasting industries. In the wake of the breakup of American Telephone & Telegraph Company, the FCC has allowed smaller nonmonopoly phone companies to change prices or add services without approval and has used lotteries as a method of distributing licenses for new services such as cellular mobile telephones. In regard to broadcasting, it has relaxed regulations on television programming aimed at children, loosened guidelines requiring programming on community issues, and eliminated time and frequency limits on television commercials. There has been some backlash from both the public and Congress on these issues, but by far the most controversial move of the FCC has been its permissive stand on rules governing station ownership. Under the chairmanship of Reagan appointee Mark Fowler, the Commission sought to allow increased concentration of economic power in the industry by raising the limit on the number of stations that may be owned by a single company. Fowler argued for complete elimination of such restrictions by 1990, but he met stiff opposition in Congress.[18] Still, the number of stations a company could own was increased by 70 percent in 1984, with the stipulation that no one company could have a potential audience exceeding 25 percent of the households in the United States. One result of Fowler's policies has been that "takeover wars," sometimes involving financially questionable deals, have erupted in the broadcasting industry.[19]

■ ■ ■ ■ ■ ■

[17] James C. Miller, III, "First Report Card on Trucking Deregulation," *The Wall Street Journal*, March 8, 1982, p. 22. (Mr. Miller was chairman of the FTC when this article was written.)

[18] "Has the FCC Gone Too Far?" *Business Week* (August 5, 1985), pp. 48–54.

[19] Another recent practice of the broadcasting industry that has come under attack by the Federal Trade Commission has been that of airing "infomercials" considered to be misleading. Infomercials are half-hour or hour-long programs that are essentially commercials, although they are sometimes presented as informational programs. See "FTC Zaps Misleading Infomercials," *The Wall Street Journal*, June 19, 1990, pp. B1, B6.

By 1990, some notes of caution were being sounded regarding over-zealous deregulation of economic life. The telecommunications industry was still unsettled as rival firms vied for market share. While consumers had more choices, they were often confronted with a confusing array of options that was not easy to analyze. Independent truckers feared that the deregulation they had counted on for access to routes would simply run them out of business as giant firms freely expanded. The magnitude of the debacle in the savings and loan industry was beginning to be recognized, and many observers questioned whether the banks would be next to crash.[20] Republican Representative Jim Leach of Iowa called the mess "the single greatest regulatory lapse of this century." [21] Even Alfred Kahn was worried when a wave of mergers swept through the airline industry. In a television interview, he remarked that he had favored de-regulation to foster competition but that he had never suggested that the antitrust laws be repealed. By the spring of 1990 a number of airlines (including People Express, Air Florida, and World Airways) had gone out of business, and a number of the remaining airlines had merged so that the eight remaining major domestic airlines had 95 percent of the landing slots. Moreover, by the spring of 1991, Continental Airlines and Pan American had filed for protection from creditors under Chapter 11 of the federal Bankruptcy Code, and Eastern Airlines had ceased operations.[22]

Partially a result of a scarcity of airport gates and landing slots, the barriers to entry for new carriers had become quite high. Moreover, al-though the initial effect of deregulation was lower fares, by the 1990s fares were once again beginning to rise.[23] It was clear that deregulation and its impacts would be the subject of much more debate and controversy.

■ ■ ■ ■ ■ ■ ■ ■   REGULATION OF "UNREGULATED INDUSTRIES"

The relationship between many businesses and the regulatory agencies they must deal with is quite different from that enjoyed by firms in the so-called regulated industries (public utilities, communications, transpor-

■ ■ ■ ■ ■ ■

[20] "Bonfire of the S & Ls," *Newsweek* (May 21, 1990), pp. 20–32.

[21] Ibid., p. 27.

[22] "The Lorenzo Legacy Haunts Continental," *Business Week* (December 17, 1990), p. 28; "Pan Am Seeks Chapter 11 Shield, Gets UAL-Backed Cash Infusion," *The Wall Street Journal*, January 9, 1991, p. A3; and "Eastern Airlines Shuts Down Operations," *San Antonio Express-News*, January 19, 1991, pp. 1-B, 4-B.

[23] See "Can These Upstart Airlines Handle the Heavy Weather?" *Business Week* (October 1, 1990), pp. 122–123; "Control of Major Airports by Carriers Is Focus of Justice Department Inquiry," *The Wall Street Journal*, June 18, 1990, p. A3; "One Sure Result of Airline Deregu-lation: Controversy About Its Impact on Fares," *The Wall Street Journal*, April 19, 1990, pp. B1, B4; "Skies Are Deregulated, But Just Try Starting a Sizable New Airline," *The Wall Street Journal*, July 19, 1989, pp. A1, A8; and "Who Wins the Air Wars?" *Newsweek* (September 18, 1989), p. 41.

tation). In manufacturing, for example, such agencies as the Occupational Safety and Health Administration (OSHA), the Environmental Protection Agency (EPA), and the Equal Employment Opportunity Commission (EEOC) are often viewed as unwelcome interlopers who both limit and *add costs to* the process of production.

Actually, the costs of regulation are borne by all of us in several ways. First, if the regulations implement policies that affect the production (and cost) functions of the firms they oversee, the likely result will be lower output and higher prices for the products of the regulated firms. Such a result would follow any time the marginal cost curve (*MC*) of a firm shifts upward. If the shift merely represents internalization of costs that were formerly borne (via externalities) by third parties, we know, from our earlier analysis of social costs and benefits in Chapter 15, that the resultant adjustment in output and price may be a socially acceptable result.

Of course, managers of profit-oriented firms are unlikely to take kindly to regulatory internalization of costs, even when the objective of such internalization is one with obvious social merit, such as pollution control or noise control. Installation of equipment that has no effect on the final product but involves substantial investment and adds to both fixed and variable costs of production is not the sort of change that managers can be expected to welcome. Often, regulatory standards call for strict policing of the production process. The costs of such monitoring have frequently been shifted away from the regulatory agency to the firms themselves, necessitating the hiring of "compliance officers" and cadres of specially trained personnel.

From the point of view of the consuming and taxpaying public, it is not always clear that the course of regulatory agencies leads to social gains. The great debates over such regulatory innovations as cars that will not start when seat belts are unfastened and the use of saccharin as a sugar substitute are cases in point. Further, some regulatory agencies have tended to duplicate the activities of others or to proliferate their rules and reporting requirements to an absurd degree. OSHA, which has been in existence only since 1971, provides a splendid example of the latter. In 1978, it was reported that OSHA had decided to repeal 1,100 of the more than 10,000 rules it had generated since its inception.[24] Moreover, a 1976 study reported that OSHA had placed in the Code of Federal Regulations about 140 standards pertaining to wooden ladders used on construction jobs.[25]

■ ■ ■ ■ ■ ■
[24] "The Regulation Mess," *Newsweek* (June 12, 1978), p. 86.

[25] Richard B. McKenzie and Gordon Tullock, *Modern Political Economy* (New York: Mc-Graw-Hill, 1978), p. 330. Also see Robert Stewardt Smith, *The Occupational Safety and Health Act: Its Goals and Its Achievements* (Washington, D.C.: American Enterprise Institute for Public Policy Research, 1976), p. 11.

After 1980, many of the regulatory agencies became less aggressive under the leadership of Reagan appointees. This certainly occurred at OSHA, which began its retrenchment by backing off on numerous "nuisance" regulations. Between 1981 and 1985, OSHA produced only two standards on toxic substances. In 1985, it was reported that the AFL-CIO viewed the agency as nearly "irrelevant" in the effort to control workplace hazards. Business firms, which at first had criticized OSHA for excessive regulation, were reported to have become tired of waiting for OSHA to come up with standards for such dangers as chemical exposure. Some had resorted to setting strict standards on their own.[26] Their incentive, of course, was fear of litigations brought against them by workers and the general public.

The Reagan Administration certainly substituted a national trend toward deregulation for the more interventionist posture taken by the federal government during the 1970s. However, by the 1990s it was becoming clear that deregulation itself could become excessive. The pace of deregulation was slowing down, and voices from business, labor, and the public at large were cautioning that the time had come to carefully reassess the entire regulation issue. Whereas the number of federal regulators had declined by 15 percent during the first Reagan administration, it appeared that the Bush administration was going to pursue a policy of at least somewhat more aggressive regulation.[27]

■ ■ ■ ■ ■ ■ ■ ■ ■ LAWS, REGULATIONS, AND THE FIRM'S STRATEGY

Regulatory changes can produce both costs and benefits for the firm. In the short run, when a regulatory change causes an adjustment of the firm's marginal cost or marginal revenue function, it is likely that profit maximization will require a change in either output or price or both. At a minimum the firm's managerial strategy should include evaluation of the impact of current or expected regulatory changes on its short-run price-output decision. Other short-run strategies may include efforts to influence the regulatory process itself through participation on government advisory committees, support of trade organizations, and lobbying efforts. However, it is in the firm's long-run planning that analysis of the legal and regulatory environment often is of major importance.

From Chapters 13 and 14, we know that the present value of the firm's activities depends on what new undertakings it chooses to pursue and how these projects contribute to its future stream of profits. Obviously,

[26] "The Pressure on OSHA to Get Back to Work," *Business Week* (June 10, 1985), pp. 55–56.

[27] "Regulation Rises Again," *Business Week* (June 26, 1989), pp. 58–59.

when a firm's managers analyze a new investment venture, they may find that legal or regulatory variables could substantially affect the venture's outcome. A decision to accept or reject a project could easily depend on anticipated costs attributable to laws or regulations or merely uncertainty regarding the regulatory environment.

What questions should management ask regarding legal and regulatory variables in the process of capital project evaluation? The following are some of the more obviously important ones:

1. What *currently existing laws and regulations* have particular bearing on the project's outcome?
2. What are the *anticipated changes* in laws or regulations that will affect the project?
3. What *regulatory agencies* have jurisdiction over the proposed project?
4. Do rival firms enjoy *regulatory privileges,* and how will they react toward a new entrant into their territory?
5. Are firms that *supply inputs* for the projected activity or that *purchase* its *output* subject to peculiar regulatory constraints?
6. Will a successful undertaking of the project require substantial expenditures on *litigation* or *representation* before regulatory agencies?
7. In general, to what extent do regulatory uncertainties add to the project's *risk?*

Once a thorough survey of the possible regulatory impacts on a given capital project is completed, the net present value (*NPV*) of the project can be appropriately adjusted for regulatory variables. This can be accomplished in a number of ways. For example, regulatory costs can be deducted from the project's annual flow of receipts if they recur each year, or they can be added to the price of the project if they are relevant only to getting it started. Anticipated future benefits from regulation can be added to project inflows. Finally, the matter of regulatory risks can be handled through adjustment of the discount rate. The important point is to make certain that legal and regulatory impacts are not overlooked, since they often can make or break a given business venture.

■ ■ ■ ■ ■ ■ ■ ■ ■   ## SUMMARY

The Legal Environment and Managerial Economics

In this chapter we have emphasized how the legal and regulatory environment affects the economic decisions made by managers of business firms. Our major focus has been the avoidance of mistakes that may occur because of indifference toward or ignorance of the firm's obligations under the law. We briefly surveyed the types of laws affecting the firm in its everyday relationships with other firms, with individual persons, and with the various levels of government. *Antitrust law* was reviewed, with emphasis on some of the kinds of business activities that constitute *per se violations* of the federal law (price fixing, division of markets, group boycotts, and tying agreements).

The last half of this chapter dealt with the important issue of *administrative or regulatory agencies* and their relation to the firm. We noted that such agencies both make and enforce laws and that the expertise of their administrators is seldom overturned by the courts. From the historical record of the so-called regulated industries (public utilities, transportation, communications), we found that the relationship between private business and the regulators is not always adverse and that, in fact, regulatory agencies may have actually promoted the concentration of economic power in many sectors of the economy.

A feature of our discussion of the regulated industries was the extension of the monopoly model to the question of *price-setting by regulatory commissions,* a common approach in public utilities management. In general, we found that such commissions emphasize a *fair return on investment* in public utilities capacity and allow price discrimination in the rate schedules of public utilities firms.

The final sections of this chapter dealt with the effects of miscellaneous regulatory measures on the operations of firms outside the regulated industries. The impact of such measures on production and prices was discussed, and we questioned whether *regulatory costs* might exceed the social benefits gained from some recent rules and standards. The chapter closed with a discussion of *strategies* the firm might employ to bring regulatory variables into the decision process. It was argued that in the short run the firm's managers should pay special attention to the *effects of regulation* on *marginal cost* and *marginal revenue*, being prepared to alter price and output in order to maximize profit under changing constraints. Our prescription for the firm's long-run strategy was that *regulatory variables should be explicitly included in capital project analyses* through adjustment of project prices, inflows, and discount rates.

■ ■ ■ ■ ■ ■ ■ ■ ■ ■ ■ ■ ■ ■   Questions   ■ ■ ■ ■ ■ ■ ■ ■ ■ ■ ■ ■ ■ ■

1. What is the difference between a crime and a tort? Give some examples of business activities that may result in litigation because a tort has occurred.
2. What kinds of contracts must generally be evidenced by a writing? Are oral agreements ever recognized as contracts? What are the usual remedies for breach of contract?
3. What are the principal antitrust laws of the United States, and what kinds of activities do they prohibit?

4. For what kinds of penalties do the federal antitrust laws provide? Is it possible to find corporate executives guilty of crimes when the antitrust laws are violated?

5. Do government administrative agencies have legislative or judicial powers? What is the relationship of Congress and the courts to administrative agencies and their activities?

6. What means can administrative agencies use to enforce their regulations? How is action against violations of business regulations initiated in cases where administrative agencies have jurisdiction?

7. Explain why firms such as electric utilities are viewed as natural monopolies.

8. What is marginal cost pricing? Use a diagram to explain why a marginal cost pricing policy might make subsidization of a public utility firm a necessity.

9. What is average cost pricing? How is average cost pricing related to the regulatory concept of a fair rate of return?

10. What kinds of price discrimination are used by public utilities? Why do regulators permit the utilities to discriminate?

11. Why does the imposition of new regulations often result in reductions in output and increases in the prices charged by firms? Use a diagram to explain how the profit-maximizing output of a single firm would change because of the imposition of new costs related to regulation.

12. Discuss some of the steps that managers of firms can take to ensure that regulatory variables are taken into account when long-run decisions are being made.

■ ■ ■ ■ ■ ■ ■ ■ ■ ■ ■ **Selected References** ■ ■ ■ ■ ■ ■ ■ ■ ■ ■ ■

Anderson, Ronald A., Ivan Fox, and David P. Twomey. *Business Law: Principles, Cases, Environment*, 8th ed. Cincinnati: South-Western, 1983, Parts 1 and 6.

"Antitrusters Are Updating the 'Failing Company' Doctrine," *Business Week* (June 25, 1984), p. 38.

Areeda, Phillip. *Antitrust Analysis: Problems, Text, Cases*, 3d ed. Boston: Little, Brown, 1981, especially Chapter 1.

Blair, John M. *Economic Concentration: Structure, Behavior, and Public Policy.* New York: Harcourt, Brace, Jovanovich, 1972, Chapters 21–24.

Breit, William, and Kenneth G. Elzinga. *The Antitrust Casebook.* Chicago: The Dryden Press, 1982.

Howell, Rate A., John R. Allison, and N. T. Henley. *Business Law: Text and Cases.* Chicago: The Dryden Press, 1985, Parts 1 and 7.

Liebhafsky, H. H. *American Government and Business.* New York: Wiley, 1971, Chapters 23–28.

Mintz, Morton, and Jerry S. Cohen. *America, Inc.: Who Owns and Operates the United States?* New York: Dial Press, 1971, Chapters 1 and 2.

Moore, Gary A., Arthur M. Magaldi, and John A. Gray. *The Legal Environment of Business: A Contextual Approach.* Cincinnati: South-Western, 1987.

"Now the Antitrust Guidelines Are Clearer—and Looser," *Business Week* (June 25, 1984), p. 38.

Truett, Lila J., and Dale B. Truett. *Economics.* St. Louis: Times Mirror/Mosby, 1987, Chapter 27.

"U.S. Eases Merger Guidelines, Allowing Somewhat More Concentrated Markets," *The Wall Street Journal,* June 25, 1984, p. 38.

C H A P T E R 17

The Firm and the Future

Throughout this book we have attempted to emphasize decision making by American managers under the traditional private sector assumption that their objective is to maximize the profits of their firms. Early in our discussion, we took a simplistic, short-run view of profit maximization, which disregarded the important fact that firms usually exist over a substantial time span. Later, we expanded our techniques to view the firm's profit as a net inflow of periodic receipts that can be evaluated in present value terms.

Our analysis of the profit-maximizing firm has encompassed many elements of the decision-making environment in which managers must play their assigned roles. Production relationships, costs, demand, and pricing problems were examined in detail. Thereafter, we extended our discussion to the questions of new investment undertakings and the analysis of public sector managerial decisions. In general, factors external to the firm became increasingly important as the topics of discussion gained both complexity and realism. Rival behavior, input market conditions, and laws and regulations all make the manager's job more challenging. In addition, as our international capsules have shown, the decision to operate in a foreign environment brings with it new complications, but many familiar economic tools can be employed to analyze and deal with them. In the future we can expect technology and market conditions to change. These adjustments will not affect the *conditions* for profit maximization, but they will alter the *data* that managers must analyze. Changes in laws and regulations and in the structure of firms are perhaps the kinds of adjustments that will most tax administrative abilities in the years to come. In our concluding chapter we survey some likely changes in the environment in which both private and public sector managers will have to function as decision makers.

■ ■ ■ ■ ■ ■ ■ ■ ■ **REGULATION, DEREGULATION, AND PRIVATIZATION**

Efforts to reduce the role of the federal government in controlling the microeconomy have constituted the most striking change affecting business in the United States over the past decade or so. During the 1960s and 1970s, the productive activities of both business and government became increasingly constrained by laws and regulations intended to promote the general welfare through internalization of costs formerly associated with, but not allocated to, the production of specific goods and services. Thus businesses were confronted with the task of responding to many new regulations involving far-ranging issues from control of environmental pollution to the establishment of new worker-safety codes. The 1980s, on the other hand, brought us deregulation and privatization (sale of government-owned enterprises to the private sector), both with mixed—but still not fully understood—results. In the 1990s, we are still assessing these comparatively new policies.

Deregulation and privatization are intended to improve economic activity by increasing competition and fostering productive efficiency. The United States took the lead on deregulation in transportation and banking. The result was a flurry of activity in the form of expansion of old firms into new markets as well as entry by new firms. At the present time, it is not clear that the gains from these changes will outweigh the losses that may eventually follow. In air transportation, there appears to be a real danger that monopoly problems will result from the numerous mergers that have been allowed to take place.[1] In trucking, expansion of large firms that have the staying power to remain in marginally profitable markets for long periods of time may lead to reduced competition as smaller firms fail. In banking, the number of failures increased markedly when firms aggressively made loans on ill-conceived or excessively risky projects. By late 1990, the government's Resolution Trust Corporation (RTC), an entity set up to manage and ultimately get rid of properties that reverted to government entities after foreclosure, claimed assets valued at $186 billion were under its wing. In Texas alone, over 18,000 properties were being overseen by the RTC.[2]

■ ■ ■ ■ ■ ■

[1] "One Sure Result of Airline Deregulation: Controversy About Its Impact on Fares," *The Wall Street Journal,* April 19, 1990, pp. B1, B4.
[2] "S&L Property Taken Over by Government," *San Antonio Express-News,* October 21, 1990, p. 1-E.

While deregulation has yielded some problems that its proponents did not anticipate, very few results are in on the movement toward privatization of government-owned firms or of activities formerly carried out by government agencies. Some cities have contracted with private firms for provision of such services as public transportation, street sweeping, and landfill management.[3] Also relatively new on the American scene is the private enterprise prison. Its backers claim that it reduces the cost of operating a penal system, while its detractors fear that the search for efficiency may impose real costs on prison inmates and, eventually, on the community at large. To some critics, the idea of running a prison for private profit is just too distasteful.

In Britain, a major step was taken toward privatization with the de-nationalization of British Gas, which occurred in late 1986. While the move definitely raised some revenue for the British government, it is not clear that any efficiency gains have occurred. British Gas historically has been an efficient supplier from a technical standpoint, and the change is unlikely to bring any significant competitors into the market. The Conservative Party government continued on its private enterprise course into the 1990s, when state sell-offs either were being proposed or were actually taking place in areas such as water supply, railroads, and highways.[4] In France, a wave of privatization occurred during the brief tenure (only two years) of conservative Prime Minister Jacques Chirac. However, a Socialist government less friendly to such policies was elected in 1988 and began in 1990 to restructure shareholding and reshuffle the chief officers of several privatized firms. In July of that year, the Socialists launched a proposal to nationalize a private firm in the nuclear power plant construction business.[5]

It is likely that the future will bring more experimentation with deregulation and privatization. Governments and businesses will have a lot of learning and relearning to do as the fallout from this process continues. In all probability, some of the newly private endeavors will provide impressive results as obsolete organizational structures and modes of production are replaced with others that are more rational. However, rational behavior responds to incentives, and sometimes the incentives built into a government policy are not those that were intended by its formulators. Where unexpected or undesirable results are obtained, we can be sure that further modification of policy will occur.

■ ■ ■ ■ ■ ■

[3] "Public Service, Private Profits," *Time* (February 10, 1986), pp. 64–66.
[4] "Thatcher's New Revolution," *Business Week* (May 1, 1989), pp. 42–43.
[5] "World Wire: New French Nationalization," *The Wall Street Journal*, July 2, 1990, p. A6.

■ ■ ■ ■ ■ ■ ■ ■ ■ THE LDCs AND THE EASTERN BLOC

The move toward rationalizing economic activity has swept contagiously through many less-developed countries and has won advocates in the Eastern Bloc as well. Countries that spent much of the past 50 years developing centrally controlled economic systems fraught with incentive-stifling bureaucracies and mismanaged government-owned enterprises have searched for ways to rescue their faltering economies. In the West, LDCs like Mexico have begun to privatize government enterprises and deregulate economic life. (Mexico privatized 230 government-owned entities between 1983 and 1990.) Some have lifted trade barriers, and many have become more open to foreign investment and joint domestic/foreign ventures.[6] Meanwhile, the Pacific Rim countries have turned supplying the United States consumer market into an economic bonanza. The flourishing economies of ministates like Hong Kong, Taiwan, Singapore, and some of their neighbors certainly have suggested that development has as much to do with organization and incentives as it does with resources. The region's giant, China, has shown that it still has substantial political obstacles to overcome before more rapid growth can occur.[7]

The opening of the Eastern Bloc in 1989 and 1990 is bound to have important consequences for the world economy. The West Germans have taken the bull by the horns in reunification, and while the costs of developing the eastern part of Germany will be tremendous, few people doubt that an economically more powerful state will emerge. In fact, Germany will provide, no doubt, a laboratory for determining the kinds of steps that can be taken in places like Poland, Bulgaria, Romania, and, of course, the Soviet Union to both speed up development and integrate an economically depressed population into the mainstream of the world economy. Whether what Germany does for its underdeveloped east will transfer to culturally different countries is open to question. It is unlikely that any Eastern European state will be able to integrate itself with the West on terms anything like those the East Germans have enjoyed.[8]

Whatever else occurs in Eastern Europe, joint private-state ventures are very likely to become a driving force in the economic integration of industrialized countries with both the LDCs and the noncapitalist economies. These do not constitute a new strategy, for there have been some joint ventures in many of these countries for a long time. However, the barriers to establishment of such ties appear to be falling, with the public sector in the host countries making foreign participants more and more

■ ■ ■ ■ ■ ■

[6] "Mexico: The New Model Debtor," *Economist* (October 6, 1990), pp. 85–87.

[7] For more on the Pacific Rim, see *Fortune Special Issue: Asia in the 1990s*, Time Magazines Inc. (Fall 1989).

[8] "The Wealth of a Nation," *Newsweek* (July 9, 1990), pp. 31–36.

welcome. All of this is cause for optimism as well as a veritable fountain of both challenges and opportunities for present and future managers. It will be important for managers in this new environment to be not only analytical, but also flexible and innovative.[9]

■ ■ ■ ■ ■ ■ ■ ■ ■   ## SOCIAL COSTS AND "ACCOUNTABILITY"

For three decades now, there has been widespread public concern about third-party costs imposed on consumers by both business and government. Individuals and interest groups have demanded reforms aimed at internalizing economic costs that were shifted to them as goods and services were produced. High on the list of consumer complaints have been the damaging effects of pollution and other environmental and health hazards. While many reform measures have been taken, these kinds of problems are far from solved. Further, the awakening of consumers to the possibility of holding businesses liable for external costs has precipitated legal action on a broader front. The number of product liability and malpractice suits has skyrocketed, as have the settlements obtained by plaintiffs in such litigations.

The emergence of massive liability claims against businesses has made it clear that some new policies regarding the way torts are handled are likely to be developed. At issue is the question of fairness, both to injured parties and to those who damaged them. These issues were dramatically brought to light by several cases that were in their settlement phases during the latter half of the 1980s. One was that of Manville Corporation (formerly Johns-Manville), a manufacturer of asbestos-based building materials. As the connection between asbestos and lung cancer (asbestosis) became firmly established, Manville was hit with thousands of lawsuits from both workers and consumers. It became clear to management that court findings in favor of the plaintiffs would bankrupt the company, so they filed for bankruptcy in advance of settlement of the claims. Finally, Manville emerged as a reorganized company, and a trust fund of $2.5 billion was set up to compensate victims of asbestosis. This fund was much smaller than the total claims of plaintiffs ($50 billion), and legal problems continued to plague the reorganized company.[10]

Two other major liability cases against private companies also made headlines during the latter half of the 1980s. The first involved A. H. Robins Company, makers of the Dalkon Shield (an intrauterine contraceptive device). Massive claims were filed against the company by women

■ ■ ■ ■ ■ ■

[9] "In Eastern Europe, the Big Sell-Off is About to Begin," *Business Week* (August 6, 1990), pp. 42–43.
[10] "Back in Jeopardy at Manville," *Business Week*, June 25, 1990, pp. 28–29.

who apparently had suffered internal damage from using the device. Like Manville, A. H. Robins filed for bankruptcy, and subsequent deliberations included both the question of the firm's reorganization and provision for compensation of the plaintiffs.[11] The second case, that of Union Carbide, involved a deadly gas leak at its pesticide plant in Bhopal, India. Thousands were killed, blinded, or maimed as the gas cloud wafted through heavily populated areas near the plant. Carbide did not file for bankruptcy, but instead waged a legal campaign to limit its liability. It made an offer to the Indian government, but that offer was rejected. Eventually a settlement was reached, but it was viewed as unsatisfactory to many in India, and at the start of the 1990s attempts were being made to have it overturned.[12]

While businesses have been taken to task for damages, governments have not been immune. Both the U.S. government and Morton Thiokol were sued in the aftermath of the *Challenger* spacecraft disaster (1986), and the Soviet Union faced claims from neighboring European countries following the Chernobyl nuclear reactor meltdown. It seems most likely that sovereign governments will negotiate damages settlements in the interests of goodwill but are unlikely to be forced to pay compensation by some outside agency.

An Insurance Crisis?

As liability claims and judgments have mounted, business insurers have moved to protect themselves from losses. In certain cases, this has meant outright refusal to insure against losses from certain activities or certain types of products. In recent years, there have been many news accounts of medical practitioners leaving some fields because of the excessive costs of insurance. Businesses, and even small local governments, were from time to time denied insurance coverage. Critics of the insurance industry cited substantial profits as evidence that the industry was not in trouble. They argued that the firms' greed led them to refuse to deal in certain types of risks.

The hue and cry about liability judgments has led many politicians (including former President Reagan) to call for legislation providing a cap on settlements. Most congressional experts doubt that any widespread legislation of this sort will be forthcoming soon. However, those who need insurance have begun to look for alternatives, displaying just the kind of market response that most economists would predict. For example, a significant number of corporations, industry groups, and nonprofit orga-

■ ■ ■ ■ ■ ■
[11] "A. H. Robins Gets a New Start," *Chemical Week*, Nov. 15, 1989, pp. 16–17, and "The Department of Justice Dropped Its Criminal Investigation of A.H. Robins Co.," *The Wall Street Journal*, January 12, 1990, p. B-2.
[12] "India Pushes to Overturn Bhopal Settlement," *Chemical Engineering News*, June 4, 1990, pp. 5–6.

nizations have turned to financing their own risks by setting up "captive" insurance companies. The corporations that have taken this route include well-known names like AT&T and Hewlett-Packard. Over 150 such captives have been set up in Vermont, which has designed legislation friendly to them. Both industry and the private sector have set up risk-pooling schemes to become self insured.[13] In California, beach communities banded together to form a self-insurance pool when private companies refused to extend their insurance against claims resulting from injuries and deaths at public beaches and recreational areas. The lesson here is that there is usually a rational solution available for an economic problem, and that if existing firms in the private sector do not come up with a solution, someone else probably will. The future is likely to bring us some limitations on tort liability, but it is also likely to be marked by significant innovations in the way firms and governments provide in advance for such contingencies.[14]

Accountability and the Manager

In Chapter 16, we noted how important it is for managers to understand the legal environment that affects the firm in regard to the questions addressed by antitrust and business practices laws. Here, we have seen that tort liability has recently become increasingly important to the business sector. Further, it is an area where changes in laws and regulations, and in the options available to both firms and their customers, may be imminent. As these changes unfold, the competent manager will have to be both knowledgeable about them and flexible enough to adjust the firm's operations in ways appropriate to the new circumstances. This may mean modifying products or processes, or even withdrawing certain lines from the market. Clearly, it also means that new capital projects can be accurately evaluated only when all of the potential changes in the legal and regulatory environment are taken into account.

As we have pointed out a number of times in preceding chapters, it is increasingly true that managerial responsibility extends beyond the firm's income statement to the consequences of virtually all of its activities. Today, "accountability" has become a major issue in both business and government, and the courts are tending to deal more harshly with corporate lawbreaking and those deemed responsible for it. Thus managers, for their *own protection* as well as that of their firms and stockholders, must keep abreast of legal and regulatory matters falling within the scope of their operations and seek competent advice when treading on unfamiliar ground.[15]

■ ■ ■ ■ ■ ■
[13] "Vermont: Land of Green Mountains and Self-Insurance," *Business Week* (August 21, 1989), p. 77.

[14] For more, see "Insurers Under Siege," *Business Week* (August 21, 1989), pp. 72–79.

[15] See: "Soon Corporate Crime May *Really* Not Pay," *Business Week* (February 12, 1990), p. 35.

■ ■ ■ ■ ■ ■ ■ ■   STRUCTURE AND ORGANIZATION OF FIRMS

While the increasing complexity of the environment surrounding managerial decisions has provided some real challenges to decision makers, it also has contributed to some structural and organizational adjustments in today's firms. Corporate managers have realized that the environment of modern business has made it increasingly risky to pursue a nondiversified strategy. A firm with all of its eggs in one basket, in terms of product line or markets, leaves itself open not only to swings in profits caused by changing rules and regulations, but also often to the uncertainties of the international marketplace and high-level international politics. Prior to the 1980s, many firms in the steel and petroleum industries of the United States constituted cases in point. Since they were vertically integrated and had not diversified their investments as much as some other large firms, they became highly dependent on government policy, both domestic and international, to ensure continued profitability. This was not entirely the doing of the firms themselves, since some of their international rivals were paragovernment firms that did not have to sell their output at profit-maximizing prices.

In the United States, two of the primary reactions of management to contemporary regulatory and international trade and investment complexities have been the conglomerate movement and the multinationalization of the corporate sector. The conglomerate movement has broadly diversified the assets of many large corporations through mergers and acquisitions that tend to insulate firms from profit fluctuations attributable to dependency on a narrow product base. On the other hand, "going multinational" for many firms has meant diversifying markets for traditional lines of products. Presumably, for a significant number of firms, both of these approaches may serve their growth, profit, and stability objectives better than other strategies.

A third approach to the contemporary business environment is the joint government/private-sector investment project. It is likely that U.S. firms have had more experience with this means of diversifying risk in their overseas operations than in their domestic activities. The reason for this is the strong presence of American private investment in such developing areas as Latin America and Africa. Rising nationalism in these parts of the world has caused governments to prohibit or at least severely constrain firms that are completely owned by foreign interests. Although U.S. firms have often resisted attempts to force them into a joint-venture format, it is clear that the joint-venture approach can reduce risk and increase bargaining clout with local government agencies.

More recently, U.S. firms have formed joint ventures with foreign private interests to produce goods both in the United States and abroad. The most conspicuous cases have been the joint ventures of U.S. automobile firms with Japanese interests. In newly industrializing countries, joint venturing has also taken on some innovative dimensions. In 1986, for example, Volkswagen and Ford merged their Argentine and Brazilian production facilities (some 15 plants) into a venture that would eventually have an output capacity of 900,000 motor vehicles per year and would export 100,000 units to the United States. Naturally, this could not have been accomplished without government cooperation, and the two governments signed new automobile trade agreements to facilitate the firms' plans.

Perhaps the most interesting development in U.S. international business is the rapid increase in the number of export trading companies formed under a provision of the Trading Association Act of 1980. The Act was intended to foster development of big U.S. trading companies that would be similar to C. Itoh and Mitsubishi of Japan. It allowed banks to take equity positions in the trading companies and provided antitrust exemptions that would allow firms to cooperate on export pricing, division of foreign markets, and joint foreign selling operations. In 1983, big companies like Sears and General Electric started trading companies that flopped. However, 1988 and 1989 saw a flurry of new activity, especially by smaller firms and manufacturers' associations. (In a six-month period, the number of such companies expanded from 700 to 4,180.)[16] With a falling dollar and fast growth abroad, U.S. export opportunities looked much brighter in 1990. In fact, the U.S. posted an export surplus with Europe for the first four months of 1990.[17]

Despite the recent developments in deregulation and privatization, it is evident that government and business will become increasingly entwined in the future. We can expect to see very close communication between the public and private sectors and even joint government/private sector investment projects. Government participation and worker purchases of shares in some corporations may blur the notion of ownership. Nevertheless, we believe that private initiative will remain important because of the driving force of technology and the key role that individual managers and small firms play in fostering innovation.

∎ ∎ ∎ ∎ ∎ ∎ ∎ ∎ ∎ **ECONOMICS AND TOMORROW'S MANAGER**

This chapter has been about change and, more specifically, about the kinds of changes that we think will shape the environment of tomorrow's managers. We did not predict any great changes in economic analysis that would revolutionize the role of the manager or managerial economist. No such changes are expected. Rather, we have emphasized trends and recent

∎ ∎ ∎ ∎ ∎ ∎

[16] "The Little Guys Are Making It Big Overseas," *Business Week* (February 27, 1989), pp. 94–96.

[17] "Selling American: In a Major Turnaround, U.S. Is Posting Surplus In Trade With Europe," *The Wall Street Journal*, July 10, 1990, pp. A1, A4.

developments in the external environment of the firm that are likely not so much to affect managerial behavior as they are to affect the data and constraints managers must work with. Clearly, the tasks of managers will become more difficult as these factors multiply and as the organizational structure of the firm increases in complexity.

We believe that the basic principles and the approaches to problem solving that we have tried to teach in this text constitute important economic foundations for tomorrow's managers. Students who understand what we have said and can solve the kinds of problems found in the preceding chapters have attained a degree of economic know-how and literacy that will help them to analyze future problems in a managerial setting. The techniques learned here should have enduring application to future problems.

Of course, managerial economics does not end with this chapter or this book. We have only scratched the surface, particularly where techniques of quantitative analysis are concerned. We hope that students who have found this book interesting will endeavor to push their knowledge of the subject considerably further. We also hope that those who cannot devote more time to the study of managerial economics will be able to remember and use in their future careers what they have learned here.

Integrating Case 5

Bayville Convention Center

The Board of Supervisors of the city of Bayville is faced with a dilemma. For a number of years, there has been an undercurrent of community interest in building a convention center on a large downtown tract of land that has remained vacant since dilapidated public housing was torn down. (The former tenants were relocated to new facilities in a less congested area.) Several older downtown hotels recently have undergone renovation, and two new luxury hotels have been built. Presently, there is excess capacity in downtown hotel rooms. Although the central city's commercial and financial districts have undergone a renaissance, population has shifted to the suburbs, and downtown retail trade has declined. Finally, the downtown area has had a long-term drainage and flood control problem that recently has been improved by large public investment in several runoff canals.

The community is divided over the convention center proposal. Naturally, the hoteliers and downtown commercial interests favor construction of the convention center. They have enlisted the help of the Economic Development Alliance (EDA), a group of industrialists with a progrowth stance, to further public sector consideration of the project. The EDA, at its own expense, has prepared a feasibility study for the center. Initially, the Board of Supervisors welcomed this gesture, since city funds for such an effort were severely limited. However, when the study was released, certain civic groups and some members of the board began to criticize it. In general, they argued that the EDA had painted an overly optimistic picture of the convention center project.

The EDA investigated four possible sizes for the convention center. In their study they assumed a useful life of 20 years and no salvage value, since this approach is generally used by the city planning department. The sizes, estimated construction costs, and estimated operating costs of the alternative convention centers follow:

Convention Center Size (sq. ft.)	Construction Cost (dollars)	Annual Operating Cost (dollars)
130,000	$23,000,000	$ 900,000
160,000	30,000,000	1,500,000
210,000	43,000,000	2,000,000
240,000	50,000,000	2,700,000

The EDA projected *annual* operating revenues from the center to be $2,400,000 if the 130,000-square-foot structure were built. Revenue was expected to increase by 37.5 percent if the size of the center were increased to 160,000 square feet. The 210,000-square-foot center would provide 25 percent more operating revenue than would the 160,000-square-foot alternative, and an increase in size from 210,000 to 240,000 square feet would yield a further increment of 12 percent in annual operating revenue. Indirect benefits, attributable primarily to expenditures of conventioneers in the local economy, were also estimated for each size center. The indirect benefit estimates follow:

Convention Center Size (sq. ft.)	Annual Estimated Indirect Benefits (dollars)
130,000	$1,800,000
160,000	2,475,000
210,000	3,625,000
240,000	4,027,000

The EDA and downtown business interests have taken a strong position, advocating that the 240,000-square-foot center should be built, since it would yield net benefits to the community at discount rates of both 6 and 9 percent per annum. The EDA has argued that there is no use to building any of the smaller proposed centers when the largest one proves to be a viable alternative.

A. L. Tella, chairperson of a citizens group called the Bay Area Council of United People (BACUP) has led the opposition to the center and has appeared before the supervisors to criticize the EDA study. Tella has argued that the study has several shortcomings. Among them, Tella has listed the following:

1. The EDA is promoting too large a project, given the alternatives, particularly if the 9 percent discount rate is appropriate.
2. The 9 percent discount rate is too low for present conditions, since BACUP estimates the opportunity cost of resources withdrawn from the private sector to be approximately 12 percent.

3. The EDA's study is lopsided because it considers only the indirect benefits from the center and does not identify any indirect costs.

BACUP has demanded that the Board of Supervisors employ a consultant to evaluate the EDA's study and to indicate what modifications would be necessary to provide a more accurate assessment of the convention center proposal.

■ ■ ■ ■ ■ ■ ■ ■ ■ ■ ■ ■ ■ **Questions** ■ ■ ■ ■ ■ ■ ■ ■ ■ ■ ■ ■ ■

Suppose you were hired as a consultant to evaluate the EDA study. Using only the data given in the case, answer the following questions:

1. How would you assess the EDA's choice of the 240,000-square-foot center?
2. What would you say about the impact of using a 12 percent discount rate, rather than a 9 percent one, to evaluate the alternative projects?
3. What would be your approach to the criticisms regarding the handling of indirect costs and benefits?

Appendix A

Mathematical Appendix

It is very important that a student of economics understand what a functional relationship is and how it can be depicted graphically. Therefore, we begin this appendix with a brief review of functions and graphs. Moreover, it is helpful, though *not essential*, for a student of managerial economics using this text to have an understanding of the fundamental techniques of differential calculus and optimization. Accordingly, we review these procedures in this appendix so that those students who have had no previous formal training in calculus can achieve a working knowledge of the mathematical tools that are helpful in understanding basic economic theory.

FUNCTIONS AND GRAPHS

If we say that *y is a function of x*, we mean that some variable *y* depends upon the value of another variable *x*. For each value of *x*, there is *one and only one* value of *y*. We call *x* the *independent variable* and *y* the *dependent variable*. We can write this relationship in mathematical notation as

$$y = f(x).$$

One function commonly used in economics is the total cost function. An example of one that has constant average variable cost is

$$TC = 1,000 + 200Q,$$

where *TC* is total cost per week and *Q* is quantity produced per week. Table A–1 gives some corresponding values for *TC* and *Q*. These values are plotted in Figure A–1.

Table A–1   Some Values for Total Cost and
Quantity when
$TC = 1,000 + 200Q$

Q	TC
0	$1,000
5	2,000
10	3,000
15	4,000
20	5,000

An example of a total cost function with first decreasing and then increasing unit cost is

$$TC = 50 + 20Q - 15Q^2 + 5Q^3.$$

Some values of TC and Q that satisfy this function are presented in Table A–2 and are plotted in Figure A–2.

The *slope* of a function $y = f(x)$ that can be graphed as a straight line is given by the change in y divided by the change in x, ($\Delta y/\Delta x$). Technically, as we shall see later, the slope of *any* function $y = f(x)$ is given by the derivative dy/dx, which is only approximated by $\Delta y/\Delta x$ if $y = f(x)$ *cannot* be graphed as a straight line. In Figure A–1 we observe that $\Delta TC_1/\Delta Q_1 =$

Figure A–1   A Total Cost Function, $TC = 1,000 + 200Q$

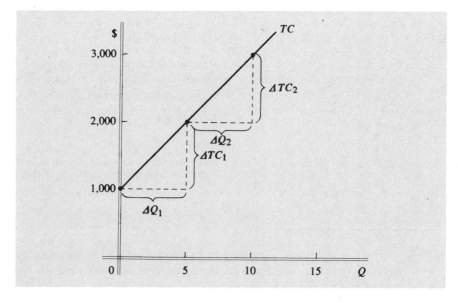

Table A–2   Some Values of Total Cost and
Output when
$TC = 50 + 20Q - 15Q^2 + 5Q^3$

Q	TC	Average Cost
0	$ 50	—
1	60	$60.00
2	70	35.00
3	110	36.67

$\Delta TC_2/\Delta Q_2 = 1{,}000/5 = 200$. Note that for our example and for any straight line (*linear*) function, the average rate of change $\Delta y/\Delta x$ of a function $y = f(x)$ is the slope of that function and is the *coefficient* of the x variable. Thus a function of the form $y = a + bx$ can be graphed as a straight line with the slope equal to b and an intersection with the y axis at a. To discuss the slope of a function such as that sketched in Figure A–2, which cannot be graphed as a straight line (*is nonlinear*), we must first define the concepts of "limit" and "derivative."

Figure A–2   A Total Cost Function, $TC = 50 + 20Q - 15Q^2 + 5Q^3$

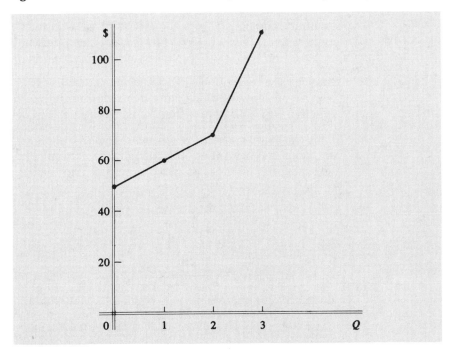

■ ■ ■ ■ ■ ■ ■ ■ **LIMITS**

The concept of the limit of a function is fairly simple. Specifically, it refers to the value, if any, that the dependent variable approaches as the independent variable approaches infinitely close to—but does not reach—a given value. Since any particular value (except $+\infty$ or $-\infty$) can be approached from either the positive or negative direction, we can define both right-hand and left-hand limits. The left-hand limit of a function $f(x)$ as x approaches some number x_0 is the value that $f(x)$ approaches as x approaches x_0 from the negative or left-hand direction and is denoted by $\lim\limits_{x \to x_0^-} f(x)$. The right-hand limit refers to the value that $f(x)$ approaches as x approaches x_0 from the positive or right-hand direction and is denoted by $\lim\limits_{x \to x_0^+} f(x)$.

These concepts can be illustrated with the function defined as follows and drawn in Figure A–3:

$$f(x) = 1, \text{ when } x < 2$$

$$f(x) = 2, \text{ when } x = 2$$

$$f(x) = 3, \text{ when } x > 2.$$

Consider $\lim\limits_{x \to 2^-} f(x)$. The value of $f(x)$ approaches 1.0 as x approaches, but does not equal, 2.0 from the left-hand side. However the value of $f(x)$ approaches 3.0 as x approaches (*but does not equal* 2) from the right-hand side, so $\lim\limits_{x \to 2^+} f(x) = 3$. Note that the right-hand and left-hand limits of this function are not equal as x approaches 2.0.

We are now in a position where we can define the overall limit of a function $f(x)$ as x approaches x_0 as $\lim\limits_{x \to x_0} f(x) = \lim\limits_{x \to x_0^-} f(x) = \lim\limits_{x \to x_0^+} f(x)$. This limit exists only when the left-hand and right-hand limits both exist and are equal to each other. To illustrate the concept of an overall limit, we will redefine the function given previously, so that

$$f(x) = 1, \text{ for } x \gtreqless 2$$

$$f(x) = 2, \text{ for } x = 2,$$

and it is graphed in Figure A–4. In this case $\lim\limits_{x \to 2^-} f(x) = 1 = \lim\limits_{x \to 2^+} f(x)$; therefore, $\lim\limits_{x \to 2} f(x)$ exists and is equal to 1. Note that $\lim\limits_{x \to 2} f(x)$ does *not* equal $f(2)$ in this case. However, $\lim\limits_{x \to x_0} f(x)$ *may* equal $f(x_0)$.

Figure A–3   Graph of the Function $y = f(x)$,
where $f(x) = 1$, when $x < 2$,
$f(x) = 2$, when $x = 2$,   and
$f(x) = 3$, when $x > 2$

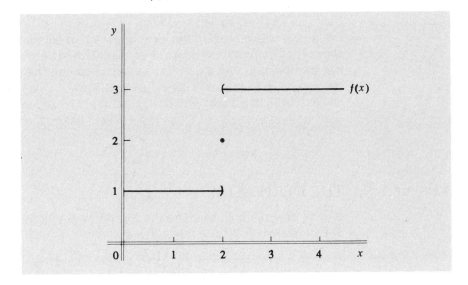

Figure A–4   Graph of the Function $y = f(x)$,
where $f(x) = 1$, for $x \gtreqless 2$,   and
$f(x) = 2$, for $x = 2$

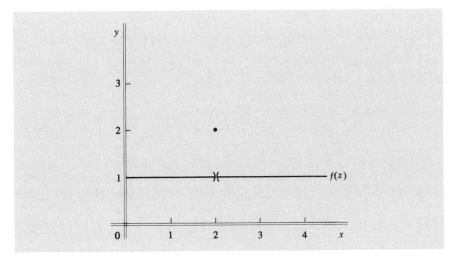

DIFFERENCE QUOTIENT

Before we proceed any further, we must develop the concept of the difference quotient. The difference quotient, $\Delta y/\Delta x$, of some function $y = f(x)$ is equal to $\dfrac{f(x_0 + \Delta x) - f(x_0)}{\Delta x}$ over some x interval $(x_0, x_0 + \Delta x)$ and gives the *average rate of change* of the function over that interval. We also indicated above that $\Delta y/\Delta x$ gives the slope of a linear function. For example, let us use the function $y = f(x) = 2x + 1$ and examine the difference quotient where $x_0 = 1$ and $\Delta x = 2$. (See Figure A–5.)

At $x = 1$, the value of $f(x) = 3$. At $x = 1 + \Delta x$, or 3, $f(x) = 7$. Thus, over the interval (1,3) for x, $\Delta y/\Delta x = \dfrac{f(x_0 + \Delta x) - f(x_0)}{\Delta x} = \dfrac{7 - 3}{2} = 2.$

THE DERIVATIVE

We are now ready to examine the concept of the derivative of a function. The derivative dy/dx of a function $y = f(x)$ at x_0 is defined as

$$\frac{dy}{dx} = \lim_{\Delta x \to 0} \frac{\Delta y}{\Delta x} = \lim_{\Delta x \to 0} \frac{f(x_0 + \Delta x) - f(x_0)}{\Delta x}.$$

Figure A–5   Graph of the Function $y = 2x + 1$

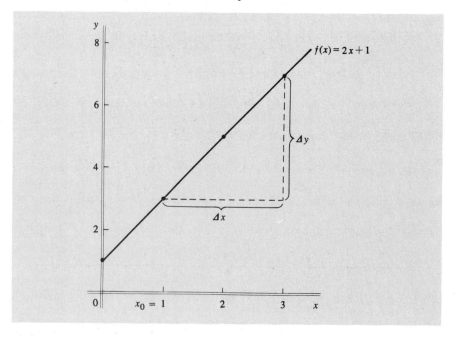

What we are saying is that the derivative dy/dx at x_0 is the limit of the difference quotient as the change in x approaches zero. Note here that it is *not* the limit of the *function $f(x)$* at x_0 with which we are concerned, but rather the *limit of the difference quotient, $\Delta y/\Delta x$*.

Examine once more the function used in Figure A–5, which is redrawn in Figure A–6. The derivative, dy/dx, of $f(x)$ where $f(x) = 2x + 1$ at $x = 1$ is thus the $\lim_{\Delta x \to 0}$ of $\dfrac{f(1 + \Delta x) - f(1)}{\Delta x}$, which is equal to $\lim_{\Delta x \to 0}$ $\dfrac{2(1) + 2\Delta x + 1 - 3}{\Delta x} = 2$. In fact, we can easily demonstrate that for any x_0 we pick, the derivative of this function at that point equals 2, or $\lim_{\Delta x \to 0}$ $\dfrac{f(x_0 + \Delta x) - f(x_0)}{\Delta x} = \lim_{\Delta x \to 0} \dfrac{2x_0 + 2\Delta x + 1 - 2x_0 - 1}{\Delta x} = 2$. In this case dy/dx will equal $\Delta y/\Delta x$, since $f(x)$ is linear and its slope is constant. The derivative is, then, the *instantaneous* rate of change of a function at a point $(x = x_0)$, whereas the difference quotient is the *average* rate of change over some interval $(x_0, x_0 + \Delta x)$. Again, we emphasize that the difference quotient and the derivative are equal in the example given above because $f(x)$ was a straight line and, therefore, its slope did not change. (The instantaneous

Figure A–6   Graph of the Function $y = 2x + 1$, Showing a Constant Difference Quotient

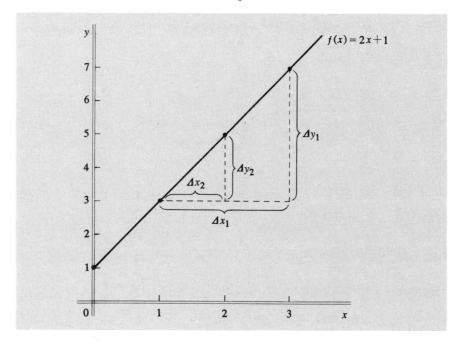

rate of change and the average rate of change of the function are, therefore, equal in this case).

We can further illustrate the relationship between the derivative dy/dx and the difference quotient $\Delta y/\Delta x$ by contrasting the slope of a line tangent to a curve at a point with that of a line connecting two points on the curve, as done in Figure A–7 for the function $y = f(x) = 10x - x^2$.

Line segment DE is tangent to $f(x)$ at point A, and its slope is equal to the value of the derivative dy/dx at point A because the tangent to $f(x)$ at point A must have the same slope or rate of change as $f(x)$ at that point. Segments AC and AB have slopes equal to $\Delta y_1/\Delta x_1$ and $\Delta y_2/\Delta x_2$, respectively. We can see that as the length of a line segment joining point A and another point on $f(x)$ gets shorter and shorter, the slope of such a line segment approaches that of the tangent DE. For example, $\Delta y_1/\Delta x_1 = 8/2 = 4$, and $\Delta y_2/\Delta x_2 = 5/1 = 5$. The derivative dy/dx at $x = 2$ is given by the

$$\lim_{\Delta x \to 0} \frac{10(x + \Delta x) - (x + \Delta x)^2 - 10x + x^2}{\Delta x}$$

$$= \lim_{\Delta x \to 0} \frac{10x + 10\Delta x - x^2 - 2x\Delta x - \Delta x^2 - 10x + x^2}{\Delta x}$$

$$= \lim_{\Delta x \to 0} \frac{10\Delta x - 2x\Delta x - \Delta x^2}{\Delta x} = 10 - 2x = 6 \text{ at } x = 2.$$

Figure A–7   The Derivative dy/dx and the Difference Quotient $\Delta y/\Delta x$ for a Nonlinear Function, $y = 10x - x^2$

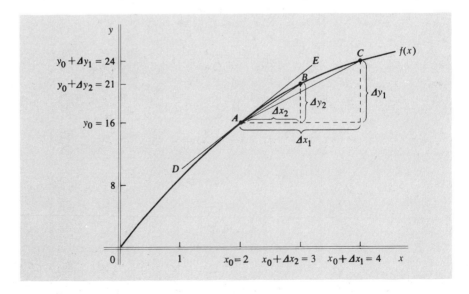

We should pause here to note the conditions required for the derivative dy/dx of $f(x)$ at x_0 to exist, which are as follows:

1. $\lim\limits_{x \to x_0} f(x)$ must exist.
2. $\lim\limits_{x \to x_0} f(x) = f(x_0)$. This condition requires that $f(x)$ be continuous; that is, it must not have a "hole" at $f(x_0)$. The function in Figure A–4 is *not* continuous at $x = 2$.
3. The function $f(x)$ must have no "sharp corners" at x_0, so that the slope of a line tangent to $f(x)$ at $x = x_0$ is defined. An example in which conditions 1 and 2 are met but the slope of the tangent is not defined at $x = x_0$ is shown in Figure A–8. The reason that the slope of the tangent is not defined at $x = x_0$ in Figure A–8 is that we could draw an infinite number of lines, each with a different slope, tangent to $f(x)$ at that point.

■ ■ ■ ■ ■ ■ ■ ■ ■ RULES FOR DIFFERENTIATION

It would be possible to derive all of the formulas given below for finding the derivative dy/dx of a function $y = f(x)$ by using the definition of a derivative and finding the limit as Δx approaches zero of the difference quotient $\Delta y/\Delta x$ for each function, as we did for the functions $f(x) = 2x + 1$ and $f(x) = 10x - x^2$ above. However, it is sufficient that students using this text be able to understand and to apply these rules, so we will not prove them here.

1. *Constant Rule*
   If $y = f(x) = C$, a constant, then $dy/dx = 0$.
   Example: If $y = 100{,}000$, then $dy/dx = 0$.

Figure A–8   Graph of a Function $y = f(x)$ that is not Differentiable at x_0

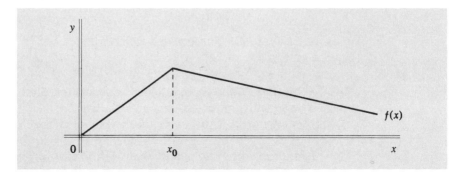

This rule is easy to comprehend if one recalls that the graph of a constant function is a horizontal line, which has a zero slope.

2. *Power Function Rule*

If $y = f(x) = Cx^n$, then $dy/dx = nCx^{n-1}$.

Examples: If $y = x$, then $dy/dx = 1x^0 = 1$.

If $y = 2x^{10}$, then $dy/dx = 10(2)x^9 = 20x^9$.

If $y = 15x^{-3}$, then $dy/dx = -45x^{-4}$.

If $y = ax^{50}$, then $dy/dx = 50ax^{49}$.

3. *Sum-Difference Rules*

a. If y equals the sum of two functions, $y = f(x) + g(x)$, then

$$dy/dx = f'(x) + g'(x), \text{ where } f'(x) = \frac{df(x)}{dx} \text{ and } g'(x) = \frac{dg(x)}{dx}.$$

Example: If $y = 10x^2 + 5x$,

$$dy/dx = 20x + 5.$$

b. If y equals the difference of two functions, $y = f(x) - g(x)$, then $dy/dx = f'(x) - g'(x)$.

Example: If $y = 4x - 10x^2$,

$$dy/dx = 4 - 20x.$$

Note that these rules can be extended to the sum or difference of any number of functions.

4. *Product Rule*

If y is the product of two functions, $y = f(x) \cdot g(x)$, then $dy/dx = f'(x) \cdot g(x) + g'(x) \cdot f(x)$.

Example: If $y = (2x + 6)(3x^4 + 1)$,

$$\begin{aligned} dy/dx &= 2(3x^4 + 1) + 12x^3(2x + 6) \\ &= 6x^4 + 2 + 24x^4 + 72x^3 \\ &= 30x^4 + 72x^3 + 2. \end{aligned}$$

5. *Quotient Rule*

If y is a quotient of two functions, $y = f(x)/g(x)$, then $dy/dx = \dfrac{f'(x) \cdot g(x) - g'(x) \cdot f(x)}{[g(x)]^2}$.

Example: If $y = \dfrac{5x}{2x + 1}$,

$$dy/dx = \frac{5(2x + 1) - 2(5x)}{(2x + 1)^2} = \frac{5}{(2x + 1)^2}.$$

6. *Chain Rule or Function-of-a-Function Rule*

If $y = g(z)$, where $z = f(x)$, then $dy/dx = \dfrac{dy}{dz} \cdot \dfrac{dz}{dx} = g'(z) \cdot f'(x)$.

Intuitively, the chain rule makes sense, for it indicates that a change in x will produce a change in z, which will, in turn, produce a change in y. Thus, dy/dx, or the rate of change of y with respect to x, is given by the rate of change of z with respect to x, dz/dx, multiplied by the rate of change of y with respect to z, or dy/dz.

Example: $y = 4z^2$, where $z = 3x^5 + 5$
$$dy/dx = 8z \cdot 15x^4 = 8(3x^5 + 5)\, 15x^4$$
$$= 120x^4(3x^5 + 5) = 360x^9 + 600x^4.$$

7. *Inverse Function Rule*

   If $y = f(x)$ defines a one-to-one mapping between x and y such that y is steadily increasing *or* steadily decreasing as x increases and if the derivative dy/dx exists, then the derivative dx/dy of the inverse function $x = f^{-1}(y)$ exists and $dx/dy = 1/(dy/dx)$. Note that here f^{-1} refers to the *inverse* function, *not* $1/[f(y)]$.

   Example: If $y = 5x + 2$, then

$$x = \frac{1}{5y} - \frac{2}{5},$$

   and

$$\frac{dx}{dy} = \frac{1}{5} = \frac{1}{dy/dx}.$$

■ ■ ■ ■ ■ ■ ■ OPTIMIZATION

Much of economics deals with optimization, or the maximization or minimization of something. For example, one important variable that firms would usually like to *maximize* is *profit*. Firms normally wish to *minimize costs*, subject to the requirement that a specific level of production is maintained.

The First Derivative Test

The derivative is quite useful as a tool in optimization—a procedure that involves finding a maximum or minimum value of some function, as indicated above. To understand how the derivative can be helpful in locating such points, observe the functions $y = f(x)$ in Figure A–9, panel (a), and $y = g(x)$ in Figure A–9, panel (b). Note that $f(x)$ reaches a (relative) maximum at x_1 and that $g(x)$ reaches a (relative) minimum at x_2. Also, note that the slope of $f(x)$ at $x = x_1$ equals the slope of $g(x)$ at $x = x_2$, which equals zero. Since the derivative dy/dx, also denoted by $f'(x)$ and $g'(x)$, respectively, gives the slopes of these functions (different for each function), then dy/dx also must equal zero at x_1 for $f(x)$ and at x_2 for $g(x)$. In fact, if dy/dx exists at such points, it is *necessary* that $dy/dx = 0$ for any function $y = f(x)$ to be at a maximum or a minimum. This result makes sense if we reflect that the function is not changing at minimum or maximum points (as long as the function is differentiable); thus, the function has a slope equal to zero at those points. That $dy/dx = 0$ at a possible maximum or minimum point is called the *first derivative test*. The graphs

Figure A–9   Graph of a Function with a Maximum and a Function
with a Minimum

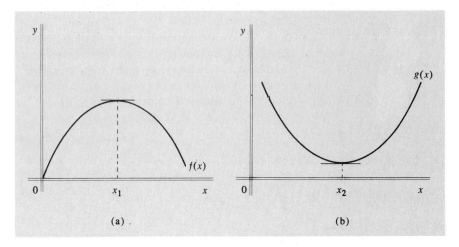

(a) (b)

of $f'(x)$ for $f(x)$ in Figure A–9, panel (a), and $g'(x)$ for $g(x)$ in Figure A–9,
panel (b), would appear similar to those drawn in Figure A–10, panels (a)
and (b), respectively.

However, $dy/dx = 0$ is not a *sufficient* condition to ensure that $f(x)$ is
at a maximum or minimum value at that point. To see why this is so,
consider the function in Figure A–11. At $x = x_0$, the slope of the function
(dy/dx) equals zero, but $f(x_0)$ is neither a relative maximum or minimum
and is an example of an *inflection point*. An inflection point of a function
$y = f(x)$ occurs at a point where the derivative dy/dx reaches a maximum

Figure A–10   The First Derivative of each of the Functions in
Figure A–9

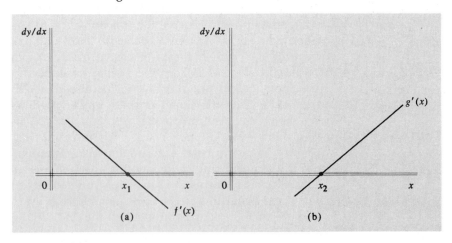

(a) (b)

Figure A–11   Graph of a Function $y = f(x)$ with an Inflection Point at x_0

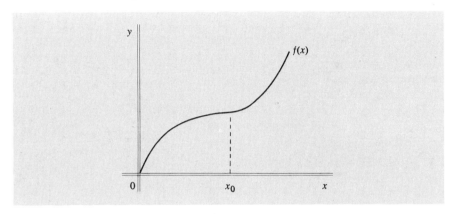

or minimum. If we were to graph dy/dx for the function $y = f(x)$ in Figure A–11, it would look similar to the curve in Figure A–12.

We emphasize that while $dy/dx = 0$ at x_0 is a *necessary* condition for the function $y = f(x)$ to be at a relative *maximum* or *minimum* at x_0, it is *not* a necessary condition for an *inflection point*. This fact is illustrated in Figure A–13. At x_0, dy/dx is at a maximum, and hence, $f(x_0)$ is an inflection point. However, dy/dx is not equal to zero at x_0.

If $dy/dx = 0$ for some $x = x_0$, one way of discriminating between an inflection point and an extreme point (maximum or minimum) of $f(x)$ is to examine the sign of dy/dx for points on either side of x_0. If dy/dx *changes signs* at x_0, the function $f(x)$ reaches an extremum (maximum or minimum) at $f(x_0)$. If dy/dx does not change signs, then $f(x)$ has an inflection point at x_0. This point can be grasped by examining Figures A–9, A–10, A–11, A–

Figure A–12   Graph of dy/dx for $y = f(x)$ in Figure A–11

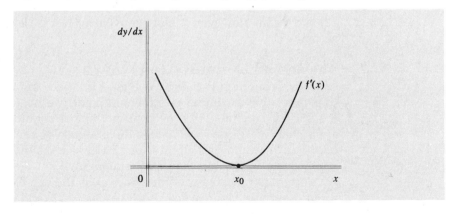

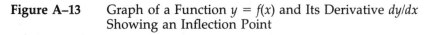

Figure A–13   Graph of a Function $y = f(x)$ and Its Derivative dy/dx
Showing an Inflection Point

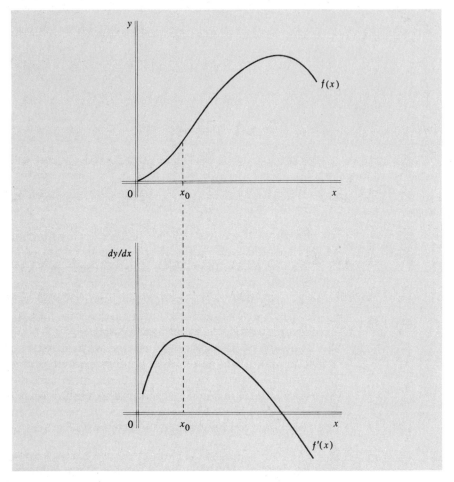

12, and A–13. However, a more convenient test is discussed in the next section.

The Second Derivative Test

While the condition that $dy/dx = 0$ at x_0 is a necessary condition for $f(x_0)$ to be a relative maximum or minimum point, we have seen that it is not a sufficient condition. We need an additional condition, convenient to apply that, when met, will ensure the presence of a relative extremum of $f(x)$ at x_0. It would be helpful if our additional condition could also discriminate between a maximum or minimum.

Fortunately, such a condition does exist and can easily be grasped by again observing Figures A–9, A–10, A–11, A–12, and A–13. Notice from

Figures A–9 and A–10 that dy/dx is *decreasing* when $f(x)$ reaches a *maximum* and is *increasing* when $g(x)$ is at a *minimum*. However, as noted above, *dy/dx itself* reaches an extreme value at an inflection point. This information suggests the usefulness of a *second derivative test*.

The second derivative of a function $y = f(x)$, denoted by $f''(x)$ or d^2y/dx^2, gives the instantaneous rate of change or the slope of the *first* derivative, $f'(x)$. It is found by taking the derivative of $f'(x)$ in the same manner as one finds $f'(x)$ by taking the derivative of $f(x)$. For example, if $y = 3x^3 - 4x^2 + 5$, then $f'(x) = 9x^2 - 8x$, and $f''(x) = 18x - 8$.

The second derivative test asserts that the function $y = f(x)$ reaches a *maximum* at some point $x = x_0$ if $f'(x_0)$ is equal to zero *and* $f''(x_0)$ is negative, which indicates $f'(x)$ is decreasing at x_0. Similarly, $f(x)$ reaches a *minimum* at x_0 if $f'(x_0)$ equals zero and $f''(x)$ is positive. We have graphed $f''(x)$ and $g''(x)$ for Figure A–9, panels (a) and (b), respectively, in Figure A–14, panels (a) and (b).

Example: $f(x) = x^3 - 6x^2 + 10$
$f'(x) = 3x^2 - 12x$
$f'(x) = 0$ when $x^2 - 4x = 0$ or $x = 0, 4$
$f''(x) = 6x - 12$
At $x = 0$, $f''(x) = -12$ and $f(0)$ is a relative maximum.
At $x = 4$, $f''(x) = 12$ and $f(4)$ is a relative minimum value.

The second derivative test is inconclusive, however, if $f'(x_0)$ *and* $f''(x_0)$ equal zero. Such a result may indicate an inflection point, as would be the case for the functions in Figures A–11 and A–13. However, it may also

Figure A–14   The Second Derivative of each of the Functions in Figure A–9

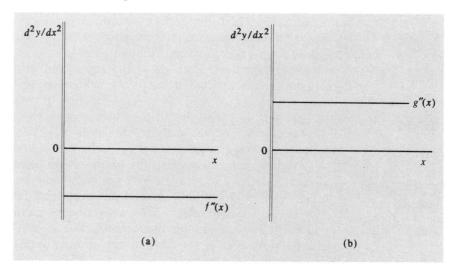

(a)   (b)

indicate a relative extremum. For example, at $x = 0$ for the function $f(x) = Cx^4$, $f'(x_0) = f''(x_0) = 0$, but $x = 0$ is a minimum point of $f(x)$.

■ ■ ■ ■ ■ ■ ■ ■ ■ ■ TOTAL, AVERAGE, AND MARGINAL RELATIONSHIPS

In economics we deal with many total, average, and marginal relationships—such as total, average, and marginal cost and total, average, and marginal profit. Since the total, average, and marginal functions for all of these variables have basically the same relationships with each other, we shall briefly discuss those relationships here. The total function states the relationship between an independent variable and the total amount of some other variable, such as output to total dollar cost of production, output to total dollar profit of a firm, or the amount of an input to the total output of the firm. The average function is obtained by dividing the total function by the independent variable. The marginal function is obtained by taking the derivative of the total function with respect to the independent variable. Graphically, the value of the *average* function for some value of the independent variable is given by the *slope of the line drawn from the origin of the graph of the total function to the corresponding point on the total function*. The value of a *marginal* function for some value of the independent variable is given by the *slope of the total function at that point*. When the average function reaches a maximum or minimum, the line drawn from the origin to the corresponding point on the total curve is tangent to the total curve at that point, and the value of the average function is thus equal to the value of the marginal function at that point. Examples of the relationships among total, average, and marginal product of an input and those among total, average, and marginal cost are shown in Figure A–15 and Figure A–16, respectively.

Note that when the average function is *decreasing*, the marginal function, whether decreasing or increasing, is taking on values *smaller than* those of the average function. This relationship is necessary for the average function to diminish. Similarly, if the average function is *increasing*, the marginal function, whether increasing or decreasing, must be taking on values *larger than* those of the average function. If the average function is not changing in value, it must be at a maximum, a minimum, or an inflection point; and the marginal function must be at a value equal to that of the average function.

A student can easily grasp the nature of the relationship between a marginal function and an average function if grade point averages (GPAs) are considered. Consider your current semester GPA to be a marginal function and your cumulative GPA to be an average function. It is a well-known fact among students that if the GPA achieved during the current semester (say, 2.50) is smaller than the cumulative GPA (say, 3.00 up to that semester), the cumulative GPA will have fallen at the end of the

Figure A–15   Relationships Among Total, Average, and Marginal Product Functions

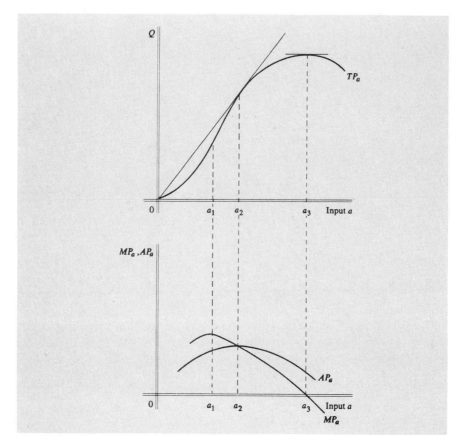

current semester. The cumulative GPA will *still fall* at the end of the next semester if the GPA for that semester rises (say, to 2.60) but is still below the cumulative GPA at the beginning of that semester. On the other hand, if the current semester GPA (say, 3.70), is greater than the cumulative GPA (say, 3.00), the cumulative GPA will rise at the end of the semester. Only when the current semester's GPA is equal to the cumulative GPA will the cumulative GPA remain the same.

■ ■ ■ ■ ■ ■ ■ ■ PARTIAL DERIVATIVES

We shall conclude this appendix with a brief discussion of partial derivatives and optimization conditions for a function with two independent variables and a few remarks about the total differential. We are interested

Figure A–16 Relationships Among Total, Average, and Marginal Cost Functions

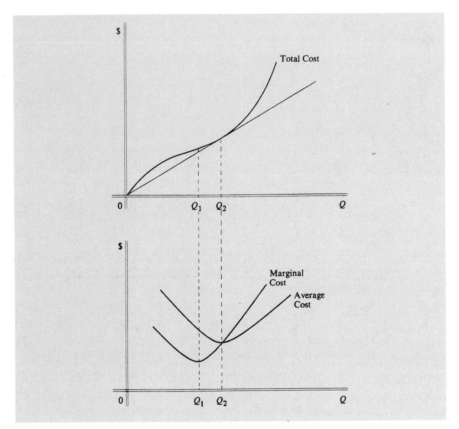

in a partial derivative when we have a dependent variable that is a function of two or more independent variables, and we wish to know the individual effect that a change in one independent variable (while the other is held constant) will have on the dependent variable. To find a partial derivative, take the derivative of the function with respect to the variable in question, treating the other independent variable or variables in the same manner as a constant. Several examples of the procedure follow:

Example 1:

$$\text{If } y = f(x,z) = x^3 + 5x^2z + 3xz^2 + 10z^3 + 10, \quad \text{then}$$
$$\partial y/\partial x = 3x^2 + 10xz + 3z^2, \quad \text{and}$$
$$\partial y/\partial z = 5x^2 + 6xz + 30z^2.$$

Example 2:

$$\text{If } y = \frac{6x^2}{z}, \quad \text{then}$$

$$\frac{\partial y}{\partial x} = \frac{12x}{z}, \quad \text{and}$$

$$\frac{\partial y}{\partial z} = \frac{-6x^2}{z^2}. \quad \text{(Use the quotient rule for } \partial y/\partial z.)$$

Example 3:

$$\text{If } Q = f(K,L) = 15K^{2/3} L^{1/3}, \quad \text{then}$$
$$\partial Q/\partial K = 10K^{-1/3} L^{1/3}, \quad \text{and}$$
$$\partial Q/\partial L = 5K^{2/3} L^{-2/3}.$$

If $Q = f(K,L)$ is a production function with inputs capital (K) and labor (L), then $\partial Q/\partial K$ and $\partial Q/\partial L$ can be interpreted as the marginal products of capital and labor, respectively.

∎ ∎ ∎ ∎ ∎ ∎ ∎ ∎ ## OPTIMIZATION CONDITIONS WITH TWO INDEPENDENT VARIABLES

The optimization conditions for a function with two independent variables are similar to those with one independent variable. The *first order* condition for a maximum or a minimum of a function $y = f(x,z)$ is that

$$\partial y/\partial x = f_x = 0, \text{ and}$$
$$\partial y/\partial z = f_z = 0.$$

The *second order* condition for a *maximum* is that

$$\frac{\partial(f_x)}{\partial x} = f_{xx} < 0,$$

$$\frac{\partial(f_z)}{\partial z} = f_{zz} < 0,$$

and

$$f_{xx} \cdot f_{zz} > \left[\frac{\partial(f_x)}{\partial z}\right]^2 = (f_{xz})^2.$$

The *second order* condition for a *minimum* is that

$$f_{xx} > 0,$$
$$f_{zz} > 0,$$

and

$$f_{xx} \cdot f_{zz} > (f_{xz})^2.$$

The condition that $f_{xx} \cdot f_{zz}$ be greater than $(f_{xz})^2$ ensures (assuming the other conditions are met) that the point in question is a relative maximum or minimum rather than a *saddle point*, which is roughly the three-dimensional counterpart of an inflection point. Again, satisfaction of the second order conditions is not *necessary* for an extremum to exist at a point, but their satisfaction together with that of the first order conditions ensures that a relative extremum *does* exist at that point.

For example, consider the function $y = f(x,z) = x^2 - 4x - 2xz - 8z + 2z^2$. Then

$$f_x = 2x - 4 - 2z, \quad \text{and}$$
$$f_z = -2x - 8 + 4z.$$

To find a maximum or minimum point(s), we first set f_x and f_z equal to zero and solve the two equations simultaneously, as follows:

$$2x - 2z - 4 = 0$$
$$-2x + 4z - 8 = 0$$
$$2z - 12 = 0$$
$$z = 6.$$

Solving for x from the first equation, we find

$$2x - 2(6) - 4 = 0,$$
$$2x - 12 - 4 = 0,$$
$$2x - 16 = 0, \quad \text{and}$$
$$x = 8.$$

To check the second order conditions for the point $f(x,z) = f(8,6)$ we find

$$f_{xx} = 2,$$
$$f_{zz} = 4, \quad \text{and}$$
$$f_{xz} = -2.$$

Since f_{xx} and f_{zz} are greater than zero and $f_{xx} \cdot f_{zz} > (f_{xz})^2$ or $2(4) > 4$, $f(x,z) = f(8,6)$ is a *minimum* point.

■ ■ ■ ■ ■ ■ ■ ■ **TOTAL DIFFERENTIAL**

We shall close with a brief discussion of the total differential. The total differential of a function attempts to measure the change in the value of a function as a result of infinitely small changes in all independent variables. If $y = f(x,z)$, the total differential, dy, is defined as

$$dy = f_x dx + f_z dz,$$

where dx and dz represent infinitely small changes in x and z, respectively. The total differential can be approximated at a specific point by using discrete (but small) changes in x and z as

$$\Delta y = f_x \Delta x + f_z \Delta z.$$

Example 1:

$$\text{If } Q = 15K^{2/3} L^{1/3}, \quad \text{then}$$
$$dQ = 10K^{-1/3} L^{1/3} \, dK + 5K^{2/3} L^{-2/3} \, dL.$$

Example 2:

$$\text{If } Q = K^2 + 10KL, \quad \text{then}$$
$$dQ = (2K + 10L) \, dK + 10K \, dL.$$

We can approximate dQ at $K = 10$ and $L = 5$ by substituting in those values for K and L in the preceding equation for dQ and substituting $\Delta K = \Delta L = .01$ for dK and dL, respectively. Thus we obtain

$$\Delta Q = [2(10) + 10(5)] \, (.01) + 10(10)(.01)$$
$$70(.01) + (100)(.01) = 1.7.$$

Such a procedure can be useful, for example, in estimating the effect that changes in the quantities of factors of production will have on total output produced by the firm. In fact, in our example above, $\Delta Q = 1.7$ could be interpreted as the *estimated* change in total output if capital and labor were to be changed from 10 and 5 to 10.01 and 5.01 units, respectively.

■ ■ ■ ■ ■ ■ ■ ■ ■ ■ **Selected References** ■ ■ ■ ■ ■ ■ ■ ■ ■ ■

Brennan, Michael J. *Preface to Econometrics*, 3d ed. Cincinnati: South-Western, 1973.

Bressler, Barry. *A Unified Introduction to Mathematical Economics*. New York: Harper and Row, 1975.

Chiang, Alpha C. *Fundamental Methods of Mathematical Economics*, 3d ed. New York: McGraw-Hill, 1984.

Dinwiddy, Caroline. *Elementary Mathematics for Economists*. Cambridge: Oxford University Press, 1967.

Appendix B

Interest Factor Tables

Table B–1   Compound Amount of $1 (CVF)

Period	1%	2%	3%	4%	5%	6%	7%	8%	9%	10%	12%
1	1.0100	1.0200	1.0300	1.0400	1.0500	1.0600	1.0700	1.0800	1.0900	1.1000	1.1200
2	1.0201	1.0404	1.0609	1.0816	1.1025	1.1236	1.1449	1.1664	1.1881	1.2100	1.2544
3	1.0303	1.0612	1.0927	1.1249	1.1576	1.1910	1.2250	1.2597	1.2950	1.3310	1.4049
4	1.0406	1.0824	1.1255	1.1699	1.2155	1.2625	1.3108	1.3605	1.4116	1.4641	1.5735
5	1.0510	1.1041	1.1593	1.2167	1.2763	1.3382	1.4025	1.4693	1.5386	1.6105	1.7623
6	1.0615	1.1262	1.1941	1.2653	1.3401	1.4185	1.5007	1.5869	1.6771	1.7716	1.9738
7	1.0721	1.1487	1.2299	1.3159	1.4071	1.5036	1.6058	1.7138	1.8280	1.9487	2.2107
8	1.0829	1.1717	1.2668	1.3686	1.4774	1.5938	1.7182	1.8509	1.9926	2.1436	2.4760
9	1.0937	1.1951	1.3048	1.4233	1.5513	1.6895	1.8385	1.9990	2.1719	2.3579	2.7731
10	1.1046	1.2190	1.3439	1.4802	1.6289	1.7908	1.9671	2.1589	2.3673	2.5937	3.1058
11	1.1157	1.2434	1.3842	1.5395	1.7103	1.8983	2.1048	2.3316	2.5804	2.8531	3.4785
12	1.1268	1.2682	1.4258	1.6010	1.7958	2.0122	2.2522	2.5182	2.8126	3.1384	3.8960
13	1.1381	1.2936	1.4685	1.6651	1.8856	2.1329	2.4098	2.7196	3.0658	3.4522	4.3635
14	1.1495	1.3195	1.5126	1.7317	1.9799	2.2609	2.5785	2.9372	3.3417	3.7975	4.8871
15	1.1610	1.3459	1.5580	1.8009	2.0789	2.3965	2.7590	3.1722	3.6424	4.1772	5.4736
16	1.1726	1.3728	1.6047	1.8730	2.1828	2.5403	2.9522	3.4259	3.9703	4.5949	6.1304
17	1.1843	1.4002	1.6528	1.9479	2.2920	2.6927	3.1588	3.7000	4.3276	5.0544	6.8660
18	1.1961	1.4282	1.7024	2.0258	2.4066	2.8543	3.3799	3.9960	4.7171	5.5599	7.6899
19	1.2081	1.4568	1.7535	2.1068	2.5269	3.0256	3.6165	4.3157	5.1416	6.1158	8.6127
20	1.2202	1.4859	1.8061	2.1911	2.6533	3.2071	3.8697	4.6609	5.6043	6.7274	9.6463
21	1.2324	1.5157	1.8603	2.2788	2.7859	3.3995	4.1405	5.0338	6.1087	7.4002	10.8038
22	1.2447	1.5460	1.9161	2.3699	2.9252	3.6035	4.4304	5.4365	6.6585	8.1402	12.1003
23	1.2571	1.5769	1.9736	2.4647	3.0715	3.8197	4.7405	5.8714	7.2578	8.9542	13.5523
24	1.2697	1.6084	2.0328	2.5633	3.2250	4.0489	5.0723	6.3412	7.9109	9.8496	15.1786
25	1.2824	1.6406	2.0938	2.6658	3.3863	4.2918	5.4274	6.8485	8.6229	10.8346	17.0000
26	1.2952	1.6734	2.1566	2.7725	3.5556	4.5493	5.8073	7.3963	9.3990	11.9180	19.0400
27	1.3082	1.7069	2.2213	2.8834	3.7334	4.8223	6.2138	7.9880	10.2449	13.1098	21.3248
28	1.3213	1.7410	2.2879	2.9987	3.9200	5.1116	6.6488	8.6271	11.1669	14.4208	23.8838
29	1.3345	1.7758	2.3565	3.1186	4.1160	5.4183	7.1142	9.3172	12.1719	15.8629	26.7498
30	1.3478	1.8113	2.4272	3.2434	4.3218	5.7434	7.6122	10.0626	13.2674	17.4491	29.9598
35	1.4166	1.9999	2.8138	3.9461	5.5159	7.6859	10.6765	14.7853	20.4135	28.1019	52.7994
40	1.4888	2.2080	3.2620	4.8010	7.0398	10.2855	14.9743	21.7244	31.4085	45.2583	93.0506
45	1.5648	2.4378	3.7816	5.8412	8.9847	13.7643	21.0022	31.9203	48.3257	72.8888	163.9868
50	1.6446	2.6915	4.3838	7.1067	11.4670	18.4197	29.4566	46.9013	74.3549	117.3878	289.0005
55	1.7285	2.9716	5.0821	8.6463	14.6350	24.6496	41.3143	68.9134	114.4037	189.0539	509.3174
60	1.8166	3.2809	5.8915	10.5196	18.6784	32.9867	57.9454	101.2563	176.0238	304.4724	897.5906

Period	14%	15%	16%	18%	20%	24%	28%	30%	32%	36%	40%
1	1.1400	1.1500	1.1600	1.1800	1.2000	1.2400	1.2800	1.3000	1.3200	1.3600	1.4000
2	1.2996	1.3225	1.3456	1.3924	1.4400	1.5376	1.6384	1.6900	1.7424	1.8496	1.9600
3	1.4815	1.5209	1.5609	1.6430	1.7280	1.9066	2.0972	2.1970	2.3000	2.5155	2.7440
4	1.6890	1.7490	1.8106	1.9388	2.0736	2.3642	2.6844	2.8561	3.0360	3.4210	3.8416
5	1.9254	2.0114	2.1003	2.2878	2.4883	2.9316	3.4360	3.7129	4.0075	4.6526	5.3782
6	2.1950	2.3131	2.4364	2.6995	2.9860	3.6352	4.3980	4.8268	5.2898	6.3275	7.5295
7	2.5023	2.6600	2.8262	3.1855	3.5832	4.5077	5.6295	6.2748	6.9826	8.6054	10.5413
8	2.8526	3.0590	3.2784	3.7588	4.2998	5.5895	7.2057	8.1573	9.2170	11.7034	14.7579
9	3.2519	3.5179	3.8030	4.4354	5.1598	6.9310	9.2234	10.6044	12.1665	15.9166	20.6610
10	3.7072	4.0455	4.4114	5.2338	6.1917	8.5944	11.8059	13.7858	16.0597	21.6465	28.9254
11	4.2262	4.6524	5.1173	6.1759	7.4301	10.6571	15.1115	17.9215	21.1988	29.4392	40.4955
12	4.8179	5.3502	5.9360	7.2875	8.9161	13.2148	19.3428	23.2979	27.9825	40.0373	56.6937
13	5.4924	6.1528	6.8858	8.5993	10.6993	16.3863	24.7587	30.2873	36.9368	54.4508	79.3711
14	6.2613	7.0757	7.9875	10.1472	12.8392	20.3190	31.6912	39.3734	48.7566	74.0531	111.1195
15	7.1379	8.1370	9.2655	11.9736	15.4070	25.1956	40.5647	51.1854	64.3587	100.7122	155.5673
16	8.1372	9.3576	10.7480	14.1289	18.4884	31.2425	51.9228	66.5410	84.9535	136.9685	217.7942
17	9.2764	10.7612	12.4676	16.6721	22.1861	38.7407	66.4612	86.5033	112.1385	186.2770	304.9116
18	10.5751	12.3754	14.4625	19.6730	26.6233	48.0384	85.0703	112.4541	148.0229	253.3367	426.8760
19	12.0556	14.2317	16.7765	23.2142	31.9479	59.5676	108.8900	146.1903	195.3902	344.5378	597.6267
20	13.7433	16.3664	19.4607	27.3927	38.3375	73.8638	139.3791	190.0474	257.9150	468.5715	836.6768
21	15.6674	18.8214	22.5744	32.3234	46.0050	91.5912	178.4052	247.0614	340.4475	637.2573	
22	17.8608	21.6446	26.1863	38.1416	55.2060	113.5730	228.3587	321.1794	449.3909	866.6689	
23	20.3613	24.8913	30.3761	45.0070	66.2472	140.8306	292.2991	417.5330	593.1960		
24	23.2119	28.6249	35.2363	53.1083	79.4966	174.6298	374.1428	542.7930	783.0186		
25	26.4615	32.9187	40.8741	62.6677	95.3958	216.5408	478.9026	705.6304			
26	30.1661	37.8565	47.4139	73.9478	114.4750	268.5107	612.9951	917.3188			
27	34.3894	43.5349	55.0001	87.2584	137.3700	332.9531	784.6340				
28	39.2039	50.0652	63.8002	102.9649	164.8440	412.8621					
29	44.6924	57.5749	74.0082	121.4985	197.8128	511.9485					
30	50.9493	66.2111	85.8495	143.3682	237.3754	634.8164					
35	98.0982	133.1740	180.3130	327.9907	590.6653						
40	188.8793	267.8601	378.7190	750.3613							
45	363.6697	538.7612	795.4382								
50	700.2131										
55											
60											

Table B–2   Compound Amount of an Annuity of $1 ($CVF_a$)

Period	1%	2%	3%	4%	5%	6%	7%	8%	9%	10%	12%
1	1.0000	1.0000	1.0000	1.0000	1.0000	1.0000	1.0000	1.0000	1.0000	1.0000	1.0000
2	2.0100	2.0200	2.0300	2.0400	2.0500	2.0600	2.0700	2.0800	2.0900	2.1000	2.1200
3	3.0301	3.0604	3.0909	3.1216	3.1525	3.1836	3.2149	3.2464	3.2781	3.3100	3.3744
4	4.0604	4.1216	4.1836	4.2465	4.3101	4.3746	4.4399	4.5061	4.5731	4.6410	4.7793
5	5.1010	5.2040	5.3091	5.4163	5.5256	5.6371	5.7507	5.8666	5.9847	6.1051	6.3528
6	6.1520	6.3081	6.4684	6.6330	6.8019	6.9753	7.1533	7.3359	7.5233	7.7156	8.1152
7	7.2135	7.4343	7.6625	7.8983	8.1420	8.3938	8.6540	8.9228	9.2004	9.4872	10.0890
8	8.2857	8.5830	8.8923	9.2142	9.5491	9.8974	10.2598	10.6366	11.0284	11.4359	12.2997
9	9.3685	9.7546	10.1591	10.5828	11.0265	11.4913	11.9780	12.4875	13.0210	13.5794	14.7756
10	10.4622	10.9497	11.4639	12.0061	12.5778	13.1808	13.8164	14.4866	15.1929	15.9374	17.5487
11	11.5668	12.1687	12.8078	13.4863	14.2067	14.9716	15.7836	16.6455	17.5602	18.5311	20.6546
12	12.6825	13.4121	14.1920	15.0258	15.9171	16.8699	17.8884	18.9771	20.1406	21.3842	24.1331
13	13.8093	14.6803	15.6178	16.6268	17.7129	18.8821	20.1406	21.4953	22.9532	24.5226	28.0291
14	14.9474	15.9739	17.0863	18.2919	19.5985	21.0150	22.5504	24.2149	26.0190	27.9748	32.3925
15	16.0968	17.2934	18.5989	20.0236	21.5784	23.2758	25.1290	27.1520	29.3607	31.7723	37.2796
16	17.2578	18.6392	20.1568	21.8245	23.6573	25.6724	27.8880	30.3242	33.0031	35.9495	42.7532
17	18.4303	20.0120	21.7615	23.6975	25.8402	28.2127	30.8401	33.7501	36.9734	40.5444	48.8835
18	19.6146	21.4122	23.4143	25.6454	28.1321	30.9055	33.9989	37.4501	41.3010	45.5988	55.7496
19	20.8107	22.8404	25.1168	27.6712	30.5387	33.7598	37.3788	41.4461	46.0180	51.1587	63.4395
20	22.0188	24.2972	26.8703	29.7780	33.0656	36.7853	40.9953	45.7618	51.1596	57.2746	72.0522
21	23.2390	25.7831	28.6763	31.9691	35.7189	39.9924	44.8650	50.4227	56.7639	64.0020	81.6985
22	24.4713	27.2988	30.5366	34.2479	38.5048	43.3919	49.0055	55.4566	62.8727	71.4021	92.5023
23	25.7160	28.8447	32.4527	36.6178	41.4300	46.9954	53.4359	60.8931	69.5311	79.5423	104.6026
24	26.9732	30.4216	34.4263	39.0825	44.5015	50.8151	58.1763	66.7645	76.7889	88.4965	118.1549
25	28.2429	32.0300	36.4591	41.6458	47.7265	54.8640	63.2487	73.1057	84.6998	98.3461	133.3335
26	29.5253	33.6706	38.5528	44.3116	51.1128	59.1558	68.6761	79.9541	93.3227	109.1806	150.3335
27	30.8205	35.3440	40.7094	47.0841	54.6684	63.7051	74.4834	87.3504	102.7217	121.0986	169.3735
28	32.1287	37.0509	42.9306	49.9675	58.4017	68.5274	80.6972	95.3385	112.9666	134.2085	190.6983
29	33.4499	38.7919	45.2186	52.9661	62.3218	73.6390	87.3459	103.9655	124.1335	148.6292	214.5821
30	34.7844	40.5677	47.5751	56.0848	66.4378	79.0573	94.4601	113.2827	136.3054	164.4921	241.3319
35	41.659	49.994	60.461	73.651	90.318	111.432	138.234	172.314	215.705	271.018	431.658
40	48.886	60.402	75.401	95.026	120.797	154.758	199.630	259.052	337.872	442.580	767.080
45	56.479	71.891	92.718	121.027	159.695	212.737	285.741	386.497	525.840	718.881	1358.208
50	64.461	84.577	112.794	152.664	209.341	290.325	406.516	573.756	815.051	1163.865	2399.975
60	81.670	114.05	163.05	237.99	353.58	533.12	813.52	1253.2	1944.7	3034.8	7471.6

Period	14%	15%	16%	18%	20%	24%	28%	30%	32%	36%	40%
1	1.0000	1.0000	1.0000	1.0000	1.0000	1.0000	1.0000	1.0000	1.0000	1.0000	1.0000
2	2.1400	2.1500	2.1600	2.1800	2.2000	2.2400	2.2800	2.3000	2.3200	2.3600	2.4000
3	3.4396	3.4725	3.5056	3.5724	3.6400	3.7776	3.9184	3.9900	4.0624	4.2096	4.3600
4	4.9211	4.9934	5.0665	5.2154	5.3680	5.6842	6.0155	6.1870	6.3624	6.7251	7.1040
5	6.6101	6.7424	6.8771	7.1542	7.4416	8.0484	8.6999	9.0431	9.3983	10.1461	10.9456
6	8.5355	8.7537	8.9775	9.4420	9.9299	10.9801	12.1359	12.7560	13.4058	14.7986	16.3238
7	10.7305	11.0668	11.4139	12.1415	12.9159	14.6153	16.5339	17.5828	18.6956	21.1261	23.8533
8	13.2327	13.7268	14.2401	15.3270	16.4991	19.1229	22.1634	23.8576	25.6782	29.7315	34.3947
9	16.0853	16.7858	17.5185	19.0858	20.7989	24.7124	29.3691	32.0149	34.8952	41.4349	49.1525
10	19.3372	20.3037	21.3214	23.5212	25.9586	31.6434	38.5925	42.6193	47.0617	57.3514	69.8135
11	23.0444	24.3492	25.7328	28.7550	32.1503	40.2378	50.3984	56.4050	63.1214	78.9979	98.7388
12	27.2706	29.0016	30.8501	34.9309	39.5804	50.8948	65.5099	74.3265	84.3202	108.4372	139.2343
13	32.0885	34.3518	36.7861	42.2184	48.4965	64.1096	84.8527	97.6244	112.3027	148.4745	195.9280
14	37.5808	40.5045	43.6719	50.8177	59.1958	80.4959	109.6114	127.9117	149.2395	202.9253	275.2991
15	43.8421	47.5802	51.6594	60.9649	72.0349	100.8149	141.3026	167.2851	197.9961	276.9783	386.4185
16	50.9800	55.7172	60.9249	72.9385	87.4419	126.0104	181.8673	218.4705	262.3547	377.6904	541.9856
17	59.1172	65.0748	71.6728	87.0674	105.9303	157.2529	233.7901	285.0115	347.3081	514.6589	759.7798
18	68.3935	75.8360	84.1405	103.7395	128.1164	195.9936	300.2512	371.5146	459.4465	700.9358	
19	78.9686	88.2113	98.6029	123.4125	154.7396	244.0320	385.3213	483.9687	607.4692	954.2725	
20	91.0241	102.4430	115.3794	146.6267	186.6875	303.5996	494.2112	630.1589	802.8594		
21	104.7675	118.8094	134.8401	174.0194	225.0250	377.4634	633.5901	820.2063			
22	120.4348	137.6308	157.4145	206.3428	271.0298	469.0544	811.9951				
23	138.2957	159.2754	183.6008	244.4843	326.2356	582.6274					
24	158.6570	184.1667	213.9769	289.4912	392.4827	723.4578					
25	181.8689	212.7916	249.2132	342.5994	471.9792	898.0874					
26	208.3304	245.7103	290.0872	405.2668	567.3750						
27	238.4966	283.5667	337.5010	479.2146	681.8499						
28	272.8857	327.1016	392.5010	566.4729	819.2197						
29	312.0896	377.1665	456.3010	669.4377	984.0637						
30	356.7817	434.7412	530.3091	790.9360							
35	693.552	881.152	1120.699	1816.607							
40	1341.979	1779.048	2360.724	4163.094							
45	2590.464	3585.031	4965.191	9531.258							
50	4994.301	7217.488									
60	18535.	29219.									

Table B-3 Present Value of $1 (*PVF*)

Period	1%	2%	3%	4%	5%	6%	7%	8%	9%	10%	12%
1	0.9901	0.9804	0.9709	0.9615	0.9524	0.9434	0.9346	0.9259	0.9174	0.9091	0.8929
2	0.9803	0.9612	0.9426	0.9246	0.9070	0.8900	0.8734	0.8573	0.8417	0.8264	0.7972
3	0.9706	0.9423	0.9151	0.8890	0.8638	0.8396	0.8163	0.7938	0.7722	0.7513	0.7118
4	0.9610	0.9238	0.8885	0.8548	0.8227	0.7921	0.7629	0.7350	0.7084	0.6830	0.6355
5	0.9515	0.9057	0.8626	0.8219	0.7835	0.7473	0.7130	0.6806	0.6499	0.6209	0.5674
6	0.9420	0.8880	0.8375	0.7903	0.7462	0.7050	0.6663	0.6302	0.5963	0.5645	0.5066
7	0.9327	0.8706	0.8131	0.7599	0.7107	0.6651	0.6228	0.5835	0.5470	0.5132	0.4523
8	0.9235	0.8535	0.7894	0.7307	0.6768	0.6274	0.5820	0.5403	0.5019	0.4665	0.4039
9	0.9143	0.8368	0.7664	0.7026	0.6446	0.5919	0.5439	0.5002	0.4604	0.4241	0.3606
10	0.9053	0.8204	0.7441	0.6756	0.6139	0.5584	0.5084	0.4632	0.4224	0.3855	0.3220
11	0.8963	0.8043	0.7224	0.6496	0.5847	0.5268	0.4751	0.4289	0.3875	0.3505	0.2875
12	0.8875	0.7885	0.7014	0.6246	0.5568	0.4970	0.4440	0.3971	0.3555	0.3186	0.2567
13	0.8787	0.7730	0.6810	0.6006	0.5303	0.4688	0.4150	0.3677	0.3262	0.2897	0.2292
14	0.8700	0.7579	0.6611	0.5775	0.5051	0.4423	0.3878	0.3405	0.2992	0.2633	0.2046
15	0.8614	0.7430	0.6419	0.5553	0.4810	0.4173	0.3624	0.3152	0.2745	0.2394	0.1827
16	0.8528	0.7285	0.6232	0.5339	0.4581	0.3936	0.3387	0.2919	0.2519	0.2176	0.1631
17	0.8444	0.7142	0.6050	0.5134	0.4363	0.3714	0.3166	0.2703	0.2311	0.1978	0.1456
18	0.8360	0.7002	0.5874	0.4936	0.4155	0.3503	0.2959	0.2502	0.2120	0.1799	0.1300
19	0.8278	0.6864	0.5703	0.4746	0.3957	0.3305	0.2765	0.2317	0.1945	0.1635	0.1161
20	0.8196	0.6730	0.5537	0.4564	0.3769	0.3118	0.2584	0.2145	0.1784	0.1486	0.1037
21	0.8114	0.6598	0.5376	0.4388	0.3589	0.2942	0.2415	0.1987	0.1637	0.1351	0.0926
22	0.8034	0.6468	0.5219	0.4220	0.3419	0.2775	0.2257	0.1839	0.1502	0.1228	0.0826
23	0.7955	0.6342	0.5067	0.4057	0.3256	0.2618	0.2109	0.1703	0.1378	0.1117	0.0738
24	0.7876	0.6217	0.4919	0.3901	0.3101	0.2470	0.1971	0.1577	0.1264	0.1015	0.0659
25	0.7798	0.6095	0.4776	0.3751	0.2953	0.2330	0.1843	0.1460	0.1160	0.0923	0.0588
26	0.7721	0.5976	0.4637	0.3607	0.2812	0.2198	0.1722	0.1352	0.1064	0.0839	0.0525
27	0.7644	0.5859	0.4502	0.3468	0.2679	0.2074	0.1609	0.1252	0.0976	0.0763	0.0469
28	0.7569	0.5744	0.4371	0.3335	0.2551	0.1956	0.1504	0.1159	0.0896	0.0693	0.0419
29	0.7494	0.5631	0.4243	0.3207	0.2430	0.1846	0.1406	0.1073	0.0822	0.0630	0.0374
30	0.7419	0.5521	0.4120	0.3083	0.2314	0.1741	0.1314	0.0994	0.0754	0.0573	0.0334
35	0.7059	0.5000	0.3554	0.2534	0.1813	0.1301	0.0937	0.0676	0.0490	0.0356	0.0189
40	0.6717	0.4529	0.3066	0.2083	0.1420	0.0972	0.0668	0.0460	0.0318	0.0221	0.0107
45	0.6391	0.4102	0.2644	0.1712	0.1113	0.0727	0.0476	0.0313	0.0207	0.0137	0.0061
50	0.6081	0.3715	0.2281	0.1407	0.0872	0.0543	0.0339	0.0213	0.0134	0.0085	0.0035
55	0.5786	0.3365	0.1968	0.1157	0.0683	0.0406	0.0242	0.0145	0.0087	0.0053	0.0020
60	0.5505	0.3048	0.1697	0.0951	0.0535	0.0303	0.0173	0.0099	0.0057	0.0033	0.0011

Period	14%	15%	16%	18%	20%	24%	28%	30%	32%	36%	40%
1	0.8772	0.8696	0.8621	0.8475	0.8333	0.8065	0.7813	0.7692	0.7576	0.7353	0.7143
2	0.7695	0.7561	0.7432	0.7182	0.6944	0.6504	0.6104	0.5917	0.5739	0.5407	0.5102
3	0.6750	0.6575	0.6407	0.6086	0.5787	0.5245	0.4768	0.4552	0.4348	0.3975	0.3644
4	0.5921	0.5718	0.5523	0.5158	0.4823	0.4230	0.3725	0.3501	0.3294	0.2923	0.2603
5	0.5194	0.4972	0.4761	0.4371	0.4019	0.3411	0.2910	0.2693	0.2495	0.2149	0.1859
6	0.4556	0.4323	0.4104	0.3704	0.3349	0.2751	0.2274	0.2072	0.1890	0.1580	0.1328
7	0.3996	0.3759	0.3538	0.3139	0.2791	0.2218	0.1776	0.1594	0.1432	0.1162	0.0949
8	0.3506	0.3269	0.3050	0.2660	0.2326	0.1789	0.1388	0.1226	0.1085	0.0854	0.0678
9	0.3075	0.2843	0.2630	0.2255	0.1938	0.1443	0.1084	0.0943	0.0822	0.0628	0.0484
10	0.2697	0.2472	0.2267	0.1911	0.1615	0.1164	0.0847	0.0725	0.0623	0.0462	0.0346
11	0.2366	0.2149	0.1954	0.1619	0.1346	0.0938	0.0662	0.0558	0.0472	0.0340	0.0247
12	0.2076	0.1869	0.1685	0.1372	0.1122	0.0757	0.0517	0.0429	0.0357	0.0250	0.0176
13	0.1821	0.1625	0.1452	0.1163	0.0935	0.0610	0.0404	0.0330	0.0271	0.0184	0.0126
14	0.1597	0.1413	0.1252	0.0985	0.0779	0.0492	0.0316	0.0254	0.0205	0.0135	0.0090
15	0.1401	0.1229	0.1079	0.0835	0.0649	0.0397	0.0247	0.0195	0.0155	0.0099	0.0064
16	0.1229	0.1069	0.0930	0.0708	0.0541	0.0320	0.0193	0.0150	0.0118	0.0073	0.0046
17	0.1078	0.0929	0.0802	0.0600	0.0451	0.0258	0.0150	0.0116	0.0089	0.0054	0.0033
18	0.0946	0.0808	0.0691	0.0508	0.0376	0.0208	0.0118	0.0089	0.0068	0.0039	0.0023
19	0.0829	0.0703	0.0596	0.0431	0.0313	0.0168	0.0092	0.0068	0.0051	0.0029	0.0017
20	0.0728	0.0611	0.0514	0.0365	0.0261	0.0135	0.0072	0.0053	0.0039	0.0021	0.0012
21	0.0638	0.0531	0.0443	0.0309	0.0217	0.0109	0.0056	0.0040	0.0029	0.0016	0.0009
22	0.0560	0.0462	0.0382	0.0262	0.0181	0.0088	0.0044	0.0031	0.0022	0.0012	0.0006
23	0.0491	0.0402	0.0329	0.0222	0.0151	0.0071	0.0034	0.0024	0.0017	0.0008	0.0004
24	0.0431	0.0349	0.0284	0.0188	0.0126	0.0057	0.0027	0.0018	0.0013	0.0006	0.0003
25	0.0378	0.0304	0.0245	0.0160	0.0105	0.0046	0.0021	0.0014	0.0010	0.0005	0.0002
26	0.0331	0.0264	0.0211	0.0135	0.0087	0.0037	0.0016	0.0011	0.0007	0.0003	0.0002
27	0.0291	0.0230	0.0182	0.0115	0.0073	0.0030	0.0013	0.0008	0.0006	0.0002	0.0001
28	0.0255	0.0200	0.0157	0.0097	0.0061	0.0024	0.0010	0.0006	0.0004	0.0002	0.0001
29	0.0224	0.0174	0.0135	0.0082	0.0051	0.0020	0.0008	0.0005	0.0003	0.0001	0.0001
30	0.0196	0.0151	0.0116	0.0070	0.0042	0.0016	0.0006	0.0004	0.0002	0.0001	0.0001
35	0.0102	0.0075	0.0055	0.0030	0.0017	0.0005	0.0002	0.0001	0.0001	0.0000	0.0000
40	0.0053	0.0037	0.0026	0.0013	0.0007	0.0002	0.0001	0.0000	0.0000	0.0000	0.0000
45	0.0027	0.0019	0.0013	0.0006	0.0003	0.0001	0.0000	0.0000	0.0000	0.0000	0.0000
50	0.0014	0.0009	0.0006	0.0003	0.0001	0.0000	0.0000	0.0000	0.0000	0.0000	0.0000
55	0.0007	0.0005	0.0003	0.0001	0.0000	0.0000	0.0000	0.0000	0.0000	0.0000	0.0000
60	0.0004	0.0002	0.0001	0.0000	0.0000	0.0000	0.0000	0.0000	0.0000	0.0000	0.0000

Table B-4   Present Value of an Annuity of $1 ($PVF_a$)

Period	1%	2%	3%	4%	5%	6%	7%	8%	9%	10%	12%
1	0.9901	0.9804	0.9709	0.9615	0.9524	0.9434	0.9346	0.9259	0.9174	0.9091	0.8929
2	1.9704	1.9416	1.9135	1.8861	1.8594	1.8334	1.8080	1.7833	1.7591	1.7355	1.6901
3	2.9410	2.8839	2.8286	2.7751	2.7233	2.6730	2.6243	2.5771	2.5313	2.4869	2.4018
4	3.9020	3.8077	3.7171	3.6299	3.5460	3.4651	3.3872	3.3121	3.2397	3.1699	3.0373
5	4.8534	4.7135	4.5797	4.4518	4.3295	4.2124	4.1002	3.9927	3.8897	3.7908	3.6048
6	5.7955	5.6014	5.4172	5.2421	5.0757	4.9173	4.7665	4.6229	4.4859	4.3553	4.1114
7	6.7282	6.4720	6.2303	6.0021	5.7864	5.5824	5.3893	5.2064	5.0330	4.8684	4.5638
8	7.6517	7.3255	7.0197	6.7327	6.4632	6.2098	5.9713	5.7466	5.5348	5.3349	4.9676
9	8.5660	8.1623	7.7861	7.4353	7.1078	6.8017	6.5152	6.2469	5.9953	5.7590	5.3282
10	9.4713	8.9826	8.5302	8.1109	7.7218	7.3601	7.0236	6.7101	6.4177	6.1446	5.6502
11	10.3677	9.7869	9.2526	8.7605	8.3064	7.8869	7.4987	7.1390	6.8052	6.4951	5.9377
12	11.2551	10.5754	9.9540	9.3851	8.8633	8.3839	7.9427	7.5361	7.1607	6.8137	6.1944
13	12.1338	11.3484	10.6350	9.9856	9.3936	8.8527	8.3577	7.9038	7.4869	7.1034	6.4235
14	13.0038	12.1063	11.2961	10.5631	9.8987	9.2950	8.7455	8.2442	7.7862	7.3667	6.6282
15	13.8651	12.8493	11.9380	11.1184	10.3797	9.7123	9.1079	8.5595	8.0607	7.6061	6.8109
16	14.7180	13.5778	12.5611	11.6523	10.8378	10.1059	9.4467	8.8514	8.3126	7.8237	6.9740
17	15.5623	14.2919	13.1661	12.1657	11.2741	10.4773	9.7632	9.1216	8.5437	8.0216	7.1196
18	16.3984	14.9921	13.7535	12.6593	11.6896	10.8276	10.0591	9.3719	8.7557	8.2014	7.2497
19	17.2261	15.6785	14.3238	13.1339	12.0854	11.1582	10.3356	9.6036	8.9502	8.3649	7.3658
20	18.0457	16.3515	14.8775	13.5903	12.4623	11.4700	10.5940	9.8181	9.1286	8.5136	7.4694
21	18.8571	17.0113	15.4151	14.0292	12.8212	11.7641	10.8355	10.0168	9.2923	8.6487	7.5620
22	19.6605	17.6581	15.9369	14.4511	13.1631	12.0416	11.0613	10.2007	9.4425	8.7716	7.6446
23	20.4559	18.2923	16.4436	14.8568	13.4887	12.3034	11.2722	10.3711	9.5803	8.8832	7.7184
24	21.2435	18.9140	16.9356	15.2470	13.7987	12.5504	11.4694	10.5288	9.7067	8.9848	7.7843
25	22.0233	19.5235	17.4132	15.6221	14.0940	12.7834	11.6536	10.6748	9.8226	9.0771	7.8431
26	22.7953	20.1211	17.8768	15.9828	14.3753	13.0032	11.8258	10.8100	9.9290	9.1610	7.8957
27	23.5597	20.7070	18.3270	16.3296	14.6431	13.2106	11.9867	10.9352	10.0266	9.2373	7.9425
28	24.3166	21.2813	18.7641	16.6630	14.8982	13.4062	12.1371	11.0511	10.1162	9.3066	7.9844
29	25.0659	21.8444	19.1884	16.9837	15.1412	13.5908	12.2777	11.1584	10.1983	9.3696	8.0218
30	25.8078	22.3965	19.6004	17.2920	15.3726	13.7649	12.4091	11.2578	10.2737	9.4269	8.0552
35	29.4087	24.9987	21.4872	18.6646	16.3743	14.4983	12.9477	11.6546	10.5669	9.6442	8.1755
40	32.8349	27.3555	23.1147	19.7927	17.1592	15.0464	13.3317	11.9246	10.7574	9.7791	8.2438
45	36.0948	29.4902	24.5186	20.7199	17.7741	15.4559	13.6056	12.1084	10.8813	9.8628	8.2825
50	39.1964	31.4237	25.7297	21.4820	18.2560	15.7620	13.8008	12.2335	10.9617	9.9148	8.3045
55	42.1476	33.1749	26.7743	22.1084	18.6335	15.9906	13.9400	12.3186	11.0141	9.9471	8.3170
60	44.9555	34.7610	27.6754	22.6233	18.9293	16.1615	14.0392	12.3765	11.0481	9.9672	8.3240

Period	14%	15%	16%	18%	20%	24%	28%	30%	32%	36%	40%
1	0.8772	0.8696	0.8621	0.8475	0.8333	0.8065	0.7813	0.7692	0.7576	0.7353	0.7143
2	1.6467	1.6257	1.6052	1.5656	1.5278	1.4568	1.3916	1.3609	1.3315	1.2760	1.2245
3	2.3216	2.2832	2.2459	2.1743	2.1065	1.9813	1.8684	1.8161	1.7663	1.6735	1.5889
4	2.9137	2.8550	2.7982	2.6901	2.5887	2.4043	2.2410	2.1662	2.0957	1.9658	1.8492
5	3.4331	3.3522	3.2743	3.1272	2.9906	2.7454	2.5320	2.4356	2.3452	2.1807	2.0352
6	3.8887	3.7845	3.6847	3.4976	3.3255	3.0205	2.7594	2.6427	2.5342	2.3388	2.1680
7	4.2883	4.1604	4.0386	3.8115	3.6046	3.2423	2.9370	2.8021	2.6775	2.4550	2.2628
8	4.6389	4.4873	4.3436	4.0776	3.8372	3.4212	3.0758	2.9247	2.7860	2.5404	2.3306
9	4.9464	4.7716	4.6065	4.3030	4.0310	3.5655	3.1842	3.0190	2.8681	2.6033	2.3790
10	5.2161	5.0188	4.8332	4.4941	4.1925	3.6819	3.2689	3.0915	2.9304	2.6495	2.4136
11	5.4527	5.2337	5.0286	4.6560	4.3271	3.7757	3.3351	3.1473	2.9776	2.6834	2.4383
12	5.6603	5.4206	5.1971	4.7932	4.4392	3.8514	3.3868	3.1903	3.0133	2.7084	2.4559
13	5.8424	5.5832	5.3423	4.9095	4.5327	3.9124	3.4272	3.2233	3.0404	2.7268	2.4685
14	6.0021	5.7245	5.4675	5.0081	4.6106	3.9616	3.4587	3.2487	3.0609	2.7403	2.4775
15	6.1422	5.8474	5.5755	5.0916	4.6755	4.0013	3.4834	3.2682	3.0764	2.7502	2.4839
16	6.2651	5.9542	5.6685	5.1624	4.7296	4.0333	3.5026	3.2832	3.0882	2.7575	2.4885
17	6.3729	6.0472	5.7487	5.2223	4.7746	4.0591	3.5177	3.2948	3.0971	2.7629	2.4918
18	6.4674	6.1280	5.8178	5.2732	4.8122	4.0799	3.5294	3.3037	3.1039	2.7668	2.4941
19	6.5504	6.1982	5.8775	5.3162	4.8435	4.0967	3.5386	3.3105	3.1090	2.7697	2.4958
20	6.6231	6.2593	5.9288	5.3528	4.8696	4.1103	3.5458	3.3158	3.1129	2.7718	2.4970
21	6.6870	6.3125	5.9731	5.3837	4.8913	4.1212	3.5514	3.3198	3.1158	2.7734	2.4979
22	6.7430	6.3587	6.0113	5.4099	4.9094	4.1300	3.5558	3.3230	3.1180	2.7746	2.4985
23	6.7921	6.3988	6.0442	5.4321	4.9245	4.1371	3.5592	3.3253	3.1197	2.7754	2.4989
24	6.8352	6.4338	6.0726	5.4510	4.9371	4.1428	3.5619	3.3272	3.1210	2.7760	2.4992
25	6.8729	6.4642	6.0971	5.4669	4.9476	4.1474	3.5640	3.3286	3.1220	2.7765	2.4994
26	6.9061	6.4906	6.1182	5.4804	4.9563	4.1511	3.5656	3.3297	3.1227	2.7768	2.4996
27	6.9352	6.5135	6.1364	5.4919	4.9636	4.1541	3.5669	3.3305	3.1233	2.7771	2.4997
28	6.9607	6.5335	6.1520	5.5016	4.9697	4.1566	3.5679	3.3312	3.1237	2.7773	2.4998
29	6.9831	6.5509	6.1655	5.5098	4.9747	4.1585	3.5686	3.3317	3.1240	2.7774	2.4998
30	7.0027	6.5660	6.1772	5.5168	4.9789	4.1601	3.5692	3.3321	3.1242	2.7775	2.4999
35	7.0701	6.6166	6.2153	5.5386	4.9915	4.1644	3.5708	3.3330	3.1248	2.7777	2.4999
40	7.1051	6.6418	6.2335	5.5482	4.9966	4.1659	3.5712	3.3332	3.1249	2.7777	2.5000
45	7.1232	6.6543	6.2421	5.5523	4.9986	4.1664	3.5714	3.3333	3.1250	2.7778	2.5000
50	7.1327	6.6605	6.2462	5.5541	4.9994	4.1666	3.5714	3.3333	3.1250	2.7778	2.5000
55	7.1376	6.6636	6.2482	5.5549	4.9998	4.1666	3.5714	3.3333	3.1250	2.7778	2.5000
60	7.1401	6.6651	6.2491	5.5553	4.9999	4.1666	3.5714	3.3333	3.1250	2.7778	2.5000

Appendix C

Answers to Selected Odd-Numbered Problems

Chapter 2

1. c. $e_p = -4.33$; $e_p = -0.45$.

3. b. Marginal revenue would equal price; marginal revenue would be less than price.

5. a. $Q_2 = 23,590$.   **b.** $\Delta TR = +\$87,200$.

7. a. 56,000 stuffed animals.   **b.** Total revenue would increase by $48,000.

9. 7,600 cars

11. $TR = 120Q - 1.5Q^2$; $MR = 120 - 3Q$; $AR = 120 - 1.5Q$

13. a. $AR = P = 142 - .05Q$; $TR = Q(P) = 142Q - .05Q^2$;
   $MR = \Delta TR/\Delta Q = 142 - 0.1Q$ **b.** max. $TR = \$100,820$.   **c.** Inelastic; $|e_p| = 0.78$.
   d. $e_p = -1.70$; TR will increase if price is cut, since $|e_p| > 1$.

15. a. 0.72   **b.** Normal; $e_I > 0$ **d.** -10 **e.** Elastic; $|e_p| > 1$

17. a. $Q_x = 1,228 - 20P_x$.   **b.** Complements, since the coefficient of P_y is negative.
   c. -4.39 **d.** Total revenue will be maximized at $Q_x = 614$; $P_x = \$30.70$, and total
   revenue will be $18,849.80.

Appendix 3

1. a. The slope, b, is -237.84 and the intercept, a, is 287.57.   **b.** $R^2 = .97$
   d. $147.26 < Y < 190.04$ **e.** The estimates should be more reliable in a large sample
   since both $\hat{\sigma}_a$ and $\hat{\sigma}_b$ become smaller as the sample size becomes larger.

Chapter 4

1. **a.** The robots are more productive per dollar spent and probably should be bought.
   b. $96/P_L = 0.25$; $0.25P_L = 96$; $P_L = 96/0.25 = \$384$ **c.** Does she expect any change in the wage rate of artists or in the operating costs of robots? Either or both will affect her decision.

3. Use more capital, less labor, since $\dfrac{MP_K}{P_K} > \dfrac{MP_L}{P_L}$.

5. Purchase the machine

7. **a.** Constant returns to scale; doubling the inputs results in a doubling of the level of output.   **d.** This is not a least cost combination because output per additional dollar spent is greater for capital.

9. **d.** 30 units and 20 units of input a, respectively.   **e.** Immediately after $a = 20$ units.

11. Robot, because additional output per additional \$1 is greater for the robot.

13. **a.** $100 = 4KL + 3L^2 - (1/3)L^3$
    b. $dQ = 4L\,dK + (4K + 6L - L^2)dL = 0,$
    $-4L\,dK = (4K + 6L - L^2)dL$

    $$\frac{dK}{dL} = \frac{4K + 6L - L^2}{-4L}$$

    This expression can also be derived using

    $$\frac{dK}{dL} = -\frac{MP_L}{MP_K}$$

    $$MP_L = \frac{\partial Q}{\partial L} = 4K + 6L - L^2,$$

    $$MP_K = \frac{\partial Q}{\partial K} = 4L, \text{ so}$$

    $$\frac{dK}{dL} = \frac{-(4K + 6L - L^2)}{4L}$$

    c. From (b), $MP_L = 4K + 6L - L^2$.
       When $K = 5$, $MP_L = 20 + 6L - L^2$.
    d. $L = 3$.

15. **a.** $Q = 576$ **b.** $L = 6$ **c.** $Q = 234.67$ at $L = 4$.

Appendix 4

1. $Q = 55{,}200$ units; $K = 10$; $L = 190$; $\lambda = 96$.

Chapter 5

3. a. $900 **b.** $3.00 **c.** 400 **d.** $700 **e.** $3.50

5. b. Between 40 and 100 units of output; between 40 and 100 units of output and 2 and 4 units of labor.

9. a. *LAC* will decrease since there are increasing returns to scale. **b.** Combination is least cost, since *MP/P* = 2.5 for both inputs. **c.** In the table, *TFC* = $Z(P_z)$ = 48, and *TVC* = $Y(P_y)$ = $Y(14)$.

11. a. *AFC* = $502/180 = $2.80. **b.** P_b = $42.

13. a. $SMC = 240 - 8Q + Q^2$; $AVC = 240 - 4Q + (1/3)Q^2$; $SAC = (1,000/Q) + 240 - 4Q + (1/3)Q^2$ **b.** $Q = 4$ **c.** $Q = 6$

15. a. *AFC* = 800/20 = 40. **b.** $Q = 10$. **c.** $Q = 15$; *AVC* = 26.25.

Chapter 6

1. Profit-maximizing price = $14.67; output = 6.

3. Profit-maximizing price = $3.50; output = 50; profit = $50.

5. Profit-maximizing price = $600; output = 60; profit = $10,000.

7. b. Profit-maximizing price = $140; output = 6,000.

9. a. 30,000 cases per month. **b.** Yes, because the net increase in profit contribution is $144,000

11. a. $Q = 20$; P = $290. **b.** Profit = $1,333.33.

13. a. $Q = 10.5$. **b.** $Q = 6$. **c.** Profit = $66.

15. a. $P = 220 - Q$; $TR = 220Q - Q^2$. **b.** $Q = 14$; P = $206. **c.** Profit = $437.33.

17. a. *AFC* = 194. **b.** $Q = 12.5$. **c.** $Q = 18.75$. **d.** $Q = 50$; Profit = 1400.

Chapter 7

1. a. 500,000 raw pineapples and 2,500,000 cans of pineapple. **b.** $725,000.

5. b. The opportunity costs associated with the road grader, roller and power trowel are $100, $0, and $200, respectively. **c.** 0; 0. Because at the profit-maximizing point, both asphalt and concrete paving should be done, which implies that L_A and L_C = 0.

7. a. $Q_A = 2$; $Q_B = 4$ **b.** Since process C is not employed, total output = $Q_A + Q_B$ = 6.

9. b. $165,000; $S_1 = 15,000$; $S_2 = S_3 = 0$. **c.** $0; $0.3125.

Chapter 8

3. Total profit = −$6,160, so by producing, the firm will lose more than the $4,000 fixed costs. It should shut down.

7. a. $Q = 56$ is optimal output.   **b.** Profit = −$468, a loss minimum.

9. $127.50

11. a. $Q = 480$; $P = 60.80.   **b.** Profit = $16,780.

13. a. $Q = 100$; $P = 195.   **b.** $2,450

Chapter 9

3. a. $.10   **b.** Price = $.07. Each booth will sell 1,667 kisses and earn $116.69.
   c. Yes, if firms cooperated, each could produce 1,250 kisses at a unit price of $.10

5. a. $280   **b.** 10,000 units   **c.** 15,000 units

7. Firms 1, 2, and 3 should be allocated 23,000, 19,250, and 11,700 barrels per year, respectively.

9. a. $P = 8.75; $Q = 7,500$ homes   **b.** $16,125   **c.** $P = 8.00; $Q = 6,000$ homes
   d. Profit is decreased by $5,125 when advertising expenditures are cut by $5,000.
   e. Restore advertising to its original level.

11. a. $Q = 12$ **b.** $508

13. a. Large firm will maximize profit at $Q = 3,000$ and charge a price of $44.   **b.** Small firms' quantity supplied will be 1,220.   **c.** For Aqualor, profit will be $14,000.

Chapter 10

5. b. Profit is maximized with two shifts, producing 100% B

7. a. Yes.   **b.** 3,800 carryout servings; 2,400 eat-in servings.   **c.** Price for carryout is $3.10, and price for eat-in is $3.60.

9. a. $Q_z = 2,000$; $Q_b = 1,900$.   **b.** $P_z = 800; $P_b = $1,900$.

11. The firm should produce 3,620 units of the joint products but sell only 3,000 units of vinegar. $P_w = 83.80; $P_v = 15; Profit = $154,670.40.

13. a. $Q_g = 1,340$; $Q_c = 820$.   **b.** $P_g = 150.20; $P_c = 99.60.   **c.** Profit = $37,884.
   d. Price will be $114.05 in both markets. $Q_g = 2,063$; $Q_c = 97$; Profit is $1,292.

Chapter 12

1. The firm should produce 84 sweatshirts because at that point, the MRP_L = $4.50 = the wage rate.

3. Forty workers should be employed. Because employment of its members would likely decrease, a union would not necessarily bargain for the highest wage.

5. a. Four bartenders should be employed, and the average price of one drink set at $2.70.   b. $7.00/hour.

7. L = 9.25, so use 9 workers.

Chapter 13

1. a. $67,019   b. $38,276   c. $15,568

3. The greatest present value in Problem 2 = $286,825.

5. The project is not acceptable at a discount rate of 9% as the NPV is −$93,306. At a discount rate of 6%, the NPV is $18,709 so the project is acceptable.

7. a. Not acceptable   b. Not acceptable   c. Acceptable

9. a. About 13%.   b. Since the NPV is $50,314, management should be advised to accept the project (assuming there is no further adjustment of the discount rate for risk).

Appendix 13

1. $61,316

3. $13,951

5. $407,124

7. $11,754

Chapter 14

3. Variance = σ^2 = 835,687,500
   Std. Deviation = σ = 28,908.26

5. Belco will choose the U.S. refinery. The Latin American project has a negative net present value.

7.

Level of Risk (σ)	Certainty Equivalent Adjustment Factor (α)
400	0.4286
300	0.5714
200	0.7143
100	0.8571

11. a. $E(R_T) = 0.28$; $E(R_M) = 0.170$.   **b.** $\sigma_T = 0.16$; $\sigma_M = 0.09$.   **c.** He would choose in accordance with his preferences regarding risk and return.

Chapter 15

3. Projects B, E, and F are acceptable. The others are not acceptable.

5. The Southeast project has the highest B/C and net differential benefits. Also, $\Delta B/\Delta C$ is less than 1.0 for higher cost projects. Therefore the Southeast project should be chosen.

7. Project D has the highest benefit-cost ratio, so it would be ranked first. The other two acceptable projects, A and E, have approximately the same B/C ratios, so they would be ranked equally behind project D.

Glossary

antitrust laws: Laws regulating any business practices and agreements that intensify monopoly power or otherwise restrict trade.

autoregressive integrative moving average models: A general class of statistical models often used in forecasting time series. They are based on the hypothesis that adequate forecasts of future values of a time series can be obtained from past values of the series.

average benefit-cost ratio: Total differential benefits of a project divided by total differential costs.

average fixed cost: Fixed cost per unit of output. Average fixed cost is equal to total fixed cost divided by level of output.

average/marginal relationship: The average cannot rise unless the related marginal value is above it; the average cannot fall unless the corresponding marginal value is below it; the average value must equal the marginal value when the average is at a maximum or a minimum.

average product (of a variable input): Total output divided by the number of units of the input in use. It gives output per unit of input.

average profit: Profit per unit of output. Average profit is found by dividing total profit by quantity of output.

average revenue: Revenue per unit sold. Average revenue is equal to total revenue divided by quantity sold, and as long as only one price is charged, average revenue is equal to price.

average (total) cost: Cost per unit of output. Average total cost is equal to total cost divided by quantity of output and is also equal to average fixed cost plus average variable cost.

average variable cost: Variable cost per unit of output. Average variable cost is equal to total variable cost divided by level of output.

barometric forecasting: Forecasting techniques that involve the use of current values of certain economic variables, called indicators, to predict the future values of other economic variables.

benefit-cost ratio (B/C): The present value of the benefits divided by the present value of the cost of a project. A project is acceptable from a social welfare point of view if and only if its B/C is greater than or equal to 1.

bilateral monopoly: A market structure characterized by having only one buyer and one seller of a particular good or service.

break-even analysis: A method whereby a firm can determine the quantity of output that it must sell to cover its costs, or "break even." It is assumed that price and average variable cost are constant.

capital budgeting: The process by which a firm determines how to allocate investment expenditure among alternative projects.

cartel: A group of firms that have joined together to make agreements on pricing and market strategy.

certainty equivalent approach to project analysis: An approach to project evaluation whereby each future cash flow associated with the project is separately adjusted for risk and a risk-free discount rate is used in the present value calculation.

change in demand: A shift in the demand curve for a good or service caused by a change in some variable other than the price of the given good or service.

change in quantity demanded: A change in the amount of a good or service that consumers are willing to purchase over some time period, which is caused by a change in the price of the good or service.

complementary goods: Products or services that are usually used with one another and have a negative cross price elasticity of demand.

compounding: The process of computing the value of a current sum of money at some future date.

consent decree: A statement of certain provisions agreed to by both the government and the defendant.

consumption spending: Expenditures by individuals for newly produced goods and services (excluding housing).

contract: A binding agreement between two or more parties in which one of the parties is obliged to do or refrain from doing a specific act and the obligation incurred is recognized or enforced by law.

contract law: Laws that pertain to the establishment of contractual obligations and to wrongful acts in breach of contract.

criminal law: Laws that pertain to acts that are viewed as offenses against a federal, state, or local government.

cost-benefit analysis: An extension of capital project analysis to public sector project decisions that attempts to take into account the economic criteria for an optimal allocation of society's resources.

cross price elasticity of demand: The cross price elasticity of demand for Product X with respect to the price of Product Y is a measure of the relative responsiveness of quantity demanded of X to changes in P_Y.

cross-section data: Observations of a particular variable at a single point in time.

cyclical factors: Factors related to fluctuations in the general level of economic activity.

demand curve: Graphical representation of the relationship between the quantity demanded of a good and its price.

demand function: Relates the quantities of a product that consumers will purchase during some specific period to the variables that influence their decisions to buy or not to buy the good or service. Examples of such variables include the price of the good or service, prices of related goods or services, and income of potential consumers.

determinants of demand: Those variables other than a good's own price that affect the amount of the good buyers are willing and able to buy at some point in time. Some examples are income, prices of related goods, tastes, and advertising.

determinants of supply: Those variables other than a good's own price that affect the amount of the good sellers are willing and able to sell at some point in time. Some examples are input prices, technology, and various kinds of taxes.

direct benefits: The benefits obtained by the users of a project or activity.

direct costs: The costs directly associated with the project or activity.

discount rate: The rate of interest used to compute a present value.

discounting: The process of computing the present value of a sum of money to be received in the future.

diseconomies of scale: Technological and organizational disadvantages that accrue to the firm as it increases output in the long run. Diseconomies of scale increase long-run average costs.

economies of scale: Technological and organizational advantages that the firm encounters as it increases output in the long run. Economies of scale reduce long-run average costs.

economic region of production: The region on an isoquant map where the marginal products of both inputs are nonnegative.

efficient portfolio: A project or a combination of investments that will involve the least risk for a given rate of return.

efficient set: The set of all efficient portfolios.

equilibrium price: The price at which the quantity demanded by consumers of a product is equal to the quantity supplied by sellers of a product.

exclusive dealing: A situation wherein a firm buying or leasing the goods of one firm agrees not to deal with competing suppliers.

expansion path: The line connecting all of the least cost combinations of input points for a particular ratio of input prices.

expected value: A weighted average of the possible outcomes, which is obtained by multiplying each outcome by the probability associated with it and then summing the resulting values.

explicit costs: Those costs of production that involve a specific payment by the firm to some person, group, or organization outside the firm.

external benefits or costs: Benefits or costs resulting from a market transaction that affect parties who did not engage in the original market transaction.

fixed costs: Those costs that cannot be eliminated in the short run.

forecasting: The process of analyzing available information regarding economic variables and relationships and then predicting the future values of certain variables of interest to the firm or to economic policymakers.

free entry: The absence of barriers to entry into a market. In a market characterized by free entry, greater than normal profit serves the function of drawing new firms into the industry.

future value: The amount that would be accumulated at some future date if a sum of money held today were invested now at a particular rate of interest.

government expenditures: Expenditures for newly produced goods and services, including government investment expenditures, by all levels of government.

gross national product: The market value of final goods and services produced in a country during some time period, usually one year.

historical costs: Costs of the firm for which explicit payment has been made sometime in the past or for which the firm is committed in the future.

implicit (opportunity) costs: Costs that do not involve actual payment by a firm to factors of production but nevertheless represent costs to the firm in the sense that in order to use certain inputs in the production process, the firm has had to abandon opportunities to use them elsewhere.

income elasticity of demand: A measure of the relative responsiveness of the quantity demanded of a product to changes in income.

incremental benefit-cost ratio: The change in total benefits divided by the change in total costs, obtained by moving to the project with the next higher level of price or initial outlay.

incremental costs: The additional costs that will be incurred by the firm if it undertakes a new project or produces an additional batch of output.

incremental profit: Incremental revenue minus incremental cost resulting from an activity of the firm.

incremental revenue: The additional revenue that a firm will receive by undertaking a particular project.

indirect benefits: External, or third party, benefits associated with a project.

indirect costs: External, or third party, costs associated with a project.

inferior good: A product or service with a negative income elasticity of demand.

input-output table: Indicates the connection between the demand for final output and the productive effort required of individual industries and their interrelationships.

internal rate of return: The net annual percentage yield of a project, obtained by solving for the discount rate that will cause the net present value of a project to be equal to zero.

investment spending: (GNP definition) All purchases of capital goods—including buildings, equipment, and inventories—by private businesses and nonprofit institutions. Includes all expenditures for residential housing.

isocost line: Gives all combinations of two inputs that can be utilized for a given dollar cost to the firm, assuming given and fixed input prices.

isoprofit curve: Indicates the different combinations of two products that will result in equal profit for the firm.

isoquants: Indicate the various combinations of two inputs that would enable a firm to produce a particular level of output.

kinked demand curve: Occurs when rival firms will not follow the price increase of a single firm in an oligopoly but will cut prices when another firm does so. Such a demand curve is relatively elastic for prices above the going market price and much less elastic for lower prices.

law of diminishing returns: A technological proposition which asserts that if equal increments of one variable input are added while the amounts of all other inputs remain fixed, total product may increase, but after some point, the *additions* to total product will decrease.

least cost combination of inputs: That input combination that will enable a firm to produce a given level of output at the lowest possible cost or to produce the greatest output for a given dollar cost.

linear programming: A mathematical technique whereby a firm can make optimizing decisions in a situation where the function to be maximized or minimized is linear and subject to linear constraints that are in the form of inequalities.

long run: Time period sufficiently long that all inputs are variable.

long-run average cost: Long-run total cost divided by the level of output. Measures cost per unit of output when all inputs are variable.

long-run marginal cost: The rate of change of long-run total cost as the level of output changes.

long-run total cost: The minimum economic cost of producing each possible level of output when the time period is sufficiently long to change all inputs in the firm's production function.

marginal cost: The rate of change of total cost with respect to changes in level of output. *Arc* marginal cost can be found by dividing the change in total cost by the change in quantity of output produced by the firm or by dividing the change in total variable cost by the change in quantity of output.

marginal cost of an input: The rate of change of a firm's total cost with respect to a change in the amount of an input. *Arc* marginal cost of an input is given by the change in a firm's total cost divided by the change in the input.

marginal cost of capital: The discount rate that represents the marginal cost of investment funds to the firm. Calculated as a weighted average of the after-tax cost of funds from each source.

marginal product (of a variable input): The rate of change of total output with respect to changes in the variable input—other inputs kept fixed. *Arc* marginal product is an approximation to marginal product and is given by the change in the total product divided by the change in the variable input.

marginal profit: The rate of change of total profit with respect to changes in the level of the firm's output. *Arc* marginal profit is found by dividing the change in total profit by the change in quantity of output. Marginal profit is also equal to marginal revenue minus marginal cost.

marginal rate of (technical) substitution of two inputs: Indicates the rate at which two inputs can be substituted for each other while a constant level of production is maintained. The marginal rate of substitution is equal to minus one times the slope of an isoquant.

marginal revenue: The rate of change of total revenue with respect to quantity sold. Marginal revenue indicates to a firm how total revenue will change if there is a change in the quantity sold of a firm's product. An approximation to marginal revenue is the change in total revenue divided by the change in quantity sold. We call this value *arc marginal revenue*.

marginal revenue product of an input: The rate of change of total revenue with respect to a change in a variable input. The marginal revenue product of an input is equal to the marginal product of the input multiplied by the net marginal revenue of the input.

marginal social benefit: The marginal private benefit of a good or service (usually measured by its price) plus any marginal external or third-party benefits.

marginal social cost: Marginal private cost plus marginal external cost.

market segmentation: See price discrimination.

markup pricing: A pricing technique whereby a certain percentage of cost of goods sold or of price is added to cost of goods sold, in order to obtain the market price.

mean: The mean for a set of data is found by adding together the values of all the separate observations and dividing the resulting total by the number of observations.

monopolistic competition: A market structure characterized by the existence of many firms in the industry (but with an element of product differentiation so that each firm has some control over price) and by free entry into and exit from the industry.

monopoly: A market structure characterized by the existence of only one firm in the industry. For a firm to retain monopoly control, there must be complete barriers to entry into the industry.

monopsonistic competition: A market with many buyers of a differentiated product.

monopsony: A market structure characterized by the existence of only one buyer of a product or service.

natural monopoly: An industry where the existence of only one firm is a matter of public convenience and allows for the maximum benefits of economies of scale.

net cash flow: Any increase in revenues brought about by the project less any increase in operating expenses and depreciation, multiplied by $(1 - T)$, where T is the firm's marginal income tax rate. The incremental depreciation associated with the project is then added to the preceding sum.

net exports: Value of newly produced U.S. goods and services purchased by foreigners (exports) less the value of newly produced foreign goods purchased by the United States (imports).

net marginal revenue: The marginal revenue from the sale of final output minus the marginal cost attributable to component costs.

net marginal revenue of an input: The marginal revenue received from selling one more unit of output less the cost of raw materials and intermediate products required for it.

net present value (NPV): The present value of the net cash inflows minus the present value of the cost outlays of an investment. An investment project is acceptable if its NPV is greater than or equal to zero.

net social benefit: The total social benefit less the total social cost of an activity.

normal good: A product or service with a positive income elasticity of demand.

normal profit: The rate of profit just sufficient, under conditions of free entry, to keep firms from leaving a given industry in the long run.

oligopoly: A market structure characterized by the existence of a few dominant firms in an industry (each of which recognize their mutual interdependence) and by substantial barriers to entry into the industry.

oligopsony: A market with a few buyers, or a few dominant buyers.

perfect competition: A market structure in which (a) the firm takes market price as given, since an individual firm produces only a small fraction of total industry output; (b) the products of all firms are undifferentiated; (c) there is freedom of entry into or exit from the industry; (d) there are no artificial interferences with the activities of buyers and sellers; and

(e) all buyers and sellers have perfect knowledge of market conditions.

present value: The value today of a stream of receipts to be received in the future. Present value is obtained by discounting the stream of receipts using an appropriate discount rate.

price discrimination: Charging consumers in different markets different prices for the same product (based on the price elasticity of demand in each market).

price elasticity of demand: A measure of the relative responsiveness of quantity demanded of a product to a change in its price. The price elasticity of demand indicates how total revenue will change as a result of a change in price.

price fixing: The practice of a group of firms agreeing to set the price of a product at a specific level.

price leadership: Occurs when a firm in an oligopoly sets a price that subsequently determines what other members of the industry will charge for their products.

private costs of a firm: The sum of the explicit and implicit costs that the firm incurs.

product differentiation: A wide variety of activities, such as design changes and advertising, that rival firms employ to attract customers by distinguishing their product from competitors' products.

product transformation curve: Indicates the various combinations of two products that can be produced for a given dollar cost to the firm.

production function: A mathematical statement of the way that the quantity of output of a product depends on the quantities used of various inputs or resources.

profit maximization: Making the greatest economic profit possible.

profit-maximizing rule: Produce up to the point where marginal revenue is equal to marginal cost and at higher output levels marginal revenue is less than marginal cost, as long as price is greater than or equal to average variable cost in the short run or long-run average cost in the long run.

pure public good: A product or service that is indivisible and nonexcludable.

returns to scale: Refers to how output changes when all inputs are increased by the same multiple (e.g., doubled or tripled).

ridge lines: The lines connecting the points where the marginal product of an input is equal to zero (one line for each input) in the isoquant map and forming the boundary for the economic region of production.

risk: A project is characterized by risk if the outcome is uncertain.

risk-adjusted discount rate: The appropriate discount rate for a project characterized by risk. The rate is found by adding a risk premium (determined by the level of risk involved) to the discount rate for a risk-free project.

risk averse investor: An investor who, given a choice between two investments with the same expected return, will always prefer the less risky one.

risk neutral investor: An investor who is indifferent between two investments with the same expected return, regardless of their risk.

risk seeker: An investor who, given a choice between two investments with the same expected return, will always prefer the riskier one.

seasonal factors: Factors connected with a specific season of the year.

semivariable costs: Costs that are fixed over some ranges of output and variable over others.

social costs of a firm: The costs that society in general incurs because of a firm's activities. Social costs include private costs plus any additional costs that the firm imposes on society but for which it does not pay.

social rate of discount: The rate of discount appropriate for evaluating public sector projects.

short run: A time period sufficiently short that at least one input is fixed.

short-run average total cost: Cost per unit of output in the short run. Equal to short-run total cost divided by the level of output. Also equal to average fixed cost plus short-run average variable cost for each level of output.

short-run average variable cost: The variable cost per unit of output produced in the short run. Equal to short-run total variable cost divided by the level of output.

short-run marginal cost: The rate of change of either short-run total cost or short-run total variable cost as the level of output changes in the short run.

short-run total cost: All of the private economic costs of the firm in the short run. Equal to total fixed cost plus short-run total variable cost.

short-run total variable cost: The sum of all private economic costs of the firm that vary with its level of output in the short run.

standard deviation: Square root of the variance. (See variance.)

substitute goods: Products or services that can be substituted for one another and that have a positive cross price elasticity of demand.

superior good: A product or service with an income elasticity of demand greater than one.

supply curve: A graphical representation of the relationship between quantity supplied of a product and the price that sellers expect to receive.

time series data: Observations of a specific variable over a number of time periods.

tort law: Laws that deal with injuries sustained by private parties as a result of nonperformance of a duty created by law.

total cost: Total dollar costs of the firm over some time period. Total cost is equal to total fixed cost plus total variable cost.

total fixed cost: Total dollar amount of costs that do not vary with the level of output.

total product (of one variable input): Indicates the maximum output that can be obtained from different amounts of one variable input, while all other inputs are kept fixed.

total profit: Total revenue minus total costs, including opportunity costs.

total revenue: Total dollar sales volume of a firm, which is equal to price times quantity sold.

total variable cost: Total dollar amount of costs that vary with the level of output.

transfer price: Accounting price charged one division of a firm for a product that is produced by another division of the same firm.

trend analysis: A forecasting technique that relies primarily on historical data to predict the future.

trend factors: Factors related to movements in economic variables over time.

tying agreement: Occurs when a firm agrees that goods sold or leased will be used only with other goods of the seller or lessor.

variable costs: Those costs that vary with the level of a firm's output.

variance: One measure of the dispersion about the expected value or mean of a set of data or possible outcomes of a project.

Index